Investment Protection Standards and the Rule of Law

Investment Protection Standards and the Rule of Law

Edited by

AUGUST REINISCH AND STEPHAN W. SCHILL

Great Clarendon Street, Oxford, OX2 6DP,
United Kingdom

Oxford University Press is a department of the University of Oxford.
It furthers the University's objective of excellence in research, scholarship,
and education by publishing worldwide. Oxford is a registered trade mark of
Oxford University Press in the UK and in certain other countries

First Edition published in 2023

Impression: 1

Published in the United States of America by Oxford University Press
198 Madison Avenue, New York, NY 10016, United States of America

British Library Cataloguing in Publication Data

Data available

Library of Congress Control Number is on file at the Library of Congress

ISBN 978–0–19–286458–1

DOI: 10.1093/oso/9780192864581.001.0001

Printed and bound in the UK by
TJ Books Limited

Preface and Acknowledgements

The present book was developed in close connection with the Committee on Rule of Law and International Investment Law of the International Law Association (ILA), which started working at the ILA's Johannesburg conference in August 2016. The Committee, which is chaired by August Reinisch, has the mandate 'to study rule-of-law implications of international investment law on both substantive and procedural matters'.[1] The Committee first devoted considerable attention to the difficulties related to defining the notion and content of the rule of law,[2] and subsequently issued a report on relevant practices and recommendations concerning the impact of the rule of law on substantive standards of treatment contained in international investment agreements.[3] Its work subsequently turned to implications of the rule of law for investor-State dispute settlement.[4] This edited volume, which counts among its contributors several members of the ILA Committee, expands on and deepens the Committee's mandate to analyse how 'substantive protections found in treaties attempt to ensure government decision-making based on the rule of law'.[5] It discusses both the extent to which the most important substantive standards of treatment reflect rule-of-law elements and critically evaluates the rule-of-law gaps those standards leave.

In preparation for this book, two author workshops were held: one in December 2018 in Vienna, and one in June 2019 in Paris. Subsequently, the Covid-19 pandemic disrupted work on this project and caused considerable delay in the finalization of the manuscript. But a group of highly dedicated contributors managed to see the process through despite the pandemic-related difficulties and an exacting editorial process with several rounds of comments and requests for revision by the editors. We are grateful to our contributors for their continued support, endurance, and patience and hope the result will be an important addition to the scholarly debate on the investment treaty regime, its benefits, and shortcomings.

We are further particularly grateful to Johannes Tropper who assisted not only in arranging the various Committee meetings, as well as the author workshops, but who was also crucial to the successful organization of the editorial process of this volume. He was joined by Maximilian Weninger and Nina Öllinger who both did an excellent job at copy-editing. Stephan Schill would like to acknowledge support, in the early phases of the project, from a European Research Council Starting Grant: 'Transnational Private–Public Arbitration as Global Regulatory Governance: Charting and Codifying the *Lex Mercatoria Publica*' (LexMercPub, Grant agreement no: 313355). August Reinisch is grateful to the Law School of the University of Vienna for its financial support to host workshops during which the chapters of this book were discussed. At Oxford University Press, we would like to thank

---

[1] See ILA Committee on the Rule of Law and International Investment Law: Report 2018 (2018) 78 International Law Association Reports of Conferences 380.

[2] ibid 381–412.

[3] Interim Report for the 2022 Lisbon conference (on file with the authors).

[4] ibid para 116.

[5] ILA Committee (n 1) 380–81.

Imogen Hill, Paulina dos Santos Major, and Kathryn Plunkett, who have supported this book project from start to finish. We are also particularly grateful to the copy-editors at Newgen KnowledgeWorks for their diligent work, namely Ashirvad Moses, Lakshmi Amritha, Kiruthiga, and Nandhini Saravanan.

August Reinisch and Stephan Schill
Vienna and Amsterdam, May 2022

Table of Contents

Table of Cases

I. INVESTOR-STATE ARBITRATIONS

ICSID Additional Facility (ICSID AF)

International Chamber of Commerce (ICC)

Stockholm Chamber of Commerce (SCC)

II. INTERNATIONAL COURTS AND TRIBUNALS

Permanent Court of International Justice

International Court of Justice

World Trade Organization Dispute Settlement Body

European Court of Human Rights

Inter-American Court of Human Rights

Court of Justice of the European Union

III. NATIONAL COURTS

Ireland

United States of America

Table of Instruments

NATIONAL LAWS

Bolivia

Canada

France

Germany

Italy

Japan

Kazakhstan

Mexico

Morocco

List of Abbreviations

I. General

ACHPR	African Charter on Human and Peoples' Rights
ACHR	American Convention on Human Rights
ACIA	ASEAN Comprehensive Investment Agreement
AIFC	Astana International Financial Centre
ASEAN	Association of Southeast Asian Nations
BIT	bilateral investment treaty
CEO	chief executive officer
CETA	Comprehensive and Economic Trade Agreement between Canada and the European Union
CFR	Charter of Fundamental Rights of the European Union
CIFA	Cooperation And Investment Facilitation Agreement
CJEU	Court of Justice of the European Union
CPTPP	Comprehensive and Progressive Agreement for Trans-Pacific Partnership
CSR	corporate social responsibility
CUP	Cambridge University Press
DR–CAFTA	Dominican Republic–Central America Free Trade Agreement
EBRD	European Bank for Reconstruction and Development
ECHR	European Convention on Human Rights
ECT	Energy Charter Treaty
ECtHR	European Court of Human Rights
ESIL	European Society of International Law
EU	European Union
FAT	fair administrative treatment
FCPA	Foreign Corrupt Practices Act
FCTC	WHO Framework Convention on Tobacco Control
FDI	foreign direct investment
FET	fair and equitable treatment
FIT	feed-in-tariff
FPS	full protection and security
FTA	free trade agreement
GATT	General Agreement on Tariffs and Trade
GHG	greenhouse gas
IACtHR	Inter-American Court of Human Rights
ICCPR	International Covenant on Civil and Political Rights
ICESCR	International Covenant on Economic, Social and Cultural Rights
ICJ	International Court of Justice
ICS	investment court system
ICSID	International Centre for Settlement of Investment Disputes
IFC	international finance corporation
IIA	international investment agreement
IIL	international investment law

IILJ	Institute for International Law and Justice
ILA	International Law Association
ILC	International Law Commission
ILO	International Labour Organization
INE	National Ecology Institute of Mexico
Iran–USCTR	Iran–United States Claims Tribunal Report
ISA	investor-State arbitration
ISDS	investor-State dispute settlement
JRP	joint review panel
MFN	most-favoured nation
NAFTA	North American Free Trade Agreement
NGO	non-governmental organization
NT	national treatment
OECD	Organisation for Economic Co-operation and Development
OIC	Organization of the Islamic Conference
OIC Agreement	Agreement on Promotion, Protection and Guarantee of Investments among Member States of the Organization of the Islamic Conference
OUP	Oxford University Press
PCA	Permanent Court of Arbitration
RCEP	regional comprehensive economic partnership
RTA	regional trade agreement
SADC	Southern African Development Community
SCBC	Supreme Court of British Columbia
SPR	single presentation requirements
UDHR	Universal Declaration of Human Rights
UN	United Nations
UNASUR	Union of South American Nations
UNCITRAL	United Nations Commission on International Trade Law
UNCTAD	United Nations Conference on Trade and Development
UNGA	United Nations General Assembly
UNSC	United Nations Security Council
UNTS	United Nations Treaty Series
USMCA	United States–Mexico–Canada Agreement
VAT	value added tax
VCLT	Vienna Convention on the Law of Treaties
WGIII	UNCITRAL Working Group III: Investor-State Dispute Settlement Reform
WHO	World Health Organization
WJP	World Justice Project
WTO	World Trade Organization

II. Journals

Adel L Rev	Adelaide Law Review
Adm L Rev	Administrative Law Review
AJIL	American Journal of International Law
Alta L Rev	Alberta Law Review
Am J CompL	American Journal of Comparative Law
Am J Jurisp	American Journal of Jurisprudence
Am Rev Intl Arb	American Review of International Arbitration

Am U Intl L Rev	American University International Law Review
Arb Intl	Arbitration International
Asper Rev Intl Bus & Trade Law	Asper Review of International Business and Trade Law
Austl J Legal Phil	Australian Journal of Legal Philosophy
BCL Rev	Boston College Law Review
Brit J Pol Sci	British Journal of Political Science
Brooklyn JIL	Brooklyn Journal of International Law
Buff CLR	Buffalo Criminal Law Review
BUL Rev	Boston University Law Review
BYIL	British Yearbook of International Law
Chin J Comp L	Chinese Journal of Comparative Law
CILJ	Cambridge International Law Journal
CJGG	Chinese Journal of Global Governance
CLJ	Cambridge Law Journal
CLP	Current Legal Problems
Colum J Transnatl L	Columbia Journal of Transnational Law
Colum L Rev	Columbia Law Review
Duke LJ	Duke Law Journal
Econ J	The Economic Journal
EJIL	European Journal of International Law
Emory LJ	Emory Law Journal
Envl L	Environmental Law
EPL	European Public Law
EYIEL	European Yearbook of International Economic Law
Fordham Intl LJ	Fordham International Law Journal
Foreign Aff	Foreign Affairs
Georgia L Rev	Georgia Law Review
Go JIL	Goettingen Journal of International Law
Harv Intl LJ	Harvard International Law Journal
Harv L Rev	Harvard Law Review
Hastings Intl & Comp L Rev	Hastings International and Comparative Law Review
HJRL	Hague Journal on the Rule of Law
ICLQ	International and Comparative Law Quarterly
ICSID Rev—FILJ	ICSID Review—Foreign Investment Law Journal
IILJ	Institute for International Law and Justice
IJAL	Indian Journal of Arbitration Law
Intl A LR	International Arbitration Law Review
Int Rev Law & Econ	International Review of Law and Economics
Intl L Practice	International Legal Practice
IRLE	International Review of Law and Economics
JEPP	Journal of European Public Policy
JIDS	Journal of International Dispute Settlement
JIEL	Journal of International Economic Law
J Institutional Econ	Journal of Institutional Economics
J Intl Arb	Journal of International Arbitration
JLC	Journal of Law and Courts
J Mod Hist	Journal of Modern History
JöR	Jahrbuch des öffentlichen Rechts der Gegenwart
J Political Ideol	Journal of Political Ideology
JWIT	Journal of World Investment & Trade
Law & Phil	Law and Philosophy

LIEI	Legal Issues of European Integration
LJIL	Leiden Journal of International Law
LRIL	London Review of International Law
LS	Legal Studies
Mich JIL	Michigan Journal of International Law
Mich L Rev	Michigan Law Review
Minn JIL	Minnesota Journal of International Law
MLR	Modern Law Review
NC J Intl L & Com Reg	North Carolina Journal of International Law and Commercial Regulation
NELR	North East Law Review
NILR	Netherlands International Law Review
Notre Dame L Rev	Notre Dame Law Review
NYU Env L J	New York University Environmental Law Journal
NYU J Intl L & Pol	New York University Journal of International Law and Politics
NYU L Rev	New York University Law Review
NZ L Rev	New Zealand Law Review
OJLS	Oxford Journal of Legal Studies:
Or L Rev	Oregon Law Review
Pac McGeorge Global Bus & Dev LJ	Pacific McGeorge Global Business & Development Law Journal
Publ L	Public Law
RdC	Recueil des Cours de l'Académie de Droit International de La
RECIEL	Review of European, Comparative and International Environmental Law
Rev Intl Organ	Review of International Organizations
Rev Intl Stud	Review of International Studies
RGDIP	Revue Générale de Droit International Public
Royal Inst Phil Supps	Royal Institute of Philosophy Supplements
Sing JLS	Singapore Journal of Legal Studies
Southwest JIL	Southwestern Journal International Law
Stan L Rev	Stanford Law Review
Syracuse J Intl L & Com	Syracuse Journal of International Law and Commerce
TDM	Transnational Dispute Management
Tex Intl LJ	Texas International Law Journal
TL & D	Trade, Law and Development
Transnatl L & Contemp Probs	Transnational Law and Contemporary Problems
UCLA L Rev	UCLA Law Review
Univ Pa L Rev	University of Pennsylvania Law Review
U Pa JIL	University of Pennsylvania Journal of International Law
U Pa L Rev	University of Pennsylvania Law Review
UTLJ	University of Toronto Law Journal
Utrecht L Rev	Utrecht Law Review
Vand J Transnatl L	Vanderbilt Journal of Transnational Law
Va JIL	Virginia Journal of International Law
WAMR	World Arbitration and Mediation Review
World Pol	World Politics
Yale LJ	Yale Law Journal
ZaöRV	Zeitschrift für ausländisches öffentliches Recht und Völkerrecht
ZEuS	Zeitschrift für Europarechtliche Studien

List of Contributors

Julian Arato is a Professor of Law at the University of Michigan Law School. His research focuses on public international law, international economic law, and private law. Professor Arato serves as Chair of the Academic Forum on Investor-State Dispute Settlement, and as an Observer Delegate to the United Nations Commission on International Trade Law Working Group III (ISDS Reform). He also serves on the editorial board of the American Journal of International Law.

Marc Bungenberg is the Director of the Europa-Institut; Professor of Public Law, European Law, Public International Law and International Economic Law at Saarland University in Germany; permanent visiting professor at the University of Lausanne, Switzerland. He also holds a Jean Monnet Chair with the title 'EU Constitutional Framework for International Dispute Settlement and the Rule of Law'. Marc received his doctorate in law from the University of Hannover and wrote his dissertation at the Friedrich-Schiller-University Jena. He holds an LLM from Lausanne University. He has also taught and researched at universities in Australia, Denmark, Germany, Switzerland, and Uzbekistan. His main fields of research are European (Common Commercial Policy, public procurement, and State aid law) and international economic law, particularly international investment and WTO law.

Manjiao Chi is Professor and Founding Director of the Center for International Economic Law and Policy, Law School, University of International Business and Economics, Beijing. His research focuses on international economic law and policy, sustainable development, and dispute settlement. He is the author of numerous books and papers, a founding editor of the Asian Yearbook of International Economic Law, and a frequent speaker in international law conferences. He is Deputy Chair, the Academic Forum on ISDS; Co-Chair, Standing Council Member, Chinese Society of International Law, and visiting professor of many law schools around the world. He has rich experience of commercial and investment arbitration, WTO litigation, treaty negotiation, and national policymaking.

Caroline Henckels is an Associate Professor in the Faculty of Law at Monash University. She is a member of the Editorial Board of the Journal of International Economic Law and is an Associate Editor of The Journal of World Investment & Trade. Caroline is qualified to practise law in Australia and New Zealand and directs Monash University's TradeLab clinical programme in international economic law.

Steffen Hindelang is Professor of International Investment and Trade Law at Uppsala University in Sweden. He teaches and researches in the areas of international economic law, especially international investment law, EU law, and German public law. He is also faculty member at SDU-University of Southern Denmark and adjunct faculty member at Humboldt-Universität zu Berlin and Technical University Berlin, a senior fellow at the Walter Hallstein Institute of European Constitutional Law at Humboldt-Universität zu Berlin and academic adviser to the International Investment Law Centre Cologne. He co-edits the YSEC Yearbook of Socio-Economic Constitutions series (Springer). Furthermore, he has advised, inter alia, European governments on investment screening regulation as well as in international investment disputes and international organizations. He was also involved in the *Achmea* proceedings, in particular in the German courts, and served as legal expert in ICSID proceedings, and in US and Swedish courts. He acted also as ICSID arbitrator and serves on the ICSID Panel of Conciliators designated by the Federal Republic of Germany (2019–25).

Martin A. Jarrett is a Senior Research Fellow at the Max Planck Institute for Comparative Public Law and International Law and an adjunct lecturer at the University of Heidelberg. His research activities focus on international investment law, particularly the topic of investor misconduct. He is the author of *Contributory Fault and Investor Misconduct in Investment Arbitration* (CUP 2019).

Susan L. Karamanian is the Dean of the College of Law at Hamad Bin Khalifa University in Doha, Qatar. She has served as the Associate Dean for International and Comparative Legal Studies and the Burnett Family Professorial Lecturer in Law and Policy at George Washington University Law School, and as a vice president of the American Society of International Law.

Ursula Kriebaum is Professor of Public International Law at the University of Vienna. She is a member of the Permanent Court of Arbitration, a member of the Panel of Arbitrators under the Agreement on the Withdrawal of the United Kingdom of Great Britain and Northern Ireland from the European Union, an alternate member of the Court of Conciliation and Arbitration within the OSCE, a member of the Panel of Conciliators maintained by the ICSID, and a member of the Arbitration Panel for the Protocol on Cultural Cooperation to the Free Trade Agreement between the European Union and its Member States and the Republic of Korea. She researches and teaches international law, investment law, and human rights law at the University of Vienna, and acts as legal expert in international investment law and human rights law cases, and as consultant for law firms and adviser to governments on investment law and arbitration issues.

Niels Lachmann is a research assistant at the Department of Law at SDU-University of Southern Denmark, Odense. His research interests span public international law—especially international investment law, but also international human rights protection and international space law—and include issues of constitutional law of the European Union, and topics of history—from Ottoman diplomacy to Quebec and Canada—whenever there is opportunity and time. He holds an LLM from SDU, a PhD in political science/international relations from Sciences Po Bordeaux and a Magister Artium in Modern and Contemporary History and Political Sciences from Albert-Ludwigs-Universität, Freiburg im Breisgau.

Sebastián Mantilla Blanco is a postdoctoral researcher at the University of Bonn in Germany and a postdoctoral global fellow at New York University. He is also an independent counsel of Zuleta Abogados (Colombia) and has been a visiting professor at the Universidad de La Sabana (Colombia). His main areas of research are general public international law and international economic law. He holds a doctorate in law from the University of Bonn, an LLM from the University of Bonn, and a law degree from the Pontificia Universidad Javeriana in Bogotá (Colombia).

Krista Nadakavukaren Schefer is Vice Director of the Swiss Institute of Comparative Law and senior fellow at the World Trade Institute, Bern. Formerly a Swiss National Science Foundation professor of international law at the University of Basel's Faculty of Law, she continues to teach as an adjunct at that faculty as well as on the law programmes of the universities of Bern, Fribourg, and Zurich. In 2020, Krista was appointed to be on Switzerland's ICSID List of Conciliators. She graduated from the University of Chicago with dual AB degrees in political science and public policy studies, and received her JD from Georgetown University Law School. Following her bar exam, she moved to Switzerland, where she obtained her doctorate and her *habilitation* from the University of Bern.

Arnaud de Nanteuil is Full Professor at Paris-Est University, in France. He is the author of numerous books and articles in the fields of international law and investment law, and he serves as counsel, expert, or arbitrator in investor-State arbitration.

Martins Paparinskis is Professor of Public International Law at University College London. Martins is a member of the Permanent Court of Arbitration, the OSCE Court of Conciliation and Arbitration, and the Implementation Committee of the UNECE Water Convention, and a member elect of the International Law Commission.

August Reinisch is Professor of International and European Law at the University of Vienna. He is a member of the International Law Commission and of the Court of the Permanent Court of Arbitration, as well as the Institut de droit international. He serves as arbitrator in investment cases and is listed on the ICSID Panel of Arbitrators.

Mavluda Sattorova is a Reader at the School of Law and Social Justice and Director of Liverpool Economic Governance Unit, University of Liverpool and a British Academy Mid-career Fellow. Her research primarily focuses on international investment law. Her most recent work examines the impact of investment treaty law on national policymaking and governance. Among other projects, Mavluda has explored an empirically driven approach to investigating the interaction between investment treaty rules with national law and policy, in particular in developing countries. She works closely with international organizations and government agencies involved in the design and reform of international investment treaties and national investment policies.

Stephan W. Schill is Professor of International and Economic Law and Governance at the University of Amsterdam. He is admitted to the Bar in Germany and New York, is a Member of the ICSID Panel of Arbitrators, and regularly acts as arbitrator in international investment arbitrations. He is also General Editor of the Publications of the International Council for Commercial Arbitration (ICCA) and Co-Editor-in-Chief of The Journal of World Investment & Trade.

Esmé Shirlow is an Associate Professor at the Australian National University College of Law. She teaches and researches in the fields of public international law, international dispute settlement, and international investment law and arbitration. Esmé is the General Editor of the Australian Year Book of International Law and an Associate Editor with the ICSID Review and Kluwer Arbitration Blog. She is Vice-President (Australia) of the Australian and New Zealand Society of International Law, and Co-Chair of the Society's International Economic Law Interest Group. Esmé is admitted as a solicitor in the Australian Capital Territory and maintains a practice in the field of international law advising parties to investment treaty claims and in proceedings before the International Court of Justice. Prior to joining the ANU, Esmé worked in the Australian Government's Office of International Law.

Patricia Sarah Stöbener de Mora is Director of European Law and International Economic Law at the Association of German Chambers of Industry and Commerce (Deutscher Industrie- und Handelskammertag). Her publications concern matters of international investment law, competition law, the rule of law, and international economic law, in particular in connection with the European Union.

Elizabeth Whitsitt is an Associate Professor at the University of Calgary, Faculty of Law where she teaches various courses in international law and dispute resolution. She received her LLM in international legal studies from New York University and her PhD from the University of Calgary. Dr Whitsitt has published and presented extensively in the areas of international trade and investment law. She is appointed to Canada's USMCA Chapter 10 Roster and is a Canadian Member of the USMCA's Joint Public Advisory Committee to the Commission for Environmental Cooperation.

Velimir Živković, LLM (Belgrade), MJur (Oxford) is an Assistant Professor and Director of the LLM International Commercial Law at University of Warwick School of Law. He completed his PhD in law at the London School of Economics and was previously a Research Fellow with Humboldt University Berlin. His research, teaching, and consultancy work concern investment and commercial law and arbitration, contract law, and the rule of law.

1

Introduction

August Reinisch and Stephan W. Schill

I. The Rule of Law as Normative Yardstick for the Investment Treaty Regime

In the controversies about international investment law and policy, the 'rule of law' is developing into one of the principles that both supporters and critics use to evaluate the investment treaty regime. While itself a vague and ambiguous, some even say essentially contested, concept,[1] which lacks a universally agreed definition, the rule of law is widely accepted as a normative benchmark that should inform the practice of investor-State dispute settlement, the application of rights and obligations of investors and States, and the reform of international investment law.[2] Supporters argue that investment treaties 'embody norms that all countries committed to the rule of law should follow', allow for the enforcement of such norms through investor-State arbitration, and thereby 'contribute greatly to institutional quality in host countries'.[3] Critics, by contrast, emphasize the rule-of-law deficits of the investment treaty regime, pointing out that 'investment treaties generally do not establish coherent, non-contradictory rules that are capable of being known and thus followed on a reasonably reliable basis'[4] and 'appear not to deliver on a core component of fair process, especially the demands of independence (and impartiality)'.[5]

---

[1] Jeremy Waldron, 'Is the Rule of Law an Essentially Contested Concept (in Florida)?' (2002) 21 Law & Phil 137.

[2] For an overview, see Stephan W Schill, 'International Investment Law and the Rule of Law' in Jeffrey Jowell, J Christopher Thomas and Jan van Zyl Smit (eds), *Rule of Law Symposium 2014: The Importance of the Rule of Law in Promoting Development* (Academy Publishing 2015) 81; Peter-Tobias Stoll, 'International Investment Law and the Rule of Law' (2018) 9 Go JIL 267. See also Mavluda Sattorova, *The Impact of Investment Treaty Law on Host States: Enabling Good Governance?* (Hart 2018) 21–25.

[3] Kenneth J Vandevelde, 'Model Bilateral Investment Treaties: The Way Forward' (2011) 18 Southwest JIL 307, 313. See alsoRudolf Dolzer, 'The Impact of International Investment Treaties on Domestic Administrative Law' (2005) 37 NYU J Intl L & Pol 972; Susan D Franck, 'Foreign Direct Investment, Investment Treaty Arbitration, and the Rule of Law' (2006) 19 Pac McGeorge Global Bus & Dev LJ 337; Thomas W Wälde, 'The Specific Nature of Investment Arbitration' in Philippe Khan and Thomas W Wälde (eds), *New Aspects of International Investment Law* (Martinus Nijhoff 2007) 43, 78; Nicholas J Birch, Borzu Sabahi and Ian Laird, 'International Investment Law Regime and the Rule of Law as a Pre-Condition for International Development' in Todd Weiler and Freya Baetens (eds), *New Directions in International Economic Law* (Brill 2011) 309, 319–22; Roberto Echandi, 'What Do Developing Countries Expect from the International Investment Regime?' in José E Alvarez and others (eds), *The Evolving International Investment Regime: Expectations, Realities, Options* (OUP 2011) 3, 13; Benjamin K Guthrie, 'Beyond Investment Protection: An Examination of the Potential Influence of Investment Treaties on Domestic Rule of Law' (2013) 45 NYU J Intl L & Pol 1151, 1186–98; Locknie Hsu, 'The Rule of Law and Foreign Investment: Treaty Contexts and the Rule of Law' in Jowell, Thomas and van Zyl Smit (n 2) 129; Schill (n 2); Stephan W Schill and Vladislav Djanic, 'Wherefore Art Thou? Towards a Public Interest-Based Justification of International Investment Law' (2018) 33 ICSID Rev—FILJ 25; Stoll (n 2); Jeswald W Salacuse, *The Law of Investment Treaties* (3rd edn, OUP 2021) 147–48.

[4] Gus Van Harten, 'Investment Treaty Arbitration, Procedural Fairness, and the Rule of Law' in Stephan W Schill (ed), *International Investment Law and Comparative Public Law* (OUP 2010) 627, 628.

[5] ibid 629. See further Thomas Buergenthal, 'The Proliferation of Disputes, Dispute Settlement Procedures and Respect for the Rule of Law' (2006) 22(4) Arb Int L 495, 497–98; David Schneiderman, *Constitutionalizing Economic Globalization: Investment Rules and Democracy's Promise* (CUP 2008) 205–22; Kyla Tienhaara, *The*

August Reinisch and Stephan W. Schill, *Introduction* In: *Investment Protection Standards and the Rule of Law.* Edited by: August Reinisch and Stephan W. Schill, Oxford University Press. © August Reinisch and Stephan W. Schill 2023. DOI: 10.1093/oso/9780192864581.003.0001

For a long time, these controversies were largely academic, but recently they have reached the constitutional courts in a number of jurisdictions.[6] In those proceedings, compliance of investment treaties and investor-State dispute settlement mechanisms with constitutional safeguards connected to the rule of law, among other constitutional principles, is at stake. This includes concerns related to the independence and impartiality of adjudicators in dispute resolution, access to justice for disputes brought by and against foreign investors, equality of treatment, legal certainty, and predictability. Constitutional courts so far have not, however, found international investment agreements to be contrary to constitutional guarantees of the rule of law. On the contrary, the Colombian Constitutional Court even went as far as stating, in a 2019 decision concerning the constitutionality of a treaty containing rules on investment protection, that investment treaties 'contribute to the materialization of constitutional principles of the rule of law'.[7]

Expropriation of Environmental Governance: Protecting Foreign Investors at the Expense of Public Policy (CUP 2009) 121ff and 275–78; Gus Van Harten, 'Perceived Bias in Investment Treaty Arbitration' in Michael Waibel and others (eds), *The Backlash against Investment Arbitration: Perceptions and Reality* (Kluwer 2010) 433, 452–53; Thomas Schultz and Cédric Dupont, 'Investment Arbitration: Promoting the Rule of Law or Over-Empowering Investors? A Quantitative Empirical Study' (2015) 25 EJIL 1147; Kate Miles, 'Investor-State Dispute Settlement: Conflict, Convergence, and Future Directions' in Marc Bungenberg and others (eds), *European Yearbook of International Economic Law 2016* (Springer 2016) 273, 278, and 290–94; Alessandra Arcuri, 'The Great Asymmetry and the Rule of Law in International Investment Arbitration' in Lisa E Sachs, Lise J Johnson and Jesse Coleman (eds), *Yearbook on International Investment Law and Policy 2018* (OUP 2020) 394, 411–13; see also the literature discussed in Franck (n 3) 365–67; see further Alfred-Maurice de Zayas, 'Report of the Independent Expert on the Promotion of a Democratic and Equitable International Order' (14 July 2015) UN Doc A/HRC/30/44 and 'Report of the Independent Expert on the Promotion of a Democratic and Equitable International Order' (5 August 2015) UN Doc A/70/285. See also the criticism voiced by numerous academics from across the globe in a 2010 public statement by Gus Van Harten and others, 'Public Statement on the International Investment Regime' (*Osgoode*, 31 August 2010) <www.osgoode.yorku.ca/public-statement-international-investment-regime-31-august-2010/> accessed 14 April 2022 (positing, inter alia, that '[i]nvestment treaty arbitration as currently constituted is not a fair, independent, and balanced method for the resolution of investment disputes and therefore should not be relied on for this purpose'); similarly, Gus Van Harten and others, 'An Open Letter from Lawyers to the Negotiators of the Trans-Pacific Partnership Urging the Rejection of Investor-State Dispute Settlement' (*TPP Legal*, 8 May 2012) <https://tpplegal.wordpress.com/open-letter/> accessed 14 April 2022 (stating, inter alia, that '[t]he current regime's expansive definition of covered investments and government actions, the grant of expansive substantive investor rights that extend beyond domestic law, the increasing use of this mechanism to skirt domestic court systems and the structural problems inherent in the arbitral regime are corrosive of the rule of law and fairness').

[6] See eg Constitutional Chamber of the Supreme Court of Costa Rica, Resolution No 2007-09469 (3 July 2007) (on the Central America Free Trade Agreement); Constitutional Court of Colombia, Judgment C-252/19 (6 June 2019) (on the 2014 France–Colombia BIT) and Judgment C-254/19 (6 June 2019) (on the 2013 Israel–Colombia Free Trade Agreement). The Constitutional Court of Ecuador has, in a series of cases between 2010 and 2014, concluded that several bilateral investment treaties (BITs) providing for investor-State arbitration were contrary to art 422 of the Ecuadorian Constitution, which prohibits the State from concluding international treaties or instruments that yield sovereign jurisdiction to international arbitration institutions for contractual and commercial disputes between the State and foreign natural persons or legal entities. A further request for interpretation, lodged in 2018, asking whether the prohibition set forth in art 422 of the Ecuadorian Constitution also applies to international investment disputes that are neither contractual nor commercial in nature, has been rejected by the Court as inadmissible, see Constitutional Court of Ecuador, Judgment No 2-18-IC/22 (12 January 2022). The Comprehensive Economic and Trade Agreement (CETA) concluded between Canada and the European Union (EU) has occupied several national courts, see eg German Constitutional Court, Case No 2 BvR 1368/16, 2 BvR 1444/16, 2 BvR 1482/16, 2 BvR 1823/16, 2 BvE 3/16, Judgment (13 October 2016), Case No 2 BvR 1444/16, 2 BvR 1482/16, 2 BvR 1823/16, 2 BvE 3/16, Order (7 December 2016) (both concerning provisional measures), Case No BvR 1368/16, 2 BvR 1444/16, 2 BvR 1482/16, 2 BvR 1823/16, 2 BvE 3/16, Order (9 February 2022); Conseil constitutionnel (France), Decision No 2017-749 DC (31 July 2017); High Court of Ireland, *Costello v Government of Ireland and ors* [2021] IEHC 600; Federal Court of Canada, *The Honourable Paul Helleyer, PC et al v Justin Trudeau et al*, Case No T-1789-16 (registered 21 October 2016, discontinued 13 June 2017). A challenge against the Trans-Pacific Partnership (TPP) before the Tokyo District Court was unsuccessful, see 'District Court Strikes Down Suit Aimed at Keeping Japan Out of TPP' (*The Japan Times*, 8 June 2017) <www.japantimes.co.jp/news/2017/06/08/national/crime-legal/district-court-strikes-suit-aimed-keeping-japan-tpp/> accessed 7 March 2022.

[7] Constitutional Court of Colombia, Judgment C-252/19 (6 June 2019) para 93; see also the discussion of the elements of the rule of law ibid paras 94–95 and para 203.

Much of the debate, as well as constitutional litigation addressing the interrelations between the investment treaty regime and the rule of law, concern the institution and functioning of investment treaty arbitration, whether it renders independent, impartial, neutral, predictable, and overall fair justice and hence advances the rule of law, or whether it would be preferable, or even necessary, from a rule-of-law perspective to settle disputes before domestic courts or a to-be-established international court.[8] The present book does not focus on the rule-of-law implications of investment arbitration, but zooms in on the substantive standards of treatment contained in international investment agreements and their interrelation with the rule of law. It builds on approaches in investment law scholarship that have used the rule of law to justify the existence of certain standards of treatment as a substitute of, or compensation for shortcomings in, domestic law and governance,[9] and to inform their interpretation, and application, most notably as far as fair and equitable treatment (FET) is concerned,[10] and expands those approaches to other standards of treatment. In addition, the book engages with rule-of-law-based criticism of how substantive standards of treatment are interpreted and applied.[11] Relevant criticism concerns the lack of consistency, predictability, and legal certainty in the interpretation of substantive standards of treatment, insufficient attention to regulatory space and competing rights and interests, difficulties in how investment law interacts with domestic law and other international legal regimes, ignorance of domestic investors, and governance gaps in respect of obligations of foreign investors.

This book therefore has three objectives: (1) to develop a more systematic assessment of the extent to which substantive standards of treatment reflect rule-of-law elements; (2) to set out how substantive standards of treatment under investment agreements interact with the host State's law and its domestic court system, as well as contractual and other commitments under international law and thereby further the rule of law; and (3) to analyse critically the rule-of-law problems or rule-of-law lacunae that substantive standards of treatment raise. The book combines doctrinal analysis of the core substantive standards of treatment and their connection to the concept of the rule of law with discussion of the potential the rule of law has in guiding the interpretation and application of substantive standards of treatment and in elucidating the rule-of-law blind spots that substantive standards

---

[8] See for example Van Harten (n 4) 627 (stating that '[i]nvestment treaty arbitration is often promoted as a fair, rules-based system and, in this respect, as something that advances the rule of law. This claim is undermined, however, by procedural and institutional aspects of the system that suggest it will tend to favour claimants and, more specifically, those states and other actors that wield power over appointing authorities or the system as a whole'). For further discussion and references on the relationship between investment arbitration and the rule of law, see August Reinisch, 'The Rule of Law in International Investment Arbitration' in Photini Pazartzis and others (eds), *Reconceptualising the Rule of Law in Global Governance, Resources, Investment and Trade* (Hart 2016) 291.

[9] See Tom Ginsburg, 'International Substitutes for Domestic Institutions: Bilateral Investment Treaties' (2005) 25 IRLE 107. For further discussion of investment law as a form of compensatory constitutionalism, see Joshua Paine, 'Investment Protection Standards as Global Constitutional Law' in Stephan W Schill and Christian J Tams (eds), *International Investment Protection and Constitutional Law* (Edward Elgar 2022) 255.

[10] See eg Marc Jacob and Stephan W Schill, 'Fair and Equitable Treatment: Content, Practice, Method' in Marc Bungenberg and others (eds), *International Investment Law: A Handbook* (Hart 2015) 700, 710; August Reinisch and Christoph Schreuer, *International Protection of Investments. The Substantive Standards* (CUP 2020) 342; Kenneth J Vandevelde, 'A Unified Theory of Fair and Equitable Treatment' (2010) 43 NYU J Intl L & Pol 43; Nicolas Angelet, 'Fair and Equitable Treatment' in Rüdiger Wolfrum (ed), *Max Planck Encyclopedia of Public International Law* (online edn, March 2011) para 5 ('the standard is essentially concerned with the rule of law in international investment protection').

[11] For criticism, see the reference above in n 5.

of treatment leave. This approach, in our view, is important for a comprehensive assessment and evaluation of the rule-of-law implications of international investment agreements.

II. Working Concept of the Rule of Law

One of the key challenges for any project dealing with the rule of law, in particular multi-author projects, is to provide a working definition of the concept that can be shared among contributors and that is acceptable to a broad audience without becoming entirely meaningless. The concept of the rule of law is highly complex and its precise content open-ended, ambiguous, and contested.[12] Moreover, the precise concept of the rule of law may differ from one legal regime to another.

Despite these challenges to developing a definition, certain conceptual commonalities or models of the rule of law can be identified.[13] Broadly speaking, two conceptions of the rule of law are generally distinguished. These are, on the one hand, procedural conceptions of the rule of law (which are often also referred to as the 'thin' or 'formal' rule of law) and, on the other hand, substantive conceptions of the rule of law (which are often also referred to as the 'thick' or 'material' rule of law). While the former conception focuses on formal qualities of the law (such as supremacy of the law, predictability, and certainty of the law) and procedural guarantees (such as due process and access to justice), the latter conception encompasses, in addition to formal characteristics, content-related aspects of the law (such as compliance with human rights or standards of democratic decision-making).

Which conception to follow for the inquiry in this book may have a great impact on the analysis and evaluation of different standards of treatment and the rule-of-law blind spots addressed. A formal approach to the rule of law, for example, while appropriately capturing the content of certain standards of treatment, will have difficulties in capturing the engagement of substantive investment protection standards with competing human rights and other non-investment concerns. In turn, a material approach to the rule of law, while being well equipped to qualify shortcomings of the investment treaty regimes as rule-of-law concerns, could result in materially expanding the content of substantive standards of treatment and reduce the greater regulatory space host States may enjoy if the same standard of treatment was understood to only require compliance with formal rule-of-law elements. This may call for flexibility and nuance depending on the context of the inquiry.

In light of the controversies about the different conceptions and content of the rule of law, and the need for flexibility, we suggest that, for purposes of the analysis in this book, a working definition of the rule of law should not be limited to a purely formal understanding, but encompass elements of the material rule of law as well. This has the advantage that substantive standards of treatment in international investment treaties can be measured against a more demanding and broader conception of the rule of law, thus giving investment treaty standards full exposure to a broad set of rule-of-law elements. Adopting a narrower, thin

---

[12] See eg Lon L Fuller, *The Morality of Law* (Yale UP 1964); Joseph Raz, *The Authority of Law* (2nd edn, OUP 2009); Jeremy Waldron, *The Law* (Routledge 1990); David Dyzenhaus (ed), *Recrafting the Rule of Law: The Limits of Legal Order* (Hart 1999); Brian Z Tamanaha, *On the Rule of Law: History, Politics, Theory* (CUP 2004); Tom Bingham, *The Rule of Law* (Penguin 2011).

[13] For further discussion on this and the following, see ILA Committee on the Rule of Law and International Investment Law: Report 2018 (2018) 78 ILA Reports of Conferences 380.

version of the rule of law, by contrast, would, from the outset, restrict the analysis of the substantive standards of treatment, and thereby also influence the outcome of the analysis. At the same time, adopting a broader working concept does not mean that using a narrower version of the rule of law would not be appropriate for the specific inquiry in question. The broader working definition, in other words, has the purpose of allowing exposure of investment treaty disciplines to the broadest possible rule-of-law inquiry, but does not suggest in any way that investment treaty disciplines should be understood or interpreted in light of a thick concept of the rule of law, or would necessarily need to be measured against the demands flowing from it.

Furthermore, it is important to stress that this book does not attempt to inquire into, let alone answer, the question of whether investment treaty disciplines comply with a specific constitutional system and its understanding of the rule of law. The present inquiry is broader and takes place on a conceptual–theoretical level, rather than at the level of constitutional law. Consequently, the working concept of the rule of law must be independent of how the concept is used and understood in any specific domestic legal system. We therefore consider it most appropriate to rely on concepts found in an international or transnational context. Such concepts are not only better suited for the conceptual–theoretical inquiry of this book, they are also more broadly—ideally even universally—acceptable than any specific national conception of the rule of law.

The working concept we suggest to adopt against the background of these considerations is the rule-of-law definition developed by the United Nations. This definition is broadly accepted and reflects both aspects that are generally considered to be part of the thin rule of law, as well as aspects generally associated with a thick version of the rule of law. In the UN Secretary-General's 2004 report 'The Rule of Law and Transitional Justice in Conflict and Post-Conflict Societies', the following rule-of-law elements are identified:

> The 'rule of law' … refers to a principle of governance in which all persons, institutions and entities, public and private, including the State itself, are accountable to laws that are publicly promulgated, equally enforced and independently adjudicated, and which are consistent with international human rights norms and standards. It requires, as well, measures to ensure adherence to the principles of supremacy of law, equality before the law, accountability to the law, fairness in the application of the law, separation of powers, participation in decision-making, legal certainty, avoidance of arbitrariness and procedural and legal transparency.[14]

While this UN report was adopted in a very specific transitional justice context, the same definition was later transposed by the UN Secretary-General in its 2012 report 'Delivering Justice: Programme of Action to Strengthen the Rule of Law at the National and International Levels' to formulate rule-of-law demands vis-à-vis national legal systems generally.[15] The 2012 UN General Assembly Declaration on the Rule of Law[16] contains similar principles,

---

[14] UNSC, 'The Rule of Law and Transitional Justice in Conflict and Post-Conflict Societies, Report of the Secretary-General' (23 August 2004) UN Doc S/2004/616, para 6.

[15] See United Nations, 'Delivering Justice: Programme of Action to Strengthen the Rule of Law at the National and International Levels, Report of the Secretary General' (16 March 2012) UN Doc A/66/749, para 2.

[16] UNGA Res 67/1 'Declaration of the High-level Meeting of the General Assembly on the Rule of Law at the National and International Levels' (30 November 2012) UN Doc A/RES/67/1.

albeit on a more abstract level, when it calls for 'an effective, just, non-discriminatory and equitable delivery of public services pertaining to the rule of law, including criminal, civil and administrative justice',[17] expresses the need for judicial independence and impartiality as 'an essential prerequisite for upholding the rule of law',[18] and demands effective 'access to justice'.[19] In addition to these mostly 'procedural' rule-of-law aspects, the 2012 Declaration also endorses a more substantive concept of the rule of law when it refers to 'just, fair and equitable laws' as well as to 'equal protection of the law' 'without any discrimination'.[20]

It is against the broad working definition of the rule of law, as used by the UN, that the contributors to this book have been asked to scrutinize the substantive standards of treatment contained in international investment treaties, and to assess to what extent these reflect, further, or limit the rule of law. Contributors were also invited to assess in their contributions what kind of rule-of-law definition the substantive standard in question conforms or does not conform to and what rule-of-law concept should serve as an appropriate yardstick against which to measure a certain substantive investment protection standard. Leaving these definitional questions deliberately open appeared the most appropriate way to ensure a comprehensive assessment of the relationship between the substantive standards of treatment and the rule of law and to allow for different views and conclusions to be drawn by different contributors depending on the rule-of-law concept used. After all, forcing contributors into a conceptual straitjacket by fixing them to just one possible definition of the rule of law would not have been appropriate, as the evaluation of international investment treaties may well differ depending on whether a formal or a material version of the rule of law is used as a normative yardstick, and it is a matter of controversy which version of the rule of law would be appropriate for this purpose and why.

III. The Contributions to this Book

The contributions to this book are structured along the lines of the different sets of issues set out above. Part I addresses the 'positive' relationship between the substantive standards of treatment in international investment agreements and the rule of law, and explores to what extent specific standards of treatment—the rules on expropriation, FET, full protection and security (FPS), etc.—reflect elements that form part of the rule of law, concentrating on host State executive and legislative conduct. Part II looks at how investment protection standards impact the enforcement of, and shape the host State's compliance with, domestic law,

[17] ibid para 12 ('We reaffirm the principle of good governance and commit to an effective, just, non-discriminatory and equitable delivery of public services pertaining to the rule of law, including criminal, civil and administrative justice, commercial dispute settlement and legal aid').

[18] ibid para 13 ('We are convinced that the independence of the judicial system, together with its impartiality and integrity, is an essential prerequisite for upholding the rule of law and ensuring that there is no discrimination in the administration of justice').

[19] ibid para 14 ('We emphasize the right of equal access to justice for all, including members of vulnerable groups, and the importance of awareness-raising concerning legal rights, and in this regard we commit to taking all necessary steps to provide fair, transparent, effective, non-discriminatory and accountable services that promote access to justice for all, including legal aid').

[20] ibid para 2 ('We recognize that the rule of law applies to all States equally, and to international organizations, including the United Nations and its principal organs, and that respect for and promotion of the rule of law and justice should guide all of their activities and accord predictability and legitimacy to their actions. We also recognize that all persons, institutions and entities, public and private, including the State itself, are accountable to just, fair and equitable laws and are entitled without any discrimination to equal protection of the law').

contractual commitments, and other international commitments, both in domestic courts and in investment treaty arbitration. Part III contains contributions that address rule-of-law problems or rule-of-law lacunae that exist in the application of substantive standards of treatment.

A. Part I: Standards of Treatment as Rule-of-Law Demands for Domestic Regulatory Action

Part I focuses on the extent to which the substantive standards of treatment reflect rule-of-law elements for host State regulatory (administrative and legislative) action. It opens with Martins Paparinskis's analysis of FET, a standard that appears in most international investment agreements and that arbitral tribunals most frequently find to have been violated by host State conduct.[21] Paparinskis shows that arbitral jurisprudence on FET reflects several elements that form part of a formal version of the rule of law. This holds true in particular for the prohibition of arbitrariness, the protection of legitimate expectations, and the requirement of due process. At the same time, Paparinskis warns of the dangers of conflating FET with (comparative) domestic analogies of the rule of law, as this may erode trust in normal methods of public international law reasoning, namely recourse to the sources of international law, in particular the customary international law minimum standard of treatment, and to accepted canons of treaty interpretation. Thus, while there are good reasons to understand FET as a positive expression of the rule of law, this should not allow for 'conceptual looseness' in analysing what obligations States have undertaken under public international law in including FET provisions in investment treaties. While the rule of law is therefore powerful in reconstructing arbitral jurisprudence on FET, it should be treated with caution in providing normative guidance for the interpretation and application of FET.

Caroline Henckels then focuses on one specific element of FET, namely the protection of legitimate expectations.[22] Unlike Paparinskis, Henckels attributes normative guidance to the rule of law for justifying and delimiting the contours of legitimate expectations. She insists, however, that such guidance should be limited to the elements associated with the thin or formal conception of the rule of law, rather than the thick or substantive version, as this avoids conflating the rule of law with political or moral ideals about the rule of good law. Given the ambiguity of FET clauses, a thick rule-of-law approach would risk reading such clauses to encompass good governance obligations that reflect the ideals and interests of capital-exporting, but not those of capital-importing countries. Against this background, Henckels argues that the protection of legitimate expectations can be justified based on two elements of the formal rule of law: legal certainty and the prohibition of arbitrariness. The combination of both of these elements means that host States can make changes to the law or legal entitlements as long as these are not arbitrary. This, in turn, depends on the type of government conduct that generated the expectation and the reasons for their frustration. The resulting spectrum will range from retroactive changes to individual promises only exceptionally complying with the protection of legitimate expectations, at one end, to

---

[21] Martins Paparinskis, 'The Rule of Law and Fair and Equitable Treatment' (in this volume) 23.
[22] Caroline Henckels, 'Legitimate Expectations and the Rule of Law in International Investment Law' (in this volume) 43.

prospective changes to general government policy only exceptionally frustrating legitimate expectations, at the other end, with several intermediate categories in between. This shows how the rule of law can usefully be employed to tailor the content of how to apply the concept of legitimate expectations to host State administrative and legislative action.

Marc Bungenberg turns to an analysis of the provisions on expropriation contained in international investment agreements. He argues that the prohibition of unlawful expropriations is an implementation of the rule of law itself.[23] Drawing comparisons with human rights treaties and case law by regional human rights courts, and adopting a broad conception of the rule of law, he highlights that the protection of property is closely associated with the concept of rule of law. Bungenberg also finds several discrete elements of the rule of law in the conditions that the provisions in investment agreements typically impose for the legality of expropriations, such as non-discrimination and due process. While the requirement of due process and non-discrimination is a 'clear expression of core rule-of-law demands',[24] he argues that also the 'requirements of public purpose and the obligation to compensate investors are reflective of the rule of law'.[25] The criterion of public purpose excludes arbitrary measures; the obligation to compensate ensures that the public at large is not unjustly enriched at the expense of individual investors. Bungenberg also addresses how arbitral tribunals have relied on rule-of-law criteria to distinguish between indirect expropriations that require compensation and regulatory action that are based on a State's exercise of its police powers and its right to regulate and that do not require compensation. In this respect, he emphasizes the importance of the principle of proportionality, which helps distinguish between legitimate regulatory action and indirect expropriations by providing for a test to balance the interests of foreign investors and public interests pursued by the State. Finding its origins in US and European constitutional law, and being reflected in the texts of recent investment agreements, including the Comprehensive Economic and Trade Agreement (CETA) concluded between Canada and the European Union, proportionality, Bungenberg argues, is also an important 'element of the rule of law'.[26]

Sebastián Mantilla Blanco analyses the connections between FPS, a standard that is included, often alongside FET, in most international investment agreements, and the rule of law.[27] Drawing on comparative constitutional law analysis, Mantilla Blanco maintains that FPS can be analogized with the security function that constitutional law and constitutional theory attribute to the State. Being a prerequisite for States to enact and maintain a legal system that functions under the rule of law, the idea of the security function is that the State monopolizes the use of force and guards investments against private offences and other sources of risk that do not emanate from the State itself. It is in this context that Mantilla Blanco considers the rule of law as 'a useful explanatory tool of the main features of the FPS standard and the risks it covers'.[28] The rule of law supports a wide reading of the risks against which FPS provisions protect, including interferences by private individuals, counterinsurgency operations, and foreign States, and clarifies what the host State's obligation to exercise due diligence in protecting against these risks as part of FPS means: ensuring treating

---

[23] Marc Bungenberg, '(Direct and Indirect) Expropriation and the Rule of Law' (in this volume) 61.
[24] ibid 64.
[25] ibid.
[26] ibid 63.
[27] Sebastián Mantilla Blanco, 'Full Protection and Security and the Rule of Law' (in this volume) 81.
[28] ibid 91.

foreigners and nationals equally in preventing harm, offering possibilities for redress, and complying with the applicable domestic law in the host State, while also taking into consideration the host State's duty to protect the public interest.

Next, Elizabeth Whitsitt examines the two types of non-discrimination provisions regularly included in international investment agreements—national treatment and most-favoured-nation (MFN) clauses—from the perspective of the rule of law.[29] Drawing on Dworkin's notion of the rule of law, which encompasses elements of thin and thick versions of the rule of law, and overlaps with the UN definition set out above, Whitsitt explains that equal treatment constitutes a core element of the rule of law. Investment treaties pick up this concern and ensure equal treatment for foreign investors to compete on equal footing with investors from the home as well as any third State. Such an understanding of the rule of law can then be used, Whitsitt posits, to provide solutions to many of the difficult issues that have befuddled arbitral tribunals and scholars of international investment law in respect of the interpretation and application of MFN and national treatment clauses. Rule-of-law arguments, Whitsitt suggests, can be used, inter alia, to support, their wording permitting, the application of MFN clauses to questions of dispute settlement and standards of treatment afforded under investment treaties with third States, and to provide proper solutions as to when investors are in like circumstances and are subject to less favourable treatment (eg whether they have to operate in the same business sector or not), or have to accept differential treatment because of the regulatory purpose at stake. Notably, Whitsitt argues that a Dworkinian approach to the rule of law is open to a government intervening and regulating bona fide in order to address market externalities and market distortions. As Whitsitt shows, a rule-of-law approach to national treatment and MFN provisions therefore allows the interests of investors in protection and that of States in efficient market regulation to be balanced.

In the final chapter in Part I, Manjiao Chi analyses how demands for transparency of a State's regulatory action interact with the rule of law.[30] Transparency obligations can arise from specific provisions in international investment agreements that require the publication of relevant legal instruments, mandate openness between foreign investors and host States in respect of, sometimes even the participation of foreign investors in, lawmaking and standard-setting, or require the establishment of contact points in the host State for concerns of foreign investors. Alternatively, transparency obligations, in particular in respect of the administration of domestic laws and regulations, may arise in the context of obligations to ensure FET. Modern and more detailed FET clauses at times expressly mention transparency; older FET clauses, in turn, are at times interpreted accordingly, as some examples in arbitral practice show. Chi argues that regulatory transparency is indeed an element of the rule of law; it forms part of the formal rule of law, such as predictability and legal certainty, and fosters further-reaching goals of good governance, participation, and democracy. Transparency, as a consequence, should not be seen one-sidedly as an investment protection standard, but rather as a standard that is supportive of government under the rule of law.

---

[29] Elizabeth Whitsitt, 'International Investment Law's Non-Discrimination Norms and the Rule of Law' (in this volume) 105.
[30] Manjiao Chi, 'Regulatory Transparency in International Investment Law: From an Investment Protection Requirement to a Rule-of-Law Requirement' (in this volume) 127.

All in all, the contributions in Part I of the book demonstrate that the core standards of treatment in international investment agreements reflect various elements of the rule of law. While mostly including elements of the thin or formal version of the rule of law, such as predictability, the prohibition of arbitrariness, or due process, elements of a thick or material version of the rule of law are equally present. This holds true in respect of the protection of legitimate expectations, transparency, and equal treatment. Overall, the rule-of-law content of investment treaty standards is remarkable, and supports the vision that these substantive standards of treatment aim at implementing the rule of law in investor-State relations.

B. Part II: Standards of Treatment as Interfaces between International and Domestic Rule of Law

The contributions in Part II of the book look at how the substantive standards of treatment function as interfaces between the international and the domestic rule of law in holding host States, as well as foreign investors, to commitments either under domestic law, in investor-State contracts or similar instruments, or other international legal frameworks, thereby contributing itself to the rule of law.

Ursula Kriebaum opens this part of the analysis with a chapter setting out the requirements that different standards of treatment in investment treaties set for the functioning of domestic courts, namely the prohibition of denial of justice as an element of FET, rules on expropriation, and specific treaty clauses requiring host States to provide effective means for the assertion of claims and the enforcement of rights.[31] This reflects the idea that the domestic judiciary fulfils an important function in ensuring that both host States and foreign investors comply with the (principally domestic) law governing their relationship, thus serving as 'gatekeepers of the rule of law'[32] in any legal system. Kriebaum spells out how the three standards of treatment in question aim at ensuring that domestic courts, or more precisely, the domestic court system as a whole, forms part of, and acts in accordance with, the rule of law. Frequently drawing parallels to the fair trial obligations contained in international human rights law, notably the European Convention on Human Rights, Kriebaum shows that the three substantive standards of treatment she addresses, while not mentioning the rule of law explicitly, impose a number of rule-of-law obligations in respect of the domestic judiciary. They require, inter alia, that access to justice is ensured, that justice is administered by independent and impartial courts, without undue delay, in good faith, in a non-arbitrary fashion, without discrimination, and in compliance with due process (in particular as regards the right to be heard and the right to a reasoned decision), and results in enforceable judicial decisions. At the same time, the investment treaty disciplines in question are generally deferential in respect of judicial conduct, with violations requiring that domestic remedies must have been exhausted in principle, and only exceptionally allowing for the review of the outcome of judicial decisions.

Another type of provision that can have the effect of ensuring compliance of host States with specific legal commitments made to foreign investors in legal instruments other

---

[31] Ursula Kriebaum, 'Rule-of-Law Demands and the Domestic Judiciary: Denial of Justice, Judicial Expropriation, Effective Means' (in this volume) 145.
[32] ibid.

than the investment treaty itself, are umbrella clauses, which are analysed by Arnauld de Nanteuil.[33] De Nanteuil conceptualizes these clauses as tools to ensure foreign investors' access to justice—albeit before investment treaty tribunals, not domestic courts—by allowing for the adjudication of disputes as to whether host States comply with specific legal commitments made vis-à-vis foreign investors. This fulfils, his argument goes, one of the core demands of the rule of law. De Nanteuil's analysis is not limited, however, to pointing to this important rule-of-law effect of umbrella clauses. He also uses the rule-of-law function of umbrella clauses to provide arguments on several of the hotly contested issues that arose in arbitral jurisprudence in connection with the interpretation and application of these clauses. De Nanteuil argues, for example, that the rule-of-law effect of umbrella clauses favours a broad interpretation of the clauses, as applying to contractual commitments and specific unilateral undertakings of host States under domestic law or other international legal instruments, and to cover sovereign as well as commercial conduct that is claimed to contravene commitments the host State made. Such interpretations, of course, are always subject to the proviso that the wording of the clause in question permits such a broad interpretation.

The interplay between investment treaty commitments, the domestic rule of law, and compliance of the host State with other international legal commitments that are relevant for an investment project are also dealt with by Velimir Živković.[34] He addresses how different substantive standards of treatment—including FET, umbrella clauses, and provisions on expropriation—can be used by foreign investors to ensure that host States comply with their own domestic law and commitments under other international legal regimes, such as international human rights treaties or treaties protecting human health or environmental concerns. Surveying arbitration proceedings that have used substantive standards of treatment to this effect, and analysing how investment tribunals engage with such outside norms, Živković points to the important function of investment treaty standards not only to give rise to autonomous obligations that host States have to live up to in their treatment of foreign investors and their investments, but to provide mechanisms to enforce commitments made by host States in domestic and international legal instruments beyond the four corners of the investment treaty in question. Such a use of substantive investment treaty disciplines, Živković argues, is a positive development that 'can bolster the international and the national rule of law and offer credibility to claims that treaty standards are actually "good-governance standards embodied in investment protection treaties"'.[35] Živković also notes, however, that the use of substantive standards of treatment to engage and ensure compliance with domestic law and other international legal regimes cuts both ways: it applies to host State compliance, just as it applies to investor compliance with the different layers of the legal framework in question.

Martin Jarrett then shifts perspective from the host State's compliance with its legal obligations as a rule-of-law demand to that of the investor.[36] He addresses to what extent an investor's compliance with domestic law is relevant for the interpretation and application of

---

[33] Arnaud de Nanteuil, 'Umbrella Clauses and the Rule of Law' (in this volume) 173.

[34] Velimir Živković, 'The Use of Investment Treaty Standards to Enforce Other International Legal Regimes and Domestic Law' (in this volume) 193.

[35] ibid 194.

[36] Martin A Jarrett, 'Legality Requirements: Managing the Tension between the Domestic and the International Rule of Law' (in this volume) 215.

substantive standards of treatment in investment treaties. Jarrett's focus, in this context, is on legality clauses that condition the application of the substantive standards of treatment on the investor's, or the investment's, compliance with domestic law. In Jarrett's view, such conditioning and the connected denial of investment treaty protection, has the effect of holding investors accountable for breaches of domestic law. While this contributes to ensuring compliance with the domestic rule of law, it also limits the extent to which the rule-of-law components of the substantive standards of treatment in investment treaties can guide and limit host State treatment of illegal investments. Against the background of this dilemma, Jarrett advocates a narrow reading of legality clauses, opposes the construction of implicit legality clauses, and engages critically with the mainstream approach of arbitral tribunals to sanction corruption by denying investors any protection under investment treaties. Overall, Jarrett argues, it is preferable to allow tribunals to assess both the investor's compliance with the domestic rule of law and the host State's compliance with the international rule of law by going to the merits of a dispute, rather than declining jurisdiction to sanction investor misconduct.

All in all, the contributions in Part II of the book show that the standards of treatment in international investment agreements have an important function in ensuring that the host State complies with its own law, contractual commitments made vis-à-vis foreign investors and their investments, and international legal obligations other than those arising from an investment agreement. Such compliance is an important component of the rule of law and investment agreements further it by ensuring access to justice either before domestic courts or investment treaty tribunals. Importantly, however, this rule-of-law function is not restricted to holding the host State to the rule of law; investment treaties also contain other mechanisms to enhance the domestic rule of law, in particular legality provisions, which limit protection under investment treaties to investments made in compliance with domestic law and thus sanction non-compliance of foreign investors with the rule of law.

C. Part III: Rule-of-Law Concerns in the Application of Substantive Standards of Treatment

Part III of the book turns from assessing to what extent the substantive standards of treatment reflect rule-of-law requirements for host States and foreign investors to the rule-of-law problems or rule-of-law lacunae that exist in respect of the interpretation and application of substantive standards of treatment. Contributions in this part focus on six rule-of-law-related issues: problems connected to the lack of consistency and predictability in the interpretation and application of substantive standards of treatment; concerns connected to arbitral tribunals replacing domestic courts in reviewing government conduct and further developing, through their jurisprudence, the content of substantive standards of treatment or even openly acting as lawmakers in international investment law; the concern that arbitral tribunals may not have sufficient regard in their interpretation and application of substantive standards of treatment to competing public and private interests, to the State's right to regulate, or to competing obligations of the host State arising under other international legal regimes; the rule-of-law shortcomings connected to the inexistence of investor obligations in international investment agreements; the rule-of-law concerns arising from the fact that investment treaties are concerned only with foreign, not domestic investors; and finally the issue whether substantive standards of treatment actually have spill-over effects in domestic governance and are complied with by host States.

Julian Arato starts the analysis of rule-of-law lacunae by exploring the problem of inconsistent interpretations and applications of substantive standards of treatment.[37] Inconsistencies are problematic from the perspective of the rule of law because they negatively impact legal certainty and predictability, two core components of the rule of law. Considering that a lack of legal certainty and predictability in the treatment of foreign investors by the host State may violate the State's investment treaty obligations, in particular the obligation to provide FET, inconsistent interpretations of substantive standards of treatment may undermine the very claim that investment treaty disciplines are rule-of-law instruments. Drawing on a Fullerian approach to the rule of law, Arato cautions against overemphasizing, or 'fetishiz[ing]'[38] consistency and attributing to it a superior rule-of-law value. Instead, consistency is only one among several rule-of-law values. While optimal consistency will be impossible to achieve—as in any, even the most advanced domestic legal system—the yardstick for the investment treaty regime should rather be, Arato claims, to distinguish between tolerable and intolerable inconsistencies. Inconsistencies in interpreting bright-line rules—for example concerning the scope of application of MFN provisions or the distinction between treaty and contract claims—would be less tolerable than inconsistencies in the application of broadly framed standards—such as FET. As Arato argues, achieving some of the societal goals that form part of (a thick notion of) the rule of law may require trade-offs in respect of other (thin) rule-of-law goals, such as consistency. In the end, Arato muses, the rule of law is itself an ambiguous concept that ties States to broadly framed standards rather than a bright-line rule.

Esmé Shirlow considers the impact of arbitral tribunals' reviews of host State conduct under investment treaty standards on another core component of the rule of law, namely the separation of powers.[39] Subjecting host State conduct to such review comes with two concerns for the separation of powers: first, review of host State conduct by arbitral tribunals risks replacing judicial review of government conduct, which customarily is exercised by domestic courts and fulfils an important role in tying host States to the rule of law; and, second, the involvement of arbitral tribunals in interpreting and applying substantive standards of treatment, in particular standards as open as the ones found in international investment treaties, may lead to arbitral tribunals not restricting themselves to resolving individual disputes before them, but actively developing the applicable law further and acting as lawmakers in international investment law. The former risks unsettling the functioning of the domestic separation of powers, whereas the latter blurs the international separation of powers between arbitral tribunals as adjudicators and States as lawmakers. Focusing on the first rule-of-law concern, Shirlow argues, that the solution lies in developing appropriate standards of review for how arbitral tribunals engage in reviewing host State conduct. These standards have to strike a meaningful balance between domestic and international legal review. Theories of deference, Shirlow shows, are the key to striking that balance and indicating where decision-making authority should rest. Theories of deference would allow arbitral tribunals to tailor the extent of their review on a case-by-case

[37] Julian Arato, 'Two Moralities of Consistency' (in this volume) 235.
[38] See ibid 236.
[39] Esmé Shirlow, 'The Rule of Law, Standards of Review, and the Separation of Powers' (in this volume) 259.

basis—taking account, inter alia, of the legitimacy of the domestic actor whose conduct is reviewed (eg legislative versus administrative action) and whether specific expertise (eg scientific or local knowledge) is involved in the domestic decision under review. This has the promise of resulting in arbitral tribunals and domestic actors jointly ensuring that review of host government conduct abides by the rule of law, without abdicating that role entirely to the international level.

Achieving the right balance between sufficient space for host State conduct and international review is also the topic explored by Steffen Hindelang, Patricia Sarah Stöbener de Mora, and Niels Lachmann.[40] They assess to what extent the review of host State conduct that arbitral tribunals undertake affects the balance between investment and non-investment concerns. Their starting point is the fact that the substantive standards of treatment confer protection on foreign investments, without expressly dealing with the role of competing, non-investment concerns—such as human rights or sustainable development—or the host State's right to regulate. As the authors point out, it constitutes a rule-of-law concern if arbitral tribunals, in interpreting and applying substantive standards of treatment, have insufficient regard to competing concerns, as this results in a one-sided rule of law for investors, rather than for all those subject to the host State's regulatory authority. One-sided results, however, risk undermining the normative foundations of the rule of law, in particular, but not limited to, observance of human rights. At the same time, the authors point out, international law provides the tools to avoid negative rule-of-law impacts, most notably the principle of systemic integration, as laid down in Article 31(3)(c) of the Vienna Convention on the Law of Treaties.[41] Systemic integration can, and in many cases actually does, avoid the concern of one-sided applications of substantive standards of treatment. Still, investment law remains a field of law with a much stronger enforcement mechanism than those available for competing concerns.[42] Thus, the connected rule-of-law concerns go much deeper than the focus of traditional investment treaties on substantive investment protection standards and are more of a structural nature: they are a function of the generally fragmented and unevenly judicialized system of international law.[43]

The chapter by Susan Karamanian turns to a closely related topic: it addresses to what extent granting protection to foreign investors under investment treaties without imposing duties on them, in particular to protect human rights, or even just to abide by obligations under the host State's domestic legal system, falls short of the rule-of-law aspirations of investment treaties.[44] Karamanian argues that the lack of explicit investor obligations indeed results in a rule-of-law gap: while foreign investors are not exempt from complying with domestic law, they can use the substantive standards of treatment in investment treaties

[40] Steffen Hindelang, Patricia Sarah Stöbener de Mora and Niels Lachmann, 'Risking the Rule of Law? The Relationship between Substantive Investment Protection Standards, Human Rights, and Sustainable Development' (in this volume) 279.

[41] Vienna Convention on the Law of Treaties (opened for signature 23 May 1969, entered into force 27 January 1980) 1155 UNTS 331.

[42] See also Anne Orford, 'A Global Rule of Law' in Jens Meierhenrich and Martin Loughlin (eds), *The Cambridge Companion to the Rule of Law* (CUP 2021) 538, 551.

[43] See Benedict Kingsbury, 'International Courts: Uneven Judicialisation in Global Order' in James Crawford and Martti Koskenniemi (eds), *The Cambridge Companion to International Law* (CUP 2012) 203; Jochen von Bernstorff, 'Reflections on the Asymmetric Rule of Law in International Relations' in James Crawford and Sarah Nouwen (eds), *Select Proceedings of the European Society of International Law*, vol 3 (Hart 2012) 381.

[44] Susan L Karamanian, 'International Investment Agreements, Investor Obligations, and the Rule of Law' (in this volume) 301.

to argue that in enforcing such duties the host State violates its investment treaty commitments. This concern is exacerbated if investment treaties result in regulatory chill, that is, if host States prospectively refrain from imposing duties on foreign investors for fear that such impositions may result in breaches of investment treaty disciplines. Karamanian also notes, however, that the sensitivity among all States for holding investors accountable for misconduct is increasing, both in finding ways to use tools under existing agreements to this effect, including the applicable-law clauses to bring in domestic law obligations or having recourse to counterclaims, but also in recent developments in treaty-making. Newer treaties increasingly contain language that mandates investor accountability or even imposes investor obligations under international law. Arbitral tribunals in interpreting investment treaties, and States in making and reforming them, are therefore involved in closing the rule-of-law gap that results from shortcomings in holding investors accountable.

Krista Nadakavukaren Schefer turns to a further, but overall little discussed rule-of-law concern, which is connected to the personal scope of application of international investment treaties and the substantive standards of treatment they contain.[45] She questions how the 'unequal treatment' of domestic investors, who regularly lack the protection that international investment agreements offer to foreign investors, can be squared with the rule-of-law's demand for equal treatment. In a way, the limitation of investment treaty protections to foreign investors is owed to the field's history in diplomatic protection and the still widespread lack of concern of international law, with the exception of human rights, for how States treat their own nationals. What is more, Nadakavukaren notes, whether the different treatment between national and foreign investors is in tension with the principle of equal treatment depends on whether both categories of investors—foreign and domestic—are truly in like circumstances. If there are reasons why international investment protections should be limited to foreign investors, equality could not be said to be affected. Indeed, several constitutional and international courts which have been asked for such reasons found that foreign and domestic investors were not in similar circumstances, either because the protection of the foreign investor at home was the corollary of seeking protection of domestic investors abroad[46] or because foreign investors did not have the same rights, in particular those of political participation, as domestic investors.[47] Alternatively, any inequality that may result from foreign investors being granted rights that domestic investors are lacking could be resolved by elevating the protection of domestic investors under domestic law to that afforded to foreign investors under international law.[48] Formally speaking, therefore, that the substantive standards of treatment are limited to benefit foreign, not domestic investors is neither an equality nor a rule-of-law problem. However, as soon as international law protections are seen as genuine privileges for foreign investors, rather than as compensation for a less-than-equal legal position compared to domestic investors, that perspective becomes brittle.

Finally, Mavluda Sattorova critically assesses to what extent investment treaty disciplines, and particularly the substantive standards of treatment they contain, have a positive

---

[45] Krista Nadakavukaren Schefer, 'Domestic Investors, the Rule of Law, and Equality' (in this volume) 327.

[46] See Conseil constitutionnel (n 6) paras 38–39 (English translation available at <www.conseil-constitutionnel.fr/en/decision/2017/2017749DC.htm> accessed 7 March 2022); Constitutional Court of Colombia (n 7) para 377.

[47] See *Lithgow and ors v United Kingdom*, ECtHR, App no 9006/80, 8 July 1986, para 116; CJEU, Opinion 1/17 (*CETA*) [2019] ECLI:EU:C:2019:341, para 180.

[48] Constitutional Court of Colombia (n 7) paras 120–21. See also High Court of Ireland (n 6) para 166.

spill-over effect on domestic governance, so that the rule-of-law elements of investment treaties actually take root in the host States' domestic legal system.[49] Sattorova acknowledges that, from a conceptual–theoretical perspective, such spill-over effects should happen. Yet, broad empirical analysis and evidence of such effects are still limited. Drawing on her own case studies of eight developing and transitioning economies—Georgia, Jordan, Kazakhstan, Kyrgyzstan, Nigeria, Turkey, Ukraine, and Uzbekistan—involving among others interviews with State officials on the impact of investment treaty disciplines, as well as qualitative studies by colleagues on India and Myanmar, Sattorova casts doubt on whether spill-over effects of investment treaty disciplines can be shown to exist empirically. She identifies a number of problems in the transmission of rule-of-law standards from the international to the national level. These include limited awareness of host State officials of investment treaty disciplines, lack of translating internationally required rule-of-law elements into domestic law reform, a disconnect between investment treaty disciplines and actual law reform even in respect of domestic investment governance, and domestic reforms that mistakenly overreach by overprotecting foreign investors at the expense of systemic improvements. All of these aspects cast doubt on whether investment treaty disciplines actually impact domestic governance. To remedy these rule-of-law lacunae, investment law's rule-of-law ambitions may need to be made clearer and remedies for breach of investment disciplines may need to be adapted to prefer specific performance over monetary damages and compensation. Further, better domestic implementation mechanisms in tandem with capacity-building may be needed in tackling investment-treaty-driven law reform. The answer to the rule-of-law problem Sattorova points to would thus be to have a more complete rule-of-law system, in which the international components are complemented with domestic implementation mechanisms that aim at enhancing the rule of law for all, rather than undoing the (albeit limited) rule-of-law elements the present investment treaty regime exhibits for the sole benefit of foreign investors.

As the contributions in Part III of the book show, investment treaty disciplines are therefore not only reflective of the rule of law; the rule of law is also a powerful tool for critically assessing the treaties' substantive standards of treatment, pointing out shortcomings in the existing regime, and developing improvements to the investment treaty regime that address those shortcomings.

IV. Concluding Remarks: The Rule of Law between Practice and Ideal

The contributions in this book put the substantive standards of treatment contained in international investment treaties to the test of the rule of law. They do so by applying different concepts of the rule of law—partly thin, partly thick—and with different objectives. On the one hand, the contributions explore the positive impact substantive standards of treatment have on the rule of law, addressing to what extent rule-of-law elements are reflected in the substantive standards of treatment and how these standards have an impact

---

[49] Mavluda Sattorova, 'The Impact of Investment Protection Standards on the Rule of Law: Strengthening or Weakening the Domestic Rule of Law?' (in this volume) 353.

on host State compliance with domestic law, contractual undertakings, and other obligations under international law. On the other hand, several contributions expose rule-of-law limits of substantive investment treaty disciplines, whether in respect of inconsistencies in their application, disregard of competing rights and interests, regulatory space, domestic investors, or investor obligations.

What transpires from these studies is that all substantive investment treaty standards analysed reflect core elements of the rule of law—including in particular the principle of legality, due process, the prohibition of denial of justice, arbitrariness and discrimination, access to justice, legal certainty, and predictability—and thus align with core values that any system of law deserving of the name, whether domestic or international, aims for. This also shows that, at least as a matter of principle, investment treaty disciplines do not impose obligations on host States that are alien to other legal systems, including under domestic administrative and constitutional law. Furthermore, the connections between substantive standards of treatment and rule-of-law elements provide a solid basis for using the rule of law, notably when supported with detailed comparative law studies, to guide the interpretation of substantive standards of treatment and avoid both overly broad, but also overly narrow applications of those standards.

The rule-of-law concept most contributors to this book use to concretize substantive standards of treatment—in particular as regards FET, FPS, and expropriation—are thin or formal versions of the rule of law. This correlates with the objective of reading the content of investment treaty obligations in a narrower, rather than broader fashion, and limiting the power of arbitral tribunals in reviewing government conduct, except in cases of arbitrariness, to issues of procedural propriety. This excludes second-guessing value judgements made by host States, including in the way they balance competing rights and interests. Only in respect of the non-discrimination standards—MFN and national treatment—a broader rule-of-law concept may be appropriate, as this would allow tribunals to probe deeper into whether differentiations among foreign investors, or between foreign and national investors, reflect legitimate policy choices, rather than formal pretexts that veil illegitimate discrimination.

As far as the interface function of a rule-of-law analysis of investment treaty disciplines is concerned, one of the principal and recurring arguments is the expansion of access to justice in favour of a broader interpretation of investment treaty standards. This is particularly true in respect of the interpretation of umbrella clauses and legality requirements, or the use of FET and FPS to enforce non-investment-related obligations. These interpretations generally have the effect of opening up investment treaty arbitration for the enforcement of claims that otherwise have to be brought either before domestic courts, another contractually agreed forum, such as commercial arbitration, or have no forum at all to which investors could turn. Such a relegation of claims to investment treaty arbitration comes with tangible benefits for foreign investors, in particular when no other comparably effective forum is available; but it may also raise tensions as different fora—domestic courts, commercial arbitration, and investment arbitration—compete with each other and may reserve certain disputes to themselves. Moreover, opening recourse before investment treaty tribunals also points to the important issue that investment treaty arbitration itself needs to conform to, and function by respecting, the rule of law. This is particularly important as far as the independence and impartiality of investment arbitrators, respect for due process, and transparency in dispute settlement are concerned.

All in all, drawing on the rule of law to analyse substantive standards of treatment appears to be a powerful instrument for informing the determination of mutual rights and obligations in investor-State relations and investor-State dispute settlement, namely in respect of the limits of government interference with foreign investment, host State duties to adapt their domestic laws and institutions to rule-of-law demands, and compliance by host States and investors with other legal commitments, whether under contract or other international legal regimes.

However, the rule of law is not only useful in concretizing the content of investment treaty disciplines and guiding the interpretation and application of specific standards of treatment. The rule of law is also highly valuable in conceptualizing shortcomings in the set-up of substantive investment treaty disciplines and their interpretation and application. Notably in its thick version, the rule of law captures a broader set of concerns with how investment treaty disciplines operate. Recourse to the rule of law brings together various problems that have been identified in respect of international investment law—in particular the lack of predictability, overly broad standards of review, insufficient regard to competing rights and interest, the lack of investor obligations, the lack of protection for domestic investors, and shortcomings in the domestic implementation of investment treaty disciplines—and articulate them as problems that go beyond issues related to policy, but concern one of the core legal values any system of law needs to conform to. Furthermore, recourse to the rule of law offers means to address the problems identified and bring investment law and dispute settlement closer to the ideal the rule of law epitomizes, not only in respect of substantive disciplines investment treaties imposes on host States, but also in respect of the need of investment law and dispute settlement itself to abide by rule-of-law standards themselves.

This immediately raises the question of how and by whom the rule-of-law gaps identified in the present book can be addressed. Some of the gaps can be addressed, if not closed, by arbitral tribunals when interpreting and applying investment treaty disciplines. Tribunals can, for example, tailor their standards of review so as to avoid separation-of-powers concerns, strive for more consistent and predictable jurisprudence, use investment treaty disciplines to address investor misconduct, or ensure due regard for competing concerns, including human rights and sustainable development, as well as the host State's right to regulate. Other rule-of-law gaps, by contrast, cannot be closed through adapting the interpretation and application of investment treaty disciplines, but require changes to investment treaties and have to be tackled by States, whether as part of the ongoing reform processes relating to international investment law or independently of it. Such changes include, for example, imposing more encompassing obligations on foreign investors under international law, developing mechanisms to ensure domestic application and enforcement of investment treaties, and protecting domestic investors against State conduct that does not conform to the rule-of-law treatment due to foreign investors.

Despite the considerable rule-of-law lacunae that investment treaty disciplines exhibit, and the significant room for improvement, one should also be conscious of the limitations of international investment law. Investment treaty disciplines tackle specific problems that exist in investor-State relations if host State conduct does not conform to specific rule-of-law elements, such as arbitrary or discriminatory conduct or expropriations without compensation. Investment treaties aim at remedying rule-of-law shortcomings that exist at the domestic level, by functioning as an international law substitute for such shortcomings;

investment treaties do not, by contrast, aim at providing a complete governance framework or government programme for all possible issues arising in investor-State relations and do not determine a State's investment policy as a whole. They leave States comprehensive autonomy in determining economic and social policy and merely require that those policies respect basic rule-of-law standards. Many problems in investor-State relations will therefore remain problems that call for political, rather than strictly legal solutions. Similarly, not all concerns that international investment law raises are rule-of-law problems, but may relate to other values and interests, for example democratic legitimacy.[50]

Finally, it is important to realize that the rule of law remains an ideal and aspiration that needs to be put into practice and lived in international investment law and dispute settlement on a day-to-day basis. It remains a goal that all law and legal practice should always strive for, even if it will never be perfectly and permanently achieved. Abiding by the rule of law is a practice as much as it is an ideal that the investment treaty regime constantly and continuously has to aspire to, just as any other system of law and adjudication.

---

[50] See eg Andreas Kulick, 'International Investment Arbitration, Treaty Interpretation, and Democracy' (2015) 4 CILJ 441; Lorenzo Cotula, 'Democracy and International Investment Law' (2017) 30 LJIL 351.

PART I

STANDARDS OF TREATMENT AS RULE-OF-LAW DEMANDS FOR DOMESTIC REGULATORY ACTION

2

The Rule of Law and Fair and Equitable Treatment

Martins Paparinskis

I. Introduction

The rule of law[1] is a contested concept, possibly even an essentially contested one.[2] Fair and equitable treatment (FET) is, in a structural sense, a rule of much more modest ambition: merely a legal term of art regarding a primary rule well known in the field of overseas investment protection.[3] However, what the primary obligation of FET lacks in conceptual importance,[4] it makes up in the considerable practical effect in international dispute settlement on the basis of investment treaties. Judging from publicly available awards, this is the obligation that investment treaty tribunals are most likely to find to have been breached.[5] Of course, to suggest that a contested concept and a specific primary obligation occupy different places in the architecture of the international legal order is not particularly original— one could make a similar point about many, if not all, concepts, principles, and rules. But there may be something more that catches the eye in the particular instance, which makes it an important topic for analysis.

The starting point of this chapter is that there is a certain amount of State practice and a significant amount of materials falling under subsidiary means for determination of rules of law, particularly legal writings but also some arbitral practice, that explicitly link FET to the rule of law. A plausible positive and normative claim can be made regarding FET as a positive expression of the rule of law more generally. Jeremy Waldron makes the point briskly in 'The Rule of Law' entry of the *Stanford Encyclopaedia of Philosophy* that '[t]heorists of the Rule of Law are fond of producing laundry lists of the principles it comprises ... which may loosely be divided into principles that address the formal aspects of governance by law; principles that address its procedural aspects; and principles that embrace certain

---

[1] This chapter draws upon earlier writing on the topic, including Martins Paparinskis, *The International Minimum Standard and Fair and Equitable Treatment* (OUP 2013).

[2] Jeremy Waldron, 'Is the Rule of Law an Essentially Contested Concept (in Florida)?' (2002) 21 Law & Phil 137; David Collier and others, 'Essentially Contested Concepts: Debates and Applications' (2006) 11 J Political Ideol 211, 228–33; Jeremy Waldron, 'The Rule of Law' (22 June 2016) *Stanford Encyclopaedia of Philosophy* <https://plato.stanford.edu/entries/rule-of-law/> accessed 1 July 2021, s 2.

[3] *Oil Platforms (Iran v US)* (Preliminary Objections: Separate Opinion Judge Higgins) [1996] ICJ Rep 803, 847 para 39.

[4] The reading of FET as a conceptually unremarkable primary obligation is not shared by everyone. For example, an argument for viewing FET as a gateway for systemic integration of other sources of international law appears in Roland Kläger, *'Fair and Equitable Treatment' in International Investment Law* (CUP 2011) ch 4.

[5] UNCTAD, 'Investor-State Dispute Settlement Cases Pass the 1,000 Mark: Cases and Outcomes in 2019' IIA Issues Note 2/2020 <https://unctad.org/system/files/official-document/diaepcbinf2020d6.pdf> accessed 1 July 2021, 5 ('In the decisions holding the State liable, tribunals most frequently found breaches of the fair and equitable treatment (FET) provision').

Martins Paparinskis, *The Rule of Law and Fair and Equitable Treatment* In: *Investment Protection Standards and the Rule of Law*. Edited by: August Reinisch and Stephan W. Schill, Oxford University Press. © Martins Paparinskis 2023.
DOI: 10.1093/oso/9780192864581.003.0002

substantive values'.[6] Many entries on the laundry list regarding the formal and procedural aspects of the rule of law (also known as 'thin', as opposed to the 'thick' rule of law that engages with substantive values), such as publicity, prospectivity, intelligibility, consistency, and stability, and the right to a hearing by an impartial tribunal,[7] parallel the language and concepts in the laundry lists compiled for FET.[8] It is not a particular stretch to build upon the similarities and argue for rule of law as an explanatory framework for FET, FET as a positivized expression of rule of law, or even speak, as one tribunal recently did in passing, of 'rule of law-elements flowing from fair and equitable treatment'.[9]

This chapter takes a more qualified position. Some people will think that explicit conceptualization of FET (decisions) as the rule of law is either unpersuasive or superfluous, and that explicit reliance on concepts drawn from it has limited long-term effects. Interpretation and application of FET certainly raises hard questions of sources and interpretation. Ordinary meaning of particular treaty terms is, in the technical sense of principles of interpretation, vague; arbitral decisions are occasionally suboptimal on the nature of relationship between treaties and customary law on the issue; subsidiary means for determination of custom are mostly constituted by archaic arbitral decisions; and many modern decisions leave something to be desired. But these are perfectly normal challenges for international legal reasoning and international dispute settlement, which can be resolved by diligent engagement with rules on sources and interpretation, with an eye to the judicial function in a substantively and procedurally decentralized field of international law. Not every field of international law comes pre-equipped with detailed rules and thick institutions—indeed, most do not—so there is no obvious reason for setting aside usual techniques of legal reasoning for this particular challenge. Reliance on rule-of-law language familiar from domestic law and regional economic orders may provide *an* answer to hard legal questions besetting those tasked with interpreting and applying rules on FET, but it is less clear that it is *the* answer called for by the international legal vocabulary of sources and interpretation. For some, rule of law will seem to have played, for investment law, the role of Ian Brownlie's metaphorical bank of fog on a still day, obscuring rather than illuminating—or perhaps even falsely illuminating what the technical law purposefully left ambiguous.[10]

I will make my argument in two steps. First, I will introduce the concept of FET, identify the elements in practice that support the argument for reading it in rule-of-law terms, and distinguish various ways of making that argument (Section II).[11] Second, I will address in

---

[6] Waldron, 'The Rule of Law' (n 2) s 5.

[7] ibid ss 5.1–5.2.

[8] See eg *Glencore International AG and CI Prodeco SA v Colombia*, ICSID Case No ARB/16/6, Award (27 August 2019) para 1310; *Belenergia SA v Italy*, ICSID Case No ARB/15/40, Award (6 August 2019) para 570; *Joshua Dean Nelson and Jorge Blanco v Mexico*, ICSID Case No UNCT/17/1, Award (5 June 2020) para 322 ('State misconduct that is (i) arbitrary, (ii) grossly unfair, unjust or idiosyncratic; (iii) discriminatory or; (iv) absent of due process'); *ESPF Beteiligungs GmbH, ESPF Nr 2 Austria Beteiligungs GmbH, and InfraClass Energie 5 GmbH & Co KG v Italy*, ICSID Case No ARB/16/5, Award (14 September 2020) paras 443–44 ('FET is made up of several components, including the duty to create stable conditions, to act in a transparent and consistent manner (with due process and in good faith), and to refrain from taking arbitrary or discriminatory measures or from frustrating investors' legitimate expectations regarding the legal, regulatory, and legislative framework and adversely affecting their investments ... the FET standard includes multiple sub-standards, including the protection of legitimate expectations, consistency, and transparency, and good faith').

[9] *Casinos Austria International GmbH and Casinos Austria Aktiengesellschaft v Argentina*, ICSID Case No ARB/14/32, Decision on Jurisdiction (29 June 2018) para 243.

[10] Ian Brownlie, 'Recognition in Theory and Practice' (1982) 53 BYIL 197, 197.

[11] I caveat one aspect of rule-of-law perspective that I will not discuss in the chapter, which would limit its impact to describing the content of applicable customary law or aspects of application of treaty obligations. I will leave open the question of whether this is a concern for the rule of law, even in the broadest sense—perhaps compliance

turn the more important instances of its application—arbitrariness (Section III.A), protection of expectations (Section III.B), and due process (Section III.C)—and show how the rule-of-law(-inspired) notions have been articulated in their regard (I will be brief in description and selective in examples since impact on the judiciary and protection of expectations is dealt with by other authors in this volume in greater detail).[12] The main claim is that reading FET through rule-of-law lenses is plausible but may be conflating positive and normative claims as well as understating the potential and benefits for answering public international law questions in public international law terms. In short, this is an optimistic chapter about what international law can do, even without dipping into the rich reservoir of domestic, regional, and jurisprudential debates on rule of law.

II. '[R]ule of law-elements flowing from fair and equitable treatment'

The 2018 decision on jurisdiction in *Casinos Austria International GmbH and Casinos Austria Aktiengesellschaft v Argentina*, from which the quote in this section title is taken, provides a helpful entry point for discussion of FET and rule of law:

> 242. Fair and equitable treatment has been interpreted, *inter alia*, to protect covered investors and their investments against the arbitrary exercise of public powers, as well as against harassment by public authorities, to require public authorities to administer the applicable law in good faith, to entitle foreign investors and their investments to due process, and to protect an investor's legitimate expectations.

> 243. These rule of law-elements flowing from fair and equitable treatment have been found to apply not only to action taken directly vis-à-vis the claimant-investor, but also to action the host State has taken in relation to a company in which the investor is a shareholder. In such situations, the shareholder-investor has been considered to have a right, and consequently standing, under the fair and equitable treatment standard that the company in which she has invested is treated in accordance with the above mentioned rule of law-elements.[13]

Casinos Austria is not the only case to have explicitly connected FET with rule of law. In the early 2005 award in the *Petrobart Limited v Kyrgyzstan* case, the tribunal noted that

---

of law with the secondary rules of recognition acts necessarily precedes engagement with the formal aspects of rules of law. The concern, however, is a different one: is there anything more to it than the proposition that FET is a primary rule of international law, to be interpreted, identified, and applied in accordance with meta-rules on sources and interpretation? As far as I can see, no actor in the international legal process has ever challenged this position (whatever their views may have been about the quality with which interpreters have carried out their mandate), so the argument leaves itself open to the charge of superfluity.

[12] See Caroline Henckels, 'Legitimate Expectations and the Rule of Law in International Investment Law' (in this volume) 43 and Ursula Kriebaum, 'Rule- of-Law Demands and the Domestic Judiciary: Denial of Justice, Judicial Expropriation, Effective Means' (in this volume) 145.

[13] *Casinos Austria* (n 9) paras 242–43 (footnotes omitted). The decision was adopted by a majority but the dissenting arbitrator did not comment on rule-of-law aspects and indeed seemed to accept the substance of the decision on the point of FET, Dissenting Opinion on Respondent's Second Preliminary Objection and Declaration of Dissent concerning its First and Third Preliminary Objections of Arbitrator Santiago Torres Bernárdez (20 June 2018) para 217.

'[g]overnment intervention in judicial proceedings is not in conformity with the rule of law in a democratic society and that it shows a lack of respect for Petrobart's rights as an investor having an investment under the Treaty' and accordingly found a breach of FET.[14] More recently, arbitrator Gary Born's 2016 dissenting opinion in the award in *Philip Morris v Uruguay* repeatedly referred to rule of law when discussing denial of justice as part of FET:

> 40.... this amounted to 'Heads, I win; tails, you lose' treatment, without affording Abal the possibility of subsequent judicial recourse, which is contrary to Article 3(2)'s guarantee of fair and equitable treatment and the rule of law.

> 42. The rule of law serves to ensure predictability, stability, neutrality, and objectivity; it ensures that generally applicable legal rules, rather than personal or political expedience, govern human affairs. Where different courts within a single legal system adopt contradictory interpretations for the same law, the rule of law is undermined, exposing individuals to inconsistent, unpredictable, and arbitrary treatment.

> 51.... The concept of the rule of law implies regularity, stability, and lack of arbitrariness.

> 57. In my view, it is something very different for the law to be interpreted in diametrically opposed ways in the *same* dispute, involving the *same* party. This latter result involves a state, through its courts, holding that the same law means exactly opposite things as applied to the same litigant in the same dispute. That is the antithesis of the rule of law: it constitutes a much more direct and immediate instance of arbitrariness, incapable of explanation by differences in the identities of the litigants, the circumstances of the parties or their dispute or the parties' litigation conduct.

> 61.... I find it very difficult to avoid concluding that these contradictory decisions, rendered against the same party in closely-related proceedings, violate guarantees of access to justice and adherence to the rule of law.

> 62.... that is arbitrary and irrational, denying parties the basic legal certainty, predictability and the fundamental fairness that the rule of law serves to ensure.

> 69.... That is not consistent with either Uruguay's commitment to the rule of law or rules of international law.

> 81.... That denial of access to a judicial forum is a denial of justice, which both the BIT and Uruguay's commitment to the rule of law proscribe.

> 133. One of the central elements of the guarantee of 'fair and equitable treatment' is a protection against arbitrary treatment. This guarantee reflects a fundamental aspect of the rule of law: citizens are entitled to treatment, by their government, which is rational and proportionate. Irrational or arbitrary governmental measures, which are unrelated to any legitimate governmental objective, or which are gravely disproportionate to the achievement of such an objective, are neither fair nor equitable, and they betray, rather than advance, the rule of law.[15]

---

[14] *Petrobart Limited v Kyrgyzstan*, SCC Case No 126/2003, Award (29 March 2005) para 75. It may be that the language was used in response to the State's earlier argument to the effect '[t]hat Petrobart, an allegedly foreign investor, was able to obtain a judgment against a state-owned company testifies to the Republic's adherence to the rule of law' (ibid para 38).

[15] *Philip Morris Brands Sàrl, Philip Morris Products SA and Abal Hermanos SA v Oriental Republic of Uruguay*, ICSID Case No ARB/10/7, Award (8 July 2016) Concurring and Dissenting Opinion of Arbitrator Born (28 June 2016) (emphasis in the original).

There is also a number of examples where the rule of law has been considered, as it were, contiguously to FET. The OECD 1967 Draft Convention on the Protection of Foreign Property, which provided the starting point for many of the bilateral investment treaty (BIT) programmes, makes the following point regarding due process of law in takings, which in its own turn trails the language used in description of FET:

> In essence, the contents of the notion of due process of law making it akin to the requirements of the 'Rule of Law', and Anglo-Saxon notion, or of the 'Rechsstaat', as understood in continental law ... whenever a State seizes property, the measures taken must be free from arbitrariness. Safeguards existing in its Constitution or other laws or established by judicial precedent must be fully observed; administrative or judicial machinery used or available must correspond at least to the minimum standard required by international law. Thus, the term contains both substantive procedural elements.[16]

The International Court of Justice (ICJ) in the *ELSI* case also, famously, explained arbitrariness as 'not so much something opposed to a rule of law, as something opposed to the rule of law';[17] a proposition that was used in a number of decisions by investment treaty tribunals to interpret and apply FET (or obligation regarding arbitrary and unreasonable conduct, which is treated for the purposes of this chapter as being equivalent in this respect).[18] In the 2008 award in *Amto v Ukraine*, the tribunal discussed the 'effective means' obligation in the Energy Charter Treaty, often read as somewhat similar to denial of justice as part of FET, and noted that '[t]he fundamental criteria of an "effective means" for the assertion of claims and the enforcement of rights within the meaning of Article 10(2) is law and the rule of law' and 'Article 10(12) is not only a rule of law standard, but also a qualitative standard'.[19]

Finally, there is the harder-to-determine relationship between FET and the rule of law in a looser sense, whether as a tool for conceptualizing and systematizing seemingly disparate arbitral practice, most prominently made in academic setting by Stephan Schill[20] and Kenneth Vandevelde,[21] or as a source of inspiration for arbitrators facing the infuriatingly vague language of fairness and equity. As August Reinisch and Christoph Schreuer put it, '[w]hile express references to the concept of the rule of law may be limited in arbitral practice, the more specific jurisprudence on the due process element of FET ... demonstrates that investment tribunals are often taking inspiration from rule of law concepts'.[22] To sum it

---

[16] OECD, 'Draft Convention on the Protection of Foreign Property, Text with Notes and Comments' art 3 Commentary 5(a), (b), art 1 Commentary 4(a) <www.oecd.org/investment/internationalinvestmentagreements/39286571.pdf> accessed 1 July 2021.

[17] *Elettronica Sicula SpA (ELSI) (US v Italy) (Judgment)* [1989] ICJ Rep 15 para 128.

[18] See eg *Noble Ventures v Romania*, ICSID Case No ARB/01/11, Award (12 October 2005) para 176; *Duke Energy v Ecuador*, ICSID Case No ARB/05/19, Award (18 August 2008) para 378; *Alghanim v Jordan*, ICSID Case No ARB/13/38, Award (14 December 2017) para 277; *Mercer International Inc v Canada*, ICSID Case No ARB(AF)/12/3, Award (6 March 2018) para 778.

[19] *Amto v Ukraine*, SCC Arbitration no 080/2005, Award (26 March 2008) para 87.

[20] In various places, including Benedict Kingsbury and Stephan W Schill, 'Investor-State Arbitration as Governance: Fair and Equitable Treatment, Proportionality and the Emerging Global Administrative Law' (2009) NYU School of Law, Public Law Research Paper No 09–46; Stephan W Schill, 'International Investment Law and Comparative Public Law' in Stephan W Schill (ed), *International Investment Law and Comparative Public Law* (OUP 2010).

[21] Kenneth J Vandevelde, 'A Unified Theory of Fair and Equitable Treatment' (2010) 43 NYU J Intl L & Pol 43.

[22] August Reinisch and Christoph Schreuer, *International Protection of Investments: The Substantive Standards* (CUP 2020) 344.

up, some actors in investment law draw the connection explicitly, others may have adopted the framing by necessary implication, and at a certain degree of loose abstraction both concepts may be responding to similar normative instincts. What relates to rule of law itself seems to be somewhat uncertain: apparently according to the *Casino Austria* tribunal, a list of cases relied upon by the investor illustrate application of rule-of-law elements (even though they do not mention 'rule of law' once).[23]

In short, rule of law plays a role in and around FET *and* it may be doing quite a lot of different things. It is helpful to spell that difference out.

First, the rule of law is one of the ideals of political morality, conceived and primarily contested in relation to domestic political communities. Arbitrator Gary Born's opinion in *Philip Morris v Uruguay* may have employed the notion of the rule of law in this sense, as a related but ultimately different benchmark from FET under public international law, for example by speaking about 'Uruguay's commitment to the rule of law or rules of international law' and 'a denial of justice, which both the BIT and Uruguay's commitment to the rule of law proscribe'.[24] Second, 'rule of law' may be a drafting shorthand for describing the content of a primary obligation as requiring the quality of domestic law and practice to correspond to a particular conception of political morality. The OECD Draft Convention's introduction of 'rule of law' seems to have served that role, and the other way of reading Born's opinion may be as suggesting that FET necessarily requires conduct in line with the rule of law (elaborated in that case by reference to regional judgments on human rights under the auspices of the Council of Europe). Third, the rule of law is employed in an *ex post facto* explanatory manner, bringing order to the decentralized arbitral practice on FET that in a fit of absent-mindedness disperses itself around roughly the same laundry list categories. The *Casinos Austria* decision may be read consistently with this argument, first identifying on the basis of arbitral practice what protections '[f]air and equitable treatment has been interpreted' as entailing, and then describing them as 'rule of law-elements flowing from fair and equitable treatment'.[25] The fourth argument, the flip side of the third, is inspiration by the rule of law, plausibly suggested by Reinisch and Schreuer.[26] Finally, the 'rule of law' may be a descriptive shorthand for the complex legal argument of identification of general principles of law, either derived from national legal systems in the field of public law or formed within the

---

[23] *Casino Austria* (n 9) fn 223 ('*El Paso Energy International Company v Argentine Republic*, ICSID Case No ARB/03/15, Award (31 October 2011) para 348 (CL-016); *Electrabel SA v The Republic of Hungary*, ICSID Case No ARB/07/19, Decision on Jurisdiction, Applicable Law and Liability (30 November 2012) part VII, para 7.75 (CL-020); *CME Czech Republic BV (The Netherlands) v The Czech Republic*, UNCITRAL, Partial Award (13 September 2001) para 611 (CL-021); *Saluka Investments BV (The Netherlands) v The Czech Republic*, UNCITRAL, Partial Award (17 March 2006) para 309 (CL-018); *Plama Consortium Limited v Republic of Bulgaria*, ICSID Case No ARB/03/24, Award (27 August 2008) paras 175, 176 (CL-118); *Metalclad Corporation v The United Mexican States*, ICSID Case No ARB(AF)/97/1, Award (30 August 2000) para 99 (CL-011); *Tecnicas Medioambientales Tecmed SA v The United Mexican States*, ICSID Case No ARB(AF)/00/2, Award (29 May 2003) para 153 (CL-008); *Waguih Elie George Siag and Clorinda Vecchi v The Arab Republic of Egypt*, ICSID Case No ARB/05/15, Award (1 June 2009) para 450 (CL-024); *Frontier Petroleum Services Ltd v The Czech Republic*, UNCITRAL, Final Award (12 November 2010, para 300 (CL-025); *Siemens AG v Argentine Republic*, ICSID Case No ARB/02/8, Award (6 February 2007) para 308 (CL-034); *Waste Management Inc v United Mexican States*, ICSID Case No ARB(AF)/00/3, Award (30 April 2004) para 98 (AL RA 119); *Eureko BV v Republic of Poland*, Partial Award (19 August 2005) paras 231–33 (AL RA 30); *Biwater Gauff (Tanzania) Ltd v United Republic of Tanzania*, ICSID Case No ARB/05/22, Award (24 July 2008) paras 597–99 (CL-031); *Joseph Charles Lemire v Ukraine*, ICSID Case No ARB/06/18, Award (28 March 2011) paras 158, 159 (CL-090)'). Others would, no doubt, disagree with this taxonomy, at least if the language suggests more self-conscious engagement of arbitrators than in the case of Molière's Mr Jourdain.

[24] *Philip Morris* Born (n 15) paras 69, 81

[25] *Casino Austria* (n 9) paras 242–43.

[26] Reinisch and Schreuer (n 22) 344.

international legal system,[27] and then taken into account in interpretation of investment treaties.[28] Perhaps this is what *Casinos Austria*'s language of 'rule of law-elements flowing from fair and equitable treatment' is really getting at.[29] In short, while I would not want to overstate the separateness of these arguments, perhaps better to be read as imprecise points on a spectrum rather than neatly distinct categories, they are nevertheless different and stand and fall against different benchmarks.

It is helpful to consider counter-arguments or at least explicitly identify the costs for these claims. At the philosophical end of the spectrum, the concern is about conflation of distinct intellectual inquiries. Similarities in language should not disguise the extent to which debates are fundamentally different, in terms of substance and focus and also in terms of basic disciplinary assumptions and techniques. That a recent ICSID decision and Aristoteles used similar language does not mean that they are both speaking to the same issue. Another hurdle is justifying the rule of law in public international investment law. Jeremy Waldron, for example, has famously doubted whether the ideal of rule of law, formulated against the background of overreaching public authority from which individuals need protection, fits within the classically horizontal inter-State model of public international law.[30] There is reasonable debate to be had about various aspects of the argument[31]—is it affected by the great material inequalities between the juridically equal sovereigns? Are the multilateral elements of the international legal order reflective of a gradual emergence of a properly public international law? Is the procedural role of non-State actors the qualitative difference for fields like investment law? But it suggests that a number of legal and normative propositions need to be established in the first place for the rule of law to be defensible as a relevant perspective for discussing FET.

At the lawyerly end of the spectrum, some will be concerned that 'rule of law' language sidesteps hard questions about identification of public international law. A brisk nod to 'investors' expectations', the Vienna Convention on the Law of Treaties or 'international law' will not impress everybody,[32] and even on general principles a demonstration of commonalities rather than their assertion is expected.[33] Why should 'rule of law' be treated any more gently? The least charitable take is that either invocation of rule of law adds something to what vocabulary of sources and interpretation does not usually provide, in which case it raises hard questions about proper applicable law, or it does not, in which case it is a harmless metaphor, to be evaluated solely in aesthetic terms and without any legal relevance. Indeed, the rule-of-law approaches may raise normative concerns precisely due to their apparent tension with the universalist assumptions underpinning (however imperfectly) the doctrine of sources and interpretation—the conceptual framework and particular

---

[27] ILC, 'Second Report on General Principles of Law by Marcelo Vázquez-Bermúdez, Special Rapporteur' (9 April 2020) UN Doc A/CN.4/74. 59, Draft conclusion 3.

[28] Vienna Convention on the Law of Treaties (opened for signature 23 May 1969, entered into force 27 January 1980) 1155 UNTS 331, art 31(3)(c).

[29] *Casino Austria* (n 9) para 243.

[30] Jeremy Waldron, 'Are Sovereigns Entitled to the Benefit of the International Rule of Law?' (2011) 22 EJIL 315.

[31] Jeremy Waldron, 'Response: The Perils of Exaggeration' (2011) 22 EJIL 389.

[32] Respectively *MTD Equity Sdn. Bhd. and MTD Chile SA v Chile*, ICSID Case No ARB/01/7, Decision on Annulment (21 March 2007) para 67; *Industria Nacional de Alimentos, SA (previously Empresas Lucchetti, SA) and Indalsa Perú, SA (previously Lucchetti Perú, SA) v Peru*, ICSID Case No ARB/03/4, Decision on Annulment, Dissenting Opinion Berman (13 August 2007); *Venezuela Holdings BV and ors v Bolivarian Republic of Venezuela*, ICSID Case No ARB/07/27, Decision on Annulment (9 March 2017) paras 155–60.

[33] Vázquez-Bermúdez's Second Report (n 27) para 44.

authorities of rule of law seem to pull away from the search for general consensus in international or domestic legal traditions and towards one particular regional approach.[34]

III. Rule-of-Law-Inspired Application of Fair and Equitable Treatment

Explicit reliance and hard-to-determine inspiration by rule of law sometimes seem to be driven by apparently insolvable queries raised by the vagueness of FET. There is nothing wrong with the international legal process being inspired by arguments from domestic legal orders or other fields of international law. Significant parts of the contemporary law of treaties, State responsibility, and territorial title have been inspired by shared assumptions and approaches in domestic law.[35] But ultimately the question is not where the inspirations came from but whether the solution proved helpful and was endorsed by international law— or was rather qualified or rejected in the normal international legal process. Vagueness of applicable law is not a reason for moving beyond the usual canons of legal reasoning but a perfectly ordinary challenge in various fields, perhaps most obviously maritime delimitation and equitable and reasonable utilization in the law of international watercourses.[36] In short, the relevant question is what States, international organizations, review institutions in dispute settlement, and inter-State tribunals made of the inspiration of investor-State arbitration tribunals in the 2000s.

There is ground for reasonable disagreement about the precise legal character of arbitral statements on FET—arbitral awards can be plausibly read as relating to treaty interpretation, identification of customary law, or identification of general principles. In my view, these cases are best read as related to application of rules, rather than determination of their content, and the key methodological question is identifying the good examples of application of the relevant considerations. Reasonable people may disagree which of the efforts to capture the elusive essence of FET has been most successful, but the award in *Waste Management v Mexico (II)* is certainly one of the most cited on this point, and its description of conduct breaching the FET standard will be taken as a convenient point of departure of the traditional position in 2004:

---

[34] As one tribunal noted, in the particular context of expropriation but with a sentiment similarly applicable to FET:

> this factor [the proportionality between the means employed and the aim sought to be realized] was relied upon in *Técnicas Medioambientales Tecmed S.A. v United Mexican States*, ICSID Case No ARB(AF)/00/2, Award (29 May 2003) paras 122 *et seq.*, available at: <http://ita.law.uvic.ca/ documents/Tecnicas_001. pdf> accessed 1 July 2021. The factor is used by the European Court of Human Rights, at n 140, and *it may be questioned whether it is a viable source of interpreting Article 1110 of the NAFTA.*

Fireman's Fund Insurance Company v Mexico, ICSID Case No ARB(AF)/02/1, Award (17 July 2006, fn 161 (emphasis added)

[35] Hersch Lauterpacht, *Private Law Sources and Analogies of International Law* (Longmans 1927).
[36] Massimo Lando, *Maritime Delimitation as a Judicial Process* (CUP 2019); Lucius Caflisch, 'Equitable and Reasonable Utilization and Factors Relevant to Determining Such Utilization (Articles 5 and 6)' in Laurence Boisson de Chazournes and others (eds), *The UN Convention on the Law of Non-Navigational Uses of International Watercourses: A Commentary* (OUP 2019); Stephen McCaffrey, *The Law of International Watercourses* (3rd edn, OUP 2019) ch 9.

conduct [that] is arbitrary, grossly unfair, unjust or idiosyncratic, is discriminatory and exposes the claimant to sectional or racial prejudice, or involves a lack of due process leading to an outcome which offends judicial propriety—as might be the case with a manifest failure of natural justice in judicial proceedings or a complete lack of transparency and candour in an administrative process. In applying this standard it is relevant that the treatment is in breach of representations made by the host State which were reasonably relied on by the claimant.[37]

The 2018 Investment Protection Agreement between the European Union (EU) and Singapore is a recent example of State practice that is broadly in line with this arbitral statement, identifying instances of proper application of FET as:

(a) denial of justice in criminal, civil and administrative proceedings;
(b) a fundamental breach of due process;
(c) manifestly arbitrary conduct;
(d) harassment, coercion, abuse of power or similar bad faith conduct.[38]

The next sections will consider in turn the temptation of FET by the rule of law in relation to arbitrariness (Section A), protection of expectations (Section B), and due process (Section C). (I will not address transparency because it has attracted less attention both in arbitral decisions and State practice.)[39]

A. Arbitrariness

The leading modern case on the obligation of non-arbitrariness in the treatment of foreign investment is *ELSI*, where arbitrariness was described as 'not so much opposed to a rule of law, as something opposed to *the* rule of law ... a wilful disregard of due process of law, an act which shocks, or at least surprises, a sense of judicial propriety'.[40] The examination of appropriateness and reasonableness was limited to the very deferential statement that '[i]t cannot be said to have been unreasonable or merely capricious'.[41] The availability of the formal and procedural safeguards—recitation of reasons and legal bases, existence of broader competence, availability of functioning remedies—were decisive in rejecting the US claim.[42] *ELSI* provides methodology for approaching the claim of arbitrariness, identifying topics that should be considered (first)—formal and procedural safeguards in particular—and those that are less relevant or to be considered in a deferential manner—legitimacy of purpose and appropriateness of means chosen. *ELSI* is in line with the postwar position of the ICJ's

---

[37] *Waste Management v Mexico (II)*, ICSID Case No ARB(AF)/00/3, Award (30 April 2004) para 98.
[38] Investment Protection Agreement between the European Union and its Member States and the Republic of Singapore (signed 15 October 2018), art 2.4(2).
[39] See further Reinisch and Schreuer (n 22) 453–61; Manjiao Chi, 'Regulatory Transparency in International: From an Investment Protection Requirement to a Rule-of-Law Requirement' (in this volume) 127.
[40] *ELSI* (n 17) para 1282 (emphasis in the original).
[41] ibid para 129.
[42] ibid paras 128–29, and more generally 123–30. While decided on the obligation of arbitrariness, it has been endorsed in arbitral practice as an authority for approaching arbitrariness in application of FET (Reinisch and Schreuer (n 22) 441).

Asylum judgment (explicitly referred to in *ELSI*), which had been elaborated in an intra-Latin American dispute with reference to denial of justice, a rule historically not focused on substantive merits or commensurability of policy choices but rather procedural safeguards, and even then applied in a markedly deferential manner.[43] The methodology and leading examples of its application in international law were distinctly unfavourable to an inquiry into merits and means and ends. *ELSI* is instructive as well for the limited effects that rule-of-law language had on standard legal reasoning: the Chamber did not derive international standards on arbitrariness from analysis of domestic or regional traditions but instead applied a vague international law rule to particular factual circumstances. There is no obvious reason why investment arbitration tribunals, equipped with much richer arbitral practice of the last two decades, should not be able to approach the question in a similar manner.

Recent practice is mixed, and there is support for the traditional approach.[44] The award in *Philip Morris v Uruguay* may be read consistently with *ELSI*, taking it as the explicit starting point, leaving aside policy choices, and focusing on the formal and evidentiary aspects relating to particular measures.[45] Still, as Reinisch and Schreuer note, 'more and more often tribunals resort to a proportionality analysis', building on concepts developed mostly in continental European legal doctrine and jurisprudence and then spread within regional European regimes and constitutional courts internationally.[46] An interesting intermediate example is *RREEF v Spain,* which also takes *ELSI* as the starting point but then reads reasonableness and proportionality as closely related, with proportionality even providing the main test for reasonableness.[47] The clearest case of rule-of-law-inspired proportionality derived from domestic and regional traditions is *Occidental v Ecuador.* In that case, the tribunal challenged not only the traditional approach to the issue in general but also the special rule that international wrongfulness of contractual breaches was to be judged by reference to its character, rather than its content and extent, by basing Ecuador's responsibility on the lack of proportionality in its conduct.[48] *Occidental* is a complex case, both at the level of domestic law as well as primary and secondary rules of international law,[49] and one should evaluate its reasoning with great care, but there is something to be said for pausing before one substitutes and rewrites contractual terms and consequences by reference to such a general and vague standard as proportionality.[50] A caution against proportionality review, particularly of an intrusive character, applies also more generally: investment obligations are not directed at disciplining policy debates and choices, but at the manner in

---

[43] *Colombian–Peruvian Asylum Case (Colombia/Peru)* [1950] ICJ Rep 266, 284 ('in the guise of justice, arbitrary action is substituted for the rule of law. Such would be the case if the administration of justice were corrupted by measures clearly prompted by political aims').

[44] *Anglo American plc v Bolivarian Republic of Venezuela,* ICSID Case No ARB(AF)/14/1, Award (18 January 2019) para 470.

[45] *Philip Morris* (n 15) paras 389–420.

[46] Reinisch and Schreuer (n 22) 446, 447–51.

[47] *RREEF Infrastructure (GP) Limited and RREEF Pan-European Infrastructure Two Lux Sàrl v Spain,* ICSID Case No ARB/13/30, Decision on Responsibility and on the Principles of Quantum (30 November 2018) paras 460–64.

[48] *Occidental Petroleum Corporation, Occidental Exploration and Production Company v Ecuador,* ICSID Case No ARB/06/11, Award (5 October 2012) paras 384–452.

[49] *Occidental Petroleum Corporation, Occidental Exploration and Production Company v Ecuador* (n 48) paras 297–452, 662–87.

[50] This is a loose paraphrase of a well-known passage that makes a similar point regarding legitimate expectations: '[r]eference to a general and vague standard of legitimate expectations is no substitute for contractual rights. The relevance of legitimate expectations is not a licence to arbitral tribunals to rewrite the freely negotiated

which these policies are formulated and applied; it is by elaboration of requirements that non-arbitrariness imposes on form and procedure that this can be best achieved, as leading arbitral decisions have done.[51]

The approach of *Occidental* has not been endorsed by State practice. The United States, a leading participant in the customary lawmaking in the area, has explicitly reacted to invocations of *Occidental* by arguing against the general obligation of proportionality.[52] The EU—familiar with proportionality from its own legal order—has studiously avoided that language and instead apparently endorsed in its treaty practice the 'arbitrariness' of *ELSI*, further buttressed by qualification of 'manifest' nature.[53] In short, rule-of-law-inspired reasoning on this point has been received in a lukewarm manner, unevenly among the tribunals and resisted explicitly or by necessary implication by States and the EU.

B. Expectations

The first case to advance a claim on legitimate expectations and FET was *Técnicas Medioambientales Tecmed, SA v Mexico* (*Tecmed*):

> The Arbitral Tribunal considers that this provision of the Agreement, in light of the good faith principle established by international law, requires the Contracting Parties to provide to international investments treatment that does not affect the basic expectations that were taken into account by the foreign investor to make the investment. The foreign investor expects the host State to act in a consistent manner, free from ambiguity and totally transparently in its relations with the foreign investor, so that it may know beforehand any and all rules and regulations that will govern its investments, as well as the goals of the relevant policies and administrative practices or directives, to be able to plan its investment and comply with such regulations. Any and all State actions conforming to such criteria should relate not only to the guidelines, directives or requirements issued, or the resolutions approved thereunder, but also to the goals underlying such regulations. The foreign investor also expects the host State to act consistently, i.e. without arbitrarily revoking any preexisting decisions or permits issued by the State that were relied upon by the investor to assume its commitments as well as to plan and launch its commercial and business activities. The investor also expects the State to use the legal instruments that govern the actions of the investor or the investment in conformity with the function usually assigned to such instruments, and not to deprive the investor of its investment without the required

---

terms of investment contracts' (J Crawford, 'Treaty and Contract in Investment Arbitration' (2008) 24 Arb Intl 351, 372).

[51] See eg *Achmea BV v Slovak Republic*, PCA Case No 2008-13, Final Award (7 December 2012) para 294 ('The Contracting Parties are free to adopt the policies that they choose. The Treaty focuses on the manner in which policies may be changed and implemented, not on the policies themselves'); *Blusun SA, Jean-Pierre Lecorcier and Michael Stein v Italian Republic*, ICSID Case No ARB/14/3, Final Award (27 December 2016) para 318; *Jürgen Wirtgen, Stefan Wirtgen, Gisela Wirtgen and JSW Solar (zwei) GmbH & Co KG v Czech Republic*, PCA Case No 2014-03, Final Award (11 October 2017) paras 43–46.

[52] *Al Tamimi v Oman*, ICSID Case No ARB/11/33, Award (3 November 2015) para 261.

[53] EU–Singapore Investment Protection Agreement (n 38) art 2.4(2)(c).

compensation. In fact, failure by the host State to comply with such pattern of conduct with respect to the foreign investor or its investments affects the investor's ability to measure the treatment and protection awarded by the host State and to determine whether the actions of the host State conform to the fair and equitable treatment principle. [54]

It is fair to say that the *Tecmed* tribunal did not link the particular passage with rule-of-law considerations, and rather bracketed it by nods to good faith in public international law and *ELSI*.[55] But it did refer to the European Court of Human Rights (ECtHR) elsewhere in the award,[56] and the ascertainment of legitimate expectations by a comparative law method was employed in a number of well-known subsequent decisions, including by the dissenting arbitrator in *Thunderbird v Mexico* and the tribunals in *Total v Argentina* and *Gold Reserve v Venezuela*.[57]

Other chapters in this volume address protection of expectations and stability in greater detail,[58] so I will not go into the minutiae of various decisions that have addressed the concept. Taking stock of recent practice, there is broad consensus among tribunals that frustration of an investment made in reliance upon representations can breach FET.[59] There is somewhat less agreement regarding the scope and meaning of particular elements of this proposition,[60] and considerable divergence regarding a broader principle that would call for general stability of the legal order in the absence of specific representations.[61] The interesting question for the present purpose is how these developments have been received by the international legal process. In short, what was the ultimate reception of this rule-of-law-inspired innovations in dispute settlement review institutions (annulment committees), inter-State tribunals, and treaty-making?

The reaction has been mixed. The *MTD v Chile* annulment committee had this to say about the fit of *Tecmed* within the traditional structure of sources:

> 66. According to the Respondent, 'the TecMed programme for good governance' is extreme and does not reflect international law. The *TECMED* dictum is also subject to strenuous criticism from the Respondent's experts, Mr. Jan Paulsson and Sir Arthur Watts. They note,

---

[54] *Técnicas Medioambientales Tecmed, SA v The United Mexican States*, ICSID Case No ARB (AF)/00/2, Award (29 May 2003) para 154.

[55] ibid paras 153–54.

[56] ibid paras 116, 122.

[57] See respectively *International Thunderbird Gaming Corporation v The United Mexican States*, UNCITRAL Case, Award (26 January 2006), Separate Opinion Thomas Wälde, 1 December 2005) paras 27–30; *Total SA v Argentine Republic*, ICSID Case No ARB/04/1, Decision on Liability (27 December 2010) paras 128–29; *Gold Reserve Inc v Bolivarian Republic of Venezuela*, ICSID Case No ARB(AF)/09/1, Award (22 September 2014) para 576. As to the scholarly version of the argument, see Elizabeth Snodgrass, 'Protecting Investors' Legitimate Expectations—Recognizing and Delimiting a General Principle' (2006) 21 ICSID Rev—FILJ 1; Michele Potestà, 'Legitimate Expectations in Investment Treaty Law: Understanding the Roots and the Limits of a Controversial Concept' (2013) 28 ICSID Rev—FILJ 88.

[58] See Caroline Henckels, 'Legitimate Expectations and the Rule of Law in International Investment Law' (in this volume) 43.

[59] *United Utilities (Tallinn) BV and another v Estonia*, ICSID Case No ARB/14/14, Award (21 June 2019) paras 575–79; *Glencore* (n 8) paras 1310, 1368.

[60] *Greentech Energy Systems A/S and ors v Italy*, SCC Arbitration V (2015/095), Final Award (23 December 2018) paras 445–55; ibid Dissenting Opinion Sacerdoti (5 December 2018); *SolEs Badajoz GmbH v Spain*, ICSID Case No ARB/15/38, Award (31 July 2019) paras 312–13.

[61] *South American Silver Limited v Bolivia*, Award (PCA Case No 2013-15) 22 November 2018) para 650; *Voltaic Network GmbH v Czech Republic*, PCA Case No 2014-20, Award (15 May 2019) paras 487–88; *Glencore* (n 8) paras 1310, 1368.

inter alia, the difference between the TECMED standard and that adopted in other cases, including one the Tribunal also cited in a footnote but without comment.

67. The Committee can appreciate some aspects of these criticisms. For example the *TECMED* Tribunal's apparent reliance on the foreign investor's expectations as the source of the host State's obligations (such as the obligation to compensate for expropriation) is questionable. The obligations of the host State towards foreign investors derive from the terms of the applicable investment treaty and not from any set of expectations investors may have or claim to have. A tribunal which sought to generate from such expectations a set of rights different from those contained in or enforceable under the BIT might well exceed its powers, and if the difference were material might do so manifestly.[62]

The ICJ in the recent *Obligation to Negotiate Access to the Pacific Ocean* judgment (having one member of the *MTD* annulment committee as a judge) did not seem overly impressed either:

> The Court notes that references to legitimate expectations may be found in arbitral awards concerning disputes between a foreign investor and the host State that apply treaty clauses providing for fair and equitable treatment. It does not follow from such references that there exists in general international law a principle that would give rise to an obligation on the basis of what could be considered a legitimate expectation. Bolivia's argument based on legitimate expectations thus cannot be sustained.[63]

State practice is mixed but generally unenthusiastic. The 2018 EU–Singapore Investment Agreement provides that:

> In determining whether the fair and equitable treatment obligation, as set out in paragraph 2, has been breached, a Tribunal may take into account, where applicable, whether a Party made specific or unambiguous representations to an investor so as to induce the investment, that created legitimate expectations of a covered investor and which were reasonably relied upon by the covered investor, but that the Party subsequently frustrated.[64]

The 2018 Comprehensive and Progressive Agreement for Trans-Pacific Partnership (CPTPP) states that:

> For greater certainty, the mere fact that a Party takes or fails to take an action that may be inconsistent with an investor's expectations does not constitute a breach of this Article, even if there is loss or damage to the covered investment as a result.[65]

---

[62] *MTD* Annulment (n 32) paras 66–67.

[63] *Obligation to Negotiate Access to the Pacific Ocean (Bolivia v Chile)* (Judgment) [2018] ICJ Rep 507 para 161.

[64] EU–Singapore Investment Protection Agreement (n 38) art 2.4(3). A footnote adds that, '[f]or greater certainty, the frustration of legitimate expectations as described in this paragraph does not, by itself, amount to a breach of paragraph 2, and such frustration of legitimate expectations must arise out of the same events or circumstances that give rise to the breach of paragraph 2'.

[65] 2018 Comprehensive and Progressive Agreement on Trans-Pacific Partnership <www.mfat.govt.nz/assets/Trade-agreements/TPP/Text-ENGLISH/9.-Investment-Chapter.pdf> accessed 1 July 2021, art 9.6(4).

The 2020 Regional Comprehensive Economic Partnership (RCEP) adopts a very narrow reading of FET, seemingly limiting it to denial of justice.[66] Finally, in a 2020 non-disputing party submission, the United States suggested, by reference to its long-standing practice, that:

> The concept of 'legitimate expectations' is not a component element of 'fair and equitable treatment' under customary international law that gives rise to an independent host State obligation. The United States is aware of no general and consistent State practice and *opinio juris* establishing an obligation under the minimum standard of treatment not to frustrate investors' expectations. An investor may develop its own expectations about the legal regime governing its investment, but those expectations impose no obligations on the State under the minimum standard of treatment. The mere fact that a Party takes or fails to take an action that may be inconsistent with an investor's expectations does not constitute a breach of this Article, even if there is loss or damage to the covered investment as a result.[67]

These instances of practice speak to different instruments and are often carefully crafted not to prejudge positions on broader questions of treaty or customary law. Still, the common thread running through is suspicion of rule-of-law-inspired notions, either rejecting them wholesale or confining them within extremely narrow boundaries. There is nothing wrong with legal arguments failing to be endorsed *verbatim* by the international legal process—the messy transposition and refinement of domestic notions into a rule suited to public international law, crafted with an eye to properly international practice and techniques (eg estoppel),[68] is precisely how one expects the legal process to work. But to the extent that the intellectual inquiry is into how rule-of-law-inspired decisions have fared, legitimate expectations, just as with respect to proportionality (Section A above), is probably not the most successful example of reception.

C. Due Process

Unlike arbitrariness and protection of expectations with their apparent tension between rule-of-law-inspired approaches in arbitral practice and a significantly more qualified attitude by States, reliance on domestic and international standards seems to give rise to less tension on due process. A recent example on the arbitral side is the award in the well-known *Chevron v Ecuador (II)* case:

> 8.56 ... the Tribunal has found that Judge Zambrano acted corruptly, in return for a bribe promised to him by certain of the Lago Agrio Plaintiffs' representatives. Judge Zambrano's

---

[66] 2020 Regional Comprehensive Economic Partnership <www.dfat.gov.au/sites/default/files/rcep-chapter-10.pdf> accessed 1 July 2021, art 10.5(2)(a), (c). cf art 10.5(2)(a) ('fair and equitable treatment *requires* each Party not to deny justice in any legal or administrative proceedings') (emphasis added) with CPTPP art 9.6(2)(a) ('"fair and equitable treatment" *includes* the obligation not to deny justice in criminal, civil or administrative adjudicatory proceedings in accordance with the principle of due process embodied in the principal legal systems of the world') (emphasis added).

[67] *Omega Engineering LLC and Oscar Rivera v Panama*, ICSID Case No ARB/16/42, Third Submission of the USA (3 February 2020) para 24.

[68] *Chagos Marine Protected Area Arbitration (Mauritius v United Kingdom)* (2015) 31 RIAA 359 paras 435–38.

collusive conduct in the 'ghostwriting' of the Lago Agrio Judgment was not authorised under Ecuadorian law. Nor was it under judicial standards long established under international law. He was far from acting as an independent or impartial judge deciding the Lago Agrio Litigation fairly between the parties, under minimum standards for judicial conduct long recognized under international law.

8.57 Article 10 of the Universal Declaration of Human Rights, adopted by the UN General Assembly on 10 December 1948, provides: 'Everyone is entitled in full equality to a fair and public hearing by an independent and impartial tribunal, in the determination of his rights and obligations and any criminal charges against him'. Article 14 of the International Covenant on Civil and Political Rights, adopted by the UN General Assembly on 16 December 1966 (in force from 23 March 1976), to which the Respondent is a party, provides, in material part: 'All persons shall be equal before the courts and tribunals. In the determination of any criminal charge against him, or of his rights and obligations in a suit at law, everyone shall be entitled to a fair and public hearing by a competent, independent and impartial tribunal established by law'. Article 2 of the UN Basic Principles on the Independence of the Judiciary, adopted by the UN General Assembly in November-December 1985, provides: 'The judiciary shall decide matters before them impartially, on the basis of facts and in accordance with the law, without any restrictions, improper influences, inducements, pressures, threats or interferences, direct or indirect, from any quarter or for any reason'. Article 6 of these Basic Principles provides: 'The principle of the independence of the judiciary entitles and requires the judiciary to ensure that judicial proceedings are conducted fairly and that the rights of the parties are respected'.

8.58 The Tribunal does not understand from the Parties' respective submissions that these international standards for judicial conduct are materially disputed between them. Moreover, in addition to the Universal Declaration of 1948 and the International Covenant of 1966, the Constitutional Court's Judgment cites Article 8 of the American Convention on Human Rights of 1969 on the right to a fair trial 'by a competent, independent and impartial tribunal'. As to Ecuadorian law, the Constitutional Court's Judgment also cites the constitutional rights under Articles 75 and 76(7)(k) of the Respondent's Constitution 'to the effective, impartial and speedy protection of his or her rights and interests' and 'to be tried by an independent, impartial and competent judge'.[69]

This is not an isolated case. For example, in the 2002 award in *Mondev v United States*, the tribunal repeatedly referred to the case law of the ECtHR by analogy to inform its reasoning on FET regarding an alleged denial of justice by denial of access to court due to immunity.[70] In the 2008 award in *Victor Pey Casado and President Allende Foundation v Chile (I)*, the tribunal again relied on the European Court's case law to confirm its reasoning on denial of justice by excessive length of proceedings.[71] In general terms, Reinisch and Schreuer have

---

[69] *Chevron Corporation and Texaco Petroleum Company v Ecuador*, PCA Case No 2009-23, Second Partial Award on Track II (30 August 2018) paras 8.56–8.58.
[70] *Mondev International Ltd v US*, ICSID Case No ARB(AF)/99/2, Award (11 October 2002) paras 138, 141, 143–44.
[71] *Victor Pey Casado and President Allende Foundation v Chile (I)*, ICSID Case No ARB/98/2, Award (8 May 2008) para 662. *Pey Casado (I)* was partially annulled but not on this point, Decision on the Application for Annulment (18 December 2012) paras 281–87.

recently noted that '[d]ue process corresponds to domestic law concepts, often guaranteed on the level of constitutional law or at least civil and administrative procedural law. Because of this, it is legitimate for investment tribunals to identify and assess the due process requirements on a comparative basis.'[72]

How did States react to these developments? The difference between at best lukewarm State practice on appropriateness of comparative public law inspiration regarding arbitrariness and legitimate expectations, considered above, and the broadly positive endorsement regarding due process is striking. Indeed, the contrasting dynamic was evident in the very first serious engagement in the *Mondev* case, where the United States invoked by analogy the practice of the ECtHR, and it was the tribunal that emphasized the various differences between investment law and regional human rights that limited the usefulness of such claims:

> 141. The parties sought to draw analogies for the present case from the field of foreign State immunity . . . in a series of decisions the European Court of Human Rights has held that the conferral of immunity in ways recognised in international practice does not involve a denial of access to a court, contrary to Article 6(1) of the European Convention of Human Rights. By analogy, the United States argued, the recognition of a limited statutory immunity for certain torts could not be considered a violation of the international minimum standard or a denial of justice, given the lack of any clear or consistent State practice requiring the denial of immunity.

> 144. These decisions concern the 'right to a court', an aspect of the human rights conferred on all persons by the major human rights conventions and interpreted by the European Court in an evolutionary way. They emanate from a different region, and are not concerned, as Article 1105(1) of NAFTA is concerned, specifically with investment protection. At most, they provide guidance by analogy as to the possible scope of NAFTA's guarantee of 'treatment in accordance with international law, including fair and equitable treatment and full protection and security'. But the Tribunal would observe that, as soon as it was decided that BRA was covered by the statutory immunity (a matter for Massachusetts law), then the existence of the immunity was arguably to be classified as a matter of substance rather than procedure in terms of the distinction under Article 6(1) of the European Convention.[73]

Treaty practice has not sought to challenge the arbitral approaches either. The EU–Singapore Investment Protection Agreement lists 'denial of justice in criminal, civil and administrative proceedings' as one example of the breach of FET (with the uncontroversial footnote that 'the sole fact that the covered investor's claim has been rejected, dismissed or unsuccessful does not in itself constitute a denial of justice').[74] RCEP seems to make a similar point from the perspective of obligation, rather than breach: 'fair and equitable treatment requires each Party not to deny justice in any legal or administrative proceedings'.[75] CPTPP directs the interpreter to comparative engagement with domestic law, explaining that FET 'includes the obligation not to deny justice in criminal, civil or administrative adjudicatory

---

[72] Reinisch and Schreuer (n 22) 377.
[73] *Mondev* (n 70) paras 141, 144.
[74] EU–Singapore Investment Protection Agreement (n 38) art 2.4(2)(a), fn 2.
[75] RCEP (n 66) art 10.5(2)(a).

proceedings *in accordance with the principle of due process embodied in the principal legal systems of the world*.[76] This is very different from the treatment of other aspects of FET in State practice, where most 'for greater certainty' footnotes and new subparagraphs nod disapprovingly towards particular bits of arbitral practice, often precisely those inspired by the rule of law. With a veil of ignorance drawn over the last two decades of investment law, one might have expected that claims about due process would be, just as they had been since time immemorial, the most controversial aspect of the field. Why has this plausible expectation not materialized?

Let me suggest a number of possible reasons. First, denial of justice is a comparatively robust rule, building on a great amount of nineteenth- and early twentieth-century practice and well understood in the pre–Second World War international law.[77] Debates about arbitrariness and protection of expectations do not seriously date to times before the 1990s, so perhaps contestation is something that is inevitable in the foundational decades, just as it was for denial of justice a century ago. The second and related point is that modern practice has closely followed early twentieth-century approaches. The continuity is reflected in the routine footnoting of authorities from the 1910s to the 1930s, not waved aside as odd anachronisms as would often be the case on other aspects of FET.[78] The third point is the greater extent of global consensus on basic expectations regarding judicial conduct. It does not mean that human rights instruments can always be easily articulated as admissible interpretative materials[79] but, as the *Chevron* award quoted at the beginning of this section illustrates, there is a great deal of normative material at various levels and settings that address judicial conduct, unlike the highly uneven protection of property rights at the level of universal rules. The fourth point is an amalgam of the first three: if the basic structure of the rule is established, then States are content to see it fleshed out by reference to globally shared expectations. The final point will perhaps sound slightly cynical but even when States explicitly direct interpreters to domestic public law, it is not meant to be taken too seriously. A 2019 US non-disputing party submission is a good example, explaining 'the obligation not to deny justice … in accordance with the principle of due process embodied in the principal legal systems of the world' over three pages of extensively footnoted references to international law authorities *and* one sentence on US law.[80] The limited effect of explicit pointers to domestic public law put into perspective how enthusiastically international legal process is likely to treat rule-of-law-inspired approaches flowing from rules silent on the matter.

---

[76] CPTPP (n 65) art 9.6(2)(a) (emphasis added).

[77] Alwyn V Freeman, *International Responsibility of States for Denial of Justice* (Longmans, Green and Company 1938).

[78] *Gramercy Funds Management LLC and Gramercy Peru Holdings LLC v Peru*, ICSID Case No UNCT/18/2, Submission of the USA, 21 June 2019, fns 74, 82 (Borchard, 1919), 78 (Harvard Draft, 1929), 85 (Baty, 1930; Freeman, 1938).

[79] *Toto Construzioni Generali Spa v Lebanon*, ICSID Case No ARB/07/12, Decision on Jurisdiction, 11 September 2009) para 157 ('Article 6 of the ECHR certainly covers the question to which extent lengthy court proceedings are a breach of the right to due process and to a fair and equitable trial. This matter has been extensively subject of decisions from domestic courts and from the European Court of Human Rights. However, as Lebanon is not party to the ECHR and lies outside the territorial scope of the ECHR, these decisions are not relevant in this case').

[80] cf *Gramercy* US Submission (n 78) paras 42–47, fn 85.

IV. Conclusion

FET may be the strongest candidate for a positive expression of the rule of law in international investment law. For some, the proposition seems self-evidently true, like the *Casinos Austria* tribunal that recently spoke of the 'rule of law-elements flowing from fair and equitable treatment'.[81] As ever in a discussion conducted with an eye to a legal setting, it is helpful to be clear about what the argument is, how its validity may be tested, and what benefits and costs flow from accepting it. Section II argued that vagueness as well as intuitive normative appeal, even inevitability of the rule of law—one might as well argue against gravity and apple pie—may be leading to some conceptual looseness of the manner of its introduction into investment law debates. At the jurisprudential end of the spectrum, the rule of law is employed as a benchmark of political morality or a shorthand for describing the content of an international obligation complying with that benchmark. At the lawyerly end of the spectrum, the rule of law systematizes the chaos of arbitral practice that roughly follows the laundry list from political morality treatises or refers to the legal argument of bringing general principles into the interpretative process.

There may be advantages for relying on rule of law: it inspires solutions where the usual vocabulary of international law seems unpromising and will, for some, provide a source of legitimacy. But there are also costs, and even if one is ultimately ready to bear them, it is important to acknowledge them. One cost is conflation of philosophical and legal inquiries, with the danger of producing bad philosophy and bad law. The other is erosion of trust in normal methods of public international law reasoning, which in investment law, just as in other specialist fields, are capable of providing answers to even hard questions. There is also the more basic concern about conflating very different debates: we know what rule-of-law-inspired institutions and debates look like regionally,[82] and that is very different indeed from the decentralized international investment law. Indeed, even consequentialists will wonder whether the right takeaway from the European experience of the last few years is that the implementation of the rule of law in an institutionalized setting will always be received by universal consensus in a spirit of perfect tranquillity.

The benefit of writing this chapter in 2020 is that the analysis can take into account how rule-of-law-inspired approaches to FET have fared in the international legal process. What did States ultimately make of these elegantly written awards? Section III considered in turn three aspects of the application of FET: arbitrariness, protection of expectations, and due process, which seemed to have been received in two distinct ways. For arbitrariness and protection of expectations, arguments explicitly or by necessary implication drawing upon domestic legal traditions—respectively proportionality and legitimate expectations—have been treated with considerable scepticism, with States and the EU rejecting or at the very least framing them in the narrowest possible terms. Conversely, the traditionally contentious arbitral practice on denial of justice has been broadly endorsed, with States invoking human rights arguments by analogy and including references to domestic legal traditions in their treaties. It is hard to read this practice other than suggesting a sceptical reception

---

[81]   *Casinos Austria* (n 9) para 243.
[82]   See eg in Europe, the Council of Europe <www.coe.int/en/web/portal/rule-of-law> accessed 1 July 2021, and the European Commission, '2020 Rule of Law Report' (30 September 2020) <https://ec.europa.eu/info/publicati ons/2020-rule-law-report-communication-and-country-chapters_en> accessed 1 July 2021.

of rule-of-law elements by positivist international investment law when it goes against or significantly beyond the grain of traditional rules and assumptions. This scepticism does not mean that rule-of-law inquiry has no role to play, either in normative terms or in providing a descriptively helpful taxonomy for this supremely decentralized field of dispute settlement. But to the extent that the argument is employed to make a difference in a strictly legal debate, it has to explain why the rule of law is more than an ingenious solution to hard questions in the 2000s that was rejected by (the ultimate masters of) the international legal process as the 2010s unfolded. This chapter remains respectfully unpersuaded that such an explanation can be successfully provided.

3

Legitimate Expectations and the Rule of Law in International Investment Law

*Caroline Henckels**

I. Introduction

At its foundation, the concept of the rule of law means that law, rather than the whim of a person or persons, should structure and order the exercise of public authority. As Dicey opined, 'the rule of law is contrasted with every system of government based on the exercise by persons in authority of wide, arbitrary, or discretionary powers'.[1]

One well-known way of categorizing different interpretations of the concept is to divide it into the formal and the substantive. This distinction is relevant in terms of both determining the normative content of the rule of law, and using the rule of law as a yardstick to evaluate a legal system. Briefly stated, a formal approach addresses not the substance of the law, but rather factors such as the manner in which the law was enacted, the clarity and certainty of the law, whether the law operates retroactively, and the avoidance of arbitrariness.[2] The substantive approach grafts certain ideals onto these formal aspects, such as protecting personal liberties and property rights. For this reason, this approach has been criticized for its inextricable connection to the moral dimension of laws.[3] According to Raz, 'the rule of law is just one of the virtues which a legal system may possess and by which it is to be judged'; equating the rule of law to 'the rule of the *good* law', is to conflate the rule of law with 'a complete social philosophy'.[4]

Another concern is that the protean nature of the rule of law renders it vulnerable to the accusation that it functions as an empty vessel in which to pour one's own ideology about which norms should control government action.[5] In the context of international investment

* Thank you to the organizers and fellow participants of the Rule of Law and International Investment Law Workshop in Vienna in December 2018, and to Jonathan Bonnitcha and Patrick Emerton for helpful discussions. Thanks are also due to Adem Ahmed and Julia Wallace for excellent research assistance. Cases cited are up to date to 31 December 2018. Any errors are mine.

[1] Albert Venn Dicey, *Introduction to the Study of the Law of the Constitution, with Introduction by E.C.S. Wade* (10th edn, Macmillan 1959) 188.
[2] See eg Paul Craig, 'Formal and Substantive Conceptions of the Rule of Law: An Analytical Framework' (1997) PL 467, 470–71.
[3] Jeremy Waldron, 'The Rule of Law' (22 June 2016) *Stanford Encyclopaedia of Philosophy* <https://plato.stanford.edu/entries/rule-of-law/> accessed 8 November 2018.
[4] Joseph Raz, *The Authority of Law: Essays on Law and Morality* (Clarendon Press 1979) 211 (emphasis added). See also Raz, 'The Law's Own Virtue' (2019) 39 OJLS 1; Craig (n 2) 487.
[5] See Jeremy Waldron, 'Is the Rule of Law an Essentially Contested Concept (in Florida)?' (2002) 21 Law & Phil 137, 140; Muthucumaraswamy Sornarajah, *Resistance and Change in International Investment Law* (CUP 2015) 295: the rule of law is 'an abstraction that can be manipulated to serve the neoliberal cause'; Muthucumaraswamy Sornarajah, 'Mutations of Neo-Liberalism in International Investment Law' (2011) 3 TL & D 203, 218: 'disguising of the rules of investment protection in the garbs of the rule of law seeks to give it legitimacy by transference'.

Caroline Henckels, *Legitimate Expectations and the Rule of Law in International Investment Law* In: *Investment Protection Standards and the Rule of Law*. Edited by: August Reinisch and Stephan W. Schill, Oxford University Press. © Caroline Henckels 2023.
DOI: 10.1093/oso/9780192864581.003.0003

law, the suggestion that international investment law should comply with a substantive conception of the rule of law risks foisting legal doctrines that evolved primarily in capital-exporting countries onto capital-importing countries that, in some instances, go above and beyond what the legal systems of capital-exporting countries oblige of governments and in other instances, are unachievable as a matter of institutional capacity.[6] As Daniels and Trebilcock put it, adopting a formal approach to the rule of law 'avoids or at least mitigates charges of cultural imperialism in transplanting vast bodies of substantive law ... to developing country contexts where distinctive social, cultural, and historical conditions may render such universalistic prescriptions inappropriate'.[7] This has particular resonance in relation to fair and equitable treatment (FET), where the textual ambiguity of typical treaty provisions has allowed the obligation to function as a back door to bring in 'good governance' obligations that originate from legal systems with highly developed systems of administrative law.

One potential concern that arises under a substantive approach is the relevance of human rights. According to Bingham, a notable proponent of the substantive approach, respect for the rule of the law requires that a legal system provide for 'adequate protection of fundamental human rights'.[8] Investment tribunals have deployed the language of rights to describe investors' enjoyment of investment protections,[9] which (whether intentionally or not) operates to heighten the moral force with which we should view investment claims vis-à-vis other public interests and concerns that are involved in governmental decision-making. In other words, deploying the language of rights (that a foreign investor has certain 'rights' that should be guaranteed by the host State) risks elevating the moral justification for their protection to the detriment of competing public welfare interests.

For the purpose of this chapter, therefore, I restrict myself to identifying elements of a formal, largely Razian, understanding of the rule of law that may provide justification for the protection of legitimate expectations in international investment law. According to Raz, the rule of law is rooted in the autonomy of the individual. The law should operate prospectively only, be open and clear, and be relatively stable. Individuals should be able to discern the law so they may plan and organize their lives according to it, and the law should not be promulgated or applied in an arbitrary manner.[10] From these attributes, I focus on *reliance* on government conduct, *legal certainty*, and the avoidance of *arbitrariness*, for reasons that will become evident.

Section II discusses potential theoretical justifications for the protection of legitimate expectations, concluding that the theory of legal certainty provides the most plausible justification. Section III identifies various circumstances that may give rise to a claim for the protection of legitimate expectations, and assesses their strength from the standpoint of legal certainty. This analysis permits the development of a continuum of situations ranging from the retroactive revocation of a legal right or administrative decision at one end, and prospectively operating changes to government policy at the other. Section IV argues that the relevant basis for protecting legitimate expectations turns on whether the frustration of

---

[6] Carol Harlow, 'Global Administrative Law: The Quest for Principles and Values' (2006) 17 EJIL 187, 193, 210, 211; Ronald J Daniels and Michael Trebilcock, 'The Political Economy of Rule of Law Reform in Developing Countries' (2004) 26 Mich JIL 99, 105.

[7] Daniels and Trebilcock (n 6) 105.

[8] Tom Bingham, 'The Rule of Law' (2007) 66 CLJ 67, 75.

[9] See Nicolás Perrone, 'The Emerging Global Right to Investment: Understanding the Reasoning behind Foreign Investor Rights' (2017) 8 JIDS 673.

[10] Raz, *Authority of Law* (n 4) 213–14, 219–20.

them amounts to arbitrary conduct, and contends that the justificatory burden on government correlates to the strength of the claim to protection of expectations.

II. Legitimate Expectations in Theory and Practice

A. The Nature of Legitimate Expectations

1. Legitimate expectations in comparative perspective

The doctrine of legitimate expectations provides individuals with a remedy in certain circumstances where the conduct of a public authority conveys an understanding that the individual will receive (or continue to receive) a substantive benefit or commodity of some kind, and then acts inconsistently with this prior conduct.[11] Relevant conduct may include formal decisions, promises, or representations, as well as extant laws, policies, and practices. In legal systems that recognize substantive legitimate expectations, the applicable remedy is the realization of a particular benefit or advantage,[12] rather than the procedural form of protection for legitimate expectations that is recognized in many other domestic legal systems.[13] Many European States,[14] together with countries including India, South Africa, and some Caribbean countries[15] recognize substantive legitimate expectations. The protection of substantive legitimate expectations is also a general principle of European Union (EU) law,[16] and such expectations are treated as a component to the right to property under the European Convention on Human Rights.[17]

Although legal systems apply a variety of tests to determine whether an individual's expectations will be protected, at a general level, two related questions must be asked (although they are not always disaggregated in this way):

1. In which circumstances can government conduct generate a legitimate expectation?
2. In which circumstances will the law protect a legitimate expectation?

The first question is addressed to the various types of government conduct that may form a basis for a claim of legitimate expectations, and the question whether the expectation is reasonable (legitimate) in the circumstances. The second question, which concerns the circumstances in which the law will intervene to protect those expectations, gives rise to two competing imperatives. On one hand, there are various normative reasons (discussed

---

[11] See Paul Craig, *Administrative Law* (7th edn, Sweet & Maxwell, 2012) 677; Farah Ahmed and Adam Perry, 'The Coherence of the Doctrine of Legitimate Expectations' (2014) 73 CLJ 61, 67.

[12] On the distinction between procedural and substantive legitimate expectations, see Craig (n 11) 350–53.

[13] Courts in some jurisdictions (such as Australia and Canada) have rejected substantive legitimate expectations for a variety of reasons pertaining to the separation of powers and other incompatibilities with constitutional principles: see further Matthew Groves and Greg Weeks (eds), *Legitimate Expectations in the Common Law World* (Hart 2017).

[14] See further Jürgen Schwarze, *European Administrative Law* (rev 1st edn, Sweet & Maxwell 2006) ch 6.

[15] See Josef Ostřanský, 'An Exercise in Equivocation: A Critique of Legitimate Expectations as a General Principle of Law under the Fair and Equitable Treatment Standard' in Andrea Gattini, Attila Tanzi and Filippo Fontanelli (eds), *General Principles of Law and International Investment Arbitration* (Brill 2018) 344, 353 (with further references).

[16] Paul Craig, *EU Administrative Law* (2nd edn, OUP 2012) 549–50.

[17] See eg Luzius Wildhaber and Isabelle Wildhaber, 'Recent Case Law on the Protection of Property in the European Convention of Human Rights' in Christina Binder and others (eds), *International Investment Law for the 21st Century: Essays in Honour of Christoph Schreuer* (OUP 2009) 657.

further below) as to why an individual's expectations ought to be recognized in certain circumstances. On the other hand, governments need to retain their lawful discretionary powers and be able to deviate from a previous course of conduct where circumstances so dictate.[18] In other words, determining whether an individual's expectations deserve legal protection will involve some form of balancing between the relevant public and private interests in order to ensure that the protection of the individual's expectations does not unduly constrain the exercise of public authority.

2. The emergence of legitimate expectations in international investment law

The emergence of legitimate expectations as a principle of FET[19] illustrates the increasing influence of both domestic and supranational law in the interpretation of international investment law. The genesis and development of legitimate expectations in international investment law is already well documented, so I will only briefly discuss it here.[20] The academic literature[21] began to assert the existence of legitimate expectations as an element of FET in parallel with its emergence in the decided cases[22] in the early 2000s.

Yet, the legal foundations of the doctrine in international investment law are contested.[23] Not only does the text of the overwhelming majority of investment treaties not refer to the concept,[24] but it has no apparent grounding in customary international law[25] and, in light of its patchy application in domestic law, it is not a general principle of law.[26] As Paparinskis observes, the concept 'seems vulnerable ... [the] legal approaches of a limited number of

[18] Paul Craig, 'Substantive Legitimate Expectations in Domestic and Community Law' (1996) 55 CLJ 289, 307, 310.

[19] The concept of legitimate expectations has also appeared in investment decisions concerning the question whether a claimant holds an 'investment' and whether a measure amounts to an indirect expropriation. This chapter addresses only legitimate expectations as an element of FET. I also note that some tribunals have relied on the concept of legitimate expectations as the organizing principle of FET in the sense that a claimant has a legitimate expectation of being afforded FET. As Bonnitcha notes, this approach is circular: Jonathan Bonnitcha, *Substantive Protection Under Investment Treaties* (CUP 2014) 169. See also Mārtiņš Paparinskis, *The International Minimum Standard and Fair and Equitable Treatment* (OUP 2013) 257.

[20] See eg Michele Potestà, 'Legitimate Expectations in Investment Treaty Law: Understanding the Roots and the Limits of a Controversial Concept' (2013) 28 ICSID Rev—FILJ 88.

[21] Francisco Orrego Vicuña, 'Regulatory Authority and Legitimate Expectations: Balancing the Rights of the State and the Individual under International Law in a Global Society' (2003) 5 International Law Forum Du Droit International 188, 194; Francisco Orrego Vicuña, 'Foreign Investment Law: How Customary Is Custom?' (2005) 99 Proceedings of the ASIL 97, 99–100; Rudolf Dolzer, 'Fair and Equitable Treatment: A Key Standard in Investment Treaties' (2005) 39 International Lawyer 87, 103; Christoph Schreuer, 'Fair and Equitable Treatment in Arbitral Practice' (2005) 6 JWIT 386; Elizabeth Snodgrass, 'Protecting Investors' Legitimate Expectations: Recognizing and Delimiting a General Principle' (2006) 21(1) ICSID Rev—FILJ 1.

[22] Starting with *Metalclad Corporation v United Mexican States*, ICSID Case No ARB(AF)/97/1, Award (30 August 2000) para 85; *CME Czech Republic BV v Czech Republic*, UNCITRAL, Partial Award (13 September 2001) para 611; *Técnicas Medioambientales Tecmed SA v The United Mexican States*, ICSID Case No ARB(AF)/00/2, Award (29 May 2003) paras 154–55; *Waste Management v United Mexican States*, ICSID Case No ARB(AF)/00/3, Award (30 April 2004) para 98.

[23] See for a critical view on the emergence of legitimate expectations as an element of FET, Sornarajah, *Resistance and Change* (n 5) 257–68. See also Ostřanský (n 15); Teerawat Wongkaew, 'The Transplantation of Legitimate Expectations in Investment Treaty Arbitration: A Critique' in Shaheeza Lalani and Rodrigo Polanco Lazo (eds), *The Role of the State in Investor-State Arbitration* (Brill 2015) 69; Christopher Campbell, 'House of Cards: The Relevance of Legitimate Expectations under Fair and Equitable Treatment Provisions in Investment Treaty Law' (2013) 30 J Intl Arb 361; Trevor Zeyl, 'Charting the Wrong Course: The Doctrine of Legitimate Expectations in Investment Treaty Law' (2011) 49 Alberta L Rev 203.

[24] See in particular, the Separate Opinion of Arbitrator Nikken in *Suez, Sociedad General de Aguas de Barcelona, SA and Vivendi Universal, SA v Argentine Republic*, ICSID Case No ARB/03/19, Decision on Liability (30 July 2010).

[25] Sornarajah, *Resistance and Change* (n 5); Paparinskis (n 19).

[26] Sornarajah, *Resistance and Change* (n 5) 253: 'The hint that ... the rule on legitimate expectations constitutes a general principle of law has not been convincingly demonstrated'; Zeyl (n 23); Campbell (n 23); Ostřanský

developed traditionally home States are attributed direct legal influence on international law that the traditional approaches to sources *prima facie* do not support'.[27]

Tribunal decisions in this area are typically sparsely reasoned, relying on neither the tools of treaty interpretation nor the sources of international law to explicate their reasons for holding that legitimate expectations are an element of FET.[28] While some tribunals have tried to ground the concept of legitimate expectations in a comparative public law analysis,[29] most tribunals have simply cited earlier decisions to establish the existence of the doctrine, without demarcating its rationales, contours and outer limits.[30] Likewise, to the extent that the literature identifies rationales for the protection of legitimate expectations, it is under-theorized and does not analyse in detail the relevant underlying principle or principles that inform the doctrine. Today, this phenomenon resembles a feedback loop: like tribunals, almost all commentators list legitimate expectations as an element of FET.[31]

B. In Search of a Justification for the Protection of Legitimate Expectations

It is not only in international investment law that legitimate expectations might be said to lack a clear theoretical and doctrinal anchor. In English law, for example, Elliot argues that the doctrine risks becoming 'an unnecessary envelope capable of being placed around intervention on any ground', and Forsyth argues that '[t]here is a real danger that the concept ... will collapse into an inchoate justification for judicial intervention'.[32] These criticisms are also apt to describe the genesis and rapid evolution of legitimate expectations in

---

(n 15). See also *Obligation to Negotiate Access to the Pacific Ocean (Bolivia v Chile)* (Judgment) [2018] ICJ Rep 507, para 162.

[27] Paparinskis (n 19) 255–56.

[28] See eg *MTD Equity Sdn. Bhd. and MTD Chile SA v Republic of Chile*, ICSID Case No ARB/01/7, Award (25 May 2004) para 180; *Azurix Corp v The Argentine Republic*, ICSID Case No ARB/01/12, Award (14 July 2006) para 372; *CMS Gas Transmission Company v The Republic of Argentina*, ICSID Case No ARB/01/8, Award (12 May 2005) para 279; *Occidental Petroleum and Production Co v The Republic of Ecuador*, LCIA Case No UN 3467, Final Award (1 July 2004) para 185. As Arbitrator Nikken in *AWG v Argentina* opined, the development of the doctrine 'is the result of the interaction of the claims of investors and their acceptance by arbitral tribunals, buttressed by the presumed moral authority of the decided cases' rather than 'the terms that the Parties themselves used to define their commitments': *Suez, Sociedad General de Aguas de Barcelona, SA and Vivendi Universal, SA v Argentine Republic*, ICSID Case No ARB/03/19, Separate Opinion Nikken (30 July 2010) para 27. Moreover, the annulment committee in *MTD v Chile* held that:

> The obligations of the host State towards foreign investors derive from the terms of the applicable investment treaty and not from any set of expectations investors may have or claim to have. A tribunal which sought to generate from such expectations a set of rights different from those contained in or enforceable under the BIT might well exceed its powers, and if the difference were material might do so manifestly.

MTD v Chile, Decision on Annulment (21 March 2007) para 67.

[29] *International Thunderbird Gaming Corporation v Mexico*, UNCITRAL, Separate Opinion Wälde (1 December 2005) paras 27–30; *Total SA v Argentine Republic*, ICSID Case No ARB/04/1, Decision on Liability (27 December 2010) para 129; *Gold Reserve Inc v Bolivarian Republic of Venezuela*, ICSID Case No ARB(AF)/09/1, Award (22 September 2014) para 576.

[30] See Bonnitcha (n 19) 161–62; Potestà (n 20) 91; Ostřanský (n 15) 348–49 (with further references).

[31] See eg Andrew Newcombe and Lluis Paradell, *Law and Practice of Investment Treaties* (Kluwer 2009) 275; Rudolf Dolzer and Christoph Schreuer, *Principles of International Investment Law* (2nd edn, OUP 2012) 145; Roland Kläger, *'Fair and Equitable Treatment' in International Investment Law* (CUP 2011) 117–18.

[32] Mark Elliott, 'Legitimate Expectations, Consistency, and Abuse of Power: the *Rashid* Case' (2005) 10 JR 281, 283; Christopher Forsyth, 'Legitimate Expectations Revisited' (2011) 16 JR 429, 429.

international investment law into what is now regarded as the 'dominant element'[33] of the FET standard.

Several different accounts of legitimate expectations emerge from the decided cases and the (mainly non-international investment law) literature. Arguably, no single theory offers a complete justification for the protection of legitimate expectations in international investment law or elsewhere. Rather, it is possible to identify a justification for the protection of legitimate expectations in certain circumstances that would accord with a formal understanding of the rule of law.

1. Good faith

A number of international investment cases advert to the international law principle of good faith as a basis for the protection of legitimate expectations.[34] In this regard, there is some analogy between legitimate expectations and the international law doctrines of estoppel and the binding nature of certain unilateral acts in international law, in relation to which the International Court of Justice (ICJ) has held are both grounded in good faith.[35] However, the ICJ has also cautioned that the principle of good faith cannot itself generate a legal obligation where none would otherwise exist.[36] Like the concept of the rule of law, good faith is a rather nebulous concept that risks being deployed after the fact to rationalize a decision,[37] and is capable of being manipulated to serve different objectives. As such, it seems that good faith cannot by itself offer a justification for the protection of legitimate expectations in international investment law.

2. Protection from arbitrary conduct, abuse of power or unfairness

Three related theories have been offered as a justification for the protection of legitimate expectations: protection of the individual against arbitrary conduct,[38] abuse of power,[39] and

---

[33] See *Saluka Investments BV (The Netherlands) v The Czech Republic*, UNCITRAL, Partial Award (17 March 2006) para 302.

[34] See eg *Técnicas Medioambientales TECMED, SA v The United Mexican States*, ICSID Case No ARB (AF)/00/ 2, Award (29 May 2003) para 154; *International Thunderbird Gaming Corporation v Mexico*, UNCITRAL, Separate Opinion Wälde (1 December 2005) para 25; *Sempra Energy International v Argentine Republic*, ICSID Case No ARB/02/16, Award (28 September 2007) para 298; *Waguih Elie George Siag & Clorinda Vecchi v Arab Republic of Egypt*, ICSID Case No ARB/05/15, Award (1 June 2009) para 450; *Total SA v Argentine Republic*, ICSID Case No ARB/04/1, Decision on Liability (27 December 2010) paras 128, 130; *El Paso Energy International Company v Argentine Republic*, ICSID Case No ARB/03/15, Award (31 October 2011) para 348; *Gold Reserve Inc v Bolivarian Republic of Venezuela*, ICSID Case No ARB(AF)/09/1, Award (22 September 2014) para 576; *CC/Devas (Mauritius) Ltd, Devas Employees Mauritius Private Limited and Telcom Devas Mauritius Limited v Republic of India*, PCA Case No 2013-09, Award on Jurisdiction and Merits (25 July 2016) para 458.

[35] See James Crawford, *Brownlie's Principles of Public International Law* (8th edn, OUP 2012) 420–21.

[36] See *Case Concerning the Border and Transborder Armed Actions (Nicaragua v Honduras)* (Judgment) [1988] ICJ Rep 69, para 94; *Case Concerning the Land and Maritime Boundary between Cameroon and Nigeria (Cameroon v Nigeria: Equatorial Guinea intervening)* (Preliminary Objections) [1998] ICJ Rep 275, para 39.

[37] See Muthucumaraswamy Sornarajah, 'Introduction' in Andrew D Mitchell, Muthucumaraswamy Sornarajah and Tania Voon (eds), *Good Faith and International Economic Law* (OUP 2015) 1.

[38] In international investment law, see *Técnicas Medioambientales TECMED, SA v The United Mexican States*, ICSID Case No ARB (AF)/00/2, Award (29 May 2003) para 154; *Frontier Petroleum Services v Czech Republic*, UNCITRAL, Final Award (12 November 2010) para 285; Ostřanský (n 15) 356, 370; Mārtiņš Paparinskis, 'Good Faith and Fair and Equitable Treatment in International Investment Law' in Mitchell and others (n 37) 169. See also Paul Reynolds, 'Legitimate Expectations and the Protection of Trust in Public Officials' (2011) PL 330, 339; Philip Sales and Karen Steyn, 'Legitimate Expectations in English Public Law: An Analysis' (2004) PL 564, 582.

[39] In international investment law, see *Total v Argentine Republic*, Decision on Liability (27 December 2010) para 129; Orrego Vicuña (n 21) 194; Ostřanský (n 15) 357; Ivar Alvik, *Contracting with Sovereignty: State Contracts and International Arbitration* (Hart 2011) 159–237. See also eg CSJ Knight, 'Expectations in Transition: Recent Developments in Legitimate Expectations' (2009) PL 15, 17–18 (describing English courts' approach); Timothy Endicott, *Administrative Law* (2nd edn, OUP 2011) 285–86.

unfairness.[40] Arbitrary conduct captures a far broader category of government action than frustrating legitimate expectations. Likewise, the concept of abuse of power does not tell us specifically why, and in which circumstances, an individual's expectations deserve legal protection. At least in common law systems, abuse of power is better understood as a general organizing principle for judicial review of administrative action or a conclusory statement, rather than a justification for judicial intervention.[41] And while fairness is relevant to the question whether to protect an individual's expectations in a given case, it is likewise relevant in many other situations.[42]

Therefore, although the need to prevent arbitrary conduct, abuse of power, and unfairness provide a partial justification for protecting legitimate expectations, none of these theories gives much assistance in delimiting its contours.[43] That is, these theories offer no particular basis for identifying values underlying legitimate expectations in particular, as opposed to controlling government action in a general sense. However, as will be discussed below in Section IV.A, the concept of arbitrariness is relevant to the question of when government conduct will be inconsistent with the FET standard, both in a general sense and in the specific context of determining whether it will be possible to frustrate legitimate expectations.

3. Reliance

A number of investment tribunals[44] and commentators[45] consider that an individual's reliance on the conduct of the host State provides the basis for the protection of legitimate expectations, or refer to reliance when stating the relevant legal test. To be sure, foreign investors can only recover damages in relation to loss incurred as a result of government

[40] In international investment law, see Campbell McLachlan, Laurence Shore and Matthew Weiniger, *International Investment Arbitration: Substantive Principles* (2nd edn, OUP 2017) para 7.179; Orrego Vicuña, 'Regulatory Authority and Legitimate Expectations' (n 21) 194. See also Søren J Schønberg, *Legitimate Expectations in Administrative Law* (OUP 2000) 2; Craig, 'Substantive Legitimate Expectations' (n 18) 297; Paul Daly, 'A Pluralist Account of Deference and Legitimate Expectations' in Groves and Weeks (n 13) 101, 106–07; Craig, *EU Administrative Law* (n 16) 554; TRS Allan, *Law, Liberty, and Justice: The Legal Foundations of British Constitutionalism* (Clarendon Press 1994) 197; TRS Allan, 'Pragmatism and Theory in Public Law' (1988) 104 LQR 422, 435.

[41] See eg Daly (n 40) 105.

[42] Ahmed and Perry (n 11) 69; Reynolds (n 38) 332–33.

[43] Reynolds (n 38) 332–33.

[44] See eg *International Thunderbird Gaming Corporation v United Mexican States*, UNCITRAL, Award (26 January 2006) para 147; *Waste Management, Inc v United Mexican States*, ICSID Case No ARB(AF)/00/3, Award (30 April 2004) para 98; *Enron Creditors Recovery Corporation and Ponderosa Assets, LP v Argentine Republic*, ICSID Case No ARB/01/3, Decision on Jurisdiction (14 January 2004) paras 262 and 264; *LG&E Energy Corp, LG&E Capital Corp and LG&E International Inc v Argentine Republic*, ICSID Case No ARB/02/1, Decision on Liability (3 October 2006) para 130; *Duke Energy Electroquil Partners and Electroquil SA v Republic of Ecuador*, ICSID Case No ARB/04/19, Award (18 August 2008) paras 365 and 340; *BG Group plc v The Republic of Argentina*, UNCITRAL, Final Award (24 December 2007) para 308; *Suez, Sociedad General de Aguas de Barcelona SA and Interagua Servicios Integrales de Agua SA v Argentine Republic*, ICSID Case No ARB/03/17, Decision on Liability (30 July 2010) para 207; *Parkerings-Compagniet AS v Lithuania*, ICSID Case No ARB/05/8, Award (11 September 2007) para 331; *PSEG Global Inc, The North American Coal Corporation, and Konya Ingin Electrik Uretim ve Ticaret Limited Sirketi v Turkey*, ICSID Case No ARB/02/5, Award (19 January 2007) paras 241–43; *GAMI Investments, Inc v Mexico*, UNCITRAL (NAFTA), Final Award (15 November 2004) para 76; *Jan de Nul NV v Arab Republic of Egypt*, ICSID Case No ARB/04/13, Award (6 November 2008) para 263; *Metalclad Corporation v United Mexican States*, ICSID Case No ARB(AF)/97/1, Award (30 August 2000) paras 85, 87, 89; *Antin Infrastructure Services Luxembourg Sàrl. and Antin Energia Termosolar BV v Kingdom of Spain*, ICSID Case No ARB/13/31, Award (15 June 2018) para 532; *Bear Creek Mining Corporation v Republic of Peru*, ICSID Case No ARB/14/21, Award (30 November 2017) para 522; *Rusoro Mining Ltd v Bolivarian Republic of Venezuela*, ICSID Case No ARB(AF)/12/5, Award (22 August 2016) para 444; *Peter A. Allard v The Government of Barbados*, PCA Case No 2012-06, Award (27 June 2016) paras 217–18.

[45] McLachlan, Shore and Weiniger (n 40) para 7.179; Todd J Grierson-Weiler and Lan A Laird, 'Standards of Treatment' in Peter Muchlinski, Federico Ortino and Christopher Schreuer (eds), *The Oxford Handbook on International Investment Law* (OUP 2008) 275.

action. In other words, reliance is necessary in order for a claim to succeed. But this is a separate issue to the question whether reliance itself is a justification for the protection of legitimate expectations.

There are good reasons why the law should afford protection to an individual where a public authority engages in a conduct upon which an individual has reasonably relied, and detriment is caused when the public authority resiles from that conduct.[46] In some circumstances, we might say that the public authority has created moral, promissory obligations that the law should step in to enforce.[47] As Raz observes, the rule of law can be violated when an individual has relied on a particular legal situation and those plans are frustrated by subsequent government conduct.[48] Reliance is also connected to legal certainty, which is discussed below.

However, an argument can be made that the reliance theory alone is under-inclusive, because the question whether an individual can receive a remedy depends on whether they can prove that they had relied on the government's conduct to their detriment. Schønberg, for instance, argues that a requirement of detrimental reliance 'may lead to unjustified distinctions between similar cases', because 'whether a person relies on the representation or not may be entirely fortuitous', and those who have not (or not yet) acted in reliance on the conduct may nevertheless be affected by it.[49] As such, the reliance theory is not itself capable of providing a normative basis for protection of legitimate expectations in all circumstances in this context.[50]

4. Legal certainty

Proponents of the legal certainty rationale[51] view the protection of legitimate expectations as normatively grounded upon recognizing the autonomy and dignity of individuals which, according to Raz, 'entails treating humans as persons capable of planning and plotting their future'.[52] As such, the conduct of public authorities ought to be reasonably certain so that individuals can ascertain their legal entitlements and obligations and plan their affairs accordingly.[53] Legal certainty also operates to protect the trust that individuals repose in governments in circumstances where a public authority has undertaken to act in a certain way.[54]

---

[46] See Schønberg (n 40) 10; Daphne Barak-Erez, 'The Doctrine of Legitimate Expectations and the Distinction between the Reliance and Expectation Interests' (2005) 11 EPL 583, 590–92.

[47] Those who liken legitimate expectations to a type of public law estoppel usually rely on this justification: see eg Alexandra Diehl, *The Core Standard of International Investment Protection: Fair and Equitable Treatment* (Kluwer 2012) 340–48. As to why estoppel is not a suitable analogy to legitimate expectations, see Chester Brown, 'The Protection of Legitimate Expectations as a "General Principle of Law": Some Preliminary Thoughts' (2009) 6(1) TDM 1, 9–10; Ostřanský (n 15) 352. See also Sales and Steyn (n 38) 564, 570–72; Endicott (n 39) 287–88.

[48] Raz, *Authority of Law* (n 4) 222 (referring to retroactive decisions).

[49] Schønberg (n 40). See also Craig, *Administrative Law* (n 11) 681; Craig, *EU Administrative Law* (n 16) 554, suggesting that reliance 'cannot … be the only reason for according protection'; Reynolds (n 38) 346: 'reliance will be helpful but is in no way necessary'.

[50] William Wade and Christopher Forsyth, *Administrative Law* (10th edn, OUP 2009) 452–53. See also Schønberg (n 40) 17: 'Reliance is only relevant in so far as it strengthens the Rule of Law [legal certainty, discussed below] justification for protection of legitimate expectations.'

[51] Another way of describing this rationale is in terms of the desirability of consistency in governance: Schønberg (n 40) 13–14. Richard Clayton, 'Legitimate Expectations, Policy, and the Principle of Consistency' (2003) 62 CLJ 93, 104–05.

[52] Raz, *Authority of Law* (n 4) 221. See also, arguing that legitimate expectations are connected to dignity, Daly (n 40) 107–08, 110, 114; Raz, *Authority of Law* (n 4) 222.

[53] Schønberg (n 40) 12–16; Craig, 'Substantive Legitimate Expectations' (n 18) 304; Craig, *EU Administrative Law* (n 16) 549–50, 555; Schwarze (n 14) 946–49.

[54] Robert Thomas, *Legitimate Expectations and Proportionality in Administrative Law* (Hart 2000) 45.

In the context of legitimate expectations, a government can act inconsistently with the principle of legal certainty in two different situations. The principle of non-retroactivity preserves the legal effect of situations that took place in the past. Individuals base their decisions on existing facts and norms, and are entitled to expect that changes should operate prospectively only. Thus, where government action with *actual retroactive effect* occurs (that is, where the conduct is applied to past events in the sense of changing their legal status), there are strong arguments that support the granting of a remedy to an individual.[55] However, where a measure has *apparent retroactive effect* (where the relevant conduct is applied prospectively only, but affects or has the potential to affect an individual that has planned their actions on the basis of an existing policy),[56] the question of whether a remedy is due is more complex. Such a situation brings into play the competing imperatives of the need for a government to be able to alter a course of conduct where the public interest so dictates, and the normative desirability of legal certainty for individuals that had planned their actions on the basis of the extant legal situation.

III. Recognizing and Protecting Legitimate Expectations in Different Circumstances

In this section, I examine the different types of government conduct that investment tribunals have examined through the lens of legitimate expectations.[57] The nature of the government conduct at issue is a key consideration. It may be eminently reasonable for an individual to rely on a formal decision taken in respect that individual, whereas it will generally not be reasonable to rely on a view that legislation will remain stable and unchanged.[58] Conduct with actual (as opposed to apparent) retroactive effect also adds to the strength of the justification for the protection of an individual's legitimate expectations in all categories discussed below.

First, however, one cross-cutting issue must be addressed, which is the question of the objective reasonableness (or 'legitimacy') of an investor's expectations. In EU law, the relevant test is whether the 'prudent trader' would have held the relevant expectations insofar as the challenged conduct could have been foreseen.[59] While a standard like this has not been articulated by investment tribunals, a number have cautioned (both in relation to legitimate expectations and more generally) that investment treaties do not function as insurance policies against poor business decisions and that a prospective investor should exercise a reasonable level of due diligence. One relevant consideration is the political, socio-economic, cultural, historical, and regulatory climate of the host State.[60] In societies or in relation to areas of law that are generally less stable, a rational actor ought to factor in the potential for change, whereas a settled area of law may generate comparatively stronger expectations in

---

[55] Craig, 'Substantive Legitimate Expectations' (n 18) 304–05.

[56] See Schwarze (n 14) 1119–22: ' "Apparent retroactivity" is deemed to be the applicability of legislative acts to events which originated in the past but which have yet to be definitely concluded.'

[57] Here I adapt the classifications made by Bonnitcha (n 19); Potestà (n 20) 88; Craig, *EU Administrative Law* (n 16) 553.

[58] Charles Sampford and others, *Retrospectivity and the Rule of Law* (OUP 2006) 208–09.

[59] See Craig, *EU Administrative Law* (n 16) 631.

[60] See Bonnitcha (n 19) 182; Patrick Dumberry, 'The Protection of Investors' Legitimate Expectations and the Fair and Equitable Treatment Standard under NAFTA Article 1105' (2009) 1 Arb Intl 47, 65–66 (with further references).

stability.[61] Another factor is the investor's own conduct in terms of any wrongdoing, such as the misrepresentation to the government of the nature of the investment.[62] These are factors that investment tribunals have taken into account, and should continue to take into account when determining whether expectations were reasonably held.

A. Revocation of Legal Right or Formal Administrative Decision

The first group of cases involves interference with a specific legal right held by an investor under domestic law (such as contractual rights or rights acquired pursuant to a licence or permit),[63] or the revocation of a formal administrative decision. There are strong arguments in favour of recognizing legitimate expectations in such circumstances.[64] As noted above, the principle of legal certainty suggests that an individual is entitled to have confidence that their legal rights will not be interfered with, and that a formal decision made by government in respect of that individual has the character of finality. Interfering with a right or revoking a decision is likely to have a detrimental effect on the plans of the individual, particularly where there has been reliance on that right or decision.[65] The more formal the decision, the weightier the justification for protecting legitimate expectations arising from it.[66] Some jurisdictions that protect substantive legislate expectations generally provide that such decisions cannot be revoked unless there are exceptional circumstances that would warrant revocation.[67]

B. Conduct Inconsistent with Prior Representation or Commitment

The second category of cases involves representations or commitments made by public authority in its official capacity, that do not create legal rights or have the character of a formal decision.[68] Generally speaking, the strength of the justification for recognizing legitimate expectations in this situation depends on the specificity of the representation with respect to its subject matter and/or representee or representees.[69] An unequivocal representation made by the legally authorized person or body to a specific individual ought generally to be viewed as non-revocable in nature, provided that the material facts on which the

---

[61] See generally Jill E Fisch, 'Retroactivity and Legal Change: An Equilibrium Approach' (1997) 110 Harv L Rev 1055.

[62] See eg *International Thunderbird v Mexico* (n 44) para 148, where the investor's claim that Mexico had acted inconsistently ordering the investor to close its gambling facilities despite previous permission failed due to the investor's misrepresentation of the nature of their business as compliant with relevant laws. See for EU law, Craig, *EU Administrative Law* (n 16) 570–73.

[63] See the discussion in Bonnitcha (n 19) 169. As Potestà notes, 'resort to this concept in this situation entails the risk of equating any kind of contractual expectation with a genuine treaty claim' ((n 20) 100–03).

[64] See Craig, *EU Administrative Law* (n 16) 561; Craig, 'Substantive Legitimate Expectations' (n 18) 304–05.

[65] See Schønberg (n 40) 14; Craig, *EU Administrative Law* (n 16) 553.

[66] Craig, *EU Administrative Law* (n 16) 553.

[67] See eg in relation to EU law, Schwarze (n 14) 1024; Craig, *EU Administrative Law* (n 16), 556–61, 567–73. In relation to Germany, see Schwarze (n 14) 889–91, 894.

[68] Bonnitcha (n 19) 176–82; Craig, *EU Administrative Law* (n 16) 568.

[69] See Bonnitcha (n 19) 287: if the domestic legal regime has clear rules in place concerning the revocability of previous unilateral representations, Razian principles might not be offended, for example, if domestic law clearly treats such representations as legally insignificant.

representation was based have not changed.[70] Such a representation might also be likened to a promise, which generates a moral obligation.[71] Conversely, a less specific and formal representation is less likely to give rise to concerns with respect to legal certainty, on the basis that an imprecise (equivocal and/or non-specific) representation cannot generate a strong expectation with regard to the stability of future government conduct, nor be likened to a promise. In short, an unequivocal, precise, and specific representation made by the appropriate representor generates a strong claim for the recognition of expectations, and any interference with the expectation would require significant justification. However, governments are complex entities, and it may be reasonable to rely on the commitments of some officials but not others (in terms of factors such as the seniority of the representor and the representor's actual or ostensible authority to make the representation), as well as any other communications between the government and an individual, including at different levels of government.[72]

C. Departure from Existing Policy in Individual Case

The third category of cases concerns a public authority departing from a generally applicable policy or procedure in respect of an individual. Such cases provide a relatively strong justification for the protection of legitimate expectations. Even though policies are general in nature and therefore distinguishable from a representation made to an individual, it is arguable that the existence of a policy to guide decision-making should, in general, bind the exercise of discretion by a decision-maker.[73] It appears that many legal systems view existing policies or guidelines as generally possessing a binding character, based on equality (treating like cases alike) as well as the need for legal certainty.[74] If the exercise of discretion in a particular case involved treating like cases differently, this would raise a prima facie issue of unequal treatment,[75] which in turn suggests arbitrary conduct.[76]

---

[70] Schønberg (n 40) 14. See also Jack Watson, 'Clarity and Ambiguity: A New Approach to the Test of Legitimacy in the Law of Legitimate Expectations' (2010) 30 LS 633, 652.

[71] See Ahmed and Perry (n 11) 70; Craig, *EU Administrative Law* (n 16) 553.

[72] In *MTD v Chile*, for example, the national government had approved the import of capital to fund the redevelopment of land, but the local government refused the proposal to rezone the land for the purpose of the development. Although Chile was found to have acted inconsistently with MTD's legitimate expectations, the approval made by the national agency stipulated that the project had to comply with local laws, suggesting that the claimant ought not to have held such expectations. See further Bonnitcha (n 19) 190–91.

[73] Ahmed and Perry (n 11) 70.

[74] Craig, *EU Administrative Law* (n 16) 578–84 (discussing EU law); Schønberg (n 40) 133–42 (discussing EU, English, and French approaches).

[75] Here, I depart from a Razian approach. According to Raz, equality is not a component of the rule of law but rather part of one's moral or philosophical standpoint: 'the rule of law ... is not to be confused with ... equality (before the law or otherwise)' (*Authority of Law* (n 4) 211). Nevertheless, on Raz's approach, it may be that unequal treatment of the similarly situated will amount to arbitrary conduct. cf John Rawls, *A Theory of Justice* (Harvard UP 1971) 237: 'The rule of law ... implies the precept that similar cases be treated similarly. [People] could not regulate their actions by rules if this precept were not followed'; Timothy Endicott, 'The Impossibility of the Rule of Law' (1999) 19 OJLS 1, 3: 'Government is arbitrary if it does not treat like cases alike—if it does not treat people consistently.'

[76] Schønberg (n 40) 15. See further Karen Steyn, 'Consistency—A Principle of Public Law?' (1997) 2 JR 22, 22.

D. Change to Legal Framework, Policy, or Procedure

The fourth category of cases involves expectations arising from the existing legal frame-work, including relevant legislation, policies, and procedures—but in circumstances where no decision or representation has been made as to their stability.[77] That is, changes to existing laws, policies, and procedures may be said to frustrate expectations that the relevant norm would continue to apply. To be sure, the Razian conception of the rule of law requires that laws be 'relatively stable' and not 'changed too often', in order that people can rely on the content of the law for both short- and long-term planning.[78] But, as Bonnitcha observes, the Razian approach 'does not place substantive constraints on states' ability to enact laws that cause loss to individuals, regardless of whether the state knew of the potential for its action to cause such loss'.[79]

Other systems typically do not recognize legitimate expectations arising from the extant legal framework, or provide protection for those expectations in only limited circumstances.[80] The argument from legal certainty is weak in this situation, because protecting legitimate expectations would risk ossifying policy choices made by governments, thereby undermining their ability to pursue regulatory change in the public interest.[81] This is especially the case where changes operate prospectively only, given the broad powers of lawmakers to amend or revoke prevailing legislation and policies.[82] Recognizing legitimate expectations in this situation could also discourage governments from adopting policies to guide decision-making, which in turn risks inconsistent (and potentially arbitrary) decision-making.[83] As such, provided that the change in the law or policy is not in some way arbitrary in the sense of being repeated or erratic[84] (discussed further below), I argue that the principle of legal certainty does not demand that such expectations are recognized.

---

[77] Bonnitcha (n 19) 175.

[78] Raz, *Authority of Law* (n 4) 214–15. See also Lon Fuller, *The Morality of Law* (rev edn, Yale UP 1969) 39: rules should not change so frequently that persons are unable to plan their behaviour based on them.

[79] Bonnitcha (n 19) 278.

[80] For example, changes in laws and policies do not engage the doctrine of legitimate expectations in English law. Under EU law, no legitimate expectations relating to policy and legislative changes are recognized, unless the claimant is party to a bargain with the authorities or there is a specific assurance on the part of the authorities that the measure would not be changed: Craig, *EU Administrative Law* (n 16) 573–78. In Germany, retroactively operating changes to laws are justifiable only in exceptional circumstances, whereas prospectively operating provisions receive comparatively less protection: Schwarze (n 14) 898–900.

[81] See eg Craig, 'Substantive Legitimate Expectations' (n 18) 305; Craig, *EU Administrative Law* (n 16) 573; Sampford and others (n 58) 90.

[82] In EU law, retroactive changes are more difficult to justify than prospective changes: Craig, *EU Administrative Law* (n 16) 550–52.

[83] Jason Varuhas, 'In Search of a Doctrine: Mapping the Law of Legitimate Expectations' in Groves and Weeks (n 13) 17, 21.

[84] See Bonnitcha (n 19) 283.

Prospectively operating changes to law, policy or practice		Retroactive revocation of legal right or formal decision
Very weak justification for protection		*Very strong justification for protection*

Figure 3.1 Strength of justification for protection of legitimate expectations

IV. The Permissibility of Frustrating Legitimate Expectations

Recalling that two questions or themes are common to the legal systems that recognize legitimate expectations—in which circumstances can government conduct *generate* a legitimate expectation, and under which circumstances will the law *protect* a legitimate expectation—it should be noted that the recognition that an individual holds a legitimate expectation is provisional, in the sense that it may yield to overriding public interest considerations.[85] Although this is not the place to engage in a detailed review of other legal systems' approaches,[86] it is evident that the strength of the argument for protecting legitimate expectations will depend on the context in which it arises in the sense of type of government action at issue. This can be depicted, as shown in Figure 3.1, by a continuum bounded at one end by retroactive revocations of rights and formal decisions, in relation to which there is a very strong justification for protection of legitimate expectations, and bounded at the other end by prospectively operating changes to the existing regulatory framework, for which there is only a very weak justification for protection.

A. The Threshold for Illegality Depends on the Legal System at Issue

In Section II.B.2, I noted that the related issues of unfairness, abuse of power, and arbitrariness were able to provide a partial justification for legitimate expectations. In English law, for example, unfairness and abuse of power are the relevant touchstones for judicial control of government action, including legitimate expectations.[87] But the threshold at which the law will intervene to protect legitimate expectations depends on the relevant legal system. This begs the question how this test might be framed in international investment law. One of the unresolved interpretive questions concerning the FET standard is the applicable threshold in relation to which government action will be inconsistent with the standard.

In relation to FET clauses that refer to treatment in accordance with international law or customary international law, the prevailing view seems to be that FET operates to control *arbitrary* treatment. Investment tribunals have held, for example, that government conduct would be arbitrary in situations where the State had arbitrarily reneged on undertakings

---

[85] See eg Watson (n 70) 365; Richard Moules, *Actions Against Public Officials: Legitimate Expectations, Misstatements and Misconduct* (Sweet & Maxwell 2009) 64, 66.
[86] As to which see eg Snodgrass (n 21) 25–52, Ostřanský (n 15) 356–69, Potestà (n 20) 93–98; Zeyl (n 23) 211–16.
[87] See eg Reynolds (n 38) 339; Elliott (n 32) 200.

made as to the stability of the legal framework,[88] or had arbitrarily revoked administrative decisions or permits.[89]

In relation to FET clauses that do not refer to customary international law or to principles of international law, tribunals' prevailing approach has been that states must conform to more exacting standards of conduct in relation to the treatment of foreign investments, and that conduct that would not be inconsistent with the customary international law standard might nevertheless fall foul of an FET clause that is not bound to customary international law. In other words, it seems to be accepted that conduct short of arbitrariness may be inconsistent with the FET standard in relation to this type of clause. Yet, as Paparinskis has argued, the correctness of this approach is open to doubt, and FET provisions that do not refer to customary international law arguably ought to be interpreted in light of custom.[90] And expansive interpretations of this type of FET clause by tribunals has led many States to change their treaty practice to instead explicitly adopt the customary international law formulation.[91]

I therefore suggest that limiting the protection of legitimate expectations to circumstances where it would be arbitrary to frustrate them comports with a formal conception of the rule of law.[92]

B. What Amounts to Arbitrary Conduct?

According to Raz, the rule of law prohibits governments engaging in arbitrary conduct including changing the law retroactively,[93] abruptly, or secretly; acting with an improper purpose; or acting with indifference as to whether conduct is directed to the purpose of the law.[94] For Endicott, arbitrary government 'lacks constraint, consistency, or certainty'.[95] A prohibition on arbitrariness as an element of the rule of law also corresponds with Fuller's principle that decisions should be made according to rules rather than in an arbitrary manner.[96]

Yet, arbitrariness is a term that has various meanings depending on the context. The decided investment cases do not clarify the circumstances in which government conduct will

---

[88] *Frontier Petroleum Services v Czech Republic*, UNCITRAL, Final Award (12 November 2010) para 285.

[89] *Técnicas Medioambientales TECMED, SA v The United Mexican States*, ICSID Case No ARB (AF)/00/2, Award (29 May 2003) 154.

[90] Paparinskis (n 19) 95–96, 166–67; Mārtiņš Paparinskis, 'Fair and Equitable Treatment (FET)' in Thomas Cottier and Krista Nadakavukaren Schefer (eds), *Elgar Encyclopedia of International Economic Law* (Elgar 2017). See also UNCTAD, 'Fair and Equitable Treatment: A Sequel' (2012) xiv.

[91] Discussed further in Section C below.

[92] Limiting the threshold for relief to arbitrary conduct also accords with the International Law Commission's Guidelines on Unilateral Acts, which provide that States maintain the power to terminate a unilateral act so long as that termination is not arbitrary: International Law Commission, 'Yearbook of the International Law Commission 2006, Volume II Part Two: Report of the Commission to the General Assembly on the Work of Its Fifty-Eighth Session' (2006) UN Doc A/CN.4/SER.A/2006/Add.1 (Part 2), principle 10.

[93] Although retroactivity generally offends the principle of legal certainty, I prefer the view of Sampford and others (n 58) 229–56, who argue that retroactive laws are justifiable in some cases. One example Sampford offers is retroactive legislation that sought to rectify large-scale tax avoidance that has caused an unequal distribution of tax burdens, or to permit the prosecution of war criminals (ibid 93–94).

[94] Raz, *Authority of Law* (n 4) 219. See also Endicott (n 75) 2; Dicey (n 1).

[95] Endicott (n 75) 3.

[96] Fuller (n 78) 39. Fuller's concept of the law required, among other things, both a degree of legal certainty and a prohibition on arbitrariness: decisions should not be made on an ad hoc basis but according to rules, and legislation should not be retroactive.

be arbitrary; rather, the term is often used as a conclusory statement. Investment tribunals have frequently cited the ICJ's decision in the *ELSI* case, where the ICJ interpreted a clause prohibiting arbitrary measures in the US–Italy Friendship, Commerce and Navigation Treaty. In that case, the ICJ stated that arbitrary conduct was something more grave than simple unlawfulness: 'To identify arbitrariness with mere unlawfulness would be to deprive it of any useful meaning in its own right ... Arbitrariness is not so much something opposed to a rule of law, as something opposed to the rule of law'.[97] UNCTAD's 2012 report on FET defines arbitrary conduct as that 'derived from mere opinion', 'capricious', 'unrestrained', 'despotic', or 'founded on prejudice or preference rather than on reason or fact'.[98] Arbitrary decision-making 'has to do with the motivations and objectives behind the conduct concerned', such as government conduct that has no legitimate purpose or rational explanation 'but that instead rests on prejudice or bias'.[99] Each of these interpretations has a different emphasis and nuance, but the common thread among all is that the concept has a high threshold—that the relevant act is irrational, not explicable by coherent reasons, or taken for an improper purpose.

In Section III, I identified the different contexts in which a legitimate expectations claim might be made. Above, I observed that the strength of a claimant's interests from the perspective of legal certainty will depend on where the type of impugned government action is located on the continuum. In order to determine whether a given legitimate expectation warrants protection, a tribunal would need to assess the government's justification and whether, in the circumstances, the treatment of the claimant (ie the frustration of the claimant's expectations) was arbitrary. The focus here is not what the investor expected, but the rationality of the government conduct. The extent of the justificatory burden on government would correlate to the strength of the claim for legitimate expectations. For example, government conduct inconsistent with a prior formal decision would require a weighty justification so as to avoid a finding of arbitrariness.[100]

Admittedly, it is difficult in the abstract to prescribe a standard or formula for what amounts to arbitrary conduct, although we can take Raz as a starting point: conduct with actual retroactivity, acting for an improper purpose, and acting without regard to the objective of the relevant governing legislation. Examples might include a situation where a government retroactively revokes a decision conferring a benefit on the claimant, without a rational justification; or where a government resiles from previous assurances made to the investor where this conduct was not explicable by rational governance–related reasons, but perhaps to favour a domestic competitor.

Figure 3.2 depicts again the continuum of conduct, adding the concomitant burden of justification required in order to mitigate a claim of arbitrary conduct.

---

[97] *Elettronica Sicula SpA (ELSI) (US v Italy)* (Judgment) [1989] ICJ Rep 15, paras 124–28.

[98] UNCTAD, 'Fair and Equitable Treatment: UNCTAD Series on Issues in International Investment Agreements II' (2012) UN Doc UNCTAD/DIAE/IA/2011/5, 78.

[99] ibid. See also Patrick Dumberry, 'The Prohibition Against Arbitrary Conduct and the Fair and Equitable Treatment Standard under NAFTA Article 1105' (2014) 15 JWIT 117, 121–25.

[100] Daly (n 40) 117: 'the relative strength of the expectation would require more or less by way of explanation from the decision-maker seeking to resile from its previous representation'; Mark Elliott, 'From Heresy to Orthodoxy: Substantive Legitimate Expectations in English Public Law' in Groves and Weeks (eds) (n 13) 220: 'the circumstances of the particular case may warrant the decision-maker being placed under a more or less onerous justificatory burden'.

Prospectively operating changes to law, policy or practice

Very weak justification for protection

Low justificatory burden on government

Retroactive revocation of legal right or formal decision

Very strong justification for protection

High justificatory burden on government

Figure 3.2 Strength of justificatory burden on government

C. Post-2016 Treaty Developments that Require Arbitrary Conduct to Establish Breach

The view that the applicable threshold for frustrating legitimate expectations is arbitrary conduct is buttressed by developments in treaty-making since 2016, which specifically refer to arbitrariness as the touchstone for review in relation to legitimate expectations.

Treaties have attempted to constrain tribunal discretion in relation to FET since 2001, when the NAFTA[101] parties issued a binding Note of Interpretation clarifying that NAFTA's FET clause did not require treatment over and above that required by the customary international law minimum standard of treatment.[102] Many treaties negotiated since then have followed suit.[103] However, the Comprehensive and Progressive Agreement for Trans-Pacific Partnership goes further, explicitly adopting the customary international law formulation and providing that 'the mere fact that a Party takes or fails to take an action that may be inconsistent with an investor's expectations does not constitute a breach ... even if there is loss or damage to the covered investment as a result'.[104] This clarifies that a government may frustrate legitimate expectations so long as the conduct is not so grave as to be inconsistent with the customary international law minimum standard of treatment (ie arbitrary conduct).

The FET clause in the Canada–EU Comprehensive Economic and Trade Agreement is more specific, providing that a State will act inconsistently with the FET standard where its conduct is, inter alia, 'manifestly arbitrary'. When making this determination, a tribunal 'may take into account whether a Party made a specific representation to an investor to induce a covered investment ... upon which the investor relied ... but that the Party subsequently frustrated'.[105] This suggests that the negotiating parties did not view legitimate

---

[101] North American Free Trade Agreement (NAFTA) (signed 17 December 1992, entered into force 1 January 1994) 32 ILM 289.

[102] NAFTA Free Trade Commission, 'Note of Interpretation of Certain Chapter 11 Provisions' (2001); NAFTA, art 133(2) provides that notes of interpretation issued by the Commission shall be binding on arbitral tribunals. Note that the awards discussed in this chapter, in some cases, relate to a treaty provision that refers to 'international law' but not specifically customary international law.

[103] See eg Agreement between the Government of the Kingdom of Bahrain and the Government of the United Mexican States on the Promotion and Reciprocal Protection of Investments (signed 21 November 2012, entered in force 30 July 2014): art 4(2): 'For greater certainty: (a) the concepts of "fair and equitable treatment" and "full protection and security" do not require treatment in addition to or beyond that which is required by the customary international law minimum standard of treatment of aliens.' UNCTAD has identified 97 treaties that qualify the FET clause with reference to customary international law or the customary international law minimum standard of treatment of aliens. Of these, 91 were concluded after the NAFTA parties' Note of Interpretation.

[104] Comprehensive and Progressive Agreement for Trans-Pacific Partnership (signed 8 March 2018, entered into force 30 December 2018) art 9.5(4).

[105] Canada–European Union Comprehensive Economic and Trade Agreement (signed 30 October 2016, provisionally applied since 21 September 2017) art 8.10(4).

expectations as a standalone element of FET, but rather as one situation that may amount to manifestly arbitrary conduct.[106] The EU–Singapore Agreement is similarly phrased, but provides that only 'specific *or unambiguous* representations to an investor' could engender legitimate expectations.[107] These treaty provisions introduce significant constraints upon arbitral discretion, by limiting the type of conduct that can engender a legitimate expectation to certain forms of representation made to induce the making of an investment.[108]

V. Conclusion

This chapter has examined the relationship between the rule of law and legitimate expectations in international investment law. In particular, it has focused on how two elements of a formal approach to the rule of law—legal certainty and non-arbitrariness—may provide a justification for the protection of legitimate expectations in international investment law.

Through the lens of legal certainty, the different situations in which legitimate expectations claims arise in international investment law can be placed on a continuum ranging from a strong claim (retroactive revocation of legal rights and formal administrative decisions) to a weak claim (prospectively operating changes to the regulatory environment). The chapter then argued that arbitrariness ought to be the organizing principle for breach of FET, both in general and relation to the frustration of legitimate expectations. The justificatory burden on government would correlate to the strength of the claim for protection of legitimate expectations. That is to say, the stronger the claim for the protection of legitimate expectations on the basis of legal certainty, the more compelling the government's reasons for its actions should be; in other words, the greater the burden of justification. The analysis suggests, largely in line with more recent decisions by investment tribunals,[109] that individualized, specific decisions and representations are far more likely to provide justification for protecting legitimate expectations than non-specific representations or changes to the extant legal framework.

However, this approach also gives rise to a more fundamental issue. It may have the effect of displacing a specific doctrine of legitimate expectations in favour of a general test of arbitrary conduct, with frustrating legitimate expectations being one possible way in which the State might act arbitrarily. This approach places the applicable test for breach of FET in line with emerging State practice, whereby in certain post-2016 treaties, legitimate expectations are subsumed under the more general prohibition of arbitrary (or manifestly

---

[106] See also *Waste Management, Inc v United Mexican States*, ICSID Case No ARB(AF)/00/3, Award (30 April 2004) para 98: 'the minimum standard of treatment of fair and equitable treatment' was infringed when State conduct was 'arbitrary, grossly unfair, unjust or idiosyncratic, is discriminatory … or involves a lack of due process … in applying this standard it is relevant that the treatment is in breach of representations made by the host State which were reasonably relied on by the claimant', but see the Separate Opinion of Thomas Wälde, paras 1, 37.

[107] Investment Protection Agreement between the European Union and its Member States and the Republic of Singapore (signed 15 October 2018) (hereafter EU–Singapore IPA) arts 2.4(2)–(3) (emphasis added). See also ch 17 (Investment), art 15(2), (4), Agreement-in-principle for the EU–Mexico Free Trade Agreement, <http://trade.ec.europa.eu/doclib/press/index.cfm?id=1833>.

[108] The EU–Singapore IPA clarifies that 'representations made so as to induce the investments include the representations made in order to convince the investor to continue with, not to liquidate or to make subsequent investments': art 2.4(3), fn 2.

[109] See McLachlan, Shore and Weiniger (n 40) 316–17.

arbitrary) conduct, and do not constitute a standalone element of FET.[110] This approach is sensible: the proscription on arbitrary conduct has a clear connection to the customary international law minimum standard of treatment, whereas the doctrine of legitimate expectations as a self-standing legal obligation has been heavily criticized since its inception. Focusing on arbitrariness would comport not only with the Razian understanding of the rule of law, but would also respond to criticisms that the concept of legitimate expectations lacks any grounding in the sources of international law.

---

[110] Paparinskis (n 19) 259: 'in many instances the focus on expectations seems to distract attention from the sophisticated criteria for evaluating different forms of arbitrariness already in existence'; Paparinskis, 'Good Faith' (n 38) 169, '[the] practice on protection of expectations is better read as an elaboration of a particular aspect of arbitrariness than as a separate perspective'; Ostřanský (n 15) 356, 370: 'the protection of legitimate expectations may thus be conceptualized within the broader notion of arbitrariness'.

4

(Direct and Indirect) Expropriation and the Rule of Law

Marc Bungenberg[*]

I. Introduction

International investment agreements (IIAs) have long since established a number of requirements—public purpose, non-discrimination, due process, and compensation—that must be fulfilled for an expropriation to be lawful. These requirements impose limits upon a State's legislative and executive branches, and thus serve as a yardstick under international law 'for the (legal) exercise of the host State's administrative, judicial, and legislative activity vis-à-vis foreign investors'.[1] Simultaneously, these requirements are closely related to the concept of rule of law as established by the United Nations (UN),[2] which will serve as a reference point for analysis in this chapter. This chapter will thus focus on the examination of the means by which the rule of law informs the prohibition of unlawful expropriation established under international investment law. In addition, it will discuss how arbitral tribunals have relied on the traditional legality criteria to distinguish between indirect expropriations and regulatory action in the exercise of a State's police powers.

The UN has devoted considerable attention to the rule of law in different resolutions, beginning with the 1970 Friendly Relations Declaration, through which the General Assembly emphasized the 'paramount importance of the Charter of the United Nations in the promotion of the rule of law among nations'.[3] The 2012 Rule of Law Declaration similarly calls for 'an effective, just, non-discriminatory and equitable delivery of public services pertaining to the rule of law, including criminal, civil and administrative justice'.[4] Both conceptualizations are understood to refer mostly to the 'procedural' conception of rule-of-law aspects but equally add certain substantive elements of the rule of law. Accordingly, the 2012 Rule of Law Declaration refers to 'just, fair and equitable laws' as well as to 'equal protection of the

---

[*] The author would like to thank Dr Fabian Blandfort for his support in preparing a first version of this chapter, as well as Bianca Böhme and Shaun Fu for further assistance.

[1] Stephan W Schill, 'Fair and Equitable Treatment, the Rule of Law, and Comparative Public Law' in Stephan W Schill (ed), *International Investment Law and Comparative Public Law* (OUP 2010) 151, 154.

[2] On the UN concept of rule of law, see August Reinisch, 'The UN Concept of the Rule of Law' (2019) 3 Z Eu S 337, 339, referring to Joseph Raz, *The Authority of Law* (OUP 1979) 211, and Tom Bingham, *The Rule of Law* (2010) 67.

[3] United Nations General Assembly, 'Declaration on Principles of International Law Friendly Relations and Cooperation among states in accordance with the Charter of the United Nations' (24 October 1970) UN Doc A/RES/2625(XXV).

[4] UNGA, 'Declaration on the Rule of Law at the National and International Levels' (30 November 2012) UN Doc A/RES/67/1 para 12 ('We reaffirm the principle of good governance and commit to an effective, just, non-discriminatory and equitable delivery of public services pertaining to the rule of law, including criminal, civil and administrative justice, commercial dispute settlement and legal aid').

Marc Bungenberg, *(Direct and Indirect) Expropriation and the Rule of Law* In: *Investment Protection Standards and the Rule of Law*. Edited by: August Reinisch and Stephan W. Schill, Oxford University Press. © Marc Bungenberg 2023. DOI: 10.1093/oso/9780192864581.003.0004

law' 'without any discrimination.'[5] Moreover, a 2004 UN Secretary-General's report mentions substantive elements, such as the adherence to international human rights norms, in its definition of the rule of law,[6] thus referring to a broad conception of the rule of law. It is this broader definition that is also the basis for discussions in the present chapter.

Separately, the recognition and observance of (individual) fundamental rights, in particular property rights, is an element of the rule of law in numerous domestic jurisdictions.[7] In parallel, a similar requirement known as the standard of 'no expropriation without compensation' can be found in various international human rights treaties. Indeed, at the global level, a right to property was first recognized in Article 17 of the 1948 Universal Declaration of Human Rights,[8] even though neither the 1966 International Covenant on Economic, Social and Cultural Rights[9] nor the 1966 International Covenant on Civil and Political Rights[10] subsequently adopted this approach. At the regional level, the right to property was included in Protocol No 1 to the European Convention for the Protection of Human Rights and Fundamental Freedoms (ECHR),[11] the American Convention on Human Rights,[12] the African Charter on Human and Peoples' Rights,[13] and the Charter of Fundamental Rights of the European Union (CFR).[14]

Originally, the ECHR did not contain a provision on the protection of property, but the Council of Europe delegated the decision on a European right to property to a special committee constituted in 1951. Finally, such a right was included in Article 1 of Protocol No 1 to the ECHR of 20 March 1952, which states that '[n]o one shall be deprived of his possessions except in the public interest and subject to the conditions provided for by law and by the general principles of international law'.[15] Even though the Convention does not explicitly provide for the requirement to pay compensation, the European Court of Human Rights (ECtHR) considered such a condition to be implicit, observing that 'under the legal systems of the Contracting States, the taking of property in the public interest without payment of compensation is treated as justifiable only in exceptional circumstances'.[16]

In addition, the ECtHR stated with regard to the protection of property that:

> the first and most important requirement of Article 1 of Protocol No. 1 is that any interference by a public authority with the peaceful enjoyment of possessions should be

---

[5] ibid para 2 ('We recognize that the rule of law applies to all States equally, and to international organizations, including the United Nations and its principal organs, and that respect for and promotion of the rule of law and justice should guide all of their activities and accord predictability and legitimacy to their actions. We also recognize that all persons, institutions and entities, public and private, including the State itself, are accountable to just, fair and equitable laws and are entitled without any discrimination to equal protection of the law').

[6] Report of the Secretary General, 'The Rule of Law and Transitional Justice in Conflict and Post-Conflict Societies' (23 August 2004) UN Doc S/2004/616, para 6.

[7] From a German perspective, see Eberhard Schmidt-Aßmann, 'Der Rechtsstaat' in Josef Isensee and Paul Kirchhof (eds), *Handbuch des Staatsrechts Band II: Verfassungsstaat* (3rd edn, CF Müller 2004) 541, para 5.

[8] UNGA Res 217 A (III) (10 December 1948) UN Doc A/RES/3/217 A.

[9] 993 UNTS 3.

[10] 999 UNTS 171.

[11] 213 UNTS 221.

[12] 1144 UNTS 123.

[13] 1520 UNTS 217.

[14] OJ 2010 C83/389.

[15] On the conditions for a justification of expropriations according to the ECHR, see Ursula Kriebaum, *Eigentumsschutz im Völkerrecht: Eine vergleichende Untersuchung zum internationalen Investitionsschutzrecht sowie zum Menschenrechtsschutz* (Duncker & Humblot 2008) 431ff.

[16] *James and ors v UK* App no 8793/79 (ECtHR, 21 February 1986) para 54.

lawful: the second sentence of the first paragraph authorises a deprivation of possessions only 'subject to the conditions provided for by law' and the second paragraph recognises that the States have the right to control the use of property by enforcing 'laws'. Moreover, the rule of law, one of the fundamental principles in a democratic society, is inherent in all the articles of the Convention ... and entails a duty on the part of the State or other public authority to comply with judicial orders or decisions against it.[17]

Accordingly, the protection of property on the international level is closely related to the rule of law, both in the field of human rights protection and in international investment law. With regard to the latter, on which this chapter focuses, the above-mentioned UN concept of a broad understanding of the rule of law is of high relevance. Referencing, in particular, the above-cited UN Secretary-General's 2004 report[18] and the 2012 UN General Assembly declaration,[19] it appears that international investment law's adoption of requirements that impose conditions on the lawfulness of expropriations can be connected with other fields of international law, especially the protection of human rights.

A rule-of-law understanding is especially important when considering the emerging discussion of proportionality as an element that is taken into account in the assessment of whether a foreign investor has been expropriated. The principle of proportionality has been particularly relevant in the jurisprudence of regional human rights courts, and is now increasingly referred to in IIAs and arbitral practice based thereon. Therefore, the subsequent analysis is based on the concept that the principle of proportionality,[20] as a legal restriction on the State's interferences with fundamental rights, can be qualified as an additional element of the rule of law.

At the domestic level, some courts derive the proportionality principle directly from (national) rule-of-law principles.[21] At the international level, rule-of-law considerations are reflected at least in the jurisprudence of the ECtHR[22] and the Court of Justice of the European Union (CJEU).[23] In addition, the WTO Appellate Body applies this principle, albeit not expressly and without further discussing its origin.[24] Finally, the above-mentioned UN reports refer to the notions of 'just' and 'fair', thus equally indicating that a proportional treatment is required under a broad rule-of-law concept.

---

[17] *Iatridis v Greece* App no 31107/96 (ECtHR, 25 March 1999) para 58.

[18] Report of the Secretary General (n 6) para 6.

[19] UNGA (n 4) para 2.

[20] See on the criteria of legitimate expectations and proportionality, eg August Reinisch, 'Expropriation' in Peter Muchlinski, Federico Ortino and Christoph Schreuer (eds), *Oxford Handbook of International Investment Law* (OUP 2008) 407, 448ff, pointing to the importance of the jurisprudence of the ECtHR.

[21] See for Germany, German Constitutional Court, BVerfGE 19, 342 (348ff) (25 December 1965): 'In der Bundesrepublik Deutschland hat der Grundsatz der Verhältnismäßigkeit verfassungsrechtlichen Rang. Er ergibt sich aus dem Rechtsstaatsprinzip, im Grunde bereits aus dem Wesen der Grundrechte selbst' ('In the Federal Republic of Germany, the principle of proportionality has constitutional rank. It arises from the principle of the rule of law, basically already from the very essence of fundamental rights') (translation by the author).

[22] See on this Johannes Saurer, 'Die Globalisierung des Verhältnismäßigkeitsgrundsatzes' (2012) 51 Der Staat 3; Joseph Cremona, 'The Proportionality Principle in the Jurisprudence of the European Court of Human Rights' in Ulrich Beyerlin and others, *Recht zwischen Umbruch und Bewahrung* (Springer 1995) 323ff.

[23] See Takis Tridimas, 'The Principle of Proportionality' in Robert Schütze and Takis Tridimas (eds), *Oxford Principles of European Union Law: The European Union Legal Order*, vol I (2018) 243ff.

[24] WTO, *European Communities: Measures Prohibiting the Importation and Marketing of Seal Products—Report of the Appellate Body* (22 May 2014) WT/DS400/AB/R and WT/DS401/AB/R, para 5.169; WTO, *United States: Measures Affecting the Cross-Border Supply of Gambling and Betting Services—Report of the Appellate Body* (7 April 2005) WT/DS285/AB/R, para 292.

As will be discussed, the requirement to compensate investors for regulatory measures can be seen as an element of a proportional interference in their property rights. In fact, the obligation to compensate is not only upheld in human rights law, but also as a matter of general international law.[25] As the obligation to compensate is part of the protection of property under human rights law, it qualifies as an element of the substantive rule-of-law concept. Moreover, the principle of proportionality is becoming increasingly relevant in the assessment of whether an indirect expropriation took place, balancing the interests of the foreign investor and the policy goals pursued by the host State.

Following this introduction, Section II will discuss the requirements established in IIAs for an expropriation to be lawful and explain how each requirement is closely connected to the concept of rule of law, as reflected in the various UN documents. Section III will discuss the impact of the rule of law on the assessment of whether a measure constitutes an indirect expropriation. It will also demonstrate how national constitutional law has influenced the regulation of indirect expropriation in recent IIAs, with the Comprehensive Economic and Trade Agreement (CETA) serving as an example. Section IV will conclude.

II. Conditions for the Lawfulness of Expropriations

This section is aimed at illustrating the extent to which the requirements established in IIAs and developed in arbitral practice for the lawfulness of expropriations relate to the concept of the rule of law. In general, an expropriation of foreign investment is only lawful when certain conditions are fulfilled. These conditions are public purpose, due process, non-discrimination, and the payment of compensation. The requirements of due process and non-discrimination are particularly clear expressions of core rule-of-law demands.[26] However, it will also be argued that the other requirements of public purpose and the obligation to compensate investors are reflective of the rule of law. In the following subsections, each of these requirements will be addressed in turn to discuss the extent to which they foster the UN concept of rule of law.

A. Public Purpose and Rule of Law

As a first condition, an expropriation must serve a public purpose to be lawful. This condition, which is reflected in nearly all investment treaties, excludes arbitrary State measures, thereby requiring all public institutions to act in the general interest.[27]

---

[25] August Reinisch, 'Legality of Expropriations' in August Reinisch (ed), *Standards of Investment Protection* (OUP 2008) 170, 194ff.

[26] OECD Draft Convention on the Protection of Foreign Property, 12 October 1967, 7 ILM 117 (1968), Notes and Comments to Article 3 (Taking of Property), 5. a ('In essence, the contents of the notion of due process of law make it akin to the requirements of the "Rule of Law", an Anglo-Saxon notion, or of "Rechtsstaat", as understood in continental law. Used in an international agreement, the content of this notion is not exhausted by a reference to the national law of the parties concerned. The "due process of law" of each of them must correspond to the principles of international law').

[27] *Norwegian Shipowners' Claims (Norway v United States)* (1921) 1 RIAA 307, 332 (referring to the 'power of a sovereign state to expropriate, take or authorize the taking of any property within its jurisdiction which may be required for the "public good" or for the "general welfare" ').

Investment tribunals are rather flexible in their assessment of whether a State measure serves a public purpose,[28] according the host State broad discretion in the determination of what constitutes such a public purpose.[29] As noted by the Tribunal in *Teinver v Argentina*[30] 'a State must be accorded a certain amount of deference in determining how to best advance its public interest'. However, the host State is not allowed to act arbitrarily, hiding under the guise of a public purpose.[31] Therefore, tribunals have scrutinized whether a public purpose was truly a prime motivator for an expropriation in a particular case.[32] In *ADC v Hungary*,[33] the Tribunal explained that:

> a treaty requirement for '*public interest*' requires some genuine interest of the public. If mere reference to '*public interest*' can magically put such interest into existence and therefore satisfy this requirement, then this requirement would be rendered meaningless since the Tribunal can imagine no situation where this requirement would not have been met.[34]

As pointed out in the 2004 UN Secretary-General's report, non-arbitrariness can be considered as a fundamental element of the rule of law.[35] The requirement of a public purpose serves as a limitation of a State's sovereign right to expropriate in order to prevent the arbitrary exercise of such power.[36] Public purpose and non-arbitrariness are, therefore, closely linked and cannot be seen in isolation. This close connection demonstrates that the requirement of a public purpose is essentially aimed at fostering the rule of law. Host States may not merely justify an expropriation indicating a public purpose, as any disguised arbitrariness covered under the veil of a public purpose must be prevented.

---

[28] See eg Jeswald W Salacuse, *The Law of Investment Treaties* (2nd edn, OUP 2015) 349.

[29] See eg *Antoine Goetz and ors v Republic of Burundi*, ICSID Case No ARB/95/3, Decision on Liability (2 September 1998) para 126; *Copper Mesa Mining Corporation v The Republic of Ecuador*, PCA Case No 2012-2, Award (15 March 2016) para 6.64; *Quiborax SA and Non Metallic Minerals SA v Plurinational State of Bolivia*, ICSID Case No ARB/06/2, Award (16 September 2015) paras 243ff; *Vestey Group Ltd v Bolivarian Republic of Venezuela*, ICSID Case No ARB/06/4, Award (15 April 2016) para 294.

[30] *Teinver SA, Transportes de Cercanías SA and Autobuses Urbanos del Sur SA v The Argentine Republic*, ICSID Case No ARB/09/01, Award (21 July 2017) para 985.

[31] *Hulley Enterprises v Russia*, PCA Case No 2005-03/AA226; *Yukos Universal v Russia*, PCA Case No 2005-04/AA227; *Veteran Petroleum v Russia*, PCA Case No 2005-05/AA228, Award (18 July 2014) para 1581; see also *ADC Affiliate Limited and ADC & ADMC Management Limited v The Republic of Hungary*, ICSID Case No ARB/03/16, Award (2 October 2006) para 432; August Reinisch and Christoph Schreuer, *International Protection of Investments: The Substantive Standards* (CUP 2020) 194–204.

[32] See Reinisch and Schreuer (n 31) paras 391ff. *Waguih Elie George Siag & Clorinda Vecchi v The Arab Republic of Egypt*, ICSID Case No ARB/05/15, Award and Dissenting Opinion (1 June 2009) paras 431ff; *British Caribbean Bank Ltd v Government of Belize*, PCA Case No 2010-18/BCB-BZ, Award (19 December 2014) paras 247ff; *UP and CD Holding Internationale v Hungary* (formerly: *Le Chèque Déjeuner and CD Holding Internationale v Hungary*), ICSID Case No ARB/13/35, Award (9 October 2018) paras 414ff.

[33] *ADC Affiliate Limited and ADC & ADMC Management Limited v The Republic of Hungary*, ICSID Case No ARB/03/16, Award (2 October 2006) .

[34] ibid para 432.

[35] Report of the Secretary-General (n 6) para 6.

[36] Reinisch and Schreuer (n 31) 194–204.

B. Non-Discrimination and Rule of Law

The second condition of a lawful expropriation is non-discrimination. Arbitral tribunals have interpreted this requirement as a prohibition of unjustifiable discrimination[37] or discrimination on the basis of particularly condemned grounds, such as race or ethnicity, gender, or religious beliefs.[38] In certain instances, tribunals have equally held that differential treatment may be rationally justified and thus may not constitute discrimination.[39]

In practice, most discriminations concern the unjustified distinction between foreigners and nationals.[40] As the Restatement (Third) of The Foreign Relations Law of the United States, often understood as reflective of US positions on international law issues, explains, 'a program of taking that singles out aliens generally, or aliens of a particular nationality, or particular aliens, would violate international law'.[41] Since expropriatory measures directed against foreigners, as opposed to nationals, may be regarded as unlawful,[42] a differential treatment of investors in comparable circumstances invariably requires a justification.[43] Discriminatory measures directed (solely) against foreign investors that are not justified must be qualified as arbitrary[44] meaning not guided by any reason and being derived from mere opinion or being capricious.[45] Since non-arbitrariness is a fundamental element of the rule of law, the prohibition of unjustified discriminatory expropriations appears as a further expression of the rule of law.

This understanding is equally confirmed in the 2012 UN General Assembly Declaration on the Rule of Law, which explicitly refers to the element of a 'non-discriminatory and equitable delivery of public services'[46] as pertaining to the rule of law. Similarly, the 2004 UN Secretary-General's report emphasizes the elements of 'equality before the law' and the 'avoidance of arbitrariness'.[47] Hence, by requiring the host State to justify any expropriatory measures that discriminate against foreign investors, IIAs implement another core element of the rule of law as understood by the UN.

---

[37] *GAMI Investments v Mexico*, UNCITRAL, Final Award (15 November 2004) para 114; *Kardassopoulos and Fuchs v Georgia*, ICSID Case Nos ARB/05/18 and ARB 07/15, Award (3 March 2010) para 393.

[38] See eg *Bernhard von Pezold and ors v Republic of Zimbabwe*, ICSID Case No ARB/10/15, Award (28 July 2015); *Mike Campbell (Pvt) Ltd and ors v Republic of Zimbabwe*, Southern African Development Community Tribunal (SADC Tribunal), SADC (T) Case No 2/2007, Judgment (28 November 2008).

[39] *Amoco v Iran* (1987) 15 Iran–USCTR 189, 232, para 142 ('[it] finds it difficult, in the absence of any other evidence, to draw the conclusion that the expropriation of a concern was discriminatory only from the fact that another concern in the same economic branch was not expropriated. Reasons specific to the non-expropriated enterprise, or to the expropriated one, or to both, may justify such a difference in treatment').

[40] See eg *ADC* (n 31) paras 441ff.

[41] Restatement of the Law Third: The Foreign Relations Law of the United States, vol 2 (1987) para 712, comment f.

[42] *Liberian Eastern Timber Corporation (LETCO) v Republic of Liberia*, ICSID Case No ARB/83/2, Award (31 March 1986) 2 ICSID Reports 343, paras 366ff; *Eureko v Republic of Poland*, Partial Award (19 August 2005) para 242; *ADC* (n 31) para 443; *Ampal-American Israel Corp et al v Egypt*, ICSID Case No ARB/12/11, Decision on Liability and Heads of Loss (21 February 2017) para 344.

[43] See eg Ursula Kriebaum, 'Expropriation' in Marc Bungenberg and others (eds), *International Investment Law: A Handbook* (Hart 2015) 1025, para 245.

[44] Rudolf Dolzer and Christoph Schreuer, *Principles of International Investment Law* (2nd edn, OUP 2012) 100 ('The measure must not be arbitrary and discriminatory within the generally accepted meaning of the terms').

[45] *Black's Law Dictionary* (10th edn, 2014) 125, 1772.

[46] UNGA (n 4) para 12.

[47] Report of the Secretary-General (n 6) para 6.

C. Due Process and Rule of Law

Another requirement of lawful expropriations found in most IIAs is due process of law. Due process is often regarded as an expression of the rule of law or 'Rechtsstaatlichkeit'.[48] In this sense, the Tribunal in *Kardassopoulos v Georgia*,[49] when scrutinizing the host State's compliance with due process, relied on the definition of the commentary to the 1967 OECD Draft Convention on the Protection of Foreign Property, which provides that:

> [i]n essence, the contents of the notion of due process of law make it akin to the requirements of the 'Rule of Law', an Anglo-Saxon notion, or of 'Rechtsstaat', as understood in continental law. Used in an international agreement, the content of this notion is not exhausted by a reference to the national law of the parties concerned. The 'due process of law' of each of them must correspond to the principles of international law.[50]

The notion of 'due process' embodies various elements of the rule of law,[51] especially formal legality in the sense of requiring authorities to act on the basis of law. The supremacy of law, ie the idea that State authorities are held accountable to laws that are publicly promulgated, is at the very heart of the concept of rule of law.[52] In addition, due process involves legal and procedural transparency as well as independent adjudication.[53]

Accordingly, IIAs often provide that due process implies the right to have the legality of the expropriation reviewed by the domestic courts or administrative agencies of the host State.[54] Arbitral tribunals have equally recognized access to justice to be inherent in the requirement of due process.[55]

Numerous tribunals have detailed instances by which access to independent adjudication is required. By way of example, the Tribunal in *ADC v Hungary* stated that:

> [s]ome basic legal mechanisms, such as reasonable advance notice, a fair hearing and an unbiased and impartial adjudicator to assess the actions in dispute, are expected to be readily available and accessible to the investor to make such legal procedure meaningful.[56]

Furthermore, the Tribunal in *Teinver v Argentina*[57] examined whether:

---

[48] Reinisch and Schreuer (n 31) para 1039.

[49] *Kardassopoulos and Fuchs* (n 37) para 394.

[50] OECD Draft Convention (n 26) Notes and Comments to Article 3.5. a.

[51] *ADC* (n 31) para 435. Regarding the contents of the due process of law, the Tribunal in *ADC v Hungary* stated that '[s]ome basic legal mechanisms, such as reasonable advance notice, a fair hearing and an unbiased and impartial adjudicator to assess the actions in dispute, are expected to be readily available and accessible to the investor to make such legal procedure meaningful'.

[52] Report of the Secretary-General (n 6) para. 6.

[53] On these aspects, see also Kriebaum (n 43) 1025, paras 248ff.

[54] See eg art 13(2) ECT (1994) ('The Investor affected shall have a right to prompt review, under the law of the Contracting Party making the Expropriation, by a judicial or other competent and independent authority of that Contracting Party, of its case, of the valuation of its Investment, and of the payment of compensation, in accordance with the principles set out in paragraph (1)').

[55] *Waguih Elie George Siag and Clorinda Vecchi v The Arab Republic of Egypt*, ICSID Case No ARB/05/15, Award and Dissenting Opinion (1 June 2009); *Bernhard von Pezold and ors v Republic of Zimbabwe*, ICSID Case No ARB/10/15, Award (28 July 2015); *OI European Group BV v Bolivarian Republic of Venezuela*, ICSID Case No ARB/11/25, Award (10 March 2015); *Rusoro Mining Limited v The Bolivarian Republic of Venezuela*, ICSID Case No ARB(AF)/12/5, Award (22 August 2016); as well as further cases discussed in Reinisch and Schreuer (n 31) 216–22.

[56] *ADC* (n 31) para 435.

[57] *Teinver* (n 30) .

the expropriation process provided [the investor] with a legal procedure that granted a reasonable chance within a reasonable time to claim its legitimate rights and have its claims heard.[58]

Independent adjudication must, therefore, be regarded as a central condition for an expropriation to be lawful. Investment tribunals have considered this condition to be a core element of the rule of law under international law. Accordingly, the Tribunal in *OI European Group v Venezuela*[59] highlighted that the rule-of-law-based concept of 'due process' must be interpreted in accordance with the requirements of international law. It is this minimum regulatory standard commonly accepted in all States governed by the rule of law, guaranteeing that any decision affecting those subject to the State's authority will be adopted after having gone through a fair and equitable process.

From this standpoint, scholars[60] stress the close link of the due process requirement with rule-of-law demands to conduct orderly legal proceedings, a feature that equally played a crucial role in the due process assessments by some of the *Yukos* tribunals.[61] As Rudolf Dolzer pointed out:

The need for an 'orderly process' of government and respect for the rule of law as a protection against the danger of favouring or disproportionally burdening one or the other segment of society may underlie this trend to require a fair process of decision-making in the context of the law governing regulation and expropriation.[62]

In addition, some IIAs emphasize another 'rule of law' aspect of due process, namely conformity with national law.[63] For example, Article 4(1)(b) of the Chinese Model BIT provides that an expropriation has to be carried out in accordance with 'domestic legal procedure'.[64] Such an understanding of the rule of law, which requires authorities to act on a statutory basis when taking specific expropriating measure, corresponds to a specifically German aspect of 'Rechtsstaatlichkeit'.[65] Some tribunals therefore found that expropriations carried out in violation of the host State's own law breached the legality requirement and were therefore unlawful. One example is the Tribunal in *Tenaris v Venezuela*, which stated:

the failure of Venezuela to observe the requirements of its own nationalisation legislation is sufficient to constitute a breach of Article 4(a) of the Portuguese Treaty, which has an

---

[58] ibid para 1002.

[59] *OI European Group* (n 55) para 387.

[60] Reinisch and Schreuer (n 31) para 1042.

[61] See *Hulley Enterprises v Russian Federation; Veteran Petroleum v Russian Federation; Yukos v Russian Federation*, Final Award (18 July 2014) paras 1583, 1598. On these aspects, see also Kriebaum (n 43) 1025, paras 248ff.

[62] Rudolf Dolzer, 'Indirect Expropriations: New Developments?' (2002) 11 NYU Env LJ 64, 75.

[63] See eg art 4(3) China–Poland BIT (1998); art 4(a) Portugal–Venezuela BIT (1994).

[64] See Wenhua Shan and Norah Gallagher, 'China' in Chester Brown (ed), *Commentaries on Selected Model Investment Treaties* (OUP 2013) 131, 163; and in-depth Norah Gallagher and Wenhua Shan, *Chinese Investment Treaties: Policies and Practice* (OUP 2009) paras 7.42ff.

[65] Gallagher and Shan (n 64) para 8.

explicit *renvoi* to Venezuelan domestic law through the language: '*in accordance with the legislation in force*'.[66]

The requirements of due process and procedural fairness are equally emphasized in the 2004 UN Secretary-General's report and the 2012 UN General Assembly Declaration on the Rule of Law. The latter refers to 'the independence of the judicial system, together with its impartiality and integrity' as 'an essential prerequisite for upholding the rule of law and ensuring that there is no discrimination in the administration of justice'[67] as well as the 'right to equal access to justice for all'.[68] In the same vein, the 2004 UN Secretary-General's report highlights the importance of independent adjudication and fair application of the laws and 'procedural and legal transparency' as elements of the rule of law.[69]

D. Compensation and Rule of Law

A further condition for a lawful expropriation is compensation. The prohibition of expropriation without compensation dates back to the discussion of a minimum standard as part of the law of aliens under customary international law.[70] The amount of compensation to be paid in this context constitutes one of the main controversies in public international law, as driven by two opposing doctrines, that of Carlos Calvo and Cordell Hull.[71] According to Hull, compensation must be prompt, adequate, and effective as part of an international minimum standard of the treatment of aliens. He connected this idea directly to the rule of law, stating that:

> The Government of the United States merely adverts to a self-evident fact when it notes that the applicable and recognized authorities on international law support its declaration that, under every rule of law and equity, no government is entitled to expropriate private property, for whatever purpose, without provision for prompt, adequate and effective payment therefore.[72]

Today, most IIAs apply the Hull formula. This holds true, for example, for Article 13(1) and (2) of the Energy Charter Treaty (ECT) of 1994.[73] The Hull formula is also reflected in a number of recent model bilateral investment treaties (BITs),[74] such as Article 7(1)(d) of

---

[66] *Tenaris SA and Talta Trading e Marketing Sociedade Unipessoal Lda v Bolivarian Republic of Venezuela I*, ICSID Case No ARB/11/26, Award (29 January 2016) para 494 (emphasis in original); see similar *Olin Holdings Limited v State of Libya*, ICC Case No 20355/MCP, Final Award (25 May 2018) para 171.

[67] UNGA (n 4) para 13.

[68] ibid para 14.

[69] Report of the Secretary-General (n 6) para 6.

[70] See Kate Miles, *The Origins of International Investment Law: Empire, Environment and the Safeguarding of Capital* (CUP 2013) 19ff; Andreas Hans Roth, *The Minimum Standard of International Law Applied to Aliens* (Leiden Sijthoff 1949) 49ff; Edwin M Borchard, *The Diplomatic Protection of Citizens Abroad or the Law of International Claims* (Banks Law Publishing 1925) 3ff.

[71] See Rudolf Dolzer, *Eigentum, Enteignung und Entschädigung im geltenden Völkerrecht* (Springer 1985) 35ff.

[72] GH Hackworth, *Digest of International Law*, vol III (1942) 658, para 288.

[73] 2080 UNTS 100.

[74] For an overview, see the contributions in Chester Brown (ed), *Commentaries on Selected Model Investment Treaties* (OUP 2013).

the Austrian Model BIT 2008,[75] Article 4(2) of the German Model BIT 2009 ('equivalent to the value of the expropriated investment'),[76] or Article 6(1)(c) of the 2012 United States Model BIT.[77]

By contrast, many capital-importing countries, especially those in Latin America, invoked the Calvo doctrine, which dates back to the mid-nineteenth century.[78] Back then, Calvo considered national treatment under domestic laws to be sufficient, claiming that a host State is not breaching its international law obligations so long as the foreigner is not treated less favourably than its own citizens, which includes the possibility that a foreigner is not compensated at all—just like the nationals of an expropriating State.[79] Since nationals of the host State are, at best, only entitled to seek judicial redress against an expropriation before the State's courts, Calvo also rejected the right of the foreigner to demand diplomatic protection, thereby adhering to a stringent national treatment approach.[80] From a 'rule of law' approach, this can be problematic in multiple ways. The central issue is that domestic laws themselves may not conform to the rule of law, regardless of whether they apply to both own nationals and aliens. In addition, national courts may not be sufficiently independent and robust to afford due process to aliens.

The concept that an investor cannot be deprived of its investment without any compensation at all also reflects the basic notion that a State should not be unjustly enriched at the expense of the person/entity that is expropriated. Furthermore, an uncompensated expropriation burdens the expropriated owner in a discriminatory way, since the general community would benefit to the detriment of the affected investor, which violates the central rule-of-law principle of equal treatment,[81] or, as UN Special Rapporteur Garcia-Amador has expressed: '[t]he very *raison d'être* of compensation for expropriation ordered in the public interest is the idea that the State, i.e. the community, must not benefit (unduly) at the expense of private individuals'.[82]

In sum, the obligation to pay compensation reflects the State's obligation to respect the individual's fundamental right to property, since the host State may only deprive owners of their property if the latter are compensated for their loss. Even in 1938, the US government had already connected compensation to the rule of law, stating that 'under every rule of law and equity, no government is entitled to expropriate private property ... without provision for prompt, adequate and effective payment therefore'.[83] Hence, the requirement to compensate foreign investors in the case of expropriation is equally closely related to the rule of law, and in particular to the proportionality analyses conducted within regional human rights systems and national constitutional courts.

---

[75] See August Reinisch, 'Austria' in Chester Brown (ed), *Commentaries on Selected Model Investment Treaties* (OUP 2013) 15, 32.

[76] See Rudolf Dolzer and Yun-I Kim, 'Germany' in Chester Brown (ed), *Commentaries on Selected Model Investment Treaties* (OUP 2013) 289, 311.

[77] See Lee M Caplan and Jeremy K Sharpe, 'United States' ibid 755, 792.

[78] Rudolf Dolzer, Ursula Kriebaum and Christoph Schreuer, *Principles of International Investment Law* (3rd edn, OUP 2022) 4.

[79] Carlos Calvo, *Droit international théorique et pratique*, vol 3 (1888) 138.

[80] See eg *Max Planck Encyclopedia of Public International Law* (2007) para 3.

[81] See Bin Cheng, 'The Rationale of Compensation for Expropriation' (1984) 78 AJIL 121, 297.

[82] FV Garcia-Amador, 'Fourth Report on State Responsibility' UN Doc A/CN.4/119 (1959) para 14.

[83] Hackworth, *Digest of International Law*, vol III (n 72) 658–59, para 288.

III. Limitations of Indirect Expropriation

The previous section has shown that the requirements IIAs impose for expropriations to be lawful are closely related to the UN concept of the rule of law. This section will now focus on the concept of indirect expropriation and how formulations introduced in recent IIAs can be understood as a reflection of the rule of law. This is important to note since practically all expropriation provisions in IIAs protect against direct as well as indirect, creeping, or de facto expropriations.

In examining whether an indirect expropriation took place, arbitral tribunals first determine whether there was a permanent and substantial deprivation of the investment and its legitimately expected economic use. In some early cases, arbitral tribunals solely relied on the effects of a State measure to determine whether an investor had been indirectly expropriated.[84] Pursuant to this 'sole effects' doctrine, an expropriation would have taken place if a State measure's interference was substantial, therefore depriving an investor of all or most of the benefits of its investment permanently or for a substantial period of time.[85] In *Metalclad*, the Tribunal emphasized that it:

> need not decide or consider the motivation or intent of the adoption of the Ecological Decree. Indeed, a finding of expropriation on the basis of the Ecological Decree is not essential to the Tribunal's finding of a violation of NAFTA Article 1110. However, the Tribunal considers that the implementation of the Ecological Decree would, in and of itself, constitute an act tantamount to expropriation.[86]

Hence, the Tribunal considered the State's motivation behind the allegedly expropriatory measure to be irrelevant.[87] Other tribunals have taken similar approaches.[88]

By contrast, numerous domestic courts have taken a different direction from early on. For example, in 1922, the US Supreme Court found in *Pennsylvania Coal Company c. Mahon et al.* that:

> Government hardly could go on if to some extent values incident to property could not be diminished without paying for every such change in the general law. As long recognized, some values are enjoyed under an implied limitation and must yield to the police power.

---

[84] See on this Federico Ortino, *The Origin and Evolution of Investment Treaty Standards* (OUP 2019) 61; see eg *Certain German Interests in Polish Upper Silesia (Germany v Poland)* (Judgment) PCIJ Rep Series A No 6, 22; *Norwegian Shipowners' Claims* (n 27).

[85] See eg Dolzer, *Eigentum, Enteignung und Entschädigung im geltenden Völkerrecht* (n 71) 79–80; Kriebaum (n 43) 959, paras 37ff. Examples of cases where tribunals applied the sole effects doctrine are: *Tippetts, Abbett, McCarthy, Stratton v TAMS-AFFA Consulting Engineers of Iran* (1984) 6 Iran–USCTR 219; *Phelps Dodge Corp, et al v Iran* (1986) 10 Iran–USCTR 121; *Biloune and Marine Drive Complex Ltd v Ghana Investments Centre and the Government of Ghana* (1989) YCA (1994) 11; *Southern Pacific Properties (Middle East) Ltd v Egypt*, ICSID Case No ARB/84/3, Award (20 May 1992); *Metalclad Corp v Mexico*, ICSID Case No ARB(AF)/97/1, Award (30 August 2000); *Compañia de Aguas del Aconquija SA and Vivendi Universal v Argentina (Vivendi II)*, ICSID Case No ARB/97/3, Award (20 August 2007) paras 7.5.20, 7.5.21; *Merrill & Ring Forestry LP v Canada*, ICSID Case No UNCT/07/1, Award (30 March 2012) para 143.

[86] *Metalclad* (n 85) para 111.

[87] Ortino (n 84) 64.

[88] *Saar Papier Vertriebs GmbH v Poland*, UNCITRAL, Award (16 October 1995) para 84; *Goetz v Burundi*, ICSID Case No ARB/95/3, Decision on Liability (2 September 1998) para 124; also—but more open for police powers—*Pope & Talbot v Canada*, UNCITRAL, Interim Award (26 June 2000) para 102.

But obviously the implied limitation must have its limits, or the contract and due process clauses are gone. One fact for consideration determining such limits is the extent of the diminution. When it reaches a certain magnitude, in most if not in all cases there must be an exercise of eminent domain and compensation to sustain the act. So the question depends upon the particular facts. The greatest weight is given to the judgment of the legislature, but it always is open to interested parties to contend that the legislature has gone beyond its constitutional power.[89]

Hence, domestic courts have long taken into account numerous elements when determining whether a State measure has an expropriatory effect or not.

Over time, a similar line of argumentation has arisen in international investment law. Accordingly, a number of investment tribunals have limited the scope of indirect expropriations by acknowledging the sovereign right of the State to exercise its police powers—an approach that is often seen as diametrically opposed to the said 'sole effects' doctrine.[90] In this respect, (national) constitutional law concepts have gained more relevance in international (investment) law. According to this approach, it is not the case that every national measure that has a negative effect on an investment automatically qualifies as an expropriation and leads to an obligation to compensate. In this regard, the Tribunal in *Feldman v Mexico* emphasized in December 2002:

> At the same time, governments must be free to act in the broader public interest through protection of the environment, new or modified tax regimes, the granting or withdrawal of government subsidies, reductions or increases in tariff levels, imposition of zoning restrictions and the like. Reasonable governmental regulation of this type cannot be achieved if any business that is adversely affected may seek compensation, and it is safe to say that customary international law recognizes this.[91]

Other tribunals also stressed the public purpose of many regulations, concluding that in such cases an automatic obligation to compensate would not apply.[92] According to the police powers doctrine, a State's regulation in the public interest does not normally amount to an indirect expropriation. Several investment tribunals regard the police powers doctrine to be based on customary international law.[93] Accordingly, these tribunals assert that a sovereign State 'has the inherent right to regulate its affairs and adopt laws in order to protect the common good of its people, as defined by its Parliament and Government'.[94]

This emphasis on the right to regulate as a relevant factor in the determination of an indirect expropriation is arguably linked to the rule of law. Interestingly, the carve-out from

---

[89] *Pennsylvania Coal Company c Mahon et al*, 260 US 393, 413.

[90] See Catharine Titi, 'Police Powers Doctrine and International Investment Law' in Filippo Fontanelli, Andrea Gattini and Attila Tanzi (eds), *General Principles of Law and International Investment Arbitration* (Brill 2018) 323ff.

[91] *Marvin Roy Feldman Karpa v Mexico*, ICSID Case No ARB(AF)/99/1, Award (16 December 2002) para 103.

[92] See inter alia *Continental Casualty v Argentine Republic*, ICSID Case No ARG/03/9, Award (5 September 2008) para 276; *S.D. Myers, Inc. v Government of Canada*, UNCITRAL, Award on Damages (21 October 2002).

[93] See *Marvin Roy Feldman Karpa v Mexico*, ICSID Case No ARB(AF)/99/1, Award (16 December 2002) para 103; *Methanex Corporation v United States of America*, UNCITRAL, Final Award on Jurisdiction and Merits (3 August 2005), pt IV D, para 7; *Saluka Investments BV (The Netherlands) v The Czech Republic*, UNCITRAL, Partial Award (17 March 2006) para 255.

[94] *Lemire v Ukraine (II)*, ICSID Case No ARB/06/18, Decision on Jurisdiction and Liability (14 January 2010) para 505.

indirect expropriations by the police powers doctrine is conditioned by the same rule-of-law-based concepts of public interest, non-discrimination, and due process as discussed above. But these elements are used in a different manner when it comes to differentiating between indirect expropriations and regulatory measures taken on the basis of the host State's police powers. Accordingly, investment tribunals have used a measure's public interest as a reason to conclude that there was no indirect expropriation as long as the interference was non-discriminatory and in accordance with due process of law,[95] irrespective of whether the conditions for a lawful expropriation were fulfilled or not.[96] In this sense, the Tribunal in *Methanex v United States* stated that:

> as a matter of general international law, a non-discriminatory regulation for a public purpose, which is enacted in accordance with due process and, which affects, inter alios, a foreign investor or investment is not deemed expropriatory and compensable unless specific commitments had been given by the regulating government to the then putative foreign investor contemplating investment that the government would refrain from such regulation.[97]

Moreover, regulation in the public interest is not only an expression of the sovereign right to regulate but can also be qualified as a decisive requirement so that the exercise of police powers does not amount to indirect expropriation, as long as such exercise conforms to principles of proportionality. This understanding again can be seen as an element of the substantive 'rule of law' concept. Both the right to regulate and the rule of law require the host State's regulations to be made for a public purpose. This requirement however directly leads to the difficult task of precisely delimiting regulatory expropriations and (legitimate) regulatory measures,[98] as only the former would be subject to an analysis of lawfulness according to the conditions listed in Section II above. As pointed out by the Tribunal in *ADC v Hungary*, the rule of law may serve as a decisive factor to delimit both concepts. Accordingly, the Tribunal pointed out that:

> while a sovereign State possesses the inherent right to regulate its domestic affairs, the exercise of such right is not unlimited and must have its boundaries. As rightly pointed out by the Claimants, the rule of law, which includes treaty obligations, provides such boundaries.[99]

This rule-of-law-based boundary may come in the form of a rationality or a proportionality test.[100] With regard to the first option, Federico Ortino points out that one 'approach of examining the existence of an indirect expropriation according to the police powers

---

[95] See eg *Chemtura Corporation v Canada*, UNCITRAL, Award (2 August 2010) para 266.
[96] Restatement of the Law Third: The Foreign Relations Law of the United States, vol 2) para 712, comment g; Katia Yannaca-Small, 'Indirect Expropriation and the Right to Regulate: Has the Line Been Drawn?' in Katia Yannaca-Small (ed), *Arbitration under International Investment Agreements: A Guide to the Key Issues* (2nd edn, OUP 2018) 562, paras 22.85ff; Campbell McLachlan, Laurence Shore and Matthew Weiniger, *International Investment Arbitration: Substantive Principles* (2nd edn, OUP 2017) paras 8.139ff.
[97] *Methanex Corporation* (n 93) pt IV D, para 7.
[98] See on this Reinisch and Schreuer (n 31) paras 391ff.
[99] *ADC* (n 31) para 423; see also *Mobil Exploration v Argentina*, ICSID Case No ARB/04/16, Decision on Jurisdiction and Liability (10 April 2013) paras 815–21.
[100] Ortino (n 84) 172.

doctrine is to determine whether the allegedly expropriatory measure is rationally re-lated to a public policy objective'.[101] Similarly, the *Saluka* tribunal applied a reasonableness test,[102] and the *Gold Reserve* tribunal reviewed whether the reasons for the termination of certain concessions were 'sufficiently well founded'.[103] Regardless of these approaches, the dominant method in investment agreements and arbitral practice now seems to be the pro-portionality test, as demonstrated below.

Traditionally, the principle of proportionality had little relevance in international eco-nomic law in general and in international investment law in particular.[104] However, this has changed,[105] considering that arbitral tribunals are now frequently invoking the principle of proportionality in assessing the host State's right to regulate, when scrutinizing its poten-tial liability under investment agreements. Moreover, States are increasingly implementing these two concepts—the right to regulate and the principle of proportionality—in the wording of recent IIAs. They do so either explicitly or implicitly through the requirement of a public purpose and the criteria of non-discrimination and non-arbitrariness with regard to regulatory deprivations.

As argued earlier in the introduction, the principle of proportionality can be seen as an element of the rule of law. It is a method of legal interpretation and adjudication in situ-ations where different interests or legal principles may clash.[106] In international investment law, it provides for a balance between the economic interests of a foreign investor and the public objectives pursued by the host State.[107] Through the inclusion of a proportionality test in recent investment treaties and arbitral practice, a new element of the rule of law is being implemented in the protection against unlawful expropriations.[108]

The methodological approach of applying a proportionality test in the assessment of the expropriatory nature of regulatory deprivations[109] can limit the scope of indirect expropri-ations. A State measure is qualified as either an indirect expropriation or a simple regulation by reviewing whether it was enacted for a public purpose (1) and in a proportional manner (2). Accordingly, this balancing between the (sovereign) right to regulate, on the one hand, and the protection of property, on the other hand, through a proportionality analysis can be considered as a further expression of the rule of law.

Multiple tribunals have applied a proportionality test to assess whether a State measure constitutes a mere regulation or a regulatory expropriation.[110] They have referred, among

---

[101] ibid 154.

[102] *Saluka* (n 93) para 272.

[103] *Gold Reserve v Venezuela*, ICSID Case No ARB(AF)/09/1, Award (22 September 2014) para 666.

[104] See Thomas Cottier and others, 'The Principle of Proportionality in International Foundations and Variations' (2017) 18 JWIT 628, 644ff, 655.

[105] On proportionality in WTO law, see eg Peter Van den Bossche, 'Looking for Proportionality in WTO Law' (2008) 35(3) LIEI 283.

[106] Benedict Kingsbury and Stephan W Schill, 'Investor-State-Arbitration as Governance: Fair and Equitable Treatment, Proportionality and the Emerging Global Administrative Law' (2009) New York University Public Law and Legal Theory Working Papers 21.

[107] Cottier and others (n 104) 656.

[108] See in general Gebhard Bücheler, *Proportionality in Investor-State Arbitration* (OUP 2015) 122ff; See also Kingsbury and Schill (n 106) 22ff; Cottier and others (n 104) 657ff.

[109] On the difficulties of the concept of indirect expropriation, see inter alia Jan Paulsson and Zachary Douglas, 'Indirect Expropriation in Investment Treaty Arbitrations' in Norbert Horn (ed), *Arbitrating Foreign Investment Disputes: Procedural and Substantive Legal Aspects* (Kluwer Law International 2004) 145; an overview on the case law is provided in McLachlan, Shore and Weiniger (n 96) paras 8.94ff.

[110] *Marfin Investment Group Holdings SA, Alexandros Bakatselos and ors v The Republic of Cyprus*, ICSID Case No ARB/13/27, Award (26 July 2018) para 826 ('the economic harm consequent to the non-discriminatory ap-plication of generally applicable regulations adopted in order to protect the public welfare do not constitute a

others, to the 'proportionality between the means employed and the aim sought to be real-ized'[111] and inquired 'whether such actions or measures are proportional to the public interest presumably protected thereby and the protection legally granted to investments, taking into account that the significance of such impact, has a key role upon deciding the proportionality'.[112] The often cited starting point in this discussion in international invest-ment law was the *Tecmed* award. The Tribunal in *Tecmed v Mexico*, relying extensively on ECtHR jurisprudence,[113] employed a proportionality analysis in the assessment of whether a State measure had an effect equivalent to an expropriation.[114] The approach has since been followed by multiple tribunals,[115] reflecting the increasing reception of the jurisprudence of the ECtHR and other human rights courts in investment arbitration.[116]

To establish whether an expropriation took place, these tribunals first determined whether the investor had been substantially deprived of its investment. Only if that was the case, would they then turn to analysing whether the interests of the investor in protection were appropriately balanced against the public purpose at stake. By way of example, the award in *Tecmed*[117] balanced the public interest presumably pursued by the interference against the charge imposed on the investor.[118] In doing so, the Tribunal applied a propor-tionality test and therefore established a relationship between the two criteria—the 'effect' and 'purpose' of the interference.[119] In the specific case, the Tribunal held that the measure did not respond to a serious and urgent situation, crisis or social emergency:

compensable taking, provided that the measure was taken in good faith, complied with due process and was pro-portionate to the aim sought to be achieved'); *Fireman's Fund Insurance Company v The United Mexican States*, ICSID Case No ARB(AF)/02/01, Award (17 July 2006) para 176; *LG&E Energy Corp, LG&E Capital Corp, LG&E International Inc v The Argentine Republic*, ICSID Case No ARB/02/1, Decision on Liability (3 October 2006) para 195.

[111] *Fireman's Fund* (n 110) para 176 ('To distinguish between a compensable expropriation and a noncompensable regulation by a host State, the following factors (usually in combination) may be taken into ac-count: whether the measure is within the recognized police powers of the host State; the (public) purpose and ef-fect of the measure; whether the measure is discriminatory; the proportionality between the means employed and the aim sought to be realized and the *bona fide* nature of the measure').

[112] *LG&E Energy* (n 110) para 195 ('With respect to the power of the State to adopt its policies, it can generally be said that the State has the right to adopt measures having a social or general welfare purpose. In such a case, the measure must be accepted without any imposition of liability, except in cases where the State's action is obvi-ously disproportionate to the need being addressed. The proportionality to be used when making use of this right was recognized in *Tecmed*, which observed that "whether such actions or measures are proportional to the public interest presumably protected thereby and the protection legally granted to investments, taking into account that the significance of such impact, has a key role upon deciding the proportionality."').

[113] *James and ors* App no 8793/79 (ECtHR, 21 February 1986) paras 50ff; but also *Mellacher and ors v Austria* App nos 10522/83; 11011/84; 11070/84 (ECtHR, 19 December 1989) para 48; *Pressos Compañia Naviera and ors v Belgium* App no 17849/91 (ECtHR, 20 November 1995) paras 38ff.

[114] *Tecnicas Medioambientales Tecmed SA v Mexico*, ICSID Case No ARB(AF)/00/2, Award (29 May 2003) para 122.

[115] See eg *Tecmed* (n 114); *Azurix Corp v Argentina (I)*, ICSID Case No ARB/01/12, Award (14 July 2006) paras 311–12, 322; *LG&E Energy* (n 110) paras 189, 194–95; *El Paso Energy International Company v Argentina*, ICSID Case No ARB/03/15, Award (31 October 2011) paras 233, 237–43, 297–99; *Philip Morris v Uruguay*, ICSID Case No ARB/10/7, Award (8 July 2016) para 287; *Continental Casualty* (n 92) para 276.

[116] See also Yannaca-Small, 'Indirect Expropriation and the Right to Regulate' (n 96) paras 22.97ff.

[117] *Tecmed* (n 114).

[118] ibid para 122. It based itself on the judgment in *Matos e Silva, Lda and ors v Portugal* App no 15777/89 (ECtHR, 27 August 1996) para 92. See Ursula Kriebaum 'Regulatory Takings: Balancing the Interests of the Investor and the State' (2007) 8 JWIT 717.

[119] *Tecmed* (n 114) para 122.

the Arbitral Tribunal will consider, in order to determine if they are to be characterized as expropriatory, whether such actions or measures are proportional to the public interest presumably protected thereby ... such situation does not prevent the Arbitral Tribunal ... from examining the actions of the State in light of Article 5(1) of the Agreement to determine whether such measures are reasonable with respect to their goals, the deprivation of economic rights and the legitimate expectations of who suffered such deprivation.[120]

Accordingly, the Tribunal weighed the public interest against the deprivation of the economic value of the investment, concluding that the disproportionality of the interference in the case at hand resulted in the measure constituting an expropriation. It stated that three factors were of particular relevance in the balancing process: (1) the reasonableness of the governmental measures with respect to their goals; (2) the deprivation of economic rights (ie the effect of the measure); and (3) the legitimate expectations of the investor.

This line of reasoning was followed by multiple other tribunals. For instance, the Tribunal in *Fireman's Fund v Mexico*[121] held that:

[t]o distinguish between a compensable expropriation and a noncompensable regulation by a host State, the following factors (usually in combination) may be taken into account: whether the measure is within the recognized police powers of the host State; the (public) purpose and effect of the measure; whether the measure is discriminatory; the proportionality between the means employed and the aim sought to be realized and the *bona fide* nature of the measure.

The *Azurix* tribunal took a similar approach. It found that the public purpose of the measure alone was 'insufficient' to remove it from the ambit of an indirect expropriation.[122] Instead, it suggested that such criterion should be complemented by others, such as proportionality and non-discrimination, to provide 'useful guidance for purposes of determining whether regulatory actions would be expropriatory and give rise to compensation'.[123] Here the Tribunal expressly invoked the ECtHR's jurisprudence on proportionality.[124]

Similarly, in *LG&E v Argentina,* the Tribunal held that:

[i]n order to establish whether State measures constitute expropriation ... the Tribunal must balance two competing interests: the degree of the measure's interference with the right of ownership and the power of the State to adopt its policies ... with respect to the power of the State to adopt its policies, it can generally be said that the State has the right to adopt measures having a social or general welfare purpose. In such a case, the measure must be accepted without any imposition of liability, except in cases where the State's action

---

[120] ibid.
[121] *Fireman's Fund* (n 110) para 176.
[122] *Azurix* (n 115) paras 310ff.
[123] ibid para 312.
[124] ibid para 311.

is obviously disproportionate to the need being addressed. The proportionality to be used when making use of this right was recognized in *Tecmed*.[125]

Finally, the Tribunal in *Philip Morris v Uruguay*[126] stressed that:

[a]s indicated by earlier investment treaty decisions, in order for a State's action in exercise of regulatory powers not to constitute indirect expropriation, the action has to comply with certain conditions. Among those most commonly mentioned are that the action must be taken bona fide for the purpose of protecting the public welfare, must be non-discriminatory and proportionate.

All these examples show that balancing different interests of the investor and the host State and introducing the explicit notion of proportionality are becoming increasingly important for the purpose of distinguishing between non-compensable regulation and indirect expropriation. This can also be demonstrated in the field of evolving treaty language. Indeed, under the influence of developing arbitral practice, the United States and Canada have redefined the scope of protection of investments against expropriations in their investment treaties and model BITs,[127] namely by applying the method previously developed by the

---

[125] *LG&E Energy* (n 110) para 189.

[126] *Philip Morris v Uruguay*, ICSID Case No ARB/10/7, Award (8 July 2016) para 305.

[127] Annex B.13(1) Canada Model BIT 2004 <https://investmentpolicy.unctad.org/international-investment-agreements/treaty-files/2820/download> last accessed 18 November 2022. Expropriation reads in this regard:

The Parties confirm their shared understanding that:
a) Indirect expropriation results from a measure or series of measures of a Party that have an effect equivalent to direct expropriation without formal transfer of title or outright seizure;
b) The determination of whether a measure or series of measures of a Party constitute an indirect expropriation requires a case-by-case, fact-based inquiry that considers, among other factors:
   i) the economic impact of the measure or series of measures, although the sole fact that a measure or series of measures of a Party has an adverse effect on the economic value of an investment does not establish that an indirect expropriation has occurred;
   ii) the extent to which the measure or series of measures interfere with distinct, reasonable investment-backed expectations; and
   iii) the character of the measure or series of measures;
c) Except in rare circumstances, such as when a measure or series of measures are so severe in the light of their purpose that they cannot be reasonably viewed as having been adopted and applied in good faith, non-discriminatory measures of a Party that are designed and applied to protect legitimate public welfare objectives, such as health, safety and the environment, do not constitute indirect expropriation.

Annex B US Model BIT 2004 <https://ustr.gov/sites/default/files/U.S.%20model%20BIT.pdf> last accessed 22 September 2021, reads in this regard:
The Parties confirm their shared understanding that:
1. Article 6 [Expropriation and Compensation](1) is intended to reflect customary international law concerning the obligation of States with respect to expropriation.
2. An action or a series of actions by a Party cannot constitute an expropriation unless it interferes with a tangible or intangible property right or property interest in an investment.
3. Article 6 [Expropriation and Compensation](1) addresses two situations. The first is direct expropriation, where an investment is nationalized or otherwise directly expropriated through formal transfer of title or outright seizure.
4. The second situation addressed by Article 6 [Expropriation and Compensation](1) is indirect expropriation, where an action or series of actions by a Party has an effect equivalent to direct expropriation without formal transfer of title or outright seizure.
   (a) The determination of whether an action or series of actions by a Party, in a specific fact situation, constitutes an indirect expropriation, requires a case-by-case, fact-based inquiry that considers, among other factors:

US Supreme Court in *Penn Central Station v New York City*.[128] These (US) constitutional law considerations are also indirectly implemented in the Canadian Model FIPA.[129] In the jurisprudence of the US Supreme Court, the assessment of whether a State measure has to be qualified as a regulatory expropriation, which requires compensation, or whether it constitutes a general regulation that does not require compensation, involves a balancing or weighing of different competing interests in the sense of reasonableness.[130] A balancing test equally partly correlates to the proportionality analysis under European and German constitutional law.[131] This reception of constitutional criteria and methodological approaches in international investment law is equally reflected in the investment policy of the European Union (EU).

The EU–Canada Comprehensive and Economic Trade Agreement (CETA) serves as an example of this development.[132] Article 8.12 CETA provides for a similar prohibition of unlawful expropriation as laid down in the ECT, albeit qualifying the notion of (especially indirect) expropriation in Annex 8-A.[133] Annex 8-A of the CETA contains several prerequisites for qualifying a State act as an indirect expropriation.[134] These prerequisites reflect recent developments in international investment law, which are influenced by national and

    (i)   the economic impact of the government action, although the fact that an action or series of actions by a Party has an adverse effect on the economic value of an investment, standing alone, does not establish that an indirect expropriation has occurred;

    (ii)   the extent to which the government action interferes with distinct, reasonable investment-backed expectations; and

    (iii)   the character of the government action (b) Except in rare circumstances, non-discriminatory regulatory actions by a Party that are designed and applied to protect legitimate public welfare objectives, such as public health, safety, and the environment, do not constitute indirect expropriations.

---

[128] *Penn Central Transportation Co v New York City* (1978) 438 US 104: 'The question of what constitutes a "taking" for purposes of the Fifth Amendment has proved to be a problem of considerable difficulty. While this Court has recognized that the "Fifth Amendment's guarantee ... [is] designed to bar Government from forcing some people alone to bear public burdens which, in all fairness and justice, should be borne by the public as a whole"'; *Armstrong v United States* (1960) 364 US 40, 49, 'this Court, quite simply, has been unable to develop any "set formula" for determining when "justice and fairness" require that economic injuries caused by public action be compensated by the government, rather than remain disproportionately concentrated on a few persons'. See *Goldblatt v Hempstead* (1962) 369 US 590, 594, 'Indeed, we have frequently observed that whether a particular restriction will be rendered invalid by the government's failure to pay for any losses proximately caused by it depends largely "upon the particular circumstances [in that] case"'. *United States v Central Eureka Mining Co* (1958) 357 US 155, 168; see *United States v Caltex, Inc* (1952) 344 US 149, 156. In engaging in these essentially ad hoc, factual inquiries, the Court's decisions have identified several factors that have particular significance. The economic impact of the regulation on the claimant and, particularly, the extent to which the regulation has interfered with distinct investment-backed expectations are, of course, relevant considerations. See *Penn Central Transportation Co. v New York City* (1978) 438 US 104, 124 , 'So, too, is the character of the governmental action. A "taking" may more readily be found when the interference with property can be characterized as a physical invasion by government, see eg *United States v Causby* (1946) 328 US 256, than when interference arises from some public program adjusting the benefits and burdens of economic life to promote the common good.'

[129] Céline Lévesque and Andrew Newcombe, 'Canada' in Chester Brown (ed), *Commentaries on Selected Model Investment Treaties* (OUP 2013) 53, 95.

[130] *Penn Central Transportation Co* (n 128) 123ff.

[131] On the US jurisprudence, see also AJ van der Walt, *Constitutional Property Clauses: A Comparative Analysis* (Kluwer Law International 1999) 410ff.

[132] On this see Marc Bungenberg, 'Investment Protection at Crossroads' in Josiane Auvret-Finck, *Vers un Partenariat Transatlantique de l'Union Européenne* (Larcier 2015) 123ff.

[133] Comparable provisions can be found inter alia in Annex 4 of the EU–Vietnam Investment Protection Agreement (IPA) and Annex 1 of the EU–Singapore IPA alike. See also inter alia arts 5.3 and 5.4 Indian Model BIT 2016; art 12.8 Netherlands Draft Model BIT 2018.

[134] On art 8.12 CETA, see in detail Ursula Kriebaum, 'Article 8.12' in Marc Bungenberg and August Reinisch (eds), *CETA Investment Law: Article-by-Article Commentary* (Hart 2022).

supranational law. In para 3, the Annex partially lays down the 'proportional police powers doctrine', as it has developed in arbitral practice,[135] by stating:

> except in the rare circumstance when the impact of a measure or series of measures is so severe in light of its purpose that it appears manifestly excessive, non-discriminatory measures of a Party that are designed and applied to protect legitimate public welfare objectives, such as health, safety and the environment, do not constitute indirect expropriations.

This approach limits the discretion of tribunals when balancing the legitimate expectations of investors with the public interest of the interfering State measure.

In sum, non-arbitrariness and non-discrimination are particularly relevant as components of the rule-of-law principle within the assessment of whether a measure qualifies as an indirect expropriation, which requires compensation, or whether it qualifies as a general regulation in the public interest, which does not require compensation, as reflected by the police powers doctrine and modern investment treaties, such as CETA. Furthermore, the principle of proportionality and the doctrine of legitimate expectations[136] have gained importance in the assessment of whether State measures can be deemed as expropriatory. In this regard, the EU approach is influenced to a large degree by the EU Charter of Fundamental Rights, the ECHR, EU Member States' laws,[137] as well as US jurisprudence.

IV. Conclusion

The protection of property is a fundamental right, which is reflected in numerous constitutional orders and public international law alike. The prohibition of unlawful expropriation has become a fundamental guarantee that implements a broad conception of the rule of law in international investment law. This has resulted from various developments since the evolution of the international minimum standard of protecting aliens under customary international law.

Today, the conditions for the lawfulness of expropriations are laid down in detail in IIAs, in investment chapters in free trade agreements (FTAs), such as the CETA, and in recent model BITs. These conditions reflect elements of a broad concept of the rule of law, as understood by the UN. Expropriations are permitted on the condition that different rule-of-law requirements—public purpose, due process, non-discrimination, and payment of compensation—are fulfilled.

---

[135] See Section II.A above; see also inter alia Ben Mostafa, 'The Sole Effects Doctrine, Police Powers and Indirect Expropriation under International Law' (2008) 15 Aust ILJ 267, 272ff; Pascale Accaoui Lorfing and Maria Beatriz Burghetto, 'The Evolution and Current Status of the Concept of Indirect Expropriation in Investment Treaties and Arbitration' (2018) 6 IJAL 98, 115ff; Bücheler (n 108) 127ff; on arbitral jurisprudence, see *Methanex Corporation* (n 93) pt IV D, para 7; *Saluka* (n 93) para 255; *Tecmed* (n 114) para 119.

[136] See *Metalclad* (n 85) para 107; *Tecmed* (n 114) para 150. On legitimate expectations, see in detail Caroline Henckels, 'Legitimate Expectations and the Rule of Law in International Investment Law' (in this volume) 43.

[137] See Burkhard Schöbener, 'Internationales Recht: Enteignung und Entschädigung im Systemvergleich' in Otto Depenheuer and Foroud Shirvani (eds), *Die Enteignung: Historische, vergleichende, dogmatische und politische Perspektiven auf ein Rechtsinstitut* (Springer 2018) 53, 76ff.

The due process requirement demands a fair procedure and thus can be seen as a core element of a formal conception of the rule of law. Elements of due process are, amongst others, reasonable advance notice and a fair hearing to claim one's legitimate rights and to have one's claims heard.

The principle of non-discrimination addresses a prohibition of an unjustifiable or unreasonable distinction on the basis of particularly condemned grounds, including the investor's nationality. In this context, unreasonableness appears to correspond to (prohibition of) arbitrary treatment, overlapping with the 'rule of law' demand not to act arbitrarily.

Any lawful expropriation must be in the public interest or for a public purpose. From a rule-of-law perspective, this requirement can be regarded as expressing the idea that State action must pursue some public good or enhance the general welfare, limiting the State's sovereign right to expropriate in order to prevent the arbitrary exercise of such power.

The obligation to provide compensation for the expropriation of investments has been controversial in regard to determining the exact amount of compensation due in a given case. The adoption of the Hull formula in bilateral and multilateral investment treaties provides for legal certainty with regard to the protection of property. Nevertheless, a number of challenges and possible inconsistencies remain with regard to the precise calculation of damages. A State may not deprive an investor of its investment without any compensation at all. Such a requirement reflects the basic notion that a State should not be unjustly enriched at the expense of the person/entity expropriated. As the obligation to compensate also conforms to the jurisprudence of regional human rights systems with regard to the protection of property, it can be viewed as a further element of a substantive rule-of-law concept.

More recent jurisprudence and investment treaties reflect the development of the principle of proportionality as a sub-element of the rule of law, emphasizing the host State's sovereign right to regulate in the assessment of indirect expropriations, especially in annexes to comprehensive FTAs or investment agreements. Proportionality gains substantial importance within a comparative public law approach, being removed from its constitutional law foundations and implemented in the jurisprudence of human rights courts and investment tribunals alike.[138]

In conclusion, this chapter has shown that the expropriation standard in international investment law is informed by different elements of the concept of the rule of law. In fact, States have begun implementing more sophisticated definitions and conditions of expropriatory State measures in recent investment agreements. These definitions often reflect elements of the rule of law. For example, the specifications in Annex 8 A of the CETA[139] reflect the foundations of the standard in a host State's treatment compliant to the rule of law, highlighting the importance of investment-backed expectations, public welfare objectives, non-discrimination, and non-arbitrariness.

---

[138] See eg *James and ors v UK* App no 8793/79 (ECtHR, 21 February 1986) para 50; *Tecmed* (n 114) para 122.
[139] See above n 134.

5

Full Protection and Security and the Rule of Law

Sebastián Mantilla Blanco

I. Introduction

One of the most basic tenets of the customary law of aliens is the State's obligation to shield foreigners within its territory from harm or injury. This protection obligation normally reaches the purview of investment arbitral tribunals through treaty clauses that guarantee 'full protection and security' (FPS) to covered investments.[1] Alleged breaches of the FPS standard refer to the most diverse factual backgrounds, from contentions that the host State failed to prevent terrorist attacks,[2] civil unrest,[3] or even revolutions,[4] to claims concerning regulatory changes causing economic detriment to the investment.[5]

The somewhat elusive wording of most FPS clauses has fostered claims where the security obligation is invoked as a catch-all provision, which is assumed to cover 'protection' against an overly broad range of risks.[6] Arguments submitted in investor-State dispute settlement proceedings often reflect not only differences regarding the application of the FPS standard to the facts of the case, but also conflicting understandings of the FPS obligation.[7] As arbitral decisions mirror these divergences, each party will find some argument of authority in support of its interpretation of the applicable FPS provision.[8] These discrepancies are often presented as a quandary between restrictive views limiting FPS to the protection of the investment against physical harm and approaches extending the standard to a reinforced guarantee of legal stability.[9] Additionally, while FPS is normally depicted as a due diligence obligation, there is still debate as to whether it could be coupled with a standard of strict liability in some scenarios.[10]

---

[1] The author has discussed the FPS standard in greater detail elsewhere: Sebastián Mantilla Blanco, *Full Protection and Security in International Investment Law* (Springer 2019). The current chapter reflects some of the arguments presented in this previous work, to the extent they are relevant for the assessment of the interplay between the rule of law and the FPS standard.

[2] *Ampal-American Israel Corp et al v Egypt*, ICSID Case No ARB/12/11, Decision on Liability and Heads of Loss (21 February 2017) paras 283ff.

[3] *Pantechniki SA Contractors & Engineers v Albania*, ICSID Case No ARB/07/21, Award (30 July 2009) paras 71ff.

[4] *Oztas Construction et al v Libyan Investment Development Co and State of Libya*, ICC Arbitration No. 21603/ZF/AYZ, Final Award (14 June 2018) paras 160–62.

[5] See eg the investors' claim in *Global Telecom Holding SAE v Canada*, ICSID Case No ARB/16/16, Award (27 March 2020) paras 653ff.

[6] See eg the investors' arguments in *Deutsche Telekom v India*, PCA Case No 2014-10, Award (13 December 2017) para 417; *Teinver et al v Argentina*, ICSID Case No ARB/09/1, Award (21 July 2017) paras 898–900.

[7] See eg the opposing views of the parties in *Belenergia SA v Italy*, ICSID Case No ARB/15/40, Award (6 August 2019) para 620.

[8] See the examples discussed in Section III. For a tribunal recognizing these discrepancies, see *Garanti Koza LLP v Turkmenistan*, ICSID Case No ARB/11/20, Award (19 December 2016) para 391.

[9] See Sections III.A and III.B.1.

[10] See Sections IV.A and IV.B.

Sebastián Mantilla Blanco, *Full Protection and Security and the Rule of Law* In: *Investment Protection Standards and the Rule of Law*. Edited by: August Reinisch and Stephan W. Schill, Oxford University Press. © Sebastián Mantilla Blanco 2023. DOI: 10.1093/oso/9780192864581.003.0005

This chapter discusses to what extent constitutional law analogies can assist scholars and practitioners in addressing these pressing questions. It argues that FPS echoes the security function of the State, guarding the investment through positive State action against private offences and other non-State sources of risk.[11] The rule of law mirrors expectations about the exercise of the State's security function, as criteria used for the assessment of due diligence in connection with FPS claims resemble elements of the rule of law (eg reasonableness and non-discrimination).

The argument has been divided into five sections. Following this introduction, the chapter starts with an overview of public law analogies in international investment law (IIL) (Section II). It then considers the potential role of domestic public law for the conceptualization of the FPS standard's scope of application, focusing particularly on the risks covered by the standard (Section III). Thereafter, it discusses the interplay between the rule of law and ongoing debates about the content of the security obligation, that is to say, the parameters it provides for the assessment of conduct (Section IV). A final section draws a general conclusion (Section V).

II. Constitutional Law Analogies in IIL

The concept of the rule of law (*Rechtsstaat*) left its domestic public law cradle long ago. For decades, scholars have recognized similarities between domestic elements of the rule of law and features of the international legal system.[12] Members of the UN General Assembly stated in 2012 that 'the rule of law applies to all States equally, and to international organizations'.[13] The rule of law is thus a telling example of a 'legal transfer'.[14] Recent studies suggest that the rule of law informs not only the relationship between the individual and the State, but moreover inter-State relations and the place of the individual within international law structures.[15] These manifold uses of the rule of law converge in IIL.[16]

In the twentieth century, international law transformed from a system fixated on the co-ordination of sovereign wills and the relations of the State vis-à-vis other States, into a legal order addressing the exercise of sovereign power in respect of persons subject to the State's jurisdiction.[17] Numerous international law regimes allow individuals direct access to international fora and bestow them with specific rights.[18] IIL is one such regime.[19]

---

[11] The author has drawn this parallel between the 'security State' and the FPS standard elsewhere: Mantilla Blanco (n 1) 611–13.

[12] See eg Simon Chesterman, 'An International Rule of Law?' (2008) 56 Am J Comp L 331, 332ff; Stéphane Beaulac, 'The Rule of Law in International Law Today' in Gianluigi Palombella and Neil Walker (eds), *Relocating the Rule of Law* (Hart 2009) 197, 197ff; William W Bishop, 'The International Rule of Law' (1961) 59 Mich L Rev 553, 553ff.

[13] Declaration of the High-Level Meeting of the General Assembly on the Rule of Law at the National and International Levels (30 November 2012) UNGA Res 67/1, UN Doc A/RES/67/1, para 2.

[14] On 'rule of law transfers', see Till Patrick Holterhus, 'A Theoretical Introduction and Legal Perspective on Rule of Law Transfers' in Till Patrick Holterhus (ed), *The Law Behind Rule of Law Transfers* (Nomos 2019) 9, 16ff.

[15] Velimir Živković, 'Pursuing and Reimagining the International Rule of Law through International Investment Law' (2019) 12 HRLJ 1, 23.

[16] ibid.

[17] For a historical study of the place of the individual in international law, see Anne Peters, *Jenseits der Menschenrechte: Die Rechtsstellung des Individuums im Völkerrecht* (Mohr Siebeck 2014) 7ff.

[18] See ibid 1ff.

[19] See Tillmann Rudolf Braun, *Ausprägungen der Globalisierung: Der Investor als partielles Subjekt im internationalen Investitionsrecht* (Nomos 2014) 71ff, 302ff.

Investment treaty claims refer to allegations that actions or omissions of public authorities caused damage to individuals or corporations.[20] The factual setting of investment cases thus resembles that of administrative disputes at the domestic level.[21] Therefore, IIL is often characterized as an example of 'global administrative law'[22] or 'international administrative law'.[23] Not surprisingly, IIL constitutes a fertile ground for public law analogies.[24] The function and structure of IIL open the door for analogies pertaining to 'specific institutions', that is, 'micro-comparisons' between international investment protection standards and principles commonly associated with the rule of law.[25] In this sense, it has been argued that '[i]n terms of their content, these standards correspond, or at least are analogous in some respects, to the rights and principles governing State–market relations found in the domestic legal orders of many countries, mostly at the constitutional level'.[26]

Studies about the interactions between IIL and the rule of law have chiefly focused on the fair and equitable treatment (FET) standard.[27] It has been suggested that, as understood in arbitral decisions, the FET standard encompasses substantive and procedural guarantees resembling rule-of-law principles, including legality, procedural fairness, proportionality, and protection of expectations.[28] Advocates for this public law approach argue that the FET standard 'embodies' the rule of law.[29] Micro-comparisons with the rule of law are not necessarily limited to FET.[30] As this chapter shows, they can also be useful with regard to other standards of investment protection, such as the FPS standard.

[20] See generally Gus Van Harten and Martin Loughlin, 'Investment Treaty Arbitration as a Species of Global Administrative Law' (2006) 17(1) EJIL 121, 127ff.

[21] ibid 145ff. See also Daniel Kalderimis, 'Investment Treaty Arbitration as Global Administrative Law: What this Might Mean in Practice' in Chester Brown and Kate Miles (eds), *Evolution in Investment Treaty Arbitration* (CUP 2011) 145, 155.

[22] Santiago Montt, *State Liability in Investment Treaty Arbitration* (Hart 2009) 4, 16; Van Harten and Loughlin (n 20) 148ff; Kalderimis (n 21) 159; Benedict Kingsbury and Stephan W Schill, 'Investor-State Arbitration as Governance: Fair and Equitable Treatment, Proportionality and the Emerging Global Administrative Law' (2009) 6 IILJ Working Paper 1, 50–51.

[23] Aniruddha Rajput, 'Advent of Investment Arbitration and Evolution of International Administrative Law' (2012) 54 JILI 232, 233, 245–46 (arguing that 'global administrative law' refers chiefly to 'procedural set ups' of international organizations and pleading for the use of the term 'international administrative law').

[24] See generally Daniel Peat, 'International Investment Law and the Public Law Analogy: The Fallacies of the General Principles Method' (2018) 9 JIDS 654, 656–62; Daniel Peat, *Comparative Reasoning in International Courts and Tribunals* (CUP 2019) 107ff; Stephan W Schill, 'Introduction' in Stephan W Schill (ed), *International Investment Law and Comparative Public Law* (OUP 2010) 3, 10ff.

[25] On the use of 'micro-comparisons' in investment law, see Valentina Vadi, *Analogies in International Investment Law and Arbitration* (CUP 2016) 8, 85–86. See also the critical discussion in Valentina Vadi, *Proportionality, Reasonableness and Standards of Review in International Investment Arbitration* (Edward Elgar 2018) 20–23.

[26] Stephan W Schill, 'International Investment Law and the Rule of Law' in Jeffrey Jowell and others (eds), *Rule of Law Symposium 2014* (Academy Publishing 2015) 81, 90. See also the analysis in *Cairn Energy PLC et al v India*, PCA Case No 2016-17, Award (21 December 2020) para 1715.

[27] See eg Kenneth Vandevelde, 'A Unified Theory of Fair and Equitable Treatment' (2010) 43 NYU J Intl L & Pol 43, 49ff; Stephan W Schill, 'Fair and Equitable Treatment, The Rule of Law, and Comparative Public Law' in Schill (n 24) 155ff.

[28] Schill (n 26) 91; Vandevelde (n 27) 49–53. For a critical discussion, see also Fulvio Maria Palombino, *Fair and Equitable Treatment and the Fabric of General Principles* (Springer 2018) 42–52.

[29] Marc Jacob and Stephan W Schill, 'Fair and Equitable Treatment: Content, Practice, Method' in Marc Bungenberg and others (eds), *International Investment Law* (Nomos 2015) 700, 761; Schill (n 27) 155ff. On the micro-comparison between the rule of law and the FET standard, see Vadi, *Analogies* (n 25) 86.

[30] Schill (n 26) 90.

III. Constitutional Analogies and the Scope of Application of FPS

Recognizing that a guarantee of security must refer to some risk against which protection is afforded,[31] this section considers to what extent constitutional law concepts can be a tool for the determination of the risks covered by the FPS standard.[32] It begins by examining the main criteria used in arbitral decisions to define the FPS standard. Based on this analysis, it submits that an analogy between the FPS standard and the security function of the State in constitutional theory, which is a precondition for the rule of law, provides a useful resource to distinguish FPS from other IIL obligations.[33]

A. Broad Approaches

A first line of arbitral decisions posits that the FPS standard is a general obligation, which requires protection of the investment from a strikingly broad and virtually boundless array of risks. Notably, covered risks would include the risk of regulatory change. In *CME v Czech Republic*, the arbitrators explained that, under the FPS standard, 'the host State is obligated to ensure that neither by amendment of its laws nor by actions of its administrative bodies is the agreed and approved security and protection of the foreign investor's investment withdrawn or devalued'.[34] This broad approach can hardly serve as the basis of a general understanding of FPS's scope of application. There are four reasons for this.[35]

First, there is insufficient authority supporting broad interpretations of the FPS standard. Most tribunals have rejected this interpretation.[36] Decisions following this extensive view normally avoid making general statements about the customary standard, emphasizing the specific wording of the applicable treaty.[37] In *Global Telecom v Canada*, for example, the arbitrators held that the adjective 'full', used 'without any exclusion or limitation', warranted a broad interpretation of the protection obligation 'as set in the BIT'.[38] This interpretation is doubtful itself, as the term 'full' is usually employed to designate the customary FPS standard and clauses using this language are normally interpreted in a more restrictive fashion.[39] In other awards, the broad approach was justified on the use of the adjective 'legal' (eg the phrase 'full legal protection and security' in some Argentinean treaties).[40]

---

[31] See generally David Baldwin, 'The Concept of Security' (1997) 23 Rev Intl Stud 5, 17; Rhonda Powell, 'The Concept of Security' (2012) 1 Oxford Socio-Legal Review 1, 6.

[32] On the use of the rule of law as a conceptual tool in IIL, see Peter-Tobias Stoll, 'International Investment Law and the Rule of Law' in Till Patrick Holterhus (ed), *The Law Behind Rule of Law Transfers* (Nomos 2019) 271, 296.

[33] The author has advanced this argument elsewhere: Mantilla Blanco (n 1) 145ff (particularly at 197ff, 269ff).

[34] *CME Czech Republic BV v Czech Republic*, UNCITRAL, Partial Award (13 September 2001) para 613. See also *Global Telecom* (n 5) para 664.

[35] On the flaws of the extensive approach, see also Mantilla Blanco (n 1) 279–89.

[36] *Belenergia* (n 7) para 621; see also *AES Summit Generation Ltd v Hungary*, ICSID Case No ARB/07/22, Award (23 September 2010) para 13.3.2 (also cited in the *Belenergia* award).

[37] See *Global Telecom* (n 5) para 664.

[38] ibid.

[39] On the use of this clause as an expression of the customary standard, see *Windstream Energy LLC v Canada*, PCA Case No 2013-22, Award (27 September 2016) para 357. For the restrictive interpretation of this treaty language, see *UAB E Energija (Lithuania) v Latvia*, ICSID Case No ARB/12/33, Award (22 December 2017) para 840 (physical security); *El Paso Energy International Co v Argentina*, ICSID Case No ARB/03/15, Award (31 October 2011) paras 522–25 (third-party violence).

[40] *Siemens AG v Argentina*, ICSID Case No ARB/02/8, Award (6 February 2007) para 303, interpreting Article 4(1) of the Germany–Argentina BIT. For a treaty using the adjective 'legal', see also Argentina–Denmark BIT (1992), art 3(2).

Even in the face of this treaty language, adjudicators must be cautious in accepting a too broad understanding of the protection obligation. In some treaty frameworks, the adjective 'legal' was merely intended to emphasize that the host State was not only obliged to prevent injuries to aliens, but also to provide adequate means of redress for such injuries.[41]

Second, the broad approach leaves the risks covered by the security obligation undefined, turning it into an all-encompassing obligation. It thus fails to provide a meaningful distinction between the FPS standard and other international standards of investment protection, such as the FET standard.[42] For instance, in *Occidental v Ecuador*, the arbitrators held that 'treatment that is not fair and equitable automatically entails an absence of full protection and security of the investment'.[43] In other cases, the arbitrators have briefly acknowledged the existence of intersections between the FET and the FPS standard, without addressing the extent of the overlap.[44] An absolute correspondence between the FPS and the FET standards suggests that the interpretation of FPS as an all-embracing obligation is inaccurate. If an IIA contains both an FPS clause and an FET clause, it can be reasonably inferred that the contracting parties intended each provision to have a different meaning and to produce separate legal effects (*effet utile*).[45]

Third, there is no sufficient State practice underpinning an extensive understanding of the customary FPS standard. Broad definitions of FPS are normally used to support the extension of the standard to legal security, in the sense of a right to an enhanced stability of the investment's regulatory environment.[46] There is no consistent State practice indicating that FPS covers expectations of legal stability. On the contrary, States have expressed doubts as to whether frustration of such expectations suffices to establish a breach of customary law.[47] There is therefore little basis for an extensive interpretation of FPS clauses which define the standard by reference to customary law.[48] Even without a direct reference to custom, the customary security obligation is among the 'relevant rules of international law applicable in the relations between the parties' to be used in the interpretation of the BIT under Article 31(3)(c) of the VCLT.[49]

Finally, the fourth reason is that this broad approach fails to explain the role of due diligence in the assessment of FPS claims. It is generally accepted that FPS is not an absolute guarantee of protection, but merely requires host authorities to be diligent.[50] FPS can be

---

[41] See eg the analysis of US practice regarding FCN treaties in Anthony Benton, 'The Protection of Property Rights in Commercial Treaties of the United States' (1965) 25 ZaöRV 50, 64.

[42] See *Plama Consortium Ltd v Bulgaria*, ICSID Case No ARB/03/24, Award (27 August 2008) para 180.

[43] *Occidental Exploration and Production Co v Ecuador*, LCIA Case No UN 3467, Final Award (1 July 2004) para 187. Other tribunals address FPS as an element of the FET standard: *Interocean Oil Development Co et al v Nigeria*, ICSID Case No ARB/13/20, Award (6 October 2020) para 357 (referring to 'fair and equitable treatment standard, including a duty to provide full protection and security').

[44] See eg *Anatolie Stati et al v Kazakhstan*, SCC Case No V116/2010, Award (19 December 2013) paras 1256–57.

[45] *Oxus Gold v Uzbekistan*, UNCITRAL, Award (17 December 2015) para 354; *Ulysseas, Inc v Ecuador*, PCA Case No 2009-19, Final Award (12 June 2012) para 272.

[46] See eg the claimant's argument in *Nord Stream 2 AG v European Union*, PCA Case No 2020-07, Claimant's Memorial (3 July 2020) para 44.

[47] See eg *Vento Motorcycles Inc v Mexico*, ICSID Case No ARB(AF)/17/3, Submission of the USA (23 August 2019) para 17.

[48] See eg United States–Mexico–Canada Agreement (USMCA) (adopted 30 November 2018, entered into force 1 July 2020) art 14.6(2).

[49] See Campbell McLachlan, 'The Principle of Systemic Integration and Article 31(3)(c) of the Vienna Convention' (2005) 54(2) ICLQ 279, 312.

[50] See generally August Reinisch, *Advanced Introduction to International Investment Law* (Edward Elgar 2020) 72.

characterized as a *délit d'omission*, where the legal duty is an obligation to act and responsibility attaches on account of the State's passivity.[51] In cases concerning legal stability, both facts and legal analysis revolve around State action (eg a legal reform). As a rule, responsibility is not built upon the breach of a legal duty by omission.

Arbitral decisions pursuing a broad interpretation of the standard have sometimes acknowledged this interweaving between FPS and due diligence.[52] However, these decisions normally fail to specify how a breach of legal stability can be assessed through the prism of due diligence.[53] In response to these shortcomings, it is often claimed that due diligence plays no role in the assessment of injuries that directly originate in acts of the host State.[54] This view runs against a fairly coherent line of cases indicating that FPS imposes no strict liability.[55]

B. Restrictive Approaches

As soon as the borderless understanding of the FPS standard as an all-encompassing security obligation is rejected, it becomes necessary to determine the contours of the standard. The following sections consider the two main approaches emerging from the practice of arbitral tribunals, namely, the definition of FPS as 'physical security' and the restriction of the standard to injuries inflicted by third parties.

1. The 'physical security' approach

Numerous arbitral tribunals confine FPS to 'physical security'. Thus, in *Indian Metals v Indonesia*, the arbitrators underscored that '[u]nless the relevant treaty clause explicitly provides otherwise, the standard of full protection and security does not extend beyond physical security'.[56] In *Olin Holdings v Libya*, the tribunal rejected an FPS claim because 'the physical integrity and the use of force were not directly at stake'.[57] While this criterion seems to be clear-cut at first sight, it has significant flaws.

It has been rightly pointed out that this view is inconsistent with the definition of investment provided in most investment treaties.[58] The term 'investment', as used in numerous IIAs, normally covers both physical and nonphysical assets. For example, the Australia–Uruguay BIT of 2019 defines 'investment' broadly, covering inter alia 'tangible

---

[51] On the notion of *délit d'omission* in international law, see Roberto Ago, 'Le délit international' (1939) 68 RdC 415, 501.

[52] *Global Telecom* (n 5) para 664 (adopting a broad notion of FPS) and paras 667–68 (characterizing FPS as an obligation of due diligence). See also paras 675, 677. For another example see *Consutel Group SpA v Algeria*, PCA Case No 2017-33, Sentence Finale (3 February 2020) para 413.

[53] See the references above n 52.

[54] These views are discussed in Section IV.A.

[55] See *Mamidoil Jetoil Greek Petroleum Products SA v Albania*, ICSID Case No ARB/11/24, Award (30 March 2015) para 821 (referring to arbitral practice on this point as a '*jurisprudence constante*').

[56] *Indian Metals et al v Indonesia*, PCA Case No 2015-40, Award (29 March 2019) para 267. For other examples, see *Crystallex International Corporation v Venezuela*, ICSID Case No ARB(AF)/11/2, Award (4 April 2016) para 632; *Deutsche Bank AG v Sri Lanka*, ICSID Case No ARB/09/02, Award (31 October 2012) paras 535, 538.

[57] *Olin Holdings Limited v Libya*, ICC Case No 20355/MCP, Final Award (25 March 2018) para 365.

[58] Nartnirun Junngam, 'The Full Protection and Security Standard in International Investment Law: What and Who Is Investment Fully[?] Protected and Secured from?' (2018) 7(1) AUBLR 1, 89–90; Thimoty Foden, 'Back to Bricks and Mortar: The Case of a "Traditional" Definition of Investment that Never Was' in Ian Laird and others (eds), *Investment Treaty Arbitration and International Law, Volume 8* (Juris Net 2015) 125, 139–66.

and intangible property, including rights such as mortgages, liens and other pledges' as well as 'intellectual property rights'.[59] A treaty guaranteeing 'protection and security' to nonphysical assets cannot be reasonably construed as referring exclusively to 'physical' protection. As noted in *Siemens v Argentina*, '[i]t is difficult to understand how the physical security of an intangible asset would be achieved'.[60]

Moreover, the physical security approach does not reflect the customary FPS standard. International law treatises published prior to the Second World War gave no importance to the physical nature of the injury sustained by an alien, emphasizing only the distinction between 'acts of individuals' and other sources of injury.[61] G. F. Martens posited in 1796 that the State is under an obligation to exercise vigilance to protect the honour of foreign citizens against slander and smear, which are clear examples of nonphysical impairment.[62] J. J. Moser had advanced a similar argument as early as 1750.[63] In the mid-twentieth century, some academic studies focused precisely on the host State's duty to protect foreigners from reputational damage.[64] Most importantly, State practice offers examples of cases where the customary protection obligation was invoked in respect of nonphysical harm, such as slander campaigns against foreign nationals.[65] For the identification of the applicable legal duty, it is therefore immaterial whether the State failed to protect a foreigner against a mob that burned down her property or against slanderous pamphlets leading to economic sabotage and financial ruin.

Modern examples of nonphysical risks triggering the security obligation could refer, for example, to inadequate supervision of financial entities, failure to enforce domestic antitrust law against competitors, or omissions in the prevention of cyberattacks.[66] The physical security approach is utterly incapable of addressing these realities. Widespread fixation on 'physical security' has led scholars to suggest, for example, that the FPS standard is only relevant where a cyberattack results in damage to physical servers.[67] These intricacies do not result from the complexity of the FPS standard, but rather suggest that the physical security approach is misplaced.

It must be cautioned, however, that certain treaty clauses link FPS to the notion of physical security. Thus, for instance, the Regional Comprehensive Economic Partnership (RCEP) of 2020 provides that 'full protection and security requires each Party to take such

---

[59] Australia–Uruguay BIT (2019), art 1(a)(i), (iv).

[60] *Siemens* (n 40) para 303.

[61] See eg Clyde Eagleton, *The Responsibility of States in International Law* (NYU Press 1928) chs III ('Acts of Agents') and IV ('Acts of Individuals').

[62] Georg Friedrich von Martens, *Einleitung in das positive Europäische Völkerrecht auf Verträge und Herkommen gegründet* (Johann Christian Dieterich 1796) 98–99.

[63] Johann Jakob Moser, *Grundsätze des jetzt üblichen Europäischen Völkerrechts in Friedenszeiten* (Hanau 1750) 398 (para 42).

[64] See eg Edward Zellweger, *Die völkerrechtliche Verantwortlichkeit des Staates für die Presse unter besonderer Berücksichtigung der schweizerischen Praxis* (Polygraphischer Verlag 1949) 7ff.

[65] See eg 'Mr. Bonham to Commissioner Seu (13 March 1849)' (1862) 38(1) British and Foreign State Papers 856, 856–57 (protection of British subjects in Hong Kong from defamation); 'Mr. Wu to Mr. Hill (6 July 1901)' (1901) Papers Relating to the Foreign Relations of the United States, with the Annual Message of the President Transmitted to Congress December 3, 1901 100 (failure to protect Chinese subjects living in Montana from slander).

[66] See eg the investor's argument in *Hesham Talaat M. Al-Warraq v Republic of Indonesia*, UNCITRAL, Final Award (15 December 2014) para 627 (unsuccessful claim referring to omissions in the supervision of a financial entity).

[67] Robert Reyes Landicho, 'Enforcing a State's International IP Obligations through Investment Law Standards of Protection—An Ill-Fated Romance' in Ian Laird and others (eds), *Investment Treaty Arbitration and International Law, Volume 11* (Juris 2018) 111, 127–28.

measures as may be reasonably necessary to ensure the *physical protection and security* of the covered investment.[68] This wording manifests a regressive force that creates unnecessary obstacles for the application of FPS in challenging contexts, such as cybersecurity.

2. The third-party approach

In addition to the physical security and all-encompassing approaches, there is a third strand of cases that define the scope of FPS by reference to the source of the covered risks. In *El Paso v Argentina*, the arbitrators described FPS as 'a residual obligation provided for those cases in which the acts challenged may not in themselves be attributed to the Government, but to a third party'.[69] The third-party approach has also emerged in cases under the Energy Charter Treaty[70] and the North American Free Trade Agreement.[71] This approach draws a fairly clear line between the risks covered by FPS and those addressed by other standards. Thus, in *Oxus Gold v Uzbekistan*, the arbitrators held that 'FET and expropriation involve the investor and the host State, whereas the full protection and security standard concerns the host State's obligation to exercise reasonable care in protecting the investment from actions of third parties'.[72]

Besides cases clearly following the third-party approach, there are also arbitral awards that lean towards this criterion but are not entirely conclusive. Some tribunals avoid making straightforward statements about the scope of FPS. Thus, in *Krederi Ltd v Ukraine*, the arbitrators rejected an FPS claim and explained that 'this claim more aptly falls under a fair and equitable treatment claim since it does not concern allegations of host State organs failing to protect the investment against a third party attack, but rather alleges that Ukraine's officials harassed the investor'.[73] However, they cautiously added that FPS 'may also be viewed as extending to prevent attacks on investments by organs of the host State'.[74]

Other awards combine the third-party approach with the physical security criterion. In *Eskosol v Italy*, for example, the arbitrators referred to the 'original customary international law dimensions' of FPS in terms of 'a due diligence obligation to protect the physical security of Eskosol's investment from harm by third parties'.[75] This approach is misguided. The problems associated with the use of the physical security criterion, identified above,[76] do not vanish by mingling this criterion with the third-party approach.

The understanding of FPS as an obligation embodying a guarantee of protection against third-party injuries reflects the rationale of the security obligation in the customary law of aliens.[77] As in these cases the immediate source of the injury is not attributable to the host

---

[68] RCEP (adopted 15 November 2020, in force 1 January 2022) art 10.5(2)(b) (emphasis added). For other examples see EU–Vietnam Investment Agreement (adopted 30 June 2019) art 2.5(5); Korea–Vietnam FTA (adopted 05 March 2015, in force 20 December 2015) art 9.5(2)(b). See also Netherlands Model BIT (2019) art 9(1).

[69] *El Paso* (n 39) para 522.

[70] *Electrabel SA v Republic of Hungary*, ICSID Case No ARB/07/19, Decision on Jurisdiction, Applicable Law and Liability (30 November 2012) paras 7.83, 7.145.

[71] *Mercer International Inc v Canada*, ICSID Case No ARB(AF)/12/3, Award (6 March 2018) para 7.80. NAFTA was in force from 1994 to 2020.

[72] *Oxus Gold* (n 45) para 354. See also *Gemplus et al v Mexico*, ICSID Case No ARB(AF)/04/3 and ARB(AF)/04/4, Award (16 June 2010) paras 9.11–9.12; *Krederi Ltd v Ukraine*, ICSID Case ARB/14/17, Award (2 July 2018) para 652.

[73] *Krederi* (n 72) para 655; see also para 651.

[74] ibid para 656.

[75] *Eskosol SpA v Italy*, ICSID Case No ARB/15/50, Award (4 September 2020) para 479.

[76] See Section III.B.1.

[77] For a detailed analysis of the origins and contours of the customary security obligation, see Mantilla Blanco (n 1) 39ff.

State, responsibility cannot be established other than for an omission in the protection of foreigners. In 1625, Hugo Grotius submitted that there were two possible causes of action in cases involving private injuries to foreign subjects.[78] The first one was toleration (*patientia*) and occurred where the State was aware of the threat and failed to take preventive action.[79] The second one was refuge (*receptus*), which referred to a failure to punish or allow punishment of the offender upon request of the injured party.[80] The closeness of these notions to the present-day understanding of FPS standard is striking. Thus, in *Ulysseas v Ecuador*, the arbitrators explained that FPS comprises 'a duty of due diligence [on the State] for the prevention of wrongful injuries inflicted by third parties to persons or property of aliens in its territory or, if not successful, for the repression and punishment of such injuries'.[81]

The rationale underpinning the third-party approach is, therefore, that the FPS standard pertains to the reaction of the host State to a threat produced by external sources of risk. While private injuries are the most common and obvious example, this category does not exhaust the FPS standard. The protection obligation covers other external risks, such as the risk of harmful acts of third States in the territory of the receiving State. Thus, in *Toto Costruzioni v Lebanon*, it was suggested that alleged omissions of Lebanon in preventing Syrian troops from obstructing the investor's construction site could be assessed through the prism of the FPS standard.[82]

Early cases where FPS clauses were applied in connection with harm inflicted by military personnel do not necessarily defy the logic of the third-party approach. In *AMT v Zaire*, for example, a group of soldiers had plundered the investment.[83] The arbitrators found 'an omission by Zaire to take every measure necessary to protect and ensure the security of the investment'.[84] It might appear counterintuitive to declare responsibility for an omission where damage was directly caused by Zairian soldiers. The key to this reasoning is the tribunal's finding that the acts in question were committed in a merely private capacity:

> The nature of the looting and the destruction of property which were [*sic*] looted show clearly that it was not 'the army' or 'the armed forces' that acted as such in the circumstance.... On the contrary, ... they were separate individuals and not the forces that performed the action.[85]

In other cases, the FPS standard has been applied with regard to omissions in the mitigation of collateral damage by the armed forces. In *AAPL v Sri Lanka*, the tribunal found that authorities failed to 'minimize the risks' arising from a counterinsurgency operation.[86] It

---

[78] Hugo Grotius, *Rights of War and Peace in Three Books* (1625) (trans printed for W Inns/R Manby 1738) 454 (bk II, ch XXI: II.2).

[79] ibid.

[80] ibid 454 (bk II, ch XXI: II.1). The English translation used here employs the word *protection* instead of *refuge*, which is the term preferred in more recent English translations. See eg Hugo Grotius, *On the Law of War and Peace* (Stephen Neff tr, CUP 2012) 292.

[81] *Ulysseas* (n 45) para 272.

[82] See *Toto Costruzioni Generali SpA v Lebanon*, ICSID Case No ARB/07/12, Award (7 June 2012) paras 171, 195–200.

[83] *American Manufacturing & Trading Inc v Zaire*, ICSID Case No ARB/93/1, Award (21 February 1997) paras 3.04, 6.08–6.11.

[84] ibid para 6.11.

[85] ibid para 7.09.

[86] *Asian Agricultural Products Ltd v Sri Lanka*, ICSID Case No ARB/87/3, Final Award (27 June 1990) para 85(b).

declared that 'Respondent through said inaction and omission violated its due diligence obligation which requires undertaking all possible measures that could be reasonably expected to prevent the eventual occurrence of killings and property destruction'.[87] Here, while the direct source of harm was State action, the FPS standard was still applied to evaluate the host State's reaction towards an external security threat (insurgency).[88]

3. Assessment: FPS as an embodiment of the State's security function

The doctrinal evolution of the FPS standard has not been isolated from the history of political and constitutional ideas. The ever-present question about the source of political and legal authority gave rise to well-known contractualist narratives about the origins of organized society and sovereign power.[89] The recognition of consent of the governed as the source of the sovereign's authority poses significant challenges when it comes to the foreigner, who is not properly a member of the *polis*, and yet requires protection from the State and must abide by its laws.[90] In the seventeenth and eighteenth centuries, Samuel Pufendorf, Christian Wolff, and Emer de Vattel developed a contractualist narrative as a legal–philosophical justification of the security obligation, using the fiction of a 'tacit agreement' between the host sovereign and the foreigner entering into its territory.[91] This agreement consisted in a promise of protection on the part of the ruler and a pledge of obedience on the part of the alien.[92]

This narrative is a reminder that the problems addressed by the law of aliens are not far from traditional questions of constitutional theory, as they both refer to the exercise of public authority over private individuals. There might therefore be some functional equivalence between constitutional law notions and institutions of the law of aliens.[93] This is precisely the case of the FPS standard.

The evolution of Western States has been aptly described as a development in three conceptual steps.[94] The process began with the 'security State' in charge of ensuring peace among the people, that is to say, the *neminem laedere* principle.[95] This is the archetypal function of the State according to Thomas Hobbes.[96] The Hobbesian stage prepared the ground for the next step, where the State—having gained its monopoly over the use of force—was subjected to the law.[97] This idea represents the inception of the rule of law or *Rechtsstaat*, in

---

[87] ibid.

[88] For a detailed analysis of this scenario, see Mantilla Blanco (n 1) 259–63.

[89] For an overview of contractualist theories, see Herfried Münkler and Grit Straßenberger, *Politische Theorie und Ideengeschichte* (Beck 2016) 191ff; Anthony Kenny, *A New History of Western Philosophy* (OUP 2010) 712ff.

[90] See eg the discussion of the problem of foreignness in Locke's political philosophy in A John Simmons, 'Denisons and Aliens: Locke's Problem of Political Consent' (1998) 24(2) Soc Theory & Prac 161, 162ff.

[91] Samuel Pufendorf, 'Of the Law of Nature and of Nations in Eight Books' (1672) in Craig Carr (ed), *The Political Writings of Samuel Pufendorf* (Michael Seidler tr, OUP 1994) 171; Christian Wolff, 'Jus gentium methodo scientifica pertractatum' (1749) in James Brown Scott (ed), *Classics of International Law* (Joseph Drake tr, Clarendon Press 1934) 536–37 (§1063); Emer de Vattel, *Le droit des gens, Volume 1* (1758) (Carnegie Institution of Washington 1916) 329, 331.

[92] See the references above n 91.

[93] See Schill (n 26) 90 (discussed in Section II above).

[94] Josef Isensee, *Das Grundrecht auf Sicherheit* (De Gruyter 1983) 17–18. See also the discussion of the three stages in Deutscher Bundestag/Wissenschaftliche Dienste, 'Zum "Grundrecht auf Sicherheit"' (2008) WD 3-3000-180/08, 8–9 <www.bundestag.de/resource/blob/423604/6bc141a9713732fc4bb4334b6d02693b/wd-3-180-08-pdf-data.pdf> accessed 28 October 2021.

[95] See Isensee (n 94) 6–7, 17. For a study of the security function of the State in the history of political ideas, see Markus Möstl, *Die staatliche Garantie für die öffentliche Sicherheit und Ordnung* (Mohr Siebeck 2002) 5ff.

[96] Thomas Hobbes, *Leviathan* (1651) (Clarendon Press 1909) 131 (pt 2, ch 17, para 87).

[97] Isensee (n 94) 17.

the sense of a State that is not above the law, but abides by the law.[98] Finally, the third stage was the social State, which attends social needs and looks after the material well-being of the people.[99] These steps should be viewed as a conceptual resource rather than as an accurate depiction of historical processes. As each of these three stages presupposes the accomplishment of the previous stage, they coexist similarly as the different wooden figures of a Russian matryoshka doll.[100]

In essence, the scope of the customary core of FPS standard mirrors the 'security State'.[101] An analogy with the security function of the State provides a useful explanatory tool of the main features of the FPS standard and the risks it covers, such as protection of aliens from private individuals and foreign States. The duty to mitigate collateral damage in contexts such as counterinsurgency operations is also intrinsically linked to the security function of the State. As noted by the tribunal in *AAPL v Sri Lanka* when addressing this issue, 'the failure to resort to such precautionary measures acquires more significance when taking into consideration that such measures fall within the normal exercise of governmental inherent powers—as a public authority—entitled to order undesirable persons out from security sensitive areas'.[102]

The analogy with the security or police State allows identification of a well-defined category of risks covered by the FPS standard. As opposed to the FET standard, the central function of FPS is not to shield the investment from State action, but from risks that do not originate directly in the host State's conduct. The functional interaction between the FPS and the FET standards is comparable to the conceptual interplay between the security function of the State and the subjection of public authority to the rule of law.[103] In the nineteenth century, emerging notions of the rule of law or *Rechtsstaat* were predominantly concerned with protection from State abuse.[104] Notwithstanding the manifold definitions of the rule of law in constitutional theory,[105] absence of arbitrariness and the reduction of administrative discretion remain at the very heart of the concept.[106]

The 'security State' and the rule of law are not mutually exclusive. Rather, there is a synergic interplay between them. On the one hand, security is a precondition for the enjoyment of fundamental liberties. A State that complies with the law is of little value if it holds no real control over the territory. On the other hand, while authoritarian States might certainly

---

[98] ibid. For a discussion of the differences and possible equivalences between the continental notion of the *Rechtsstaat* and the common law concept of the rule of law, see Martin Loughlin, *Foundations of Public Law* (OUP 2010) 312ff; Danilo Zolo, 'The Rule of Law: A Critical Reappraisal' in Pietro Costa and Danilo Zolo (eds), *The Rule of Law: History, Theory and Criticism* (Springer 2007) 3, 3ff; Klaus Thomalla, *Herrschaft des Gesetzes, nicht des Menschen* (Mohr Siebeck 2019) 387–98. See also Dietmar von der Pfordten, 'On the Foundations of the Rule of Law and the Principle of the Legal State/Rechtsstaat' in James R Silkenat and others (eds), *The Legal Doctrines of the Rule of Law and the Legal State (Rechtsstaat)* (Springer 2014) 15, 25ff.

[99] Isensee (n 94) 17.

[100] See ibid 18.

[101] Mantilla Blanco (n 1) 574–76 and 612; 257ff.

[102] *Asian Agricultural Products* (n 86) para 85(b).

[103] Mantilla Blanco (n 1) 574–76.

[104] See Thomalla (n 98) 387ff; Michaela Wittinger, 'Das Rechtsstaatsprinzip—vom nationalen Verfassungsprinzip zum Rechtsprinzip der europäischen und der internationalen Gemeinschaft?' (2009) 57(1) JöR 427, 428; Udo Di Fabio, *Risikoentscheidungen im Rechtsstaat* (Mohr Siebeck 2019) 11ff.

[105] See Katharina Sobota, *Das Prinzip Rechtsstaat* (Mohr Siebeck 1997) 21ff.

[106] On the opposition between the rule of law and arbitrariness, see *Elettronica Sicula SpA (ELSI)* (Judgment) [1989] ICJ Rep 15, 76, para 128; German Federal Constitutional Court, Decision (2 May 1967) BVerfGE 21, 362 (372); Thomalla (n 98) 389 (on the continental notion of *Rechtsstaat*) and 394–95 (on the common law idea of the rule of law); Robert von Mohl, *Encyklopädie der Staatswissenschaften* (Mohr 1872) 106 ('*Rechtsstaat*' as the 'opposite of despotism'). On the reduction of discretion, see Tom Bingham, *The Rule of Law* (Penguin 2011) ch 4.

have the ability to ensure peace among individuals, the rule of law introduces basic expectations about the manner in which the State exercises its fundamental security function.[107]
The following sections explore the extent to which the rule of law permeates the evaluation
of State conduct through the lens of the FPS standard.

IV. The Rule of Law and the Content of FPS

Analogies to the rule of law constitute an important ingredient for ongoing discussions
about the content of the protection obligation. This section examines three uses of such
constitutional law analogies in academic discourse and arbitral practice, namely: (1) FPS
and the positive and negative functions of fundamental rights; (2) FPS and the creation of
rule-of-law-based institutions; and (3) due diligence as an anchor for rule-of-law analogies.

A. FPS and the Positive and Negative Functions of Fundamental Rights

The protection of fundamental rights is a key feature of the rule of law.[108] The subjection of
the State to the law is intrinsically intertwined with the recognition of legal rights or liberties of individuals as legal subjects.[109] Such recognition gives rise to a law-based relationship
between private individuals and public authorities.[110] In the tradition of Georg Jellinek, this
relationship crystallizes in a threefold function of fundamental rights, namely, protection
from the State (*status negativus*), protection through the State (*status positivus*), and political participation rights (*status activus*).[111] These three statuses are in constant interplay
with the obligations of the individual towards the State (*status subjectionis*).[112] The obligation to provide protection against third parties under the FPS standard has been compared
with Jellinek's *status positivus*.[113] Adherents of this approach do not, however, normally
limit the FPS standard to the *status positivus*. Rather, they assume a two-faced character of
FPS, which is said to encompass both protection through and from the State.[114]

The claimed duality of the standard is sometimes translated into a duality of standards of
responsibility. It has been argued that responsibility for breaches of the duty of abstention
(ie the obligation concerning direct injuries of the State) is absolute or strict, whereas responsibility for damages inflicted by third parties is subject to due diligence.[115] An example
of this approach appears in *Cengiz Insaat Sanayi ve Ticaret AS v Libya*:

---

[107] See generally Möstl (n 95) 9ff, 14ff and 655ff.
[108] Sobota (n 105) 65ff.
[109] See Georg Jellinek, *System der subjektiven öffentlichen Rechte* (Mohr 1892)76ff, particularly 79–81.
[110] ibid 82.
[111] ibid.
[112] ibid 81.
[113] Helge Elisabeth Zeitler, 'Full Protection and Security' in Schill (n 24) 212. See also Julian Scheu, *Systematische Berücksichtigung von Menschenrechten in Investitionsschiedsverfahren* (Nomos 2017) 194ff (dual standard, but always subject to due diligence).
[114] See the references above n 113.
[115] See eg Ralph Lorz, 'Protection and Security (Including the NAFTA Approach)' in Bungenberg and others (n 29) 764, 777–78; Eric de Brabandere, 'Host State's Due Diligence Obligations in International Investment Law' (2015) 42 Syracuse J Intl L & Com 319, 333 (duty to abstain) and 337–41 (duty to protect). See also Rudolf Dolzer and Christoph Schreuer, *Principles of International Investment Law* (OUP 2012) 162 (irrelevance of due diligence in cases of direct harm by the State).

FPS thus entails a two-fold obligation for the host State: a negative obligation to refrain from directly harming the investment by acts of violence attributable to the State, plus a positive obligation to prevent that third parties cause physical damage to such investment. *The FPS standard thus combines an obligation of result and an obligation of means:* (i) The *obligation of result* requires that the State and its organs abstain from directly causing physical harm ... (ii) the second leg of the standard requires the State to exercise *reasonable care* to prevent damage caused by third parties.[116]

The idea that the FPS standard encompasses two different standards of liability—one for the duty of abstention and one for the duty of protection—is most problematic.[117] As far as the scope of FPS is restricted to external sources of risk, there will be no place for an absolute 'duty of abstention' within the standard.[118] Moreover, most sources reject the understanding of FPS as the source of 'absolute' or 'strict' liability.[119] The due diligence element cannot be easily dismissed, even where the scope of the standard is defined broadly.[120] In *Eskosol v Italy*, the arbitrators noted that 'even tribunals that might see constant protection and security as including some component of legal stability should accept that the obligation would not require some absolute freezing of regulatory frameworks in place, but simply that due diligence (or reasonable care) be taken'.[121]

The potential broadness of the FPS standard, coupled with the idea that it could impose some form of absolute responsibility, played a fairly important role in the assessment of the FPS clause of the Colombia–France BIT by the Colombian Constitutional Court in 2019.[122] The General Civil Attorney considered that the FPS standard implied that the State would 'assume objective responsibility for any risk'.[123] Based on this premise, he argued that the FPS clause contravened the principle of national convenience (ie foreign relations should serve the national interest) and could impact fiscal sustainability (ie prevention of unsustainable expenditure policies affecting macroeconomic stability).[124] The Court disagreed. It noted that FPS merely requires the State to 'preserve normal conditions of security and public order'.[125] It further underscored that FPS does not entail strict responsibility.[126]

---

[116] *Cengiz Insaat Sanayi ve Ticaret AS v Libya*, ICC Case No 21537/ZF/AYZ, Award (7 November 2018) paras 403–06 (emphasis added).

[117] For a more detailed discussion of these theories, see Mantilla Blanco (n 1) 349ff. See also 257ff (discussing parallels to the *status positivus*).

[118] See Sections III.B.2 and III.C.

[119] See *Bernhard von Pezold and others v Zimbabwe*, ICSID Case No ARB/10/15, Award (28 July 2015) para 596; *Toto Costruzioni Generali* (n 82) para 227; *Tulip Real Estate v Republic of Turkey*, ICSID Case No ARB/11/28, Award (10 March 2014) para 430.

[120] See the analysis in *Convial Callao SA v Peru*, ICSID Case No ARB/10/2, Final Award (21 March 2013) paras 642–43, 651.

[121] *Eskosol* (n 75) para 481.

[122] Constitutional Court of Colombia, Judgment C-252/19 (6 June 2019). The author discloses his participation in these proceedings with an *amicus curiae* brief (*intervención ciudadana*) on another treaty clause.

[123] ibid paras 175, 213.

[124] ibid. On the principle of convenience under Article 226 of the Constitution, see Constitutional Court of Colombia, Judgment C-269/14 (2 May 2014) s 6. On fiscal sustainability, see Constitutional Court of Colombia, Judgment C-288/12 (18 April 2012) paras 30ff.

[125] Constitutional Court of Colombia, Judgment C-252/19 (n 122) para 213.

[126] ibid.

B. FPS and the Creation of Rule-of-Law-Based Institutions

Academic studies have suggested that the FPS standard requires the host State not only to act diligently in the protection of investments, but also to create adequate legal and administrative structures of protection.[127] It has been contended that this obligation is not a duty of due diligence.[128] If these views were correct, the FPS standard could arguably provide the basis for an international law obligation to develop institutions coherent with the rule of law. This understanding of the FPS standard is, however, misplaced. It can be objected to on three grounds.[129]

The first objection is that this view confuses the conditions for a State to be in a position to fulfil an international obligation with the object of the obligation. There can be no doubt that compliance with international obligations presupposes that certain municipal law institutions or administrative mechanisms are in place. As a rule, failure to create those institutions or structures does not, however, entail per se a breach of international law. In principle, as rightly observed by Dionisio Anzilotti in 1906, international law does not predetermine the specific content of domestic law.[130] Each State is free to choose the municipal law institutions it deems appropriate to fulfil its international commitments.[131] In 1899, Heinrich Triepel depicted those national law instruments as an 'internationally indispensable domestic law'.[132] The mere absence of such 'indispensable domestic law' is not an international wrongful act.[133] Rather, failure to design and implement those institutions will often result in the State's inability to abide by its international obligations.[134] When a breach of international law occurs, the State cannot rely on its own failure to adopt such necessary legislation to escape international responsibility.[135]

The second objection is that State and arbitral practice provide little support to the proposition that 'full protection and security' entails an abstract obligation to create domestic institutions that ensure the protection of aliens. The decisions normally cited in support of this view typically refer to the redress element of the FPS standard.[136] The argument of authority is however weak. Even arbitral decisions stating that FPS encompasses an 'obligation to make a functioning system of courts and legal remedies to the investor' have not declared the State responsible for the mere absence of such system.[137] Rather, they normally emphasize that the FPS standard 'does not create an obligation of result or absolute liability'.[138] Breaches of FPS on account of malfunctions of the justice system are never assessed on an abstract level, detached from the manner in which they operated in a specific case.[139] Due diligence is at the centre of this analysis. Thus, in *AMF v Czech Republic*, the tribunal held

---

[127]   de Brabandere (n 115) 324–25, 341–45.

[128]   ibid 325, 360.

[129]   On this approach and its flaws, see also Mantilla Blanco (n 1) 353ff.

[130]   Dionisio Anzilotti, 'La responsabilité internationale des états a raison des dommages souffert par des étrangers' (1906) 13 RGDIP 285, 294.

[131]   ibid.

[132]   Heinrich Triepel, *Völkerrecht und Landesrecht* (Hirchfeld 1899) 301.

[133]   ibid 301–04.

[134]   ibid 303–04.

[135]   ibid. See also *American Manufacturing* (n 83) para 6.05.

[136]   de Brabandere (n 115) 341ff.

[137]   *Frontier Petroleum Services v Czech Republic*, UNCITRAL, Final Award (12 November 2010) para 273.

[138]   ibid paras 269–70. See also *AMF Aircraftleasing Meier & Fischer GmbH et al v Czech Republic*, PCA Case No 2017-15, Final Award (11 May 2020) para 661.

[139]   See Mantilla Blanco (n 1) 362ff.

that FPS requires the host State to exercise 'due diligence in maintaining a functioning judicial system that is available to foreign investors seeking redress'.[140] In *Levy v Peru*, even though the tribunal adopted a broad understanding of FPS,[141] it rejected a claim requiring examination of the 'very organization structure' of the judiciary.[142]

Third, a breach of the FPS standard can only occur where actual damage has been inflicted.[143] Damage, albeit not a general precondition for international responsibility, is a condition for the breach of certain international obligations.[144] The FPS standard is one such obligation. This holds true for both the redress and the preventive dimensions of the standard. It is tautological that a breach of an obligation of redress can only be established where there is an injury or wrong to be redressed.[145]

The prevention obligation is more complex. The idea that a violation of FPS could occur even in the absence of actual damage seems to stem from the depiction of the FPS standard as an obligation of means or conduct.[146] International law sources commonly describe due diligence duties as obligations of conduct.[147] In the civil law tradition, an obligation of conduct is that which requires the debtor to pursue a result.[148] Responsibility attaches on account of negligence, regardless of whether the result was actually achieved.[149] Thus, a breach of an obligation of means—triggering responsibility—can occur even in the absence of damage.

The International Law Commission (ILC) discussed the distinction between obligations of conduct and result in the 1970s,[150] as Roberto Ago sought to introduce it into the law of State responsibility.[151] Ago's use of the terms differed significantly from their original meaning in domestic legal systems.[152] In fact, he posited that responsibility for obligations of conduct required not only negligence, but moreover the actual occurrence of harm.[153] One of Ago's preferred examples was precisely the customary obligation to protect foreign citizens.[154] The Report of the 30th Session of the ILC states:

> Both at the diplomatic and at the international judicial or arbitral levels, therefore, the State claiming injury has not normally complained of an internationally wrongful act until after

---

[140] *AMF Aircraftleasing* (n 138) para 661.

[141] *Renée Rose Levy v Peru*, ICSID Case No ARB/10/17, Award (26 February 2014) para 406.

[142] ibid para 442.

[143] See generally Mantilla Blanco (n 1) 339ff.

[144] See generally James Crawford, *State Responsibility: The General Part* (CUP 2013) 59.

[145] See the analysis of the obligation of redress in Eagleton (n 61) 92–93.

[146] For an example of the use of the notion of 'obligations of conduct' ('*obligation de moyens*') in this context, see *LESI SpA et al v Algeria*, ICSID Case No ARB/05/3, Award (12 November 2008) para 153. Other awards refer to a 'best efforts obligation': *Deutsche Bank AG v Sri Lanka*, ICSID Case No ARB/09/02, Award (31 October 2012) para 537.

[147] *The Environment and Human Rights*, Advisory Opinion OC-23/17, Inter-American Court of Human Rights Series A No 23 (15 November 2017) para 123.

[148] See René Demogue, *Traité des obligations en general, Volume 5* (Rousseau 1925) 538–39.

[149] ibid.

[150] See particularly, the records of the 30th session of the ILC in 1978: ILC, 'Summary Records of the Thirtieth Session, Held at Geneva from 8 May to 28 July 1978' (1978) ILC YB, vol I, 4ff (1476th meeting), 9ff (1477th meeting), 206ff (1513th meeting).

[151] ILC, 'Sixth Report on State Responsibility by Mr. Roberto Ago, Special Rapporteur: The Internationally Wrongful Act of the State, Source of International Responsibility (Continued)' (1977) ILC YB, vol II, Pt One, 4–43, paras 1ff.

[152] James Crawford, 'Revisiting the Draft Articles on State Responsibility' (1999) 10 EJIL 435, 441.

[153] ILC, 'Seventh Report on State Responsibility by Mr. Roberto Ago, Special Rapporteur' (1978) ILC YB, vol II, Pt One, 31, 32ff, paras 4ff.

[154] ibid.

the event, represented by the attack emanating from private individuals or other sources, has actually occurred.[155]

This statement unveils a remarkable metamorphosis of the concept of obligations of conduct, which has been portrayed as a case where 'the effect of a national law analogy has been reversed in the course of transplantation'.[156] That is why the ILC preferred the term 'obligations of event'.[157] The breach of an obligation of this type requires fulfilment of two necessary and non-sufficient conditions, namely, the occurrence of the event (ie the infliction of harm) and the failure to exercise due diligence.[158]

These three reasons show that the FPS standard cannot be read as the source of an obligation to create rule-of-law-based institutions. An abstract failure to create said institutions provides no basis for an FPS claim. Still, the FPS standard could be an incentive for the implementation of proper protection mechanisms, consistent with the rule of law. It is in the interest of the host State to create tools that place it in a position to comply with the security obligation.

C. Due Diligence as an Anchor for Rule-of-Law Analogies?

Analogy is a deeply rooted component of international legal arguments.[159] Analogies often refer to domestic law, including both public law[160] and private law.[161] The notion of due diligence, which is a firmly etched element of the FPS standard, certainly invites analogical arguments. Diligence and negligence are present in virtually every area of the law, from family law to administrative and criminal law. This section begins by exploring the use of domestic law concepts in connection with due diligence, providing evidence of an ongoing shift from private law to public law (and, particularly, rule-of-law) analogies. It then considers the extent to which specific features of due diligence, as applied in connection with the FPS standard, resemble elements of the rule of law.

1. From private law analogies to public law analogies?
a) Due diligence and private law analogies
Prior to the BIT era, it was common to build a bridge between private law notions of diligence and the customary obligation to provide security to foreigners. This private law benchmark precedes present-day uses of reasonableness and other elements of the rule of law in the assessment of FPS claims. The use of rule-of-law analogies in the analysis of due diligence must therefore be considered against the background of the private law analogy, which had a shaping influence over the due diligence element of the FPS standard.

---

[155] ILC, 'Report of the International Law Commission on the Work of Its Thirtieth Session, 8 May–28 July 1978' (1978) ILC YB, vol II, pt Two, 74, 84, para 12 (Draft Article 23, Commentary para 12).

[156] Crawford (n 152) 441.

[157] ILC (n 155) 81ff (Draft Article 23, Commentary).

[158] See Ago's statement in ILC (n 150) 5, para 9.

[159] See generally, Albert Bleckmann, *Grundprobleme und Methoden des Völkerrechts* (Verlag Karl Alber 1982) 219ff.

[160] See generally Peat, 'International Investment Law and the Public Law Analogy' (n 24) 654ff.

[161] See generally Hersch Lauterpacht, *Private Law Sources and Analogies of International Law* (Longmans, Green and Co 1927) 5ff.

The very definition of the content of the host State's obligation to protect aliens in terms of due diligence stems from the Grotian theory of fault, which was in turn essentially based on an analogy with Roman law.[162] Grotius compared the responsibility of the sovereign for the acts of its subjects with that of parents for wrongs committed by their children.[163] The core of his argument was that, in those scenarios, State responsibility could only arise if the State was at fault.[164] The Grotian concept of fault unleashed decades of academic debate.[165] The objective theory of State responsibility eventually led to the rejection of fault as one of the elements of the internationally wrongful act.[166] This did not imply, however, the acceptance of an absolute responsibility of the State for third-party injuries to aliens. Instead of conditioning international responsibility through the private law–inspired notion of fault, it was submitted that the content of the protection obligation was a positive duty of due diligence.[167] Therefore, responsibility for breach of the security obligation was not fault-based, but a form of objective responsibility for breach of an obligation to exercise due diligence.[168]

The rejection of the notion of fault did not entail an emancipation from private law analogies and a turn to public law concepts, such as the rule of law. Debate revolved around the civil law notions of *diligentia quam in suis rebus* (ie the diligence a person displays in her own affairs) and *diligens paterfamilias* (ie an objectivized head of family).[169] The opposition of these two standards reflects the debate on the subjective–objective character of due diligence.

From a present-day perspective, subjective parameters analogous to the private law *diligentia quam in suis rebus* criterion are inadequate for the assessment of FPS claims.[170] These criteria require *per definitionem* a comparison between the host State's acts for the protection of aliens and the measures which the host State's authorities have adopted in their own affairs. In practice, this exercise leads to a comparison of the measures adopted for the protection of the host State's nationals and those adopted in respect of foreigners.[171] The FPS standard would be effectively reduced to national treatment.[172]

The problem lies in the fact that FPS is generally recognized as an element of the customary minimum standard of treatment.[173] The 'minimum standard' is both historically

---

[162] On the Grotian analogy, see ibid 135ff.

[163] Grotius (n 78) 454 (bk II, ch XXI: II.1).

[164] ibid.

[165] See generally, Roberto Ago, *La colpa nell'illecito internazionale* (CEDAM 1939) 3ff. For discussion of these views and the subsequent turn from fault-based responsibility to an objective theory of State responsibility, see Mantilla Blanco (n 1) 388ff (also discussing Grotius at 386ff).

[166] ILC, 'Draft Articles on Responsibility of States for Internationally Wrongful Acts, with Commentaries' (2001) ILC YB, vol II, pt Two, 31, 34 (art 2).

[167] Anzilotti (n 130) 290–91; Hans Kelsen, *General Theory of Law and State* (1945) (Anders Wedberg tr, Lawbook Exchange 2009) 66.

[168] See the references above n 167.

[169] For an example of the use of the *diligentia quam in suis* criterion, see *Affaire des biens britanniques au Maroc espagnol (Spain v UK)* (1925) 2 RIAA 615, 644, para 4; Paul Guggenheim, 'Les principes de droit international public' (1952) 80 RdC 2, 148–49. For an example of the use of the *diligens paterfamilias* criterion, see 'Mr. Bayard, Sec. of State, to Mr. Sutphen (6 January 1888)' in John Bassett Moore, *A Digest of International Law, Volume 6* (Government Printing Office 1906) 961–62. For a detailed discussion of the objective or subjective character of due diligence, see also Mantilla Blanco (n 1) 432ff.

[170] For a critical perspective on the subjective notion of due diligence, see Riccardo Pisillo Mazzeschi, *"Due diligence" e responsabilità internazionale degli stati* (Giufrè Editore 1989) 398ff.

[171] See eg Arnold D McNair, *International Law Opinions, Volume 2* (CUP 1956) 245 (specifically referring to damages inflicted during insurrections).

[172] See eg the interpretation advanced by the respondent in *Pantechniki* (n 3) para 74.

[173] See Helge Elisabeth Zeitler, 'The Guarantee of Full Protection and Security in Investment Treaties Regarding Harm Caused by Private Actors' (2005) 3 SIAR 1, 21; Zeitler (n 113) 201; Mantilla Blanco (n 1) 435–36.

and conceptually the counterpart of the doctrine of equality.[174] It rests on the fundamental idea that States are under an obligation to afford aliens an absolute and objective minimum treatment, regardless of whether the host State's own nationals receive such treatment.[175] Explaining the essence of the minimum standard, Elihu Root stated in 1910 that '[i]f any country's system of law and administration does not conform to that standard, although the people of the country may be compelled to live under it, no other country can be compelled to accept it as furnishing a satisfactory measure of treatment to its citizens.'[176]

References to a 'subjective' standard of due diligence have re-emerged recently, as an increasingly growing number of scholars have expressed support for a standard of due diligence that takes into consideration the conditions of the host State.[177] This terminology is used to express the idea that the assessment of diligence must include circumstances such as the resources at the disposal of the State.[178] The use of the label 'subjective' and the maxim *diligentia quam in suis rebus* in this context is inaccurate.

The idea that the diligence required under the protection obligation must be commensurate with the capacities of host authorities looks back on a long tradition in the international law of aliens. Already Grotius recognized that 'it is required that in Conjunction with the Knowledge there is sufficient power to prevent'.[179] In 1896, US Secretary of State Richard Olney referred to State responsibility for revolutionary damages in the following terms:

> The general position is that the responsibility of an established government for acts committed by rioters or insurgents depends upon the failure of the constituted authorities to exercise due diligence for protection of alien property *when in a position to protect it and the imminence of danger is known.*[180]

This feature of due diligence does not coincide with the notion of *diligentia quam in suis rebus*. There is a long way between the idea that the conditions of the host State should have a bearing on the assessment of diligence and the proposition that host authorities' conduct in their own affairs is the ultimate measure of the diligence required under international law.[181]

Other sources conveyed this very same idea through the objective standard of a *diligens paterfamilias*. Perhaps, the clearest example of this approach appears in a communication

---

[174] See generally Hollin Dickerson, 'Minimum Standards' *Max Planck Encyclopedia of Public International Law* (October 2010) <https://opil.ouplaw.com/view/10.1093/law:epil/9780199231690/law-9780199231690-e845?prd=EPIL> accessed 27 October 2021, para 6; Raúl Emilio Vinuesa, 'National Treatment, Principle' ibid (April 2011) <https://opil.ouplaw.com/view/10.1093/law:epil/9780199231690/law-9780199231690-e1540?prd=EPIL> accessed 27 October 2021, para 20.

[175] See Edwin Borchard, 'The "Minimum Standard" of the Treatment of Aliens' (1940) 38 Mich L Rev 445, 452ff.

[176] Elihu Root, 'The Basis of Protection of Citizens Residing Abroad' (1910) 4(3) AJIL 517, 521–22.

[177] See eg Eric de Brabandere, 'Fair and Equitable Treatment and (Full) Protection and Security in African Investment Treaties Between Generality and Contextual Specificity' (2017) 18 JWIT 530, 553 and 555. See also Finnur Magnússon, 'Full Protection and Security in International Law' (Dissertation, University of Vienna 2012) 197; Marua Fanou and Vassilis Tzevelekos, 'The Shared Territory of the ECHR and International Investment Law' in Yannick Radi (ed), *Research Handbook on Human Rights and Investment* (Edward Elgar 2018) 93, 128.

[178] Andrew Newcombe and Lluís Paradell, *Law and Practice of Investment Treaties: Standards of Treatment* (Kluwer 2009) 310.

[179] Grotius (n 78) 455 (bk II, ch XXI: II.4).

[180] 'Mr. Olney, Sec. of State, to Messrs. Lauman & Kemp (13 January 1896)' in Bassett Moore (n 169) 961, 967 (emphasis added).

[181] See Mantilla Blanco (n 1) 450–51.

of US Secretary of State Thomas Bayard concerning the *Negrete* affair of 1888. Referring to injuries inflicted by insurgents on foreigners, Bayard stated that '[t]o adopt the rule stated in the Code of Justinian the law requires *diligentia qualem diligens paterfamilias suis rebus adhibere solet*'.[182] He further observed that the notion of *paterfamilias* 'served to illustrate the relations of the government to the state'.[183] Emphasizing the use of the word *solet*, which refers to custom in Roman sources, he concluded that international law requires the 'the diligence good governments are accustomed to exercise under the circumstances'.[184] Bayard's understanding of the customary standard of diligence was based on the premise that 'custom depends on conditions', so that:

> [T]he degree of diligence customary and reasonable in a newly and sparsely settled region of (sic) country where the police force is weak and scattered, where armed forces cannot be maintained and where custom throws on the individual, in a large degree, not only the preservation of order but the vindication of supposed rights, is very different from the degree of diligence customary in a center of population under a well-organized police, and in which armed forces could be promptly summoned in support of the law.[185]

This statement bears remarkable resemblance to the 'modified objective standard' of due diligence, as used in contemporary arbitral decisions.[186] This term was coined precisely to underscore that the assessment of diligence must give weight to the conditions and resources of the receiving State.[187] This fundamental principle, which is nowadays detached from private law analogies, enjoys general acceptance in IIL. For instance, in *Strabag v Libya*, the tribunal stated:

> Respondent's obligation under the Treaty to accord constant protection exists in a setting of weak and uncertain State authority, recurring armed conflict, and widespread breakdown of the law in wide areas of the country. The reality of these circumstances cannot be ignored in assessing Respondent's obligations.[188]

The legacy of the private law analogy is a due diligence standard that is objective rather than subjective, and which remains adaptable to the specific conditions of the host State. Accurate rule-of-law analogies must be able to preserve these defining features of due diligence.

b) Due diligence and public law analogies
Private (Roman) law analogies have been abandoned gradually, paving the way for a public law turn and rule-of-law analogies. Critics of the use of the private law analogy have pointed out that shortcomings of State action could stem from circumstances that cannot be accurately grasped through the concept of a Roman *paterfamilias*, such as the distribution of

---

[182] Mr. Bayard (n 169) 961–62.
[183] ibid.
[184] ibid.
[185] ibid.
[186] *Joseph Houben v Burundi*, ICSID Case No ARB/13/7, Award (12 January 2016) para 163; *Pantechniki* (n 3) para 81.
[187] Newcombe and Paradell (n 178) 310.
[188] *Strabag SE v Libya*, ICSID Case No ARB(AF)/15/1, Award (29 June 2020) para 234.

competences between State organs under domestic law.[189] In the 1930s, Hans Kelsen criticized the then widespread analogy with the private law concept of fault in international law, stating that '[the State]—as it is no human being and has no soul—can never have the mindful conduct of a diligent family father'.[190]

Instead of drawing parallels to a Roman *paterfamilias*, investment tribunals normally address due diligence by reference to notions that recall principles and concepts of domestic public law.[191] This shift to public law can be evidenced in awards that define due diligence through the idea of a 'well-organized modern State',[192] a 'well-administered government',[193] or a 'democratic State'.[194] This approach may be an important step but, in the final analysis, it says little about the benchmark against which State omissions are being measured. Moreover, acts that do not conform to the expected conduct of an idealized State cannot be automatically characterized as breaches of the FPS standard.[195] The FPS standard is generally regarded as an element of the international minimum standard, which sets a low bar— a minimum—that could lie far below the expectations associated with a 'well-organized modern State'.[196]

Another concept employed to describe the diligence required under the FPS standard is reasonableness.[197] For example, in *Consutel v Algeria* the arbitrators portrayed FPS as a 'duty of diligence' (*devoir de diligence*), noting that this duty required the State to adopt 'reasonable measures' (*mesures raisonnables*) to prevent the injury, provided that such measures fall within the host State's authority.[198] The RCEP of 2020 incorporated reasonableness into the very text of the FPS clause, creating an obligation to adopt 'reasonably necessary' measures of protection.[199]

In principle, the concept of reasonableness lacks a higher degree of precision, consistency, or certainty than the notion of due diligence.[200] The mere redefinition of due diligence in terms of reasonableness is therefore unsatisfactory.[201] References to reasonableness could however serve a practical purpose by building a bridge to public law, facilitating references to specific aspects of the rule of law in the assessment of FPS claims.[202] In fact, reasonableness is a shared concept of most national legal orders, particularly in the areas of constitutional and administrative law.[203]

---

[189] See Dionisio Anzilotti, *Lehrbuch des Völkerrechts, Volume 1* (De Gruyter 1929) 393.

[190] Author's translation. Hans Kelsen, 'Unrecht und Unrechtsfolge im Völkerrecht' (1932) 12 ZöR 481, 544–45.

[191] On the apparently interchangeable use of these notions, see Riccardo Pisillo-Mazzeschi, 'The Due Diligence Rule and the Nature of the International Responsibility of States' in René Provost (ed), *State Responsibility in International Law* (Ashgate 2002) 97, 133. On the many standards used to define due diligence in connection with FPS claims, see Mantilla Blanco (n 1) 440ff.

[192] *Asian Agricultural Products* (n 86) para 77.

[193] *Al-Warraq* (n 66) para 628.

[194] *Técnicas Medioambientales TECMED SA v Mexico*, ICSID Case No ARB(AF)/00/2, Award (29 May 2003) para 177.

[195] Mantilla Blanco (n 1) 439–40.

[196] For this understanding of the minimum standard, see *Grand River Enterprises Six Nations Ltd et al v United States of America*, UNCITRAL, Award (12 January 2011) paras 214–15.

[197] See Federico Ortino, *The Origin and Evolution of Investment Treaty Standards: Stability, Value, and Reasonableness* (OUP 2020) 117ff.

[198] *Consutel Group* (n 52) para 415. See also *Joseph Houben* (n 186) para 160; *TECMED* (n 194) para 177.

[199] RCEP (adopted 15 November 2020, in force 1 January 2022) art 10.5(2)(b).

[200] On the indeterminacy of the notion of reasonableness, see Caroline Henckels, *Proportionality and Deference in Investor-State Arbitration* (CUP 2015) 118–19.

[201] See Mantilla Blanco (n 1) 444–45.

[202] ibid.

[203] Stephan W Schill, 'Fair and Equitable Treatment, the Rule of Law, and Comparative Public Law' in Schill (n 24) 151, 169.

2. The use of rule-of-law notions in the assessment of FPS claims

Due diligence provides a flexible parameter for the assessment of the host State's conduct, leaving a fairly wide margin of discretion to adjudicators.[204] It cannot be condensed in a rule providing an *ex ante* solution for every individual case.[205] As expressed by the tribunal in *Tulip v Turkey*, '[t]he question of whether the State has failed to ensure FPS is one of fact and degree, responsive to the circumstances of the particular case'.[206] Nonetheless, conformity with basic rule-of-law principles provides a strong indication that the State acted within the margin permitted or required by international law. In this sense, the rule of law reflects basic expectations about the exercise of the host State's security function. Four examples confirm this observation.

A first example is the redress obligation. Compliance or non-compliance with basic tenets of due process in proceedings for the redress of private injuries to aliens are strong indications of whether the State has acted with the diligence required under the FPS standard. This element of analysis is closely linked to the rule of law.[207] It mirrors and complements procedural guarantees emanating from other IIL standards commonly associated with the rule of law, such as the FET standard.[208] Thus, in *Frontier Petroleum v Czech Republic*, the arbitrators held:

> [N]early all of the decisions dealing with procedural propriety and due process in the context of fair and equitable treatment have concerned proceedings involving disputes with the host state or with state entities. This may suggest that complaints about lack of due process in disputes with private parties are better dealt with in the context of the full protection and security standard.[209]

The principle of non-discrimination provides a second example of the potential synergies between the rule of law and due diligence. The risks covered by the FPS standard often affect not only the investor, but also other individuals or corporations. Divergences in the treatment afforded to different stakeholders placed in a similar situation could lead to the conclusion that the State had the means and opportunity to protect the investment.[210] If the State unjustifiably denies the investor the protection it was able to grant to others, there is a strong argument for a finding of liability under the FPS standard.[211] By contrast, evidence of non-discriminatory treatment indicates absence of arbitrariness, conformity with the rule of law, and diligence. Following this line of argument, the tribunal in *LESI v Algeria* explained:

---

[204] See generally Mantilla Blanco (n 1) 456–57 (also discussing the factual elements of analysis considered in the assessment of diligence at 456ff). For a more general study of the notion of due diligence, see Joanna Kulesza, *Due Diligence in International Law* (Brill 2016) 262ff.

[205] See ILC, 'International Responsibility, Second Report by Francisco García Amador, Special Rapporteur' (1957) ILC YB, vol II, 104, 122, para 7.

[206] *Tulip* (n 119) para 430.

[207] See eg *Enkev Beheer BV v Poland*, PCA Case No 2013–01, First Partial Award (29 April 2014) para 377.

[208] On this aspect of the FET standard, see Schill (n 203) 151, 172–73.

[209] *Frontier Petroleum* (n 137) para 296.

[210] See Mantilla Blanco (n 1) 477–78.

[211] See *LESI* (n 146) para 154.

[I]l n'a pas été prouvé par les Demanderesses que leur chantier bénéficiait d'un traitement discriminatoire par rapport aux autres chantiers en Algérie. Enfin, les décisions prises par l'Etat algérien en matière de sécurité ne sont pas arbitraires.[212]

Third, an analysis of due diligence must take into consideration that the State has a duty to protect the public interest. Thus, in *Eskosol v Italy*, the tribunal gave weight to the fact that the host State's policies 'were reasonably related to a rational policy goal.'[213] The idea of a balancing exercise is closely entangled with the basic expectation of rationality of State action, as understood in constitutional theory.[214] It is the State who is in a position to balance the interests of different stakeholders and decide on the most appropriate course of action. In *South American Silver v Bolivia*, the investor argued that Bolivia breached the FPS standard inter alia by failing to militarize a mining zone in the face of a social conflict allegedly led by illegal miners.[215] The tribunal dismissed the argument, noting that 'militarization of the area has not been shown to be an adequate measure conducive to resolving the social conflict.'[216] It further underscored that 'the *experience of the State* in this regard shows that the measure is not only ineffective, but that it may also have fatal consequences.'[217] In *Peter Allard v Barbados*, the tribunal recognized that the environmental measures challenged by the investor responded to a complex situation of fact, which required consideration of 'the interests of all stakeholders.'[218] The arbitrators dismissed the FPS claim, stressing that the decisions of Barbados were 'part of its governance of the entire area' and '[did] not fall short of what was appropriate and sufficient for purposes of the duty of due diligence.'[219]

A fourth example refers to compliance with applicable domestic regulations. There are many situations where domestic law determines the measures required to prevent some type of injury or to mitigate its effects. Municipal law regulations could define, for example, the procedure that police forces must follow when they receive information about a security threat or the manner in which antitrust authorities respond to complaints about unfair market practices. Depending on the circumstances of the case, tribunals could give weight to the fact that the State followed or disregarded those procedures. Municipal law does not release States from responsibility. Still, it can at least explain the State's actual course of action and be considered in the assessment of due diligence.[220] It might be difficult for a State that fails to abide by its own laws to present itself as a diligent host State in the face of an FPS claim. This aspect of due diligence is intrinsically interlocked with the essence of the rule of law, namely, the idea that the State is subject to—rather than above—the law.

These examples show that the evaluation of due diligence in arbitral decisions already incorporates elements of analysis analogous to the rule of law, which reflect basic expectations about the exercise of sovereign authority in the protection of foreign investors. The rule of law manifests itself in the practical application of the due diligence standard of liability

---

[212] ibid.

[213] *Eskosol* (n 75) para 482. See also *AES* (n 36) para 13.3.2.

[214] See generally Matthias Herdegen, *Staat und Rationalität* (Schöningh 2010) 59ff.

[215] *South American Silver Ltd v Bolivia*, PCA Case No 2013-15, Award (30 August 2018) paras 677 and 690.

[216] ibid para 690.

[217] ibid (emphasis added).

[218] *Peter Allard v Barbados*, PCA Case No 2012-06, Award (27 June 2016) para 248.

[219] ibid para 249.

[220] See eg *Marion Unglaube et al v Costa Rica*, ICSID Cases ARB/01/1, ARB/09/20, Award (16 May 2012) para 286 (noting that 'court proceedings were conducted in accordance with Costa Rican law'); *Interocean Oil* (n 43) para 356 (underscoring that there was no evidence that an arrest had been unlawful).

through notions such as due process and non-discrimination, balancing exercises, and examination of compliance with municipal law.

V. Concluding Remarks

There is abundant evidence indicating functional and teleological similarities between standards of investment protection and constitutional law notions, including the rule of law.[221] The Colombian Constitutional Court stated in 2019 that the goals of the Colombia–France BIT 'contribute to the materialization of constitutional principles of the rule of law'.[222] While micro-comparisons between the rule of law and specific IIL standards normally refer to the FET standard, there is also a synergic interplay between public law principles and the FPS standard. This interplay is twofold.

On the one hand, the customary FPS standard mirrors the security function of the State.[223] This is particularly relevant for the identification of the risks covered by the standard. FPS requires the State to protect investments from others but, in essence, is not concerned with the protection of investments from the State itself.[224] As such, its overall function corresponds to the preservation of peace as a precondition of the rule of law.[225]

On the other hand, the rule of law influences the manner in which the State is expected to exercise this security function. There are strong parallels between rule-of-law principles and the content of the FPS standard. FPS requires the host State to act with due diligence. For a long time, international lawyers resorted to private law analogies to define the diligence required under the customary protection obligation, using Roman law yardsticks such as *diligentia quam in suis rebus* and *diligens paterfamilias*.[226] Notwithstanding the strong influence of private law, there has been a gradual change of paradigms. Depictions of due diligence in investment arbitral decisions are now dominated by references to public law notions, such as reasonableness or the idea of a 'well-organized State'.[227] More importantly, the criteria actually used for the assessment of due diligence are closely related to specific elements of the rule of law, including due process, non-discrimination, and the protection of public interests.[228] Measures of protection that contravene basic rule-of-law principles will likely fall short of the degree of diligence required under the FPS standard. In this sense, the FPS standard incentivizes the expansion of the rule of law.

---

[221] Schill (n 26) 90–93.

[222] Constitutional Court of Colombia, Judgment C-252/19 (n 122) para 93. See also the discussion of the elements of the rule of law at paras 94–95.

[223] Section III.C.

[224] Sections III.B.2 and III.C.

[225] Section III.C.

[226] Section IV.C.1(a).

[227] Section IV.C.1(b).

[228] Section IV.C.2.

6

International Investment Law's Non-Discrimination Norms and the Rule of Law

Elizabeth Whitsitt[*]

I. Introduction

Lawyers across the world and in all manners of discipline are captivated by the idea of the 'rule of law'. Whether wittingly or unwittingly, the sound of this phrase can stir up our inner-most sense of occupational meaning and purpose. The rule of law makes us think about the positive qualities that law should have and the positive qualities that we as lawyers should promote within a system of law and our respective societies. Given its instinctual appeal to those of us who study and practise law, it is not surprising that the rule of law has a long lin-eage in the ancestral charts of legal systems that span the globe.[1] Despite this pedigree, the rule of law—and more importantly what it requires—is highly contested. Even more funda-mentally, there are issues associated with transposing the notion of the rule of law, a concept developed and applied within States, to the international arena.[2] These foundational ques-tions are undoubtedly important. But this contribution suspends, at least for the time being, discussion of these threshold considerations.

The aim of this chapter is more targeted. The primary purpose of this contribution is to evaluate whether inclusion of the most-favoured-nation (MFN) and national treatment (NT) standards of protection in bilateral investment treaties (BITs) and regional trade agreements (RTAs) that contain investment provisions reflect, influence, further, or limit the rule of law. More particularly, this chapter considers how the MFN and NT disciplines promote the rule of law by ensuring that foreign investors have an equal opportunity to compete in the global marketplace. In so doing, this chapter looks to Ronald Dworkin and his theory about the rule of law, which, as discussed in Section II, contemplates both thin and thick conceptions of the rule of law similar to the definition that ground many other chapters this book and has been articulated by the United Nations (UN) Secretary General.[3] This chapter begins by explaining Dworkin's rule-of-law ideal (Section II). It then moves to a discussion of the MFN and NT disciplines in the IIL regime (Sections III and IV, respect-ively). In so doing, these sections discuss the constituent elements of each discipline and the

[*] I wish to thank several people for their support in the writing of this chapter. I want to express my gratitude to Professors Stephan Schill and August Reinisch for inviting me to participate in this project and for their thoughtful comments on earlier drafts of this chapter. I also want to express my gratitude to all those who provided insightful comments at a workshop hosted by the University of Vienna and the University of Amsterdam on investment pro-tection standards and the rule of law. All errors are my own.

[1] See eg Simon Chesterman, 'An International Rule of Law' (2008) 56 Am J Comp L 331, 333–40.
[2] See eg Jeremy Waldron, 'Are Sovereigns Entitled to the Benefit of the International Rule of Law?' (2011) 22 EJIL 315; Samantha Besson, 'Sovereignty, International Law and Democracy' (2011) 22 EJIL 373.
[3] See n 9 below.

Elizabeth Whitsitt, *International Investment Law's Non-Discrimination Norms and the Rule of Law* In: *Investment Protection Standards and the Rule of Law*. Edited by: August Reinisch and Stephan W. Schill, Oxford University Press. © Elizabeth Whitsitt 2023. DOI: 10.1093/oso/9780192864581.003.0006

jurisprudence interpreting these requirements in relation to the rule of law. Following this discussion, Section V provides my concluding remarks.

II. Evaluating IIL's Non-Discrimination Norms: Choosing a Dworkinian Account of the Rule of Law

Conceptions of the rule of law are often placed into one of two categories. Jurists have conceptualized the rule of law in either formal/procedural ('thin') or substantive ('thick') terms.[4] Those who define the rule of law in more formal (or thin) terms do so by carving out from their definitions, considerations of legitimacy, fairness, justice, or democracy.[5] Instead, thin accounts distil the rule of law into a set of procedural requirements. There is no definitive catalogue of these requirements, but it is generally agreed that the rule of law requires that laws be set out in general and clear terms in advance so that those subject to the law can comply with it. In that same vein, many agree that laws should be sufficiently stable over time. Thin conceptions of the rule of law also demand that laws have prospective— rather than retrospective—application and that compliance with one law does not preclude compliance with other laws. They also contemplate the existence of procedural rules where adjudicators are tasked with interpreting and applying law. In such circumstances, the rule of law requires that those subject to the law have access to an impartial forum governed by due process in which disputes can be resolved.[6] Evaluating laws, including the MFN and NT disciplines, with reference to these procedural aspects is certainly one of the means by which to assess whether the IIL regime operates in accordance with the rule of law. For example, it may be said that aspects of the rule of law so conceived are met by inclusion of the MFN and NT disciplines in investment treaties that are made publicly available.

Nonetheless, when the rule of law is only conceptualized in such thin terms, it is possible—at least in principle—for a legal system to satisfy the demands of the rule of law even though there are weaknesses in the system with respect to other values, such as legitimacy, fairness, justice, or democracy.[7]

Consideration of the impact that the MFN and NT disciplines have on the rule of law in the IIL regime demands that we consider such other values and their relationship to the rule of law. After all, inclusion of NT and the MFN obligations in investment treaties reflect the rules of 'fair play' underpinning the IIL regime; they point at equality of competition that facilitates investment flows to the most efficient markets.[8] Discussion of how

---

[4] Leading authorities include: AV Dicey, *Introduction to the Study of the Law of the Constitution* (10th edn, Macmillan 1959) ch 4; Ronald Dworkin, *A Matter of Principle* (Harvard UP 1985) ch 1; Richard H Fallon, 'The Rule of Law as a Concept in Constitutional Discourse' (1997) 97(1) Colum L Rev 1; Lon Fuller, *The Morality of Law* (Yale UP 1964) ch 2; Joseph Raz, *The Authority of Law* (Clarendon Press 1979) 210; John Rawls, *A Theory of Justice* (Belknap Press 1971) 55–60 and 235–41; Brian Tamanaha, *On the Rule of Law: History, Politics and Theory* (CUP 2004).

[5] See generally John Tasioulas, 'The Rule of Law' in John Tasioulas (ed), *The Cambridge Companion to the Philosophy of Law* (CUP 2020) 117–34.

[6] Fuller (n 4); Raz (n 4) 214–18; John M Finnis, *Natural Law and Natural Rights* (2nd edn, OUP 2011); Margaret Jane Radin, 'Reconsidering the Rule of Law' (1989) 69 BU L Rev 781.

[7] See Tasioulas (n 5) 123 where the author highlights that this is a consequence of the way in which 'thin' accounts of the rule of law address the pluralism constraint (ie that the rule of law is just one of many standards used to evaluate law and legal institutions).

[8] See Stephan W Schill, *The Multilateralisation of International Investment Law* (CUP 2009) ch IV. See also Stephan W Schill, 'MFN Clauses as Bilateral Commitments to Multilateralism: A Reply to Simon Batifort and J. Benton Heath' (2018) 111(4) AJIL 914, 934.

these non-discrimination norms reflect, influence, further, or limit the rule of law therefore requires us to look beyond the thin and more formal indicia of the rule of law and also consider other, more substantive, formulations.[9] In so doing, I examine the MFN and NT disciplines with reference to Ronald Dworkin's conception of the rule of law, who advocates for a thick conception of the rule of law, but acknowledges that laws must also meet formal rule-of-law requirements.

Dworkin espouses a so-called rights conception of the rule of law. Conceived of and developed within a domestic law context, Professor Dworkin's rule of law assumes that individuals have rights and duties vis-à-vis each other and the State as a whole.[10] In his view, the rule of law requires that those rights be recognized in positive law so that individuals can demand enforcement of those rights through courts or other judicial institutions.[11] By this measure, the rule of law is the ideal of an accurate public conception of individual rights.[12] Dworkin's conception of the rule of law is not separate from substantive justice. Rather, it connotes an ideal of law that requires justice.[13] In Dworkin's view, equality is one of the constituting features of justice and requires that government treat all those in its charge as equals—that is entitled to equal concern and respect.[14]

For Dworkin defining what constitutes 'equal concern and respect' is intimately tied to questions about the role of government within a State. More precisely put, Dworkin considers that governments should intervene via laws and policies to ensure greater distribution of wealth and opportunity within its community.[15] The rationale for this view cannot, in Dworkin's view, be grounded in the idea of laissez-faire economics or notions of utilitarianism.[16] Both of these responses to the challenge of ensuring all are treated with 'equal concern' within a State respect the idea that private actors have responsibility for the choices they make, but neither of them really provides any guidance about what it is to ensure that those within a State are treated equally.[17] Dworkin is also critical of welfare accounts justifying government regulation in favour of equality as such accounts erode personal responsibility and impose sweeping value judgements on what counts as well-being or what opportunities are important.[18]

For Dworkin, the key to ensuring that private actors within a State are treated with equal concern is tied to resources.[19] Here Dworkin is clear that resources refers to 'impersonal

---

[9] See for example the UN Secretary General's 2004 report on the rule of law and transnational justice in conflict and post-conflict societies which posits a conception of the rule of law that encapsulates both thin and thick considerations:

> [The rule of law] refers to a principle of governance in which all persons, institutions and entities, public and private, including the State itself, are accountable to laws that are publicly promulgated, equally enforced and independently adjudicated, and which are consistent with international human rights norms and standards. It requires, as well, measures to ensure adherence to the principles of supremacy of law, equality before the law, accountability to the law, fairness in the application of the law, separation of powers, participation in decision-making, legal certainty, avoidance of arbitrariness and procedural and legal transparency.

(23 August 2004) S/2004/616, 4.

[10] See Dworkin (n 4) 11.

[11] ibid

[12] ibid

[13] ibid 11–12.

[14] See generally ibid chs 8–9.

[15] Ronald Dworkin, *Justice for Hedgehogs* (Harvard UP 2013) ch 16.

[16] ibid 352–54.

[17] ibid 354.

[18] ibid 354–55.

[19] ibid 355–58.

resources' or wealth measured in abstract terms as these types of resources are capable of being distributed through economic transaction and without any underlying welfare assumptions.[20] A society governed by the rule of law is, therefore, one that attempts to provide opportunities for it citizens to be equal in those resources.[21] In Dworkin's view, the mechanism by which this takes place is a capitalist economy that reflects the true opportunity cost of resources acquired by other market participants. In this case, opportunity cost is the incremental cost of applying such resources for alternative uses. Where such costs are corrupted by market distortions, such as monopolies or other externalities (eg unregulated pollution), Dworkin supports government intervention as a means by which to better match people's resources to the opportunity cost of what they do or consume in the market.[22] For example, Dworkin would support government intervention to regulate greenhouse gas emissions since absent such regulation those emissions are not fully reflected in the true opportunity cost of using the underlying resources.

While Dworkin's ideas about the rule of law, including equality and justice, are developed and tested in a domestic law context, they nonetheless have application in the international economic law context. I expand on this in later sections of the chapter. For now, we must acknowledge some important nuances between Dworkin's ideal and the realities of the IIL regime. To begin, the source and definition of the rights that a foreign investor enjoys within the global economic order is different from those that individuals enjoy within a State. In the IIL regime, foreign investors do not have rights and obligations as between each other. Instead, a foreign investor enjoys rights that are defined with reference to, and enforced against, States. Moreover, those rights are neither inherent nor assumed. With the exception of customary international law standards of treatment that may evolve over time as State practice and *opinio juris* dictate, the rights and obligations governing foreign investors and States are articulated in thousands of treaties and thus derived through their home State as a treaty party. These differences, while important to acknowledge, do not prevent us from using Dworkin's theory to examine the rule of law in the global investment law context. Even in his theoretical framework in which individuals have inherent or assumed rights Dworkin acknowledges that those rights should be articulated in positive law and that such articulation is an important aspect of the rule of law.[23] The majority of investment treaties expressly recognize that equality—or non-discrimination—is central to global economic governance. Likewise, such investment treaties also expressly provide for host States' regulatory space and in doing so align with Dworkin's recognition that government intervention may be justified in a free market if it indeed addresses market distortions that obfuscate the true opportunity cost of resources. As a result, Dworkin's notion of the rule of law, with its emphasis on equality, is a very useful lens through which to consider IIL's MFN and NT disciplines.

---

[20] ibid 355.
[21] ibid
[22] ibid 356–57.
[23] Dworkin (n 4).

III. Equality through MFN Treatment

The MFN discipline is one of the keystone obligations that establishes the rules of 'fair play' or equality in the global economy.[24] MFN clauses in investment treaties come in a variety of formulations, of which the International Law Commission (ILC) has identified six types.[25] These are: (1) where the MFN obligation relates to 'treatment' accorded to the investor or the investments;[26] (2) where the scope of treatment provided to the investor is broadened to 'all' treatment;[27] (3) where the term 'treatment' is related to specific aspects of the investment process, such as 'management', 'maintenance', 'use', and 'disposal' of the investment;[28] (4) where MFN treatment is related to specific obligations under the treaty (eg fair and equitable treatment (FET));[29] (5) where MFN treatment is limited to investors or investments that are 'in like circumstances' or 'in similar situations' to comparator investors or investments;[30] and (6) where MFN treatment is explicitly limited by territory.[31] To be fair, these six categories most likely do not encapsulate all of the textual varieties of MFN provisions in investment treaties, given the thousands of investment treaties that have been entered into over the past several decades. The ILC even acknowledges that some investment treaties may combine these different types of obligation in a single MFN provision.[32]

It is trite to say, but important to acknowledge, that textual variations in various BITs and RTAs must be accounted for when interpreting MFN provisions.[33] Nonetheless, the equality guarantee grounded in MFN clauses generally requires consideration of (Section A) the scope of MFN clauses, which often concerns the proper construction of 'treatment' in the relevant MFN clause, (Section B) whether a foreign investor is in *like circumstances* relative to other foreign investors, (Section C) whether a foreign investor is treated *less favourably* than such other foreign investors and (Section D) whether there is an underlying *regulatory purpose* that justifies this differential treatment. Here it is important to highlight that the equality guarantee housed in MFN clauses is not absolute. The sections below highlight how each of these constituent criteria relate to the rule of law as constructed in Dworkinian terms. As discussed below, an investor's right to be treated equally vis-à-vis

---

[24] Schill, *Multilateralisation* (n 8); Schill, 'MFN Clauses' (n 8).

[25] ILC, 'Final Report of the Study Group on the Most-Favoured-Nation Clause' (2015) ILC YB, vol II, pt Two, paras 59–65.

[26] ibid para 60 (citing Austria–Czechoslovakia BIT).

[27] ibid para 61 (citing Agreement on the Reciprocal Promotion and Protection of Investments (Spain–Argentina), art IV(2) ('In all matters governed by this Agreement, such treatment shall be no less favourable than that accorded by each Party to investments made in its territory by investors of a third country')).

[28] ibid para 62 (citing the North America Free Trade Agreement (NAFTA), art 1103(2) ('Each Party shall accord to investments of investors of another Party treatment no less favourable than that it accords, in like circumstances, to investments of investors of any other Party or of a non-Party with respect to the establishment, acquisition, expansion, management, conduct, operation, and sale or other disposition of investments')).

[29] ibid para 63.

[30] ibid para 64 (citing NAFTA, art 1103 and Agreement between the Republic of Turkey and Turkmenistan concerning the reciprocal promotion and protection of investments, 16 March 1995, art II(2) ('Each Party shall accord to these investments, once established, treatment no less favourable than that accorded in similar situations ... to investments of investors of any third country').

[31] ibid para 65 (citing the Agreement between the Government of the Hashemite Kingdom of Jordan and the Government of the Italian Republic on the promotion and protection of investments).

[32] ibid para 59.

[33] Vienna Convention on the Law of Treaties (opened for signature 23 May 1969, entered into force 27 January 1980 1155 UNTS 331; 8 ILM 679 (1969) art 31(1): '[a] treaty shall be interpreted in good faith in accordance with the ordinary meaning to be given the terms of the treaty in their context and in the light of its object and purpose'.

other foreign investors is constrained by each of these constituent criteria in ways that are consistent with the rule of law as constructed in Dworkinian terms.

A. Scope of MFN Clauses

The invocation of an MFN clause in IIL often engages interpretive questions about whether the rights and guarantees granted in a host State's investment treaties with third States constitute 'treatment' in the relevant MFN clause. Investors have most often invoked the equality protections housed in MFN clauses as a means by which to find refuge in another investment treaty's substantive protections or its dispute settlement provisions.[34] Investors have sought to import standards of protection from third-party treaties in a variety of ways. Tribunals have been asked to: (1) replace investment treaty provisions (eg FET clauses tied to customary law) with less restrictive provisions (eg free-standing FET clauses);[35] (2) import entirely new treaty provisions;[36] (3) remove treaty provisions;[37] and (4) extend the scope of an investment treaty.[38]

Much of the jurisprudence about the MFN clause has taken place in circumstances where investors have invoked the MFN clause as a way of accessing dispute settlement provisions in third-party investment treaties. Jurisprudence considering the MFN clause in this context can be placed into three categories: those circumstances in which an investor has used the MFN clause (1) to invoke a dispute settlement process not available under a BIT, (2) as a way of vesting arbitral tribunals with jurisdiction over classes of claims not contemplated or expressly excluded under a BIT, or (3) to gain access to an expedited arbitration process. For a while, arbitral jurisprudence regarding the scope and applicability of equality as articulated in MFN clauses seemed to cohere (at least in result) around the use investors sought to put MFN clauses to. Arbitral tribunals were willing to extend the scope of the MFN clause where an investor sought expedited arbitral processes.[39] They were not willing to extend the

---

[34] For a recent discussion on whether the MFN should be interpreted to permit import of substantive treaty protections, see Simon Batifort and J Benton Heath, 'The New Debate on the Interpretation of MFN Clauses in Investment Treaties: Putting the Brakes on Multilateralization' (2018) 111 AJIL 873.

[35] See eg *ADF Group Inc v United States of America*, ICSID Case No ARB (AF)/00/1, Award (9 January 2003). See also *CME Czech Republic BV v Czech Republic*, UNCITRAL, Final Award (14 March 2003) para 500 (where the investor was permitted to import the 'fair market value' criterion as a basis for determining compensation in cases of expropriation).

[36] See eg *Bayindir Insaat Turizm Ticaret Ve Sanayi AS v Islamic Republic of Pakistan*, ICSID Case No ARB/03/29, Award (27 August 2009); *MTD Equity Bhd and MTD Chile SA v Republic of Chile*, ICSID Case No ARB/01/7, Award (25 May 2004); *White Industries Australia Limited v Republic of India*, UNCITRAL, Award (30 November 2011).

[37] See *CMS Gas Transmission Company v The Argentine Republic*, ICSID Case No ARB/01/8, Award (12 May 2005) para 377 (where the tribunal refused to permit the investor to delete the necessity clause in the Argentina– US BIT on grounds that it resulted in the investor suffering 'less favourable' treatment).

[38] See eg *Técnicas Medioambientales Tecmed, SA v United Mexican States*, ICSID Case No ARB(AF)/00/02, Award (29 May 2003) para 69; *MCI Power Group LC and New Turbine, Inc v Republic of Ecuador*, ICSID Case No ARB/03/6, Award (31 July 2007) paras 118–28 (where the investors in both cases unsuccessfully invoked the MFN clause to secure retroactive application of their respective investment treaties). See also *Société Générale in respect of DR Energy Holdings Limited and Empresa Distribuidora de Electricidad del Este, SA v Dominican Republic*, UNCITRAL, LCIA Case No UN 7927, Award on Preliminary Objections to Jurisdiction (19 September 2008) para 41 (where the tribunal rejected arguments that an MFN clause could be used to import more favourable definitions of investment from other investment treaties).

[39] See eg *Emilio Agustín Maffezini v Kingdom of Spain*, ICSID Case No ARB/97/7, Award (13 November 2000); *Siemens AG v Argentine Republic*, ICSID Case No ARB/02/8, Decision on Jurisdiction (3 August 2004); *Suez Sociedad General de Aguas de Barcelona SA and Interagua Servicios Integrales de Agua SA v Argentine Republic*, ICSID Case No ARB/03/17, Decision on Jurisdiction (16 May 2006); *Gas Natural v Argentina*, ICSID Case No

scope of the MFN clause where an investor sought to vest an arbitral tribunal with jurisdiction over a class of claims for which such jurisdiction was specifically excluded under a BIT or where an investor sought to substitute international arbitration for dispute settlement before domestic courts.[40] However, this pattern of outcomes was disrupted by subsequent arbitral awards.[41] In fact, questions regarding the MFN clause and its application to dispute settlement continue to produce divergent decisions both in outcome and in analysis.[42]

As one might expect, the scope and application of the MFN clause in IIL has generated an abundance of literature.[43] For example, some experts have expressed concerns that a broad interpretation of the MFN clause—as seen in *Maffezini*—would permit investors to claim a violation of FET because of disparities in MFN clauses across investment treaties.[44] In other instances, commentators try to resolve issues about the scope and application of the MFN clause by emphasizing a particular treaty interpretation technique. For example, Yannick Radi has argued that by virtue of the *effet utile* principle, an MFN clause should always cover dispute settlement, unless the opposite intention can be demonstrated.[45] In contrast, others stress the *ejusdem generis* principle to contend that an MFN clause should only extend to dispute settlement clauses where treaty parties explicitly provide for that possibility.[46] Of the many observations made about the application of the MFN clause to dispute settlement clauses, perhaps the most prescient one for our purposes is that which illuminates the underlying tension between consent and compulsion in the settlement of

---

ARB/03/10, Decision of the Tribunal on Preliminary Questions of Jurisdiction (17 June 2005); *National Grid plc v Argentina*, UNCITRAL, Decision on Jurisdiction (20 June 2006).

[40] *Salini Costruttori SpA and Italstrade SpA v Hashemite Kingdom of Jordan*, ICSID Case No ARB/02/13, Decision on Jurisdiction (9 November 2004); *Plama Consortium Limited v Republic of Bulgaria*, ICSID Case No ARB/03/24, Decision on Jurisdiction (8 February 2005); *Telenor Mobile Communications AS v Republic of Hungary*, ICSID Case No ARB/04/15, Award (13 September 2006).

[41] See *RosInvestCo UK Ltd v Russian Federation*, SCC Case No V079/2005, Award on Jurisdiction (1 October 2007) paras 130–35; *Wintershall Aktiengesellschaft v Argentine Republic*, ICSID Case No ARB/04/14, Award (8 December 2008) paras 160–97.

[42] *Teinver SA, Transportes de Cercanías SA and Autobuses Urbanos del Sur SA v The Argentine Republic*, ICSID Case No ARB/09/1, Decision on Jurisdiction (21 December 2012) para 186 (the tribunal concluded that the claimant could rely on the MFN clause to make use of more favourable dispute resolution provisions contained in another BIT between Argentina and Australia); cf *Daimler Financial Services AG v Argentine Republic*, ICSID Case No ARB/05/1, Award (22 August 2012) paras 224, 230–31, 236 (the tribunal found that the MFN clause in the Argentina–United Kingdom BIT did not apply in such a way as to permit the claimant to avail itself of the dispute resolution provisions of the Argentina–Lithuania BIT). See also *Garanti Koza LLP v Turkmenistan*, ICSID Case No ARB/11/20, Decision on the Objection to Jurisdiction for Lack of Consent (3 July 2013) paras 74–75 (where the majority of the tribunal permitted the claimant to avail itself of ICSID arbitration by virtue of the MFN clause in the United Kingdom–Turkmenistan BIT).

[43] Literature on this jurisprudence is plentiful. See eg August Reinisch, 'How Narrow Are Narrow Dispute Settlement Clauses in Investment Treaties?' (2011) 2 JIDS 115; Dana Freyer and David Herlihy, 'Most-Favoured-Nation Treatment and Dispute Settlement in Investment Arbitration: Just How "Favoured" Is "Most-Favoured"?' (2005) 20 ICSID Rev—FILJ 58; Jürgen Kurtz, 'The Delicate Extension of Most-Favoured-Nation Treatment to Foreign Investors: *Maffezini v Kingdom of Spain*' in Todd Weiler (ed), *International Investment Law and Arbitration: Leading Cases from the ICSID, NAFTA, Bilateral Treaties and Customary International Law* (Cameron May 2005) 523–55; Rudolf Dolzer and Terry Myers, 'After *Tecmed*: Most-Favoured-Nation Clauses in Investment Protection Agreements' (2004) 19 ICSID Rev—FILJ 49. For a thorough discussion of the MFN clause and its multilateralizing implications for the IIL regimes, see Schill, *Multilateralisation* (n 8) particularly ch IV and the references therein.

[44] Ruth Teitelbaum, 'Who's Afraid of *Maffezini*? Recent Developments in the Interpretation of Most Favored Nation Clauses' (2005) 22 J Intl Arb 225.

[45] Yannick Radi, 'The Application of the Most-Favoured-Nation Clause to the Dispute Settlement Provisions of Bilateral Investment Treaties: Domesticating the "Trojan Horse"' (2007) 18 EJIL 757.

[46] Stephen Fietta, 'Most Favoured Nation Treatment and Dispute Resolution under Bilateral Investment Treaties: A Turning Point?' (2005) 8 Intl A LR 131.

IIL disputes.[47] Decisions such as that in the *Maffezini* case evidence a movement away from consent as the grounding principle justifying an arbitral tribunal's jurisdiction in favour of more compulsory forms of dispute settlement.[48]

Dworkin's conception of the rule of law is a useful lens through which to discuss interpretation of the MFN clause and its implications for investment treaty arbitration. For Dworkin one of the important features of the rule of law is that individuals can enforce their rights through courts or other judicial institutions.[49] To be clear, Dworkin's account of the rule of law would not permit an interpretation of 'treatment' in an MFN clause to include dispute settlement where States have expressly articulated a different intention in their investment treaties. But, where there is ambiguity about what constitutes 'treatment' within an MFN clause, Dworkin's conception of the rule of law supports an interpretation of 'treatment' that is more consistent with the reasoning of the tribunals in *Maffezini* and its progeny. In this way, the rule of law is both reflected and furthered by the trend towards compulsory forms of dispute settlement where constraints (eg likeness and less favourable treatment) on the MFN's equality guarantee are satisfied.

Until recently, uncertainty about the scope and application of MFN protection remained largely limited to questions about its impact on dispute settlement. No one questioned that MFN clauses in investment treaties permitted an investor to access and seek shelter under substantive treaty standards contained in investment treaties concluded between the host State and a third State. But the decision in *Içkale v Turkmenistan*[50] calls this thinking into question.

In this case the Turkish claimant contended that a series of actions and omissions related to contracts it had with Turkmenistan-owned companies amounted to violations of investment treaty standards, namely FET, full protection and security (FPS), and/or the umbrella clause. However, none of these standards were housed in the Turkey–Turkmenistan BIT.[51] Instead, Içkale sought to import those standards of protection from other investments treaties Turkmenistan concluded with third parties. The means through which such importation was sought was the MFN clause in the Turkey–Turkmenistan BIT.[52] Turkmenistan challenged this assertion.[53] In its view, violation of the MFN clause required Içkale to show factual discrimination. More specifically, Içkale had to identify an investment of a similarly situated investor who was 'actually receiving more favourable treatment'.[54] The Tribunal ultimately agreed with Turkmenistan on this latter point and refused to incorporate substantive treaty standards from other investment treaties by way of the MFN clause in the Turkey-Turkmenistan BIT.[55]

---

[47]   See Brigitte Stern, 'ICSID Arbitration and the State's Increasingly Remote Consent: Apropos the *Maffezini* Case' in Steve Charnovitz (ed), *Law in the Service of Human Dignity: Essays in Honour of Florentino Feliciano* (CUP 2005). See also Elizabeth Whitsitt, 'Application of MFN Clauses to the Dispute Settlement Provisions of BITs: An Updated Assessment of the Jurisprudence since *Wintershall*' (2011) 2 Journal of Arbitration and Mediation 21–50.

[48]   Stern (n 47); Whitsitt (n 47).

[49]   Dworkin (n 4) 11.

[50]   *Içkale Insaat v Turkmenistan*, ICSID Case No ARB/10/24, Award (8 March 2016).

[51]   ibid para 148(ii)–(iv).

[52]   See Agreement between Turkey and Turkmenistan concerning the Reciprocal Promotion and Protection of Investments (signed 2 May 1992, entered into force 13 March 1997) art II(2) which reads:

> Each Party shall accord to these investments, once established, treatment no less favourable than that accorded in similar situations in investments of its investors or to investors of any third country whichever is the most favourable.

[53]   ibid paras 320–21.

[54]   ibid para 322.

[55]   ibid para 329.

This decision renewed the scholarly debate about the proper scope and application of MFN clauses. For example, Simon Batifort and J. Benton Heath have called for renewed attention to 'bottom-up' approaches that emphasize treaty text. In their view, focusing on the details of the MFN clauses in a given investment treaty dispute avoids adoption of more contested interpretive approaches that engage questions about the objectives of the IIL regime more generally.[56] Stephan Schill, by contrast, contends that the interpretation of MFN clauses, while grounded in the text of the provision, must consider the meaning of MFN provisions in general international law. More particularly, Schill argues that the work of the International Law Commission and decisions of the International Court of Justice support the proposition that MFN clauses 'apply to more favourable treatment that the granting state extends to third states and their subjects, including investors, in international agreements'.[57]

Here, we find ourselves in the all-too-familiar position of trying to determine which of these interpretive approaches is correct. More importantly for our purposes, the question is better put thus: which of these interpretations best accords with Dworkin's rule-of-law ideal? As in the case of dispute settlement, Dworkin's account of the rule of law would not permit an interpretation of 'treatment' in an MFN clause to include substantive protections from other investment treaties where States have expressly limited the MFN clause. However, where the language of an MFN clause is vague with respect to incorporation of substantive treaty standards, Dworkin supports an application of the MFN clause grounded in equality and justice.

Here, the fundamental purpose of MFN clauses as articulated by Stephan Schill bears repeating: 'MFN clauses are essential pieces of the multilateral structures that underlie international investment law ... [and] [s]uch multilateral structures are the prerequisite for equal competition that allows capital to flow to where it is allocated most efficiently and national economies to specialize in areas where they enjoy a comparative advantage.'[58] In Dworkinian terms, MFN clauses are fundamental to ensuring that governments treat investors with 'equal concern' in the global market. As a result, any application of an ambiguous MFN clause that permits a government to discriminate between similarly situated foreign investors by limiting their substantive rights would permit undue government intrusions in the global marketplace. Limiting the MFN's equality guarantee in this manner would be, for Dworkin, inconsistent with the rule of law.

B. Like-Circumstances Criteria

Where an MFN clause stipulates that investments or investors must be in 'like' circumstances or situations, arbitral tribunals have insisted that such comparisons limit a foreign investor's discrimination claims.[59] Even where MFN clauses do not explicitly require a comparison between foreign investors on the basis of 'likeness', arbitral tribunals have insisted on such comparisons grounding MFN claims. Consider, for example, the tribunal's

---

[56] Simon Batifort and J Benton Heath, 'The New Debate on the Interpretation of MFN Clauses in Investment Treaties: Putting the Brakes on Multilateralization' (2018) 111 AJIL 873.

[57] Schill, 'MFN Clauses' (n 8).

[58] ibid 934.

[59] See eg *Bayindir* (n 36) paras 415–20 (where the tribunal rejected Bayindir's MFN claim on the basis that there was no evidence to meaningfully compare Bayindir with other similarly situated contractors).

decision in *Parkerings v Lithuania*.[60] In this case the Norwegian claimants contended that the municipality's refusal to authorize construction of its parking facility was, among other things, a violation of the MFN obligation because the municipality had authorized the construction of parking facilities in the same area by another Dutch investor.[61] In addressing the claimants' discrimination arguments, the tribunal indicated that '[a] comparison is *necessary* with an investor in like circumstances'.[62] Thus, it seems clear that the MFN obligation, whether explicitly stated or not, guarantees investors equal treatment, but such rights are not limitless. They are notionally confined by the concept of 'likeness' as a basis for comparison.

The decision in *Windstream Energy LLC v Government of Canada*[63] provides more discussion of the 'likeness' criteria in the MFN context than the other prior cases. In this case, the claimant was a US investor involved in the development of an offshore wind electricity generation project in the Canadian province of Ontario.[64] In an attempt to support a transition to renewable energy and develop its provincial economy, the Ontario government instituted a feed-in-tariff (FIT) programme in 2009.[65] Under this programme, Windstream was initially successful in securing an FIT contract to sell renewable energy into Ontario's electricity grid.[66] However, Windstream alleged that its efforts to develop an offshore wind generation facility were stymied when the provincial government put a moratorium on offshore wind projects and did not offer Windstream another opportunity to participate in Ontario's clean energy sector.[67] Windstream argued that this was a violation of NAFTA's MFN clause because the Ontario government had provided alternative opportunities to other foreign investors (ie Samsung) to participate in Ontario's clean energy sector.[68]

The Tribunal, however, disagreed.[69] In its view, there were important distinctions between Windstream and foreign counterparts like Samsung. The key distinction between these investors was that Windstream had an FIT contract for the development of offshore wind, while other investors, such as Samsung, did not. Samsung was therefore not affected by the moratorium placed on Ontario's FIT programme and could not be used as a basis for comparison in this case.[70] The Tribunal noted:

> [T]he moratorium only applied to offshore wind and that it was not applied in a non-discriminatory manner in that it resulted in the cancellation of all offshore wind projects, with the exception of that of the Claimant, which was the only holder of a FIT Contract. The Tribunal is therefore unable to agree that the Claimant was treated less favorably than

---

[60] *Parkerings-Compagniet AS v Republic of Lithuania*, ICSID Case No ARB/05/8, Award (11 September 2007).
[61] ibid paras 195–204.
[62] ibid para 369 (emphasis added).
[63] *Windstream LLC v Government of Canada*, PCA Case No 2013-22, Award (27 September 2016).
[64] ibid paras 1–2.
[65] ibid paras 96ff.
[66] ibid paras 117ff.
[67] *Windstream LLC v Government of Canada*, PCA Case No 2013-22, Memorial of Claimant (19 August 2014) paras 634, 645.
[68] ibid.
[69] *Windstream* (n 63) paras 414–15.
[70] ibid para 414.

other prospective developers of offshore wind projects, which were the only proponents that could be said to have been in 'like circumstances'.[71]

The Tribunal's reasoning is important to the rule of law for several reasons. First, it reiterates that the equality guarantee in the MFN discipline is relative—determination that there has been a violation of this guarantee requires comparisons to be drawn between foreign investors. Moreover, not just any comparison will do; only those made between foreign investors who are 'like' can ground an MFN claim. The Tribunal's decision is also important to the rule of law because it highlights the flexible nature of the 'likeness' criterion. The fact that two investors are operating within the same industry sector may (or may not) be enough to establish that they are comparators upon which to base an MFN claim. Here we see the Tribunal move beyond the industry sector (ie renewable energy) in which the relevant investors (ie Windstream and Samsung) operate to consider the legal frameworks that apply to them as a way of assessing whether they are in 'like circumstances'. Thus, the Tribunal's decision confirms that determinations of 'like circumstances' are context-dependent and vary across a gamut of factual circumstances.

All of these observations become important when considering how the 'like circumstances' criteria impacts the rule of law. As a starting point, it is important to note that recognition of the necessity of 'likeness' as a basis for determining whether an investor is given 'equal concern' vis-à-vis other foreign investors is once again supported by Dworkin's rule-of-law ideal. For Dworkin, treating an investor with 'equal concern' vis-à-vis other foreign investors is tied to the idea that these market participants are responsible for the choices they make in conducting their business. Respect for such choices and responsibility within the market implicitly recognize that not all market participants (eg investors) will make the same decisions about the industries in which they choose to participate, where they do business, and how they do business, which would include the domestic regulatory regime applicable to their investment (ie FIT programme). Where, for example, a foreign investor decides to participate in an industry that is highly regulated (eg nuclear energy) versus a much less regulated industry (eg retail sales) that investor bears the responsibility for the consequences of its decision. Consequently, holding a foreign investor responsible for its market entry decision that distinguishes it from other foreign investors when assessing 'likeness' under an MFN claim again both reflects and furthers the rule of law.

C. No-Less-Favourable-Treatment Criteria

A violation of the MFN discipline also requires a foreign investor to suffer 'less favourable' treatment. There is little MFN jurisprudence that expands upon this criterion, although, de jure or de facto differences in treatment may ground an MFN claim.[72] Applying Dworkin's conception of the rule of law to the question of what constitutes 'less favourable' treatment requires us to consider whether differences in treatment between similarly situated foreign

---

[71] ibid (emphasis added).
[72] See UNCTAD, 'Most Favoured Nation Treatment' UNCTAD Series on Issues in International Investment Agreements II (UN 2010) 26.

investors affect the efficient functioning of the marketplace. This is a factual determination, which should be assessed by an adjudicator on a case-by-case basis.

Where the MFN clause is used to import dispute settlement clauses from third-party investment treaties, several arbitral awards appear to accept that access to arbitration without first going to domestic courts constituted 'more favourable' treatment without much discussion about differences in timelines, costs, and remedies of the varying dispute settlement processes.[73] This was not the case, however, in *Daimler v Argentina*. In this dispute the Tribunal was reluctant to rely on the investor's subjective preferences as compelling evidence of 'less favourable' treatment.[74] The Tribunal ultimately found that the investor would not suffer any competitive disadvantage by having to enforce its rights through a procedural route (ie 18-month court submission requirement) that was different from other foreign investors.[75] In so finding, the Tribunal noted that an investor may spend more money and be forced to engage in more protracted processes when pursuing investment treaty arbitration as opposed to domestic court proceedings in Argentina.[76] The Tribunal also found that should the investor be dissatisfied with Argentina's domestic court process, it 'could add to its other claims an additional claim concerning its treatment in the Argentine courts, which if proven would be fully compensable, with interest, in the same manner as any other treaty violation'.[77] In the Tribunal's view all of these factors worked to ensure that the claimant enjoyed 'fundamental equality without discrimination among all of the [foreign investors] concerned'.[78]

Whether or not the specific facts in *Daimler* ought to constitute 'less favourable' treatment is an interesting question but beyond the scope of this chapter. Rather the *Daimler* case is helpful in that it illustrates the factual spectrum upon which debates about what constitutes 'less favourable treatment' might play out and the corresponding consequence for the rule of law. For example, a required three-month summary domestic court process might not constitute 'less favourable' treatment. In my opinion, a de minimis distinction would be of no consequence to the rule of law because it is unlikely to materially impact the efficient functioning of the marketplace. On the other hand, it is also possible to conceive of circumstances in which the less favourable treatment criteria might demand a different conclusion in order to respect the rule of law. Consider for example, a precedent domestic court process that would reasonably be expected to last several years and risk remedies being precluded in the subsequent arbitration as *res judicata*. At that end of the spectrum, a tribunal could find that the claimant meets the less favourable treatment criteria. In doing so, the tribunal's decision would reflect and further the rule of law by requiring that the claimant's rights be recognized in positive law and enforced arbitration incorporated via the MFN provision.

---

[73] See eg *Maffezini, Suez Sociedad, Gas Natural, National Grid* (n 39).
[74] *Daimler* (n 42) paras 245–46.
[75] ibid paras 249–50.
[76] ibid para 245.
[77] ibid paras 247–48.
[78] ibid para 249.

D. Regulatory-Purpose Justification

The role and scope of regulatory purpose arises, though infrequently, in the context of the MFN discipline. Where tribunals do address regulatory purpose, they have done so with regard to NT jurisprudence.[79] More particularly, tribunals have linked this discussion to the comparative equality-based analysis of 'like circumstances'. For example, consistent with NT jurisprudence under NAFTA, the Tribunal in *Parkerings v Lithuania* found that an assessment of 'like circumstances' must account for circumstances that would justify governmental regulations that treat investors differently in order to protect the public interest. Recall that in this case the claimant argued that a municipality's refusal to authorize its parking facility was an MFN violation because the municipality had permitted development of a similar facility by another foreign investor. But the Tribunal rejected this claim, and the basis for that decision was that the investors were not 'like' and could be distinguished on the basis of regulatory purpose. The Tribunal observed:

[T]he fact that the [Claimant's] MSCP [multi-storey car park] project in Gedimino extended significantly more into the Old Town as defined by the UNESCO, is decisive. Indeed, the record shows that the opposition raised against the [Claimant's] projected MSCP were important and contributed to the Municipality decision to refuse such a controversial project. The historical and archaeological preservation and environmental protection could be and in this case were a justification for the refusal of the project. The potential negative impact of the [Claimant's] project in the Old Town was increased by its considerable size and its proximity with the culturally sensitive area of the Cathedral. Consequently, [Claimant's] MSCP in Gedimino was not similar with the MSCP constructed by [the other investor].[80]

Thus, the tribunal in *Parkerings* accepted that the MFN obligation may be inapplicable where governments differentiate between foreign investors (or their investments) for legitimate public policy reasons. To that end, more recently concluded RTAs expressly contemplate some role for regulatory purpose by incorporating WTO law exceptions into their investment chapters.[81]

At first glance, it may seem as though inclusion of the objective 'regulatory purpose' criterion—either via interpretation of the 'likeness' factor or via inclusion of treaty exceptions—detracts from the rule of law as it contemplates that legitimate public policies passed by host States may impact foreign investors participating in the same industry sector differentially and thereby challenge the equality guarantee articulated in MFN clauses. However, even Dworkin would acknowledge that government ought to intervene in the market where the market is distorted by externalities and does not reflect true opportunity cost.[82] Bona fide host State regulation of externalities, such as land use impeding on culturally sensitive areas as was the case in *Parkerings*, or industrial air or water emissions, provide a useful illustration of how addressing market distortions that obfuscate the true

---

[79] See eg *Bayindir* (n 36) para 416; *Parkerings* (n 60) paras 366–71.

[80] *Parkerings* (n 60) para 392.

[81] See eg Canada–European Union Comprehensive Economic and Trade Agreement (signed on 30 October 2016, provisionally entered into force 21 September 2017) art 28.3(1)(2) (hereafter CETA).

[82] Dworkin (n 15).

opportunity cost of resources may necessarily result in distinguishing between foreign investors and/or their investments. Thus, to the extent that the MFN 'regulatory purpose' criterion facilitates a host State's right to so regulate, it reflects and furthers the rule of law.

IV. Equality through National Treatment

National treatment clauses, like MFN clauses, are a mainstay of most BITs and RTAs. And, like MFN, the NT standard of protection helps to ensure that foreign investors are treated equally within the IIL regime. Its articulation in treaty clauses varies. Sometimes the NT and the MFN standard of treatment are housed in the same treaty provision. Consider its formulation in the United Kingdom's most recent Model BIT:

> Neither Contracting Party shall in its territory subject investments or returns of nationals or companies of the other Contracting Party to treatment less favourable than that which it accords to investments or returns of its own nationals or companies or to investments or returns of nationals or companies of any third State.[83]

In other instances, States specify that the clause will only apply where foreign investors (investments) are in 'like situations'[84] or 'like circumstances'[85] to domestic investors (investments).[86] Consider, for example, its articulation in the United States–Mexico–Canada Agreement (USMCA):

> Each Party shall accord to investors of another Party treatment no less favorable than that it accords, in like circumstances, to its own investors with respect to the establishment, acquisition, expansion, management, conduct, operation, and sale or other disposition of investments in its territory.[87]

Such clauses prevent a host State from securing for its own investors more favourable competitive opportunities than it secures for foreign investors.[88] The NT standard thus precludes host States from discriminating against foreign investors on the basis of nationality but offers no refuge to foreign investors if a host State's domestic investors are also treated badly.[89] As is the case with MFN clauses, inclusion of NT clauses in investment treaties evidences a concern for equality that reflects and furthers the rule of law.

---

[83]   United Kingdom Model BIT (2008) art 3.

[84]   See eg United States Model BIT (1994) art II(1). See also CETA (n 81) art 8.6(1).

[85]   See eg United States Model BIT (2004) art 3 and US Model BIT (2012) art 3. See also Comprehensive and Progressive Agreement for Trans-Pacific Partnership (signed on 8 March 2018, entered into force 14 January 2019) art 9.4 (hereafter CPTPP).

[86]   The United States changed the language of its NT clause from 'in like situations' in its 2004 Model BIT to 'in like circumstances' in its 2012 Model BIT. The rationale for this change is unknown.

[87]   United States–Mexico–Canada Agreement (signed on 30 November 2018, entered into force 1 July 2020) art 14.4(1).

[88]   Rudolf Dolzer and Christoph Schreuer, *Principles of International Investment Law* (2nd edn, OUP 2012) 198–204.

[89]   Here, it is important to note that the meaning of the NT obligation in the IIL regime has evolved over time. Our current understanding of the NT obligation is fundamentally different from the concept of NT as it was known during the postcolonial era.

The broad interpretive questions that arise when determining whether a host State has violated the NT discipline are similar to those discussed above in relation to the MFN standard of protection. Jurisprudence discussing discrimination on the basis of the NT discipline addresses questions about the meaning and application of 'like circumstances', 'less favourable treatment', and 'regulatory purpose'. Despite these similarities, jurisprudence interpreting and applying the NT discipline differs from arbitral decisions that consider the MFN discipline.

The main point of analytical divergence that we see between these two equality obligations lies in the interpretation of 'treatment'. As discussed above, the appropriate interpretation to be given to (the term) 'treatment' in MFN clauses has generated a string of controversial rulings (particularly in relation to dispute settlement). This same controversy has not played a role in NT jurisprudence. The primary reason for this has to do with the different comparators engaged in analyses of MFN and NT violations. As evidenced by the above discussion, foreign investors invoking the equality guarantee grounded in an MFN clause do so on the basis that other foreign investors whose relationship with the host State is governed by another investment treaty are appropriate comparators (ie in like circumstances). For the most part, arbitral tribunals have accepted this proposition with the paramount interpretive issue being the multilateralizing effect of the MFN obligation through interpretation of 'treatment'. This same issue is not part of the calculus that informs interpretation of the NT discipline. In the MFN context, 'treatment' engages questions about a host State's treatment of different foreign investors under different investment treaties, respectively. In the NT context, the comparative treatment is a foreign investor as against a domestic investor, the latter of which is not governed by a BIT or RTA insofar as its domestic investment is concerned. Consequently, the issue of what constitutes 'treatment' in the NT context is easier to define and less controversial. NT disputes have, for example, related to a host State's differential tax treatment of foreign investors[90] or a host State's differential treatment of foreign investors via its own environmental legislation.[91] Rather than focus on what constitutes 'treatment', the bulk of NT jurisprudence addresses the proper interpretation of 'like circumstances', what constitutes 'less favourable' treatment, and 'regulatory purpose'. These NT criteria and their relationship to the rule of law are briefly described below (Sections A–C).

A. Like-Circumstances Criteria

As in the case of the MFN clause, claims to equal treatment under the NT clause are grounded in comparison. In the case of the NT obligation, such comparisons are made between a domestic investor that is 'like' the foreign investor. However, the precise meaning of 'like circumstances' is subject to varying interpretations.[92] Tribunals have, for example, considered whether investors operate in the same business or economic sector,[93] whether

---

[90] See eg *Marvin Roy Feldman Karpa v Mexico*, ICSID Case No ARB(AF)/99/1, Award (16 December 2002).

[91] *SD Myers Inc v Canada*, UNCITRAL, Partial Award (13 November 2000).

[92] See generally August Reinisch, 'National Treatment' in Marc Bungenberg and others (eds), *International Investment Law: A Handbook* (Hart 2015) 856.

[93] *Feldman* (n 90) paras 171–72; *Archer Daniels Midland Co v Mexico* (No 5), ICSID Case No ARB(AF)/04/5, Award (21 November 2007) para 198; *Grand River Enterprises Six Nationals Ltd v United States of America*, UNCITRAL, Award (12 January 2011) para 165.

investors are in competition with each other,[94] and whether investors operate within the same regulatory environment.[95] Other factors that have been considered in discussions about 'like circumstances' include end-user preferences,[96] geographical location of investment,[97] economic context in which investors operates, business portfolio and relative size of proposed comparators,[98] and the economic circumstances in which investors operate.[99] A thorough examination of all of these cases, while useful, falls outside the parameter of this study. Suffice it to say that scholars have suggested a variety of analytical approaches to clarify the interpretation and application of the 'like circumstances' requirement in IIL.[100]

For our purposes, the following cases juxtapose two approaches, with opposite consequences for the rule of law, that tribunals have adopted when determining whether investments need to operate within the same business sector in order to be considered 'like' for the purpose of establishing appropriate comparators in NT cases.

Marvin Roy Feldman Karpa v Mexico[101] arose out of concerns regarding Mexico's application of certain tax laws to companies operating in Mexico that were in the business of reselling/exporting tobacco products. Marvin Roy Feldman Karpa, a US citizen, who owned and operated such a business alleged that Mexico provided excise tax rebates to other cigarette resale/export companies that were Mexican owned but refused to do so for his company. As a result, he claimed that this difference in treatment breached, among other things, the NT standard in NAFTA (art 1102).[102] The Tribunal agreed with Feldman in finding that Mexico had indeed breached the NT standard.[103] The issue of 'like circumstances' in this case was not controversial. Both of the disputing parties and the Tribunal accepted that foreign-owned and domestic-owned firms in the same business of reselling/exporting cigarettes all qualified as firms in like circumstances.[104]

The Tribunal's ruling in *Occidental Exploration and Production Company v Ecuador* (*OEPC I*) provides an interesting contradistinction.[105] In this case, the US investor and Petroecuador were involved in oil exploration and production activities in Ecuador.[106] Until 2001, the US investor had received value-added tax (VAT) refunds on purchases

[94] *SD Myers* (n 91) paras 250–51.

[95] See eg *Apotex Holdings Inc v United States of America*, ICSID Case No ARB(AF)/12/1, Award (25 August 2014) paras 2.30, 2.60, 2.62; *Pope & Talbot v Canada*, UNCITRAL, Award on the Merits of Phase 2 (10 April 2001) paras 83–95.

[96] See eg *Corn Products International, Inc v United Mexican States*, ICSID Case No ARB(AF)/04/1, Decision on Responsibility (15 January 2008) para 126 (where the tribunal found likeness between CPI and Mexican sugar producers because high fructose corn syrup (HFCS) and sugar were indistinguishable to end users).

[97] See eg *Merrill & Ring Forestry LP v Canada*, ICSID Case No UNCT/07/1, Award (31 March 2010) para 91 (where the tribunal rejected that the claimant, a forestland management company operating in British Columbia, was 'like' log producers operating in other Canadian provinces).

[98] *Renée Rose Levy de Levi v Republic of Peru*, ICSID Case No ARB/10/17, Award (26 February 2014) para 398 (where the tribunal distinguished between banks operating in Peru on the basis of their market share and client base).

[99] *Cargill v United Mexican States*, ICSID Case No ARB(AF)/05/2, Award (18 September 2009) paras 204–07 (where the tribunal discusses whether the difference in economic circumstances of sugar industry and HFCS industry in Mexico affect the 'likeness' of US and Mexican investors in the sweetener industry).

[100] See eg Jürgen Kurtz, *The WTO and International Investment Law: Converging Systems* (CUP 2016).

[101] *Feldman* (n 90).

[102] ibid

[103] ibid paras 173, 110, respectively.

[104] ibid para 171.

[105] *Occidental Exploration and Production Company v The Republic of Ecuador*, LCIA Case No UN3467, Award (1 July 2004).

[106] ibid para 1.

required to perform its services under its contract with Petroecuador.[107] Ecuadorian tax law provided that exporters were entitled to such refunds on the purchase of goods as part of their export activities.[108] With the conclusion of a new contract between the US investor and Petroecuador, those VAT refunds ceased. The Ecuadorian tax authority explained this change by pointing to new contractual provisions that remunerated Occidental based on a percentage of its oil production.[109] The tax authority determined that VAT refunds had already been accounted for as part of this new formula.[110]

Occidental initiated arbitral proceedings and alleged breach of NT under the United States–Ecuador BIT. More precisely, Occidental claimed that VAT refunds were given to domestic companies involved in the export of non-oil-related goods, such as flowers and seafood products.[111] Ecuador, by contrast, contended that reference to 'in like situations' in the NT obligation restricted the operation of the clause to companies competing in the same economic sector.[112] In that vein, Ecuador noted that Petroecuador—the primary exporter of oil under the contract—had also been refused VAT refunds.[113] The tribunal ultimately sided with the US investor and stated:

> 'in like situations' cannot be interpreted in the narrow sense advanced by Ecuador as the purpose of national treatment is to protect investors as compared to local producers, and this cannot be done by addressing exclusively the sector in which the particular activity is undertaken.[114]

The narrower, industry sector–specific formulation of like circumstances found in *Feldman* is difficult to reconcile juristically with the much broader approach taken in *OEPC I* and leads to opposite consequences for the rule of law. As discussed above in relation to the MFN standard of protection, inclusion of the 'likeness' criteria in helping to frame equality guarantees do not in and of themselves detract from the rule of law. On the contrary, inclusion of the 'likeness' criterion as a means by which to compare foreign investors and domestic investors for purposes of determining whether a State has violated its NT commitments conforms with Dworkin's conception of the rule of law in that it respects an investor's choice and responsibility in the marketplace.[115] For example, a foreign entity choosing to invest in a personal firearms retail business should not be compared to a domestic entity choosing to invest in a chocolatier business. The greater regulations imposed on a personal firearms business as opposed to a chocolatier business is a direct consequence of the investor's choice of market in which to participate. This perspective on equality is useful when considering some of the jurisprudence outlined above on the interpretation of 'like circumstances'. Unlike the narrower formulation in *Feldman*, decisions that define an investor's comparators too broadly to include all exporters regardless of industry sector, such as *OEPC I*, ignore the fact that equality is not absolute and that an investor ought to bear responsibility for the

---

[107] ibid paras 1–3.
[108] ibid para 133.
[109] ibid paras 26–30.
[110] ibid para 3.
[111] ibid para 168.
[112] ibid paras 171–72.
[113] ibid
[114] ibid para 173.
[115] Dworkin (n 15) 354.

market entry choices it makes. Put another way, an investor should only be compared to other participants it actually competes against.[116] In doing so, the decision in *OEPC I* detracts from the rule of law and its equality guarantee.

B. Less-Favourable-Treatment Criteria

The NT obligation, like the MFN discipline, requires that a foreign investor be treated 'no less favourably' than a 'like' domestic investor. Determinations of 'less favourable' treatment is inextricably linked to the 'like circumstances' criterion because NT is a relative concept.[117] Where appropriate comparators are established, 'less favourable treatment' encapsulates both de facto and de jure differences.[118] As a result, the NT obligation may be violated where a measure is discriminatory on its face or where a measure has a disparate impact on foreign investors vis-à-vis a host State's own investors.[119] From a Dworkinian rule-of-law perspective, the issue of less favourable treatment is better understood by asking whether differences in treatment affect the true opportunity cost of resources acquired by market participants. This is a factual determination, which should be assessed on a case-by-case basis. While government intervention may be needed to correct market distortions and may be justifiable under the regulatory purpose criteria discussed below, government intervention (ie regulation) should not in and of itself create market distortions that favour 'like' domestic investors.[120] With that in mind, the test for less favourable treatment should clearly identify whether a gap exists between a foreign investor's situation and the market's most efficient use of resources subject to bona fide regulation (see Section C).

For example, some tribunals have found that a foreign investor has suffered 'less favourable' treatment when it does not receive the best level of treatment available to 'like' domestic investors.[121] This was the case in *Archer Daniels Midland et al (ADM) v Mexico* where a NAFTA Tribunal found that a tax imposed on non-cane sugar sweeteners violated NAFTA's NT obligation.[122] In so finding the Tribunal observed:

> [T]he Tax was indirectly imposed on non-cane sugar sweeteners, as it subjects the distribution of a certain group of soft drinks -including those containing fructose, but not

---

[116] It is notable that the requirement to show actual competition under the NT less favourable treatment criteria is, in my view, not as critical in the MFN context. Where the normative question pertains to the scope and application of a non-discrimination provision like an MFN clause, insistence on an investor identifying a comparator that is competing and actually receiving more preferential treatment under a third-party BIT (eg *Içkale* (n 50)) is not as relevant and may even detract from Dworkin's rule-of-law ideal.

[117] Where a claimant is unable to establish that it is 'like' the domestic entity receiving the allegedly more favourable treatment, its NT claims will fail: see eg *ADF* (n 35) para 156; *Methanex Corporation v United States of America*, Final Award (3 August 2005) Part IV, ChB, paras 18, 22.

[118] See eg *Corn Products* (n 96) para 138.

[119] Dolzer and Schreuer (n 88) 200–01.

[120] ibid.

[121] Todd J Grierson-Weiler and Ian A Laird, 'Standards of Treatment' in Peter Muchlinski and others (eds), *The Oxford Handbook of International Investment Law* (OUP 2008) 293; Andrea K Bjorklund, 'National Treatment' in August Reinisch (ed), *Standards of Investment Protection* (OUP 2008) 54–56.

[122] *Archer Daniels* (n 93) paras 205–13. See also *Pope & Talbot v Canada* (n 95) para 42; *Loewen v United States of America*, ICSID Case No ARB(AF)/98/3, Award (26 June 2003) para 140: 'What Article 1102(3) requires is a comparison between the standard of treatment accorded to a claimant and the most favourable standard of treatment accorded to a person in like situation to that claimant'; *Methanex* (n 117) paras 20–21 'the investor or investment of another party is entitled to the most favourable treatment accorded to some members of the domestic class'.

cane sugar, to the payment of a 20 percent ad valorem tax. Therefore, HFCS was taxed in excess of like domestic products (cane sugar). Cane sugar was the only sweetener exempted from the Tax.[123]

The US claimants could not receive the best available treatment (ie exemption) afforded to Mexican sugar producers under the impugned tax regime. As a result, the Tribunal found that the effect of the tax resulted in the claimants (producers and distributors of non-sugar cane sweeteners) receiving less favourable treatment than that accorded to Mexican sugar producers.[124]

Other tribunals have applied a disproportionate disadvantage test when determining what constitutes 'less favourable' treatment. While this test is more often seen in the international trade law context and requires an assessment of the effects of a measure on the group of domestic and foreign investors (as defined by the 'likeness' criteria),[125] it was also applied in the investment law context by the Tribunal in *SD Myers Inc v Government of Canada*.[126] In this case, the claimant, a polychlorinated biphenyls (PCB) waste remediation company, asserted that an interim order preventing it from exporting PCB-contaminated waste to its US facility was discriminatory. More particularly, the claimant contended that the interim order did not allow US waste disposal companies to operate in Canada in the same manner as Canadian waste disposal companies.[127] The Tribunal agreed with the claimant.[128] In so doing it indicated that one of the factors to consider in NT cases is 'whether the practical effect of the measure is to create a disproportionate benefit for nationals over non-nationals'.[129]

Whether by application of the disproportionate disadvantage test or the best available treatment test, so long as the tribunal is able to clearly identify that differential government intervention (ie regulation) has created a gap in treatment favouring domestic investors over a foreign investor, and thus a distortion of the true opportunity cost of resources acquired by market participants, then the rule of law from a Dworkinian perspective is eroded.

C. Regulatory-Purpose Justification

As in the case of the MFN equality guarantee, regulatory purpose is relevant to considerations about whether a host State has violated the NT obligation. In jurisprudence considering the NT obligation tribunals have considered regulatory purpose as part of the 'like circumstances' analysis. *SD Myers v Canada* is an example of this approach.[130] While the tribunal in this case ultimately found Canada liable for discriminating against the US claimant, a PCB waste management company, it did recognize that interpretation of 'like circumstances' must account for a number of factors, including 'circumstances that would

---

[123] *Archer Daniels* (n 93) para 206.
[124] ibid para 211.
[125] See Nicolas F Diebold, 'Standards of Non-Discrimination in International Economic Law' (2011) 60 ICLQ 831, 842–44, fn 48.
[126] *SD Myers* (n 91).
[127] ibid paras 130–33.
[128] ibid paras 255–56.
[129] ibid para 255.
[130] ibid.

justify governmental regulations that treat [investors] differently in order to protect the public interest'.[131] Regulatory purpose has also formed part of the 'less favourable' treatment assessment requiring evidence of a host State's protectionist intention in order to establish a violation of the NT discipline.[132] Still other tribunals seem to discuss regulatory purpose as a distinct element within the NT obligation.[133]

Until recently most investment treaties have not contained provisions that exempt a host State from liability for otherwise discriminatory measures where the purpose of those measures is to achieve legitimate public policy goals.[134] Such express recognition of the circumstances in which a host State may intrude into the market would undoubtedly accord with the rule of law. And even absent such textual clarity, a Dworkinian approach to the rule of law could still accommodate government intervention in an NT analysis. Dworkin accepts that a government ought to intervene in the market where the market is distorted by externalities and does not reflect true opportunity cost.[135] Consequently, bona fide host State regulation of externalities, may necessarily result in distinguishing foreign investors and their investments from 'like' domestic investors.

Climate change policy and regulation provides a useful and timely frame of reference for this discussion. It appears that the world has now largely moved past the climate change question of whether to regulate greenhouse gas (GHG) emissions, and on to the more contentious question how best to do so. A variety of regulatory options are often discussed, and some have even been implemented, including financial incentives, emission limits, cap-and-trade programmes, and carbon taxes. GHG emissions are typically viewed as an externality in a market-based economy since, absent regulation, the volume of GHG emissions released by a market participant has no direct impact on the realized value of their production. In that case, the market does not reflect the true opportunity cost of such GHG emissions, and Dworkin would acknowledge that government intervention to address such a market distortion is indeed required and does not offend the rule of law.

For our consideration of the NT standard and the rule of law, the salient question is whether a regulatory measure redresses this market externality by requiring market participants to bear the true opportunity cost of GHG emissions. That will involve a factual determination. However, if answered in the affirmative, then a GHG regulation that would otherwise violate the NT standard but can be saved on the basis of its regulatory purpose, would enhance the rule of law in spite of a host State's differential treatment of foreign versus domestic investors.

Consider, for example, the cap-and-trade regime established by the government of Alberta (Canada).[136] The Alberta government has established emission limits for various regulated facilities. It also issues 'emission offsets' for qualifying GHG offset and sequestration projects, and 'emission performance credits' for GHG emissions reductions against a regulated facility's baseline.[137] Both emission offsets and emission performance credits may be sold to a third party and ultimately used for compliance (ie netted off against actual emissions) by a regulated facility in Alberta to meet its regulated emission limit. Notably, however, both emission offsets and emission performance credits must be generated by

---

[131] ibid para 250.
[132] See eg *Methanex* (n 117) paras 46–60.
[133] *Pope & Talbot* (n 95) para 78.
[134] See eg CETA (n 81) art 28.3(1)(2).
[135] See Section II above.
[136] <www.alberta.ca/alberta-emission-offset-system.aspx> accessed 1 February 2022.
[137] <https://alberta.csaregistries.ca> accessed 1 February 2022.

facilities located in Alberta.[138] So a foreign investor cannot use GHG emission reductions attributable to offsets, sequestration or performance improvements from its investments outside of Alberta. To the extent that domestic investors are more likely to have more regulated facilities in Alberta than foreign investors, then arguably Alberta's cap-and-trade regime treats domestic investors better than foreign investors. Consequently, the regime may prima facie violate the NT standard, but it can be saved by its bona fide regulatory purpose. That result, however, would not offend Dworkin from a rule-of-law perspective given that the Alberta regime corrects market distortions by reflecting the true opportunity cost of GHG emissions.

V. Concluding Remarks

This chapter considers the extent to which the MFN and NT standards of protection in IIL reflect, influence, further, or limit the rule of law, and it has done so by drawing upon Dworkin's ideal of the rule of law. In so doing, this chapter has demonstrated that the MFN and NT disciplines, along with their component features, largely reflect and further the rule of law within the IIL regime. The MFN and NT disciplines are essential equality guarantees that operate to ensure an efficient global market. That is, one in which an investor's cost of participating in the market truly reflects opportunity cost and permits government intervention to address market distortions. Regardless of variations in the scope of MFN and NT clauses, these provisions remain at their core equality doctrines that ground the rules of fair play and justice in the IIL regime.

The MFN and NT clauses with their requisite components enshrine rights and curtail host State behaviour in a manner consistent with equality. Recall that Dworkin's conception of equality is grounded in the impersonal resources each individual has within a State with government intervention required to redistribute those resources so that they better align with the opportunity cost of each individual's market decisions. The rule of law is therefore more likely to be achieved in societies that strive towards this type of equality. These same ideas have relevance at the global level and provide a useful framework with which to think about the MFN and NT obligations. Consistent with a rejection of purely laissez-faire economics, inclusion of the MFN and NT disciplines in investment law signals a desire by States to balance foreign investor responsibility with a redistribution of resources in the global marketplace. At their core, the MFN and NT disciplines seek to ensure that foreign investors are put on equal footing to use their resources to make decisions about their business operations (ie how they structure their investments, in what industry sector they invest, etc.) in the global economy without a host State government redistributing those resources (ie by way of subsidization, taxation, etc.) to their own investors or to foreign investors whose nationality is connected to States which are more favoured political allies. MFN and NT disciplines therefore support the idea that foreign investors operating within the global economy are responsible for their market choices and that those choices should not be unduly constrained by host State interference.

---

[138] *Technology Innovation and Emissions Reduction Regulation*, Alta. Reg. 133/2019, s 19. See also the Government of Ontario's announcement on 26 January 2022 directing research and a report on the design of a provincial clean energy credit registry that 'would allow for the simplified creation, trading, and retirement of CECs in Ontario' <https://news.ontario.ca/en/release/1001486/new-ontario-clean-energy-registry-will-make-province-even-more-attractive-for-investment> accessed 1 February 2022.

This desire to ensure that foreign investors operating within the IIL regime are given 'equal concern' is not and should not be an absolute guarantee. The above discussion highlights this as it considers the constituent requirements that must be met if an investor is to successfully assert a violation of the MFN or NT disciplines. We see, for example, that comparisons—essential to any equality discussion—require a foreign investor to be 'like' its foreign or domestic counterpart, respectively. The MFN and NT disciplines also require an investor to show proof of treatment that is 'less favourable' than that accorded to other 'like' foreign or domestic investors. These requirements, while subject to varying interpretations, largely reflect and further the rule of law. Moreover, accounting for a foreign investor's choice and responsibility within the market implicitly recognizes that not all market participants, foreign or domestic, will make the same decisions about the industries, including the specific sector and applicable regulatory regime, in which they choose to participate. These choices appropriately affect the 'equal concern' calculus. However, arbitral decisions, such as *OPEC I*, which define an investor's comparators too broadly to include all exporters regardless of industry sector when assessing the NT likeness criteria detract from the rule of law and its equality guarantee by undermining the fact that equality is not absolute and that an investor bears responsibility for the choices it makes such as participation in a specific industry sector.

The 'less favourable' treatment requirement is also an important constraint that reflects and furthers the rule of law. This criterion has been addressed more frequently in cases assessing the NT obligation. In those cases, we see some tribunals adopt the 'best available treatment' standard (*ADM*) while others adopt the 'disproportionate disadvantage' test (*SD Myers*) to assess whether there is less favourable treatment. Both standards work fundamentally to ensure that government intervention (ie regulation) does not in and of itself create market distortions—a result that furthers the rule of law. Nonetheless, the above discussion highlights that a Dworkinian account of the rule of law would favour the 'best available treatment' standard given the potential market inefficiencies that are permissible under the disproportionate disadvantage test.

This is not to say that governments should never intervene in the market. Dworkin accepts that government ought to intervene in the market where the market is distorted by externalities and does not reflect true opportunity cost. The 'regulatory purpose' criterion in the analyses of both the MFN and NT disciplines recognizes the importance of such interventions and is therefore consistent with the rule of law.

Lastly, Dworkin's conception of the rule of law is also a useful lens through which to discuss the ongoing controversy about the scope of MFN clauses, including the proper interpretation of 'treatment' in MFN jurisprudence. For Dworkin one of the important features of the rule of law is that individuals can enforce their rights through courts or other judicial institutions. Dworkin's account of the rule of law would not permit an interpretation of 'treatment' in and MFN clause to include dispute settlement or substantive treaty protections where States have expressly articulated a different intention in their investment treaties. But, where there is ambiguity about what constitutes 'treatment' within an MFN clause, Dworkin's conception of the rule of law supports a broad interpretation of such clauses so that investors have access to the same substantive treaty protections and dispute settlement processes.

7

Regulatory Transparency in International Investment Law

From an Investment Protection Requirement to a Rule-of-Law Requirement

Manjiao Chi[*]

I. Introduction

Transparency plays an important role in international economic governance. It is fair to say that it has entered into almost all fields of international economic law.[1] While transparency has been established as a basic principle of the law of the World Trade Organization (WTO),[2] and is viewed as a key indicator and guarantee of international trade governance,[3] it remains premature to claim that an internationally uniform transparency standard in international investment law (IIL) has been formed, despite the growing acceptance of transparency in certain areas of law.[4]

Existing literature seems to suggest that the issue of transparency in IIL has been discussed mainly in relation to two aspects, namely publication of national laws and regulations relevant to a State's foreign investment governance, and transparency relating to investor-State dispute settlement (ISDS), investor-State arbitration (ISA) in particular, covering a wide range of issues, such as publication of arbitral awards and other decisions, opening of hearings to the public, and participation of third parties in ISA proceedings.[5] Over time, transparency rules concerning the two aspects have been codified in a growing

[*] The author thanks Andrea Bjorklund, Marc Bungenberg, Caroline Henckels, Marcin Menkes, August Reinisch, and Stephan Schill for their comments on earlier drafts. All errors remain the author's.

[1] See Andrea Bianchi, 'On Power and Illusion: The Concept of Transparency in International Law' in Andrea Bianchi and Anne Peters (eds), *Transparency in International Law* (CUP 2013) 1–2.

[2] General Agreement on Tariffs and Trade (opened for signature 30 October 1947, entered into force 1 January 1948) 55 UNTS 187, art X.

[3] See eg Padideh Ala'i, 'From the Periphery to the Center? The Evolving WTO Jurisprudence on Transparency and Good Governance' (2008) 11 JIEL 779, 794–95; Andrew D Mitchell, Elizabeth Sheargold and Tania Voon, 'Good Governance Obligations in International Economic Law: A Comparative Analysis of Trade and Investment' (2016) 17 JWIT 7, 7–46.

[4] For instance, in regard to public procurement law, which is closely connected with investment governance, the European Union (EU) requires a high level of transparency in granting public procurement contracts. See Irena Georgieva, *Using Transparency against Corruption in Public Procurement: A Comparative Analysis of the Transparency Rules and Their Failure to Combat Corruption* (Springer 2017) 5–49; see also, *Parking Brixen GmbH v Gemeinde Brixen and Stadtwerke Brixen AG* [2005] ECLI:EU:C:2005:605.

[5] See generally Cristoffer Nyegaard Mollestad, 'See No Evil? Procedural Transparency in International Investment Law and Dispute Settlement' (2014) PluriCourts Research Paper No 14-20 <https://papers.ssrn.com/sol3/papers.cfm?abstract_id=2516242> accessed 9 February 2022, 19–75.

Manjiao Chi, *Regulatory Transparency in International Investment Law* In: *Investment Protection Standards and the Rule of Law*. Edited by: August Reinisch and Stephan W. Schill, Oxford University Press. © Manjiao Chi 2023. DOI: 10.1093/oso/9780192864581.003.0007

number of international investment agreements (IIAs), including bilateral investment treaties (BITs) and investment chapters of various forms of free trade agreements (FTAs).[6]

There is also a third aspect of transparency in IIL, namely 'regulatory transparency', which could be defined as 'transparency that involves both the accessibility and intelligibility of laws on the one hand and the openness and consistency of the processes by which they are made, on the other, which is about both the law-making process and the implementation and enforcement of the resulting laws'.[7] In the context of IIL, 'regulatory transparency' could be understood as a requirement that the implementation of national laws and measures relating to foreign investment regulation should meet certain transparency standards.

Up to the present, regulatory transparency seems to have been underexplored. This is mainly because States are often of the view that the primary purpose of IIAs is to secure adequate, prompt, and effective compensation to foreign investors in case of expropriation, and regulatory transparency was not a major concern in IIA-making.[8] This situation has gradually changed. Since the conclusion of the North American Free Trade Agreement (NAFTA) in 1994, in particular, regulatory transparency has received growing attention in IIA-making and ISA practice, predominantly through the application and interpretation of the fair and equitable treatment (FET) standard.[9] NAFTA Member States expect IIAs to also play a helpful role in ensuring a sound investment environment in addition to protecting investment, and regulatory transparency is a major element of a sound investment environment.[10]

Against such a background, this chapter discusses the development of regulatory transparency in IIL, with a focus on IIAs and ISA practice. Section II summarizes the major types of regulatory transparency provisions in existing IIAs. Section III explores regulatory transparency obligations in the context of FET claims in ISA practice. Section IV first outlines the relevance of regulatory transparency to the rule of law in global investment governance, then analyses some typical regulatory transparency provisions in recent IIAs, which could be deemed also as a rule-of-law requirement in addition to a mere investment protection requirement. Section V provides a brief conclusion.

II. Major Types of Regulatory Transparency Provisions in Existing IIAs

It seems to be 'standard' practice for IIAs to include certain transparency provisions, either in the form of a standalone clause (sometimes entitled 'transparency') or scattered in

---

[6] See generally Manjiao Chi, *Integrating Sustainable Development in International Investment Law: Normative Incompatibility, System Integration and Governance Implications* (Routledge 2017) 120–21.

[7] Rex Deighton-Smith, 'Assuring Regulatory Transparency: A Critical Overview' <www.apeccp.org.tw/htd ocs/doc/APEC-OECD/2002-10/002%20paper.pdf> accessed 9 February 2022, 6; Lorenzo Betolini, 'How to Improve Regulatory Transparency' (2006) <https://openknowledge.worldbank.org/bitstream/handle/10986/10733/375470Gridline1ransparency01PUBLIC1.pdf?sequence=1&isAllowed=y> accessed 9 February 2022.

[8] Akira Kotera, 'Regulatory Transparency' in Peter Muchlinski, Federico Ortino and Christoph Schreuer (eds), *The Oxford Handbook of International Investment Law* (OUP 2008) 617, 625–28.

[9] Julie A Maupin, 'Transparency in International Law' in Andrea Bianchi and Anne Peters (eds), *Transparency in International Law* (CUP 2013) 170.

[10] Kotera (n 8) 625–28.

different sections and clauses of the IIAs.[11] These provisions cover both substantive and procedural aspects, enabling States to have a number of ways to define and fulfil their transparency obligations.[12] As observed by the United Nations Conference on Trade and Development (UNCTAD), existing transparency provisions mostly focus on the publication of laws and regulations of the host State, as well as arbitral awards or decisions, which reflect the traditional concerns of foreign investors regarding the transparency of host States' conduct, statements, policies, regulations, and decision-making.[13]

Provisions that focus on regulatory transparency remain infrequently seen in IIAs. Existing regulatory transparency provisions in IIAs can be roughly categorized into the following three major types, entailing obligations on States that are different in nature, content, and scope.

First, declaratory provisions. This type of provision often appears in the form of a State's statement of maintaining a transparent investment governance regime, typically found in the preambles or initial clauses of IIAs. For instance, Article 1 of the ASEAN [Association of Southeast Asian Nations] Comprehensive Investment Agreement (ACIA) lists several objectives of the treaty, including transparency. The relevant part of this provision reads 'the objective of this Agreement is to create a free and open investment regime in ASEAN', through 'improvement of transparency and predictability of investment rules, regulations and procedures conducive to increased investment among Member states'.[14] Under the Vienna Convention on the Law of Treaties (VCLT), treaty preambles often do not confer contractual rights or obligations on the contracting parties or their investors, though they may reflect rules of customary law and form an integral part of a treaty.[15] However, treaty preambles could play various roles in the interpretation of the treaty, as they are particularly important for establishing a treaty's object and purpose.[16] Therefore, from a treaty law perspective, the effectiveness of such provisions contained in IIA preambles in promoting the rule of law in a State is limited.

Second, engagement provisions. While the publication of laws and regulations is an indispensable element of a State's transparency obligation, some IIAs take a step further to include certain provisions that require States to provide formal or informal means to the stakeholders, such as foreign investors, with regard to making laws and regulations, setting up standards or taking regulatory measures. A major type of these provisions requires States to establish a contact point to address concerns and enquiries from the other contracting

---

[11] For instance, the 2012 US Model BIT probably hosts some of the most comprehensive and complicated transparency provisions that can be found in modern IIAs, which are scattered in several standalone clauses, mainly including art 10 (Publication of Laws and Decisions Respecting Investment), art 11 (Transparency), and art 29 (Transparency of Arbitral Proceedings). Likewise, the transparency provisions of the ACIA can also be found in three different sections, including the preamble and two standalone clauses: ASEAN Comprehensive Investment Agreement (opened for signature 26 February 2009, entered into force 29 March 2012) <http://investasean.asean.org/files/upload/Doc%2005%20-%20ACIA.pdf> accessed 10 February 2022, preamble, art 21 (Transparency), art 39 (Transparency of Arbitral Proceedings).

[12] UNCTAD, 'Transparency: UNCTAD Series on Issues in International Investment Agreements' (2004) UN Doc UNCTAD/ITE/IIT/2003/4 <https://unctad.org/system/files/official-document/iteiit20034_en.pdf> accessed 10 February 2022, 13–47.

[13] UNCTAD, 'Transparency in IIAs: UNCTAD Series on Issues in International Investment Agreements II' (2012) UN Doc UNCTAD/DIAE/IA/2011/6 <http://unctad.org/en/PublicationsLibrary/unctaddiaeia2011d6_en.pdf> accessed 10 February 2022, 15.

[14] ACIA (n 11), art 1(c).

[15] See generally Gerald Fitzmaurice, 'The Law and Procedure of the International Court of Justice 1951–1954' (1957) 33 BYIL 229.

[16] See Mark E Villiger, *Commentary on the 1969 Convention on the Law of Treaties* (Nijhoff 2008) 44.

State, potential investors or the public, such as the one contained in the 2012 US Model BIT,[17] and in the ACIA.[18] Another type requires States to consult with stakeholders or to provide them an opportunity to comment on the proposed laws or measures, such as the transparency provision in the 2012 US Model BIT.[19] A third type, also known as standard-setting provisions, requires States to allow persons of the other party to participate in the development of standards and technical regulations by its central government bodies, and to take measures to facilitate their participation in the standard-setting.[20] In general, these provisions serve different purposes, and are helpful in creating a transparent regulatory environment. However, as most of these provisions are carved out of the scope of ISA, as is the case of the 2012 US Model BIT, they usually cannot be enforced by private investors through ISA.[21]

Third, some IIAs, limited in number, incorporate transparency obligations in FET clauses. A typical example is the Energy Charter Treaty (ECT), which provides in relevant part:

> Each Contracting Party shall, in accordance with the provisions of this Treaty, encourage and create stable, equitable, favourable and transparent conditions for Investors of other Contracting Parties to make Investments in its Area. Such conditions shall include a commitment to accord at all times to Investments of Investors of other Contracting Parties fair and equitable treatment.[22]

Similarly, the investment chapter of the Comprehensive and Economic Trade Agreement between Canada and the European Union (CETA), unlike the majority of existing IIAs, provides an exhaustive list of situations of FET violations, including, inter alia, 'fundamental breach of due process, including a fundamental breach of transparency, in judicial and administrative proceedings'.[23] This list could not only provide more certainty to the contracting parties and investors, but also potentially limits the interpretive power of adjudicators in applying the FET standard. Besides, the Dutch Model BIT 2019 also explicitly lists transparency as an FET obligation, which provides in part that 'fundamental breach of due process, including a fundamental breach of transparency, in judicial and administrative proceedings' by a contracting State shall be deemed to be a breach of the FET obligation.[24]

III. Regulatory Transparency as an Investment Protection Standard

Considering that, as discussed above, most of the regulatory transparency provisions that are enforceable for foreign investors are included in IIAs as part of the FET standard, the

---

[17] US Model BIT (2012), art 11.5 (a).
[18] ACIA (n 11), art 21.1 (d).
[19] US Model BIT (2012), art 11.2 (b).
[20] ibid art 11.8.
[21] ibid art 24.1(a).
[22] Energy Charter Treaty (opened for signature 17 December 1994, entered into force 16 April 1998) 2080 UNTS 95, art 10 (1).
[23] Comprehensive Economic and Trade Agreement (CETA) between Canada, of the one part, and the European Union and Its Member States, of the other part [2017] OJ L11/23, art 8.10.2.
[24] Dutch Model BIT (2019), art 9.2 (b).

issue of regulatory transparency is dealt with in ISA predominantly in the context of FET claims.[25] In a number of ISA cases, the investors claimed that the host State had breached the 'transparency obligation', which constituted a violation of the FET clause in the applicable IIAs. It is of interest to briefly analyse these ISA cases to explore whether and to what extent regulatory transparency is accepted as an obligation of the host State in foreign investment governance.

At the outset, as discussed earlier, some IIAs expressly refer to transparency in their FET clauses. In ISA cases where such IIAs have been invoked, it seems that tribunals could fairly easily determine that transparency constitutes an element of the FET obligation. For instance, in *Electrabel v Hungary*, the ECT was the applicable IIA. The tribunal held that the FET clause contained in the ECT, as mentioned above, not only spoke of equitable and stable conditions, but it also referred to 'favourable and transparent conditions'.[26] On this basis, the tribunal held:

> The reference to transparency can be read to indicate an obligation to be forthcoming with information about intended changes in policy and regulations that may significantly affect investments, so that the investor can adequately plan its investment and, if needed, engage the host state in dialogue about protecting its legitimate expectations.[27]

Unlike the ECT, many IIAs do not clearly refer to transparency as an element of FET. In ISA cases where such IIAs have been invoked, tribunals faced similar tasks of determining, first, whether the host State bears a transparency obligation under the FET clause at all, and, second, if so, whether the host State has violated such an obligation. These questions essentially require tribunals to ascertain the existence, content, scope, and extent of the alleged transparency obligation in light of the applicable IIAs. In this respect, a series of cases is worth mentioning.

Metalclad v Mexico[28] is deemed as an early and classical case in which a tribunal found that a lack of transparency (of local laws and procedures) constituted a violation of the FET obligation.[29] Metalclad invested in a hazardous waste landfill project in Mexico. It was granted a construction permit by the federal government of Mexico. A few months after the construction started, Metalclad was notified by the local government that the project was in unlawful operation as it had not obtained a local permit. Yet, when Metalclad applied for a local permit, it was rejected by the local government. The rejection effectively barred the operation of Metalclad's project and led to an ISA claim under the Additional Facility of the International Centre for Settlement of Investment Disputes (ICSID).[30] Metalclad claimed, inter alia, that the conduct of Mexico violated the minimum standard of treatment under NAFTA, Article 1105, which required the contracting States to treat foreign investment 'in

[25] See Catharine Titi, 'International Investment Law and Good Governance' in Marc Bungenberg and others (eds), *International Investment Law: A Handbook* (Hart 2015) 1771–73.

[26] *Electrabel SA v Republic of Hungary*, ICSID Case No ARB/07/19, Decision on Jurisdiction, Applicable Law and Liability (30 November 2012), para 7.79.

[27] ibid.

[28] *Metalclad Corporation v The United Mexican States*, ICSID Case No ARB (AF)/97/1, Award (30 August 2000).

[29] See eg Shotaro Hamamoto, 'Domestic Review of Treaty-Based International Investment Awards: Effects of the *Metalclad* Judgment of the British Columbia Supreme Court' in Machiko Kanetake and André Nollkaemper (eds), *The Rule of Law at the National and International Levels: Contestations and Deference* (Hart 2016) 101.

[30] William S Dodge, 'International Decisions: *Metalclad Corp. v. Mexico and Mexico v. Metalclad Corp*' (2001) 95 AJIL 910, 911.

accordance with international law, including fair and equitable treatment and full protection and security'. As this FET provision did not expressly refer to transparency, treaty interpretation was needed. In this respect, the tribunal made a clear reference to the objective of NAFTA, as enshrined in its Article 102(1), finding that 'an underlying objective of NAFTA is to promote and increase cross-border investment opportunities and ensure the successful implementation of investment initiatives'.[31] The tribunal found that FET included a transparency obligation, holding that 'prominent in the statement of principles and rules that introduces the Agreement [NAFTA] is the reference to "transparency"'.[32] Then, the tribunal addressed the transparency issue straightforwardly. It analysed the scope and content of the transparency obligation under NAFTA Article 1105 and held:

> The Tribunal understands this to include the idea that all relevant legal requirements for the purpose of initiating, completing and successfully operating investments made, or intended to be made, under the Agreement should be capable of being readily known to all affected investors of another Party. There should be no room for doubt or uncertainty on such matters. Once the authorities of the central government of any Party (whose international responsibility in such matters has been identified in the preceding section) become aware of any scope for misunderstanding or confusion in this connection, it is their duty to ensure that the correct position is promptly determined and clearly stated so that investors can proceed with all appropriate expedition in the confident belief that they are acting in accordance with all relevant laws.[33]

The tribunal, based on the above analysis, held that Mexico violated the transparency obligation under the FET provision in NAFTA, Article 1105. It stated:

> The absence of a clear rule as to the requirement or not of a municipal construction permit, as well as the absence of any established practice or procedure as to the manner of handling applications for a municipal construction permit, amounts to a failure on the part of Mexico to ensure the transparency required by NAFTA.[34]

As can be seen, the tribunal in *Metalclad v Mexico* not only determined that FET included a transparency obligation, despite the lack of clear mentioning thereof in NAFTA, Article 1105, but it also held that the transparency obligation should include several interrelated aspects: first, all relevant legal instruments shall be made publicly available; second, such instruments shall be sufficiently clear and easily understandable by the investor; and, third, the host State shall promptly clarify to the investor any misunderstanding or confusion of the instruments when necessary.

The decision in *Metalclad v Mexico* was highly contentious. As observed by the ILA Committee, the transparency obligation established by the tribunal in this case is probably 'too high'.[35] Because the seat of the arbitration proceeding was in Canada, Mexico sought

---

[31] *Metalclad Corporation* (n 28) para 75.
[32] ibid para 76.
[33] ibid para 76.
[34] ibid para 88.
[35] International Law Association 'Sydney Conference (2018): Rule of Law and International Investment Law' (2018) <www.ila-hq.org/images/ILA/DraftReports/DraftReport_Investment_RuleofLaw.pdf> accessed 10 February 2022, 30 (hereafter ILA Committee Report).

to set aside the award before the Supreme Court of British Columbia (SCBC). The SCBC examined whether the *Metalclad* tribunal had made decisions on matters beyond the scope of NAFTA, ch 11. On this issue, the SCBC disagreed with the tribunal on the existence of a transparency obligation under NAFTA, Article 1105. The SCBC analysed the structure and objective of NAFTA, and found that the tribunal erred in expansively interpreting Article 1105. It held:

> The arbitrator crafted the argument by assuming that the words 'international law' in Article 1105 were not intended to have their routine meaning and should be interpreted in an expansive manner to include norms that have not yet technically passed into customary international law. However, the arbitrator did not decide the point because it had not been fully argued in the arbitration and he was not aware of the argument having been made in any earlier case law or academic literature. In my view, such an argument should fail because there is no proper basis to give the term 'international law' in Article 1105 a meaning other than its usual and ordinary meaning.[36]

While rejecting the tribunal's interpretive approach, the SCBC found that the tribunal had determined matters beyond the scope of NAFTA, ch 11. With regard to the transparency issue, the SCBC held:

> The Tribunal made its decision on the basis of transparency. This was a matter beyond the scope of the submission to arbitration because there are no transparency obligations contained in Chapter Eleven.[37]

Consequently, the SCBC partly set aside the award. The SCBC's interpretation of FET under NAFTA, Article 1105 was later confirmed by the joint interpretation issued by the NAFTA Free Trade Commission.[38]

Despite these controversies, the decision in *Metalclad v Mexico* has exerted profound impact on ensuing ISA practices with regard to the understanding of the transparency component of FET. This is particularly the case considering that many IIAs contain an FET provision similar or even identical to Article 1105.

As a matter of fact, since *Metalclad v Mexico*, a number of ISA cases involving the issue of regulatory transparency have been decided, many applying FET provisions. For instance, in *Tecmed v Mexico*,[39] the investor's hazardous waste landfill project failed to be relicensed by the National Ecology Institute of Mexico (INE), a government agency of Mexico. The investor suspected that the refusal was a result of the change of the relevant administrative process of Mexico. Similar to *Metalclad v Mexico*, the *Tecmed* tribunal criticized that the lack of predictability and transparency in the administrative process of the local government of Mexico culminated in the de facto revocation of the licence. While relying on the

---

[36] *The United Mexican States v Metalclad Corporation*, 2001 BCSC 664, Judgment (2 May 2001) <www.italaw. com/sites/default/files/case-documents/ita0512.pdf> accessed 10 February 2022, para 68.

[37] ibid para 72.

[38] NAFTA Free Trade Commission, 'Notes of Interpretation of Certain Chapter 11 Provisions' (31 July 2001) <www.sice.oas.org/tpd/nafta/commission/ch11understanding_e.asp> accessed 9 February 2022.

[39] *Técnicas Medioambientales Tecmed SA v The United Mexican States*, ICSID Case No ARB (AF)/00/2, Award (29 May 2003).

FET provision in the underlying Mexico–Spain BIT (2006), the tribunal found that INE was subject to a transparency obligation. The tribunal held:

> The foreign investor expects the host State to act in a consistent manner, free from ambiguity and totally transparently in its relations with the foreign investor, so that it may know beforehand any and all rules and regulations that will govern its investments, as well as the goals of the relevant policies and administrative practices or directives, to be able to plan its investment and comply with such regulations.[40]

The tribunal in *Tecmed v Mexico* seemed to have followed the reasoning in *Metalclad v Mexico*. Both tribunals held that an FET provision included a transparency obligation on the host States, and that such an obligation required more than merely publishing legal instruments and procedures, but further required that the legal instruments and procedures should be made known to the investor in a proper manner, which, in the view of the *Tecmed* tribunal, essentially required the host State to send 'explicit, transparent and clear warning' to the investor with regard to the revocation of the licence.[41] The tribunal found that, as INE failed to send such a warning to the investor, Mexico breached the transparency obligation, resulting in a violation of the FET obligation under the BIT.

The holding of *Tecmed v Mexico* was adopted by the tribunal in *MTD Equity v Chile*.[42] It is of interest to note that, while the tribunals in both cases adopted a test requiring the host State to act 'free from ambiguity and totally transparently', they failed to elaborate on the test in detail, especially the element of 'total transparency'.

In *Waste Management v Mexico*,[43] the tribunal opined that a transparency obligation was included in the FET obligation, but it held that only 'a complete lack of transparency and candour in an administrative process' could amount to violation of FET.[44] The tribunal failed to sufficiently elaborate on the meaning of 'complete lack of transparency', except holding that 'the [FET] standard is to some extent a flexible one which must be adapted to the circumstances of each case'.[45]

In *Parkerings v Lithuania*,[46] a Norwegian investor signed a concession agreement with the City of Vilnius in Lithuania for constructing several parking projects. The host government later amended certain laws that impacted on the concession agreement. The investor claimed, inter alia, that such changes in the host State had affected its collection of fees and charges so as to make the agreed revenue-sharing mechanism unfeasible, leading to a breach of the FET clause in the underlying BIT.[47] To substantiate its FET claim, the investor partly relied on the lack of transparency in the host State's conduct. According to the investor, 'fair and equitable treatment inherently precludes arbitrary and capricious actions against investors'.[48] As the City of Vilnius failed to disclose to it information pertaining to

---

[40] ibid para 154.
[41] ibid para 160.
[42] *MTD Equity Sdn. Bhd. and MTD Chile SA v Republic of Chile*, ICSD Case No. ARB/01/7, Award (25 May 2004) paras 114–15.
[43] *Waste Management, Inc v United Mexican States*, ICSID Case No ARB (AF)/00/3, Award (30 April 2004).
[44] ibid para 98.
[45] ibid para 99.
[46] *Parkerings-Compagniet AS v Republic of Lithuania*, ICSID Case No ARB/05/8, Award (11 September 2007).
[47] Martina Polasek and Sergio Puig, '*Parkerings-Compagniet AS v Republic of Lithuania* (ICSID Case No ARB/05/8) (Award, September 11, 2007)' (2007) 22 ICSID Rev—FILJ 446, 447–48.
[48] *Parkerings-Compagniet* (n 46) paras 293–94.

the viability of the hybrid parking fee concept prior to the execution of the Agreement, such a conduct was 'arbitrary and lack[ing] transparency', and constituted a violation of FET. The tribunal agreed that 'arbitrariness is incompatible with FET', without explicitly ruling whether FET included a transparency obligation on the host State.[49] After reviewing the facts, the tribunal decided that Lithuania had not breached its transparency obligation. It should be noted that, similar to the awards in *Tecmed v Mexico* and *Waste Management v Mexico*, the *Parkerings* tribunal failed to elaborate on the scope and extent of the transparency obligation, as it did not directly respond to the investor's claim of a 'complete lack of transparency'.

The viewpoint that a transparency obligation constitutes an implied FET requirement despite a lack of a clear reference to transparency in the applicable FET clause was adopted by a number of other tribunals.

In *Rumeli v Kazakhstan*, the tribunal found that the parties had agreed that 'that the fair and equitable treatment standard encompasses *inter alia* the following concrete principles: the State must act in a transparent manner'.[50]

In *Biwater Gauff v Tanzania*, the tribunal held that '[t]he general standard of "fair and equitable treatment" as set out above comprises a number of different components', which include 'transparency, consistency, non-discrimination'.[51]

In *Invesmart v Czech Republic*, the tribunal noted that there has been a growing jurisprudence and case law in dealing with the notion of FET, and held that the content of FET obligations 'has been variously and not consistently as including the different strands of, *inter alia*, transparency'.[52]

In *Lemire v Ukraine*, the tribunal held that in deciding on an FET breach, it was necessary to ascertain 'whether there is an absence of transparency in the legal procedure or in the actions of the state'.[53]

In *Inmaris v Ukraine*, the tribunal held that '[a] government act could be unfair or inequitable if it is in breach of specific commitments, if the investor is not treated in an objective, even-handed, unbiased, and transparent way, or for other reasons'.[54]

In *Deutsche Bank v Sri Lanka*, the tribunal held that the host State had breached the FET obligation partly because 'the actions by the Supreme Court and the Central Bank … involved excess of powers and improper motive as well as serious breaches of due process, transparency and indeed a lack of good faith'.[55]

Despite the above ISA cases, the viewpoint that a transparency obligation is an implied FET requirement has not been universally adopted.

In *Cargill v Mexico*,[56] for example, the tribunal denied the existence of 'a general duty of transparency' under the FET clause of NAFTA. In this case, a US investor, Cargill, claimed

---

[49] ibid para 300.

[50] *Rumeli Telekom AS and Telsim Mobil Telekomikasyon Hizmetleri AS v Republic of Kazakhstan*, ICSID Case No ARB/05/16, Award (29 July 2008) para 609.

[51] *Biwater Gauff (Tanzania Ltd) v United Republic of Tanzania*, ICSID Case No ARB/05/22, Award (24 July 2008) para 602.

[52] *Invesmart, BV v Czech Republic*, UNCITRAL, Award (26 June 2009) para 200.

[53] *Joseph Charles Lemire v Ukraine*, ICSID Case No ARB/06/18, Decision on Jurisdiction and Liability (14 January 2010) para 284.

[54] *Inmaris Perestroika Sailing Maritime Services GmbH and ors v Ukraine*, ICSID Case No ARB/08/8, Excerpts of Award (1 March 2012) para 265.

[55] *Deutsche Bank AG v Democratic Socialist Republic of Sri Lanka*, ICSID Case No ARB/09/2, Award (31 October 2012) para 523.

[56] *Cargill Inc v United Mexican States*, ICSID Case No ARB (AF)/05/2, Award (18 September 2009).

that its investments in the high fructose corn syrup industry in Mexico had been adversely impacted by Mexico's adoption of a tax on high fructose corn syrup in 2002. Cargill alleged that Mexico's conduct constituted, inter alia, a violation of the FET provision in NAFTA, Article 1105. To support its claim, Cargill argued that Mexico violated its transparency obligation. Cargill's transparency claim had two aspects: first, that Mexico had failed to mention the tax measure to Cargill in advance; second, that Mexico had also failed to announce criteria for acquiring a permit or respond to its alleged repeated queries for further information.[57] In response, Mexico argued that a transparency obligation could not be grounded under customary international law; instead, in Mexico's view, it was a conventional obligation, which could only be grounded in treaties.[58] The tribunal rejected the investor's arguments on transparency, ruling that a general duty of transparency could not be established under the FET provision in NAFTA, Article 1105.[59] It should be noted that, despite its above ruling, the tribunal in *Cargill v Mexico* did stress that, in order for a lack of transparency to constitute a violation of the FET obligation under NAFTA, Article 1105, it had to be 'gross', 'manifest', or 'complete'.[60] Yet, the tribunal did not further elaborate on these tests.

Several observations can be drawn from the above discussions. First, if the underlying FET clause expressly refers to transparency, as in *Electrabel v Hungary*, it is safe to conclude that the contracting States bear a transparency obligation, and a violation thereof could constitute a breach of FET. Second, even if the FET clauses do not explicitly refer to transparency, tribunals often support the viewpoint that transparency is an implied element of FET. In such cases, however, the tribunals seem reluctant to elaborate on the content, scope, and extent of the transparency obligation. Thus, whether and to what extent a host State's conduct violates the transparency obligation depends on the circumstances of the individual cases and the wording of the underlying FET clauses. Third, as shown by *Cargill v Mexico*, it is difficult to conclude that a general obligation of transparency has been established under customary international law. Thus, State transparency obligation remain 'regime-specific and typically based on treaty commitments'.[61]

IV. Regulatory Transparency as a Rule-of-Law Requirement in IIAs

As can be seen, the issue of regulatory transparency is predominantly addressed in FET claims in ISA practice. FET clauses could be deemed as 'embodying the rule of law as a standard that the legal systems of host states have to embrace in their treatment of foreign investors'.[62] Today, as IIL continues to face demands for greater transparency, openness, predictability, and fair balance between investor rights and public interest,[63] not only do a

---

[57] ibid para 263.

[58] ibid para 264.

[59] ibid para 294.

[60] ibid para 285.

[61] Stephan W Schill and Felix Boos, 'State Transparency' in Thomas Cottier and Krista Nadakavukaren Schefer (eds), *Elgar Encyclopedia of International Economic Law* (Edward Elgar 2017) 216.

[62] Stephan W Schill, 'Fair and Equitable Treatment, the Rule of Law, and Comparative Public Law' in Stephan W Schill (ed), *International Investment Law and Comparative Public Law* (OUP 2010) 159.

[63] Stephan W Schill, 'Enhancing International Investment Law's Legitimacy: Conceptual and Methodological Foundations of a New Public Law Approach' (2011) 52 Va JIL 57, 69.

growing number of IIAs incorporate regulatory transparency provisions, but these provisions are also increasingly deemed as a rule-of-law requirement on States.

A. The Relevance of Regulatory Transparency to the Rule of Law

The rule of law is viewed as a fundamental principle of governance and the foundation of civilized societies. Despite the frequent use of the term 'rule of law', it lacks a unified definition at the international level.[64] In the context of IIL, while the concept of rule of law has attracted some academic discussions, existing studies have yet to fully address the fundamental question as to whether and how IIL materializes the key elements of the rule of law.[65] As has been confirmed by the 2018 Report of the International Law Association Committee on Rule of Law and International Investment Law (ILA Committee), given that the rule of law does not have a clear and universally accepted meaning and may be particularly responsive to different cultures, it is hard to find a single institutional formula that captures all of the nuances of the rule of law.[66]

This notwithstanding, due largely to its close relationship with the principle of legal certainty, transparency is recognized as an integral part of the rule of law and contributes to the creation of a 'foreseeable' legal environment.[67] For instance, in the widely accepted descriptive definition of the rule of law put forward by the United Nations (UN) Secretary-General in a report to the UN Security Council in 2004, 'procedural and legal transparency' is explicitly listed as a core element of the rule of law.[68] The European Commission for Democracy through Law, known as the Venice Commission, has also summarized several core constituting principles of rule of law in its report, which include the principle of 'legality, including a transparent, accountable and democratic process for enacting law'.[69] Indeed, due partly to the benefits of, and the growing global need for, the rule of law, the international community is experiencing a 'transparency turn' in global governance, as there appear to be demands for more transparent institutions and procedures in almost all fields of international law, and such demands are increasingly satisfied.[70]

Up to the present, despite the growing recognition of transparency in global governance, there has been no general international treaty on transparency, and it remains doubtful whether transparency has become a principle under customary international law.[71] Existing international treaties on transparency only focus on a few specific legal fields, such as the

---

[64] See eg Robert McCorquodale, 'Defining the International Rule of Law: Defining Gravity?' (2016) 65 ICLQ 277, 277–78.

[65] Prabhash Ranjan, 'National Contestation of International Investment Law and the International Rule of Law' in Machiko Kanetake and Andre Nollkaemper (eds), *The Rule of Law at the National and International Levels: Contestations and Deference* (Hart 2016) 120.

[66] ILA Committee Report (n 35) 2–3.

[67] See Vasiliki Karageorgou, 'Transparency Principle as an Evolving Principle of EU Law: Regulative Contours and Implications' (2012) <https://www.yumpu.com/en/document/view/22492647/transparency-principle-as-an-evolving-principle-of-eu-law-> accessed 18 November 2022, 4.

[68] UNSC, 'The Rule of Law and Transitional Justice in Conflict and Post-Conflict Societies: Report of the Secretary-General' (23 August 2004) UN Doc S/2004/616, para 6.

[69] See European Commission for Democracy through Law (Venice Commission) 'Report on the Rule of Law: Adopted by the Venice Commission at Its 86th plenary session (Venice, 25–26 March 2011)' (4 April 2011) CDL-AD(2011)003rev, 10.

[70] Anne Peters, 'The Transparency Turn of International Law' (2015) 1 CJGG 3, 4, 14.

[71] ibid 5.

United Nations Convention on Transparency in Treaty-Based Investor-State Arbitration adopted in 2014.[72] As a result, the exact scope of transparency obligations of States can only be ascertained within the context of the relevant provisions of the underlying treaty.

Transparency could have a major impact on investment governance. To market players, transparency plays key governance functions, such as providing foreseeability, accessibility, and legal clarity, facilitating accountability, participation, and democracy, and supporting market effectiveness and efficiency, notably in the financial sector.[73] To State regulators, transparency can contribute to the overall legitimacy of regulatory decisions, without which the decision-making could be easily tweaked so that a cost–benefit analysis supports the option preferred by politicians, regulators, or organized interests.[74]

In the context of investment governance, transparency provisions of various types are incorporated in a growing number of IIAs. Also, claims related to regulatory transparency, ie transparency of government conduct and measures, have been frequently raised by foreign investors in ISA. Despite its increasing appearance in IIAs and ISA practices, transparency as a legal standard is difficult to be uniformly and precisely defined, and its contents and scope remain largely uncertain.[75] Besides, given the fragmentation of IIAs and laws, as well as the ad hoc nature of ISA, there remains a lack of a uniform transparency standard in IIL. In this respect, the ILA Committee has rightly observed that transparency is 'both an essential and an aspirational requirement of the rule of law that is not always easy to meet'.[76]

B. Regulatory Transparency Provisions in IIAs as a Rule-of-Law Requirement

To respond to the growing demand for the rule of law in foreign investment governance, an increasing number of regulatory transparency provisions are incorporated in IIAs. These provisions are not only integrated as an FET requirement, but also aim at playing a helpful role in ensuring the appropriateness of State regulatory acts. This is especially the case in some recent IIAs. In this sense, these provisions are expected to also impose a rule-of-law requirement on States in addition to protecting foreign investment.

A typical example of such regulatory transparency provisions could be found in the Model BIT of the Southern African Development Community (SADC).[77] As held by the drafters of the SADC Model BIT, because an FET clause is highly controversial, and is likely to be expansively interpreted in ISA practice, it is desirable to replace an FET clause with a 'Fair Administrative Treatment' (FAT) clause.[78] The FAT clause of this BIT provides that:

---

[72] United Nations Convention on Transparency in Treaty-based Investor-State Arbitration (opened for signature 10 December 2014, entered into force 18 October 2017) <https://uncitral.un.org/en/texts/arbitration/conventions/transparency> accessed 9 February 2022.

[73] Peters (n 70) 7.

[74] Susan E Dudley and Kai Wegrich, 'The Role of Transparency in Regulatory Governance: Comparing US and EU Regulatory Systems' (2016) 19 Journal of Risk Research 1141, 1143.

[75] KF Gómez, 'Rethinking the Role of *amicus curiae* in International Investment Arbitration: How to Draw the Line Favorably for the Public Interest' (2012) 35 Fordham Intl LJ 513, 528.

[76] ILA Committee Report (n 35) 20.

[77] Southern African Development Community, 'SADC Model Bilateral Investment Treaty Template with Commentary' (July 2012) <www.iisd.org/itn/wp-content/uploads/2012/10/sadc-model-bit-template-final.pdf> accessed 10 February 2022 (hereafter SADC Model BIT (2012)).

[78] ibid 23.

State Parties will progressively strive to improve the transparency, efficiency, independence and accountability of their legislative, regulatory, administrative and judicial processes in accordance with their respective domestic laws and regulations.[79]

In the eyes of the drafters of the SADC Model BIT, while the FAT clause avoids the most controversial elements of FET, it still addresses levels and types of actions by host States towards an investor that should create liability.[80] Here, it is noteworthy that the drafters acknowledged the expansion of regulatory transparency from an investment protection standard to a rule-of-law standard, as they explicitly held that 'some key elements in the approach include changing the focus of the language from investor rights to a focus of governance standards'.[81] In a sense, the inclusion of an FAT clause, instead of an FET clause, in the Model BIT sends out a clear message that SADC members are committed to regulatory transparency as a way to improve the rule of law in investment governance, in addition to investment protection.

Despite its merits and innovativeness, the FAT clause has two insufficiencies. First, the key terms used in this clause, such as 'will' (instead of 'shall'), 'progressively', and 'strive to improve', imply that the clause only creates a best-efforts obligation on the contracting States. This could limit the practical effectiveness of the FAT clause in promoting the rule of law. Second, the FAT clause aims at establishing a requirement of transparent administrative and judicial processes, while the satisfaction of the requirement is to be determined in accordance with the domestic laws and regulations of the contracting States. As SADC members may have quite different domestic laws and regulations, the helpfulness of the FAT clause could be restrained in establishing unified transparency obligations for these members at the regional level.

The Dutch Model BIT 2019 should also be mentioned. This Model BIT is probably one of the very few model IIAs, if not the only one, that incorporates a clause explicitly entitled 'Rule of Law', which includes the element of regulatory transparency. It provides:

1. The Contracting Parties shall guarantee the principles of good administrative behavior, such as consistency, impartiality, independence, openness and transparency, in all issues that relate to the scope and aim of this Agreement.
2. Each Contracting Party shall ensure that investors have access to effective mechanisms of dispute resolution and enforcement, such as judicial, quasi-judicial or administrative tribunals or procedures for the purpose of prompt review, which mechanisms should be fair, impartial, independent, transparent and based on the rule of law.[82]

As can be seen, para 1 of this Article makes clear that the contracting States have an obligation to abide by 'the principles of good administrative behavior', which includes an obligation of transparency. Paragraph 2 could be seen as a continuation of, and supplement to, para 1. In case of dispute, the contracting States should provide effective dispute settlement mechanisms to foreign investors, which should conform to rule-of-law requirements, including transparency.

---

[79] SADC Model BIT (2012), art 5.5, Option 2.
[80] ibid 24.
[81] Ibid.
[82] Dutch Model BIT (2019), art 5.

It should be noted that the Dutch Model BIT greatly enhances States' transparency obligation, since the incorporation of transparency in the standalone rule-of-law clause is in addition to the FET clause (treatment of investor and of covered investments) and a standalone transparency clause.[83] The FET clause in this BIT explicitly provides that a fundamental breach of transparency in judicial and administrative proceedings would constitute a violation of the FET obligation; while the transparency clause in this BIT requires contracting States to promptly publish relevant laws, regulations, and judicial decisions.[84] It seems that, under this Dutch Model BIT, transparency should be deemed as an investment protection requirement under the FET clause, as well as a standard for the administrative acts of the contracting States as embedded in the rule-of-law clause.

The above IIA provisions are limited in number, especially considering that there exist over 3,000 IIAs of various types nowadays.[85] Yet, the integration of transparency obligations as a rule-of-law requirement in some recent IIAs implies a tendency that regulatory transparency not only serves the purpose of investment protection, but also establishes a requirement for State administrative acts.

Such a tendency can also be found at the multilateral level. For instance, in the non-binding G20 Guiding Principles for Global Investment Policymaking adopted during the G20 Meeting in July 2016,[86] world leaders stressed the need for transparency in global investment governance. In this document, transparency is clearly referred to in the following four of the principles:

Principle II: Investment policies should establish open, non-discriminatory, transparent and predictable conditions for investment;

Principle III: ... Dispute settlement procedures should be fair, open and transparent, with appropriate safeguards to prevent abuse;

Principle IV: Regulation relating to investment should be developed in a transparent manner with the opportunity for all stakeholders to participate, and embedded in an institutional framework based on the rule of law; and

Principle VII: Policies for investment promotion should, to maximise economic benefit, be effective and efficient, aimed at attracting and retaining investment, and matched by facilitation efforts that promote transparency and are conducive for investors to establish, conduct and expand their businesses.[87]

As can be seen, the Guiding Principles strongly emphasize regulatory transparency in global investment governance. They require that transparency should be a fundamental element in various policy areas in investment governance, including policymaking, dispute settlement, institution building, and development strategy. For this reason, the Guiding

---

[83] ibid art 4 ('Each Contracting Party shall ensure that its laws, regulations, judicial decisions, procedures and administrative rulings of general application with respect to any matter covered by this Agreement are promptly published or made available in such a manner as to enable interested persons and the other Contracting Party to become acquainted with them. Whenever possible, such instruments will be made available through the internet in English').

[84] ibid arts 9 and 4.

[85] Latest statistics of existing IIAs <https://investmentpolicy.unctad.org/international-investment-agreements> accessed 9 February 2022.

[86] G20 Trade Ministers Meeting Statement (9–10 July 2016, Shanghai) <www.oecd.org/daf/inv/investment-policy/G20-Trade-Ministers-Statement-July-2016.pdf> accessed 9 February 2022.

[87] ibid.

Principles go beyond the traditional construct of IIAs, and are likely to have far-reaching implications, as the international community charts the path towards a new generation of investment policies and IIAs.[88] It is not surprising to see that not only more regulatory transparency provisions will be included in future IIAs and investment policies, but more importantly, they are also likely to be deemed as a rule-of-law requirement in addition to a mere investment protection requirement.

V. Conclusion

Transparency provisions are becoming increasingly popular in IIAs. The majority of these provisions relate to publication of laws and regulations, and participation in investment dispute settlement. While regulatory transparency provisions are not often seen in IIAs, existing ISA practices suggest that regulatory transparency has frequently been held to constitute an investment protection standard explicitly provided for, or impliedly embedded in, FET clauses. More recently, regulatory transparency has also been deemed as a rule-of-law standard that aims at regulating State administrative acts. Such a trend seems to suggest that regulatory transparency is not only a requirement of investment protection, but more importantly, it could also be deemed as a rule-of-law requirement. As indicated by some recent investment policy documents, such as the Guiding Principles, the orientation of regulatory transparency to the rule of law could have profound impact in future IIA-making and investment governance. As such IIAs remain limited in number, it is worth further studying how regulatory transparency would contribute to the rule of law in global investment governance.

---

[88] James Zhan, 'G20 Guiding Principles for Global Investment Policymaking: A Facilitator's Perspective' (2016) <www.e15initiative.org/> accessed 9 February 2022, 7.

PART II

STANDARDS OF TREATMENT AS INTERFACES BETWEEN INTERNATIONAL AND DOMESTIC RULE OF LAW

8

Rule-of-Law Demands and the Domestic Judiciary

Denial of Justice, Judicial Expropriation, Effective Means

Ursula Kriebaum

I. Introduction

Investor State arbitration is increasingly referred to as a system that protects the 'rule of law' for investors but also promotes it generally in the host States.[1] However, there is no uniform understanding among lawyers of what the 'rule of law' means. It can be defined in different ways. Legal documents as well as legal literature do not use the term uniformly.[2] Despite these differences, there is agreement that the judiciary carries an important burden in ensuring that the rule of law prevails.[3] Regular courts were already identified as the proper safeguard for lawful conduct and against arbitrariness by kings in the Magna Carta.[4] The formula 'by the law of the land' found in the Magna Carta has been identified as meaning 'due process of law'.[5]

The courts are the gatekeepers of the rule of law. To be able to fulfil this function, they themselves need to act in accordance with the rule of law. Otherwise, their acts or omissions can lead to violations of international law. Three different areas of investment protection specifically address the domestic judiciary: denial of justice, judicial expropriation, and effective means provisions included in some international investment agreements. This contribution will deal with all three of them.

Unlike human rights treaties, investment protection treaties do not contain explicit rule-of-law demands for host States or 'fair trial clauses' that would provide for a detailed set of guarantees specifying in detail which institutional guarantees national courts have to fulfil and how courts have to administer justice. In their texts on fair trial, human rights treaties contain provisions about minimum institutional guarantees that domestic courts and tribunals must fulfil and specify how these have to administer justice. An example of such a

---

[1] See eg the literature referred to in Thomas Schultz and Cédric Dupont, 'Investment Arbitration: Promoting the Rule of Law or Over-empowering Investors? A Quantitative Empirical Study' (2015) 25 EJIL 1147, 1164.

[2] Brian Z Tamanaha, *On the Rule of Law* (CUP 2004) 114.

[3] See eg André Nollkaemper, *National Courts and the International Rule of Law* (OUP 2011) 1; Helge E Kjos, 'Domestic Courts under Scrutiny: The Rule of Law as a Standard (of Deference) in Investor-State Arbitration' in Machiko Kanetake and André Nollkaemper (eds), *The Rule of Law at the National and International Levels: Contestation and Deference* (Hart 2016) 353.

[4] Tamanaha (n 2) 26.

[5] ibid.

Ursula Kriebaum, *Rule-of-Law Demands and the Domestic Judiciary* In: *Investment Protection Standards and the Rule of Law*. Edited by: August Reinisch and Stephan W. Schill, Oxford University Press. © Ursula Kriebaum 2023.
DOI: 10.1093/oso/9780192864581.003.0008

specific clause is Article 6 of the European Convention on Human Rights (ECHR).[6] It incorporates the rule-of-law aspects relevant for the judiciary.

In addition to specific requirements for courts and tribunals that decide on civil and criminal cases, the European Court of Human Rights (ECtHR) uses the concept of the rule of law directly as a guiding principle in the interpretation of the right to a fair trial. It does so to clarify further requirements in judicial proceedings that are not expressly provided for in the text of the Convention. The Court refers to the concept of the rule of law, for example when stipulating that the right of access to courts is part of the right to a fair trial.[7] The rule of law is very influential not only with regard to judicial safeguards, but also concerning the quality of laws. The Court uses it both in the context of compliance with domestic law and with regard to the quality of national law (ie accessibility, foreseeability, and legal certainty).[8]

In the field of international investment law, traditionally, countries with diverse legal backgrounds that did not trust each other's domestic legal system have concluded investment treaties. Rule-of-law conceptions prevalent in various legal systems differ considerable. They run from 'thin formal' versions of the 'rule by law' to 'thick substantive' versions encompassing social welfare.[9] States parties to investment treaties do not necessarily share the same conception of the 'rule of law'.

Despite this fact and in the absence of a generally agreed definition on the rule of law, the United Nations (UN) Secretary General's 2012 Report 'Delivering Justice: Programme of Action to Strengthen the Rule of Law at the National and International Levels' contains a definition that has gained a certain acceptance on the global level. It defines the rule of law as follows:

> a principle of governance in which all persons, institutions and entities, public and private, including the State itself, are accountable to laws that are publicly promulgated, equally enforced and independently adjudicated, and which are consistent with international human rights norms and standards. It requires, as well, measures to ensure adherence to the principles of supremacy of law, equality before the law, accountability to the law, fairness in the application of the law, separation of powers, participation in decision making, legal certainty, avoidance of arbitrariness and procedural and legal transparency (see S/2004/616).[10]

This definition contains fair trial requirements and demands a certain quality of laws. Some of these elements are of particular relevance for the domestic judiciary in the context of

---

[6] European Convention for the Protection of Human Rights and Fundamental Freedoms (opened for signature 4 November 1950, entered into force 3 September 1953) 213 UNTS 221, art 6(1) ('In the determination of his civil rights and obligations or of any criminal charge against him, everyone is entitled to a fair and public hearing within a reasonable time by an independent and impartial tribunal established by law').

[7] A large number of cases deal with this aspect. See eg *Golder v United Kingdom* App no 4451/70 (ECtHR, 21 February 1975) para 36; *Fayed v United Kingdom* App no 17101/90 (ECtHR, 21 September 1994) para 65; *Bellet v France* App no 23805/94 (ECtHR, 4 December 1995) para 38.

[8] See eg Ursula Kriebaum, 'Rule of Law Notions in Human Rights Law' (2019) 22(3) Z Eu S 369, 380 with further references.

[9] For an overview of these conceptions, see eg Tamanaha (n 2) 91ff; Simon Chesterman, 'An International Rule of Law?' (2008) 56 Am J Comp L 331–61.

[10] UNGA, 'Delivering Justice: Programme of Action to Strengthen the Rule of Law at the National and International Levels, Report of the Secretary General' (16 March 2012) UN Doc A/66/749, para 2.

investment arbitration: The independent adjudication of the laws, consistency with international human rights norms, fairness in the application of the law, avoidance of arbitrariness or discrimination, separation of powers, procedural and legal transparency, as well as laws that are accessible and independently adjudicated.

This chapter addresses the understanding of the actual and potential role of the rule-of-law criteria as a yardstick for investment tribunals when they examine whether measures taken by domestic courts constitute a denial of justice, a judicial expropriation, or a violation of effective means clauses.[11]

When reviewing measures of domestic courts only a few tribunals have relied on the rule of law explicitly in dealing with these three investment protection standards. Furthermore, when relying on the rule of law, investment tribunals have not discussed which of the various conceptions of the rule of law they are relying on. Where they rely on the rule of law, they use it to examine the conduct of the court proceedings rather than for assessing the content and outcome of the national court decisions. In general, there is a heavy burden for an investor to establish that a State has violated one of these standards through its domestic courts.

The chapter will take the criteria developed in the context of the UN, the ECHR, the *Glamis Gold* award,[12] and the *ELSI* judgment[13] as points of reference for its analysis. The

---

[11] For a critique of the variety of standards under which acts of the domestic judiciary can be challenged before investment tribunals, see Mavluda Sattorova, 'Denial of Justice Disguised? Investment Arbitration and the Protection of Foreign Investors from Judicial Misconduct' (2012) 61 ICLQ 223–46. Her critique is principally directed at the internal inconsistency of the finality requirement of denial of justice. She highlights the fact that investors can circumvent the finality requirement of denial of justice by relying on other standards. This contribution will not focus on the issue of the finality requirement in investment law. See on this topic eg James ES Fawcett, 'The Exhaustion of Local Remedies, Substance or Procedure?' (1954) 31 BYIL 452; David R Mummery, 'The Content of the Duty to Exhaust Local Judicial Remedies' (1964) 58 AJIL 389; Stephen M Schwebel and J Gillis Wetter, 'Arbitration and the Exhaustion of Local Remedies' (1966) 60 AJIL 484; AO Adede, 'A Survey of Treaty Provisions on the Rule of Exhaustion of Local Remedies' (1977) 18 Harv Intl LJ 1; Antonio A Cançado Trindade, 'Exhaustion of Local Remedies in International Law Experience Granting Procedural Status to Individuals in the First Half of the Twentieth Century' (1977) 24 NILR 373; Paul Peters, 'Exhaustion of Local Remedies: Ignored in Most Bilateral Investment Treaties' (1997) 44 NILR 233; William S Dodge, '*National Courts and International Arbitration: Exhaustion of Remedies and Res Judicata under Chapter Eleven of NAFTA*' (2000) 23 Hastings Intl & Comp L Rev 357; Andrea K Bjorklund, 'Waiver and the Exhaustion of Local Remedies Rule in NAFTA Jurisprudence' in Todd Weiler (ed), *NAFTA Investment Law and Arbitration: Past Issues Current Practice, Future Prospects* (Transnational 2004) 253; Christopher Greenwood, 'State Responsibility for the Decisions of National Courts' in Malgosia Fitzmaurice and Dan Sarooshi (eds), *Issues of State Responsibility before International Judicial Institutions* (Hart 2004) 55; Bradford K Gathright, 'Comment: A Step in the Wrong Direction: The *Loewen* Finality Requirement and the Local Remedies Rule in NAFTA Chapter Eleven' (2005) 54 Emory LJ 1093; Robert B Love, 'The Local Remedies Issue in Venezuelan Investment Treaty Disputes' (2008) 5 TDM; Ursula Kriebaum, 'Local Remedies and the Standards for the Protection of Foreign Investment' in Christina Binder and others (eds), *International Investment Law for the 21st Century* (OUP 2009) 417; Ole Spiermann, 'Premature Treaty Claims' in Christina Binder and others (eds), *International Investment Law for the 21st Century* (OUP 2009) 463; Bart Legum, 'Local Remedies and Investment Treaties: Policy Choices and Drafting Solutions' in Anne K Hoffmann (ed), *Protection of Foreign Investments through Modern Treaty Arbitration—Diversity and Harmonisation* (Association suisse de l'arbitrage 2010) 34 ASA Special Series 87; Daniel Kalderimis, 'Back to the Future: Contemplating a Return to the Exhaustion Rule' in Anne K Hoffmann (ed), *Protection of Foreign Investments through Modern Treaty Arbitration—Diversity and Harmonisation* (Association suisse de l'arbitrage 2010) 34 ASA Special Series 310; Zachary Douglas, 'International Responsibility for Domestic Adjudication: Denial of Justice Deconstructed' (2014) 63 ICLQ 867; Rudolf Dolzer, 'Local Remedies in International Treaties, A Stocktaking' in David D Caron and others (eds), *Practising Virtue: Inside International Arbitration* (OUP 2015) 280; Ursula Kriebaum, 'Previous Exhaustion of Local Remedies: Investment Arbitration', *Max Planck Encyclopedia of International Procedural Law* (November 2018) <https://opil.ouplaw.com/view/10.1093/law-mpeipro/e3332.013.3332/law-mpeipro-e3332> accessed 20 October 2021.

[12] *Glamis Gold Ltd v United States of America*, UNCITRAL, Award (8 June 2009).

[13] *Elettronica Sicula SpA (ELSI) (United States v Italy)* (Judgment) [1989] ICJ Rep 15, 76, para 128, citing the judgment of the Court in the *Asylum Case (Colombia v Peru)* [1950] ICJ Rep 266, 284, which referred to arbitrary action being 'substituted for the rule of law'.

criteria of the UN are widely accepted and largely overlap with the criteria contained in the ECHR. While one cannot simply transfer the ECtHR's case law to investment arbitration, it nevertheless provides for useful guidance to inform the understanding of what is required by the rule of law. This is especially so as, in substance, due process requirements largely correspond to the customary international law guarantee against denial of justice.[14] Furthermore, the elements of the rule of law mentioned in *ELSI v Italy* and *Glamis Gold v United States* will be used since many of those investment arbitration tribunals that explicitly dealt with rule-of-law issues have frequently referred to them. The following characteristics are mentioned in the parts of *Glamis Gold* and *ELSI* that investment tribunals typically rely on when they refer to these two cases in the context of the 'rule of law':[15]

- sufficiently egregious and shocking/an act which shocks or at least surprises a sense of judicial propriety;
- a gross denial of justice;
- manifest arbitrariness;
- blatant unfairness;
- a complete lack of due process/wilful disregard of due process of law;
- evident discrimination; or
- a manifest lack of reason.

Sections II–IV of the chapter analyse whether and how investment tribunals have made use of these criteria when assessing the existence of a denial of justice, a judicial expropriation, or a violation of the effective means clause. Although many tribunals did not refer to the rule of law explicitly, rule-of-law criteria were often the decisive reference point to assess whether national courts had violated any of the three standards. Section V contains concluding remarks, and suggests that tribunals should make it explicit when they use criteria derived from the rule of law to assess whether any of the three standards has been violated.

---

[14] See eg Clyde Eagleton, 'Denial of Justice in International Law' (1928) 22 AJIL 538, 540; Chalres de Visscher, 'Le déni de justice en droit international' (1935) 52 RdC 365, 397–98; Andrea K Bjorklund, 'Reconciling State Sovereignty and Investor Protection in Denial of Justice Claims' (2005) 45 Va JIL 809, 861f; Jan Paulsson, *Denial of Justice in International Law* (CUP 2005) 204–05; Article 9 Harvard Research Draft on the Law of State Responsibility, cited in Edwin M Borchard, 'The Law of Responsibility of States for Damage Done in Their Territory to the Person or Property of Foreigners' (1929) 23 AJIL Spec Suppl 131, 173; *Waguih Elie George Siag and Clorinda Vecchi v Egypt*, ICSID Case No ARB/05/15, Award (1 June 2009) para 452.

[15] See eg *Mondev International Ltd v United States*, ICSID Case No ARB(AF)/99/2, Final Award (11 October 2002) para 127; *The Loewen Group, Inc and Raymond L. Loewen v United States*, ICSID Case No ARB(AF)/98/3, Final Award (26 June 2003) para 132; *Jan de Nul NV and Dredging International NV v Arab Republic of Egypt*, ICSID Case No ARB/04/13, Award (6 November 2008) paras 192–93; *Chevron Corporation (USA) and Texaco Petroleum Corporation (USA) v Republic of Ecuador I*, PCA Case No AA 277, Partial Award on the Merits (30 March 2010) para 244; *GEA Group Aktiengesellschaft v Ukraine*, ICSID Case No ARB/08/16, Award (31 March 2011) paras 319, 322; *White Industries Australia Limited v Republic of India*, UNCITRAL, Final Award (30 November 2011) para 10.4.23; *Jan Oostergetel and Theodora Laurentius v Slovak Republic*, UNCITRAL, Final Award (23 April 2012) para 291; *Bosh International, Inc and B&P, PTD Foreign Investments Enterprise v Ukraine*, ICSID Case No ARB/08/11, Award (25 October 2012) para 281; *Franck Charles Arif v Republic of Moldova*, ICSID Case No ARB/11/23, Award (8 April 2013) para 447; *OAO Tatneft v Ukraine*, PCA Case No 2008-8, Award on the Merits (29 July 2014) para 475; *Fouad Alghanim & Sons Co for General Trading & Contracting, WLL and Fouad Mohammed Thunyan Alghanim v Hashemite Kingdom of Jordan*, ICSID Case No ARB/13/38, Award (14 December 2017) para 471.

II. Denial of Justice

Denial of justice, like the rule of law, has no clearly defined list of requirements, but is a flexible concept.[16] Jan Paulsson even stated: 'No enumerative approach to defining denial of justice has succeeded in the past, and there are no prospects that one will emerge in the future.'[17]

Denial of justice is originally linked to reprisals in that the former was a condition for the legality of the latter.[18] The modern theory of denial of justice has developed in the context of the law on State responsibility for injuries to aliens. Often, though not always, foreign property was at stake. The scope of the concept was disputed. Some interpreted it broadly and held that also non-judicial wrongs against foreigners were covered. A narrow interpretation focused on judicial injustices such as a lack of access to the court system, the refusal of the right to be heard, or the violation of the right to have a judgment pronounced.[19]

The prohibition of denial of justice was regarded as part of the international minimum standard.[20] In the context of human rights law, this standard crystallized in fair trial norms, such as Article 6 ECHR. This contribution only deals with those aspects of the standard that concern the judiciary directly. To be able to assess whether 'denial of justice' and the 'rule of law' have reference points in common, it is first important to set out the criteria for a denial of justice.

Traditionally, investment protection treaties do not mention denial of justice as such. Treaties therefore do not contain a definition of this standard. More recent treaties,[21] like the CETA, do mention denial of justice. CETA lists it in its Article on FET.[22] It does not, however, include a definition of it. CETA Article 8.10 relates to criminal, civil, and administrative proceedings. As in the *Glamis* list mentioned above,[23] denial of justice is mentioned

---

[16] See eg Bjorklund (n 14) 812.

[17] Paulsson (n 14) 98.

[18] See Hans W Spiegel, 'Origin and Development of Denial of Justice' (1938) 32 AJIL 63, 63ff.

[19] For an overview, see eg Visscher (n 14); Oliver J Lissitzyn, 'The Meaning of the Term Denial of Justice in International Law' (1936) 30 AJIL 632–46; Alwyn V Freeman, *The International Responsibility of States for Denial of Justice* (Longmans, Green and Company 1938).

[20] See Martins Paparinskis, *The International Minimum Standard and Fair and Equitable Treatment* (OUP 2013) 48–54.

[21] The 2004 US Model BIT is an early example of a text containing an explicit reference to denial of justice in its FET provision. Article 5(2)(2) provides:

> 'fair and equitable treatment' includes the obligation not to deny justice in criminal, civil, or administrative adjudicatory proceedings in accordance with the principle of due process embodied in the principal legal systems of the world;

[22] Comprehensive Economic and Trade Agreement (opened for signature 30 October 2016) (CETA) art 8.10: Treatment of Investors and of Covered Investments

> 2. A Party breaches the obligation of fair and equitable treatment referenced in paragraph 1 if a measure or series of measures constitutes:
> (a) denial of justice in criminal, civil or administrative proceedings;
> (b) fundamental breach of due process, including a fundamental breach of transparency, in judicial and administrative proceedings.
> (c) manifest arbitrariness;
> (d) targeted discrimination on manifestly wrongful grounds, such as gender, race or religious belief;
> (e) abusive treatment of investors, such as coercion, duress and harassment; or
> (f) a breach of any further elements of the fair and equitable treatment obligation adopted by the Parties in accordance with paragraph 3 of this Article.

[23] See above nn 12–15 and accompanying text.

in CETA's FET provision side by side with other examples of treatment that would violate the treaty such as fundamental breach of due process or manifest arbitrariness. However, Article 8.10 CETA does not specify what is to be understood by denial of justice.

Furthermore, no coherent test or list of established criteria can be deduced from the case law of investment tribunals. There is nevertheless a number of them that tribunals have resorted to repeatedly to establish whether a denial of justice has occurred, namely bad faith, finality, egregiousness, judicial propriety, and due process.

A. Bad Faith

If bad faith on the part of the authorities is proven in a case,[24] this may trigger a finding of denial of justice. However, bad faith is not a requirement for the establishment of a denial of justice claim as such.[25]

B. Failure of the Court System as a Whole: Finality Rule

It is an important characteristic of denial of justice that it requires a failure of the judicial system as a whole. This has been stated by a number of tribunals[26] and is well established in the literature.[27] The requirement of a failure of the court system as a whole implies compliance with the finality rule. The expression 'finality rule' is to be preferred over 'exhaustion of local remedies' because it is not a matter of jurisdiction or admissibility but a characteristic requirement of the substantive protection standard as has been clearly stated eg in *Flughafen Zürich*.[28]

The finality rule requires that the investor who wants to rely on denial of justice has to make sure that there is no reasonably available further recourse before domestic courts possible. It is not necessary to pursue improbable local remedies but a claimant has to demonstrate that the remedy is futile. Thus, there is an exception to the requirement to make use of all local remedies, although this is construed narrowly: *actual unavailability of a particular remedy, manifestly ineffective remedy*.[29]

---

[24] The tribunal in *Flughafen Zürich* pointed out that a violation of domestic law does not generate a denial of justice unless there is eg bad faith of the judge. *Flughafen Zürich AG and Gestión e Ingenería IDC SA v Bolivarian Republic of Venezuela*, ICSID Case No ARB/10/19, Award (18 November 2014) para 68.

[25] See eg *Loewen* (n 15) para 132.

[26] ibid para 54; *Arif* (n 15) paras. 434, 443; *Corona Materials LLC v Dominican Republic*, ICSID Case No ARB(AF)/14/3, Award (31 May 2016) para 254; *Rupert Joseph Binder v Czech Republic*, UNCITRAL, Final Award (15 July 2011) paras 449, 451; *Flughafen Zürich* (n 24) para 635; *Chevron Corporation and Texaco Petroleum Company v The Republic of Ecuador II*, PCA Case No 2009-23, Second Partial Award (30 August 2018) para 8.40.

[27] See eg Paulsson (n 14) 7.

[28] *Flughafen Zürich* (n 24) paras 391–92; see also eg *Loewen* (n 15) para 154; *Krederi Ltd v Ukraine*, ICSID Case No ARB/14/17, Award (2 July 2018) paras 473–85; see also eg Paulsson (n 14) 107ff. On the issue of exhaustion of local remedies in investment arbitration, see eg Kriebaum, 'Previous Exhaustion of Local Remedies' (n 11) with further references.

[29] See eg *Loewen* (n 15) paras 168–70.

C. Egregiousness or Judicial Propriety

Tribunals found that a State can only be held liable for denial of justice when the court system 'fundamentally failed'.[30] Therefore, an individual procedural shortcoming will often not automatically trigger a denial of justice. As the tribunal in *Vannessa Ventures* pointed out:

> [t]he question is not whether the host State legal system is performing as efficiently as it ideally could: it is whether it is performing so badly as to violate treaty obligations.[31]

Often tribunals use relatively general notions referring to severe shortcomings in judicial proceedings as yardsticks to decide whether a denial of justice has occurred. Some of them contain subjective elements. One of these is 'egregiousness'. Tribunals, ultimately negating the occurrence of a denial of justice, have held that the court decisions they had to assess were not so egregiously wrong as to trigger a denial of justice.[32] The wording they used is not identical, but similar in substance. The tribunal in *Rumeli* stated that the decision was not 'so egregiously wrong as to be inexplicable other than by a denial of justice'.[33] The tribunal in *Unglaube*, relying on Jan Paulsson, required 'a decision so egregiously wrong that no honest or competent court could possibly have given it'.[34] The tribunal in *Binder* found that 'a denial of justice normally relates to egregious procedural impropriety' and explained that a manifest deficiency in the judicial process would trigger a violation of the standard.[35] The tribunal in *Krederi v Ukraine* assessed whether a denial of justice had occurred in four court proceedings. In this context it held that when a domestic judgment is egregiously wrong and not merely erroneous this may amount to a violation of due process in turn triggering a denial of justice.[36]

A number of tribunals took inspiration from the famous quote of the International Court of Justice (ICJ) in the *ELSI* case—'willful disregard of due process of law, an act which shocks, or at least surprises, a sense of judicial propriety'[37]—and used 'judicial propriety' as a yardstick.[38]

---

[30] See eg *RosInvestCo UK Ltd v The Russian Federation*, SCC Case No V079/2005, Final Award (12 September 2010) para 279; *Liman Caspian Oil BV and NCL Dutch Investment BV v Republic of Kazakhstan*, ICSID Case No ARB/07/14, Excerpt of the Award (22 June 2010) para 279.

[31] *Vannessa Ventures Ltd v Bolivarian Republic of Venezuela*, ICSID Case No ARB(AF)04/6, Award (16 January 2013) para 227.

[32] See eg *Philip Morris Brands Sàrl, Philip Morris Products SA and Abal Hermanos SA v Oriental Republic of Uruguay*, ICSID Case No ARB/10/7, Award (8 July 2016) para 579; *OAO Tatneft* (n 15) para 392.

[33] *Rumeli Telekom AS and Telsim Mobil Telekomunikasyon Hizmetleri AS v Republic of Kazakhstan*, ICSID Case No ARB/05/16, Award (29 July 2008) para 619.

[34] *Marion Unglaube v Republic of Costa Rica*, ICSID Case No ARB/08/1, Award (16 May 2012); *Reinhard Hans Unglaube v Republic of Costa Rica*, ICSID Case No ARB/09/20, Award (16 May 2012) para 277 referring to Paulsson (n 14) 98. Similar to the finding in *Arif* (n 15) paras 442, 453.

[35] *Binder* (n 26) para 448.

[36] *Krederi* (n 28) para 449 in connection with para 468.

[37] *ELSI case* (n 13) 76 (para 128), citing the judgment of the Court in the *Asylum Case* (*Colombia v Peru*), ICJ Rep 266, 284, which referred to arbitrary action being 'substituted for the rule of law'.

[38] *Mondev* (n 15) para 127; *Loewen* (n 15) para 132; *Jan de Nul* (n 15) paras 192–93; *Chevron v Ecuador I* (n 15) para 244; *GEA* (n 15) paras 319, 322; *White Industries* (n 15) para 10.4.23; *Jan Oostergetel* (n 15) para 291; *Bosh* (n 15) para 281; *Arif* (n 15) para 447; *OAO Tatneft* (n 15) para 475; *Dan Cake (Portugal) SA v Hungary*, ICSID Case No ARB/12/9, Decision on Jurisdiction and Liability (24 August 2015) para 146; *Alghanim* (n 15) para 471.

D. Lack of Due Process

A number of tribunals mentioned lack of due process[39] as an example of a failure of the judicial system leading to a denial of justice.[40] Among the concrete procedural requirements that tribunals have referred to when assessing whether a denial of justice had occurred are access to justice, duration of proceedings, discrimination, right to be heard, lack of independence or impartiality, no arbitrariness, the right to a reasoned decision, and enforceability.

1. Access to justice

A number of investment tribunals have pointed out that the classical form of a denial of justice is denial of access to courts.[41] The tribunal in *Flughafen Zürich* described this as the most traditional form of denial of justice ('la forma más tradicional y clara de denegación de justicia').[42] However, the facts of the case did not concern a denial of access to the courts.

The tribunal in *Victor Pey Casado,* in finding a denial of justice, referred to the *Azinian* tribunal[43] and its *obiter dictum*, which stated that a refusal to entertain a suit can be a form of denial of justice.[44] In *Victor Pey Casado*, the courts had not issued a decision of first instance for seven years. The case therefore concerned an unreasonable delay rather than a lack of access to the courts.

Dan Cake, one of the rare cases in which a tribunal found that a denial of justice had occurred, concerned a slightly different situation. For finding a denial of justice, it was crucial that the Metropolitan Court of Budapest had denied the investor a composition hearing in bankruptcy proceedings. This would have provided the debtor with the possibility of securing a 'composition agreement' from a sufficient percentage of creditors to avoid liquidation. The Court had denied such a hearing even though the investor had a legal right to it.[45] Therefore, the claimant in this case was not generally denied access to the courts but the organization of a particular hearing that would have been crucial for the survival of the investment was refused. The tribunal found that, in the circumstances of the case, this constituted a denial of justice.

Access to justice concerns not only the existence of a remedy as such, but also its accessibility by the investor and the possibility to achieve redress for the original wrongful act. However, the right is not absolute. The tribunal in *Mondev* did not find a violation of Article 1105(1) NAFTA in a situation where the local law granted State agencies immunity from suit for interference with contractual relations and in this way restricted the right of access to courts. The tribunal found the rationale underlying the immunity to be acceptable:

---

[39]   *Loewen* considers a lack of due process leading to an outcome which offends a sense of judicial propriety as triggering a denial of justice ((n 15) para 132).

[40]   See eg *Liman Caspian Oil* (n 30) para 279; *Arif* (n 15) para 486; *Krederi* (n 28) para 449.

[41]   See eg *Swisslion v Macedonia*, ICSID Case No ARB/09/16, Award (6 June 2012) para 263; *Iberdrola Energy v Guatemala*, ICSID Case No ARB/09/5, Award (17 August 2012) para 432; *Arif* (n 15) para 447; *OAO Taftneft* (n 15) para 351; *Krederi* (n 28) paras 449, 451.

[42]   *Flughafen Zürich* (n 24) paras 638, 680. The same is true for the tribunal in *Krederi v Ukraine* (n 28) para 451.

[43]   *Victor Pey Casado and President Allende Foundation v Chile I*, ICSID Case No ARB/98/2, Award (8 May 2008) para 659.

[44]   *Robert Azinian, Kenneth Davitian & Ellen Baca v Mexico*, ICSID Case No ARB(AF)/97/2, Award (1 November 1999) para 102.

[45]   *Dan Cake* (n 38) paras 145, 146.

> After considering carefully the evidence and argument adduced and the authorities cited by the parties, the tribunal is not persuaded that the extension to a statutory authority of a limited immunity from suit for interference with contractual relations amounts in this case to a breach of Article 1105(1) ... within broad limits, the extent to which a State decides to immunize regulatory authorities from suit for interference with contractual relations is a matter for the competent organs of the State to decide.[46]

The approach chosen by investment tribunals is similar to that of the ECtHR. Relying on the rule of law, the Court held that the right to a fair trial covers access to courts,[47] but also decided that the right is not absolute.[48]

2. Duration of proceedings

Another factor that tribunals took into consideration when confronted with claims of denial of justice was the duration of the domestic proceedings. Tribunals invariably found that undue delays can lead to a denial of justice.[49] To assess whether the duration was justified, tribunals took the complexity of the case and the conduct of the parties,[50] the behaviour of the domestic courts as well as the need for swiftness into account.[51] In *Jan de Nul*, the tribunal decided that ten years for a first instance judgment was unsatisfactory. However, because of the complexity of the case and the number of submissions made by the parties this duration did not amount to a denial of justice.[52]

As mentioned above,[53] the tribunal in *Pey Casado* found that seven years without a decision of first instance on the merits constituted a denial of justice. It specified that significant procedural delays constituted a classic form of denial of justice and referred to the *Azinian* award.[54]

Again, the approach of investment tribunals is quite similar to that of the ECtHR.[55] Article 6 of the ECHR provides for the right to a trial within a reasonable time. Therefore, the Court did not have to rely on the rule of law, but directly referred to the text of Article 6

---

[46] *Mondev* (n 15) para 154.

[47] See eg *Golder* (n 7) para 34; *Fayed* (n 7); *Bellet* (n 7); *Janosevic v Sweden* App no 24619/97 (ECtHR, 23 July 2002) para 80.

[48] See eg *Fayed* (n 7) paras 69–82; *Janosevic* (n 47) para 80.

[49] See eg *Azinian* (n 44) para 102; *Pey Casado Chile I* (n 43) para 659; *Toto Costruzioni Generali SpA v The Republic of Lebanon*, ICSID Case No ARB/07/12, Decision on Jurisdiction (11 September 2009) para 156 (the tribunal referred for this purpose to the *Fabiani* case of the France–Venezuela Claims Commission (Antoine Fabiani no 1 (*France v Venezuela*), Moore, Arbitrations, 4878 at 4895); *Spyridon Roussalis v Romania*, ICSID Case No ARB/06/1, Award (7 December 2011) para 602; *Iberdrola* (n 41) para 432; *OAO Taftneft* (n 15) para 351; *Flughafen Zürich* (n 24) para 638; *OI European Group BV v Venezuela*, ICSID Case No ARB/11/25, Award (10 March 2015) para 525; *Krederi* (n 28) paras 449, 455. The tribunal in *Arif v Moldova* held when examining whether a denial of justice had occurred that the delays of the local proceedings were not excessive ((n 15) para 447). In the same way, the tribunal in *Amto* stated that the court decisions were delivered without undue delay (*Limited Liability Company Amto v Ukraine*, SCC Case No 080/2005, Final Award (26 March 2008) para 80).

[50] See eg *Jan de Nul* (n 15) para 204.

[51] See eg *White Industries* (n 15) paras 10.4.10–10.4.24; *Toto Costruzioni* (n 49) para 163; *Jan Oostergetel* (n 15) para 290.

[52] *Jan de Nul* (n 15) para 204.

[53] See above Section II.D.1.

[54] *Pey Casado v Chile I* (n 43) para 659; *Azinian* (n 44) para 102.

[55] When making its assessment, the Court uses the following four criteria to assess the reasonableness of the length of proceedings: (i) the complexity of the case; (ii) the complainant's conduct; (iii) the conduct of the relevant authorities; and (iv) what is at stake for the complainant. See eg, *Frydlender v France* App no 30979/96 (ECtHR, 27 June 2000) para 43.

when assessing whether due to the duration of proceedings the right to a fair trial had been violated in a particular case.

3. Discrimination

Investment tribunals also mentioned discrimination in court proceedings as being capable of leading to a denial of justice.[56] The *Loewen* tribunal pointed out that it is incumbent on States 'to ensure that litigation is free from discrimination against a foreign litigant and that the foreign litigant should not become the victim of sectional or local prejudice'.[57]

4. Right to be heard

Another violation of due process requirements that led to findings of a denial of justice was failure to hear the investor. This was for example the case in *Flughafen Zürich*.

In that case, the Constitutional Chamber of the Supreme Court of Venezuela de facto transferred the control over an airport to the central government. It did so *sua sponte* without hearing any of the affected stakeholders.[58]

5. Lack of independence or impartiality

Lack of independence and impartiality are also important benchmarks for the existence of a denial of justice. Schwarzenberger had explicitly pointed to the link between the minimum standards of international law, the rule of law, and the requirement to provide for an independent judiciary:

> In particular, the organization of every State must correspond to reasonably defined minimum requirements of the rule of law in the Anglo-Saxon sense or of the Continental *Rechtstaat*. States must, for instance, provide for an independent judiciary.[59]

In *Flughafen Zürich*, the tribunal found that the Constitutional Chamber of the Supreme Court of Venezuela was biased in favour of the government.[60] In a first judgment, the Constitutional Chamber of the Supreme Court removed various claims between the investor and a province from the lower courts, and ordered the provisional transfer of the management of an airport to a specially created oversight board. In a second judgment, the Supreme Court remitted cases back to a lower court for decision but nevertheless transferred the administration of the airport to the central government. The Supreme Court did not base the provisional transfer of control on a valid law. Although the central government's powers in airport matters were not discussed by any of the parties in the proceedings, the Chamber of the Supreme Court had *ultra petita* recognized the authority of the government to adopt measures in connection with the country's airports.[61]

The fact that the Supreme Court acted without the request of any party, without a hearing, without respecting basic due process requirements and without proper legal reasoning or

---

[56] See eg *Jan de Nul* (n 15) para 206; *OAO Tatneft* (n 15) para 351; *Flughafen Zürich* (n 24) para 638.
[57] *Loewen* (n 15) para 123.
[58] *Flughafen Zürich* (n 24) para 695. The tribunal in *Krederi* also lists a violation of the right to be heard as capable of triggering a denial of justice ((n 28) para 449).
[59] Georg Schwarzenberger, 'The Protection of British Property Abroad' (1952) 5 CLP 295, 298.
[60] *Flughafen Zürich* (n 24) para 702.
[61] ibid paras 697–708.

justification for its decision were essential elements in the tribunal's reasoning for its finding of a denial of justice.

For a finding of a denial of justice, the investor itself has to be involved in the court cases where the lack of independence and impartiality has occurred. Inferences of a general lack of independence and impartiality in the judicial system of a country are not enough for a finding of a denial of justice in a particular case.[62]

The tribunal in *Chevron II*, when examining whether a denial of justice had occurred, referred to Judge Fitzmaurice's famous quote concerning possible shortcomings in a judicial procedure that can lead to a denial of justice. Lack of impartiality is one of them. Fitzmaurice wrote:

> the only thing that can establish a denial of justice so far as a judgment is concerned is an affirmative answer, duly supported by evidence, to some such question as 'Was the court guilty of bias, fraud, dishonesty, lack of impartiality, or gross incompetence?'[63]

The *Chevron II* tribunal found that the judge in the domestic Lago Agrio case had acted corruptly in return for a bribe and was far from acting as an independent or impartial judicial organ.[64] It referred to Article 10 of the Universal Declaration of Human Rights which provides: 'Everyone is entitled in full equality to a fair and public hearing by an independent and impartial tribunal, in the determination of his rights and obligations and any criminal charges against him.' Furthermore, the tribunal quoted Article 14 of the ICCPR that enshrines the right to a fair trial under the Covenant as well as Article 2 of the UN Basic Principles on the Independence of the Judiciary adopted by the UN General Assembly in 1985. Both require that judges be impartial.[65] The tribunal decided that party representatives ghost-writing a judgment satisfied the legal test for denial of justice.[66]

As the reference to human rights instruments by the *Chevron II* tribunal in its analysis demonstrates, once again the denial of justice standard shows clear parallels to human rights provisions guaranteeing the right to a fair trial.

6. No arbitrariness: The right to a reasoned decision

The right to a reasoned decision is another core element of the right to a fair trial.[67] It demonstrates that a case has been considered properly. A failure to state reasons is listed as one of the reasons for annulment in Article 52(1) of the ICSID Convention.[68] Annulment has been provided for in the ICSID Convention to secure the legitimacy of the process and not to ensure the correctness of awards.[69] Given this fundamental importance of the duty to state reasons for the integrity of proceedings it is not surprising that investment tribunals when confronted with allegations of denial of justice inquired whether this requirement

---

[62] See eg *Vannessa Ventures* (n 31) para 228; *Swisslion* (n 41) para 268.
[63] *Chevron v Ecuador II* (n 26) para 8.37 referring to Gerald G Fitzmaurice, 'The Meaning of the Term "Denial of Justice"' (1932) 13 BYIL 93, 112–13.
[64] *Chevron v Ecuador II* (n 26) para 8.56.
[65] ibid para 8.57.
[66] ibid para 8.59.
[67] See eg Council of Europe, Consultative Council of European Judges CCEJ (2008), Opinion no 11 on 'the quality of judicial decisions', 18 December 2008.
[68] On this ground for annulment under the ICSID Convention, see eg Stephan W Schill and others (eds), *Schreuer's Commentary on the ICSID Convention* (3rd edn, CUP 2022) 1335f.
[69] ibid 1227.

had been fulfilled in domestic proceedings. *Flughafen Zürich* is an example of a case where a lack of proper reasoning was one element contributing to a finding of a denial of justice.[70]

In a number of cases investment tribunals denied the existence of a denial of justice on the facts and mentioned explicitly that the domestic courts in the cases under consideration had stated reasons for their findings.[71] The tribunal in *Krederi* explicitly mentioned that a domestic court decision made on the basis of manifestly abusive reasoning could amount to a denial of justice.[72] At the same time, the tribunals made clear in that context, that their role was not to act as courts of appeal.[73]

The obligation to state reasons is a protection against arbitrariness. It ensures that the parties understand how a court reached its decision and that it considered the arguments presented. A number of arbitral tribunals have mentioned manifest arbitrariness as a triggering criterion for a denial of justice and some of them alluded to the duty to state reasons.[74]

In exceptional cases, such as in *Al-Warraq*, investment tribunals rely directly on specific elements of the right to a fair trial as guaranteed under human rights instruments, in this case Article 14 ICCPR, to establish the occurrence of a denial of justice.[75] The dispute concerned the bailout of a bank. Indonesian courts found the investor guilty of contributing to the bank's collapse. They convicted him *in absentia* of corruption and money laundering without providing him with a possibility to participate in the criminal proceedings. The tribunal applied Article 14 ICCPR, which guarantees a fair trial in criminal proceedings, and it found that a denial of justice and a violation of the FET standard had occurred. It decided that Article 14 ICCPR was binding upon Indonesia and contained rules that make it possible to decide whether a denial of justice had occurred through a trial *in absentia*. The tribunal found that Mr. Al-Warraq had neither been informed correctly of the accusation nor of his conviction and that he had not been interrogated as a suspect. Furthermore, the tribunal found that he had been deprived of the possibility to nominate a representative for his trial and the appeals proceedings. Therefore, Indonesia had violated discrete guarantees contained in the ICCPR. This amounted to a denial of justice and hence constituted a violation of the FET standard.[76]

7. Enforceability

The tribunal in *Flughafen Zürich* also mentioned non-enforcement by a host State of a favourable judgment obtained by an investor as being capable of triggering a denial of justice.[77] Once more, parallels may be drawn to the ECtHR which requires the enforceability of judgments as a component of the fair trial standard required by the rule of law.[78]

---

[70] *Flughafen Zürich* (n 24) paras 680, 692, 696–99.

[71] See eg *Arif* (n 15) para 453; *Waste Management, Inc v United Mexican States II*, ICSID Case No ARB(AF)/00/3, Award (30 April 2004) para 130.

[72] *Krederi* (n 28) para 523.

[73] See eg *Iberdrola* (n 41) paras 491–93; *Krederi* (n 28) para 486.

[74] See eg *Azinian* (n 44) para 103; *Waste Management v Mexico II* (n 71) para 130 (decisions were reasoned); *Rumeli* (n 33) para 653; *OAO Tatneft* (n 15) para 475; *Flughafen Zürich* (n 24) para 680; *Iberdrola* (n 41) paras 432, 504; *Alghanim* (n 15) para 356.

[75] *Hesham TM Al-Warraq v Republic of Indonesia*, UNCITRAL, Final Award (15 December 2014) paras 556–621.

[76] ibid para 621.

[77] *Flughafen Zürich* (n 24) para 638.

[78] See eg *Hornsby v Greece* App no 18357/91 (ECtHR, 19 March 1997) 509 para 40; *Iatridis v Greece* App no 31107/96 (ECtHR, 25 March 1999) para 58; *Immobiliare Saffi v Italy* App no 22774/93 (ECtHR, 28 July 1999) para 66; *Hasan and Chaush v Bulgaria* App no 30985/96 (ECtHR, 26 October 2000) para 87.

E. Conclusions

In sum, the criteria that tribunals have used to assess in an individual case whether a denial of justice has occurred correspond with the list of criteria taken from *Glamis* and *ELSI*.
Furthermore, the criteria also coincide with the criteria found in human rights treaties on
fair trial and the case law of the ECtHR on this issue. Access to a court, availability of remedies, due process in the sense of an impartial and independent court, and no undue delays
also figure prominently in the case law of investment tribunals.

Tribunals found that egregious breaches of fair trial, as for example those committed by
the corrupt judge who was neither independent nor impartial in the *Chevron* case, constitute at the same time a denial of justice. However, the case law concerning institutional
requirements is far less differentiated in investment law than in human rights law. For instance, no exact requirements as to how a national court system should be set up to ensure independence and impartiality have been formulated so far in investment awards. This
might be due to the fact that investment tribunals have not nearly had as many occasions to
deal with malfunctioning court systems as the ECtHR.

Findings of a denial of justice indicate a problem of the judicial system. If this problem
of the judicial system turns into a systemic failure, ie if it does not just occur in a single case,
the rule of law is endangered. The rule of law is about guaranteeing a system with certain
minimum standards not necessarily to achieve a particular outcome in each and every case,
but to make sure that overall a functioning judicial system guaranteeing certain minimum
standards is available. Findings of denial of justice are an indicator that the rule of law in a
country is at risk. Given the high threshold for a violation, it is no surprise that findings of
denial of justice are rare.

III. Judicial Expropriation

Judicial interferences with property rights raise similar problems as regulatory interferences with investments.[79] The challenge lies in drawing the line between expropriatory judicial decisions that require compensation and judicial decisions that have consequences
for property rights but do not require compensation.

Expropriation is not prohibited under international law but is subject to certain conditions. Investment protection treaties require that expropriations must be for a public purpose, must be non-discriminatory, must be in accordance with due process of law and must
be accompanied by adequate compensation.[80] Treaties for the protection of investments
typically contain provisions on expropriation that include direct as well as indirect expropriations, measures having equivalent effect, or measures tantamount to expropriation.[81]

---

[79] On the topic, see eg Mavluda Sattorova, 'Judicial Expropriation or Denial of Justice? A Note on *Saipem
v. Bangladesh*' (2010) 2 Intl ALR 35; Alexis Mourre, 'Expropriation by Courts: Is It Expropriation or Denial of
Justice?' in Arthur W Rovine (ed), *Contemporary Issues in International Arbitration and Mediation: The Fordham
Papers 2011* (Martinus Nijhoff 2012) 60; Sattorova (n 11); Hamid G Gharavi, 'Discord over Judicial Expropriation'
(2018) 33 ICSID Rev—FILJ 349; Sara Mansour Fallah, 'Drawing the Line between Adjudication and Expropriation'
(2019) 2 TDM; Johanne M Cox, *Expropriation in Investment Treaty Arbitration* (OUP 2019) 238.
[80] See eg Ursula Kriebaum, 'Expropriation' in Marc Bungenberg and others (eds), *International Investment Law*
(Hart 2015) 959 with further references.
[81] Rudolf Dolzer and Margarete Stevens, *Bilateral Investment Treaties* (Martinus Nijhoff 1995) 99.

Most treaties do not go beyond a broad generic reference to indirect expropriation or measures equivalent or tantamount to expropriation. The reason is the great variety of possible measures amounting to an indirect or de facto taking of foreign-owned property, which defies a more specific description.[82] The 2004 and 2012 Model BITs of the US and the 2004 Model BIT of Canada[83] as well as BITs and investment chapters in FTAs concluded by these two countries in recent years and treaties negotiated by the EU point to a new direction. They specify the criteria for the existence of an indirect expropriation in their annexes. The clauses in these annexes state that regulatory interferences are generally not to be regarded as expropriations. There is rich international judicial practice dealing with indirect expropriation, measures having equivalent effect, and measures tantamount to expropriation. That practice demonstrates that international courts and tribunals have held a large variety of measures to amount to indirect expropriations. The common feature of all these instances of indirect expropriation is that the investor has suffered a substantial deprivation of the economic benefits of its investment while retaining formal title to it.

Therefore, the investor need not be deprived of its title but the interference must have the effect of depriving the investor in whole or in significant part of the economic benefit of its investment.[84]

Most of the proprietary interests that can be affected by court decisions—such as property *in rem*, shares, contractual rights, concessions, and other rights granted under public law, intellectual property rights, and other claims to money in the context of an investment—may at the same time constitute investments under an investment protection treaty.[85] Court

---

[82] ibid (fn omitted); UNCTAD, *Series on Issues in International Investment Agreements: Taking of Property* (United Nations Publications 2000) 41.

[83] Agreement between Canada and ... for the Promotion and Protection of Investments—Foreign Investment Promotion and Protection Agreements (FIPA):

Article 13 Expropriation
1. Neither Party shall nationalize or expropriate a covered investment either directly, or indirectly through measures having an effect equivalent to nationalization or expropriation (hereinafter referred to as 'expropriation'), except for ...

Annex B.13(1) Expropriation
The Parties confirm their shared understanding that

a) Indirect expropriation results from a measure or series of measures of a Party that have an effect equivalent to direct expropriation without formal transfer of title or outright seizure;
b) The determination of whether a measure or series of measures of a Party constitute an indirect expropriation requires a case-by-case, fact-based inquiry that considers, among other factors:
   i) the economic impact of the measure or series of measures, although the sole fact that a measure or series of measures of a Party has an adverse effect on the economic value of an investment does not establish that an indirect expropriation has occurred;
   ii) the extent to which the measure or series of measures interfere with distinct, reasonable investment-backed expectations; and
   iii) the character of the measure or series of measures;
c) Except in rare circumstances, such as when a measure or series of measures are so severe in the light of their purpose that they cannot be reasonably viewed as having been adopted and applied in good faith, non-discriminatory measures of a Party that are designed and applied to protect legitimate public welfare objectives, such as health, safety and the environment, do not constitute indirect expropriation.
(<www.dfait-maeci.gc.ca/tna-nac/documents/2004-FIPA-model-en.pdf> accessed 20 October 2021)

[84] See eg *Metalclad Corporation v Mexico*, ICSID Case No ARB(AF)/97/1, Award (30 August 2000) para 103. For a list of the different formulas applied, see Kriebaum (n 80) 984ff.

[85] See eg Christoph Schreuer and Ursula Kriebaum, 'The Concept of Property in Human Rights Law and International Investment Law' in Stephan Breitenmoser and others (eds), *Liber Amicorum Luzius Wildhaber, Human Rights Democracy and the Rule of Law* (Dike 2007) 743–62.

decisions in administrative proceedings can deprive an investor for example of a conces-sion. Even civil proceedings between private parties can have an 'expropriatory effect' where a court awards the proprietary interest to one party and deprives the other party of it.

In the context of judicial measures there will often be no transfer of title to the State. But this transfer is not a requirement for an expropriation.[86] Therefore, judicial decisions can potentially lead to direct and indirect expropriations.[87] However, many of the judicial de-cisions leading to such outcomes will be legitimate judicial decisions. What is therefore ne-cessary is a distinction between legitimate judicial decisions having an expropriatory effect that do not require compensation and judicial measures that require compensation.

One method to assess whether an indirect expropriation has occurred is the 'sole effects' doctrine.[88] Judicial measures may have the effect that the losing party is deprived in whole or in substantial part of the property constituting the protected asset under the investment protection treaty. Thus, no matter how justified the court action was, this criterion would lead to the existence of an expropriation as long as the measure brought about a substantial deprivation of the asset in question. Hence, the State would have to pay compensation.

However, normally the State would not be responsible for compensating a losing party for a court judgment rendered in a fair proceeding. Therefore, the classical 'sole effects doc-trine' reaches its limits with court judgments.

This has become apparent in a number of cases.[89] The tribunal in *Saipem* recognized this problem, when it stated:

> That said, given the very peculiar circumstances of the present interference, the Tribunal agrees with the parties that the substantial deprivation of Saipem's ability to enjoy the benefits of the ICC Award is not sufficient to conclude that the Bangladeshi courts' intervention is tantamount to an expropriation. If this were true, any setting aside of an award could then found a claim for expropriation, even if the setting aside was ordered by the competent state court upon legitimate grounds.[90]

Therefore, the tribunal inquired whether the disputed court actions were illegal.[91] It held the actions of the Bangladeshi courts to be contrary to international law and found that an expropriation had occurred.[92]

---

[86] Ursula Kriebaum, *Eigentumsschutz im Völkerrecht* (Dunker & Humblot 2008) 416–21; *Tippetts, Abbett, McCarthy, Stratton v TAMS-AFFA Consulting Engineers of Iran*, Award No 141-7-2, 29 June 1984, 6 IUSCTR 219, 225, 226; *Amco Asia Corporation and ors v Republic of Indonesia*, Award (20 November 1984) 1 ICSID Reports 413, para 158; *Southern Pacific Properties (Middle East) Limited (SPP) v Arab Republic of Egypt*, ICSID Case No ARB/84/3 (National Law), Award (20 May 1992) para 163; *Wena Hotels Ltd v Arab Republic of Egypt*, ICSID Case No ARB/98/4 (United Kingdom–Egypt BIT), Award (8 December 2000) para 97; *Metalclad Mexico* (n 84) para 103; *CME v The Czech Republic*, Partial Award (13 September 2001) para 606; *Técnicas Medioambientales Tecmed, SA v United Mexican States*, ICSID Case No ARB(AF)/00/2 (Spain–Mexico BIT), Award (29 May 2003) para 113; *Rumeli* (n 33) para 707; *Sistem Mühendislik İnşaat Sanayi ve Ticaret A. v Kyrgyz Republic*, ICSID Case No ARB(AF)/06/1, Award (9 September 2009) para 118.

[87] See eg *Eli Lilly and Company v The Government of Canada*, UNCITRAL, ICSID Case No UNCT/14/2, Final Award (16 March 2017) para 221.

[88] See eg Rudolf Dolzer, 'Indirect Expropriations: New Developments?' (2003) 11 NYU Env L J 65, 65, 79, 80.

[89] For an overview of many of the cases, see Mansour Fallah (n 79); Cox (n 79).

[90] *Saipem SpA v People's Republic of Bangladesh*, ICSID Case No ARB/05/07, Award (30 June 2009) para 133.

[91] ibid paras 133–70.

[92] ibid paras 170, 214.

Similarly, the tribunal in *Swisslion* found that no expropriation had occurred although the rights of the investor had been terminated by a court decision:

> The internationally lawful termination of a contract between a State entity and an investor cannot be equated to an expropriation of contractual rights simply because the investor's rights have been terminated; otherwise, a State could not exercise the ordinary right of a contractual party to allege that its counterparty breached the contract without the State's being found to be in breach of its international obligations. Since there was no illegality on the part of the courts, the first element of the Claimant's expropriation claim is not established.[93]

What tribunals were looking for was an element of illegality to distinguish judicial expropriations that required compensation from court decisions that had an expropriatory effect but did not require compensation. Courts were not always at the origin of the illegal act but sometimes validated interferences that were the result of improper actions of other State organs.[94] In such cases the judicial conduct was part of the expropriation analysis but tribunals did not require proof of illegal conduct on the part of the court itself.

To decide whether court action or inaction having an expropriatory effect qualified as expropriations tribunals either required the existence of a denial of justice[95] or mentioned several potential illegal acts that would, standing alone or in combination, lead to a compensable judicial expropriation. These additional criteria consist of due process violations, arbitrariness, discrimination, violations of domestic or international law, collusion, and egregiousness.

A. Due Process Violations

One of these criteria is due process of law. Although this is one of the criteria to distinguish between illegal and legal expropriations, here it becomes a criterion to decide whether there was an expropriation at all. The tribunal in *Middle East Cement* is an example of this approach. The tribunal stated:

> though, normally a seizure and auction ordered by the national courts do not qualify as a taking, they can be 'a measure the effects of which would be tantamount to expropriation' if they are not taken 'under due process of law'.[96]

The tribunal found this to be the case and decided that an expropriation had occurred.[97]

The tribunal in *Ares* endorsed this approach explicitly, but denied the occurrence of an expropriation on the facts.[98]

---

[93] *Swisslion* (n 41) para 314.
[94] See eg *Rumeli* (n 33) discussed below in Section E.
[95] See eg *Ares International Srl and MetalGeo Srl v Georgia*, ICSID Case No ARB/05/23, Award (26 February 2008) paras 8.3.5–8.3.6; *Arif* (n 15) para 415; *MNSS BV and Recupero Credito Acciaio NV v Montenegro*, ICSID Case No ARB(AF)/12/8, Award (4 May 2016) para 370.
[96] *Middle East Cement Shipping and Handling Co SA v Arab Republic of Egypt*, ICSID Case No ARB/99/6, Award (12 April 2002) para 139.
[97] ibid para 143.
[98] *Ares* (n 95) para 8.3.7.

B. Arbitrariness

In *Liman Caspian Oil v Kazakhstan*, the tribunal relied on a number of criteria that were also used in denial of justice cases to evaluate whether an expropriation had occurred. The tribunal held that the court's decisions were not 'arbitrary, grossly unfair, unjust, idiosyncratic, discriminatory or lacking due process' and hence one could not conclude that a transfer of rights was wrongfully annulled.[99] Therefore, no expropriation had occurred.

One of these criteria, arbitrariness, also played a role in the assessment of other cases.[100] The tribunal in *Karkey v Pakistan* decided that an arbitrary Supreme Court judgment that had declared an investor's power generation contract to be *void ab initio* had expropriated the investment.[101]

The tribunal in *Eli Lilly* explicitly stated that the decisions of the Canadian courts were neither arbitrary nor discriminatory nor expropriatory.[102] It used the criteria of arbitrariness and discrimination to assess not only whether a violation of the international minimum standard under NAFTA had been violated but also whether an expropriation had occurred.[103] Concerning the standard of arbitrariness, the tribunal discussed the criteria of unpredictability, inconsistency, and incoherence of the national case law identified by claimant as controlling without deciding whether it subscribed to them.[104] The ECtHR typically refers to these criteria when it examines the compatibility of laws with the rule of law. Notably, they have to be accessible, precise, and foreseeable in their application.[105]

C. Discrimination

Discrimination is another indicator used by tribunals often in combination with other factors when deciding whether court decisions where expropriatory. The tribunal in *Liman* only referred to discrimination as one of a number of factors to identify whether an expropriation had occurred.[106] The same is true for the award in *Schooner*.[107] Without explicitly stating that unfair proceedings would have led to a finding of an expropriation, the tribunal in *Anglia Auto* mentioned that the claimant could not complain about 'arbitrary, discriminatory and unreasonable' conduct by the national courts or a sweeping refusal to act of the courts.[108]

---

[99]   *Liman Caspian Oil* (n 30) para 431.
[100]   See eg *Vincent J Ryan, Schooner Capital LLC, and Atlantic Investment Partners LLC v Republic of Poland*, ICSID Case No ARB(AF)/11/3, Award (24 November 2015) para 495; *Anglia Auto Accessories Ltd v Czech Republic*, SCC Case No V 2014/181, Award (10 March 2017) para 301.
[101]   *Karkey Karadeniz Elektrik Uretim AS v Islamic Republic of Pakistan*, ICSID Case No ARB/13/1, Award (22 August 2017) paras 645–50.
[102]   *Eli Lilly* (n 87) para 418.
[103]   ibid paras 420–30, 442.
[104]   ibid paras 420–30.
[105]   See eg *Del Rio Prada v Spain* App no 42750/09 (ECtHR, 21 October 2013) para 125.
[106]   *Liman Caspian Oil* (n 30) para 431.
[107]   *Schooner* (n 100) para 495.
[108]   *Anglia Auto* (n 100) para 301.

D. Violations of Domestic or International Law

Illegalities stemming from mere errors in the application of domestic law did, in principle, not lead to findings of a judicial expropriation.[109] On the other hand, violations of international law have led to findings of an expropriation. The tribunals in *Saipem* and *ATA* found that a breach of the NY Convention for the Recognition and Enforcement of Foreign Arbitral Awards had occurred.[110] The tribunal in *Saipem* furthermore pointed out that the Bangladeshi courts had committed an 'abuse of right', since the Bangladesh courts abused supervisory functions:

> The revocation of an arbitrator's authority can legitimately be ordered in the case of a misconduct ... However, they cannot use their jurisdiction to revoke arbitrators for reasons wholly unrelated with such misconduct ... the standard for revocation used by the Bangladesh courts and the manner in which the judge applied that standard to the facts indeed constituted an abuse of right.[111]

In light of these findings the tribunal in *Saipem* concluded that the actions of the Bangladeshi courts were contrary to international law[112] and found that an expropriation had occurred.[113]

In *ATA v Jordan*, the tribunal found that a Jordanian court had unlawfully extinguished an arbitration clause contained in a construction contract. It held that the right to arbitrate, which it found to be a distinct investment, was not annulled with the enactment of the new Jordanian Arbitration Law, but upon the decision of the Jordanian Court of Cassation which applied it retroactively.[114] It is, however, not entirely clear which standard of the BIT had been violated since the tribunal found that the 'extinguishment of the Claimant's right to arbitration by the Jordanian Courts thus violated both the letter and the spirit of the Turkey–Jordan BIT'.[115] The tribunal referred to FET in the preamble of the BIT and in a footnote of the award to an MFN clause whereby the claimant had imported FET protection from two other BITs.[116] However, it also used the word 'extinguishment' of a right that qualified as an investment[117] several times. This would signal the occurrence of an expropriation.

---

[109] *Liman Caspian Oil* (n 30) para 431 (even if they—Kazakh court decision—might have been incorrect as a matter of Kazakh law); *Schooner* (n 100) para 491 (not for this tribunal to rule on the correctness of those decisions as a matter of Polish law); *Mohammad Ammar Al-Bahloul v The Republic of Tajikistan*, SCC Case No 064/2008, Partial Award (2 September 2009) para 284 (does not find the Court's position to be manifestly in contradiction with the Tajik legislation).

[110] *Saipem* (n 90) para 167; *ATA Construction, Industrial and Trading Company v The Hashemite Kingdom of Jordan*, ICSID Case No ARB/08/2, Award (18 May 2010) para 128.

[111] *Saipem* (n 90) para 159.

[112] ibid para 170.

[113] ibid para 214.

[114] *ATA Construction* (n 110) paras 116–20, 124–28.

[115] ibid para 125.

[116] ibid.

[117] ibid paras 116, 125.

E. Collusion

Tribunals also inquired in their decisions on judicial expropriation whether there was collusion between the local courts and either State organs or competitors[118] or between one party in the court proceedings and a State organ.[119]

Rumeli Telekom is an example of such a case. It concerned a court-ordered transfer of property rights to a third party. The tribunal relied on criteria that distinguish legal from illegal expropriations to decide whether an expropriation had occurred. It was satisfied that the Kazakh Supreme Court's decision affirming the compulsory redemption of shares held by the investor was made 'for a public purpose' and that there was no evidence that it was not made 'in accordance with due process of law'.[120]

However, it found that a creeping expropriation had occurred because of collusion of the claimant's local partner and Kazakhstan's Investment Committee that led to the court proceedings and the court's grossly inadequate decision on compensation.[121] It was important for the tribunal that the court proceedings were instigated by the State.[122]

F. Egregiousness as Standard of Review

The tribunal in *GEA* used 'egregiousness' as a standard of review when it examined whether the refusal to enforce an ICC award was tantamount to an expropriation. The tribunal considered in the first place that the ICC award was no investment and the examination of a potential expropriation is therefore an *obiter dictum*.[123] It would have denied the existence of an expropriation even if it found that an investment had existed since:

> the Tribunal has been presented with no evidence that the actions taken by the Ukrainian courts were 'egregious' in any way; that they amounted to anything other than the application of Ukrainian law; or that they were somehow deliberately taken to thwart GEA's ability to recover on the ICC Award.[124]

G. Conclusion

As in the case of denial of justice, the criteria that tribunals have used to assess whether a judicial expropriation had occurred correspond partially with those in the list of rule-of-law requirements taken from *Glamis* and *ELSI* as well as some of the criteria applied by the ECtHR:[125] no egregious court decisions, respect of due process, no arbitrariness and

---

[118] See eg *Arif* (n 15) para 415; *Saipem* (n 90) paras 147–48.
[119] *Rumeli Telekom* (n 33).
[120] ibid para 705.
[121] ibid paras 706, 708.
[122] ibid para 704.
[123] *GEA* (n 15) para 231.
[124] ibid para 236.
[125] See above n 15 and accompanying text.

no discrimination, no collusion of the courts that would lead to a lack of independence or impartiality.

From a conceptual perspective, these typical rule-of-law requirements are appropriate benchmarks for a decision on whether a judicial expropriation has occurred in situations where an investor has de facto lost the control of property because of a court decision. This is true for both situations where the existence of a property right hinges on the legality of the actions of local courts as well as for situations where deprivations of existing assets are at stake. The *Saipem* case illustrates the first situation, the *Swisslion* case the second.[126] In *Saipem*, there would have been no property to expropriate had the domestic court's actions not been illegal.[127] Therefore, rule-of-law criteria used to assess the domestic court proceedings are also used to establish whether there was an investment in the first place that could have been expropriated.

In the second illustrative example, *Swisslion*,[128] there was no question that a contractual right existed in the first place. The question was whether the court decision that determined that the other party had a right to terminate the contract led to an expropriation. In this situation the domestic court proceeding violating the rule of law led to the loss of propri-etary rights that otherwise would not have been lost and is therefore expropriatory in char-acter.[129] This would not have been the case, had the rule-of-law standards been respected in these domestic proceedings.

Therefore, rule-of-law standards provide useful criteria for deciding in both situations whether a judicial expropriation has occurred. Like the case law on denial of justice, the case law on judicial expropriation does not develop criteria on how the domestic courts would have to be organized institutionally to respect the rule-of-law requirements.

IV. Effective Means for Asserting Claims and Enforcing Rights

The third standard, the obligation to provide a system of adequate judicial protection for asserting claims and enforcing rights, is often called 'effective means' standard.[130] Clauses providing for this type of protection are not very common in investment protection treaties. They have been included predominantly in US BITs, the Energy Charter Treaty (ECT) and some other BITs.[131] Article 10(12) of the ECT provides in this regard:

---

[126] See above nn 90–93 and accompanying text.

[127] See Vid Prislan, 'Domestic Courts in Investor-State Arbitration, Partners, Suspects, Competitors' (PhD thesis, Leiden University 2019) 263.

[128] See *Swisslion* (n 41) para 314.

[129] See Prislan (n 127) 262.

[130] On this standard, see eg Oscar M Garibaldi, 'Effective Means to Assert Claims and Enforce Rights' in Meg Kinnear and others (eds), *Building International Investment Law: The First 50 Years of ICISD* (Wolters Kluwer 2015) 359; Annelise P Karreman and Kanaga Dharmananda, 'Time to Reassess Remedies for Delays Breaching "Effective Means"' (2015) 30 ICSID Rev—FILJ 118.

[131] See eg US Model BIT (1994) art II(4); Egypt–United States BIT (1986) and Protocol, art II(7); Poland–United States BIT (1990) and Protocol, art II(7); Turkey–United States BIT (1985) and Protocol, art II(8); Sri Lanka–United States BIT (1991) and Protocol, art II(6); Romania–United States BIT (1992) and Protocol, art II(6); Moldova–United States BIT (1993) and Protocol, art II(6); Kazakhstan–United States BIT (1992), art II (6); Estonia–United States BIT (1994), art II(7); Czech and Slovak Federal Republic (Czech Republic and Slovak Republic)–United States BIT (1991) and Protocol, art II(6); Bahrain–United States of America BIT (1999) art 2(4); US–Viet Nam Trade Relations Agreement (2000) art 4(1); Czech Republic–United Arab Emirates BIT (1994) art 2(10); Protocol, 2 (d), Italy–Lithuania BIT (1994) and Protocol; Algeria–Finland BIT (2005) art 2(3); Kazakhstan–Sweden BIT (2004) art 2(5); Republic of Korea–Kuwait BIT (2004) art 2(8); Ukraine–United Arab Emirates BIT (2003) art 2(10).

(12) Each Contracting Party shall ensure that its domestic law provides effective means for the assertion of claims and the enforcement of rights with respect to Investments, investment agreements, and investment authorizations.

The formulation of the treaty standard is different from the classical denial of justice standard. Rather than merely providing that justice must not be done in such a bad way that an outside observer is shocked or at least surprised,[132] it imposes a positive obligation on the State to provide an effective judicial remedy.[133] In that way, it is similar to human rights treaty clauses providing for a right to an effective remedy for human rights violations in addition to the guarantee of a fair trial in civil and criminal matters.[134]

It is remarkable that Vandevelde, the former chief negotiator of the US treaties, explained that the effective means standard was introduced into BITs in 1983 to address a lack of clarity in customary international law. The uncertainty concerned the content of the right of access to courts being part of the denial of justice standard.[135] Therefore, the United States included the effective means standard in their treaties to clarify the not sufficiently precise customary international law standard of denial of justice by a more precise treaty standard.[136] The United States deleted the judicial access provision from the substantive provisions of their Model BIT in 2004. They shifted it to the preamble since by then it had become clear that the substantive standards in the BITs prohibiting denial of justice provided adequate protection.[137]

---

[132] *ELSI case* (n 13) 76, para 128; *Chevron v Ecuador I* (n 15) para 244. See also the references above in n 38.

[133] *Chevron v Ecuador I* (n 15) para 248.

[134] See eg International Covenant on Civil and Political Rights (opened for signature 16 December 1966, entered into force 23 March 1976) 999 UNTS 171 (ICCPR) art 2(3):

> Each State Party to the present Covenant undertakes: (a) To ensure that any person whose rights or freedoms as herein recognized are violated shall have an effective remedy, notwithstanding that the violation has been committed by persons acting in an official capacity; (b) To ensure that any person claiming such a remedy shall have his right thereto determined by competent judicial, administrative or legislative authorities, or by any other competent authority provided for by the legal system of the State, and to develop the possibilities of judicial remedy; (c) To ensure that the competent authorities shall enforce such remedies when granted.

European Convention on Human Rights, art 13: 'Everyone whose rights and freedoms as set forth in [the] Convention are violated shall have an effective remedy before a national authority notwithstanding that the violation has been committed by persons acting in an official capacity'; American Convention on Human Rights, art 25:

> 1. Everyone has the right to simple and prompt recourse, or any other effective recourse, to a competent court or tribunal for protection against acts that violate his fundamental rights recognized by the constitution or laws of the state concerned or by this Convention, even though such violation may have been committed by persons acting in the course of their official duties.
> 2. The States Parties undertake:
>   a. to ensure that any person claiming such remedy shall have his rights determined by the competent authority provided for by the legal system of the state;
>   b. to develop the possibilities of judicial remedy; and
>   c. to ensure that the competent authorities shall enforce such remedies when granted.

African Charter on Human and Peoples' Rights, art 7(1): 'Every individual shall have the right to have his cause heard. This comprises: (a) The right to an appeal to competent national organs against acts of violating his fundamental rights as recognised and guaranteed by conventions, laws, regulations and customs in force.'

[135] Kenneth J Vandevelde, *U.S. International Investment Agreements* (OUP 2009) 411: 'Although customary international law guarantees an alien the right of access to the courts of the host state, disagreement among publicists concerning the content of the right prompted to United States to seek treaty protection.'

[136] Garibaldi (n 130) 359–74, 373.

[137] Vandevelde (n 135) 415.

The relative paucity of treaties containing a separate clause addressing adequate judicial protection for asserting claims and enforcing rights might be the explanation for the fact that there are fewer than a dozen cases dealing with such a provision.[138]

A first part deals with awards that explicitly linked the effective means standard to the rule of law. A second part discusses the relationship between the prohibition of a denial of justice and the effective means standard.

A. Explicit Link of the Effective Means Standard to the Rule of Law

A number of tribunals explicitly linked the effective means standard to the rule of law. Only certain of them elaborated on criteria for this standard. The first case that addressed an effective means provision was *Petrobart*.[139] The tribunal did not enter into an analysis of the standard. However, it explicitly referred to the rule of law when assessing the legal consequences of the interference of the vice prime minister in judicial proceedings concerning the stay of execution of a final judgment that the claimant had won. The tribunal found interference by the executive with court proceedings to be incompatible with the rule of law in a democratic society. Without an analysis of the requirements of the two standards, it stated that Kyrgyzstan had violated the FET standard (art 10(2) ECT) as well as the effective means guarantee (art 10(12) ECT) as a consequence of the interference.[140]

In *Amto*, the investor claimed that legislative acts adopted during bankruptcy proceedings had influenced the outcome of the proceedings and that the respondent had failed to provide the investor with effective means by which to assert its legitimate claims. The tribunal found that the 'effective means standard' in Article 10(12) of the ECT established a specific requirement for the legislator to provide for effective means to assert claims and enforce rights. Legislative failures affecting these rights could be measured against this standard:

> In Article 10(12) of the ECT there is a specific obligation to ensure that domestic law provides an effective means for the assertion of claims and the enforcement of rights. Legislative failures affecting the administration of justice in cases under the ECT can therefore be measured against the express standard established by Article 10(12).[141]

Like the tribunal in *Petrobart*, the *Amto* tribunal linked the 'effective means standard' expressly to the rule of law:

---

[138] See eg *Petrobart Limited v Kyrgyzstan*, SCC Case No 126/2003, Arbitral Award (29 March 2005); *Amto* (n 49); *Duke Energy Electroquil Partners and Electroquil SA v Republic of Ecuador*, ICSID Case No ARB/04/19, Award (18 August 2008); *Chevron v Ecuador I* (n 15); *White Industries* (n 15); *H&H Enterprises v Egypt*, ICSID Case No ARB 09/15, Excerpts of Award (6 May 2014); *Apotex Holdings Inc v United States of America*, ICSID Case No ARB(AF)/12/1, Award (25 August 2014); *OAO Tatneft* (n 15); *Marco Gavazzi and Stefano Gavazzi v Romania*, ICSID Case No ARB/12/25, Decision on Jurisdiction Admissibility and Liability (21 April 2015); *Charanne and Construction Investments v Spain*, SCC Case No V 062/2012, Award (21 January 2016).

[139] *Petrobart* (n 138).

[140] See ibid ch 8.

[141] *Amto* (n 49) para 75.

[t]he fundamental criteria of an 'effective means' for the assertion of claims and the enforcement of rights is the law and the *rule of law*. There must be legislation for the recognition and enforcement of property and contractual rights. This legislation must be made in accordance with the constitution, and be publicly available. An effective means of the assertion of claims and the enforcement of rights also requires secondary rules of procedure so that the principles and objectives of the legislation can be translated by the investor into effective action in the domestic tribunals.[142]

The tribunal used the rule of law to set out certain quality requirements for legislation providing for redress: it has to be accessible and ensure effective enforcement. The ECtHR uses a similar approach to the quality of laws relative to all provisions of the Convention. It requires them to be compatible with the rule of law, which means they have to be accessible, precise, and foreseeable in their application.[143]

The *Amto* tribunal required the State to create an effective system of enforcement but stated that it does not have to ensure that individual failures of that system do not occur:

[T]he Tribunal considers that 'effective' is a systematic, comparative, progressive and practical standard. It is systematic in that the State must provide an effective framework or system for the enforcement of rights, but does not offer guarantees in individual cases. Individual failures might be evidence of systematic inadequacies, but are not themselves a breach of Article 10(12). It is comparative in that compliance with international standards indicates that imperfections in the law might result from the complexities of the subject matter rather than the inadequacies of the legislation. It is progressive in the sense that legislation ages and needs to be modernized and adapted from time to time, and results might not be immediate.[144]

B. Relationship between Denial of Justice and Effective Means

In a number of cases tribunals discussed the relationship of the effective means standard and the prohibition of a denial of justice. The first one is *Duke Energy v Ecuador*. The tribunal explicitly related the guarantee of access to the courts and the existence of institutional mechanisms for the protection of investments to the customary international law guarantee against denial of justice:

As such, it [the effective means provision of the BIT] seeks to implement and form part of the more general guarantee against denial of justice.[145]

The tribunal did not discuss the specific requirements of this guarantee and its relationship with denial of justice.[146] Therefore, it is not surprising that the tribunal used the criteria for assessing a denial of justice to decide on a violation of the 'effective means standard'.

---

[142] ibid para 87 (emphasis added).
[143] See eg *Del Rio Prada* (n 105) para 125.
[144] *Amto* (n 49) para 88. For a critical evaluation of the case, see Garibaldi (n 130) 367.
[145] *Duke Energy* (n 138) para 391.
[146] For a criticism of this approach, see Garibaldi (n 130) 363.

The *Chevron* tribunal dealt extensively with the 'effective protection' standard.[147] The case concerned the duration of several lawsuits brought by one of the claimants against Ecuador for failure to make payments under a contract. The tribunal discussed the relationship between denial of justice and effective means. It agreed to 'some extent' with the finding in *Duke Energy* that Article II(7) of the US–Ecuador BIT 'seeks to implement and form part of the more general guarantee against denial of justice'.[148] However, it found the 'effective protection' standard to be one of 'lex specialis and not a mere restatement of the law on denial of justice'.[149] It found the standard to be 'distinct and potentially less-demanding' than the denial of justice standard.[150] Because of the 'related genesis' of the two standards it found that for purposes of interpretation and application it is 'informed by the law of denial of justice'.[151]

In line with this approach, the *Chevron* tribunal borrowed the criteria from the denial of justice standard for assessing whether an undue delay in the enforcement of the investor rights under the effective means standard had occurred. It mentioned the following factors that have to be taken into consideration for this purpose: the complexity of the case, the behaviour of the litigants involved, the significance of the interests at stake in the case, and the behaviour of the courts themselves.[152] It did not require a strict exhaustion of local remedies but found that claimant must 'have adequately utilized the means made available to them to assert claims and enforce rights in Ecuador'.[153]

The tribunal found that a breach of the effective means standard had occurred since the cases had been pending 13 and 15 years in the domestic courts.[154] Since the tribunal had found that the effective means provision of the BIT was a *lex specialis* to the customary international law prohibition of denial of justice and had found a violation of the effective means requirement, it considered it unnecessary to assess whether the denial of justice standard had also been violated.[155] Therefore, apart from the abstract statement of the differences between the two standards, the tribunal did not discuss whether in the case at stake it would have reached a different outcome on the denial of justice standard.

The *White Industries* case concerned two different proceedings that had lasted for over nine years in Indian courts. The tribunal imported the effective means standard from the India–Kuwait BIT by using an MFN clause in the India–Australia BIT.[156]

It confirmed the finding of the *Chevron I* tribunal that 'the 'effective means' standard was *lex specialis* and a distinct and potentially less demanding test in comparison to denial of justice in customary international law'.[157] It also demonstrated how 'distinct from and less demanding' the test of the 'effective means' obligation is compared to a denial of justice.[158]

The tribunal found the duration of the national proceedings overall to be 'certainly unsatisfactory'.[159] However, it did not consider them as being such 'particular serious

---

[147] *Chevron v Ecuador I* (n 15) paras 241–75.
[148] ibid para 242, referring to *Duke Energy v Ecuador* (n 138) para 391.
[149] ibid para.
[150] ibid para 244.
[151] ibid para 244.
[152] ibid para 250.
[153] ibid para 268.
[154] ibid para 270.
[155] ibid para 275.
[156] *White Industries* (n 15) paras 11.2.1–11.2.9.
[157] ibid para 11.3.2.a.
[158] ibid para 11.4.16, fn 78.
[159] ibid para 10.4.22.

shortcomings' or egregious conduct that 'shocks or at least surprises, a sense of judicial proprietary' to amount to a denial of justice.[160]

With regard to one of the proceedings, the *White Industries* tribunal decided that claimant
had been unable to prove that the courts would not have decided timely had claimant used
available appeals.[161] However, the second proceeding, and in particular the failure of India's
Supreme Court to decide an appeal for over five years, triggered a violation of the effective
means standard.[162] The tribunal fully endorsed the approach of the *Chevron I* tribunal:[163]

> the 'effective means' standard is different from and less demanding than the 'denial of
> justice' standard. Moreover, with respect to a forward looking promise by a State to
> provide 'effective means' of enforcing rights and making claims, the relevance of the State's
> population or the current operation of its court system(s) (in assessing the undueness of
> a delay) is limited. This is because the focus of such a *lex specialis* is whether the system of
> laws and institutions work effectively at the time the promisee seeks to enforce its rights/
> make its claims.[164]

Therefore, the *White Industries* tribunal also endorsed the position that there was no strict
requirement to exhaust local remedies but found that claimant must 'have adequately utilized the means made available to them to assert claims and enforce rights'.[165]

The tribunal found that the State had to establish proper remedies and that those remedies had to work effectively in the individual case under consideration:

> [T]he standard requires both that the host State establish a proper system of laws and
> institutions and that those systems work effectively in any given case.[166]

In this respect the approach differs from that of the *Amto* tribunal which had found that
under the effective means standard a State does not have to ensure that individual failures
do not occur in a system that in principle provides for an effective framework.[167]

The *White Industries* case is interesting, since the tribunal had denied a denial of justice
but had found that the effective means standard had been violated as a result of the undue
length of domestic court proceedings. In this manner it confirmed the abstract difference
set out by the *Chevron I* tribunal in a concrete case.[168]

The tribunal in *Gavazzi and Gavazzi v Romania* endorsed the reasoning of the *White
Industries* tribunal[169] enumerating and endorsing the criteria applied by the *Chevron I* tribunal.[170] It stated that due to the wide notion of the effective means provision it 'does not

---

[160] ibid paras 10.4.23–10.4.24. On the severity requirement for denial of justice, see above Section II.C.
[161] ibid paras 11.4.5–11.4.15.
[162] ibid para 11.4.19.
[163] ibid para 11.3.3.
[164] ibid para 11.4.16, fn 78.
[165] ibid para 11.3.2.g.
[166] ibid para 11.3.2.b.
[167] *Amto* (n 49) para 88.
[168] For a critical approach, see Berk Demirkol, *Judicial Acts and Investment Treaty Arbitration* (CUP 2018) 45–
50 who considers that the effective means standard does not broaden the judicial protection beyond the denial of
justice standard.
[169] *White Industries* (n 15) para 11.3.2.
[170] *Gavazzi and Gavazzi* (n 138) para 260.

guarantee that each and every decision [of a national court] is correct'.[171] The tribunal then elaborated that the claim was not that there were no effective means to assert claims or enforce rights. Rather, claimants criticized that the decision of the Romanian courts to annul an arbitral award had been wrong. The tribunal continued with an analysis whether the denial of justice standard had been violated and denied this.[172]

The tribunal in *H&H Enterprises* only provided a very short analysis of the denial of justice and effective means standards. It found that no manifestly 'unjust decisions' or 'gross deficiency' had occurred and that claimant had been able to participate in the proceedings and present its claims and counterclaims.[173] Concerning the allegedly undue delay it found, first, that there were no fixed time limits under international law, and, second, the claimant did not actively pursue its case. Therefore, it denied the occurrence of a denial of justice and explained that '[t]he same reasoning applies to the claimant's claim for denial of effective means'.[174] Therefore, the criteria of the tribunal were typical due process requirements.

C. Conclusion

In sum, in line with the other two standards, tribunals deciding on a violation of the effective means standard used typical fair trial requirements as we find them in the denial of justice standard or under human rights treaties. They assessed whether there was access to court, whether there was an undue interference by the executive, whether there were undue delays in court proceedings and whether an investor was able to present its case properly. All of these are typical due process requirements and as such form part of the list of the rule-of-law criteria taken from *ELSI* and *Glamis*. Like in the context of the other two standards we find one case that concerned the quality of a law. The tribunal in *Amto* required that the legislation providing for redress had to be accessible,[175] a requirement also often used by the ECtHR with a reference to rule-of-law considerations.

V. Concluding Remarks

This overview has collected and systematized the rule-of-law elements that arbitral tribunals have deployed when assessing the existence of a denial of justice, a judicial expropriation or a violation of the effective means clause. While the rule of law is not mentioned explicitly in any of these standards, in a large majority of cases tribunals that reviewed judicial proceedings used criteria typically associated with the rule of law: access to court, due process, independence and impartiality of courts, no arbitrariness, no undue delay of court decisions as well as the quality of laws are typically associated with the rule of law.

Therefore, the role of rule-of-law criteria for investment tribunals can be assessed in the following way: the rule of law provides a useful toolbox in the case law of investment tribunals with regard to denial of justice, judicial expropriation, and the effective means

---

[171] ibid.
[172] ibid paras 260–65.
[173] *H&H Enterprises* (n 138) para 403.
[174] ibid paras 405–06.
[175] *Amto* (n 49) para 87.

standards. This applies in particular to the procedural requirements of due process in a more technical sense. These were applied successfully with regard to the quality of laws in the context of civil law as well as common law systems.[176] Although the tribunals did not base their analysis explicitly on the rule of law, rule-of-law standards were particularly helpful for tribunals that had to decide on the existence of a judicial expropriation. Rule-of-law criteria provide a useful framework of analysis both in cases that concern the existence of property as well as in cases where property rights are terminated.

An analysis of the concrete criteria applied by investment tribunals to assess potential violations of the three standards shows that the criteria used by investment tribunals are fairly similar to the requirements of human rights treaties and those developed in the case law of the ECtHR in the context of rule of law and judicial proceedings. However, there remains an important difference between investment tribunals and the ECtHR that concerns a further potential role of the rule of law: whereas the ECtHR used the rule of law as justifying additional criteria not explicitly mentioned in the Convention when assessing measures of domestic courts, investment tribunals have not done so. For instance, the ECtHR when deciding on fair trial violations by domestic courts, referred to the rule of law when it introduced criteria for due process that were not explicitly mentioned in the text of the fair trial guarantee of the Convention. In this way the Court justified the use of them and gave its approach additional legitimacy.

Investment tribunals often did not expressly link the rule of law to the criteria they used to assess measures of domestic courts in view of the three standards. This was the case although investment protection treaties, unlike human rights treaties, only rarely contain explicit fair trial requirements in their treaty standards.[177] Therefore, it would be particularly helpful if tribunals were to point out that the standards they use are derived from the rule of law. An explicit linkage to the rule of law could give the criteria employed by tribunals to assess violations of the three standards additional authority, and highlight their importance. This is the method employed in the case law of the ECtHR. In this way, investment tribunals could also sensitize States for important problems in their domestic judiciary with regard to rule-of-law matters.

Concerning the question of how investment tribunals conceptualized the rule of law (thin formal vs thick substantive) in cases dealing with actions or omissions of the domestic judiciary, caution is needed. None of the tribunals, to the extent they mentioned the rule of law at all, discussed its rule-of-law concept. Most tribunals did not even mention the rule of law when they applied criteria commonly associated with the rule of law. Particular caution is therefore required when one extrapolates a tribunal's conceptual approach to the rule of law from the criteria applied when deciding on a violation of one of the three standards. Furthermore, all analysed cases concern the rule-of-law demands on the judiciary and the criteria in most of the cases were quite similar to those applied by human rights courts in fair trial cases. These criteria will typically be already covered by a thin (formal) rule-of-law approach. Therefore, even if the tribunals believed in a thick (substantial) one, they would often not have to apply it to the cases before them since the issue was about procedural propriety.

---

[176] See above Sections III.G and IV.C.

[177] The explicit requirement to follow due process standards when expropriating or the condition that in case of an expropriation judicial review has to be guaranteed that can be found in many investment treaties are exceptions.

Nevertheless, under all three standards, one can identify cases where tribunals resorted to a thicker conception of the rule of law looking also at substance and not only procedure. This was so when the tribunals used criteria like egregiousness not limited to procedural faults, arbitrariness that was not linked to procedural deficiencies as well as characterizations such as grossly unfair, unjust, or discriminatory, or the concept of 'abuse of rights'.[178] In most of the cases tribunals made use of criteria typically associated with the right to a fair trial and only in exceptional circumstances did they resort to criteria implying a substantive assessment of the content of the actions or omissions of domestic courts.

The approach of the investment tribunals dealing with proceedings before domestic courts is in line with the approach practised by the ECtHR in similar situations. When reviewing actions and omissions by domestic courts, the ECtHR will typically also focus on procedural guarantees enshrined in the fair trial provision of the Convention. In general, it defers to the decision of local courts in the interpretation of the domestic law or international law as incorporated into domestic law.[179] The ECtHR stresses in this context that its power to review compliance with domestic law is limited. It is for the national authorities in the first place to interpret and apply that law.[180] It accepts national court decisions unless they apply the legal provisions in question manifestly erroneously or so as to reach arbitrary conclusions.[181]

Therefore, when investment tribunals used notions that allude to a thicker conception of the rule of law in the context of one of the three standards, their approach was similar to that of the ECtHR. All tribunals made clear that they do not sit as appeal courts but only apply a limited review of the substantive decision of domestic courts.

It seems that the application of what appears like a thinner or thicker rule-of-law concept was more owed to the particularities of the cases than to a deliberate difference of opinion among tribunals on which concept of the rule of law they should apply. The approach of tribunals seems justified, not to limit their review of the domestic judiciary to a formal thin version of the rule of law, but, where appropriate, to also demand from the domestic courts that the minimum standards of a substantive conception of the rule of law are respected without, however, acting as fourth instance.

---

[178] See eg *Arif* (n 15) paras 442; *Amto* (n 49) para 87; *Rumeli* (n 33) para 619; *OAO Tafnet* (n 15) para 475; *Unglaube* (n 34) para 277; *Krederi* (n 28) paras 443 (fn 162), 449.

[179] *Anheuser-Busch Inc v Portugal* App no 73049/01 (ECtHR, 11 January 2007) para 83.

[180] *Tre Traktörer Aktiebolag v Sweden* App no 10873/84 (ECtHR, 7 July 1989) para 58; *Allan Jacobsson v Sweden* App no 10842/84 (ECtHR, 25 October 1989) para 57; *Håkansson and Sturesson v Sweden* App no 11855/85 (ECtHR, 21 February 1990) para 47; *Beyeler v Italy* App no 33202/96 (ECtHR, 5 January 2000) para 108; *Allard v Sweden* App no 35179/97(ECtHR, 24 June 2003) para 53.

[181] See eg *Beyeler v Italy* (n 180) para 108.

9

Umbrella Clauses and the Rule of Law

Arnaud de Nanteuil

I. Introduction

An umbrella clause can be defined in general as a treaty provision requiring a State party to respect the commitments it may have undertaken towards the investors of the other State party. For this reason, it is sometimes described as an 'observation of undertakings' provision.[1] There is no real dispute as to the basic meaning of such clauses. However, their exact scope and effect are probably among the most controversial topics in international investment law, giving rise to strong divisions in arbitral case law.[2]

Thus, it may be argued that umbrella clauses lead to an increased uncertainty in the legal relationships between a State party and a foreign investor. In particular, it is well known that there is no ready-made answer to the question of extending the arbitral tribunal's jurisdiction to contract claims, when this jurisdiction is founded on the treaty in which the umbrella clause is included.[3] Moreover, the scope of umbrella clauses is unclear. It is still highly debated in case law whether the clauses should only apply to specific commitments, such as contractual undertakings, or whether they also apply to unilateral commitments—such as those made by the State in a general statute.[4] Furthermore, as many cases involve a contract, it may be questioned whether any State action is covered by an umbrella clause or whether only acts performed as a sovereign (*jure imperii*) are covered by the scope of the clause. The latter position has been justified by the (not uncontroversial) statement that a breach of contract can be an internationally wrongful act only when it is the result of an act a State performed as a sovereign and not as a party to said contract.[5]

---

[1] *WNC v Czech Republic*, PCA Case No 2014-34, Award (22 February 2017) para 321.

[2] For a comprehensive, albeit a little dated presentation of the different possible trends, see in particular Katia Yannaca-Small, 'Interpretation of the Umbrella Clause in Investment Agreements' (2006) OECD Working Papers on International Investment, 2006/03. For a more recent description, see Arnaud de Nanteuil, *International Investment Law* (Edward Elgar 2020) 124–33. See (n 6) references.

[3] The well-known cases of *SGS* provide a perfect illustration of opposing solutions on the basis of two very similarly drafted treaty provisions, one tribunal having refused to give such an effect to the clause and the other having accepted, subject to some conditions, its jurisdiction over the contract claims: *SGS Société Générale de Surveillance SA v Islamic Republic of Pakistan*, ICSID Case No ARB/01/13, Decision on Objections to Jurisdiction (6 August 2003) paras 163–73; *SGS Société Générale de Surveillance SA v Republic of the Philippines*, ICSID Case No ARB/02/6, Decision on Objections to Jurisdiction (29 January 2004) paras 11–28. On this question, see (nn 12ff).

[4] Cf eg *LG&E Energy Corp LG&E Capital, LG&E International Inc v Argentine*, ICSID Case No ARB/02/1, Award (3 October 2006) paras 169ff with *Noble Ventures, Inc v Romania*, ICSID Case No ARB/01/11, Award (12 October 2005) para 51 and *Burlington Resources Inc v Republic of Ecuador*, ICSID Case No ARB/08/5, Decision on Liability (14 December 2012) para 206. In these cases, the wording of the umbrella clauses was not identical, which can explain the differences in the rulings. On this question, see Section III.A below.

[5] This is particularly the case when the breach of the contract can be qualified as an expropriation. See in particular *Consortium RFCC v Kingdom of Morocco*, ICSID Case No ARB/00/6, Award (22 December 2003) para 65. See also *Impregilo SpA v Islamic Republic of Pakistan*, ICSID Case No ARB/03/3, Decision on Jurisdiction (22 April 2005) para 278. See on this issue *Compañía de Aguas de Aconquija, SA and Compagnie Générale des Eaux v Argentine Republic*, ICSID Case No ARB/97/3, Award (21 November 2000) para 79, where the tribunal refused to impose such a requirement as it would have led to a detailed interpretation of the contract on which it had ruled

Arnaud de Nanteuil, *Umbrella Clauses and the Rule of Law* In: *Investment Protection Standards and the Rule of Law*. Edited by: August Reinisch and Stephan W. Schill, Oxford University Press. © Arnaud de Nanteuil 2023. DOI: 10.1093/oso/9780192864581.003.0009

In light of these different approaches on the interpretation of umbrella clauses, it is evident that case law is deeply divided and that it is not always possible to predict decisions of arbitral tribunals in relation to such a clause. As these questions have been analysed extensively in academic writings, there is no point in rehearsing them here.[6]

Against the backdrop of divergent case law on the scope and effect of umbrella clauses, umbrella clauses may appear at first as a threat to the rule of law. According to the UN Secretary-General in 2004, the rule of law implies a range of requirements, including legal certainty, avoidance of arbitrariness, transparency, and independent adjudication of rules.[7] Consequently, if umbrella clauses only entail a lack of foreseeability in the investment protection system, one may question whether such clauses could be helpful for the promotion of the rule of law. In addition, a general rejection of umbrella clauses has been adopted in recent treaty practice.[8] The United Nations Conference for Trade and Development (UNCTAD) noted that the absence of an umbrella clause is 'typical of new-generation treaties'.[9] This decline of umbrella clauses may be one of the manifestations of the growing hostility towards investor-State arbitration in general. However, it may also be explained by a specific reluctance vis-à-vis umbrella clauses in particular, considering the difficulty in predicting their legal effects.

That being said, one may also argue that umbrella clauses do allow for the promotion of the rule of law for several reasons. First, umbrella clauses may be helpful in securing the enforcement of the State's contractual—or other types of—commitments. Hence, such a clause may in reality introduce stability to the investor-State relationship. It can be argued that umbrella clauses are essential tools to ensure access to justice, which is an uncontested rule-of-law demand (see below Section II).[10] Since umbrella clauses are above all a means

---

not to have jurisdiction. Yet the award was partially annulled on this point, which proves that the question is much disputed. See *Compania de Aguas del Aconquija SA and Vivendi Universal SA v Argentine Republic* (formerly *Compañía de Aguas del Aconquija, SA and Compagnie Générale des Eaux v Argentine Republic*), ICSID Case No ARB/97/3, Decision on Annulment (3 July 2002) paras 95ff.

[6] See eg Emmanuel Gaillard, 'Investment Treaty Arbitration and Jurisdiction over Contract Claims—The SGS Cases Considered' in Todd Weiler (ed), *International Investment Law and Arbitration: Leading Cases from the ICSID, NAFTA, Bilateral Treaties and Customary International law* (Cameron May 2005) 334; Laura Halonen, 'Containing the Scope of the Umbrella Clause' (2008) 2 WAMR 183–94; Craig S Miles, 'Where's My Umbrella? An "Ordinary Meaning" Approach to Answering Three Key Questions that Have Emerged from the "Umbrella Clause" Debate' (2008) 2 WAMR 161–82; Andrés Rigo Sureda, 'The Umbrella Clause' in Meg Kinnear and others (eds), *Building International Investment Law: The First 50 Years of ICSID* (Wolters Kluwer 2016) 375–87; Stephan Schill, 'Enabling Private Ordering: Function, Scope and Effect of Umbrella Clauses in International Investment Treaties' (2009) 18 Minn JIL 1–97; Anthony Sinclair, 'The Origins of the Umbrella Clause in the International Law of Investment Protection' (2014) 20 Arb Int L 411–34

[7] UNSC, 'Report of the Secretary-General on the Rule of Law and Transitional Justice in Conflict and Post-Conflict Societies' (23 August 2004) UN Doc S/2004/616 (hereafter 2004 Report) para 6:

> The 'rule of law'... refers to a principle of governance in which all persons, institutions and entities, public and private, including the State itself, are accountable to laws that are publicly promulgated, equally enforced and independently adjudicated, and which are consistent with international human rights norms and standards. It requires, as well, measures to ensure adherence to the principles of supremacy of law, equality before the law, accountability to the law, fairness in the application of the law, separation of powers, participation in decision-making, legal certainty, avoidance of arbitrariness and procedural and legal transparency.

[8] See Raul Pereira de Souza Fleury, 'Closing the Umbrella: A Dark Future for Umbrella Clauses?' (*Kluwer Arbitration Blog*, 13 October 2017).

[9] See <http://investmentpolicyhub.unctad.org/Pages/mapping-of-iia-clauses#umbrella> accessed 13 December 2021.

[10] On this aspect of the rule of law, see Section II below.

to ensure that a claim based on the breach of a given commitment (eg made in a contract or statute) is adjudicated by an independent tribunal, a rule-of-law criterion might be promoted. An umbrella clause is indeed a treaty provision compelling the State to respect its commitments vis-à-vis foreign investors. Therefore, a breach of such a commitment could be considered as a breach of the treaty and then be adjudicated on the basis of the arbitration provision that is included in the treaty. Article 7 of Germany–Iran BIT provides a clear illustration of this argument as that provision stipulates that '[e]ither Contracting Party shall guarantee the observance of the commitments it has entered into with respect to investments of investors of the other Contracting Party'.[11] Even if some slight drafting differences may appear from one treaty to another,[12] all umbrella clauses share one common point: they are a commitment to respect undertakings.[13]

In practice, the main purpose of umbrella clauses is jurisdictional. Their aim is to ensure that the commitments to which they apply fall within the scope of the arbitral tribunal's jurisdiction pursuant to the investment treaty which incorporates the umbrella clause. Hence, in *Noble Ventures v Romania*, the Tribunal described the umbrella clause as an 'international secured legal remedy in respect of investment contracts'.[14] The meaning of this statement is clear: if a contract does not contain any dispute settlement provision or contains a dispute settlement clause which does not guarantee impartial and independent adjudication, a claim made on the basis of such contract could be brought before an arbitral tribunal on the basis of the umbrella clause. In this sense, an umbrella clause can play a crucial role in ensuring the effective adjudication of certain commitments, and, therefore, might prove to be an essential tool for the promotion of the rule of law.

For umbrella clauses to promote the rule of law at least some of the above-mentioned questions in relation to the scope of the provision must be answered. In order to develop a rule-of-law theory of umbrella clauses, we will first see that access to justice is a rule-of-law requirement (Section II), before assessing how umbrella clauses may be helpful in providing such access (Section III), which, as we will see, supposes a broad interpretation of umbrella clauses (Section IV). Finally, we ask whether umbrella clauses, by promoting arbitration as a priority dispute settlement mechanism to the detriment of the domestic courts, might still be a threat to the rule of law (Section V).

II. Access to Justice as a Rule-of-Law Requirement

Albeit central, the question of whether access to justice constitutes a rule-of-law requirement can be addressed quite briefly since there is no real doubt about this. This question is actually twofold: not only must access to justice be guaranteed (Section A), but also access must be granted to fair justice (Section B).

---

[11] Germany–Islamic Republic of Iran BIT (2002) art 7.
[12] The scope of the clause may vary depending on the wording of the treaty. In the example of the Germany–Iran BIT, the wording is rather narrow, limiting the obligation of respect to commitments that the State has 'entered into'.
[13] See the references above n 6.
[14] *Noble Ventures* (n 4) para 52, emphasis added.

A. The Rule of Law and Access to Justice

Access to justice is central among the requirements that are imposed upon States in the name of the rule of law. Dicey noted that the rule of law implies that 'every man, whatever be his rank or condition, is subject to the ordinary law of the realm and amenable to the jurisdiction of the ordinary tribunals'.[15] Even if this statement only recalls that no one can escape the jurisdiction of domestic courts of law, which is slightly different from stating a general right to resort to the courts, it obviously implies such a right. Today, this right is included in most national constitutional laws and in international human rights law.

For instance, several European constitutions provide that all individuals benefit from the right to recourse to the courts. This right is provided, for instance, by Article 24 of the Spanish Constitution (1976),[16] by Article 24 of the Italian Constitution (1948),[17] and by Article 19(4) of the German Constitution (1949).[18] In France, even if this right is not explicitly incorporated in the Constitution or in the Declaration of Human Rights of 1789 (which has a constitutional value), it has been considered to be a fundamental right by the Constitutional Court (Conseil constitutionnel) in several decisions.[19] Whatever the context, this right undoubtedly covers claims against State (or public body) action. Hence it is part of the rule of law as 'a principle of governance in which all persons, institutions and entities, public and private, including the State itself, are accountable to laws'.[20] Indeed, the State and public bodies or institutions can only be effectively accountable in law if individuals whose rights are affected by their action have the right to resort to a judge against them.

Beyond Europe, numerous references to the right to a judge can be found in national constitutions. This right is mentioned in Articles 46 and 47 of the Russian Constitution (1993),[21] Article 34 of the Constitution of South Africa (1996),[22] Article 118 of the Constitution of Morocco (2011),[23] Article 115 of the Constitution of Bolivia (2009),[24] Article 17 of the Constitution of Mexico (1917),[25] and Article 32 of the Constitution of Japan (1947).[26] These

---

[15]   Albert Venn Dicey, *Introduction to the Study of Law of the Constitution* (Macmillan 1885, repr Liberty Classics 1985) 114.

[16]   The original text reads: 'Todas las personas tienen derecho a obtener tutela efectiva de los jueces y tribunales en el ejercicio de sus derechos e intereses legítimos, sin que, en ningún caso, pueda producirse indefensión'. See also Spanish Constitution, art 14.1.

[17]   The original text reads: 'Tutti possono agire in giudizio per la tutela dei propri diritti e interessi legittimi'.

[18]   The original text reads: 'Wird jemand durch die öffentliche Gewalt in seinen Rechten verletzt, so steht ihm der Rechtsweg offen. Soweit eine andere Zuständigkeit nicht begründet ist, ist der ordentliche Rechtsweg gegeben'.

[19]   Conseil constitutionnel (France), Decision No 93–325 (13 August 1993); Decision No 93–335 (21 January 1994); Decision No 96–373 (9 April 1996); Decision No 96–378 DC (23 July 1996).

[20]   2004 Report (n 7) para 7.

[21]   Article 46 reads: '1. Everyone shall be guaranteed judicial protection of his rights and freedoms. 2. Decisions and acts (or omissions) of state authorities, local self-government bodies, associations and officials may be appealed against in court'. Article 47 reads: 'No one may be deprived of the right to have his case examined by the court and by the judge competent for that case' (our translation).

[22]   Article 34 reads: 'Everyone has the right to have any dispute that can be resolved by the application of law decided in a fair public hearing before a court or, where appropriate, another independent and impartial tribunal or forum'.

[23]   The original text reads: 'L'accès à la justice est garanti à toute personne pour la défense de ses droits et de ses intérêts protégés par la loi'.

[24]   The original text reads: 'Toda persona será protegida oportuna y efectivamente por los jueces y tribunales en el ejercicio de sus derechos e intereses legítimos'.

[25]   The original text reads: 'Toda persona tiene derecho a que se le administre justicia por tribunales que estarán expeditos para impartirla en los plazos y términos que fijen las leyes, emitiendo sus resoluciones de manera pronta, completa e imparcial'.

[26]   Article 32 reads: 'No person shall be denied the right of access to the courts'.

random examples, which refer to different places and different times, tend to show that the recognition of a right to a judge is widely shared.

In any case, even in States where such an explicit guarantee is absent from constitutional law, governments are still bound to ensure the right to access to courts under international and regional human rights law. In Europe, on the basis of the rules of treaty interpretation of the Vienna Convention on the Law of Treaties, the European Court of Human Rights (ECtHR) ruled in *Golder v UK* in 1975 that, pursuant to the European Convention on Human Rights (ECHR):

> in civil matters one can scarcely conceive of the rule of law without there being a possibility of having access to the courts ... It would be inconceivable, in the opinion of the Court, that Article 6 para. 1 (art. 6-1) should describe in detail the procedural guarantees afforded to parties in a pending lawsuit and should not first protect that which alone makes it in fact possible to benefit from such guarantees, that is, access to a court.[27]

The Court deduced that 'the right of access constitutes an element which is inherent in the right stated by Article 6 para. 1'.[28] The same Court also ruled, on the basis of the same provision, that 'where an individual considers himself to have been prejudiced by a measure allegedly in breach of the Convention, he should have a remedy before a national authority in order both to have his claim decided and, if appropriate, to obtain redress'.[29] The European Union Charter of Fundamental Rights also guarantees the right to resort to a judge in its Article 47.[30] In other regional human rights protection systems, the same right can be found: it is provided in Article 7 of the African Charter on Human and Peoples' Rights[31] as well as in Article 25(1) of the American Convention on Human Rights.[32]

At a universal level, the right of access to a judge is also contained in Article 9(4) of the International Covenant on Civil and Political Rights, albeit only in the context of a deprivation of liberty.[33] Nonetheless, the right of access to justice is conceived as a core element of human rights law. A glance at the United Nations instruments regarding the rule of law fully

---

[27] *Golder v United Kingdom* App no 4451/70 (ECtHR, 21 February 1975) paras 34–35.

[28] ibid para 36.

[29] *Klass v Germany* App no 5029/71 (ECtHR, 6 September 1978) para 64.

[30] Charter of Fundamental Rights of the European Union [2008] OJ C 326/391, art 47 reads:

> Everyone whose rights and freedoms guaranteed by the law of the Union are violated has the right to an effective remedy before a tribunal in compliance with the conditions laid down in this Article. Everyone is entitled to a fair and public hearing within a reasonable time by an independent and impartial tribunal previously established by law. Everyone shall have the possibility of being advised, defended and represented. Legal aid shall be made available to those who lack sufficient resources in so far as such aid is necessary to ensure effective access to justice.

[31] African Charter on Human and Peoples' Rights (adoption 27 June 1981, entry into force 21 October 1986) 1520 UNTS 217 (ACHPR) art 7 reads: 'Every individual shall have the right to have his cause heard. This comprises: a) The right to an appeal to competent national organs against acts of violating his fundamental rights as recognized and guaranteed by conventions, laws, regulations and customs in force'.

[32] American Convention on Human Rights (adoption 22 November 1969, entry into force 22 November 1969) 1144 UNTS 123 (ACHR) art 25(1) reads: ' Everyone has the right to simple and prompt recourse, or any other effective recourse, to a competent court or tribunal for protection against acts that violate his fundamental rights recognized by the constitution or laws of the state concerned or by this Convention, even though such violation may have been committed by persons acting in the course of their official duties'.

[33] International Covenant on Civil and Political Rights (opened for signature 19 December 1966, entry into force 23 March 1976) 999 UNTS 171 (ICCPR) art 9 reads: 'Anyone who is deprived of his liberty by arrest or detention shall be entitled to take proceedings before a court, in order that that court may decide without delay on the lawfulness of his detention and order his release if the detention is not lawful'.

corroborates this conclusion. For example, General Assembly Resolution 69/123 (2014), recalls:

> the commitment of the Member States to take all necessary steps to provide fair, transparent, effective, non-discriminatory and accountable services that promote access to justice for all, including legal aid, encourages further dialogue and the sharing of national practices in strengthening the rule of law through access to justice.[34]

This requirement, in the context of the rule of law, can also be found in other UN texts.[35]

On that basis, one may recognize that access to a judge is indeed a requirement imposed upon States in the name of the rule of law. As clearly stated by the Council of Europe:

> Access to justice enables individuals to protect themselves against infringements of their rights, to remedy civil wrongs, to hold executive power accountable and to defend themselves in criminal proceedings. It is an important element of the rule of law.[36]

B. The Rule of Law and the Right to a Fair Trial

The rule of law does not only require access to any judge that may exercise jurisdiction. It is also important that such a judge presents some basic guarantees. Thus, the EU Commission has identified 'generally shared traits of rule of law' among which it includes 'access to justice before independent and impartial courts'.[37] The UN Secretary-General requirement under which the rules must be 'independently adjudicated' refers to the same prerequisite.[38] This obligation can also be found in human rights law in which (for example under the ECHR) the explicit right is to a fair trial, from which the Strasbourg Court deduced the existence of a right to access to justice.[39] Human rights law in general provides for the right to access courts that respect the general rules of fair trial. This is true both for universal and regional human rights instruments.[40] For example, Article 47 of the EU Charter of Fundamental Rights includes several requirements that tribunals must meet in order to comply with the right to a judge.[41] Such requirements are also present in several domestic constitutions.[42] In any event, recognizing the right to access to courts of law without requiring such courts to act in a fair and independent fashion would be pointless.[43]

---

[34] UNGA, 'The Rule of Law at the National and International Levels' (18 December 2014) UN Doc A/RES/69/123, para 14.

[35] See eg UNGA, 'Declaration of the High-level Meeting of the General Assembly on the Rule of Law at the National and International Levels' (30 November 2012) UN Doc A/RES/67/1, para 12.

[36] European Union Agency for Fundamental Rights and Council of Europe, *Handbook on European Law Relating to Access to Justice* (Publication office of the European Union 2016) 16.

[37] Communication from the Commission to the European Parliament and the Council, 'A New EU Framework to Strengthen the Rule of Law' COM (2014) 158 final, Annexes 1–3.

[38] See UNSC (n 7) para 6.

[39] See *Golder v United Kingdom* (n 27) paras 34–35.

[40] See ICCPR art 14; ACHR art 8(1); ACHPR art 7.

[41] For the text of art 47 of the Charter, see above n 30.

[42] See eg the Constitution of South Africa (n 22) which requires tribunals to be independent and impartial.

[43] See ILA Committee on the Rule of Law and International Investment Law, Sydney Report, 'Rule of Law and International Investment Law' (2018) 28.

There is probably no need to elaborate further on this point. What matters is that the judge to which access is guaranteed respects some basic requirements, such as independence, impartiality, respect for the rights of defence, the right to be represented, the right to a judgment within a reasonable period of time, and the right to an effective remedy.[44] All of this is perfectly consistent with the general philosophy of the rule of law, but the question is now how umbrella clauses can help respect this requirement.

III. Umbrella Clauses as a Means of Ensuring Access to (Fair) Justice

Umbrella clauses have primarily a jurisdictional effect (Section A), thus ensuring access to a tribunal (Section B). In some cases, umbrella clauses could also ensure that, among different competent adjudicators, only the one that respects the fair trial requirement will actually exercise jurisdiction (Section C).

A. Jurisdictional Effects of Umbrella Clauses

In short, one could argue that the main objective of umbrella clauses is to ensure effective access to justice. These clauses may allow an investor to access an arbitral tribunal in situations where the coexistence of several applicable instruments creates gaps in jurisdictional protection. Stephan Schill rightly points out that '[t]he primary function of umbrella clauses … consists of remedying the loopholes the dualist framework has created in the enforcement of host State promises'.[45] This dualism stems from the coexistence, in some situations, of a treaty (in which the umbrella clause is included) and of a commitment of the State (be it contractual or not) undertaken within the domestic legal order. The remedy that is referred to consists in offering a competent forum for claims that may not be heard otherwise, due to differences between the domestic and the international legal orders. For example, if a contract or a domestic statute refers to domestic jurisdictions, the umbrella clause in an applicable treaty may allow for claims for breach of contract or for breach of the statute to be submitted to an arbitral tribunal founded on the basis of the treaty. This is especially important if the domestic courts are not likely to satisfy the rule-of-law requirements.[46] This simplified illustration can be sustained in more complex circumstances, as shown in the *Noble Ventures* case.

As mentioned above, the *Noble Ventures* tribunal described the umbrella clause as an 'international secured legal remedy in respect of investment contracts',[47] assuming that the foremost function of umbrella clauses was of a procedural nature. Umbrella clauses grant a remedy, but do not have any impact on the substantive rights of the investor. As stated by the arbitral tribunal in *WNC v Czech Republic* in relation to the effect of umbrella clauses:

[44] The elements are listed in EU Agency for Fundamental Rights and Council of Europe (n 36).
[45] Schill (n 6) 36.
[46] As a matter of principle, umbrella clauses generally allow access to investment arbitration even when there is no problem with the other judge, ie the judge in the domestic court. However, this chapter argues that the question of whether the other judge respects the requirements of the right to a fair trial may be introduced in the interpretation of umbrella clauses. See Section II.C below.
[47] See *Noble Ventures v Romania* (n 14) para 52.

The term 'umbrella clause' is often used as a convenient shorthand for 'observation of undertaking'. That nomenclature does not expand the scope of the obligation to observe an undertaking under international law. An undertaking is a formal and legally binding pledge to do something. States are obliged under international law to observe their undertakings. This is, *inter alia,* part of the duty of good faith and the principle of *pacta sunt servanda.*[48]

This statement suggests that the presence of an umbrella clause has no effect by itself on the binding character of the State's undertakings.[49] Indeed, the obligation to abide by an undertaking stems from general international law—here, the tribunal refers to the principle of good faith and *pacta sunt servanda*—and not from the umbrella clause. Also, in case of a domestic contract, the binding character of the commitment can generally be grounded in the domestic law that is applicable to the contract.[50] One could, therefore, assume that the commitment would be binding in and of itself, not through application of the umbrella clause.[51] Nevertheless, it is certain that umbrella clauses can have an effect at the jurisdictional level: by guaranteeing, in a treaty, that the undertakings must be respected, the clause may give the arbitral tribunal seized on the basis of that treaty the jurisdiction to hear any possible breach of the undertaking covered by the clause since any breach of the commitment might be qualified as a breach of the umbrella clause—and therefore of the treaty. In that sense, umbrella clauses may help to enhance the jurisdictional protection that is required by the rule of law.

However, this conclusion is true only if we admit that recourse to investment arbitration can be considered as access to justice as required by the rule of law, which may be questionable since treaty-based investment arbitration has faced an important criticism in recent years for falling short of the rule-of-law criteria. This opposition is mainly based on a supposed bias of investment tribunals, an alleged lack of impartiality, and on a potential structural hostility towards host States.[52] Criticism against investment arbitration is rooted in criticism against investment law in general, and the idea that the system is based on structural inequality between States.[53] However, several arguments can be made that investment

---

[48]   *WNC* (n 1) para 321.

[49]   However, see Section III.A.

[50]   We are here referring to the fact that all domestic contract rules include first a general principle recalling the binding character of contractual commitments. A reflection of this general principle can be found for example in art 1.3 of the UNIDROIT Principles of international commercial contracts, 2016 <www.unidroit.org/instruments/commercial-contracts/unidroit-principles-2016/> accessed 13 December 2021, which is supposed to reflect a universal principle of contract law: 'A contract validly entered into is binding upon the parties. It can only be modified or terminated in accordance with its terms or by agreement or as otherwise provided in these Principles.'

[51]   See in this sense and drawing the same conclusion not only about umbrella clauses but about BITs in general Jason Webb Yackee, '*Pacta Sunt Servanda* and State Promises to Foreign Investors Before Bilateral Investment Treaties: Myth and Reality' (2008) 32 Fordham Intl LJ 1550.

[52]   For a clearly hostile and probably a little excessive criticism, see Helen Burley (ed), *Profiting from Injustice: How Law Firms, Arbitrators and Financiers Are Fuelling an Arbitration Boom* (Corporate Europe Observatory and the Transnational Institute 2012) 76. Even developed States have admitted a need for some change: Armand de Mestral (ed), *Second Thoughts: Investor-State Arbitration between Developed Democracies* (CIGI 2017). An important reflexion is ongoing on the different possible ways to improve investor-State dispute settlement. See in particular Malcolm Langford and others (eds), 'Special Issue: UNCITRAL and Investment Arbitration Reform: Matching Concerns and Solutions' (2020) 21 JWIT 167.

[53]   See Andrew T Guzman, 'Why LDCs Sign Treaties that Hurt Them: Explaining the Popularity of Bilateral Investment Treaties' (1998) 38 Va JIL 639. An answer to this approach has been provided by José E Alvarez, *The Public International Law Regime Governing International Investment* (Pocketbooks of The Hague Academy of International Law 2011) 123.

arbitration as a fair system of justice, access to it being considered as an element of the rule of law.

The first series of arguments in that sense stems from a general evolution of investment arbitration in recent years. First, ICSID and UNCITRAL have recently drafted a code of conduct which aims to further ensure that arbitrators will judge impartially and avoid any conflicts of interest.[54] Second, it seems that case law has already evolved towards a better taking into account of impartiality requirements. For instance, the *Eiser Infrastructure v Spain* award has been recently annulled by an ICSID ad hoc Committee for the lack of impartiality of the arbitrator appointed by the investor claimant. In that case, one of the arbitrators had failed to disclose a relationship with a law firm and an expert that were involved in the case. The ad hoc Committee found that a third party would find an appearance of bias and, therefore, that there had been a serious departure from a fundamental rule of procedure.[55] This case can be considered as a sign of the evolution of arbitral case law: independence and impartiality are no longer formal requirements; rather they are actually enforceable and enforced through annulment proceedings. Finally, transparency has undoubtedly become a question of primary importance in investment arbitration, as shown by the adoption of the Mauritius Convention on Transparency in Treaty-based Investor-State Arbitration.[56] These developments are indications that respecting the basic requirement of the right to a fair trial is an important consideration in investment arbitration, rendering tenable the argument that investment arbitration qualifies as a form of justice consistent with the rule of law.

Furthermore, the ECtHR has already held that recourse to arbitration was to be considered access to justice as required by the rule of law. In the *Lithgow v United Kingdom* case, the ECtHR had to address the issue of whether the possibility to have recourse to an arbitral tribunal was consistent with the right to a fair trial guaranteed by Article 6(1) of the ECHR. The Court ruled that the arbitral tribunal in question met the requirements for independence and impartiality.[57] The Court of Justice of the European Union (CJEU) also found that the investor-State dispute settlement system of the Comprehensive Economic and Trade Agreement (CETA) between the EU and Canada was consistent with Article 47 of the EU Charter of Fundamental Rights.[58] We can extrapolate that arbitral tribunals *in abstracto* meet the requirements for a fair trial, especially considering the said recent developments. For the purposes of this chapter, and while keeping in mind the ongoing debate on this point, it will thus be accepted that recourse to investment arbitration can be considered as access to justice as is required by the rule of law.

---

[54] The Draft Code of Conduct for Adjudicators in Investor-State Dispute Settlement was prepared jointly by the Secretariats of ICSID and UNCITRAL and was made public during the spring of 2020 <https://icsid.worldbank.org/en/Documents/Draft_Code_Conduct_Adjudicators_ISDS.pdf>accessed 13 December 2021.

[55] *Eiser Infrastructure Limited and Energía Solar Luxembourg Sàrl v Kingdom of Spain*, ICSID Case No ARB/13/36, Annulment Decision (11 June 2020).

[56] United Nations Convention on Transparency in Treaty-based Investor-State Arbitration (opened for signature 10 December 2014, entered into force 18 October 2017). The Convention has been signed by only 23 States and has been ratified by only nine of them.

[57] *Lithgow and ors v United Kingdom* App no 9006/80 (ECtHR, 8 July 1986) paras 200–02.

[58] CJEU, Opinion 1/17 (*CETA*) [2019] ECLI:EU:C:2019:341, paras 189ff.

B. Umbrella Clauses as a Guarantee for Access to Justice

The aim of an umbrella clause is to ensure that a commitment taken by the State can be adjudicated by an arbitral tribunal seized on the basis of the treaty in which the clause is included.[59] The clause thus addresses two possible situations: either the covered commitment does not fall within the scope of any other forum's jurisdiction, in which case the only solution is then to have it adjudicated by the arbitral tribunal otherwise access to justice is not guaranteed, or the covered commitment refers to an adjudicator (which could be a domestic court or an international commercial arbitral tribunal) implying that the relationship with the treaty-based tribunal jurisdiction may be an issue.

One can address quite quickly the first situation, since it is very unlikely that a commitment of the State falls outside the scope of any jurisdiction, even when such commitment does not include a specific dispute settlement provision. Indeed, these commitments arise in almost all cases from a statute or a contract, but they may also take the form of a simple unilateral undertaking of the State, such as the granting of a permit. In any event, those commitments are expressed in legal instruments that are included within a legal order, namely that of the State. Therefore, if a dispute arises between them, even without an explicit dispute settlement provision, such a dispute would fall within the jurisdiction of the domestic courts of the host State. Therefore, the situation is as if there had been a dispute settlement provision referring to domestic courts.

When the dispute falls within the scope of a specific judge's jurisdiction, either due to a clause in the commitment or by default as explained above, the question of the relationship between that judge and the arbitral tribunal also needs to be explored. Two opposite trends can be identified in case law.

On the one hand, several arbitral tribunals have ruled that an umbrella clause could neutralize the effects of another dispute settlement clause. Those tribunals have ruled that they could exercise their jurisdiction over State commitments, be they contractual or unilateral. According to such an interpretation of the umbrella clause, the presence of a forum selection clause in the contract cannot bar the jurisdiction of the treaty-based tribunal because the arbitral tribunal in such a case is asked to assess the State's conduct only with regard to the treaty and not to the contract per se. In a different context not involving an umbrella clause (but raising the exact same question), the ad hoc Committee in *Vivendi v Argentina* has summarized this standpoint in the following manner:

> where 'the fundamental basis of the claim' is a treaty laying down an independent standard by which the conduct of the parties is to be judged, the existence of an exclusive jurisdiction clause in a contract between the claimant and the respondent state or one of its subdivisions cannot operate as a bar to the application of the treaty standard. At most, it might be relevant—as municipal law will often be relevant—in assessing whether there has been a breach of the treaty.[60]

[59]   See Section I above.

[60]   *Compañiá de Aguas del Aconquija SA and Vivendi Universal SA v Argentine Republic*, ICSID Case No ARB/97/3 (formerly *Compañía de Aguas del Aconquija, SA and Compagnie Générale des Eaux v Argentine Republic*), Decision on Annulment (3 July 2002) para 101.

Applying this standard may thus lead an arbitral tribunal, in order to rule on the alleged breach of the treaty, not to take into account a possible dispute settlement clause in the provision. Furthermore, it can be argued that if an arbitral tribunal were to refuse to exercise its jurisdiction on a contract by invoking the presence of a dispute settlement clause in said contract, this refusal would amount to a breach of the right to resort to arbitration that is recognized by the BIT.[61] That is why some arbitral tribunals have accepted that their jurisdiction be exercised on contracts on the basis of the umbrella clause of the treaty 'without regard for the dispute resolution clause in the [contract]'.[62] This approach of umbrella clauses then consists in applying strictly the dispute settlement clause of the treaty without taking account of the fact that one part of the dispute might also fall within the jurisdiction of another forum.[63]

On the other hand, some arbitral tribunals have adopted the exact opposite view. They consider that an umbrella clause does not allow an arbitral tribunal to bypass a forum selection clause in a contract or in any other commitment. According to this approach, in order to be able to assess whether the umbrella clause has been breached, arbitral tribunals should stay their proceedings pending the decision of the judge that has jurisdiction over the covered commitment. It is only if this judge identifies a breach of the commitment that the arbitral tribunal can rule that the umbrella clause has been violated. This was the position endorsed in the *SGS v Philippines* case,[64] among others.[65] The main reasons in favour of this position have been stated in the *SGS* case as follows:[66] first, the dispute settlement clause of a BIT may be qualified as a *lex generalis*, while the forum selection clause of the contract is a *lex specialis*. The latter must then be applied with priority. Second, an investment treaty is a framework instrument, made to 'support and supplement, not to override or replace' specific investment agreements such as contracts. According to this standpoint, an arbitral tribunal ruling on the basis of a treaty including an umbrella clause must, in order to assess whether such umbrella clause has been violated, ask the competent judge whether or not the commitment covered by the umbrella clause has been breached.

Therefore, there is no ready-made answer to the question of the exact jurisdictional effect of umbrella clauses. This is all the more true because the answer also depends to a large extent on the wording of the applicable umbrella clause: the narrower it is (eg as regards the covered commitments), the stricter the interpretation of the tribunal will be. However, this is precisely where the rule-of-law approach of umbrella clauses might be helpful in reaching a general understanding of the clause. Indeed, one additional factor could be taken into

---

[61] *SGS Société Générale de Surveillance SA v The Republic of Paraguay*, ICSID Case No ARB/07/29, Decision on Jurisdiction (12 February 2010) para 177.

[62] *Spyridon Roussalis v Romania*, ICSID Case No ARB/06/1, Award (7 December 2011) para 781.

[63] See also *Eureko v Poland*, Partial Award (19 August 2005) paras 112–13.

[64] *SGS v Philippines* (n 3) para 155.

[65] *Malicorp Limited v The Arab Republic of Egypt*, ICSID Case No ARB/08/18, Award (7 February 2011) para 103; *Bureau Veritas, Inspection, Valuation, Assessment and Control, BIVAC BV v The Republic of Paraguay*, ICSID Case No ARB/07/9, Further Decision on objections to Jurisdiction (9 October 2012) para 284; *Toto Costruzione Generali SpA v Lebanon*, ICSID Case No ARB/07/12, Decision on Jurisdiction (11 September 2009) paras 201–02.

[66] *SGS v Philippines* (n 3) para 141.

account, in order to determine whether the arbitral tribunal can exercise its jurisdiction on the basis of the umbrella clause, namely the question as to whether the other forum respects the right to a fair trial. In a nutshell, it could be argued that only when the forum State and the domestic courts do not respect the right to a fair trial that the extension of the arbitral tribunal's jurisdiction should be admitted. Still, the wording of the clause is the primarily relevant factor.

C. Umbrella Clauses and the Right to a Fair Trial

Depending on whether or not the judge designated by the State commitment covered by the umbrella clause respects the right to a fair trial, an arbitral tribunal may decide to extend or to refrain from extending its own jurisdiction over such commitment.[67]

If the arbitral tribunal is satisfied that the other forum, be it a domestic judge or a commercial arbitral tribunal, respects the basic requirements for a fair trial, the arbitral tribunal may accept more easily to stay its proceedings and wait for the other procedure to be carried out. An interesting statement has been made in this respect in *BIVAC v Paraguay* in which the arbitral tribunal decided to suspend the arbitral procedure for three months. This period was decided in order to give the investor the possibility to file its claims before the domestic jurisdictions designated by the contract. [68] The Tribunal stated that, if the investor did not avail itself of this possibility, the award would be rendered. However, the tribunal added the following remark, in the event that the investor would refer to domestic jurisdictions: 'the Tribunal will retain jurisdiction over these proceedings for a reasonable period of time, to allow the tribunals of Asunción to hear the Claimant's claim'.[69] What is interesting here is that the Tribunal refers to the domestic courts' jurisdiction but seems to retain the possibility to resume the arbitral proceeding in the event the national procedure takes too long. Besides, the Tribunal asked the parties to report on the status of the domestic proceeding every six months. Accordingly, it may be argued that the Tribunal accepted the jurisdiction of the domestic courts, but provided that the domestic court must rule on the case within a reasonable period of time, which is an important aspect of the right to a fair trial.[70] This is how umbrella clauses may be, in the end, an interesting tool to ensure that the right to a fair trial is guaranteed while respecting the fundamental principles of distinction of jurisdiction.

Alternatively, an arbitral tribunal may decide not to stay its proceeding and to directly address the contractual questions at stake, without taking into account the presence of a dispute settlement provision in the covered commitment. This solution has been endorsed by a certain number of tribunals, on the mere basis of a broad interpretation of

---

[67] It is understood here that the judge 'designated' by the commitment may be either designated explicitly (by a dispute settlement clause in a contract for instance) or implicitly (in the case of a legislative statute for instance, there may be an article providing the jurisdiction of an arbitral tribunal but absent such a provision, such a statute shall be by default subject to the domestic judge jurisdiction).

[68] *BIVAC BV* (n 65) para 284.

[69] ibid.

[70] See in this respect European Convention for the Protection of Human Rights and Fundamental Freedoms (opened for signature 4 November 1950, entered into force 3 September 1953) 213 UNTS 221, art 6(1) and ACHPR art 7(1)(d) which both include the right to get a decision in a reasonable period of time.

the umbrella clause.[71] Yet, this position might be further supported in situations where the judge designated by the covered commitment does not respect the basic requirements of the right to a fair trial. A good illustration can be found in *Strabag SE v Libya*, where the contracts referred to the domestic courts. However, the treaty-based arbitral tribunal decided to uphold its jurisdiction to hear the contract claims on the basis of the umbrella clause of the treaty. It did so considering the situation in the host State, which clearly excluded 'the possibility for Claimant to pursue its claims in Libyan courts in tranquillity and safety'.[72] Even if the Tribunal did not mention the rule of law as such, it is clear that the rationale of its decision was the impossibility for the investor to benefit from a fair trial. Therefore, the decision was partially informed by the rule of law. Besides, this solution was not meant to be applied as a matter of principle: on the contrary, it was issued 'in light of the protracted conditions of insecurity in Libya since 2011'.[73] Had the Libyan courts been in a position to guarantee a fair and safe trial, the tribunal might have decided not to hear the contract claims.

However, reference to a judge that does not respect the basic requirements of the right to a fair trial might be rare in practice, as an investor will hardly ever sign a contract referring to a judge which is known for being partial or lacking independence. Nevertheless, an investor may rely on an umbrella clause in a treaty to make sure that its contractual rights will be adjudicated by an arbitral tribunal. Besides, the commitment of the State may also be made in the form of a unilateral act which is not negotiated and in which the State might impose on the investor a dispute settlement provision in favour of the domestic judge. In this hypothesis, the other forum's incapacity to fulfil the basic requirements of the right to a fair trial is another argument in favour of the extensive scope of the umbrella clause. Apart from the legal basis that has been invoked by arbitral tribunals which decided to uphold their jurisdiction even in the presence of a dispute settlement provision in the commitment covered by the umbrella clause,[74] a further argument could be based on the object and purpose of BITs. These treaties aim to create an effective and efficient system of protection for foreign investment. A tribunal may, therefore, consider that the full satisfaction of this purpose implies interpreting the umbrella clause in a way that does not bar the exercise of its own jurisdiction, in order to allow investors to appeal to a jurisdiction which respects the general principles of fair trial.

Consequently, a rule-of-law approach to umbrella clauses might help reach a general conclusion: an arbitral tribunal should not exercise its jurisdiction under the umbrella clause when the forum State is competent to adjudicate the covered commitment in accordance with the requirements of fair trial; when the same forum does not respect such requirements, the arbitral tribunal should exercise its jurisdiction over the commitment. In this respect, umbrella clauses could act as a safety net for the rule of law. However, this requires a proper interpretation of umbrella clauses as discussed below.

---

[71] See references above nn 61–63.
[72] *Strabag SE v Libya*, ICSID Case No ARB(AF)/15/1, Award (29 June 2020) para 196.
[73] ibid.
[74] See references above nn 61–63.

IV. The Necessity of a Broad Interpretation of Umbrella Clauses to Promote the Rule of Law

Umbrella clauses can only be a buttress to the rule of law if they are interpreted in a certain manner. There are specifically two issues on which case law is still divided but about which reference to the role played by umbrella clauses in terms of rule of law may support one view instead of the other. These are the identification of the covered commitments (Section A) and the covered acts of the State (Section B). In both cases, it is possible to assume that only the broadest interpretation would really help umbrella clauses to serve the rule of law.

A. The Covered Commitments: Umbrella Clauses as a Means to Secure All the Commitments of the State

One of the most salient questions relative to umbrella clauses is whether they cover, in addition to contractual undertakings, unilateral commitments of States, such as those which may be taken in a domestic statute or in any other domestic legal act. For rule-of-law purposes, both contractual and unilateral commitments shall be covered.

There is no doubt that contractual undertakings fall within the scope of umbrella clauses as a contract signed with a foreign investor is a 'commitment' of the State. This is also true when the clause refers to a 'specific' commitment that the State may have entered into vis-à-vis a foreign investor, since a contract would surely be considered as such.[75] Some treaties even explicitly refer to contracts, like the Chile–Austria BIT.[76] In such a case, there is no doubt that only contractual undertakings can be covered. Nevertheless, absent such a strict wording, there is no reason to exclude, as a matter of principle, other forms of commitments.

First, some umbrella clauses are drafted in a sufficiently broad manner as to certainly include unilateral commitments. Hence, when the clause refers to 'any' obligation or commitment, it can be assumed that '[u]nder its ordinary meaning the phrase "any obligation" refers to obligations regardless of their nature' so that unilateral commitments are obviously covered.[77] That conclusion was endorsed by several arbitral tribunals even in cases where the wording of the clause was slightly different. That was the case, in particular, in *SGS v Pakistan*, in which the applicable umbrella clause covered 'the commitments' that the State had entered into.[78] Likewise, in *LG&E v Argentina*, the Tribunal admitted that the umbrella clause, which referred to 'any obligation' of the State covered the commitments made by the State through the enactment of the Gas Law and other regulations.[79]

---

[75] See eg the wording of the umbrella clause in the Switzerland–Philippines BIT (1997) art X(2): '[e]ach Contracting Party shall observe any obligation it has assumed with regard to specific investments in its territory by investors of the other Contracting Party'.

[76] Chile–Austria BIT (1997) art 2(4) stipulates that '[e]ach Contracting Party shall observe any contractual obligation it may have entered into towards an investor of the other Contracting Party with regard to investments approved by it in its territory'.

[77] *Enron Corporation, Ponderosa Assets LP v Argentine Republic*, ICSID Case No ARB/01/3, Award (22 May 2007) para 274.

[78] *SGS v Pakistan* (n 3) para 166. See Switzerland–Pakistan BIT (1995) art 11 ('Either Contracting Party shall constantly guarantee the observance of the commitments it has entered into with respect to the investments of the investors of the other Contracting Party').

[79] *LG&E Energy Corp, LG&E Capital Corp, and LG&E International, Inc v Argentine Republic*, ICSID Case No ARB/02/1, Decision on Liability (3 October 2006) para 175. Argentina–USA BIT (1991) art II(2)(c) reads: 'Each Party shall observe any obligation it may have entered into with regard to investments'.

However, the scope of umbrella clauses remains problematic as other tribunals have refused to extend them to unilateral commitments, such as in *Burlington v Ecuador*. Although the umbrella clause in that case covered 'any obligation [the State] may have entered into',[80] the Tribunal interpreted this wording as covering only contractual commitments.[81] Arguably, reference to obligations 'entered into' may justify a slightly narrower interpretation. However, it is possible that another arbitral tribunal could have accepted that the clause extended to unilateral acts. There is no reason, as a matter of principle, to exclude unilateral acts from the scope of umbrella clauses. The possibility of extending the scope of the clause to unilateral commitments seems to find roots in general international law but it can also find support by reference to the rule of law.

Pursuant to general international law, a unilateral act is generally considered to give rise to an international obligation, depending on the context in which it is adopted. As stated by the International Court of Justice, '[w]hen it is the intention of the State making the declaration that it should become bound according to its terms, that intention confers on the declaration the character of a legal undertaking'.[82] This statement suggests that the binding character of a unilateral act in international law mainly depends on the intent of the State. But the presence of an umbrella clause in a treaty is precisely a circumstance that reveals an intent of the State to give to its commitment a mandatory value in the international legal order. Hence the form of the commitment is not really relevant, or at least is less relevant than the State's intent. The mere presence of an umbrella clause may be an element in favour of covering any commitment of the State, be it contractual or not.

A rule-of-law-approach to umbrella clauses further supports the inclusion of unilateral commitments. By providing a forum for any claim based on an alleged breach of an undertaking of the State, umbrella clauses ensure that such undertakings can effectively be adjudicated. Therefore, umbrella clauses can be considered as a way of enforcing host country promises, which is an important element of legal certainty which is itself an element of the rule of law. For instance, the CJEU stated that 'the principle of legal certainty requires that Community rules enable those concerned to know precisely the extent of the obligations which are imposed on them'.[83] Yet, in order to know what the state of the law is, you have to be able to rely upon the State's commitments which precisely describe your own rights and obligations. Therefore, the actual possibility of enforcing a State's promises or commitments do support legal stability.

There is no doubt that legal stability forms part of the rule of law. In his 2004 Report, the UN Secretary-General indeed indicated that the rule of law implied 'legal certainty ... and procedural and legal transparency'.[84] The UN General Assembly also recalled in 2012 'the importance of fair, stable and predictable legal frameworks' for the purposes of the rule of law.[85] The Venice Commission stated that 'generally shared traits of the rule of law' included legality and legal certainty.[86] Yet, there can be no legal stability without States being

---

[80] Ecuador–USA BIT (1993) art II(3)(c).
[81] *Burlington* (n 4) para 206.
[82] Nuclear Tests (*Australia v France*) (Judgement) [1974] ICJ Rep 253, para 43.
[83] CJEU, Case C-345/06, *Gottfried Heinrich* [2009] ECLI:EU:C:2009:140, para 44.
[84] See UNSC (n 7) para 6.
[85] See UNGA (n 35) para 8.
[86] See Commission (n 37).

bound to respect their commitments. Therefore, the rule of law, by imposing legal stability, requires States to respect their undertakings.

In this sense, umbrella clauses can play an important role especially in cases where they are the only means to ensure that such undertakings can be actually adjudicated (ie cases where the State's commitment does not include a dispute settlement provision or includes one referring to a judge that does not present sufficient guarantees in terms of the right to a fair trial). But umbrella clauses can further the rule of law only if they cover the widest possible range of States' commitments. Indeed, if they were to be limited to contractual undertakings, there would be no full legal stability, since the State could still modify unilaterally any commitment made under another form. Hence, a true rule-of-law approach militates in favour of a broad understanding of the scope of umbrella clauses.

Of course, even though this conclusion should be applicable as a matter of principle, it may still be reversed by the umbrella clause's wording. An arbitral tribunal cannot rule *contra legem* and, for example, has no right to include unilateral commitments in the scope of an umbrella clause that would explicitly cover contracts only. Furthermore, there is an inherent limit to the scope of umbrella clauses which cannot be interpreted to cover any obligation of the State; were it otherwise, other protection clauses would be redundant.[87] Nonetheless, provided that those limits are kept in mind, umbrella clauses can be given a broad interpretation in terms of scope.

B. The Clause Protects against Any Act of the State

A rule-of-law approach to umbrella clauses also works in favour of a broad interpretation on another subject, namely the acts of the State that should be covered by an umbrella clause in the context of contractual commitments. Some tribunals have ruled that only the acts of the State adopted in a sovereign capacity (*jure imperii*) which breached the contract can be considered as a violation of the umbrella clause.[88] This point of view stems from the general principle that a violation of a contract can only be an internationally wrongful act if it is attributable to a State acting as a sovereign and not as a contractor.[89] Indeed, when a State acts as would any private contractor, the State must be treated as such and thus cannot be held liable under international law: it is only as a party having breached a contract so that the consequences must be drawn accordingly, ie in the context of the contractual provisions. As stated by the Tribunal in *Impregilo*, a:

---

[87] See *El Paso Energy International Company v Argentine Republic*, ICSID Case No ARB/03/15, Decision on Jurisdiction (27 April 2006) para 76:

> [I]f this interpretation were to be followed—the violation of any legal obligation of a State, and not only of any contractual obligation with respect to investment, is a violation of the BIT, whatever the source of the obligation and whatever the seriousness of the breach—it would be sufficient to include a so-called 'umbrella clause' and a dispute settlement mechanism, and no other articles setting standards for the protection of foreign investments in any BIT.

[88] See the references above n 2. This position has been endorsed eg in *Pan America Energy LLC and BP Argentina Exploration Company v Argentine Republic*, ICSID Case No ARB/04/8, Decision on Preliminary Objections (27 July 2006) para 105.

[89] See specifically in the context of expropriation claims, *Consortium* (n 5); *Bayindir Insaat Turizm Ticaret Ve Sanayi AS v Islamic Republic of Pakistan*, ICSID Case No ARB/03/29, Decision on Jurisdiction (14 November 2005) para 183

[h]ost State acting as a contracting party does not 'interfere' with a contract; it 'performs' it. If it performs the contract badly, this will not result in a breach of the provisions of the Treaty … unless it be proved that the State or its emanation has gone beyond its role as a mere party to the contract, and has exercised the specific functions of a sovereign authority.[90]

However, this position is also disputed, and several arbitral tribunals have refused to take into account the nature of the State action considering that, by referring to a 'commitment', an umbrella clause does not introduce any distinction based on the nature of the breach. In several cases, tribunals refused to consider the distinction, in particular because '[l]ogically, one can characterize every act by a sovereign State as a "sovereign act"—including the State's acts to breach or terminate contracts to which the State is a party'.[91] In the context of such a divided case law, it seems difficult to reach a final answer as to the relevance of the nature of the State action.[92] Here again a rule-of-law analysis of umbrella clauses is clearly opposed to taking into account the nature of the State's action.

If umbrella clauses are to be used as instruments of the rule of law in the sense that they provide for a possibility to adjudicate a claim based on a breach of a commitment of the State, such clauses have to be interpreted in such a way as to cover any acts of the State and not only those which it performs as a sovereign. If the contrary interpretation were to be retained, it would limit the investor's right to access to a judge to some acts of the State. As a consequence, it would reduce the scope of the jurisdictional protection granted by umbrella clauses. Furthermore, this distinction between the State acting as contractor or as sovereign can only be relevant, by definition, in the context of a contract and is not applicable in cases where the undertaking is made as a unilateral act.[93] Besides, in contracts, the very purpose of the clause is to ensure adjudication, by an arbitral tribunal, of a possible contract claim rather than supporting the binding character of contractual obligations that exists in any event.[94] This aim would be missed if such adjudication covered only part of the acts of the State.

Therefore, recourse to the rule-of-law purpose of umbrella clauses clearly supports the rejection of their limitation to acts performed as a sovereign. This may shed a new light on the matter and help to solve the inconsistency in case law with regard to this particular question.

V. Umbrella Clause and Access to Domestic Courts

A final issue is that of the room left to the courts in the interpretation of umbrella clauses that is defended in this chapter. Indeed, our approach is based on the assumption that the domestic judge may not respect the fair trial requirements. However, there are obviously

---

[90] *Impregilo* (n 5) para 278.

[91] *SGS v Paraguay* (n 61) para 135. The refusal to consider the distinction was also assumed eg in *Duke Energy Electroquil Partners & Electroquil SA v Republic of Ecuador*, ICSID Case No ARB/04/19, Award (18 August 2018) para 320.

[92] However, there are strong arguments in favour of the exclusion of such a distinction, see Schill (n 6) 39–40.

[93] See the references above n 5.

[94] See Schill (n 6) 36. See also *WNC* (n 1).

two limits to this: first, some domestic judges fully respect the right to a fair trial so resort to an arbitral tribunal is unnecessary. Second, one could argue that the rule of law requires, in the name of access to justice, access to domestic jurisdictions. For example, the UN General Assembly resolution on the rule of law of 2012 stated that 'the independence of the judicial system, together with its impartiality and integrity, is an essential prerequisite for upholding the rule of law and ensuring that there is no discrimination in the administration of justice'.[95] There is no doubt that the 'judicial system' here refers to the domestic system and that, above all, the rule of law implies access to independent justice within domestic legal orders. The ECtHR explicitly refers to access to domestic justice in the context of Article 6(1),[96] and the African Charter on Human and Peoples' Rights provides for a right to access to domestic justice.[97]

Hence, there is here a discrepancy between, on the one hand, the requirement that the domestic judge be accessible to all and, on the other hand, the interpretation of umbrella clauses that is supported here, which in many cases leads to bypassing the domestic judge's jurisdiction in favour of that of arbitral tribunals. One can even argue in an extreme fashion that, if umbrella clauses were to be interpreted in a manner that systematically prevented domestic judges from exercising their jurisdiction, this could present an obstacle to the rule-of-law requirement of ensuring access to domestic courts of law.

However, two remarks can be formulated in order to address this issue. First, barring the jurisdiction of another judge would be a breach of the rule of law only if such judge actually met the requirements of the right to a fair trial. If it does not, umbrella clauses could be a means to bypass such a judge's jurisdiction and to have contracts enforced by an arbitral tribunal. In this hypothesis, the umbrella clause could be used as a rule-of-law support (as described in Section II.C above). To recap: the rule of law does not imply merely a right to access to a judge, it implies a right to access to a judge that is independent and impartial.[98] Therefore, allowing investors to bypass the jurisdiction of a judge that does not meet the requirement of the fair trial principle cannot be considered as a breach of the rule of law.

Second, even though some arbitral tribunals have ignored the presence of a forum selection clause in the commitment covered by an umbrella clause and thus decided to exercise their own jurisdiction on such commitments,[99] this does not actually prevent the judge designated by the commitment from exercising jurisdiction. In fact, the latter exercises its jurisdiction on a different basis, which is totally independent of the jurisdiction of the arbitral tribunal. Barring exceptional circumstances that might lead the arbitral tribunal to issue an anti-suit injunction,[100] the judge designated by the commitment cannot be prohibited from ruling by the mere presence of an umbrella clause. That being said, it is also undesirable that two adjudicators can be in a position to rule on the same subject matter.[101] Therefore,

---

[95] See UNGA (n 35) para 13.
[96] See *Klass v Germany* (n 29) para 64.
[97] ACHPR art 7 grants 'The right to an appeal to competent national organs'.
[98] See Section I.B above.
[99] See the references above nn 61–63.
[100] Anti-suit injunctions are rather rare in investment arbitration practice. For an analysis in the context of ICSID, see Konstantinos Kerameus, 'Anti-Suit Injunctions in ICSID Arbitration' in Emmanuel Gaillard (ed), *Anti-Suit Injunctions in International Arbitration* (Juris 2005) 131.
[101] In our hypothesis, the subject matter is not strictly the same since one claim is based on the commitment of the State (ie contract) and the other on the treaty. Therefore, the cause of both actions is formally different.

if the judge designated by the commitment or the contract decided to exercise jurisdiction, the best solution would undoubtedly be the one adopted in several cases (in particular *SGS v Philippines*) where the arbitral tribunal stayed proceedings pending a decision of the domestic judge.[102] This approach is probably the best in order to reconcile both the interpretation of umbrella clauses that is consistent with the rule of law (described in Section III above), and the need to preserve access to domestic judges, as it is required by the rule of law. However, it is here argued that an additional parameter should be introduced in the analysis compared to the cases in which arbitral tribunals stayed the proceedings: the stay should be granted by the arbitral tribunal only provided that the other judge meets the standard of the fair trial principle. That is how umbrella clauses can play a major role in promoting the rule of law.

Consequently, umbrella clauses would not have the effect of automatically bypassing the domestic judges' jurisdiction so they would not be considered as a real threat to the rule-of-law requirement of access to (domestic) justice. Umbrella clauses may be a threat to the rule of law if an arbitral tribunal decided to ignore the other judge's jurisdiction without taking into account whether or not such judge meets the requirements of the fair trial principle.[103] Umbrella clauses can support the rule of law only if arbitral tribunals recognize that, in the presence of an umbrella clause that covers a commitment referring to a judge that is independent and impartial, they should stay their proceedings and refer the question of the breach of the commitment to that competent judge.

VI. Conclusion: Umbrella Clause and the Rule of Law

Umbrella clauses may be used as an essential tool to support the rule of law, and especially the necessity to guarantee access to a judge. For this purpose, umbrella clauses must be interpreted in a sufficiently broad fashion. In particular, subject to any specific wording, umbrella clauses should apply to contracts and unilateral commitments and should cover any type of government action. Accordingly, a rule-of-law approach of umbrella clauses is also a good way of bringing answers to questions that generally arise about them—namely, should they apply to contractual commitments only, or should they take into account the nature of the State action?

This conclusion does not only clarify the concept of the umbrella clause. It also helps to shed light on the content of the rule-of-law standard. Although it is not easy to determine whether umbrella clauses, as they have been described here, embody a formal ('thin') or a substantive ('thick') rule of law, access to a judge may refer to the first one but, on the other hand, the requirements that the competent judge rules in conformity with the right to a fair trial has more to do with the second one. Furthermore, we have seen in

---

However, and this is the main issue raised by umbrella clauses, in order to determine whether the umbrella clause has been breached, the arbitral tribunal has to review whether the commitment covered by the clause has been breached—which is by nature a question falling within the scope of the jurisdiction designated by the commitment. Consequently, there is some inherent overlap between the material scope of the two judges' jurisdictions.

[102] Several tribunals have accepted to do so, see the references in nn 64–65.
[103] This is what happened in the above-mentioned cases, see above nn 61–63.

this chapter that umbrella clauses have both a jurisdictional dimension (they can ensure access to justice) and a substantive one (they are a means of securing host States promises and commitments, hence promoting legal stability and certainty). This may thus reveal the somehow artificial character of the distinction between the jurisdictional and the substantive aspect of umbrella clauses since there can be no full rule of law without those complementary aspects.

10

The Use of Investment Treaty Standards to Enforce Other International Legal Regimes and Domestic Law

Velimir Živković

I. Introduction

The topic of this chapter is the use of substantive standards under investment treaties to enforce other (not investment protection–related) international obligations and domestic law, seen through the prism of the rule of law. In general, investor-State dispute settlement (ISDS) is one of the critical 'norm–interface' points[1] where different legal regimes contest for recognition. In interpreting and applying substantive standards of investment protection, diverse factual scenarios can put investment arbitrators into contact with different international and national legal regimes. The legal framework governing the applicable law and rules of interpretation allow for a considerable discretion in deciding if and how these regimes impact the reasoning process and/or outcome of a case when applying specific investment treaty standards.

From the rule-of-law perspective, diversity of scenarios and the presence of discretion presents both tangible challenges and considerable opportunities. Relationship between international investment law and other legal regimes is generally a topic of debate and often intense disagreement between States, investors, academics, and non-governmental organizations (NGOs).[2] Focusing specifically on the enforcement of non-investment legal regimes through treaty standards, arbitration case law shows an uneven approach when it comes to the scope and depth of engagement with these regimes in decision-making, which can to a large extent be attributed to the permissive framework mentioned above. In terms of the commonly recognized rule-of-law requirements, there is thus a tension between legality and predictability. In light of the still largely 'atomized' structure of international investment law, it is not a tension that is easy to tackle.

But the awards discussed in this chapter also provide grounds for optimism and leave the door open to suggesting normative paths forward. First, investment arbitrators can and do persuasively engage with different legal regimes when applying investment treaty standards, often exhibiting a deep understanding of other areas of law and admirable attention

---

[1] ILA Rule of Law and International Investment Law Committee Sydney Conference 2018 Report (2018) <www.ila-hq.org/index.php/committees> accessed 10 March 2021, 25–26 (report by Stephan W Schill) (hereafter ILA Sydney Report 2018).

[2] Malcolm Langford and others, 'Empirical Perspectives on Investment Arbitration: What Do We Know? Does It Matter?' (15 March 2019) ISDS Academic Forum Working Group 7 Paper, 22–26 and materials cited therein.

Velimir Živković, *The Use of Investment Treaty Standards to Enforce Other International Legal Regimes and Domestic Law* In: *Investment Protection Standards and the Rule of Law.* Edited by: August Reinisch and Stephan W. Schill, Oxford University Press.
© Velimir Živković 2023. DOI: 10.1093/oso/9780192864581.003.0010

to detail. This supports the idea that productive engagement with other legal regimes can be both broadly replicated across ISDS when applying substantive investment treaty standards, and also channelled towards normatively desirable goals. As argued in this chapter, the ideals of the rule of law at both international and national levels can offer such normative guidance.

The rule of law, as a globally endorsed ideal, is not just a benchmark for assessing what we have now, but also a worthy aim in itself. Bearing in mind the importance and impact of many investment awards on States and their populations, the key role of substantive investment treaty standards, and regardless of how much the future of investment law remains open to debate, this aspect is something worth focusing on. Investment arbitrators should, to the extent that this is legally and factually possible, enforce other legal regimes or at least offer clear explanations as to why such enforcement cannot take place. Such an approach can bolster the international and the national rule of law and offer credibility to claims that treaty standards are actually 'good-governance standards embodied in investment protection treaties'.[3]

The chapter proceeds as follows. Section II addresses the concept of the rule of law used in this chapter, the legal framework governing the relationship of substantive standards and other legal regimes, and how 'enforcement' is understood for present purposes. Section III highlights one side of the enforcement coin and discusses prominent examples of enforcing international, domestic, and both international and domestic legal regimes through substantive investment treaty standards. Section IV addresses the obverse of the coin, discussing some of the typical examples where enforcement, despite being possible, did not occur. Section V, building on these examples, discusses the rule-of-law tension between legality and predictability in enforcing other legal regimes and offers a potential normative path to tackle this tension through the focus on the international and national rule of law. Section VI briefly concludes.

II. 'Rule of Law' and Enforcement of Other Legal Regimes in ISDS

A. Concept of the 'Rule of Law'

The 'rule of law' is not a self-explanatory concept. As noted by the ILA Committee on investment law and the rule of law, the concept is multifaceted and open to serious disagreement.[4] Be that as it may, at least a working definition of the rule of law is desirable as a framework for analysis and evaluation of how substantive standards of investment protection interact with other legal regimes. A working definition is perhaps the most that can be hoped for when bearing in mind the debates surrounding the different understandings.

There is a considerable degree of pessimism that a true international consensus can be reached about the meaning of the 'rule of law', as it seems contingent on differing cultural and historical contexts.[5] The well-known theoretical divide between 'thinner', formal

---

[3] As famously put by the late Thomas Wälde in *International Thunderbird Gaming Corporation v The United Mexican States*, UNCITRAL, Separate Opinion Wälde (1 December 2005) para 13.

[4] ILA Sydney Report 2018 (n 1) 1–5.

[5] ibid 2–3 and 18.

understandings of the rule of law (emphasizing stability, predictability, due process) and 'thicker', substantive ones (emphasizing the relevance of substance, or 'good law') adds to the complexity.[6]

A promising way forward is to recognize that substantive understandings tend to incorporate and build upon formal ones.[7] This allows distilling a theoretical 'common core' of requirements,[8] further accompanied by empirical inquiries into the common rule-of-law denominators among national legal systems.[9] A working definition of 'the rule of law' for present purposes would thus contain the following elements:[10]

- legality and non-arbitrariness;
- legal certainty, predictability, and transparency;
- access to justice before independent and impartial adjudicators;
- non-discrimination and equality before the law.

There is no implied hierarchy of importance among these requirements, so focusing the discussion on one or more of them depends on the context. For the purposes of this chapter, the focus is on the first two requirements—legality and non-arbitrariness, on the one hand, and certainty, predictability, and transparency, on the other. These are most pertinent for a general discussion of substantive law issues concerning the interplay of different legal regimes. Requirement of access to justice is mainly a procedural one,[11] and issues of non-discrimination and equality before the law would usually refer to specific content of individual standards (eg national treatment or fair and equitable treatment (FET)). Of course, when access to (impartial) justice and non-discrimination and equality are applied as requirements of relevant standards, non-investment legal regimes can and sometimes do play a role in interpreting and applying them.[12] However, for a bird's-eye view of the rule-of-law issues surrounding enforcement of other regimes, broad requirements of legality and predictability offer the most suitable benchmarks and, as argued below, create tension points in jurisprudence. For an initial understanding of why this is so, it is necessary to briefly explore the legal framework that governs the relationship of substantive investment standards and other legal regimes.

---

[6] Brian Z Tamanaha, *On the Rule of Law: History, Politics, Theory* (CUP 2004) 91; Paul Craig, 'Formal and Substantive Conceptions of the Rule of Law: An Analytical Framework' (1997) 12 PL 467, 468; ILA Sydney Report 2018 (n 1) 3–5.

[7] See generally Peter Rijpkema, 'The Rule of Law: Beyond Thick and Thin' (2013) 32 Law & Phil 793; ILA Sydney Report 2018 (n 1) 5; Tamanaha (n 6) 65–71.

[8] Velimir Živković, 'Pursuing and Reimagining the International Rule of Law Through International Investment Law' (2020) 12 HJRL 1, 7–8.

[9] See eg ILA Sydney Report 2018 (n 1) 7–14 and 33–60; and European Commission for Democracy through Law (Venice Commission) 'Report on the Rule of Law' (4 April 2011) CDL-AD(2011)003rev.

[10] See Živković (n 8) 3–6 and materials cited there; as well as ILA Sydney Report 2018 (n 1) 16–31.

[11] The procedural ISDS element of independent and impartial access to justice is high on the reform agenda of, for example, UNCITRAL Working Group III; see Malcolm Langford and others, 'UNCITRAL and Investment Arbitration Reform: Matching Concerns and Solutions' (2020) 21 JWIT 167.

[12] On the right to fair trial and relevance of international obligations, see discussion of the *Al Warraq v Indonesia* case in Section III below.

B. Relationship of Substantive Standards and Other Legal Regimes

International investment law encompasses thousands of treaties, and substantive decision-making in ISDS can touch upon many other legal regimes due to the de facto extensive subject matter of investment agreements.[13] Such diversity makes the relevant legal framework multifaceted. Due to a number of differences, it is worth briefly examining the relationship of substantive standards in investment treaties with other international legal regimes separately from that of domestic law.

1. Substantive investment standards and other international legal regimes

Substantive investment standards are international legal provisions, contained in international treaties, and are in principle subject to public international law as applicable law.[14] The wording of these provisions is the starting point in their application, and nothing prevents treaty drafters to include therein explicit instructions as to the relationship with other regimes of international law. This, however, does not seem to be the case in practice. Rather, the potential relationship with other legal regimes can be regulated by a separate applicable law provision of the treaty.[15] These provisions, when present, usually broadly designate other rules and principles of international law as applicable.[16] At the same time, such clauses usually list potentially applicable legal regimes without specifying further when and how they are to be applied, giving investment tribunals a considerable degree of discretion.[17]

In case the investment treaty in question does not have an applicable law provision, the matter can be addressed by the applicable arbitral rules. The most famous example is Article 42(1) of the ICSID Convention,[18] stating that in the absence of agreement 'the Tribunal shall apply the law of the Contracting State party to the dispute (including its rules on the conflict of laws) and such rules of international law as may be applicable'. This provision has been a subject of considerable debate in literature and jurisprudence, but the prevailing opinion is that arbitrators have the discretion to apply either domestic or international law in their discrete domains as they see appropriate.[19] Rules of other arbitral institutions differ, but a common thread seems to be that in the absence of an agreement on substantive law the arbitrators have substantial discretion to apply the (rules of) law they see as appropriate, either through direct choice or through choosing of a suitable conflict of laws approach.[20]

---

[13] Rudolf Dolzer, 'The Impact of International Investment Treaties on Domestic Administrative Law' (2004-2005) 37 NYU J Intl L & Pol 953, 956; Dafina Atanasova, 'Applicable Law Provisions in Investment Treaties: Forever Midnight Clauses?' (2019) 10 JIDS 396, 396–97.

[14] Ole Spiermann, 'Applicable Law' in Peter Muchlinski, Federico Ortino and Christoph Schreuer (eds), *The Oxford Handbook of International Investment Law* (OUP 2008) 107–10. This excludes the substantive provisions contained in domestic statutes or individual investment contractual arrangements.

[15] Atanasova (n 13) 397–98.

[16] Research by Atanasova also shows that large number of investment agreements do not contain applicable law provisions (ibid 407). Those that do exist usually contain a list of sources which does not assign particular questions to any specific source (ibid 408–11 and materials cited therein).

[17] See generally Hege Elisabeth Kjos, *Applicable Law in Investor-State Arbitration: The Interplay between National and International Law* (OUP 2013) 61–103; see also *Total SA v Argentine Republic*, ICSID Case No ARB/04/1, Decision on Annulment (1 February 2016) paras 196–97.

[18] Convention on the Settlement of Investment Disputes between States and Nationals of Other States (opened for signature 18 March 1965, entered into force 14 October 1966) 575 UNTS 159 (hereafter ICSID Convention).

[19] See Christoph Schreuer and others, *The ICSID Convention: A Commentary* (2nd edn, CUP 2009) paras 236–44.

[20] Margaret Moses, *The Principles and Practice of International Commercial Arbitration* (3rd edn, CUP 2017) 84–85 and materials cited therein.

Another way in which other international legal regimes can impact a substantive investment standard is through interpretation. This field is primarily regulated by the Vienna Convention on the Law of Treaties,[21] which is also considered to embody customary international law principles.[22] Of primary importance here is the VCLT Article 31(3)(c), often seen as the lynchpin of 'systemic integration' in public international law.[23] It mandates that in interpreting a treaty, in addition to its context, the decision-maker 'shall' take into account 'any relevant rules of international law applicable in the relations between the parties'. Concerning investment treaty standards, if all the State parties to the investment agreement at hand are also subject to another set of international legal rules (treaty-based, arising from customary law or general principles), there is a clear legal mandate to take these rules into account.[24]

What is fairly clear is that the expressions 'relevant rules of international law' and 'taking into account' again leave a considerable amount of discretion to arbitrators. The open-ended nature of these phrases can lead to everything from an ultimate decision to reject any influence by 'extrinsic' rules on one end, to direct influence on interpretation of a treaty provision and, likely, the outcome of a dispute, on the other.[25]

Finally, investment tribunals are free to take account of other international obligations as facts.[26] The wide discretion of tribunals as to which facts they will deem relevant for their decision is common to both commercial and investment arbitration,[27] and is implicit in the decision-making power and procedural autonomy of arbitrators. Therefore, specific international legal obligations can (but are not guaranteed to) feature as determinative or at least important in assessing such matters as arbitrariness, fairness, or reasonableness of the host State behaviour.

The common thread through these various modes of interaction with other international legal regimes is the dearth of hard-and-fast rules that allows for considerable arbitral discretion. This provides welcome flexibility in light of many potential factual scenarios, but is not conducive to predictability. The situation is similar when it comes to domestic law.

2. Substantive investment standards and domestic law

The legal framework concerning engagement with domestic (municipal) law has certain similarities to the above, but also notable differences. First, it is again possible that the relevant treaty standard explicitly sets out its relationship with domestic law. This is rarely the case, but not unheard of.[28] As set out above, it is more common to find the relevant rules in

---

[21] Vienna Convention on the Law of Treaties (opened for signature 23 May 1969, entered into force 27 January 1980) 1155 UNTS 331 (hereafter VCLT).

[22] Trinh Hai Yen, *The Interpretation of Investment Treaties* (Brill 2014) 36–39.

[23] Campbell McLachlan, 'The Principle of Systemic Integration and Article 31(3)(c) of the Vienna Convention' (2005) 54 ICLQ 279; Campbell McLachlan, 'Investment Treaties and General International Law' (2008) 57 ICLQ 361.

[24] McLachlan (n 23) 369–74.

[25] Oliver Dörr, 'Article 31' in Oliver Dörr and Kirsten Schmalenbach (eds), *Vienna Convention on the Law of Treaties: A Commentary* (2nd edn, Springer 2018) paras 2, 38, 96–102 and materials cited therein.

[26] See for example *David R. Aven and ors v Republic of Costa Rica*, ICSID Case No UNCT/15/3, Award (18 September 2018) paras 417–23. See also *The Rompetrol Group NV v Romania*, ICSID Case No ARB/06/3, Award (6 May 2013) paras 172 and 251.

[27] See generally Robert B von Mehren, 'Burden of Proof in International Arbitration' in Albert Jan van den Berg (ed), *Planning Efficient Arbitration Proceedings: The Law Applicable in International Arbitration* (Kluwer Law International 1996) and William W Park, 'Arbitrators and Accuracy' (2010) 1 JIDS 25.

[28] An example is CARICOM–Cuba BIT (2000) art IV, which prescribes that FET is to be provided in accordance with domestic law.

applicable law provisions—either in investment agreements or otherwise applicable arbitral rules. Applicable law provisions usually list domestic law without specifying its particular role, and only a handful of treaties refer to domestic law to the exclusion of international law.[29] When it comes to arbitral rules, to reiterate, in both ICSID and non-ICSID settings there seems to be a considerable amount of discretion as to whether and when domestic law might apply in substantive decision-making.

One matter that is clear is that domestic law cannot formally influence the interpretation of an investment treaty standard under Article 31(3)(c) VCLT. As a more general point, and barring explicit exceptions, investment tribunals applying substantive standards are not bound by domestic law and keep for themselves the ultimate verdict on its relevance.[30] In many, if not most situations, domestic law will be treated as a fact.[31] However, as noted by Hepburn, municipal law is often treated as a 'qualitatively different' fact by the tribunals.[32] While the practice varies, the examination of domestic legality sometimes plays an important or even decisive role in establishing a breach of an investment treaty standard.[33]

Engagement with non-investment legal regimes can thus take different forms. What is then considered as 'enforcing' a regime through an investment treaty standard? A working definition of that term is necessary before engaging with the practical examples set out in Sections III–IV.

C. 'Enforcement' of Non-Investment Legal Regimes

As defined by *Black's Law Dictionary*, to 'enforce' means to either 'give force or effect' to a particular legal instrument or rule, or 'compel obedience' to the same, while 'enforcement' is 'the act or process of compelling compliance with a law'.[34] For present purposes, what is being applied in a given case is the investment treaty standard,[35] with independent normative content,[36] so it does not seem accurate to say investment arbitrators are 'compelling obedience' to another legal regime through their interpretation and application of substantive investment treaty standards—it is formally to the investment law obligations that the obedience is due. Giving 'force or effect' to a different legal regime more accurately captures the essence of 'enforcement' in this context.

Therefore, for the purposes of this chapter, enforcing non-investment regimes would mean that in interpreting and/or applying an investment treaty standard, rules of specific non-investment regime(s) played such a determinative role that the decision on whether

---

[29] Atanasova (n 13) 411–12 and materials cited therein.

[30] As well explained in *Fouad Alghanim & Sons Co for General Trading & Contracting, WLL and Fouad Mohammed Thunyan Alghanim v Hashemite Kingdom of Jordan*, ICSID Case No ARB/13/38, Award (14 December 2017) para 345; see also *Gami Investments, Inc v The Government of the United Mexican States*, UNCITRAL, Final Award (15 November 2004) para 95: ('A failure to satisfy requirements of national law does not necessarily violate international law').

[31] *Certain German Interests in Polish Upper Silesia* (Merits) PCIJ Rep Series A No 7.

[32] Jarrod Hepburn, *Domestic Law in International Investment Arbitration* (OUP 2017) 105.

[33] ibid 39–40 and 67–68.

[34] Bryan A Garner (ed), *Black's Law Dictionary* (9th edn, West 2009) 608.

[35] Campbell McLachlan, Laurence Shore and Matthew Weiniger, *International Investment Arbitration: Substantive Principles* (2nd edn, OUP 2017) paras 3.99–3.106; Zachary Douglas, *The International Law of Investment Claims* (CUP 2009) 39.

[36] Rudolf Dolzer, Ursula Kriebaum, and Christoph Schreuer, *Principles of International Investment Law* (3rd edn, OUP 2022) 187–88.

a breach of an investment standard occurred aligns with, or hinges on, what that non-investment regime required.

Enforcement understood in this way can come about via different formal paths. Taking environmental protection as an example, an investment tribunal can interpret an FET standard provision through VCLT Article 31(3)(c) and determine what 'fair and equitable' behaviour means by taking into account obligations contained in an environmental protection treaty to which both parties to the BIT at hand are also parties. But in case that Article 31(3)(c) is not applicable as there are no other relevant treaties between the parties to the investment agreement, international environmental obligations placed upon the host State or its domestic environmental legislation can feature as facts in applying the FET standard.

For example, assessing whether the State behaved in accordance with these rules can help in determining if it respected legitimate expectations or acted illegally and/or arbitrarily. The legal mechanism is different, but the ultimate outcome is not—the host State is found in breach (or not) of the investment treaty obligation primarily or for the most part because it breached (or not) an environmental obligation that was incumbent upon it.

Bearing in mind the concepts and definitions delineated above, the following two sections will respectively discuss examples of enforcement and non-enforcement of other legal regimes, aiming at illustrating the broader trends in the case law. This provides the basis for analysis and discussion of potential ways forward in Section V.

III. Examples of Enforcement of Other Legal Regimes

Examples of interaction with other legal regimes are numerous, as the number of investment awards has soared to roughly 700,[37] and factual scenarios involve diverse legal areas—constitutional law,[38] administrative law,[39] environmental law,[40] mining law,[41] criminal law and criminal procedure,[42] corporate law,[43] and tax law.[44] The merits of these awards often engage both international obligations and relevant domestic law, as many host States implement their international obligations through national legislation.

This section discusses a selection from different legal areas. The examples are structured according to the predominantly enforced legal regime(s)—obligations arising from other international law sources (Section A), intertwined international and domestic law obligations (Section B), and 'purely' domestic legal obligations (Section C). Common to these examples is a diligent engagement with and enforcement of other legal regimes. Coupled with

---

[37] UNCTAD Investment Policy Hub data <https://investmentpolicy.unctad.org/investment-dispute-settlement> accessed 22 December 2021.

[38] See *Glamis Gold, Ltd v The United States of America*, UNCITRAL, Award (8 June 2009); *Bernardus Henricus Funnekotter and ors v Republic of Zimbabwe*, ICSID Case No ARB/05/6, Award (22 April 2009).

[39] See for example *Técnicas Medioambientales Tecmed, SA v The United Mexican States*, ICSID Case No ARB (AF)/00/2, Award (29 May 2003); *Toto Costruzioni Generali SpA v The Republic of Lebanon*, ICSID Case No ARB/07/12, Award (7 June 2012).

[40] In addition to *Bilcon v Canada* and *Aven v Costa Rica* award discussed in Section III, see also *Peter A. Allard v Barbados*, PCA Case No 2012-06, Award (27 June 2016).

[41] *Gold Reserve Inc v Bolivarian Republic of Venezuela*, ICSID Case No ARB(AF)/09/1, Award (22 September 2014).

[42] *Rompetrol* (n 26).

[43] *Spyridon Roussalis v Romania*, ICSID Case No ARB/06/1, Award (7 December 2011).

[44] See eg *Yukos Universal Limited (Isle of Man) v The Russian Federation*, PCA Case No 2005-04/AA227, Final Award (18 July 2014).

the discussion of opposite examples in Section IV, this shows that the decision on whether to enforce a particular legal regime is often primarily a normative one.

A. Enforcing Other International Obligations: *Al-Warraq v Indonesia*

The *Al-Warraq v Indonesia*[45] award is centred around the bailout of the Indonesian Century Bank in 2008 and its aftermath. Briefly,[46] the claimant Hesham T.M. Al-Warraq is a Saudi national and was one of the bank's three main equity investors. Following the bailout, criminal investigations were launched against all three main shareholders concerning bank operations. Al-Warraq fled to Saudi Arabia and did not participate in the criminal proceedings and the ensuing trial. He was convicted in absentia, some of his assets were confiscated, and some were pursued for confiscation worldwide. Al-Warraq's claim was launched under the OIC Agreement on Promotion, Protection and Guarantee of Investments (OIC Agreement),[47] alleging breaches of several of its provisions, including that the bailout of the Century Bank amounted to an expropriation.[48] The key findings in relation to other legal regimes were made in relation to the alleged FET standard breach caused by the criminal proceedings and the trial.[49]

The key non-investment rules binding Indonesia in this case were those addressing the right to fair trial in Article 14 of the International Covenant on Civil and Political Rights (ICCPR),[50] which directly shaped the more general due process requirement of the FET standard in the case at hand. The tribunal considered the ICCPR a part of 'general international law', with undoubtedly binding legal provisions, and which should be obeyed in any case due to the principle of good faith that underpins them.[51] As put most clearly:

> When ratifying a treaty the State undertakes to honour its obligations under that treaty. This means in the present context its obligations to comply inter alia with the provisions of Article 14(3)(d) [of ICCPR] in all aspects. When it does not do so, it is the duty of the competent court or tribunal to so declare: even though there is no recourse to be had to the implementing agency—the Human Rights Commission—with respect to remedies.[52]

The ICCPR provisions thus shape the FET standard content through the 'vehicle' of the principle of good faith, and Article 31(3)(c) VCLT is not specifically referred to during the reasoning process. Although this is not stated, it seems likely this route was chosen by the tribunal because the ICCPR is not in force 'between the parties', regardless of whether 'the parties' are understood as all of the parties to the OIC Agreement or simply Indonesia and

---

[45] *Hesham T.M. Al-Warraq v Republic of Indonesia*, UNCITRAL, Final Award (15 December 2014).
[46] ibid paras 73–141.
[47] Agreement on Promotion, Protection and Guarantee of Investments among Member States of the Organization of the Islamic Conference (opened for signature 5 June 1981, entered into force 23 September 1986).
[48] *Al-Warraq* (n 45) paras 523–39; the claim was rejected as the bailout was a preventive measure allowed by the OIC Agreement.
[49] See generally ibid paras 556–621; the FET provision was 'imported' from the UK–Indonesia BIT (1976) through art 8 (MFN clause) of the OIC Agreement (see paras 540–55).
[50] International Covenant on Civil and Political Rights (opened for signature 16 December 1966, entered into force 23 March 1976) 999 UNTS 171.
[51] *Al-Warraq* (n 45) paras 558–60.
[52] ibid para 561 (footnotes omitted).

Saudi Arabia (as the claimant's home State). The Kingdom of Saudi Arabia is not a party to the ICCPR.[53]

Be that as it may, once Article 14 (and its para 3) was established as a relevant rule, it was systematically used by the tribunal (alongside secondary sources such as Human Rights Committee General Comments) to assess the behaviour of Indonesian police and judicial organs. On a number of issues, the tribunal also referred to the UN Convention against Transnational Organized Crime,[54] the UN Convention against Corruption,[55] and the Vienna Convention on Consular Relations,[56] although seeing them rather as relevant facts.[57] Finally, the tribunal examined domestic Indonesian law at various points to analyse the conduct of criminal investigations and the trial.[58]

Based on this complex mosaic, the tribunal found specific FET breaches as the claimant was not properly notified of the criminal charges against him; was tried and convicted in absentia; the sentence was not properly notified; he was not able to appoint legal counsel; and he was not able to appeal his sentence.[59] The ultimate failure to observe international legal obligations directly led to a finding of a breach of the FET standard, in particular through a denial of justice committed by Indonesia.[60] Finalizing its findings, the tribunal concluded 'that the Claimant did not *receive fair and equitable treatment as enshrined in the ICCPR*'.[61] Although ultimately there was no liability of Indonesia,[62] the award is a good example of enforcement as understood in this chapter.[63] The 'autonomous' requirements of the FET standard (due process/denial of justice) were both interpreted and applied in light of other legal obligations—specifically ICCPR—and breaches of these other obligations decisively contributed to finding the breach of the treaty standard.

B. Enforcing a Combination of International and National Law

In many situations, a specific subject area of the dispute (such as the environment, health protection, labour rights, cultural and natural heritage) in a given host State will be regulated by at least partially overlapping international and domestic legal instruments. Dualist systems may implement their international obligations through domestic legislation, or

---

[53] See OHCHR 'Status of Ratification: Interactive Dashboard' <https://indicators.ohchr.org> accessed 22 December 2021.

[54] United Nations Convention against Transnational Organized Crime (opened for signature 15 November 2000, entered into force 29 September 2003) 2225 UNTS 209.

[55] United Nations Convention against Corruption (opened for signature 31 October 2003, entered into force 14 December 2005) 2349 UNTS 41.

[56] Vienna Convention on Consular Relations (opened for signature 24 April 1963, entered into force 19 March 1967) 596 UNTS 261.

[57] *Al-Warraq* (n 45), paras 582–83, 590–94, 607, 612.

[58] ibid paras 584–88, 596–610.

[59] ibid para 621.

[60] ibid paras 556–621.

[61] ibid para 621 (emphasis added).

[62] Claimant's misconduct caught by OIC Agreement art 9 (mandating investors to 'refrain from all acts that may disturb public order or morals or that may be prejudicial to the public interest') eventually made the claim inadmissible (see ibid paras 631–48).

[63] For somewhat similar reliance on domestic law to exonerate the behaviour of domestic organs, see *Binder v The Czech Republic*, UNCITRAL, Final Award (Redacted) (15 July 2011) paras 448–67; for an opposite outcome, see *Chevron Corporation and Texaco Petroleum Corporation v Ecuador (II)*, PCA Case No 2009-23, Second Partial Award on Track II (30 August 2018) paras 8.56–8.60.

different aspects of the subject matter might be regulated by different (international and national sources). In those situations, it is not surprising that an arbitral tribunal might refer to both international and national law in applying substantive investment treaty standards to provide for a holistic assessment of the legal framework and also to add further persuasiveness to its findings, and thereby essentially enforce the international and national law in question. The two cases discussed in this section provide a good illustration of how this can be done effectively.

1. Phillip Morris v Uruguay

The often-discussed case of *Philip Morris v Uruguay*[64] arose from the imposition of so-called single presentation requirements (SPR) for tobacco brands in Uruguay (limiting product variety to one per brand) and the increased size of graphic health warnings on cigarette packages.[65] Claimant alleged that these regulations comprised, inter alia, an indirect expropriation of its intellectual property (specifically the use and display of trademarks) and unfair and inequitable treatment due to the arbitrariness and the lack of respect for legitimate expectations.[66]

The tribunal dismissed both claims as it found that Uruguay diligently complied with its domestic and international obligations in enacting measures aimed at preserving and improving the health of the population.[67] The legal framework surrounding tobacco control was extensively summarized by the tribunal,[68] with a particular emphasis on the WHO Framework Convention on Tobacco Control (FCTC),[69] and relied thereon for its critical findings (although it should be borne in mind that the SPR measure is not per se mandated/ supported by the FCTC). The tribunal recognized the 'police power' of the host State to protect public health as a situation different from indirect expropriation, through a process explicitly involving VCLT Article 31(3)(c).[70] It then examined the measures in question primarily by assessing their compliance with the (non-investment) legal framework. As stated at the outset, '[i]t should be stressed that the [relevant measures] have been adopted in fulfilment of Uruguay's national and international legal obligations for the protection of public health'.[71] The relevant sources used were also the Uruguayan Constitution and a number of legislative acts.[72]

The FET claim was dismissed for similar reasons. The measures were not arbitrary as they had a clear goal of public health protection and adhered to domestic and international obligations.[73] The WHO FCTC was particularly taken as 'a point of reference on the basis of which to determine the reasonableness of the two measures'.[74] There was also no breach

---

[64] *Philip Morris Brands Sàrl, Philip Morris Products SA and Abal Hermanos SA v Oriental Republic of Uruguay,* ICSID Case No ARB/10/7, Award (8 July 2016).

[65] ibid paras 108–32.

[66] ibid para 309.

[67] The expropriation claim was also dismissed as no plausible 'severe economic deprivation' occurred (see ibid paras 276–86).

[68] ibid paras 85–123; this includes, among others, the WHO Framework Convention on Tobacco Control, accompanying Guidelines for the Convention, Uruguayan Constitution, and a number of laws and decrees.

[69] WHO Framework Convention on Tobacco Control (opened for signature 21 May 2003, entered into force 27 February 2005) 2302 UNTS 166.

[70] *Philip Morris* (n 64) paras 290–301.

[71] ibid para 302.

[72] ibid paras 302–04.

[73] ibid paras 390–420.

[74] ibid para 401.

of legitimate expectations and legal stability as the claimant could not expect that Uruguay would not further legislate in this area, particularly when considering domestic constitution and international conventions.[75]

The award is also significant for the reliance on *amicus* submissions of the World Health Organization and the Pan American Health Organization to determine, inter alia, the importance of FCTC Guidelines for the application of the tobacco regulating measures;[76] support for the way Uruguay implemented its obligations;[77] and non-arbitrariness of the measures.[78] *Amicus* submissions are a topic of controversy in literature,[79] but the *Philip Morris* award provides a good example of how they can assist tribunals to persuasively enforce non-investment obligations.

Philip Morris v Uruguay also exemplifies enforcement of human rights concerning broader third-party/public interests, and not just those relating to investors individually.[80] The explicit enforcement of obligations such as the right to health is still a relative rarity,[81] but the well-reasoned discussion in *Philip Morris* shows that this by no means needs to be the case.

2. Aven v Costa Rica

Aven v Costa Rica[82] is one of a number of awards dealing with environmental issues and obligations arising from international and domestic environmental law.[83] What makes this award stand out within that field is the depth and thoroughness with which the tribunal assessed the complex legal framework of Costa Rica. The dispute arose as the development of a tourist estate on the Costa Rican coast, mostly owned by the claimants, was eventually stopped due to infringements of domestic environmental legislation and international environmental commitments, resulting also in criminal proceedings against the leading claimant Mr Aven.[84]

According to claimants, actions of Costa Rican governmental entities were completely unexpected, with ulterior motives, resulted in complete destruction of the investment, and were coupled with unjust criminal prosecution that had serious reputational effects for Aven.[85] In legal terms, this allegedly resulted in breaching Articles 10.5 (minimum standard of treatment, including FET) and 10.7 (prohibition of unlawful expropriation) of the DR–CAFTA agreement.[86] Per respondent, all of its actions were in accordance with applicable domestic law and long-standing policy of protection of environment,[87] being in addition

---

[75] ibid paras 421–34.

[76] ibid para 91.

[77] ibid paras 141–42, 362, 391, 393.

[78] ibid paras 306, 404, 407.

[79] See on this Farouk El-Hosseny, *Civil Society in Investment Treaty Arbitration: Status and Prospects* (Brill 2018) 175–84.

[80] Silvia Steininger, 'What's Human Rights Got to Do with It? An Empirical Analysis of Human Rights References in Investment Arbitration' (2018) 31 LJIL 33, 55–56.

[81] ibid 52–53; human rights are sometimes enforced more implicitly—see in that sense *South American Silver Limited v The Plurinational State of Bolivia*, PCA Case No 2013-15, Award (30 August 2018) paras 523–24, 532, 561, 565, 634, 640.

[82] *Aven* (n 26).

[83] Non-compliance with international (environmental) obligations also formed the backbone of claimant's case is *Allard* (n 40), where the claims were rejected (see paras 50–61 and 170–79).

[84] *Aven* (n 26) paras 6–7 and 93–181 for details.

[85] ibid paras 6–7.

[86] ibid para 183.

[87] ibid paras 8 and 185.

allowed under Articles 10.11 (adoption and maintaining of non-contravening environ-mental measures) and 17.2 (effective enforcement of environmental laws) of DR–CAFTA.[88] The tribunal set out that:

> [b]y signing the Treaty, Respondent has agreed that there are limits to the manner in which a Party may implement and enforce its own environmental laws. It must do so in a fair, non-discriminatory fashion, applying said laws to protect the environment, following principles of due process, not only for its adoption but also for its enforcement.[89]

The tribunal engaged with the non-investment law with exemplary thoroughness in order to assess the host State's enforcement of relevant laws. The elaboration of environmental legal framework spans some 30 paragraphs, and notes the 11 most relevant legal sources (ran-ging from international conventions, over the Constitution of Costa Rica, to implementing environmental legislation), an organogram of all relevant Costa Rican authorities and their competences and seven key principles of Costa Rican law.[90]

Various elements of the identified framework then feature in nearly 200 paragraphs of the tribunal's assessment of both the actions to stop the project and pursue criminal pro-ceedings. The conclusion reached was that the environmental measures were non-arbitrary and consistent with Costa Rican and international law,[91] and that criminal proceedings were consistent with domestic law,[92] resulting in the ultimate rejection of all claims.

The *Aven* award is an example of the potential complexity of relevant legal regimes and their interplay, as well as of how thoroughly arbitrators can disentangle this complexity to reach well-argued conclusions. From a host State perspective, awards such as this and *Phillip Morris v Uruguay* can provide welcome reassurance that diligent compliance with other legal obligations can go a long way in preventing potential liability.

C. Enforcing Domestic Law

The final possibility is that the tribunal only deals with enforcement of domestic, muni-cipal law when applying substantive investment treaty standards. This is a somewhat pecu-liar situation as in many cases domestic law (or rather its amendments) might be the very reason that an investment claim is launched in the first place. But careful assessment under otherwise uncontroversial municipal law can be a proper course of action in a range of situ-ations, especially those where the investor alleges procedural improprieties and a potential denial of justice. This was the general setting in the two examples discussed below.

1. *Bilcon v Canada*

Bilcon v Canada[93] (a NAFTA-based claim) involved a detailed examination of domestic en-vironmental and administrative law and demonstrated that invocation of environmental

---

[88] ibid paras 385 and 390.
[89] ibid para 413.
[90] ibid paras 417–46.
[91] ibid para 585.
[92] ibid paras 630–31.
[93] *William Ralph Clayton, William Richard Clayton, Douglas Clayton, Daniel Clayton and Bilcon of Delaware Inc v Government of Canada*, PCA Case No 2009-04, Award on Jurisdiction and Liability (17 March 2015).

concerns is not per se a trump card over investment protection and/or rule-of-law require-ments. The way in which Canada applied its environmental law remained critically im-portant, leading to a finding of breach of a number of substantive standards.

As for the facts, the claimant US investor was interested in pursuing mining operations in the province of Nova Scotia.[94] Canadian officials at different levels of government ex-pressed support for this project.[95] However, the operating licence was eventually denied after a negative report of an environmental joint review panel (JRP) that used 'commu-nity core values' as a critical benchmark for its assessment of the project.[96] The notion 'core values', the claimant suggested, was not a part of the applicable legal framework for the JRP's determinations.[97]

The tribunal's analysis touched upon several points concerning the relevance of domestic law for breaching the minimum standard of treatment found in Article 1105 of NAFTA. As noted, the violation of domestic law must reach a high threshold of gravity for such a breach, and mere controversy or even clear-cut mistakes may not suffice.[98] The decision of the JRP to base its decision on a previously non-existent criterion was found to be above this threshold. After an extensive scrutiny of the applicable legal framework on the federal and provincial levels, the JRP proceedings and the decision itself, the tribunal determined that the JRP report was fundamentally at variance with applicable Canadian laws,[99] reaching the level of arbitrary behaviour.[100] The gravity of misconduct led to a breach of Article 1105 of NAFTA.[101]

Notably, it is not simply the case that domestic law was breached, but that the breach was interwoven with the requirements of the international minimum standard. There were three key findings. One is the breach of a legitimate expectation that the investor and its in-vestment will be accorded 'a fair opportunity to have the specifics of [their] case *considered, assessed and decided in accordance with applicable laws*.'[102] Second, there was a breach of procedural due process in the sense that the investor was not given any fair notice about the effective change of the legal test introduced by the JRP.[103] This particular requirement of fair notice was not explicitly linked to domestic law in terms of its content by the tri-bunal, despite reliance on expert witnesses,[104] and it remains somewhat unclear what 'fair' or 'reasonable' notice would have been in concrete terms. Finally, there was a fundamental substantive breach of due process in the decision of the JRP that invented its own novel legal test, and 'thus arrived at its conclusions under both the laws of federal Canada and Nova Scotia without having fully discharged a crucial dimension of its mandated task'.[105]

The award also offers an illustration of the overlap of protection offered by different in-vestment treaty standards. The identified violation of domestic law also triggered a breach of the national treatment standard in Article 1102 of NAFTA.[106] In essence, as no other

---

[94] ibid paras 5, 8–9.
[95] ibid paras 458–71.
[96] ibid paras 502–06.
[97] ibid paras 20–24.
[98] ibid para 437.
[99] ibid paras 530–35.
[100] ibid para 591.
[101] ibid paras 598–604.
[102] ibid para 603 (emphasis added).
[103] ibid paras 451, 534–43.
[104] ibid paras 539–41.
[105] ibid para 452.
[106] ibid paras 689–725.

domestic investor was ever subjected to such prejudicial novelty as introduced by the JRP, claimant was also discriminated against.[107] However, and more troublingly for tribunals as enforcers of other legal regimes, the award was also accompanied by a powerful dissent.[108] Professor McRae as a dissenting arbitrator strongly argued that 'community core value' was actually within the mandate of the JRP as it was a shorthand for relevant human environment effects,[109] but also suggested that if Canadian law was infringed (an arguable point) this would not meet the threshold for breaching NAFTA Article 1105.[110] This last point indicates that total alignment between demands of substantive investment treaty standards and other legal regimes may not be possible—even if a breach of eg domestic law is found, an arbitral tribunal is the ultimate arbiter of whether that breach is grave enough for finding an accompanying breach of an investment treaty standard.

The dissent shows to what extent 'getting it right' when it comes to other regimes remains a demanding task, as well as that domestic (rule of) law can sometimes simply not be an important enough consideration when applying substantive standards. At some point, the autonomous international legal character of these standards can ultimately take precedence.

2. Dan Cake v Hungary

Moving to the perhaps less controversial field, to insolvency law, the *Dan Cake v Hungary*[111] award focused on insolvency proceedings against Danesita, a Hungarian confectionery manufacturer predominantly owned by the Portuguese company Dan Cake. Danesita experienced fluctuating business fortunes, and eventually faced a request for liquidation by its creditors.[112] Despite the apparent inclusion of all necessary documents for convening a meeting of creditors, the Metropolitan Court of Budapest preliminarily denied Danesita's request to stop the liquidation proceedings,[113] and ordered supplementary filings of more documents.[114] Danesita found it impossible to comply with the order for a number of reasons and its assets were eventually sold, thus ending the existence of the investment.[115]

The claimant alleged a breach of several investment treaty standards, all focusing on the illegality of the Budapest court's decisions. The tribunal centred on the FET standard and whether a breach occurred through imposition of requirements by the court which were *'obviously unnecessary or impossible to satisfy*, or in *breach of a fundamental right'*.[116] This test was the tribunal's own refinement of the denial of justice requirements for the present case.[117]

The key to the assessment was the tribunal's extensive engagement with the court decision itself, a number of relevant Hungarian laws, and their academic commentary.[118] The

---

[107] ibid paras 715–16 and 724–25.
[108] *William Ralph Clayton, William Richard Clayton, Douglas Clayton, Daniel Clayton and Bilcon of Delaware Inc v Government of Canada*, PCA Case No 2009-04, Dissenting Opinion McRae (10 March 2015).
[109] ibid paras 14, 20, 23–26.
[110] ibid paras 30–31, 34–37.
[111] *Dan Cake (Portugal) SA v The Republic of Hungary*, ICSID Case No ARB/12/9, Decision on Jurisdiction and Liability (24 August 2015).
[112] ibid paras 38–39.
[113] ibid para 54.
[114] ibid.
[115] ibid paras 59–62.
[116] ibid para 117 (emphasis in the original).
[117] ibid para 117 in conjunction with para 146.
[118] ibid paras 99–142.

tribunal insisted that it is not an appellate tribunal, even when the appeal to a particular decision was not possible.[119] Still, it then quoted the decision of the Metropolitan court in its entirety,[120] before engaging with the Hungarian legislation (including the Civil Procedure Act), jurisprudence and doctrine to establish what sort of discretion the Court might have in ordering the additional documents in liquidation proceedings.[121] After recognizing that the Court might have the power to order additional, non-statutorily mandated documents which are truly 'necessary',[122] the tribunal in the main part of the award dissects in considerable detail each of the seven requests for filing ordered by the court. The tribunal refers to the domestic legal framework, reasonableness, and actual commercial and business reality before finding that all these requests were unnecessary.[123]

This extensive analysis is a thorough build-up to concluding 'the Court simply did not *want*, for whatever reason, to do what was *mandatory*'.[124] Based on the breaches of domestic law, Hungary was found liable for breaching the FET standard and the prohibition of unjust and discriminatory measures.[125] Although the award has a rather narrow scope, it does further demonstrate the ability of investment tribunals to grapple with rather minute details of domestic law.

Taken together, the awards discussed above show that extensive and sophisticated engagement with other legal regimes is well within the grasp of investment arbitrators under different substantive standards of treatment. Yet, the enforcement of these regimes is not a simple affair. Intertwinement with specific requirements of individual standards, required degree of gravity of breach of other legal obligations, and even the basic question of whether there was a breach in the first place all complicate substantive decision-making. It is perhaps at least partly for these reasons that, as discussed in the next section, many tribunals do not enforce other legal regimes in situations where this is legally possible.

IV. Examples of Non-Enforcement

Although this chapter is dedicated to the *use* of investment treaty standards to enforce other legal regimes, it is instructive to discuss some opposite examples as well—those where enforcement did not occur despite arguably being legally and factually possible. Examining some typical scenarios where this non-enforcement took place not only provides a more holistic picture of arbitral case law, but helps illustrate the rule-of-law tension between legality of decision-making and its predictability when it comes to interaction with other legal regimes. These scenarios of non-enforcement can also offer insight into the practical or more principle-based obstacles that normative solutions proposed in Section V can encounter.

The first situation is when non-investment obligations are invoked (usually, but not exclusively, by the host State) in a cursory manner or almost as an afterthought to other

---

[119] ibid para 117.
[120] ibid para 99.
[121] ibid paras 108–16.
[122] ibid paras 113 and 116.
[123] ibid paras 118–42.
[124] ibid para 142 (emphasis in the original).
[125] ibid paras 160-161.

arguments. Arbitral tribunals in general have a duty to decide based on the actual submissions of the parties,[126] and should not (unilaterally)[127] develop or complement them even if they feel sympathetic to the idea of enforcing other legal regimes. In *Siemens v Argentina*, for example, Argentina claimed that by virtue of its 1994 Constitution, international human rights law was part of its legal framework and that upholding claimant's claims would breach human rights obligations.[128] However, the tribunal noted that '[t]his argument has not been developed by Argentina … without the benefit of further elaboration and substantiation by the parties, it is not an argument that, *prima facie*, bears any relationship to the merits of this case'.[129] In *Azurix v Argentina*, Argentina argued that BIT obligations breached human rights treaties that protected consumer rights, and that these latter treaties should have precedence.[130] The tribunal summarily noted that '[t]he matter has not been fully argued and the tribunal fails to understand the incompatibility in the specifics of the instant case'.[131] Finally, in a more recent case of *South American Silver v Bolivia*, while the tribunal was generally more open towards Bolivia's arguments involving human rights of indigenous communities,[132] it gave short shrift to upholding these rights in the context of the 'police powers' of Bolivia after Bolivia for the most part of the proceedings had not raised them at all.[133]

Another scenario, which illustrates well the discretion of the tribunals in these matters, is where the lack of engagement with other legal regimes is simply not explained. For example, in *White Industries v India*,[134] the tribunal fairly thoroughly assessed whether waiting for nine years to enforce an arbitral award was either breach of legitimate expectations, denial of justice, or breach of the requirement under the governing BIT to provide 'effective means' for claimant to enforce its rights.[135] The tribunal eventually found a breach of the 'effective means' obligation,[136] but apart from taking into account practice and circumstances in India,[137] the tribunal did *not* elaborate at all what were the actual enforcement deadlines in domestic law and to what extent this might have contributed to assessing the behaviour of Indian courts. The tribunal insisted on using a somewhat underexplained 'objective, international standard'[138] for assessing the situation, implicitly suggesting that domestic legal obligations were not a sufficiently relevant fact for its decision.

Finally, it also happens that tribunals fairly explicitly reject enforcement of other legal regimes in situations where this might be possible. A prominent example is the Procedural Order 2 in *von Pezold v Zimbabwe*, replying to an *amicus* submission requesting the consideration of human rights of indigenous peoples. The tribunal noted, inter alia, that the reference to general international law 'in the BITs does not incorporate the universe of

---

[126] See generally Phillip Landolt, 'Arbitrators' Initiatives to Obtain Factual and Legal Evidence' (2012) 28 Arb Intl 173.

[127] Tribunals do have a possibility of suggesting new lines of inquiry, but this proactivity should be the object of further communication with both parties (see Hepburn (n 32) 120).

[128] *Siemens AG v The Argentine Republic*, ICSID Case No ARB/02/8, Award (6 February 2007) paras 74–75 and 79.

[129] ibid para 79.

[130] *Azurix Corp v The Argentine Republic*, ICSID Case No ARB/01/12, Award (14 July 2006) paras 254 and 261.

[131] ibid para 261.

[132] *SAS v Bolivia* (n 81) paras 523–24, 532, 561, 565, 634, 640.

[133] ibid paras 622–25.

[134] *White Industries Australia Limited v The Republic of India*, UNCITRAL, Final Award (30 November 2011).

[135] ibid ss 10.3., 10.4, and 11.

[136] ibid para 11.4.19.

[137] ibid paras 10.3.14–10.3.15, 10.4.10, 10.4.18, 11.3.2.

[138] ibid para 11.3.2; this was also based on the claimant's contention in para 11.1.5.

international law into the BITs or into disputes arising under the BITs'.[139] Furthermore, the tribunal did not agree that 'any decision of these Arbitral tribunals which did not consider the content of international human rights norms would be legally incomplete'[140] nor that consideration of invoked human rights was 'part of their mandate under either the ICSID Convention or the applicable BITs'.[141] Such reasoning, arguably allowed by the permissible legal framework discussed in Section II above, also implies a much more limited role for systemic integration in international law.

Relatedly, there are situations where tribunals recognize the potentially contradictory obligations of host States, but consciously avoid the issue of enforcement. In *Suez v Argentina*, the tribunal noted that Argentina was subject to both investment protection and human rights obligations, which were 'not mutually exclusive' and could be fulfilled simultaneously.[142] Similar understanding seems to have motivated the *SAUR v Argentina* tribunal in concluding that Argentina's human rights and investment obligations operated 'at different levels'.[143]

In both cases, human rights considerations had no real relevance for the final outcome, and such findings imply a 'parallel life' for different obligations and a limited role for their interplay.

As both this and previous sections illustrate, the practice of investment tribunals is heterogeneous despite in many situations being based on the same or similar legal framework. In light of this, it is necessary to recognize the rule-of-law issues that arise, but also think about normative ideals that may guide the tribunals in their decision-making.

V. Substantive Standards, Other Legal Regimes, and the Rule of Law: Where Are We Now? Where Should We Go?

Investment tribunals do enforce other legal regimes beyond international investment law, and they can do so in a thorough and arguably persuasive manner. Examples in Section III show a high level of engagement with relevant legal regimes and well-argued conclusions. While it is sometimes suggested that effectively interacting with heterogeneous legal regimes might be asking too much from investment arbitrators,[144] it seems fair to say that tribunals can perform this task well.

At the same time, as seen in the examples in Section IV above, investment tribunals retain a fairly broad discretion whether and to what extent to enforce or even acknowledge other legal regimes when applying substantive standards. This leads to tensions, discussed in Section A below, between two key rule-of-law benchmarks—legality and non-arbitrariness, on the one hand, and predictability and consistency, on the other. The solution simply cannot be found in the applicable legal framework, and the exercise of the discretion given

---

[139] *Bernhard von Pezold and ors v Republic of Zimbabwe*, ICSID Case No ARB/10/15, Procedural Order No 2 (26 June 2012) para 57.

[140] ibid para 58.

[141] ibid para 59.

[142] *Suez, Sociedad General de Aguas de Barcelona, SA and Vivendi Universal, SA v Argentine Republic*, ICSID Case No ARB/03/19, Decision on Liability (30 July 2010) para 262.

[143] *SAUR International SA v Republic of Argentina*, ICSID Case No ARB/04/4, Decision on Jurisdiction and Liability (6 June 2012) para 331.

[144] Andreas Kulick, *Global Public Interest in International Investment Law* (CUP 2012) 28–29.

to the arbitrators arguably requires taking a normative stance. As argued in Section B below, broader considerations of upholding and promoting the international and/or national rule of law can offer such normative guidance for interpreting and applying the substantive investment standards.

A. Tension between Legality and Predictability in Enforcing Other Legal Regimes

From the perspective of legality and non-arbitrariness, different ways in which the arbitrators can, but are not obliged to, enforce other legal regimes make it unlikely that their actions often cross into the territory of illegality. There are, of course, examples (albeit very rare) of awards being annulled for excess of powers due to a manifest failure to apply the proper law in substantive matters.[145] But in the vast majority of situations, there is ample scope for arbitrators to decide to (not) enforce or interact with a particular source of law other than the applicable investment treaty. This is covered by the broad discretion to qualify (or not) other sources of law as relevant facts, to identify incidental issues in the way they see fit,[146] or to disregard particular rules or regimes as insufficiently relevant, eg for purposes of interpretation. Examples discussed in Sections III–IV show that different approaches do also materialize in practice—and that from the rule-of-law perspective it is not possible to simply deem one or the other as illegal or arbitrary.

This is far from ideal when the rule-of-law requirements of predictability and consistency are added to the equation. Within a legal framework which is not conducive to predictability, there is no certain way in which an investor and/or the host State can forecast if a given tribunal will, for example, see relevant international human rights provisions as indispensable for finding a breach (as in *Al Warraq v Indonesia*) or reject their relevance as a matter of general principle (*von Pezold v Zimbabwe*). Nor is there necessarily any predictability as to which particular instruments or areas of law will be taken into account by individual tribunals. This last point indicates the problem that certain legal regimes might gain special recognition and deference within investment law, while others may still fight for that recognition.[147]

Provided that this tension between legality and predictability is recognized as a problem, one solution lies in clearer drafting of international investment agreements. In addition to exception clauses which can affect the application of substantive standards,[148] there are recent examples of specifically clarifying the status of other potentially relevant legal regimes. Most prominently, Article 8.10 of the Canada–EU Comprehensive Economic and Trade Agreement (CETA), providing for an enhanced wording of the FET standard, also clarifies that breaches of domestic law or other international agreements do not automatically entail

---

[145] See for example *Venezuela Holdings, BV et al v Bolivarian Republic of Venezuela*, ICSID Case No ARB/07/27, Decision on Annulment (9 March 2017) paras 114 and 153–59.

[146] Jonathan Brosseau, 'A Choice-of-Law Approach to the Application of Domestic Law in Investment Arbitration' 10–19 (forthcoming, on file with the author).

[147] See generally also Dafina Atanasova, 'Non-Economic Disciplines Still Take the Back Seat: The Tale of Conflict Clauses in Investment Treaties' (2021) 34 LJIL 155.

[148] See on this recently Caroline Henckels, 'Permission to Act: The Legal Character of General and Security Exceptions in International Trade and Investment Law' (2020) 69 ICLQ 557.

the breach of that standard;[149] equally relevantly, Article 8.31, setting out rules on applicable law and interpretation, confirms the relevance of the VCLT for interpretation of CETA and adds that 'other rules and principles of international law applicable between the Parties' are also applicable.[150] Clarifying further the tribunal's task, the same Article also states that domestic law is to be treated as a fact, but that tribunal's decision would not settle the matter of illegality or interpretation of that law for domestic purposes.[151]

Such clarifications are welcome. They also seem to be rare. At least for now and perhaps for the foreseeable future, the majority of investment claims are likely to be made under the 'old style' investment agreements.[152] The application of substantive standards thus in most cases remains squarely within the complex framework highlighted in Section II.A above. Such a situation calls for ideas on how the tension between legality and predictability can be at least eased, if not resolved, within the existing coordinates and by arbitrators themselves. As Sections III–IV illustrate that application of particular legal regimes is often essentially a normative choice, it is worth considering what normative arguments can be put forward for a particular approach towards interpreting and applying the substantive standards. As further elaborated in the next sections, broader considerations of the international and national rule of law can provide powerful normative guidance in that sense.

B. Resolving the Tensions: International Rule-of-Law Considerations

Stepping away for the moment from the narrower topic of applicable law and interplay of legal regimes through substantive standards, an important normative point is that international investment law and ISDS are embedded into the fabric of public international law; there are good grounds to see ISDS as international law's most vibrant dispute settlement mechanism.[153] Such a comparatively powerful mechanism is potentially a good vehicle to enhance effective compliance with and coherence of international law. Although investment law has its own sphere of operation, its embeddedness in the international legal order makes it easier to argue that investment arbitrators should lend a helping hand in upholding the ideal of the international rule of law more generally.[154]

In line with the understanding in this chapter, the international rule of law would demand effective, predictable, coherent, transparent, and equal application of the whole body of international law. Taking this in principle uncontroversial normative position can also help guide decision-making. In terms of interpretation and application of substantive standards, enhancing the international rule of law would mean securing that host States

---

[149] Comprehensive Economic and Trade Agreement (CETA) between Canada of the one part, and the European Union and its Member States, of the other part (signed 30 October 2016, provisionally applied since 21 September 2017) (hereafter CETA) art 8.10(6) and (7).

[150] ibid art 8.31(1).

[151] ibid art 8.31(2).

[152] For example, UNCTAD notes that '[a]t least 55 known treaty-based investor–State dispute settlement (ISDS) cases were initiated in 2019 ... all under old-generation treaties signed before 2012' (UNCTAD, 'IIA Issues Note' (July 2020) Issue 2 <https://unctad.org/system/files/official-document/diaepcbinf2020d6.pdf> accessed 22 December 2021, 1).

[153] Langford and others (n 2) 2–5 and 22 and materials cited therein.

[154] See generally on this James Crawford and Penelope Nevill, 'Relations between International Courts and Tribunals: The "Regime Problem"' in Margaret A Young (ed), *Regime Interaction in International Law: Facing Fragmentation* (CUP 2012).

and (increasingly) investors are duly held accountable to the full range of international obligations incumbent upon them. Rule-of-law considerations would suggest heeding the call for 'systemic integration' in interpretation and relying on relevant non-investment regimes when assessing potentially problematic host State behaviour.[155] If the same legal outcome can be achieved by either a discretionary assessment under substantive standards of treatment in investment treaties or (also) by reference to other obligations of the host State to support the reasoning process, interests of legal certainty would suggest opting for the latter.

Another related normative point is that the host States should ideally fulfil all obligations they may have under other legal regimes. If substantive investment standards are clinically isolated from other obligations, this can (and in practice at least sometimes does)[156] create a dynamic in which investment protection looms disproportionately large over domestic decision-makers.[157] The threat of investment claims and their associated expenses, not to mention adverse awards, can successfully dissuade host States from pursuing goals mandated by legal regimes which do not contain similarly effective enforcement mechanisms and in that sense present less of a 'threat' for domestic lawmaking and policymaking.

This is not to say that it is always possible to avoid an explicit clash between substantive investment protection standards and other international legal regimes. Tribunals can find fulfilling other international obligations by the host State to be inconsistent with investment treaty standards, and clashes between international legal obligations are nothing new. Saying that investment standards should always be used to enforce any other international regime that claims applicability would mean that substantive standards of investment protection are essentially 'empty vessels' and could well go against the principle of effectiveness in interpretation.[158]

Perhaps the most that can be said is that an 'ideal' international rule of law is not possible in any case and that best efforts and 'good enough' is what can reasonably be expected.[159] This does not detract from the general point that, within inevitable limits, efforts to uphold the widely shared ideal of the international rule of law can guide investment arbitrators in enforcing other international legal regimes through substantive investment standards. As it seems to be one of the rare ideals on which there is a broad (even if somewhat shallow) global consensus, the international rule of law offers an excellent reference point for both legal and legitimate exercise of arbitrators' discretion.

C. Resolving the Tensions: Domestic Rule-of-Law Considerations

Taking a different perspective, substantive investment standards often effectively allow for a judicial review of sensitive domestic decision-making.[160] Investment claims are also often

---

[155] As done, for example, in *Philip Morris* (n 64) (see Section III above).
[156] This is the problem of potential 'regulatory chill', on which see Jason Bonnitcha, Lauge N Skovgaard Poulsen and Michael Waibel, *The Political Economy of the Investment Treaty Regime* (OUP 2017) 238–44.
[157] See in that sense also *Bilcon v Canada*, Dissenting Opinion McRae (n 108) paras 45–51.
[158] Dörr (n 25) para 34 and materials cited therein.
[159] See in that sense Martin Krygier (with Adam Winchester), 'Arbitrary Power and the Ideal of the Rule of Law' in Christopher May and Adam Winchester (eds), *Handbook on the Rule of Law* (Edward Elgar 2018) 75.
[160] Federico Ortino, 'The Investment Treaty System as Judicial Review' (2013) 24 Am Rev Intl Arb 437; Gus Van Harten, *Investment Treaty Arbitration and Public Law* (OUP 2007).

high-profile affairs that draw considerable domestic attention. In light of this, thorough engagement with domestic law in the awards may indicate existing problems and offer guidelines so as to help enhance the rule of law in host States.[161] As the ideal of the rule of law is so widely shared by those same States, such enhancement would be another normatively desirable goal.

However, entanglement by investment tribunals with the national rule of law raises considerable issues. It is appealing to say that substantive investment standards should help with effective, predictable, and equal application of domestic law, just as they should on the international plane. The critical caveat is that domestic law cannot contravene the relevant investment treaty standards at hand or, potentially, other international obligations that are enforced through that standard. At some point a choice may need to be made—if domestic legislation is in breach of these standards, then it cannot be enforced. Doing so would go against the very idea of foreign investment protection.[162] When outright conflict can be avoided, however, the question is how the engagement with domestic law can be made more nuanced and persuasive, with potential domestic rule-of-law benefits. Alternatively, even if the conflict is present, thorough explanation of why it occurred and how it can potentially be avoided is still a worthy normative endeavour.

Awards discussed above offer useful illustrations of potential contributions to the national rule of law or lack thereof. In *Bilcon v Canada*, a critical finding of a NAFTA Article 1105 breach relied on both an explicit infringement of domestic statutes and the fuzzier requirement of 'fair notice' that needed to be given to Bilcon that the JRP would apply a novel legal approach. To reiterate, 'Bilcon lacked reasonable notice of the "community core values" approach … [and] the Tribunal concurs that Bilcon had been denied a fair opportunity to know the case it had to meet and to address it'.[163] But it remains unclear what would suffice as 'fair notice' and the tribunal did not delve into the details of Canadian law on this issue. Nor it is clear whether sufficient 'fair notice' would have mattered as to make the arguable breach of domestic law excusable or at least not sufficiently grave from the perspective of the treaty standard. What can Canada or its provinces thus learn for the future in terms of what 'fair notice' is needed before introducing legal innovations? What is the guidance, if any, for rectifying potential rule-of-law defects?

Awards, such as *Al Warraq v Indonesia* or *Dan Cake v Hungary*, also offer different examples. Both awards, in their respective fields, clearly identify the shortcomings of the way in which domestic institutions acted and framed these shortcomings within the pre-existing legal obligations stemming from international and/or domestic law. As much as there is no guarantee that host States would necessarily adopt insights for governance reform from such awards, offering thorough analysis in terms of pre-existing legal obligations would seem to be a normatively desirable path to substantive decision-making.

---

[161] Velimir Živković 'Fair and Equitable Treatment between International and National Rule of Law' (2019) 20 JWIT 513, 519–22 and materials cited therein; it is important to note that in empirical terms the link between investment awards and the effect on domestic governance remains complex and disputed—see on this Mavluda Sattorova, *The Impact of Investment Treaty Law on Host States: Enabling Good Governance?* (Hart 2018).

[162] Ortino (n 160) 439–43.

[163] *Bilcon* (n 93) para 543.

VI. Conclusion

The relationship between substantive investment standards, non-investment legal regimes, and the rule of law is multifaceted. There are various ways of giving effect to other legal regimes—by treating them as law, fact, or interpretive guide—and the discretion of arbitrators remains considerable in this area. Importantly, investment tribunals can and do enforce other legal regimes, and can do so effectively when they choose so through interpreting and applying the substantive standards in investment treaties. The discussed cases show how critical other legal regimes can be for deciding the merits of investment claims, and how persuasively they can be applied by arbitrators.

But the practice remains uneven. In rule-of-law terms, there is a tension between disparate levels of reliance on non-investment legal regimes in investment arbitration case law, and the ideals of certainty and predictability. But the rule of law can also potentially offer a normative path out of this tension. For one, and bearing in mind the advantages of ISDS as a dispute settlement mechanism, enforcement of non-investment-related international obligations through substantive standards of treatment under investment treaties can help boost the international rule of law in terms of more consistent, coherent, and impactful application of the whole body of public international law. Second, when possible in terms of the international–municipal law hierarchy, investment tribunals should also enforce domestic law and/or thoroughly identify why this is not possible. Awards that do so can have beneficial impact on the domestic rule of law, even if that outcome might not be guaranteed.

To summarize in broad terms, as stated by Stephan Schill, 'governments need to be reminded of their role as enforcers of obligations that serve interests that compete with investment protection'.[164] The same role of enforcers can be and increasingly is ascribed to investment arbitrators. The awards discussed in this chapter show they can fulfil it well if they want to.

---

[164] Stephan W Schill, 'International Investment Law and the Rule of Law' in Jeffrey Jowell, J Christopher Thomas and Jan van Zyl Smit (eds), *Rule of Law Symposium 2014: The Importance of the Rule of Law in Promoting Development* (Singapore Academy of Law 2015) 100.

11

Legality Requirements

Managing the Tension between the Domestic and the International Rule of Law

*Martin A. Jarrett**

I. The Rule-of-Law Tension in Legality Requirements

Legality requirements are one of the few tools that arbitral tribunals have to sanction investor misconduct. They typically derive from the words 'in accordance with host state law' that are found in the definitions of 'investment' in investment treaties. And even when these words are absent from the applicable investment treaty, arbitral tribunals may read a legality requirement into the treaty, thereby creating an implicit legality requirement. Whether a legality requirement arises explicitly or implicitly, they usually stipulate that investors must establish[1] their investments in accordance with the domestic law of host States.[2] The failure to fulfil this requirement usually[3] means that an arbitral tribunal will decline to exercise jurisdiction over the investor's claim.[4]

This outcome can be seen as an enhancement of the domestic rule of law. Specifically, one of the core elements of the formal rule of law[5] is congruence between law and official action;[6] in other words, the law must be administered and enforced as it is written.[7] Acting out that idea is a matter for domestic courts and other domestic institutions. What arbitral tribunals do, when they apply legality requirements, is add another layer of law enforcement, thereby enhancing the rule of law in the host State. But this enhancement of the *domestic* rule of law in the host State may compromise the *international* rule of law. The international rule of law here refers to the legal effect of international rules; for example, the rules in

---

* The original draft of this contribution was presented at the workshop 'International Protection Standards and the Rule of Law' hosted by the University of Vienna in collaboration with the University of Amsterdam. I wish to thank the attendees of the workshop for their comments and questions on the original draft. Additionally, this chapter has greatly benefited from the review conducted by the editors of this volume. For all their efforts, I am very grateful. All errors are my own.

[1] Other verbs are also used in addition to 'establish'. For a list of them, see Thomas Obersteiner, ' "In Accordance with Domestic Law" Clauses: How International Investment Tribunals Deal with Allegations of Unlawful Conduct of Investors' (2014) 31 J Intl Arb 265, 268–69.

[2] *Muszynianka Spółka z Ograniczoną Odpowiedzialnością v The Slovak Republic*, PCA Case No 2017-08, Award (7 October 2020) para 300.

[3] As explained further in Section II.B, if the applicable legality requirement is viewed as having a merits function, then it will potentially mean that the State can use the legality requirement as a defence in respect of its breach of the applicable investment treaty.

[4] Obersteiner (n 1) 266; Rahim Moloo and Alex Khachaturian, 'The Compliance with the Law Requirement in International Investment Law' (2011) 34 Fordham Intl LJ 1473, 1475.

[5] Jeremy Waldron, 'The Rule of Law' (*Stanford Encyclopaedia of Philosophy*, 22 June 2016) para 5.1 <https://plato.stanford.edu/entries/rule-of-law/> accessed 18 February 2022.

[6] Lon Fuller, *The Morality of Law* (rev edn, Yale UP 1969) 81.

[7] David Luban, 'The Rule of Law and Human Dignity: Re-examining Fuller's Canons' (2010) 2 HJRL 29, 31.

Martin A. Jarrett, *Legality Requirements* In: *Investment Protection Standards and the Rule of Law*. Edited by: August Reinisch and Stephan W. Schill, Oxford University Press. © Martin A. Jarrett 2023. DOI: 10.1093/oso/9780192864581.003.0011

investment treaties on the treatment of investments by States. The operation of legality requirements prevents these rules from taking legal effect because when an arbitral tribunal declines jurisdiction, because of an investor's failure to satisfy a legality requirement, it means that the conduct of the host State that gave rise to the investor's investment-treaty claim will not be assessed against the investment protection standards in the applicable investment treaty. Effectively, legality requirements can stop the application of investment protection standards, which practically means that the State's treatment of the investment cannot be measured against the rule-of-law standards encapsulated in them. And herein lies the rule-of-law tension in legality requirements: on the one hand, they enhance the domestic rule of law by adding another layer of enforcement for domestic law, but, on the other hand, by preventing the application of investment protection standards, they arguably compromise the international rule of law.

This chapter is dedicated to examining how arbitral tribunals can best address this tension. That examination starts in Section II with identifying and outlining the current strategies that arbitral tribunals have developed to deal with explicit legality requirements. The main insight from Section II is that arbitral tribunals have sought to narrow the scope of explicit legality requirements. After evaluating that jurisprudential trend from the rule-of-law perspective and concluding that, on balance, it is a positive development, attention turns to the two major exceptions to it, specifically some arbitral tribunals' willingness to, one, read legality requirements into investment treaties or the ICSID Convention, where such requirements are not explicitly mentioned, and, two, more readily decline jurisdiction on account of corruption. These issues of implicit legality requirements and corruption are addressed in Section III and Section IV, respectively. In respect of implicit legality requirements, this chapter argues that they are problematic from a rule-of-law perspective, while, in respect of corruption, an evaluation of the different solutions that have been proposed to the 'corruption paradox' is completed.

II. Strategies for Managing the Rule-of-Law Tension in Legality Requirements

It can be contested whether legality requirements compromise the international rule of law because they prevent the application of investment protection standards. If the applicable investment treaty explicitly conditions States' consent to investment-treaty arbitration on investment legality, then the arbitral tribunal has to respect and apply that condition.[8] This is formally correct. But substantively speaking, things can look different. Legality requirements do in effect void investment protection standards, which can be a source of injustice for the investor, most obviously when the State has clearly breached one of these standards. This explains why legality requirements compromise the international rule of law, thereby giving rise to the rule-of-law tension. Arbitral tribunals have recognized this tension and seek to manage it by using various strategies to confine the scope of application of explicit legality requirements. In the paragraphs that follow, each of these strategies is identified and described.

---

[8] See *Fraport AG Frankfurt Airport Services Worldwide v The Republic of the Philippines*, ICSID Case No ARB/03/25, Award (16 August 2007) paras 402–03 (*Fraport (I)*).

A. Six Strategies for Narrowing Legality Requirements

The first strategy is placing a temporal limitation on legality requirements. To understand this temporal limitation, it is worth looking at a legality requirement, for example from the Argentina–Sweden BIT:

> The term 'investment' shall comprise every kind of asset, invested by an investor of one Contracting Party in the territory of the other Contracting Party, provided that the investment has been made in accordance with the laws and regulations of the other Contracting Party.[9]

The temporal limitation zeroes in on the word 'made'. It provides that illegalities falling within the period when the investor is 'making' the investment are relevant illegalities for the purposes of legality requirements. Deductively, this means that all illegalities coming after the point when the investment is 'made' fall outside the scope of legality requirements.[10] These illegalities are sometimes called 'post-establishment illegalities'.

A recent example of the activation of the temporal limitation can be seen in *Bank Melli v Bahrain*.[11] It was found that the investor's local company had been engaging in financial dealings with Iran-based financial institutions.[12] Given that the Central Bank of Bahrain had issued regulations that prohibited such conduct, the investor was found to have breached Bahraini law.[13] Bahrain contended that the investor could not satisfy the legality requirement in the applicable investment treaty because of this.[14] The arbitral tribunal dismissed this contention.[15] In its reasoning, the arbitral tribunal stated that it viewed these financial dealings as post-establishment business dealings:

> once the investment is lawfully made (and subject to other jurisdictional requirements not at issue here), the Contracting States have consented to give the treaty tribunal the competence to adjudicate the disputes arising out of such investment, including disputes about alleged subsequent illegal activities and their consequences.[16]

A second limitation is the requirement that the illegality must bear a sufficiently close relationship to the process of making the investment. This can be conveniently called the 'relation to investment' limitation. It requires that the relevant illegality go to the core the investment-making process, as opposed to some peripheral matter.[17] For example, if a

---

[9] Agreement between the Government of the Kingdom of Sweden and the Government of the Republic of Argentina on the Promotion and Reciprocal Protection of Investments (signed 22 November 1991, entered into force 28 September 1992) art 1(1).

[10] *Gustav FW Hamester GmbH & Co KG v Republic of Ghana*, ICSID Case No ARB/07/24, Award (18 June 2010) para 127.

[11] *Bank Melli Iran and Bank Saderat Iran v The Kingdom of Bahrain*, PCA Case No 2017-25, Award (9 November 2021).

[12] ibid para 502.

[13] ibid.

[14] ibid para 328.

[15] ibid para 507.

[16] ibid para 356.

[17] *Fraport (I)* (n 8) para 396 ('Another indicator that should work in favour of an investor that had run afoul of a prohibition in local law would be that the offending arrangement was not central to the profitability of the investment').

director of the investor bribes a government minister for the core permit to engage in its investment activities, this would be a 'core illegality', but the fact that this director drove over the speed limit and ran a number of red lights to submit a tender bid on time, this would amount to a 'peripheral illegality'.[18]

A third limitation is the exclusion of de minimis illegalities. The genesis of this limitation is the case of *Tokios Tokelés v Ukraine*.[19] Because the investor failed to correctly fill out certain application documents when establishing its investment, Ukraine argued that the investor could not satisfy the legality requirement.[20] The arbitral tribunal summarily dismissed this argument. It reasoned that 'to exclude an investment on the basis of such minor errors would be inconsistent with the object and purpose' of the applicable investment treaty.[21] Since this decision, arbitral tribunals have consistently held that de minimis illegalities do not fall within the scope of legality requirements.

A fourth limitation is the importation of a proportionality test. Sometimes called the 'Kim principle'[22] from the case *Kim and ors v Uzbekistan*,[23] this limitation requires that the illegality must be of such a nature that declining jurisdiction over the investor's claim is an equitable response, having regard to the value of the investor's potential investment loss. Essentially, this limitation calls for a balancing act between the gravity of the illegality and the value of the investor's potential investment loss. If the balance is not sufficiently weighed down by the gravity of the investor's misconduct, then such misconduct will not constitute an 'illegality' for the purposes of legality requirements.

A good example of this balancing process can be seen in *Anglo-Adriatic Group v Albania*.[24] There, the relevant illegality concerned the funding of the investor. The investor allegedly loaned its local company more than USD 5,000,000.[25] Under Albanian law, funding this particular local company via loans was illegal (because it was a special corporate form that was designed to be immune from insolvency).[26] To determine whether this illegality was of such weight, the arbitral tribunal examined the policy behind the rule that rendered the investor's loan unlawful. It found that the rule pursued a 'compelling public purpose' because it sought to protect ordinary Albanian citizens, who could invest in the local company, from financial risk.[27]

A fifth limitation comes through the use of the estoppel principle. The case of *Fraport v Philippines (I)* introduced this method of limiting legality requirements.[28] The relevant statement of principle reads as follows:[29]

---

[18] *Achmea BV v The Slovak Republic*, UNCITRAL, PCA Case No 2008-13, Award (7 December 2012) para 173.
[19] See Jarrod Hepburn, 'In Accordance with Which Host State Laws? Restoring the "Defence" of Investor Illegality in Investment Arbitration' (2014) 5 JIDS 559, 545.
[20] *Tokios Tokelés v Ukraine*, ICSID Case No ARB/02/18, Award (26 July 2007) para 83.
[21] ibid para 86.
[22] See eg *Cortec Mining Kenya Limited, Cortec (Pty) Limited and Stirling Capital Limited v Republic of Kenya*, ICSID Case No ARB/15/29, Award (22 October 2018) para 320.
[23] *Vladislav Kim and ors v Republic of Uzbekistan*, ICSID Case No ARB/13/6, Decision on Jurisdiction (8 March 2017).
[24] *Anglo-Adriatic Group Limited v Republic of Albania*, ICSID Case No ARB/17/6, Award (7 February 2019).
[25] The investor was ultimately unable to establish that it did loan this money, see ibid para 273.
[26] ibid paras 283–84, 290.
[27] ibid para 292.
[28] See *Fraport (I)* (n 8).
[29] ibid para 120.

Principles of fairness should require a tribunal to hold a government estopped from raising violations of its own law as a jurisdictional defense when it knowingly overlooked them and endorsed an investment which was not in compliance with its law.

This principle has been mostly invoked in cases where the investor has not complied with admission requirements for foreign investments, but also in cases where the investor is alleged to engage in misconduct. As an example, consider the case of *von Pezold v Zimbabwe*.[30] Because of alleged violations of securities law,[31] Zimbabwe contended that the legality requirement could not be satisfied. The arbitral tribunal dismissed this contention for various reasons, including because 'it is evident that any breach of the free float rule should have been dealt with by the Zimbabwe Stock Exchange'.[32]

The sixth and final limitation concerns the issue of illegalities committed prior to the investor (who is the claimant in the investment-treaty arbitration) taking ownership of the investment. The general rule on this issue is that such illegalities do not fall within the scope of legality requirements,[33] unless the investor should have known about the previous owner's conduct that constituted the illegalities.[34] The various cases that have arisen out of the Yukos–Russia dispute help to illustrate how this rule operates. In these cases,[35] the investors purchased their ownership stakes in the investments from prior owners. Russia alleged that these prior owners came to acquire the (formerly state-owned) investments via a rigged auction process. Even assuming that the auction process was rigged, the arbitral tribunals were not prepared to find that that fact could amount to an illegality.[36] They implicitly justified this ruling by emphasizing that the investors had to engage in misconduct connected to their acquisition of the investment.[37]

With the exception of the first limitation, what is most interesting about all of these moves to narrow the scope of legality requirements is that arbitral tribunals had a genuine choice to go the other way; in other words, their interpretations of legality requirements could have been legitimately broader.[38] With the sixth limitation, the arbitral tribunal could have said that it was not a question whether the *investor* committed or knew of the

---

[30] *Bernhard von Pezold and ors v Republic of Zimbabwe*, ICSID Case No ARB/10/15, Award (28 July 2015).

[31] For details, see ibid paras 364, 366–68.

[32] ibid para 419.

[33] See *Yukos Universal Limited (Isle of Man) v The Russian Federation*, UNCITRAL, PCA Case No 2005-04/AA227, Award (18 July 2014) paras 1370–71. For other investment-treaty arbitrations where this issue of the investor's knowledge of a prior illegality was a core issue, see *Churchill Mining plc and Planet Mining Pty Ltd v Republic of Indonesia*, ICSID Case No ARB/12/14 and 12/40. There, the arbitral tribunal held that unless the investor could show that it had engaged in proper due diligence, then it would be found to have knowledge of the illegality.

[34] For clarification, the relevant point is that the investor knew of the previous owner's conduct. Whether the investor knew that this conduct is illegal, this is irrelevant, as per the Latin maxim '*ignorantia legis neminem excusat*'.

[35] These three investment-treaty arbitrations are: *Hulley Enterprises Ltd v The Russian Federation*, UNCITRAL, PCA Case No 2005-03/AA226; *Veteran Petroleum Ltd v The Russian Federation*, UNCITRAL, PCA Case No 2005-05/AA228; *Yukos* (n 33). For reasons of expediency, in the footnotes below, reference is only made to the arbitral tribunals for the case of *Yukos Universal v Russia*. Other investment-treaty arbitrations have arisen out of the Yukos–Russia dispute, although the facts of these other cases (*RosInvestCo UK Ltd v The Russian Federation*, SCC Case No V079/2005 and *Yukos Capital v The Russian Federation*, PCA Case No 2013-31) are slightly different from the other cases.

[36] *Yukos* (n 33) para 1370.

[37] ibid.

[38] Same observation has also been made by Giorgio Risso and Anna Chiara Amato, see generally Giorgio Risso and Anna Chiara Amato, 'Pleas of Illegality and the Application of Domestic Law in Investment Treaty Arbitration' (2020) 9 CILJ 96.

illegality in question, but rather whether the establishment of the investment itself was tainted. Also, with respect to the jurisprudence whereby legality requirements are subjected to the estoppel principle (the fifth limitation), considerations of proportionality (the fourth limitation), and the requirement that the relevant illegality be more than minor (the third limitation), there was the real possibility to create a different jurisprudence. What is important to recognize here is that these limitations have been read into legality requirements. As previously noted, legality requirements arise from the words 'made in accordance with host state law'. Arbitral tribunals have added to these words these three limitations. By adopting a more formalistic interpretation, they could have rejected these additions to legality requirements, all of which ultimately narrow their scope. Similarly, with respect to the second limitation, a more formalistic interpretation might also be put forward, specifically that the illegality need not be a 'core element' of the investment-making process, but rather had to be only 'minimally connected' to it, for example.

B. Rule-of-Law Considerations for Narrowing Legality Requirements

What is the explanation for the trend? The suspicion is that arbitral tribunals are very conscious that the more they expand the scope of legality requirements, the more they compromise the international rule of law. The approach of limiting the scope of legality requirements is apparently a 'win' for the international rule of law. But there is an outstanding rule-of-law issue: if few illegalities fall within the scope of legality requirements, what is the fate of those many illegalities that fall outside the scope? Are these 'out-of-scope illegalities' relevant for other purposes in investment-treaty arbitrations?

There are four purposes for which they are relevant. First, they assume relevance as regards the question whether a State has breached an investment protection standard. A classic example comes from the case of *Genin v Estonia*.[39] There, Estonia revoked the investor's operating permit on account of its misconduct.[40] The investor filed a claim in investment-treaty arbitration. The arbitral tribunal considered the core issue to be whether the revocation of the operating permit was legitimate.[41] Having regard to Estonian law, the arbitral tribunal decided that this revocation was (technically) legal,[42] with the result that the investor's claim was rejected.[43]

The fact of investment illegality also assumes relevance as regards the question: does an investor still have the benefit of the investment protection standards of an investment treaty, notwithstanding the fact that some investment illegality has been committed? This is the question that preoccupied the arbitral tribunal in the merits phase of the case *Plama v Bulgaria*.[44] It held that the application of the investment protection standards of the Energy

---

[39] *Alex Genin, Eastern Credit Limited, Inc and AS Baltoil v The Republic of Estonia*, ICSID Case No ARB/99/2, Award (25 June 2001). For other cases that also followed the route of dismissing the investors' claims on the merits on account of misconduct, see *Cementownia 'Nowa Huta' SA v Republic of Turkey*, ICSID Case No ARB(AF)/06/2; and *Malicorp Limited v The Arab Republic of Egypt*, ICSID Case No ARB/08/18.

[40] *Genin* (n 39) para 57.

[41] ibid para 349.

[42] ibid paras 360, 363.

[43] ibid para 365.

[44] *Plama Consortium Limited v Republic of Bulgaria*, ICSID Case No ARB/03/24, Award (27 August 2008).

Charter Treaty were subject to a legality requirement.[45] Considering that the investor had made fraudulent misrepresentations when purchasing the investment from Bulgaria, the result was that its claim was dismissed.[46]

In a case where the State's response to the investor's misconduct breaches the applicable investment treaty, it still has another card up its sleeve, specifically the defence of contributory fault. Pleading contributory fault is the third way that investment illegality can become relevant in the merits stage. The case of *Occidental v Ecuador* provides a good example of how contributory fault works.[47] There, Ecuador's response to the investor's misconduct was found to have breached the applicable investment treaty.[48] Ecuador, however, argued that because the investor's misconduct caused it to breach the treaty, then the investor had contributed to its own injury.[49] Further, because the investor had engaged in misconduct, this contribution could be described as fault-worthy.[50] The arbitral tribunal applied contributory fault and Ecuador's international responsibility was reduced by 25%.[51]

The calculation of damages is a fourth point at which investor misconduct can assume relevance. There is a long line of jurisprudence to the effect that considerations of equity can play a role in measuring damages.[52] Under this umbrella, an arbitral tribunal might reduce the investor's damages on account of its illegal activities. For example, imagine that the investment in question is a casino. It offers its patrons the possibility of participating in various gambling activities, one of which is poker games. The investor's operating permit does not cover poker games. Thus, if this investment were unlawfully expropriated, the arbitral tribunal could calculate the damages in such a way that the value of the casino represented by the poker games should be discounted.

Circling back to the broader issue of the rule-of-law tension that legality requirements create, what should be apparent is that arbitral tribunals have struck a certain balance to manage this tension. On the one hand, they have narrowed the scope of legality requirements in order to preserve the international rule of law. Then, on the other hand, they have sought to counterbalance that movement by opening up various avenues through which investor misconduct can become relevant in the merits stage, thereby showing their commitment to the domestic rule of law.

III. The Issue of Implicit Legality Requirements

But not all the jurisprudence on legality requirements has gone in the direction of narrowing their scope. There are some jurisprudential developments that defy this trend, one of which is the practice of reading legality requirements into investment treaties or the

---

[45] ibid paras 138–39. See also *David Minnotte & Robert Lewis v Republic of Poland*, ICSID Case No ARB(AF)/10/1, Award (16 May 2014) para 131.

[46] *Plama* (n 44) para 146.

[47] *Occidental Petroleum Corporation and Occidental Exploration and Production Company v The Republic of Ecuador*, ICSID Case No ARB/06/11, Award (5 October 2012).

[48] ibid para 455.

[49] ibid para 659.

[50] ibid para 662.

[51] ibid para 687.

[52] Irmgard Marboe, *Calculation of Compensation and Damages in International Investment Law* (2nd edn, OUP 2017) para 3.343.

ICSID Convention. How arbitral tribunals execute this practice is described and analysed in the sections that follow.

A. Techniques for Reading Legality Requirements into Investment Treaties

As noted in Section II.A, in the definition of 'investment' in many investment treaties, there are words to the effect that the investment must be 'made in accordance with host state law'. However, there are also investment treaties where no such words appear in the definition of 'investment'. The question then is: can legality requirements be read into these definitions?

For those jurists who answer 'no', their task is not difficult. They can look at the treaty text of the definition of 'investment' and reasonably conclude that there is no implicit requirement, which could be derived from the ordinary meaning of the words, that an investment needs to be lawfully established. To solidify their position, they can point out that they have other tools to address any investor misconduct,[53] as discussed in Section II.A above. Further, if they can say that if an arbitral tribunal did read a legality requirement into the investment treaty, then it runs the risk that it would be defining its own jurisdictional competence, remembering that the existence of an investment is always a necessary prerequisite as regards the arbitral tribunal's jurisdiction, and an implicit legality requirement would form part of the definition of investment for this purpose.

For those jurists who answer 'yes' to this question, their task is more difficult. They have developed a number of techniques to overcome the problem that legality requirements cannot be derived from the ordinary meaning of the words in the definition of 'investment'. One such technique uses the investment protection standard on admission of investments. In this standard, the State usually promises to admit investments in accordance with its domestic law, as shown in the Greece–Kuwait BIT:

> Each Contracting Party shall, in its territory promote and admit investments by investors of the other Contracting Party, in accordance with its laws and regulations.[54]

From these words, arbitral tribunals have concluded that the applicable investment treaty only applies to 'legal investments', thereby allowing them to read a legality requirement into the definition of 'investment'. A recent example of this practice comes from the case of *Fynerdale v Czech Republic*.[55] After citing the standard on admission of investments in the applicable investment treaty, the arbitral tribunal held:

> In the view of the Tribunal, this [standard] clearly establishes that the conformity of investments with the national law of the host State of the investment is part of the notion of

---

[53] See eg *Bear Creek Mining Corporation v Republic of Peru*, ICSID Case No ARB/14/21, Award (30 November 2017) para 320 (although the arbitral tribunal did indicate that there might be an exception in cases involving fraud, see ibid para 322); *Yukos* (n 33) para 1374; *Minnotte* (n 45) para 140; *Plama Consortium Limited v Republic of Bulgaria*, ICSID Case No ARB/03/24, Decision on Jurisdiction (8 February 2005) para 229.

[54] Agreement between the Government of the Hellenic Republic and the Government of the State of Kuwait on the Promotion and Reciprocal Protection of Investments (signed 12 June 2014, entered into force 28 March 2019) art 2(1).

[55] *Fynerdale Holdings BV v The Czech Republic*, UNCITRAL, PCA Case No 2018-18, Award (29 April 2021).

investment. Accordingly, the jurisdiction of this Tribunal only covers disputes concerning legal investments.[56]

Combined with the finding that its loan-based investment was funded with fraudulently obtained monies, the arbitral tribunal went on to find that it lacked jurisdiction.

Another technique uses the governing-law clause in the applicable investment treaty. The governing-law clause in the China-Latvia BIT is a typical example of this provision:

> The arbitration award shall be based on the law of the Contracting Party to the dispute including its rules on the conflict of laws, the provisions of this Agreement as well as the universally accepted principles of international law.[57]

This technique proceeds in four steps: first, interpret the State's offer of investment-treaty arbitration with reference to the governing-law clause in the applicable investment treaty; second, note that, in that clause, one of the applicable laws is 'principles of international law'; third, identify 'good faith' as one of those principles; and fourth, reason that for an investment to be made in good faith, it must be legally made. A paradigmatic example of its application comes from *Inceysa v El Salvador*.[58] It started its analysis by extracting the governing-law clause from the applicable investment treaty and commented:

> The reference made in the Agreement to the generally recognized rules and principles of International Law obliges this Tribunal ... to determine whether, according to said principles and rules, Inceysa's investment can be considered legally made.[59]

The arbitral tribunal then went about the task of identifying 'said principles and rules'.[60] Although it insisted that it was not providing a definition, it nonetheless defined them as follows:

> [T]he Tribunal notes that, in general, they have been understood as general rules on which there is international consensus to consider them as universal standards and rules of conduct that must always be applied and which, in the opinion of important commentators, are rules of law on which the legal systems of the States are based.[61]

The arbitral tribunal then had to apply this definition and identified as the first principle: good faith.[62] In light of the misrepresentations that the investor made in establishing its investment, the arbitral tribunal concluded:

---

[56] ibid para 554.
[57] Agreement between the Government of the People's Republic of China and the Government of the Republic of Latvia on the Promotion and Protection of Investments (signed 15 April 2004, entered into force 1 February 2006) art 9(3).
[58] *Inceysa Vallisoletana SL v Republic of El Salvador*, ICSID Case No ARB/03/26, Award (2 August 2006).
[59] ibid para 224.
[60] ibid paras 224–29.
[61] ibid para 227.
[62] ibid para 230.

It is clear to this Tribunal that the investment made by Inceysa in the territory of El Salvador, which gave rise to the present dispute, was made in violation of the principle of good faith ... Faced with this situation, this Tribunal can only declare its incompetence to hear Inceysa's complaint.[63]

A third technique is a simplified variation of this second technique. It holds that the principle of good faith is part of all domestic legal systems, with the result that it is a principle of international law.[64] In this role, it must be used to interpret the provisions of investment treaties, including the meaning of the word 'investment'.[65] This means that 'investment' is always subject to a good faith requirement.[66] This conclusion is solidified by the fact that, in the core rule on treaty interpretation, it stipulates that treaties must be interpreted 'in good faith'.[67] The case that pioneered the use of this third technique was *Phoenix v Czech Republic*.[68] It reasoned that:[69]

The Washington Convention as well as the BIT have to be construed with due regard to the international principle of good faith. The principle of good faith is also recognized in most, if not all, domestic legal systems. It appears therefore as a kind of 'Janus concept', with one face looking at the national legal order and one at the international legal order ... Therefore, ICSID tribunals which have relied on this principle in order to determine whether or not there existed a protected investment have often relied on both dimensions of the principle.

Formally, this good faith requirement is distinguishable from a legality requirement,[70] but as circumstances such as corruption and fraud in the making of investments activate both of them,[71] they are substantively the same. Interestingly, it has also been opined that 'investment' as it appears in the ICSID Convention is also subject to this good faith requirement.[72] For ICSID arbitrations where the applicable investment treaty does not contain a legality requirement, and also contains a provision that clearly specifies that the States' consent to investment-treaty arbitration is unconditional, the investor might still have to satisfy a good faith requirement.

B. Doctrinal Problems with Implicit Legality Requirements

For the reasons set out below, the doctrinal correctness of all of these techniques for reading legality requirements into investment treaties is open to serious doubt. Apart from doctrinal

---

[63] ibid paras 234, 239.

[64] *Phoenix Action, Ltd v The Czech Republic*, ICSID Case No ARB/06/5, Award (15 April 2009) para 107.

[65] See ibid ('every rule of law includes an implied clause that it should not be abused').

[66] ibid para 113.

[67] ibid para 108 (citing *Amco Asia Corporation and ors v Republic of Indonesia*, ICSID Case No ARB/81/1, Decision on Jurisdiction (25 September 1983) para 14).

[68] See the references above n 65.

[69] *Phoenix* (n 64) paras 109–10.

[70] In *Phoenix*, the arbitral tribunal listed six elements that an investment needed to exhibit in order to qualify as an 'investment'. The sixth one was 'bona fide investment', while the fifth one was 'made in accordance with host state law', see ibid para 114.

[71] ibid para 113.

[72] ibid para 109.

problems, these techniques also create rule-of-law concerns. Fuller dedicates much of his discussion of the 'congruence'[73] element to this concern.[74] The congruence element is the requirement that the law must be administered and enforced as it is written.[75] Naturally, interpretation is a key part of ensuring congruence between enacted law and its subsequent enforcement.[76] Fuller concluded his discussion in the following terms:

> With all its subtleties, the problem of interpretation occupies a sensitive, central position in the internal morality of the law. It reveals, as no other problem can, the cooperative nature of the task of maintaining legality. If the interpreting agent is to preserve a sense of useful mission, the legislature must not impose on him senseless tasks. If the legislative draftsman is to discharge his responsibilities he, in turn, must be able to anticipate rational and relatively stable modes of interpretation.[77]

Accordingly, when interpreting legal text, the adjudicator needs to use 'rational and stable modes of interpretation'. What these modes of interpretation are will differ from legal system to legal system. In international law, it is universally recognized that they are found in the Vienna Convention on the Law of Treaties (VCLT), particularly Articles 31–33.[78] The techniques for reading legality requirements into investment treaties will be assessed against these 'modes of interpretation' found in the VCLT. The core rule is Article 31(1),[79] which reads as follows:

> A treaty shall be interpreted in good faith in accordance with the ordinary meaning to be given to the terms of the treaty in their context and in the light of its object and purpose.

With respect to all three techniques, there is a strong argument that they disrespect this rule. The first premise of this argument is that, under this rule, the meaning of treaty text can be derived from three sources: (1) ordinary meaning; (2) context; and (3) object and purpose. This is not a hierarchy.[80] Rather, interpreting treaty text has been described as an 'encircling process' where all three sources are used to determine meaning.[81] But when undertaking this encircling process, the foundational meaning of treaty text is its ordinary meaning.[82] When the other sources of meaning, namely context and object and purpose, are consulted to further elicit the meaning of treaty text, they cannot be used to rewrite the ordinary meaning.[83] And this is the error that all three techniques run into. What they

---

[73] See Section I above for a discussion of the congruence element.
[74] Fuller (n 6) 81–91.
[75] See Luban (n 7).
[76] See Colleen Murphy, 'Lon Fuller and the Moral Value of the Rule of Law' (2005) 24 Law & Phil 239, 241.
[77] Fuller (n 6) 91 (emphasis added).
[78] Richard Gardiner, 'The Vienna Convention Rules on Treaty Interpretation' in Duncan B Hollis (ed), *The Oxford Guide to Treaties* (2nd edn, OUP 2020) 460.
[79] Jean-Marc Sorel and Valérie Boré Eveno, 'Article 31: 1969 Vienna Convention' in Olivier Corten and Pierre Klein (eds), *The Vienna Conventions on the Law of Treaties* (OUP 2011) 807.
[80] ibid.
[81] Richard Gardiner, *Treaty Interpretation* (OUP 2015) 162.
[82] ibid 185 ('the ordinary meaning is the starting point of an interpretation').
[83] Håkan Berglin, 'Treaty Interpretation and the Impact of Contractual Choice of Forum Clauses on the Jurisdiction of International Tribunals: The Iranian Forum Clause Decisions of the Iran–United States Claims Tribunal' (1986) 21 Tex Intl LJ 39, 44 ('tribunals have usually rejected otherwise reasonable interpretations because to accept them would have been tantamount to rephrasing or otherwise altering the actual text').

effectively do is add the words 'lawfully made' before the word 'investment' wherever it appears in the applicable investment treaty.

Some more specific criticisms can also be levelled at particular techniques. As regards the first technique, where a legality requirement is derived from the standard on admission of investment, it can be criticized on the ground that it creates an obligation for the investor where none apparently exists. To illustrate this criticism, take a typical rendition of this standard from the Denmark–North Macedonia BIT:

> Each Contracting Party shall admit investments by investors of the other Contracting Party in accordance with its legislation and administrative practice and encourage such investments, including facilitating the establishment of representative offices.[84]

On any reading of this provision, it imposes an obligation on *the host State*, not *the investor*.[85] It compels the host State to admit investments in accordance with its law, for example, by forbidding the investor to pay bribes to obtain certain permits. As regards the third technique, the first point of criticism is that the reference to good faith in Article 31(1) of the VCLT does not create a free-floating obligation that attaches to all treaty text. It rather creates an obligation to interpret treaty text in good faith,[86] as opposed to interpreting treaty text in bad faith, which would happen, for example, when an arbitrator puts forward an interpretation that is designed to secure more appointments to arbitral tribunals. A second point of criticism that while good faith is a part of all legal systems, its meaning across different legal systems varies so much that it is very doubtful whether there is a unified concept of good faith. The problem is that good faith can become an empty vessel[87] into which arbitral tribunals can pour their own ideas on what constitutes good law.[88] Accordingly, this good faith–based technique not only fails because it misreads Article 31(1), but it is also problematic on account of its lack of clarity, which is concerning considering that law should reasonably precise.[89]

C. Implicit Legality Requirements and the Rule-of-Law Tension in Legality Requirements

It is suspected that the promoters of implicit legality requirements are aware of these doctrinal problems with their techniques, but they still persevere. This perseverance prompts

---

[84] Agreement between the Macedonian Government and the Government of the Kingdom of Denmark for the Promotion and Reciprocal Protection of Investments (signed 8 May 2015, entered into force 30 June 2016) art 2(1) (emphasis added).

[85] *Álvarez y Marín Corporación SA and ors v Republic of Panama*, ICSID Case No ARB/15/14, Award (12 October 2018) para 127; *SAUR International v Argentina*, ICSID Case No ARB/04/4, Decision on Jurisdiction and Liability (6 June 2012) para 307; August Reinisch, 'How to Distinguish "in Accordance with Host State Law" Clauses from Similar International Investment Agreement Provisions?' (2018) 7 IJAL 70, 82.

[86] Gardiner (n 81) 171 ('Thus, the term 'in good faith' indicates *how* the task of interpretation is to be undertaken' (emphasis added)).

[87] This idea of good faith being an 'empty vessel' is taken from Emily Houh, 'The Doctrine of Good Faith in Contract Law: A (Nearly) Empty Vessel?' (2005) Utah LR 1.

[88] See Stephan W Schill and Heather L Bray, 'Good Faith Limitations on Protected Investments and Corporate Structuring' in Andrew D. Mitchell, M Sornarajah and Tania Voon (eds), *Good Faith and International Economic Law* (OUP 2015) 88.

[89] Fuller (n 6) 63.

a basic question: why? Particularly bearing in mind that legality requirements, of whatever variety, prevent the application of rule-of-law-based investment protection standards, what is the justification for implicit legality requirements? They cannot, of course, point to the 'in accordance with host state law' and say 'we are giving effect to these words'. For this reason, they point to another rule-of-law theme: it would be an abuse of the system of investment-treaty arbitration if claims based on illegal investments could be adjudicated on.

What exactly this abuse is, is not clearly spelled out. It seems to be the case that by finding it has jurisdiction, an arbitral tribunal potentially furthers the benefit of the illegality, rather than condemning it. For example, imagine that the main permit for a particular investment is acquired via bribery. Without this bribe, the investment would not exist. The investor makes a claim for compensation under an investment treaty. The arbitral tribunal accepts that it has jurisdiction over this claim, with the implication being that, at the merits stage, the investor might be awarded compensation. 'Might' is the key word here. As detailed in Section II.B, arbitral tribunals have different options for dealing with investor misconduct of this nature at the merits stage, most particularly by deciding, because of this illegality, the investor does not have the benefit of the application of the investment protection standards.

The promoters of implicit legality requirements will counter that there will be investment-treaty claims that are so tainted by grievous illegality that they cannot be allowed to proceed to the merits phase. It would be easy to have some sympathy for this counterargument, but the evidence suggests that implicit legality requirements are not being confined to cases of the most serious illegality. The case in point is *Cortec Mining v Kenya*.[90] After reading a le-gality requirement into the applicable investment treaty,[91] the arbitral tribunal held that it could not be satisfied because a State official misapplied the law when it granted the investor a permit;[92] in other words, there was no investor misconduct at all in this case.

In summing up, implicit legality requirements are particularly problematic from a rule-of-law perspective. As explained in Section III.B, the doctrinal correctness of the tech-niques that are used to read such requirements into investment treaties is very much open to doubt. To overcome this rule-of-law pitfall, promoters claim that they are pursuing a bigger rule-of-law goal by reading legality requirements into investment treaties, specific-ally the protection of the integrity of their adjudicative function. Yet, in pursuing this rule-of-law outcome, what they also do is compromise the international rule of law, considering that investment protection standards never have the chance to take effect. Moreover, as dis-cussed in Section II.B, arbitral tribunals have a number of tools in their toolkit to address investor misconduct on the merits.

IV. The Issue of Corruption

This brings us back to the balance that arbitral tribunals have to strike when managing the rule-of-law tension created by legality requirements: narrow their scope and open out av-enues for addressing investor misconduct on the merits. This delicate balance looks dif-ferent in cases of corruption, however. It could even be argued that legality requirements are

---

[90] *Cortec* (n 22).
[91] ibid para 319.
[92] ibid para 333(c).

'read up' in cases of corruption. This is because, when corruption is proven, which is admittedly difficult,[93] arbitral tribunals invariably decline to exercise jurisdiction on the ground of the investment's illegality,[94] with the result that the investment protection standards do not apply in these cases. This could be a particularly regrettable outcome in some cases. The fact that corruption has occurred indicates that the health of the domestic rule of law is not good in the host State,[95] bearing in mind that corruption is the antithesis of the rule of law. If the health of the domestic rule of law is poor, then this is a factor in favour of proceeding to the merits. What 'proceeding to the merits' practically means is subjecting the State to the investment protection standards of the applicable investment treaty. As these standards are ultimately inspired by the idea of the rule of law, by proceeding to the merits, there is the chance to give the State 'a dose of the rule of law' via the application of the investment protection standards, which could (more generally) improve the health of the domestic rule of law. This is the corruption paradox: a State that should be subjected to rule-of-law-informed standards gets an escape pass because of a rule-of-law failing on its part, specifically the fact that corruption has occurred. Is there another approach to avoid this paradox?

A. Proposed Solutions to the Corruption Paradox

One solution to avoid the corruption paradoxes is to condition the application of legality requirements in cases involving corruption on the prior prosecution of relevant State officials.[96] By embarking on such prosecutions, the idea is that the State demonstrates its dedication to addressing the domestic rule-of-law deficit on its part. It is an idea with great merit, but it is encumbered by a doctrinal problem: by ordering the State to prosecute the persons allegedly involved in the corruption before it can argue that the investor fails the legality requirement, the arbitral tribunal might be seen to be defining its own jurisdiction.[97] It effectively adds more content to a legality requirement in an investment treaty. It demands that the State not only prove that the relevant investment was illegally made, but, if the illegality takes the form of corruption, then the State has to (additionally) prosecute it. Presumably on account of this reason, no arbitral tribunal has ever sought to apply it.

---

[93] Frédéric Gilles Sourgens, Kabir Duggal and Ian A Laird, *Evidence in International Investment Arbitration* (OUP 2018) para 5.53.

[94] The six (publicly known) cases in which the State has proven that the investor has engaged in corrupt practices are *Metal-Tech Ltd v Republic of Uzbekistan*, ICSID Case No ARB/10/3 (*Metal-Tech*); *Kim v Uzbekistan* (n 23); *Georg Gavrilovic and Gavrilovic d.o.o. v Republic of Croatia*, ICSID Case No ARB/12/39, Award (25 July 2018); *Spentex Netherlands, BV v Republic of Uzbekistan*, ICSID Case No ARB/13/26; *Littop Enterprises Limited, Bridgemont Ventures Limited and Bordo Management Limited v Ukraine*, SCC Case No V 2015/092, Award (4 February 2021); *Penwell Business Limited (by MegaCom) v Kyrgyz Republic*, PCA Case No 2017-31. In four of them (*Metal-Tech*, *Spentex*, *Littop*, and *Penwell*), the arbitral tribunals declined to exercise jurisdiction. In *Kim* and *Gavrilovic*, the arbitral tribunals did decide that they had jurisdiction, notwithstanding their findings of corruption. In *Kim*, the explanation for this outcome was that the corruption did not technically breach domestic law because the investor's counterparty was not a State official. In *Gavrilovic*, as further explained below, the arbitral tribunal carved out an exception to the general rule that corruption in the making of an investment results in declining jurisdiction.

[95] See Fuller (n 6) 81.

[96] Aloysius Llamzon, *Corruption in International Investment Arbitration* (OUP 2014) para 11.20. For further analysis of this proposal, see Charles Brower and Jawad Ahmad, 'The State's Corruption Defence, Prosecutorial Efforts, and Anti-corruption Norms in Investment Treaty Arbitration' in Katia Yannica-Small (ed), *Arbitration Under International Investment Agreements: A Guide to the Key Issues* (2nd edn, OUP 2018) paras 18.40–18.51.

[97] See *Littop* (n 94) para 462.

Having said that, some arbitral tribunals have given (some) effect to this solution, although not with the creation of a hard rule that corruption has to be prosecuted, but a softer rule to the effect that the lack of prosecution is evidence that corruption has not occurred.[98] For example, in *Glencore v Colombia*,[99] the arbitral tribunal rejected a corruption allegation in the following terms:

> <u>Summing up</u>, the Tribunal rejects Colombia's [corruption] allegation ... The dots simply do not connect ... The Tribunal's conclusion is confirmed by the fact that the Colombian criminal prosecutor and the Colombian criminal courts, which have a much higher capacity for investigation than this Arbitral Tribunal, have not initiated an investigation into the alleged corrupt practices.[100]

The second solution to avoid the corruption paradoxes comes from the case of *Gavrilovic v Croatia*.[101] There, the arbitral tribunal held that 'it is not open to Croatia to oppose the claim on the basis of an illegality that the State itself not only countenanced but likely orchestrated'.[102] The arbitral tribunal did not give additional details on the meaning of this ruling, but it is apparent that if a State official of a sufficiently high rank[103] initiates the corrupt dealing, then the State cannot object to the arbitral tribunal's jurisdiction on account of illegality. This solution has one particularly attractive aspect, specifically that it imposes legal consequences on the person who is most at fault in the corrupt dealings, which is clearly the initiator. But there is the lingering problem of wrongfulness of the investor's role. Although it is a secondary role, it is still wrongful—without it, the corrupt dealing does not happen. But as detailed in Section II.B above, there might be other ways to effectively sanction the investor for its misconduct in the merits stage or in a domestic court. A final issue with this second solution concerns its practical application in an investment-treaty arbitration. Considering that corruption is already notoriously difficult to prove, it will often be very difficult to find evidence on who is responsible for initiating it.

The third solution to avoid the corruption paradoxes was proposed by the arbitral tribunal for *Spentex v Uzbekistan*.[104] As the arbitral award for this investment-treaty arbitration has not been published, the specifics of this solution cannot be detailed.[105] But looking

---

[98] See eg *Glencore International AG and CI Prodeco SA v Republic of Colombia*, ICSID Case No ARB/16/6, Award (27 August 2019) para 738; *Unión Fenosa Gas, SA v Arab Republic of Egypt*, ICSID Case No ARB/14/4, Award (31 August 2018) para 7.111; *Wena Hotels Ltd v Arab Republic of Egypt*, ICSID Case No ARB/98/4, Award (8 December 2000) para 116; *Southern Pacific Properties v Arab Republic of Egypt*, ICSID Case No ARB/84/3, Award (20 May 1992) para 132. But see *Littop* (n 94) para 461:

> A domestic failure or inability to investigate and prosecute does not dispose of illegality allegations and criminal actions without a final determination of the facts and/or allegations, and in particular, the ramifications in an international context. In fact, an international tribunal has a duty to investigate the facts of a case 'even sua sponte' and take appropriate measures under the applicable principles of law when there are prima facie grounds for suspecting malfeasance.

[99] See the references above n 98.
[100] *Glencore* (n 98) para 738 (emphasis in the original).
[101] See the references above n 94.
[102] *Gavrilovic* (n 94) para 396.
[103] In this case, a minister was involved, see ibid para 384.
[104] See the references above n 94.
[105] The information on this case that appears in this chapter has been gleaned from the following sources: Kathrin Betz, *Proving Bribery, Fraud and Money Laundering in International Arbitration: On Applicable Criminal Law and Evidence* (CUP 2017) para 5.1.11; Luke Eric Peterson and Vladislav Djanic, 'In an Innovative Award, Arbitrators Pressure Uzbekistan—Under Threat of Adverse Cost Order—To Donate to UN Anti-Corruption Initiative; Also Propose Future Treaty-Drafting Changes that Would Penalize States for Corruption' (*IAReporter*, 22 June 2017).

at the work of others who have apparently read the arbitral award, Uzbekistan successfully challenged the arbitral tribunal's jurisdiction, but, when ordering costs, the arbitral tribunal ordered Uzbekistan to make a payment to an anti-corruption body as a form of punishment for its role in the corrupt dealing.[106] A dissenting opinion objected to this order against Uzbekistan.

Not only does this *Spentex* solution impose a meaningful legal consequence against the state: it also has the secondary benefit of directing the proceeds of the penalty that the State pays towards efforts to tackle corruption. But it is questionable whether this order is enforceable. For example, if the State refuses to pay the amount to the anti-corruption organization, does that organization have any way to sue to obtain the money? The general rule in both ICSID arbitration[107] and non-ICSID arbitration[108] is that arbitral awards (including costs orders) can only be enforced by the parties to the arbitration.

B. Rule-of-Law Evaluation of Proposed Solutions

Do these proposed solutions solve the corruption paradox? In answering this question, it should be remembered that the paradox arises because after a finding of corruption has been made, which is an instance of a rule-of-law failing on the part of the State, the State can benefit in two ways. First, and in all cases, it avoids the possibility of international responsibility under the applicable investment treaty. Second, in cases where the State has unlawfully taken the investment, it will get to keep the investment, which is objectionable for the reason that if investor-State corruption was part of the making of the investment, then the State benefits from its unlawful role in the corrupt dealing. Thus, for any solution to solve the corruption paradox, it must take away or limit this benefit that the State obtains. The first proposed solution seeks to limit the benefit by effectively forcing the State to prosecute the State officials allegedly involved in the corrupt dealing. Such prosecutions serve to strengthen the domestic rule of law. But effectively forcing prosecutions is at odds with the idea of prosecutorial discretion. By denying prosecutors their discretion, there might be unintended negative rule-of-law-related consequences; for example, limited resources are sucked into prosecuting a corruption case where there are limited chances for success, as opposed to being directed towards other prosecutions where there are good chances. Of course, the obligation to prosecute could be downgraded to an obligation to investigate, but such an obligation to investigate looks more like a symbol in the fight against corruption, rather than a meaningful measure. The same criticism might be levelled at the third solution. A payment from the State to an anti-corruption body might look good, but, for the state, it might be a payment that it is more than willing to make to avoid paying (potentially) billions of euros if it is found to be in breach of the applicable investment treaty.

---

[106] In the arbitral award, the majority arbitrators were careful not to describe their action towards Uzbekistan as an 'order', but rather an 'urging'. When the arbitral tribunal 'urged' Uzbekistan to make this payment, it also stated that if Uzbekistan did not make it, then it would have to bear all of the legal costs relating to the case. Considering that this condition was imposed, it is submitted that the majority arbitrators actually made a costs 'order'.

[107] See Convention on the Settlement of Investment Disputes between States and Nationals of other States (opened for signature 18 March 1965, entered into force 14 October 1966) 575 UNTS 129, art 54(2) (ICSID Convention) (indicates that only a party can seek recognition or enforcement of an ICSID arbitral award).

[108] Stavros L Brekoulakis, *Third Parties in International Commercial Arbitration* (OUP 2011) para 9.10.

This is a convenient point to turn to the second solution. It completely denies the State the benefit that it would otherwise receive, thereby meaning that it is exposed to the possibility of having to pay compensation to the investor. Such a payment would follow a finding that the State has breached an investment protection standard of the applicable investment treaty. Considering that investment protection standards are fundamentally informed by the rule of law, this is the principal rule-of-law benefit of the third solution. Does this rule-of-law benefit trump the rule-of-more benefits that the other proposed solutions offer? Yes. Because of the financial repercussions that a finding of international responsibility under an investment treaty has for a State, it has much more potential to improve the health of the domestic rule of law more generally. Another attractive feature of subjecting States to investment protection standards is that it deals with the problem that, in cases involving expropriation, the State would hold on to the fruits (the investment) of its unlawful conduct (its role in the corrupt dealing). If the State plays the leading role in the corrupt dealing, specifically by initiating it, the unfairness of this outcome is clear. By contrast, the other two solutions let the State hold on to its ill-gotten gains. Finally, it is important to note that the investor does not escape liability for its part in the corrupt dealing. As previously noted, there is always the potential for the arbitral tribunal to take action against the investor at the merits stage. Additionally, because of the criminal nature of the investor's corrupt acts, it may find itself as the subject of a criminal prosecution in domestic courts.

V. Conclusion

At the beginning of this chapter, it was highlighted that legality requirements give rise to a rule-of-law tension: while on the one hand they enhance the domestic rule of law, on the other hand they compromise the international rule of law. The way that arbitral tribunals have managed this tension is by narrowing the scope of legality requirements. Practically speaking, this strategy keeps investment protection standards alive, which is a favourable outcome for the international rule of law. But the domestic rule of law is not neglected; in other words, the investor can still be sanctioned for breaching host State law. This is because arbitral tribunals have opened up a number of avenues through which investor misconduct can be addressed on the merits. This 'narrowing of legality requirements, expansion of investor accountability on the merits' is the balance that has been struck between the domestic rule of law and the international rule of law.

Two developments, however, threaten this balance. The first is the practice of reading legality requirements into definitions of 'investment' when the words 'in accordance with host state law' are not there. This practice is fundamentally problematic from the rule-of-law perspective because, when they perform it, arbitral tribunals rewrite treaty text rather than interpret it. The second development is the tendency of arbitral tribunals to invariably decline to exercise their jurisdiction on account of corruption. This tendency gives rise to a paradox whereby the State obtains a benefit because of a rule-of-law failing on its own part. Different solutions have been proposed to solve this paradox, all of which have some merit, but the most attractive is the solution proposed by the arbitral tribunal for *Gavrilovic v Croatia*. This solution disqualifies the State from objecting to an arbitral tribunal's jurisdiction on account of corruption if a State official initiated such corruption. In keeping with the strategy for managing the rule-of-law tension that legality requirements give rise to, this solution keeps investment protection standards alive, with the result that the relevant investment treaty fulfils its basic purpose: to subject the State to rule-of-law-informed standards as regards its treatment of foreign investments.

PART III

RULE-OF-LAW CONCERNS IN THE APPLICATION OF SUBSTANTIVE STANDARDS OF TREATMENT

12

Two Moralities of Consistency

Julian Arato

I. Introduction

The provocative premise of this volume is that the investment treaty regime has an antinomic relationship to the rule of law. On the one hand, it is said that a key function of both international investment law (IIL) and investor-State dispute settlement (ISDS) is the promotion of the rule of law at the domestic level (at least vis-à-vis foreign investors).[1] On the other hand, sceptics have observed that the regime recreates many of the same rule-of-law problems at the international level.[2] This tension is perhaps clearest with respect to the value of consistency, which is central to advancing investment treaties' promise of fairness and predictability. This chapter examines the 'internationalized' consistency problem in ISDS and IIL from the perspective of the rule of law.[3]

A core tenet of the claim that IIL promotes the rule of law is that it enhances legal certainty for foreign investors. The idea is that investment treaties function as credible commitments, which lessen the risk of arbitrary, discriminatory, or unfair State action, and enhance the predictability of the legal framework applicable to foreign investment. Inter alia, they do this by pushing the State to act consistently towards covered investors—often under the rubric of a guarantee of 'fair and equitable treatment' (FET). ISDS tribunals typically demand a high level of consistency.[4] However, it turns out that, as interpreted, the investment treaty regime itself suffers from widespread inconsistency.[5] Thus, from a rule-of-law perspective, this regime appears to recreate the very consistency problems it purports to solve.

---

[1] See August Reinisch and Stephan W Schill, 'Introduction' (in this volume) 1; Kenneth Vandevelde, 'A Unified Theory of Fair and Equitable Treatment' (2010) 43 NYU J Intl L & Pol 43; Susan D Franck, 'Foreign Direct Investment, Investment Treaty Arbitration, and the Rule of Law' (2007) 19 Pac McGeorge Global Bus & Dev LJ 337, 340; but see Tom Ginsburg, 'International Substitutes for Domestic Institutions: Bilateral Investment Treaties and Governance' (2005) 25 IRLE 107, 119 (suggesting that by providing substitutes for domestic courts, investment treaties might counterintuitively lead to reductions in domestic governance quality); Richard C Chen, 'Bilateral Investment Treaties and Domestic Institutional Reform' (2017) 55 Colum J Transnatl L 547, 579, 586 (suggesting that investment treaties can be redesigned to better promote the rule of law).

[2] See eg Recommendations of China regarding investor-State dispute settlement reform, United Nations Commission on International Trade Law, 'Possible Reform of Investor-State Dispute Settlement (ISDS): Submission from the Government of China' (19 July 2019) UN Doc A/CN.9/WG.III/WP.177, 3 ('The numerous inconsistencies in the awards . . . and the uncertainty of arbitration results have seriously affected the expectations of the parties involved. [ISDS] clearly cannot meet the requirements for realizing the rule of law in international investment').

[3] See eg August Reinisch, 'The Rule of Law in International Investment Arbitration' in Photini Pazartzis and Maria Gavouneli and others (eds), *Reconceptualizing the Rule of Law in Global Governance, Resources, Investment and Trade* (Hart 2016) 291–307.

[4] *Técnicas Medioambientales Tecmed, SA v The United Mexican States*, ICSID Case No ARB(AF)/00/2, Award (29 May 2003) para 154; *Waste Management, Inc v United Mexican States (II)*, ICSID Case No ARB(AF)/00/3, Award (30 April 2004) para 98; but see *Eli Lilly v Canada*, ICSID Case No UNCT/14/2, Final Award (16 March 2017) para 310 (more leniently scrutinizing inconsistency in the holdings of a common law–based judicial system).

[5] See Julian Arato, Chester Brown and Federico Ortino, 'Parsing and Managing Inconsistency in Investor-State Dispute Settlement' (2020) 21 JWIT 336.

Julian Arato, *Two Moralities of Consistency* In: *Investment Protection Standards and the Rule of Law*. Edited by: August Reinisch and Stephan W. Schill, Oxford University Press. © Julian Arato 2023. DOI: 10.1093/oso/9780192864581.003.0012

In this chapter, I argue that it would be a mistake to analyse the uncomfortable relationship between investment treaties and legal certainty in zero-sum terms. Following a moderate, Fullerian conception of the rule of law, I argue that consistency should not be overemphasized. On a Fullerian view, the rule of law rests upon a set of core values—such as non-retroactivity, non-contradiction, constancy of the law through time, and congruence between official action and the declared rule—which must all be present to at least a degree, but which cannot all necessarily be maximized without perverse results, and which may well exist in considerable tension with one another.[6] On this view, there can be no rule of law—or, arguably, any law at all—without at least a basic expectation of consistency.[7] Yet this is only one rule-of-law value among many—one which cannot be secured absolutely, and should not always be pursued maximally. Striking the balance is no simple exercise in line drawing. As a matter of institutional design, I suggest that the pursuit of optimal consistency is clarified by thinking in terms of Fuller's two moralities: the morality of duty and the morality of aspiration. With that framework in mind, I suggest that interpretive consistency is more pressing with some kinds of norms than others. For instance, inconsistency tends to be more troublesome in the interpretation of bright-line *rules* than with broadly framed *standards*. And within the former set, inconsistent interpretations of *secondary rules* (ie rules that articulate the basic structure of a legal system, or 'rules about rules') are more vexing than with *primary rules* (ie rules that discipline particular conducts).[8]

From a reform perspective, I argue that the utility of enhancing consistent interpretive outcomes is greatest with respect to secondary rules with broad, systemic reach. I focus particularly on rules that determine the applicable law and decide questions of norm conflict. Specific examples where inconsistency is particularly vexing include rules articulating: whether a most-favoured-nation (MFN) provision allows the wholesale importation of procedural or substantive terms from treaties with third States; whether and how States and investors can contract out of investment treaty terms; and how to determine when investment treaties opt out of general international law (*lex specialis*) or when the two should be interpreted harmoniously (systemic integration). These sorts of rules about rules determine the scope and content of the legal framework that will structure a relationship between covered investor and host State, and make prediction and private ordering possible.

Finally, I suggest that this analysis of consistency in treaty interpretation feeds back into evaluating the demands investment treaties make of host States. On a Fullerian view,

---

[6] Fuller himself presents these values as part of a theory of law itself as a set of eight principles (including also generality, clarity, promulgation, and non-impossibility) that together reflect what he calls the 'inner morality of law'—without which no law can properly exist. See Lon Fuller, *The Morality of Law* (2nd edn, Yale UP 1969) 44–45, 79–81. However, his conception serves well (arguably even better) as a theory of the rule of law, and is 'commonly read as an attempt to provide a deeper account of that idea'. Frank Lovett, 'Lon Fuller, *The Morality of Law*' in Jacob Levy (ed), *The Oxford Handbook of Classics in Contemporary Political Theory* (OUP 2015). I rely on Fuller's conception here solely as a theory of the rule of law.

[7] See Fuller (n 6) 79–81.

[8] The distinction between primary and secondary rules is most famously articulated by HLA Hart, who refers to secondary rules as 'rules about rules'. HLA Hart, *Concept of Law* (OUP 1961) Hart focuses on three types in his opus: rules of interpretation, rules of change, and rules of recognition. However, there are many others. See Roberto Ago in ILC 'Yearbook of the International Law Commission 1970, Volume II' (1972) UN Doc A/CN.4/SER.A/1970/Add.1 306, para 66(c). Admittedly the boundary between primary and secondary rules is not always obvious, as noted by James Crawford in his first report as special rapporteur on State responsibility. ILC 'First Report on State Responsibility' (24 April 1998) UN Doc A/CN.4/490, para 14. Resolving these theoretical boundaries lies firmly beyond the present scope, as the focus on secondary rules here will be limited to relatively clear cases.

maximalist interpretations of the consistency demand embedded in FET tend to fetishize consistency and predictability rather than advance the rule of law—as in the exacting formulation in *Tecmed* and its progeny, which require strict levels of consistency, non-ambiguity, and transparency in State action.[9] If ISDS chronically *under-achieves* consistency at the international level, it can tend to *over-demand* consistency at the national level.

Section II analyses consistency as a rule-of-law value, central to the claimed purpose of the investment treaty regime. By appeal to Fuller, I emphasize the analytical purchase in keeping separate the moralities of duty and aspiration. I then set out the most glaring costs of inconsistency, as well as its oft undercounted potential benefits. In a call for moderation, I further situate consistency alongside other rule-of-law values with which it may have to trade off—including fidelity, accuracy, deliberation over time, responsiveness, and flexibility. Section III illustrates the pernicious breadth and depth of inconsistency in the investment treaty regime, while Section IV attempts to separate the more tolerable from the more troubling veins of inconsistency in the case law—with an eye to reform. In concluding, I tie the analysis back to the kinds of consistency that investment treaties can reasonably demand of internal State action.

II. Consistency as a Rule-of-Law Value

One way or another, consistency appears as a central tenet in most conceptions of the rule of law. Without consistent application, a system of legal rules slides into arbitrary rule by fiat. Yet the rule of law is itself a slippery concept, and the relative importance of consistency can vary across accounts. In this section, I first lay out the particular vision of the rule of law to which I will appeal throughout this chapter. This might be labelled a *moderate formal conception*, on the model of Lon Fuller.[10] I then situate consistency as a rule-of-law value within that conception.

A. A Moderate Formal Conception of the Rule of Law

The United Nations (UN) Secretary-General's 2004 report on the rule of law and transitional justice in conflict and post-conflict societies offers a fairly inclusive working definition of the rule of law:

> The 'rule of law' ... refers to a principle of governance in which all persons, institutions and entities, public and private, including the State itself, are accountable to laws that are publicly promulgated, equally enforced and independently adjudicated, and which are consistent with international human rights norms and standards. It requires, as well, measures to ensure adherence to the principles of supremacy of law, equality before the law, accountability to the law, fairness in the application of the law, separation of powers, participation

---

[9] See eg *Tecmed* (n 4) para 154; *Waste Management II* (n 4) para 98.
[10] Fuller (n 6).

in decision-making, legal certainty, avoidance of arbitrariness and procedural and legal transparency.[11]

This broad conception serves as a reasonable starting point, because it is general enough to capture a wide range of approaches. On the one hand, its second sentence readily accommodates most 'formal' theories of the rule of law, which emphasize qualities like legal supremacy, consistency, certainty, and predictability (sometimes called 'thin' or 'procedural' theories).[12] On the other hand, its first sentence seems to link to more robust 'material' conceptions of the rule of law, which, in addition to formal elements, also emphasize the contents of a legal system—such as norms of democratic governance and/or compliance with human rights (sometimes called 'thick' or 'substantive' theories).[13]

Fortunately, for present purposes, there is no need to choose among these branching theoretical paths. It suffices to stick to the thin, formal features of the rule of law. Consistency, certainty, and predictability are formal values which overlap most thin and thick conceptions of the rule of law.[14] I take no firm stance on whether formal or material conceptions have better explanatory power, or whether either is normatively preferable. I merely adopt the formal conception as the simplest analytical device.

Central as they may be to the rule of law, it is not obvious how far consistency and predictability should be valued. Even on a purely formal conception, the rule of law entails a constellation of values which always rest in considerable tension. Maximizing any one node can introduce its own perversions. Moreover, individual rule-of-law values may have to be traded off against one another. Hence I adopt, here, a conception of the rule of law that is not only *formal*, but also *moderate*—one not aimed at maximizing any particular value or set of values in the name of the rule of law, but at maintaining balance across a cluster of values in unstable equilibrium.

Few, if any, well-thought-out theories of the rule of law demand absolute realization of the values they feature. The differences are more a matter of degree. The difficulty lies in thinking through how far to value particular rule-of-law values between the poles, and as against other values with which they might trade off. Though there are no easy answers here, Lon Fuller's work provides a helpful heuristic.[15]

In *The Morality of Law*, Fuller develops an analytical framework for evaluating law and legal institutions. It turns on distinguishing between two moral modes—'the two moralities'—which Fuller eventually develops into two evaluative yardsticks. The 'morality of duty' refers to the minimum demands of morality, compliance with which is strictly and clearly obligatory, and which tends to be conceived in terms of individual duties. These are the bare minimum precepts of righteousness; to live otherwise would be plain moral failure. By contrast, the 'morality of aspiration' refers to the pursuit of excellence beyond those

---

[11] UNSC, 'Report of the Secretary-General on the Rule of Law and Transitional Justice in Conflict and Post-Conflict Societies' (23 August 2004) UN Doc S/2004/616, para 6.

[12] Schill and Reinisch (n 1).

[13] ibid.

[14] See Fuller (n 6) 79–81; Joseph Raz, *The Authority of Law: Essays on Law and Morality* (Clarendon Press 1979) 214–15; Margaret Jane Radin, 'Reconsidering the Rule of Law' (1989) 69 BU L Rev 781, 785, 791–92; Jeremy Waldron, 'The Concept and the Rule of Law' (2008) 43 Georgia L Rev 1. On its formal embodiment across legal systems, see Vandevelde (n 1) fn 31 ('Within common law legal systems, this principle is embodied in the maxim of *stare decisis* ("Let the decisions stand"), which requires that like cases be decided in a like manner. In civil law systems, this principle is somewhat embodied in the concept of *jurisprudence constante*').

[15] Fuller (n 6). *The Morality of Law* reflects the archetypal moderate formal conception of the rule of law.

minimums. For Fuller, 'the morality of aspiration is most plainly exemplified in Greek philosophy. It is the morality of the Good Life, of excellence, of the fullest realization of human powers'. Failure, here, is more a matter of 'shortcoming, not [of] wrongdoing'.[16] It starts 'at the top of human achievement'. By contrast, the morality of duty is 'the morality of the Old Testament and the Ten Commandments'.

> [It] starts at the bottom. It lays down the basic rules without which an ordered society is impossible, or without which an ordered society directed toward certain specific goals must fail of its mark ... It speaks in terms of 'thou shalt not' and, less frequently, of 'thou shalt'. It does not condemn men for failing to embrace opportunities for the fullest manifestation of their powers. Instead, it condemns them for failing to respect the basic requirements of social living.[17]

The line between the two moralities is never clear. 'Deciding where duty ought to leave off is one of the most difficult tasks of social philosophy. Into its solution a large element of judgment must enter and individual differences of opinion are inevitable.'[18] For Fuller, this cannot and need not be resolved. The point is rather to establish clearly that the demands of morality come in two very different flavours—a point which has its signal payoff when applied to the nature of the law (and the demands of the rule of law).

Fuller's opus is, of course, not primarily a study of individual morality, but of the morality of institutions—a study of law, and, in essence, a portrait of the rule of law. For Fuller, the two moralities are key to understanding the split moral logic of law and legal institutions. Famously, Fuller insists upon a narrow set of core values that any legal order must secure to be worthy of the name—what he calls the 'inner morality of law'. These include: (1) generality; (2) promulgation; (3) prospectivity; (4) clarity; (5) non-contradiction; (6) possibility of compliance; (7) constancy; (8) congruence (between official action and the declared rule).[19] But the key insight is that the law only *must* secure these core values to a minimum degree (morality of duty). Law and legal institutions can and should pursue them further (morality of aspiration), but perfection is an unachievable ideal, leaving room for a wide range of institutional constellations and experimentation. Herein lies the work of institutional choice.[20]

In fact, for Fuller, 'the inner morality of law lends itself badly to realization through duties'.[21] In his view, making duties out of questions of institutional choice may be sensible when it comes to the bare minimum. But it quickly devolves into frustrating line drawing problems:

> No matter how desirable a direction of human effort may appear to be, if we assert there is a duty to pursue it, we shall confront the responsibility of defining at what point that duty

---

[16] ibid 5.

[17] ibid 5–6.

[18] ibid 12.

[19] ibid ch 2. See Colleen Murphy, 'Lon Fuller and the Moral Value of the Rule of Law' (2005) 24 Law & Phil 239, 241; Benjamin Zipursky, 'The Inner Morality of Private Law' (2013) 58 Am J Jurisp 27, 28–29.

[20] Neil K Komesar, *Imperfect Alternatives: Choosing Institutions in Law, Economics, and Public Policy* (University of Chicago Press 1994); Sergio Puig and Gregory Shaffer, 'Imperfect Alternatives: Institutional Choice and the Reform of Investment Law' (2018) 112 AJIL 361.

[21] Fuller (n 6) 43.

has been violated. It is easy to assert that the legislator has a moral duty to make his laws clear and understandable. But this remains at best an exhortation unless we are prepared to define the degree of clarity he must attain in order to discharge his duty. The notion of subjecting clarity to quantitative measure presents obvious difficulties.[22]

In other words, the attempt to evaluate law and the rule of law in terms of the morality of duty would, beyond the margins, lead to arbitrary rigidity. Thus, Fuller concludes, 'the inner morality of law is condemned to remain largely a morality of aspiration and not of duty'.[23]

Fuller makes a further important observation about law and the duty of aspiration of immediate relevance here. The quality of a legal order is defined not only by its mere satisfaction of the minimum demands of the rule of law, but by its excellence in securing those values much more deeply. As a matter of institutional design, the core values of the inner morality of law can and should be pursued beyond the exigencies of duty. Yet, it is possible to go too far. It is not clear that any particular value should be pursued with abandon. Fuller expresses his main concern as a matter of marginal utility. A minimum degree of values like constancy and non-retroactivity are required as a matter of duty if there is to be law. Wherever the minimums lie, a good legal system will pursue these values further. But there may be diminishing returns in pursuing any one particular value beyond a certain point—especially to the extent that it trades off against other values. Moreover, maximizing these values can create new problems when pushed too far. For example, absolutism about non-retroactivity and constancy would undercut law's flexibility and responsiveness over time.[24]

Though he does not use the term, Fuller's elaboration of the inner morality of law can be translated into a robust formal theory of the rule of law.[25] On this view, law can only be said to properly reign where Fuller's eight desiderata are met to at least some minimum degree. But not all of them can be maximized without unduly straining the others. The distinction between the two moralities thus moderates the theory, leaving ample room for institutional diversity within the rule of law. And it is this aspect that makes Fuller's conception so fruitful for the evaluation of IIL. The Fullerian perspective sharpens the two core questions posed by this volume—how far should investment law demand that national legal orders achieve rule-of-law values as a matter of actionable legal duty, as opposed to aspiration? And likewise, as a matter of institutional design, how doggedly should those same values be pursued at the international level? As an initial matter, what is clear under Fuller's conception is that the scope of demand should, in both cases, be relatively low, even if the possibilities of aspiration abound.

B. The Benefits and Costs of Consistency

Consistency and predictability are core rule-of-law values.[26] Fuller himself gives neither of them explicit pride of place among his eight. Yet, it is clear from his analysis that these

---

[22] ibid.
[23] ibid.
[24] ibid 60.
[25] Waldron (n 14) 7; Vandevelde (n 1).
[26] See Fuller (n 6) 79–81; Raz (n 14) 214–15; Radin (n 14) 791–92; Waldron (n 14).

values straddle several of his desiderata.[27] Consistency embodies the venerable principle of 'treating like cases alike',[28] which entails elements of non-contradiction, constancy, congruence, and retroactivity. And in any case there is no reason to be beholden to the semantics of Fuller's list. What is more important is that Fuller's lesson of moderation applies with as much force to consistency as to any of his listed values. With no consistency, one could not predict legal outcomes at all—without which law cannot be rightly said to rule in any meaningful sense. As a matter of evaluating existing legal institutions or designing new ones, a degree of consistency is required (as a matter of duty). It can and should be pursued beyond the barebones minimal requirements of the rule of law (aspiration). Yet consistency absolutism can crowd out other rule-of-law values such as fidelity to the spirit and letter of the law (via course-correction), deliberation and dialogue over time, responsiveness, as well as the potential utility of flexibility in judgment.

The value of consistency can be seen in both *ex post* and *ex ante* terms. *Ex post*, consistency reflects a basic precept of natural justice—that like cases should be treated alike. From an *ex ante* perspective, consistency allows private and public actors to rely on the law in making plans. For example, public actors plan regulatory interventions around expectations set by the courts' method of judicial review. Private actors similarly rely on courts' consistent application (and interpretation) of basic commercial rules, as well as default contract terms, which reduce the need for parties to dicker over all contract terms expressly.

On the other side, widespread inconsistency has costs. From a commercial perspective, inconsistency undercuts parties' ability to plan, and to adequately allocate risk (*ex ante*).[29] It can lead to unfair surprises (*ex post*), and, *in extremis*, retroactive application of the law. From a regulatory perspective, inconsistency can also impose governance costs—making planning more difficult for regulators by increasing uncertainty about the potential costs of regulation and potentially leading to regulatory chill.[30]

The limiting cases should by now be obvious. It is hard to imagine the rule of law without any consistency in the interpretation or application of the laws. But absolute mechanical consistency would also be untenable. Such rigidity would turn the law into an iron cage, unbending yet ultimately brittle as the world it is designed to govern changes.[31] No legal system has achieved (nor likely could achieve) absolute consistency. And more importantly, none purport to.

It is not just that the pursuit of consistency eventually yields diminishing returns. Perhaps counterintuitively, the possibility of inconsistency can have its own benefits in certain contexts. The utility of some potential for inconsistency can be understood in terms of give in

---

[27] Consistency in interpretation, particularly, straddles non-retroactivity, non-contradiction, constancy, and congruence, all of which go to predictability from an *ex ante* perspective. See further Waldron (n 14) 7 ('On Fuller's account, the Rule of Law does not directly require anything substantive ... All it requires is that the state should do whatever it wants to do in an orderly, predictable way, giving us plenty of advance notice by publicizing the general norms on which its actions will be based, and that it should then stick to those norms and not arbitrarily depart from them even if it seems politically advantageous to do so').

[28] See Aristotle, *Nicomachean Ethics*, V.3 1131a10–b15; Aristotle, *Politics*, III.9.1280 a8–15, III.12 1282b18–23.

[29] Julian Arato, 'The Private Law Critique of International Investment Law' (2019) 113 AJIL 1.

[30] See eg Tarald Laudal Berge and Axel Berger, 'Do Investor-State Dispute Settlement Cases Influence Domestic Environmental Regulation? The Role of Respondent State Bureaucratic Capacity' (2021) 12 JIDS 1.

[31] In Kelsen's conception, the part of the specificity of law lies in its dynamism—its capacity for change, not only through constitutional and legislative action, but through judicial action. Hans Kelsen, *General Theory of Law and State* 112 (Anders Wedberg tr, Harvard UP 1945) (distinguishing between nomodynamnics and nomostatics). The metaphor of the iron cage is borrowed liberally from Max Weber, *The Protestant Ethic and the Spirit of Capitalism* (Talcott Parsons tr, Allen & Unwin 1930).

the legal system. First, fidelity is itself an important value, which can stand in tension with consistency when early interpretations appear wrong, or not in line with the spirit of the law. Consistency should not automatically trump independent interpretation—especially where the adjudicator believes a previous interpretation was in error. Second, consistency can stand in tension with responsiveness and dynamism. The possibility of inconsistency allows judges to develop the law through dialogue over time, amongst themselves and/or with legislators (or treaty parties). And finally, flexibility can be a virtue in itself—one which lawmakers and/or contract drafters often purposefully seek to enshrine. *Ex ante*, the possibility of some inconsistency is especially useful to parties who wish not to decide all questions up front and rather leave important questions to neutral adjudication *ex post*—for example by employing broad standards rather than bright-line rules. At some point, the dogged pursuit of consistency in institutional design begins to neutralize adjacent values like fidelity, accuracy, dialogue, flexibility, responsiveness, and compromise.

III. Disaggregating Inconsistency in ISDS

For a regime premised, in part, on disciplining inconsistent behaviour by States towards foreign investors, the level of inconsistency in the interpretation of investment treaty standards is troubling. This section illustrates the consistency problem across several perennial interpretive questions arising out of common treaty terms: FET (Section A); MFN (Section B); the treaty–contract relationship (Section C); as well as certain fundamental background norms of public international law, in the law of treaties and the law of State responsibility (Section D). Inconsistency is rife across each of these contexts. Yet its costs and potential benefits vary from norm to norm, and bear drawing out.[32]

A. FET

FET provides a basic illustration of interpretive inconsistency in ISDS. FET guarantees investors an absolute threshold of treatment irrespective of how States treat their own nationals. Most ISDS cases that reach the merits turn on the application of this provision. Yet FET clauses are typically drafted as broad and open-textured standards (often going no further than the words 'fair and equitable treatment'). Tribunals have differed widely over just what FET entails, enunciating tests for scrutinizing State action that range from the extremely strict to the highly deferential.[33] It is also the locus for the demand on States that their actions be internally consistent.

On one end of the spectrum is the *Tecmed* award, which reflects one of the most stringent interpretations of FET. In that tribunal's view, the standard requires that the State not run afoul of the investor's 'basic expectations' in making the investment:

---

[32] I draw here substantially on prior research that I have published with Chester Brown and Federico Ortino. See Arato, Brown and Ortino (n 5).

[33] See ibid 351–57.

The foreign investor expects the host State to act in a consistent manner, free from ambiguity and totally transparently in its relations with the foreign investor, so that it may know beforehand any and all rules and regulations that will govern its investments, as well as the goals of the relevant policies and administrative practices or directives, to be able to plan its investment and comply with such regulations ... The foreign investor also expects the host State to act consistently, i.e. without arbitrarily revoking any preexisting decisions or permits issued by the state that were relied upon by the investor to assume its commitments as well as to plan and launch its commercial and business activities. The investor also expects the state to use the legal instruments that govern the actions of the investor or the investment in conformity with the function usually assigned to such instruments, and not to deprive the investor of its investment without the required compensation.[34]

Among other things, the tribunal reads into FET near totalizing demands of consistency and transparency, in the service of maximizing *ex ante* predictability. The *Tecmed* interpretation of FET has been influential, and has been adopted in numerous cases.[35] But it has also proven highly controversial, described by one tribunal as 'a programme of good governance that no State in the world is capable of guaranteeing at all times'.[36]

Other tribunals have understood FET to entail more flexibility. The NAFTA tribunal in *Waste Management II* adopted a moderately scrutinizing formulation, based loosely on the *Tecmed* interpretation, but qualifying most of its prongs in a signal of deference—such as *gross* unfairness, *complete lack* of transparency and candour, *manifest* failure of natural justice, or breach of host State representations on which the investor *reasonably relied*.[37]

Still others have viewed FET as fairly deferential, taking into account the host State's right to regulate as a legitimate countervailing interest. The *El Paso* tribunal considered FET to entail 'reasonableness and proportionality' review, such that 'a foreign investor can expect that the rules will not be changed without justification of an economic, social or other nature. Conversely, it is unthinkable that a State could make a general commitment to all foreign investors never to change its legislation whatever the circumstances', though liability

---

[34] *Tecmed* (n 4) para 154.

[35] See eg *Bayindir v Pakistan*, ICSID Case No ARB/03/29, Award (27 August 2009) para 179 (accepting *Tecmed* as an ' "authoritative precedent" with respect to the doctrine of legitimate expectations'); *MTD Equity Sdn. Bhd and MTD Chile SA v Republic of Chile*, ICSID Case No ARB/01/7, Award (25 May 2004) paras 113–15; *LG&E Energy Corp v Argentine Republic*, ICSID Case No ARB/02/1, Decision on Liability (3 October 2006) para 127.

[36] *El Paso Energy International Company v The Argentine Republic*, ICSID Case No ARB/03/15, Award (31 October 2001) para 342; Zachary Douglas, 'Nothing If Not Critical for Investment Treaty Arbitration: Occidental, Eureko and Methanex' (2006) 22 Arb Intl 27, 28.

[37] The *Waste Management II* (n 4) tribunal determined at para 98 that FET prohibits conduct that is: 'arbitrary, grossly unfair, unjust, or idiosyncratic, is discriminatory and exposes the claimant to sectional or racial prejudice, or involves a lack of due process leading to an outcome which offends judicial propriety as might be the case with a manifest failure of natural justice in judicial proceedings or a complete lack of transparency and candour in an administrative process. In applying this standard, it is relevant that the treatment is in breach of representations made by the host State which were reasonably relied on by the claimant.'

Waste Management II has been highly influential both within the NAFTA context, and outside of it—including by tribunals charged with interpreting BIT provisions that do not appear to be linked to the international minimum standard of treatment. See eg *Philip Morris Brands Sàrl, Philip Morris Products SA and Abal Hermanos SA v Oriental Republic of Uruguay*, ICSID Case No ARB/10/7, Award (8 July 2016) paras 323–24. For some tribunals, the *Waste Management II* represented a welcome course correction from the too-extreme *Tecmed* approach. Yet others have viewed those two formulations as mutually supportive, relying on both as though they entailed the same level of strict review. *Oko Pankki Oyj v Estonia*, ICSID Case No ARB/04/6, Award (19 November 2007) para 242.

might still arise where a 'reasonable general regulation ... violates a specific commitment towards the investor'.[38]

These examples hardly exhaust the variety of approaches taken by tribunals in expounding the sparse FET standard, but they serves to illustrate the wide flux in the cases. Without any clear tether to differences in underlying treaty text, tribunals have ranged from viewing the standard as extremely strict (*Tecmed*) to moderate (*Waste Management II*) to fairly deferential (*El Paso*). It is not easy to draw firm lines between these approaches, and tribunals often blend them together. But, in the aggregate, it is clear that the scope and power of the lynchpin investment treaty standard remains radically unclear. This creates costs for all parties: it can lead to expensive surprises *ex post*, and, if sufficiently appreciated, can inflate transaction costs *ex ante* as States and investors try to price in the risks involved.[39]

B. MFN

MFN clauses provide another example of troubling inconsistency, where interpretations have fluctuated across a dramatic range of meanings.[40] The basic concept entails a guarantee against horizontal discrimination—that the State will not treat foreign investors from a treaty party any worse than foreign investors hailing from other nations.[41] The principal inconsistency in the cases concerns whether MFN enables an investor covered by one treaty to automatically invoke any more favourable arrangements in the host State's treaties with third States—a practice known as 'importing' treaty terms.[42] Tribunals differ markedly as to whether MFN can be used to import more favourable procedural terms, substantive terms, both, or neither.[43]

---

[38] *El Paso* (n 36) paras 372–75. See also *Saluka Investments BV v The Czech Republic*, UNCITRAL, Partial Award (17 March 2006) paras 304–05.

[39] See Arato, Brown and Ortino (n 5) 357.

[40] The divergence in approaches to MFN is well known. Inconsistency in the interpretation and application of MFN has been specifically identified by the United Nations Commission on International Trade Law (UNCITRAL) Working Group III as an example of an 'unjustified inconsistency'. UNCITRAL, 'Report of Working Group III (Investor-State Dispute Settlement Reform) on the Work of its Thirty-Fifth Session (New York, 23–27 April 2018)' (14 May 2018) UN Doc No A/CN.9/935, para 31.

[41] MFN clauses in investment treaties generally require that investors from the home State receive treatment 'no less favourable' than the treatment enjoyed by investors from other States. See eg August Reinisch, 'Most Favoured Nation Treatment' in Marc Bungenberg and others (eds), *International Investment Law* (Hart 2015) 807; Andreas Ziegler, 'Most-Favoured-Nation (MFN) Treatment' in August Reinisch (ed), *Standards of Investment Protection* (OUP 2008) 59; Pia Acconci, 'Most-Favoured Nation Treatment' in Peter Muchlinski, Federico Ortino and Christoph Schreuer (eds), *The Oxford Handbook of International Investment Law* (OUP 2008) 363. In some treaties, the obligation is framed as requiring treatment 'no less favourable' to that afforded to investors from third States 'in like circumstances'. See eg the North American Free Trade Agreement between Canada, the United States and Mexico (signed 17 December 1992, entered into force 1 January 1994) [1993] 32 ILM 1480 (NAFTA) art 1103(1).

[42] See Simon Batifort and J Benton Heath, 'The New Debate on the Interpretation of MFN Clauses in Investment Treaties: Putting the Brakes on Multilateralization' (2018) 111 AJIL 873 (adopting the term 'importation' as a widely used and convenient shorthand, while acknowledging that 'it does not precisely reflect the operation of MFN clauses'); Christopher Greenwood, 'Reflections on "Most Favoured Nation" Clauses in Bilateral Investment Treaties' in David D Caron and others (eds), *Practising Virtue: Inside International Arbitration* (OUP 2016) 556, 559–61 (emphasizing that, as a matter of law, third-party treaty provisions are neither 'written into' nor 'incorporated' into the basic treaty via an MFN clause).

[43] Spotting glaring inconsistencies in the MFN cases is not always easy on a granular case-by-case level. Unlike with FPS and FET, MFN provisions are framed in often substantially different terms across investment treaties. See ILC, 'Final Report of the Study Group on the Most-Favoured-Nation Clause' (2015) ILC YB, vol II, pt Two, paras 59–66 (identifying at typology of formulations of MFN clauses in investment treaties, which can be found alone or in combination across various treaties). And tribunals make frequent efforts to distinguish and reconcile

Most salient and controversial is the question of importing *procedural mechanisms*, such as more favourable conditions on access to ISDS, access to particular arbitral institutions and their attendant enforcement mechanisms, or even host State consent to arbitration. Here, tribunals have split relatively evenly, with some interpreting MFN clauses permissively to allow the importation of 'procedural' terms from third-party treaties,[44] and others reading MFN restrictively to exclude procedural importation.[45] Tribunals have been more consistent in interpreting MFN clauses to allow investors to import *substantive standards* from treaties with third States.[46] Yet, here too, some recent tribunals have closed off this possibility as well,[47] prompting new questions (and inconsistencies) about whether invoking MFN to import *any* third-party treaty terms is appropriate.[48]

The inconsistent case law on MFN makes the content of the clause unpredictable, within a significantly wider range of flux than with FET. The inconsistency in MFN can potentially alter every aspect of the disciplines of investment treaty protection. Uncertainty as to whether MFN clauses permit importation of procedural provisions, substantive provisions, or neither, makes it difficult for States and investors to predict the scope of the international legal framework applicable to an investment—whether it will be limited to the terms of the treaty between the host State and the investor's State of nationality, or whether it will also extend to a patchwork of favourable procedural and/or substantive terms from third-party treaties. Here again, though to a greater order of magnitude than with FET, this vast uncertainty is likely to lead to unfair surprise *ex post* and substantial price inefficiencies *ex ante*. All this also introduces substantial uncertainty into the State's regulatory process.

C. The Treaty–Contract Relationship

Most investment treaties cover contracts within the definition of investment, but rarely do they articulate the relationship between treaty and contract. Across all cases where the investment is, or includes, a contract between the State and the investor, ISDS tribunals have proven highly inconsistent on the relationship between investment treaty norms and

---

themselves with prior MFN cases—if not always successfully. See Arato, Brown and Ortino (n 5) 361. However, the distinctions in the treaties are not always clear-cut, and the lines in the case law do not neatly map on to drafting differences. See ibid ('at a high level of altitude, at least, the cases appear broadly inconsistent on the big questions, rendering the scope of MFN in any treaty uncertain at best'); see further Zachary Douglas, 'The MFN Clause in Investment Arbitration: Treaty Interpretation off the Rails' (2011) 2 JIDS 97 (casting doubt on the relevance of nuanced differences in the wording of MFN clauses for purposes of interpretation, and suggesting that all MFN clauses should be interpreted in light general international law); but see Stephan Schill, 'Allocating Adjudicatory Authority: Most-Favoured-Nation Clauses as a Basis of Jurisdiction—A Reply to Zachary Douglas' (2011) 2 JIDS 353 (concurring with Douglas as to the relevance of general international law in interpretation, but cautioning that this does not alleviate tribunals from taking a 'BIT by BIT' approach to interpretation).

[44] See eg *Maffezini v Spain*, ICSID Case No ARB/97/7, Decision on Jurisdiction (25 January 2000); *Siemens AG v Argentine Republic*, ICSID Case No ARB/02/8, Decision on Jurisdiction (3 August 2004); *RosInvestCo UK Ltd v Russian Federation*, SCC Case No V079/2005, Award on Jurisdiction (1 October 2007) paras 124–39; *Teinver SA v Argentine Republic*, ICSID Case No ARB/11/20, Decision on Jurisdiction (21 December 2012) para 186.

[45] *Salini Costruttori SpA and Italstrade SpA v Jordan*, ICSID Case No ARB/02/13, Decision on Jurisdiction (29 November 2004); *Plama Consortium Ltd v Bulgaria*, ICSID Case No ARB/03/24, Decision on Jurisdiction (8 February 2005); *Daimler AG v Argentine Republic*, ICSID Case No ARB/05/1, Award (22 August 2012) para 281.

[46] See eg *White Industries v India*, UNCITRAL, Award (30 November 2011).

[47] See eg *Muhammet Çap & Sehil v Turkmenistan*, ICSID Case No ARB/12/6, Award (4 May 2021) paras 788–98; *Içkale Insaat v Turkmenistan*, ICSID Case No ARB/10/24, Award (8 March 2016).

[48] See Batifort and Heath (n 42).

contractual terms expressly chosen by the parties.[49] Tribunals have taken entirely incompatible positions on whether treaty provisions should take precedence over express contract terms, or whether States and investors are free to contract out of treaty norms.[50]

Investment treaties effectively address many of the same things that States and investors bargain over in their contractual relations. These range from specific rights and obligations, to damages rules, defences, and forum selection. Often treaties address these matters expressly (as with clauses providing for ISDS). Other matters are addressed only implicitly (such as damages rules for breach of treaty, which tend to be drawn from general international law). ISDS has yielded highly inconsistent results not only with respect to the substantive interpretation of these provisions, but also on the second-order question of how far States and investors may contract around these treaty terms.

Absent any guidance in the underlying treaties, tribunals have taken three broadly irreconcilable approaches to the treaty–contract problem. Some have viewed investment treaty norms as effectively *mandatory*—barring States and investors from opting out of treaty terms by contract.[51] Other tribunals have understood the same kinds of treaty provisions as mere *defaults*, prioritizing parties' contractual choices over treaty rules.[52] And still others

---

[49] See Arato (n 29) 25–27; Julian Arato, 'The Logic of Contract in the World of Investment Treaties' (2016) 58 Wm & Mary L Rev 351; James Crawford, 'Treaty and Contract in Investment Arbitration' (2008) 24 Arb Intl 351; Zachary Douglas, *The International Law of Investment Claims* (CUP 2009) 17–18.

[50] Some treaties incorporate clauses that seem to expressly convert any breach of a contract between the State and the investor into a breach of the treaty (umbrella clause). Tribunals have interpreted such clauses inconsistently, in terms of both scope (application to contracts) and content (effects on a covered contract). *SGS Société Générale de Surveillance SA v Pakistan*, ICSID Case No ARB/01/13, Decision of Jurisdiction (6 August 2003) (finding that the umbrella clause did not cover contracts between State and investor); *SGS Société Générale de Surveillance SA v Philippines*, ICSID Case No ARB/02/6, Decision on Jurisdiction (29 January 2004) (finding that the umbrella clause did convert breach of contract into breach of treaty, but implicitly approaching the treaty as providing mere defaults that would not displace the choices made by the contracting parties—particularly as to forum selection); *SGS Société Générale de Surveillance SA v Paraguay*, ICSID Case No ARB/07/29, Decision on Jurisdiction (12 February 2010) paras 131, 138–42, 177–84 (finding that the umbrella clause applied, and effectively approaching the treaty's terms as mandatory rules). See further Arato (n 49) 373–75; Julian Arato, 'Corporations as Lawmakers' (2015) 56 Harv Int LJ 229, 252–56. More subtly, the same basic problem arises even absent an umbrella clause. By covering contracts under the definition of investment, practically all investment treaties apply to some kinds of contracts in some way, raising the question of how choices in contract and treaty interact. Here too, tribunals have landed all over the map. See (nn 61–63) and accompanying text. The presence of an umbrella clause seems to have little effect on how this matter is resolved.

[51] In the context of the umbrella clause, see *SGS v Paraguay* (n 50) paras 131, 138–42, 177–84. Numerous tribunals have understood treaties as effectively mandatory terms outside of the context of umbrella clauses. On ISDS as a mandatory rule, see *Compañía de Aguas del Aconquija SA and Vivendi Universal SA v Argentine Republic* ('Vivendi I'), ICSID Case No ARB/97/3, Decision on Annulment (3 July 2002) paras 101–03 (on forum selection). On treaty/international law damages as mandatory, see *Venezuela Holdings v Venezuela*, ICSID Case No ARB/07/27, Award (9 October 2014) (on damages). On substantive treaty standards as mandatory rules, see *Sempra Energy v Argentine Republic*, ICSID Case No ARB/02/16, Award (28 September 2007) para 310 (applying the stabilization requirements that it interpreted the treaty's FET provision to mandate, without reference to the contractual provisions on stabilization); *Enron Creditors Recovery Corporation v Argentine Republic*, ICSID Case No ARB/01/3, Award (22 May 2007) paras 260–61; *CMS Gas Transmission Company v Argentine Republic*, ICSID Case No ARB/01/8, Award (12 May 2005).

[52] In the context of the umbrella clause, see *SGS v Philippines* (n 50); *Bureau Veritas, Inspection, Valuation, Assessment and Control, BIVAC BV v Paraguay*, ICSID Case No ARB/07/9, Decision on Jurisdiction (29 May 2009). Outside of the context of umbrella clauses, several tribunals have understood treaties as mere default rules susceptible to opt out by contract. On forum selection, see *Oxus Gold v Uzbekistan*, UNCITRAL, Final Award (17 December 2015) para 958(ii) (recognizing contractual waiver of ISDS jurisdiction over counterclaims). On damages, see *Venezuela Holdings v Venezuela*, ICSID Case No ARB/07/27, Decision on Annulment (9 March 2017) paras 181–84 (2017) (annulling the underlying award for failing to explain why it failed to give effect to apparent contractual caps on damages); *Siag v Egypt*, ICSID Case No ARB/05/15, Award (1 June 2009) paras 577–84 (giving effect to contractual compensation provisions). On substantive standards, see *Parkerings-Compagniet AS v Lithuania*, ICSID Case No ARB/05/8, Award (11 September 2007) para 332 (finding that FET does not impose broad stabilization requirements, but that States and investors are free to ratchet up the level of protection that FET

have viewed treaty norms as *sticky defaults*—rules which parties may contract around, but only by meeting some heightened threshold, like a clear statement rule, or rules requiring use of 'magic words' to signify opt-out.[53]

Inconsistency and unpredictability with respect to the treaty–contract relationship produces harms distinct from the inconsistent interpretations FET and MFN considered above. Uncertainty as to the effect of contractual bargaining under the shadow of an investment treaty can impose substantial unnecessary costs on all parties. *Ex ante*, States and investors cannot predict whether and under what circumstances their directly bargained-for terms will prevail over the overarching treaty, or vice versa, if and when they find themselves in ISDS down the line. Such uncertainty, if fully appreciated by all parties at the negotiation stage, can lead to costly drafting exercises with inefficient effects on price—even potentially dampening the parties' willingness to contract. If unappreciated, such uncertainty is likely to lead to unfair surprise *ex post*, most likely to the detriment of host States.[54]

D. General International Law

Investment treaties are brief, generally spartan instruments that tend to focus on primary rules (substantive obligations) and procedural norms relating to dispute resolution. They are nestled within a much more comprehensive framework of general international law— secondary rules that govern agreements between States (the law of treaties), the assignment and consequences of liability (State responsibility), more basic rules about the sources of international law, the law of nationality, and so on. The relationship between investment treaties and general international law is analogous to the relationship between a contract and the law of contracts—the vast majority of these background norms are mere defaults, and investment treaties can opt out by selecting more specialized or even contradictory terms (*lex specialis*).[55] But due to their brevity, practically every investment treaty dispute requires the tribunal to apply some of these background rules. The interpretation and application of general international law has thus emerged as a further site of inconsistency, which produces both familiar and novel problems.

---

would entail by negotiating for a stabilization clause in the contract); *EDF Services Ltd v Romania*, ICSID Case No ARB/05/13, Award (8 October 2009) para 217; and *Philip Morris* (n 37) para 423.

[53] On forum selection, see *Crystallex v Venezuela*, ICSID Case No ARB(AF)/11/2, Award (4 April 2016) para 481 (considering that States and investors can contract out of ISDS, but that 'any such waiver would have to be formulated in clear and specific terms', and that waiver 'is never to be lightly admitted as it requires knowledge and intent of forgoing a right'. Here the tribunal rejected an exclusive forum selection clause which expressly required that all disputes be resolved in Venezuelan court); *Aguas del Tunari v Bolivia*, ICSID Case No ARB/02/3, Decision on Jurisdiction (21 October 2005) paras 119, 122; *Occidental v Ecuador*, ICSID Case No ARB/06/11, Decision on Jurisdiction (9 September 2008) paras 71–74. On damages, see *Kardassopoulos v Georgia*, ICSID Case Nos. ARB/05/18 and ARB/07/15, Award (3 March 2010) paras 480–81 (viewing the fair market value damages standard as a sticky default, with a strong presumption against opt-out). On contracting around substantive treaty standards, see *MNSS v Montenegro*, ICSID Case No ARB(AF)/12/8, Award (4 May 2016) para 163 (finding that 'investors may waive the rights conferred to them by treaty provided [the] waivers are explicit and freely entered into'. In this case the tribunal accepted a contractual waiver that disclaimed substantive BIT and other international legal rights by name, including FET).

[54] For a more fulsome treatment of the harms posed by this form of second-order inconsistency, see Arato (n 29) 25–27; Arato (n 49) 351.

[55] See eg ILC, 'Articles on State Responsibility of States for Internationally Wrongful Acts' UNGA Res 56/83 (12 December 2001) UN Doc A/RES/56/83 (ARSIWA) art 55.

The engagement of ISDS tribunals with public international law is rich, with many examples of inconsistency ranging in their significance. Suffice it to highlight just a few examples from the law of treaties and State responsibility. Key examples include: the rules of treaty interpretation; attribution; and circumstances precluding wrongfulness (especially necessity).

Practically every treaty-based ISDS tribunal has to interpret some aspect of the underlying treaty, and most engage expressly with the rules of treaty interpretation articulated in the Vienna Convention on the Law of Treaties (VCLT) in Articles 31–34.[56] Much of this engagement is uncontroversial, but significant inconsistencies have arisen in how tribunals understand the rules of treaty interpretation over time—particularly relating to systemic integration (VCLT, 31(3)(c)), subsequent agreements (VCLT 31(3)(a)), and subsequent practice (VCLT 31(3)(b)).

The systemic integration rule requires adjudicators to take into account, as part of the interpretive process, any 'relevant rules of international law applicable in the relations among the parties'.[57] The inconsistencies here come in two flavours. First, tribunals have divided over what kinds of extrinsic evidence the systemic integration rule admits in the interpretive process. Some tribunals have taken fairly expansive approaches, as by adopting broad interpretations of *relevance*[58] and *applicability*.[59] Other tribunals have interpreted these conditions more restrictively.[60] Second, tribunals have split over how far 31(3)(c) authorizes contorting the plain text of the treaty—or, in other words, how to resolve the tension between systemic integration and the principle of *lex specialis*. For example, many investment treaties incorporate a 'local litigation' provision, requiring an investor to pursue her claims for a limited period in domestic courts before resorting to ISDS (often 18 months). By contrast, the general international law of diplomatic protection requires injured nationals to exhaust local remedies before the State can make a claim on their behalf—except where doing so would be strictly futile.[61] Several tribunals have had to consider whether to interpret a

---

[56] Vienna Convention on the Law of Treaties (opened for signature 23 May 1969, entered into force 27 January 1980) 1155 UNTS 331 (hereafter VCLT) arts 31–34; ILA, 'Final Report, Study Group on the Content and Evolution of the Rules of Interpretation, International Law Association' (2020) 30; Julian Arato and Andreas Kulick, Annex 2, 3.

[57] VCLT (n 56) art 31(3)(c).

[58] See *Ambiente Ufficio v Argentine Republic*, ICSID Case No ARB/08/9, Decision on Jurisdiction and Admissibility (8 February 2013) para 602 (a norm of general international law is relevant within the meaning of 31(3)(c) if it is merely 'sufficiently comparable'); *Urbaser v Argentine Republic*, ICSID Case No ARB/07/26, Award (8 December 2016) paras 1204–05 (interpreting 'relevance' broadly).

[59] For example, several tribunals have invoked art 31(3)(c) to consider treaties that are opposable to only one of the parties to the treaty in question, and in some cases to neither of them, as valid extrinsic evidence for the purposes of interpretation. See eg *Vladimir Berschader v Russian Federation*, SCC Case No 080/2004, Award (21 April 2006) para 97 (considering non-party BITs as persuasive evidence of party intent for purposes of interpretation); *Tulip Real Estate v Republic of Turkey*, ICSID Case No ARB/11/28, Decision on Annulment (30 December 2015) paras 87, 90–92 (considering 'provisions in human rights instruments dealing with the right to a fair trial and any judicial practice thereto are relevant to the interpretation of the concept of a fundamental rule of procedure as used in Article 52(1)(d) of the ICSID Convention' and considering it unnecessary that the extrinsic sources be formally opposable to all parties to the Convention, including the State involved in the present dispute).

[60] See eg *RosInvest* (n 44) para 39 (reading art 31(3)(c) to allow only consideration of extrinsic rules that 'condition the performance of the specific rights and obligations stipulated in the treaty'); *European Media Ventures v Czech Republic*, UNCITRAL, Partial Award on Liability (8 July 2009) para 49 (expressing caution in what can be drawn from extrinsic treaties not in force between all parties to the investment treaty at issue); Arato and Kulick (n 56) 16–17.

[61] See eg *Claim of Finnish Shipowners (Finland v United Kingdom)* (1934) 3 RIAA 1479. Local litigation requirements and the exhaustion of local remedies rule may seem similar, but they have very different functions. The former creates merely a cooling-off period, which might allow disposing of relatively easy cases, dissuade some frivolous suits, and perhaps facilitate a restoration of the relationship between State and investor. The exhaustion

treaty's strict local litigation requirement (making no exception for futility) in light of the futility exception to the general international law exhaustion rule. The tribunal in *Ambiente* found that 31(3)(c) justified effectively importing the futility exception into the treaty's local litigation provision. However, the tribunal in *Içkale* refused to do so, finding that 'the local litigation requirement in the BIT is not a reflection or incorporation of a rule of customary international law, but rather a *lex specialis*'.[62] Though both cases involved similar BIT provisions, the tribunals came to opposite conclusions about how far 31(3)(c) allows effectively importing norms of general international law into the treaty. Similarly to the issues relating to MFN, inconsistency in the rules of systemic integration creates uncertainty as to the applicable law.[63] And analogously to the treaty–contract problem, it creates uncertainty for States about the gravitational force of general international law and the viability of opt-out via *lex specialis*. Beyond imposing *ex ante* costs, this uncertainty has further costly implications for treaty reform.

Without going into detail, further inconsistencies can be found in how tribunals engage with the rules relating to subsequent agreements and subsequent practice—both as to what counts as authoritative extrinsic sources and how far these allow interpretive drift from clear text.[64] Inconsistency here creates uncertainty as to how far States can reduce or augment treaty obligations, even in relation to an ongoing dispute, as well as how far States can be held to their previous interpretive statements.

Tribunals have also proven inconsistent in how they interpret and apply the general rules of State responsibility. For example, tribunals have differed materially over which entities qualify as organs such that their conduct would be attributable to the State under ARSIWA, Article 4.[65] Several have held that any entity with separate legal personality cannot be an organ per Article 4,[66] whereas others have held that separate legal personality is not dispositive.[67] Considering how many agencies, subnational entities, and other instrumentalities have separate legal personality from the State for at least some purposes under domestic law, the applicability of Article 4 to them has potentially vast implications for determining

---

rule, by contrast, gives States the full opportunity to resolve any potential international legal wrong committed by its organs through domestic judicial processes—however time-consuming this may be—as a matter of sovereign dignity. Though clearly good policy in the latter context, it is not so clear that a futility exception would serve the functions of a local litigation rule.

[62] *Içkale v Turkmenistan* (n 47) para 261; see further Arato and Kulick (n 56) 18.

[63] Stephan W Schill, *The Multilateralization of International Investment Law* (CUP 2009) (considering 31(3)(c) as a driver of multilateralization).

[64] See eg Arato and Kulick (n 56) 8–14.

[65] ARSIWA (n 55) art 4.

[66] See eg *Noble Ventures v Romania*, ICSID Case No ARB/01/11, Award (12 October 2005) para 69 ('Since [the entities in question] were legal entities separate from the Respondent, it is not possible to regard them as *de jure* organs'); *Bayindir* (n 35) para 119; *Jan de Nul and Dredging International NV v Arab Republic of Egypt*, ICSID Case No ARB/04/13, Award (6 November 2008) para 160.

[67] See eg *Eureko v Republic of Poland*, Partial Award (19 August 2005) para 131 ('the state is responsible for the acts of 'all the organs, instrumentalities and officials which form part of [the State's] organization and act in that capacity, *whether or not they have separate legal personality under its internal law*') (quoting then Professor Crawford in UNGA, 'Report of the International Law Commission on the Responsibility of States for Internationally Wrongful Acts' (23 April–1 June and 2 July–10 August 2001) UN Doc A/56/10, 83, para 7); *Deutsche Bank v Democratic Socialist Republic of Sri Lanka*, ICSID Case No ARB/09/2, Award (31 October 2012) para 405(a) ('the fact that [a State entity] takes the form of a separate legal entity is not decisive'); *Ampal-American Israel Corp et al v Egypt*, ICSID Case No ARB/12/11, Decision on Liability and Heads of Loss (21 February 2017) para 138. There are further inconsistencies in respect of other aspects of attributing the actions of State-owned entities to the State. See Luca Schicho, 'Attribution and State Entities: Diverging Approaches in Investment Arbitration' (2011) 12 JWIT 283.

whose actions the State is responsible for, or, put the other way, whose actions investment treaties protect investors from.

Tribunals have also famously differed on the applicability of necessity as a circumstance precluding wrongfulness, including: the relationship between treaty-based essential security clauses and the necessity rule codified in ARSIWA, Article 25; the scope of necessity under ARSIWA, Article 25; and the applicability of ARSIWA, Article 27 preserving the possibility of compensation even when necessity precludes wrongfulness.[68] These issues implicate two different kinds of consistency problems. When applied by ISDS tribunals as a pure customary defence, inconsistency as to the scope of necessity under ARSIWA, Articles 25 and 27 can create uncertainty as to when tribunals will ratify States of necessity *ex post*, and what precise consequences can be expected with respect to compensation. But where treaties incorporate provisions that seemingly deal with necessity, inconsistency as to the relationship between the treaty provision and custom raise the same broad issues of applicable law and norm priority as arise with systemic integration—sometimes explicitly in connection with VCLT 31(3)(c).[69]

Some of these inconsistencies create more systemic issues than others. Some, like inconsistency as to the scope of ARSIWA, Article 25 create uncertainty about the application of particular (important) rules. Others create more structural problems. Similar to MFN, inconsistency as to the scope of 31(3)(c) and its relationship to *lex specialis* create far-ranging uncertainty *ex ante* about the legal framework applicable to an investment. Inconsistency in the interpretation and application of general international law also creates its own special systemic problems. For instance, uncertainty about norm priority here imposes barriers to treaty reform. Where the gravitational force of general international law is unclear, the bar to reform through treaty design can go up, as it becomes difficult for treaty parties to know when opt-out will be effective. This is all the more true with inconsistency as to whether 31(3)(c) requires systemic integration with the wider constellation of pre-existing BITs.[70] Moreover, inconsistency here can fuel the fragmentation of general international law—particularly given the under-judicialized of nature public international law relative to ISDS.

ISDS has an evident consistency problem. Many facets of investment treaties are subject to churning inconsistency—from FET and MFN, to the treaty–contract relationships, and even the interpretation and application of general international law. These interpretive divergencies are difficult to predict and manage. Sometimes differences in approach turn on distinctions in treaty drafting (which is at least potentially justifiable), but not always. Even similarly or identically drafted treaty provisions are regularly interpreted in irreconcilable ways. The explanation is fairly obvious. Interpretation in the investment treaty regime occurs on a one-off basis, through ad hoc arbitral dispute resolution. Decisions and awards are often published, allowing future investors to know the reasoning of past adjudicators,

---

[68] See August Reinisch, 'Necessity in International Investment Arbitration—An Unnecessary Split of Opinions in Recent ICSID Cases? Comments on *CMS v. Argentina* and *LG&E v. Argentina*' (2007) 8 JWIT 191; Stephan W Schill, 'International Investment Law and the Host State's Power to Handle Economic Crises: Comment on the ICSID Decision in *LG&E v. Argentina*' (2007) 24 J Intl Arb 265; José Alvarez and Tegan Brink, 'Revisiting the Necessity Defense: Continental Casualty v. Argentina' in Karl P Sauvant (ed), *Yearbook of International Investment Law & Policy 2010–2011* (OUP 2012) 319; J Benton Heath, 'The New National Security Challenge to the Economic Order' (2020) 129 Yale LJ 924; Kathleen Claussen, 'The Casualty of Investor Protection in Times of Economic Crises' (2019) 118 Yale LJ 1545.

[69] *El Paso* (n 36).

[70] *Berschader* (n 59) para 97 and *Ambiente v Argentina* (n 58) para 602 (construing the systemic integration rule expansively); see contra *RosInvest* (n 44) para 39 (construing it restrictively).

but without imposing any formal precedential commitment on future adjudicators. There is, as yet, no institution capable of systematizing the jurisprudence like a unifying appellate mechanism or multilateral investment court. This state of near total interpretive flux on every important question calls into question the basic rule of law in the investment treaty regime.

IV. Consistency and the Rule of Law in Investment Law: Duty, Aspiration, and Excess

While the investment treaty regime clearly suffers from inconsistency, this might not of itself entail a significant rule-of-law deficiency. More needs to be said about where the inconsistencies arise, and about their specific consequences. In Fullerian terms, not all inconsistencies reflect a failure of duty, or even a failure of aspiration—sometimes even true inconsistency may have at least instrumental value, as where it promotes fidelity and accuracy (eg course correction from problematic early interpretations), or responsiveness to changing conditions. Thinking through these line-drawing problems is especially important insofar as enhancing consistency has emerged as a central object of States' efforts to reform the regime on a multilateral basis in the context of the United Nations Commission on International Trade Law (UNCITRAL).[71] The most difficult problem of institutional design is to decide where consistency is essential (the realm of duty), and where the possibility of inconsistency is more tolerable (the realm of aspiration), or even desirable. As Fuller cautions, no clear lines can be drawn here. But the examples of inconsistency in the investment treaty regime considered above help to make some rough distinctions.

As a first step, the classical distinction between rules and standards proves helpful in sorting out where consistency may be more or less tolerable.[72] While consistency is a core rule-of-law value, the rule of law does not necessarily abhor all interpretive discretion and flexibility over time.[73] In fact, the degree of flexibility (and thus the potential for inconsistency over time) can be a design choice. This is one way to think about rules and standards. Rules connote relatively precise, rigid legal norms. By regulating through crystalline rules legislators (or, here, treaty drafters) constrain judicial discretion *ex post*, and create a relatively strong expectation of consistent judicial behaviour among those subject to the rules *ex ante*.[74] Standards, by contrast, are open-textured, flexible directives. By regulating through muddy standards, legislators leave adjudicators wider discretion to interpret, apply, and

---

[71] See United Nations Commission on International Trade Law, 'Report of Working Group III (Investor-State Dispute Settlement Reform) on the Work of Its Thirty-Fourth Session (Vienna, 27 November–1 December 2017), Part II' (26 February 2018) UN Doc A/CN.9/930/Add.1/Rev1, paras 9–35.

[72] Frederick Schauer, 'The Convergence of Rules and Standards' (2003) NZ L Rev 303, 306. On the distinction between rules and standards generally, see Larry Alexander and Emily Sherwin, 'The Deceptive Nature of Rules' (1994) 142 U Pa L Rev 1191; Alan Chen, 'Shadow Law: Reasonable Unreasonableness, Habeas Theory, and the Nature of Legal Rules' (1999) 2 Buff CLR 535; Louis Kaplow, 'Rules versus Standards: An Economic Analysis' (1992) 42 Duke LJ 557; Duncan Kennedy, 'Form and Substance in Private Law Adjudication' (1976) 89 Harv L Rev 1685; Russel Korobkin, 'Behavioral Analysis and Legal Form: Rules vs. Standards Revisited' (2000) 79 Or L Rev 23; Pierre Schlag, 'Rules and Standards' (1985) 33 UCLA L Rev 379. See further Arato, Brown and Ortino (n 5) 339.

[73] Fuller (n 6); Lovett (n 6).

[74] See Arato, Brown and Ortino (n 5) 373; Schauer (n 19) 308; Carol Rose, 'Crystals and Mud in Property Law' (1988) 40 Stan L Rev 577, 578 (distinguishing between crystalline and muddy rules—the former being bright, clear, and rigid, and the latter leaving judges substantial *ex post* discretion).

develop the norm *ex post*, which ought to yield far more modest expectations about consistency *ex ante*. These consequences may or may not be intended at the design stage—but they are functional consequences of drafting choices nevertheless. At least under the moderate conception advanced here, the rule of law does not necessarily prefer one regulatory approach to the other. A delegation of total discretion to the courts to rule by fiat may run afoul of the rule of law, but a range of more balanced trade-offs between consistency and flexibility remain perfectly possible.

FET is typically drafted as a broad standard—as are provisions like the guarantee against indirect expropriation and full protection and security (FPS).[75] Early treaties hardly specified these standards at all. More recent treaties have added minor qualifications, but especially FET and FPS usually remain open textured. These standards can be contrasted to other substantive norms like provisions on direct expropriation, or free transfer guarantees, which entail relatively clear bright-line rules and where problems of adjudicative inconsistency appear less pervasive. These are drafting choices, against which expectations about consistency and predictability should be kept in check. Such standards cannot be applied without a healthy dose of interpretation and judgment *ex post*. Functionally, their use represents a regulatory choice to leave future adjudicators broad flexibility in working out how the obligation applies to particular facts. Use of especially broad standards also introduces flexibility into the development of the law over time—by giving adjudicators space to define their content, hopefully in dialogue with past and future adjudicators.[76]

This is not to suggest that the wide flux in the cases on FET is totally unproblematic. The point is rather that inconsistency in the interpretation and application of standards like these may be relatively tolerable—certainly from a rule-of-law perspective. Granting that consistency is an important value, the possibility of inconsistent interpretations of a broad standard over time may not be a failure of either morality if it arises out of a drafting choice to leave a degree of discretion to adjudicators *ex post*. At the least, in this context, a degree of inconsistency should be fairly predictable. Moreover, the possibility of inconsistent interpretations of broad standards has its virtues. Preserving flexibility among tribunals to develop these provisions over time reduces the stakes of drafting *ex ante*, as well as the stakes of initial efforts to interpret any particular treaty norm *ex post*. A strong consistency demand here would be paramount to a demand that future tribunals follow the prior tribunal's approach simply because it got there first—not because its interpretation was a sensible way to advance the letter or spirit of the underlying law.[77] In this way, consistency absolutism can lead to stultification and arbitrariness in the long term.

Ultimately, several of the key disciplines in the investment treaty regime are framed as broad standards, for which expectations about consistency will have to be tempered. At least in principle, this is a design choice perfectly in keeping with the rule of law. There is little reason why the legislative power cannot enlist the adjudicative power to develop the law over time, as is common enough in common law countries. Certainly a minimum level of consistency can be demanded, if FET is not to result in pure judicial discretion to assign

---

[75] Federico Ortino, 'Refining the Content and Role of Investment "Rules" and "Standards": A New Approach to International Investment Treaty Making' (2013) 28 ICSID Rev—FILJ 152.

[76] Julian Arato, 'The Margin of Appreciation in International Investment Law' (2014) 54 Va JIL 545, 571–72; Gabrielle Kaufmann-Kohler, 'Arbitral Precedent: Dream, Necessity, or Excuse?' (2007) 23 Arb Intl 357, 378; Richard Chen, 'Precedent and Dialogue in Investment Treaty Arbitration' (2019) 60 Harv L Rev 47.

[77] Arato (n 76) 571–72. UNCITRAL (n 71) para 29.

liability. But it is clear enough from the cases that the standard has a (mostly) common basic core—with most of the variation turning on the level of scrutiny it entails, or exactly how far it covers investor expectations. In Fullerian terms, it would seem that here duty is satisfied, if not necessarily aspiration.

With this said, it is not obviously good policy to leave the contents of such a potent discipline up to ad hoc arbitrators *ex post*—particularly regarding the scope of protection for legitimate expectations.[78] It may be that the use of open-textured standards to capture such a potentially broad discipline is a governance mistake, leaving too much discretion to adjudicators to decide major questions of private ordering and public regulatory choice. Even if this does not necessarily run afoul of the rule of law, it may not reflect a wise distribution of power and risk.

The dynamics are similar with necessity. Inconsistency as to the exact scope of ARSIWA, Article 25 or its standard of review is problematic. But uncertainty here is unavoidable, especially in a system of fragmented adjudication. Although the necessity defence in Article 25 is more carefully articulated and rule-like than any FET provision, it still affords adjudicators a healthy dose of discretion. More importantly, engaging with such a politically sensitive and factually complex question has to leave much to *ex post* judgment. It cannot be surprising that tribunals will come to different conclusions about even legal questions of scope and scrutiny. Here, then, is another area where uncertainty and inconsistency are likely to be endemic.

By contrast, the inconsistencies inhering in the case law on MFN, the treaty–contract relationship, and interpretive integration produce a more systemic uncertainty—one which calls into question the rule of law in the investment treaty regime more directly. This is because these inconsistencies make the rules for determining the applicable law and norm conflicts unpredictable. These secondary rules—or 'rules about rules'—articulate the scope and bounds of the entire legal relationship between States and investors—covering which sets of rules apply (contract, treaty, general international law) and how these norms interrelate.[79] Here the problem is not just uncertainty as to the interpretation of a particular rule or standard across a relatively defined range. Here, the fluctuating case law makes it near impossible for States and investors to know which legal rules apply to their relationships in the first place—whether these are limited to the treaty at hand, or are some pastiche of substantive and/or procedural norms pulled from all other treaties in force for the host State. As a result, the entire legal edifice rests on shifting sands. In Fullerian terms it is here unclear that even the basic precepts are duly satisfied—let alone aspiration.

At first glance, MFN reflects a fairly typical substantive treaty guarantee—closer to a rule than a standard. It reflects a promise not to discriminate against foreign investors vis-à-vis foreigners hailing from third States. As the experience in WTO law amply demonstrates, there is no shortage of interpretive difficulty in determining the concepts of 'likeness' and 'treatment', but the core obligation is relatively clear cut. Inconsistency as to the proper test for discrimination—whether it entailed testing for effects or aims and effects, or how to test for aims—would all be highly consequential. But it might be tolerable from a rule-of-law

---

[78] See further Caroline Henckels, 'Legitimate Expectations and the Rule of Law in International Investment Law' (in this volume) 43.

[79] See Arato, Brown and Ortino (n 5) 346 (distinguishing similarly between such structural rules as 'rules of the game' and ordinary 'norms of conduct').

perspective, similarly to the analysis of FET above. However, as things have developed, the cases have proven inconsistent on a different sort of question—to what extent the notion of treatment allows investors to import wholesale substantive and/or procedural provisions from any of the host State's treaties with third States. Inconsistency, here, goes to the systemic question of applicable law. It prevents States and investors from knowing which international legal rules will govern their relationship *ex ante*. Similar effects arise out of inconsistency in the interpretation of the rules on interpretation—particularly the rules on systemic integration and *lex specialis*, which together determine how far norms of general international law can be imported into investment treaties.[80]

The treaty–contract issue also goes to systemic issues of applicable law in a loose sense, though it more precisely implicates rules of norm conflict and opt-out. Where States and investors attempt to order their relationship through a contract, ISDS inconsistency as to how treaty and contract interact leaves unclear *ex ante* which rules will ultimately govern their relationship—their express contractual choices, norms set in the domestic law of the contract, or treaty terms. This leaves a shadow of doubt over the entire bargaining process. The cases have also proven inconsistent as to whether and how investment treaties apply to contracts between investors and municipal entities,[81] or State-owned enterprises,[82] adding a further layer of uncertainty about the relationship between treaty-based regulation and private ordering. Inconsistency here is especially offensive, because private ordering presents one of the few means available for investors and States (or State-owned enterprises) to manage concerns about unpredictability in ISDS directly for themselves. Under most legal orders, if private actors were concerned about unpredictable judicial action *ex post*, they could contract for what they care most about *ex ante*. But the utility of private ordering is diminished where parties cannot know whether their private contractual choices will be ultimately given effect.[83]

From a rule-of-law perspective, widely fluctuating inconsistency in the interpretation of systemic secondary rules is surprising and costly—particularly so with respect to applicable law, norm priority, and the possibility of opt-out. At a minimum, the expectation of consistency requires that subjects of the law are able to know the basic features of the legal regime that binds them, and to plan their affairs around the law. This is obviously so for private law and private ordering, but equally so for public law and public officialdom. The inconsistencies in the MFN and treaty–contract case law fundamentally distort the possibility of planning *ex ante*, and creates the potential for unfair surprise across all legal questions *ex post*.[84] Pervasive inconsistency as to these systemic matters may fall short of even the basic

---

[80]   Arato and Kulick (n 56).

[81]   The tribunal in Azurix found that the investor could not invoke the treaty's umbrella clause against Argentina in relation to a contract between its subsidiary and the municipality of Buenos Aires, because neither the investor nor the State were formal parties to the contract—finding that privity was lacking on either side. Yet in the next breath the tribunal held that the State was responsible for the termination of the contract as a breach of FET, see *Azurix Corp v The Argentine Republic*, ICSID Case No ARB/01/12, Award (14 July 2006). See further Arato (n 49) 256–59.

[82]   *Venezuela Holdings* (n 51).

[83]   See Arato, Brown and Ortino (n 5) 361.

[84]   My suggestion that structural inconsistencies undermine investment treaties' utility in facilitating planning and reducing transaction costs *ex ante* of course assumes that that investors are actually aware of BITs and take them into account when making their investments. However, this assumption equally underlies one of the core goals of investment treaties, namely to promote cross-border investment by providing investors with clear international law protections against future State conduct. Whether investors actually do take BITs into account in making their investments and whether States do so in planning regulatory interventions—whether, in other words, investment treaties have real world planning and price effects—is an empirical question, and one beyond

expectations of duty. It certainly undermines the commercial utility of the rule of law which investment treaties are supposed to promote.

Moreover, there is little reason to suspect that the consistency problems in the context of MFN, the treaty–contract relationship, or the rules of integrative treaty interpretation reflect intentional drafting choices. Unlike with FET, where some degree of flexibility at least arguably reflects an intentional trade-off, it seems unlikely that treaty drafters intended to delegate to adjudicators the discretion to work out secondary rules about applicable law, norm priority, and opt-out *ex post*, on a case-by-case basis.[85] Inconsistency, here, does not appear to be a by-product of enhanced flexibility or any other value. Here, then, is a failure of the rule of law.

V. Conclusion

Evidently IIL is rife with consistency problems. Here is a regime which insists on consistency in national legal orders in relation to foreign investors. As discussed above, consistency is a central discipline of FET—whether in its strong form interpretations (as in *Tecmed* or *Waste Management II*) or in more deferential incarnations (as in *El Paso*).[86] The consistency demand is often framed in terms of the rule of law,[87] and in terms of more particularized values like planning and private ordering.[88] And yet, once processed through its own international adjudicatory mechanisms, the investment treaty regime itself fails to deliver legal consistency and predictability in relation to its most basic disciplines, its scope, and even in the operation of its institutions. This inconsistency is explained easily enough. As has been well documented, it results largely from the institutional structure of the regime, and the spartan language of its underlying legal instruments.[89] The more difficult task is to evaluate these inconsistencies. In other work with Chester Brown and Federico Ortino, I have evaluated these inconsistencies through immanent critique—in light of the regime's

---

the scope of this chapter. Suffice it to say that if the objection is correct, it is difficult to see what is left of the promise that BITs promote investment at all. Either BITs do affect investment, in which case their effects on planning should be carefully considered (which counsels reforms relating to consistency), or they do not (which counsels more towards exit).

[85] It can certainly be argued that MFN provisions in BITs are meant precisely to allow importation, or, intentions aside, that importation has its benefits. As interpreted, MFN has been described as an '"ingenious" legal shorthand' (Marie-France Houde and Fabrizio Pagani, 'Most-Favoured-Nation Treatment in International Investment Law' in OECD (ed), *International Investment Law: A Changing Landscape* (OECD 2005) 142) in the sense of Georg Schwarzenberger, *International Law as Applied by International Courts and Tribunals* (3rd edn, Stevens 1957) 243 ('This drafting device ... contributes greatly to the rationalization of the treaty-making process and leads to the automatic self-revision of treaties which are based on the most-favoured-nation standard. It makes unnecessary the incorporation in the treaty between grantor and the beneficiary of the most-favoured-nation treatment of any of the relevant treaties between the grantor and third States and their deletion whenever such treaties cease to be in force. So long as this last-mentioned aspect of the matter is kept in mind, most-favoured-nation clauses are correctly described as drafting (and deletion) by reference'). Stephan Schill has famously demonstrated a related function of multilateralizing the regime, which (if pursued consistently) could enhance legal certainty over time. Schill (n 63). However, it is at least clear that States have become increasingly wary of importation through MFN, as treaty drafters have begun responding to the case law. Several more recent treaties have expressly pared back the possibility of importing procedural terms, substantive guarantees, or both. See eg Comprehensive Economic and Trade Agreement (opened for signature 30 October 2016) (CETA) art 8.7(4).
[86] See discussion above nn 34–38 and accompanying text.
[87] Vandevelde (n 1).
[88] *Tecmed* (n 4) para 154.
[89] See eg Arato, Brown and Ortino (n 5) 337; Franck (n 1); Arato (n 76) 550.

professed internal values. This chapter takes a different approach, analysing the consistency problem in ISDS from the external perspective of the rule of law. Drawing on Fuller's conception, I have argued that a moderate formal conception of the rule of law helps to reframe the consistency concern, to identify its sharpest edges and to draw out avenues where reform would be most beneficial.

From a rule-of-law perspective, the inconsistency problems in ISDS vary in their stakes and import. The key payoff of the Fullerian approach is the recognition that the rule of law does contain values, but that it does not (and cannot) require that all of its values be pursued absolutely. While consistency is surely a prime virtue, no legal system enshrines it perfectly in the interpretation and application of the law. Nor should any legal order strive for mechanical consistency. The really difficult task is in determining where such values are most critical, and where some compromise is possible or even advisable. Here Fuller's distinction between the two moralities is critical. Problematic as they all may be, some failures of consistency in ISDS appear more as shortcomings of aspiration than of duty. Even high degrees of flux in the interpretations of broad standards like FET fall into this category. Inconsistency here causes difficulties of planning *ex ante* and may lead to unfair surprise *ex post*, but this may nevertheless be relatively tolerable. After all, these standards have at least a more or less common core across most of the cases, even as their limits fluctuate to a high degree. Ultimately, inconsistency is a natural feature of all living law, and cannot be entirely avoided—particularly where legal directives take the form of broad standards. Moreover, some of the inconsistency here may be a reasonable trade-off for other values, such as flexibility and responsiveness.

But in other cases the interpretive fluctuations of ISDS fail even the most basic expectations of consistency over time. Insofar as they undermine subjects' basic ability to plan around the law, inconsistencies in the cases on MFN, the treaty–contract relationship, and systemic integration thus reflect more fundamental failures of duty—that is, failure to satisfy even the minimum threshold separating the rule of law from arbitrariness. These sorts of inconsistencies call into question not only the limits of one particular rule, but the shape and bounds of the entire legal order. They thoroughly diminish investment law's capacity to facilitate planning for the future. Here, then, are real failures of the rule of law.

Concerns about consistency rate high in the context of ISDS, in large part because a common justification for the regime is that it serves to make the domestic legal framework more predictable for business—that, in this way, it enhances the domestic rule of law. That the regime itself fails to deliver on the same value is jarring. But, as we have seen, not every inconsistency is a failure, and not all failures are equally significant. The rule of law does not require perfect consistency in the interpretation and application of legal rules. And, indeed, maximizing predictability at the expense of all other values might tend to undermine the rule of law. In thinking about inconsistency in the context of institutional design, achieving consistency in at least the systemic rules is the biggest prize, while focusing too much on consistency elsewhere may have lower marginal utility.[90]

This rule-of-law analysis can also be turned back on the substantive disciplines of the investment treaty regime. The pitfalls of consistency fetishism at the international level also counsel against absolutism at the national level. It may be that the investment treaty

---

[90] See Arato, Brown and Ortino (n 5) 373.

regime can play a role in promoting the rule of law domestically, including in promoting consistent State behaviour (at least towards foreign investors). But what kind of consistency can be demanded? Surely not the totalizing consistency demanded by the tribunal in *Tecmed*. There will certainly be cases of inconsistent treatment so unjustifiable as to represent failures of duty, and these should be actionable. But other forms of inconsistent treatment by the State might implicate only the duty of aspiration, and may trade off against other values. Fortunately, there are signs that this is where the jurisprudence is heading. For example, in two recent high-profile awards, the tribunals in *Philip Morris v Uruguay* and *Eli Lilly v Canada* both found that inconsistency in domestic judicial decisions is not necessarily actionable where it arises out of normal institutional processes. The former involved the inconsistent interpretations of two Uruguayan apex courts with discrete jurisdictional mandates—the Supreme Court of Justice and the Tribunal de lo Contencioso Administrativo.[91] The latter involved a material change in Canadian common law jurisprudence on the requirements for maintaining a patent, which the claimant (unsuccessfully) alleged to have brought about a sudden, dramatic, and fundamental change in the law of patents in that country. Both tribunals accepted that a degree of inconsistency is endemic in legal institutions.[92]

There is obviously inconsistency where a common law court develops the rules. Such changes can of course affect an investor's bottom line, in surprising and even devastating ways. But it is hardly a failure of the rule of law. If anything, such unsettled expectations may fall short of the lofty goals of aspiration, without remotely approaching a failure of the morality of duty. It is as inappropriate to demand consistency of this kind at the domestic level as it is to expect it of ISDS. Moreover, it seems perfectly reasonable that different legal orders would make different legitimate trade-offs between consistency and other values like flexibility. If the investment treaty regime is to demand consistency at the national level in the name of the rule of law, the demands of duty should be relatively modest—perhaps limited to gross inconsistencies in behaviour, rather than those casual or otherwise justifiable inconsistencies that the rule of law can stomach (granting the obvious line-drawing difficulties that this will entail). The rest must be left to aspiration, with due regard to the possibility that variety in institutional choice is legitimate, and even desirable.

---

[91] *Philip Morris* (n 37) para 529 ('The failure of the TCA to follow the Supreme Court's interpretation of Articles 9 and 24 of Law 18,256 may appear unusual, even surprising, but it is not shocking and it is not serious enough in itself to constitute a denial of justice. Outright conflicts within national legal systems may be regrettable but they are not unheard of'); but see Dissenting and Concurring Opinion Born, para 42 ('Where different courts within a single legal system adopt contradictory interpretations for the same law, the rule of law is undermined, exposing individuals to inconsistent, unpredictable, and arbitrary treatment').

[92] *Eli Lilly* (n 4) para 310 ('the Tribunal is mindful of the role of the judiciary in common law jurisdictions.... evolution of the law through court decisions is natural, and departures from precedent are to be expected').

13

The Rule of Law, Standards of Review, and the Separation of Powers

*Esmé Shirlow**

I. Introduction

The connection between investment treaties and the rule of law is subject to considerable debate. Scholars contest, for example, the impact of investment treaties on the domestic rule-of-law qualities of host State legal systems. Some argue that investment treaties assist in promoting the rule of law domestically, whereas others contend that investment treaties undermine domestic rule-of-law frameworks.[1] A further set of studies use the rule of law to critique investment arbitration itself, including by reference to an alleged lack of independence, transparency, or consistency in arbitral decision-making.[2] Scholars have also examined whether certain investment treaty obligations themselves reflect rule-of-law values.[3] A further, associated line of analysis is whether the rule of law offers a useful framework for developing, analysing, or critiquing the analytical approaches of arbitral tribunals to certain issues. This chapter addresses this latter issue, to examine more specifically to what

* The author wishes to thank the Editors for their invitation to contribute this chapter and to consider these issues as part of this volume, Johannes Tropper for his support during the production process, and Richard Harry Fenton and Savannah Still for their assistance in proofreading earlier drafts.

[1] See generally Christoph Schreuer, 'Do We Need Investment Arbitration?' (2014) 11 TDM 1, 4; Peter Muchlinski, Federico Ortino and Christoph Schreuer (eds), *The Oxford Handbook of International Investment Law* (OUP 2008) vi; Thomas Schultz and Cedric Dupont, 'Investment Arbitration: Promoting the Rule of Law or Over-Empowering Investors? A Quantitative Empirical Study' (2015) 25 EJIL 1147, 1161; Tom Ginsburg, 'International Substitutes for Domestic Institutions: Bilateral Investment Treaties and Governance' (2005) 25 IRLE 107, 121; Susan Franck, 'Foreign Direct Investment, Investment Treaty Arbitration, and the Rule of Law' (2006) 19 Pac McGeorge Global Bus & Dev LJ 337; Roberto Echandi, 'What Do Developing Countries Expect from the International Investment Regime?' in Jose E Alvarez and Karl P Sauvant (eds), *The Evolving International Investment Regime: Expectations, Realities, Options* (OUP 2011); James Crawford, 'International Law and the Rule of Law' (2003) 24 Adel L Rev 3, 8; Mavluda Sattorova, *The Impact of Investment Treaty Law on Host States: Enabling Good Governance?* (Hart 2018); Gus Van Harten, 'Five Justifications for Investment Treaties: A Critical Discussion' (2010) 2 TL & D 19, 19.

[2] See especially August Reinisch, 'The Rule of Law in International Investment Arbitration' in Photini Pazartzis and Maria Gavouneli (eds), *Reconceptualising the Rule of Law in Global Governance* (Hart 2016); Alessandra Arcuri, 'The Great Asymmetry and the Rule of Law in International Investment Arbitration' in Lisa Sachs, Lise Johnson and Jesse Coleman (eds), *Yearbook on International Investment Law and Policy 2018* (OUP 2019); Gus Van Harten, 'Investment Treaty Arbitration, Procedural Fairness, and the Rule of Law' in Stephan W Schill (ed), *International Investment Law and Comparative Public Law* (OUP 2010).

[3] See especially Stephan W Schill, 'Fair and Equitable Treatment under Investment Treaties as an Embodiment of the Rule of Law' (2006) IILJ Working Paper 2006/6 (Global Administrative Law Series); Kenneth J Vandevelde, 'A Unified Theory of Fair and Equitable Treatment' (2010) 43 NYU J Intl L & Pol 43. See also Sattorova (n 1); Sergio Puig and Gregory Shaffer, 'Imperfect Alternatives: Institutional Choice and the Reform of Investment Law' (2018) 112 AJIL 361; Reinisch (n 2); Jansen Calamita, 'The Internalisation of Investment Treaties and the Rule of Law Promise' (U Oxford, 7 May 2019) <http://podcasts.ox.ac.uk/internalisation-investment-treaties-and-rule-law-promise> accessed 27 October 2021; Velimir Zivkovic, 'International Rule of Law through International Investment Law—Strengths, Challenges and Opportunities' (2018) 16 KFG Working Paper Series.

Esmé Shirlow, *The Rule of Law, Standards of Review, and the Separation of Powers* In: *Investment Protection Standards and the Rule of Law*. Edited by: August Reinisch and Stephan W. Schill, Oxford University Press. © Esmé Shirlow 2023.
DOI: 10.1093/oso/9780192864581.003.0013

extent arbitral approaches to deference and standards of review interact with a particular feature often associated with the rule of law: the separation of powers. The chapter is in part exploratory. It responds to the potential separation of powers issues that might arise from empowering international tribunals to substantively review domestic regulatory choices under investment treaties. Such substantive review has been critiqued from a separation of powers perspective, including on the basis that it should be for States themselves to make decisions about certain issues free from outside scrutiny by investment tribunals. This concern goes to the appropriate separation of powers between domestic actors (such as courts and administrative bodies) and international tribunals. International review of domestic decisions may also compound domestic rule-of-law concerns, including because it may treat the State as a unitary actor and thus risk collapsing domestic separation of powers frameworks.[4] Against this background, the chapter examines the extent to which the rule of law (and separation of powers theories in particular) offer a useful framework to guide the approaches that tribunals take—or should take—to analyse matters of deference and standards of review when applying investment treaty obligations to assess host State conduct. It examines, in particular, the extent to which deference and standards of review may offer investment tribunals a means of respecting the separation of powers both between domestic actors, and between domestic actors and international tribunals.

Section II defines the concept of the rule of law, and links that concept to the separation of powers. Section III then explores how the rule of law—and separation of powers theories in particular—might impact the approaches adopted by investment tribunals to deference and standards of review in practice. The separation of powers recognizes that decision-makers of structurally different institutional types will hold greater capacity to decide certain questions vis-à-vis others. Such institutional considerations might be relied upon by investment arbitrators to justify adopting deferential standards of review when examining the decisions of particular domestic actors, or the decisions of domestic actors on certain topics. Deference may thus be used by investment tribunals to appraise and accommodate a separation of powers between domestic and international actors on a case-by-case basis. Section IV considers how rule-of-law frameworks, and separation of powers theories, might be more expressly leveraged by investment tribunals to inform approaches to deference in practice. Section V concludes.

II. The Rule of Law and the Separation of Powers

This section considers the meaning of the rule of law, and connects this concept to theories about the separation of powers. Section A outlines the scholarly debates concerning the contents of the rule of law to highlight the broad divide between procedural and substantive approaches to defining rule-of-law criteria. Section B introduces the concept of separation of powers, and explains why both the procedural and substantive approaches to the rule of law entail some role for a theory related to the separation of powers. This conceptual

---

[4] See further Esmé Shirlow, *Judging at the Interface: Deference to State Decision-Making Authority in International Adjudication* (CUP 2021) 207–11. See also Johannes Fahner, *Judicial Deference in International Adjudication: A Comparative Analysis* (Hart 2020) 8, 11, 190–93.

framework is developed in the remainder of the chapter by reference to the links between standards of review and a separation of powers in investment treaty arbitration.

A. The Rule of Law

The rule of law is a definitionally ambiguous concept.[5] As Jeremy Waldron notes, it is increasingly used 'as a general stand-in for everything nice one could ever want to say about a political system, or everything good one could want from it'.[6] For some commentators, this means that the concept of the rule of law has become 'meaningless'[7] or at the very least is 'essentially contestable'.[8] As August Reinisch and Stephan Schill note in this volume's introductory chapter, a distinction is frequently made between a procedural and a substantive conception of the rule of law. These two conceptions are briefly outlined in this section, in order to set the scene for the remainder of the chapter, which explores how particular rule-of-law values link to deference and standards of review in investment treaty arbitration.

A procedural conception of the rule of law focuses on the procedural or formal qualities of law and legal decision-making. Such conceptions emphasize requirements, inter alia, that law be transparent, non-arbitrary, non-contradictory and consistent, general in application, prospective, publicly promulgated, predictable and stable, procedurally fair, and clear and possible to comply with.[9] Different commentators emphasize different elements in such procedural accounts.[10] Such accounts nonetheless share in common a focus on the formal or procedural qualities of law, rather than seeking 'to pass judgment upon the actual

---

[5] See similarly Brian Tamanaha, *On the Rule of Law* (CUP 2004) 3.

[6] Jeremy Waldron, 'Is the Rule of Law an Essentially Contested Concept (in Florida)?' (2002) 21 Law & Phil 137, 140. See similarly Joseph Raz, *The Authority of Law* (OUP 1979) 210.

[7] Judith N Shklar, 'Political Theory and the Rule of Law' in Allan C Hutcheson and Patrick Monathan (eds), *The Rule of Law: Ideal or Ideology* (Carsell 1987) 1.

[8] Michel Rosenfeld, 'The Rule of Law and the Legitimacy of Constitutional Democracy' (2001) Cardozo Law School Working Paper Series, Paper No 36, 4.

[9] See variously Jeremy Waldron, 'The Rule of Law and the Importance of Procedure' (2010) New York University School of Law, Public Law & Legal Theory Research Paper Series, Paper No 10-73, 1; Raz (n 6) 214–17; Aleardo Zanghellini, 'The Foundations of the Rule of Law' (2016) 28 Yale J Law & Humanity 213, 213; Paul Gowder, 'The Rule of Law and Equality' (2013) 32 Law & Phil 565, 566; Richard H Fallon Jr , '"The Rule of Law" as a Concept in Constitutional Discourse' (1997) 97 Colum L Rev 1, 15–16; Lord Bingham, 'The Rule of Law' (2007) 66 CLJ 67; Robert S Summers, 'Principles of the Rule of Law' (1999) 74 Notre Dame L Rev 1691, 1693; Peter F Nardulli, Buddy Peyton and Joseph Bajjalieh, 'Conceptualizing and Measuring Rule of Law Constructs, 1850–2010' (2013) 1 JLC 139, 149; Benjamin Gregg, *The Human Rights State* (U Pennsylvania Press 2016) 177; Rosenfeld (n 8) 2–3; Brian Tamanaha, 'The History and Elements of the Rule of Law' (2012) Sing JLS 232, 233; Andrei Marmor, 'The Rule of Law and Its Limits' (2004) 23 Law & Phil 1, 6; Simon Chesterman, 'An International Rule of Law' (2008) 56 Am J Comp L 331, 342; Samuel L Bufford, 'Defining the Rule of Law' (2007) 46 Judges Journal 16, 19.

[10] See eg Lon Fuller, *The Morality of Law* (Yale UP 1969) (emphasizing eight qualities of the rule of law, focusing on the requirements of: generality; publicity; prospectivity; clarity; consistency; constancy/stability; practicability/possibility; congruence between the written rules and their application); Raz (n 6) 214–19 (the rule of law as reflecting an underlying requirement 'that the law should be capable of providing effective guidance', such as to generate requirements that laws be prospective, clear and stable; that there be an independent judiciary with powers of judicial review; that there be clear rules for making laws; that courts operate in an accessible way and consistent with principles of natural justice; and that there be control over crime prevention agencies); Albert V Dicey, *Introduction to the Study of the Law of the Constitution* (Liberty Fund 1982) 120–21 (an absence of arbitrary power, equality before the law, and that principles of constitutional law be derived from judicial decisions rather than written constitutions); Brian Tamanaha, 'A Concise Guide to the Rule of Law' (2007) Legal Studies Research Paper Series 3 ('law must be set forth in advance [be prospective], be made public, be general, be clear, be stable and certain, and be applied to everyone according to its terms').

content of the law itself'.[11] Joseph Raz, for example, notes that under a procedural account of the rule of law:

> [a] non-democratic legal system, based on the denial of human rights, on extensive pov-erty, on racial segregation, sexual inequalities, and religious persecution may, in principle, conform to the requirements of the rule of law better than any of the legal systems of the more enlightened Western democracies.[12]

Substantive conceptions of the rule of law typically couple the procedural qualities intro-duced above with additional, substantive, criteria.[13] This might include, inter alia, require-ments that the law be substantively just or fair, emanate from democratic procedures, protect human rights, be substantively reasonable, or secure private property rights or the operation of a free market economy.[14] Many international organizations have endorsed a substantive, and thus thicker, conception of the rule of law. The International Commission of Jurists in 1959, for example, endorsed the view that the rule of law referred to the 'so-cial, economic, educational, and cultural conditions under which man's legitimate aspir-ations and dignity may be realized'.[15] UN officials have similarly defined the rule of law as encompassing such substantive elements, including human rights and even democratic decision-making. In a 2004 report, for example, the then UN Secretary-General endorsed the view that the rule of law was a:

> principle of governance in which all persons ... are accountable to laws that are publicly promulgated, equally enforced and independently adjudicated, and which are consistent with international human rights norms and standards.[16]

Procedural and substantive conceptions of the rule of law can be informed by differing un-derlying goals. Rule-of-law values might, for instance, be derived by reference to what is necessary to support the efficiency of law.[17] An account of the rule of law informed by ob-jectives of efficiency might take the view that, to the extent that law is consistent with certain procedural requirements, it will produce a more efficient system for individual decision-making or social organization.[18] The rule of law might alternatively be valued for its cap-acity to promote individual autonomy and liberty.[19] Requirements of publicity, consistency,

---

[11] Paul Craig, 'Theory and Values in Public Law: A Response' in Paul Craig and Richard Rawlings (eds), *Law and Administration in Europe: Essays in Honour of Carol Harlow* (OUP 2003) 30. See further: Brian Tamanaha, 'The Rule of Law for Everyone?' (2002) 55 CLP 97; Jeremy Waldron, 'The Concept and the Rule of Law' (2008) 43 Georgia L Rev 1, 7; Katie R Eyer, 'Administrative Adjudication and the Rule of Law' (2008) 60 Adm L Rev 647, 655–56.

[12] Raz (n 6) 211. See similarly Tamanaha (n 9) 233–34; John Tasioulas, 'The Rule of Law' in John Tasioulas (ed), *The Cambridge Companion to the Philosophy of Law* (CUP 2019) 117–34.

[13] Zanghellini (n 9) 213; Chesterman (n 9) 340.

[14] See for descriptions of such accounts Tasioulas (n 12); Tamanaha (n 11); Raz (n 6) 227–28; Lord Bingham (n 9) 66, 75; Ronald Dworkin, *A Matter of Principle* (Harvard UP 1985) 259; Trevor Allan, *Constitutional Justice: A Liberal Theory of the Rule of Law* (OUP 2001).

[15] International Commission of Jurists, 'The Rule of Law in a Free Society' (Geneva 1959) VII.

[16] 'The Rule of Law and Transitional Justice in Conflict and Post-Conflict Societies: Report of the Secretary-General' (23 August 2004) UN Doc S/2004/616, para 6.

[17] Imelda Deinla, *The Development of the Rule of Law in ASEAN: The State and Regional Integration* (CUP 2017).

[18] Tamanaha (n 9) 240; John C Reitz, 'Export of the Rule of Law' (2003) 13 Transnatl L & Contemp Probs 429, 443; Thomas Carothers, 'The Rule of Law Revival' (1998) 77 Foreign Aff 95, 97.

[19] Randall Peerenboom, 'Varieties of Rule of Law: An Introduction and Provisional Conclusion' in Randall Peerenboom (ed), *Asian Discourses of Rule of Law* (Routledge 2003) 3.

and prospectivity, for instance, equip individuals with knowledge of how the State will exercise its regulatory powers and so allow individuals to plan their activities on the basis of the law.[20] This improves efficiency while at the same time respecting individual autonomy.[21] Substantive views of the rule of law might, instead, emphasize, a need for law to respect justice or individual dignity.[22] TRS Allan, for example, argues that '[t]he equal dignity of citizens, with its implications for fair treatment and respect for individual autonomy, is the … ultimate meaning of the rule of law'.[23] Such accounts might value the public promulgation of laws and the giving of reasons as a means for protecting individuals against arbitrariness.[24] The indicia comprising the rule of law will thus be drawn from a broader conception of the role of legal systems, and the qualities—be they efficiency, autonomy, liberty, dignity, etc.—that legal systems should strive to promote and protect.

B. Separation of Powers

The distinction between the procedural and substantive accounts of the rule of law is not rigid.[25] In fact, some qualities of law and legal systems may be emphasized in both accounts. Relevantly for present purposes, both the procedural and substantive accounts of the rule of law envisage the existence of legal systems that have institutions able to variously promulgate law, make law publicly available, and enforce and implement law consistent with procedural norms like fairness and/or equality.[26] Both accounts of the rule of law thus require the existence of institutions capable of performing these differing roles within each legal system. As Randall Peerenboom notes:

> The promulgation of law assumes a legislature and the government machinery necessary to make the laws publicly available. It also assumes rules for making laws. Congruence of laws on the books and actual practice assumes institutions for implementing and enforcing laws. While informal means of enforcing laws may be possible in some contexts, modern societies must also rely on formal means such as courts and administrative bodies.[27]

Both accounts of the rule of law thus require a set of official actors empowered to exercise diverse functions of lawmaking, law implementation, law interpretation, and law enforcement. While such tasks might be vested in a unitary organ, the nature of these tasks—and the growing complexity of the modern State—is such that a legal system is likely to require

---

[20] Raz (n 6) 214–15; Zanghellini (n 9) 213; Fallon (n 9) 14–15; Randall Peerenboom, 'Let One Hundred Flowers Bloom, One Hundred Schools Contend: Debating Rule of Law in China' (2002) 23 Mich JIL 471; Tamanaha (n 9) 240.

[21] Zanghellini (n 9) 213.

[22] Colleen Murphy, 'Lon Fuller and the Moral Value of the Rule of Law, Law and Philosophy' (2005) 24 Law & Phil 239, 250; JM Bernstein, 'The Rule of Law' in JM Bernstein, Adi Ophir and Laura Stoler (eds), *Political Concepts: A Critical Lexicon* (Fordham UP 2018) 170; Fuller (n 10) 162.

[23] Allan (n 14) 2.

[24] Peerenboom (n 19) 3; Murphy (n 22) 240; Zanghellini (n 9) 217; Fallon (n 9) 7–8; Tamanaha (n 10) 9; David Dyzenhaus, 'Proportionality and Deference in a Culture of Justification' in Grant Huscroft, Bradley W Miller and Grégoire Webber (eds), *Proportionality and the Rule of Law: Rights, Justification, Reasoning* (CUP 2014) 238.

[25] Waldron (n 11) 7.

[26] Peerenboom (n 20) 480.

[27] ibid.

differently structured organs in order to discharge such functions in an accurate and/or legitimate way.[28] Most legal systems will thus divide decision-making authority between different organs empowered to undertake distinct tasks. This might entail, for instance, the creation of organs empowered to decide the content of laws or rules of general application; those empowered to apply rules to specific persons, disputes, or cases; and those empowered to make policy decisions to support the development of law.

Any division of labour implicitly creates a 'separation of powers' between the entities empowered to exercise governance functions.[29] The degree of separation required between such organs will differ depending upon the particular account of the rule of law by reference to which such organs operate (or are expected to operate). This separation of powers may also be made more or less explicit as a requirement of the rule of law. Raz's account of the rule of law, for example, specifically requires as a component of the rule of law that judges be independent from other decision-making organs.[30] As Raz notes: '[t]he rules concerning the independence of the judiciary … are designed to guarantee that they will be free from extraneous pressures and independent of all authority save that of the law'.[31] Other accounts implicitly rely upon such a separation of powers between governance bodies as a means of achieving other express rule-of-law requirements. A legal system might, for instance, only be able to produce rules of 'generality' if it has institutional structures adapted to making general, rather than individual, decisions.[32] Such a legal system might be found deficient against this criterion of the rule of law to the extent that general, legislative, functions are allocated to organs that 'are trying to do through adjudicative forms something that does not lend itself to accomplishment through those forms'.[33] Similarly, a requirement of equality before the law entails the presence of some kind of separation of powers. Equality before the law implies that the law should apply equally to the State's organs.[34] This necessitates the creation of some independent organ/s with adjudicative functions empowered to enforce the law against other organs.[35] Equally, a requirement of non-arbitrariness might be served by a division of powers between decision-makers, insofar as such a division means that powers will not be consolidated in the hands of one actor and, moreover, will mean that the decisions of all actors are subject to some scrutiny by others.[36] The generality of laws, their fair application and administration, or the avoidance of arbitrary decision-making, might thus best be secured by a distribution of powers between different organs. A system abiding by either a procedural or substantive rule-of-law framework will thus be premised on some 'division of labor in the process of decision-making'.[37]

The structures and purposes of such separation of powers will vary from regime to regime, and ultimately will depend upon underlying understandings of the role of law and

---

[28] Eoin Carolan, *The New Separation of Powers* (OUP 2009) 27.
[29] Rosenfeld (n 8) 2–3; Summers (n 9) 1693; International Law Association, 'Rule of Law and International Investment Law: Sydney Conference (2018)' (2018) 6; Deinla (n 17); Fahner (n 4) 191.
[30] Raz (n 6) 217.
[31] ibid.
[32] ibid 216.
[33] Fuller (n 10) 46.
[34] Waldron (n 6) 155.
[35] Chesterman (n 9) 342; Waldron (n 11) 7–8; Marmor (n 9) 5; Jonathan K Van Patten, 'Judicial Independence and the Rule of Law' (1986) 2 Benchmark 117, 117; Nicholas Cowdery, 'The Rule of Law' (1999) 24 Intl L Practice 56, 56.
[36] International Law Association (n 29) 20.
[37] Thomas Christiano, *The Constitution of Equality: Democratic Authority and Its Limits* (OUP 2008) 257.

conceptions of the rule of law in a given society.[38] The goals underlying the rule of law will thus inform how powers are structured, negotiated and separated in practice. As Dimitrios Kyritsis notes, for example, efficiencies may be achieved where the powers of the various bodies empowered to govern are separated such that each body can 'respect the contributions of their fellow-participants in the joint institutional effort'.[39] A separation of powers might otherwise (or as well) be informed by desires to secure individual liberty against arbitrariness or abuses of power.[40] A separation of powers may protect individuals against arbitrariness by ensuring that those responsible for making the law are not also responsible for applying it.[41] Separation of powers might otherwise assist to prevent abuses of power by creating horizontal accountability between organs with different institutional mandates.[42]

III. Connecting Standards of Review to the Rule of Law and Separation of Powers in International Investment Arbitration

Different qualities may be associated with the concept of the rule of law depending upon the analytical use being made of it. This section explores the uses made of rule-of-law concepts in legal analysis, distinguishing between analytical uses of the rule of law as a principle of 'law' or of 'governance'. As Section A explains, this supports a connection between the rule of law and standards of review. Section B then unpacks this connection to outline how theories about the separation of powers may have implications for standards of review analysis.

A. The Rule of Law as a 'Principle of Law' or 'Principle of Governance'

The rule of law undoubtedly 'means different things to different people'.[43] As the International Law Association's Committee on the Rule of Law and International Investment Law (ILA Committee) has noted, understandings of the rule of law differ depending upon sociopolitical context.[44] Despite their differences in content, however, both the procedural and substantive conceptions of the rule of law are invoked in one of two ways as analytical concepts: either as a principle of law, or as a principle of governance. Where the rule of law is invoked as a principle of law, it is used to define what (minimal) qualities a system or a particular law must manifest in order to qualify as a legal system, or in order to be considered as law at all.[45] Under this usage, the rule of law is used analytically 'to distinguish

---

[38] Randy Peerenboom, 'Competing Conceptions of Rule of Law in China' in Peerenboom (n 19) 115; Carolan (n 28) 18.

[39] Dimitrios Kyritsis, *Where Our Protection Lies: Separation of Powers and Constitutional Review* (OUP 2017) 162

[40] Allan (n 14) 56.

[41] Christiano (n 37) 257; Allan (n 14) 48.

[42] Leonardo Morlino, 'What Is a "Good" Democracy?' (2004) 11 Democratization 10, 17–18; Philippe C Schmitter and Terry Lynn Karl, 'What Democracy Is ... and Is Not' (1991) 2 Journal of Democracy 75; Deinla (n 17); Guillermo O'Donnell, 'Why the Rule of Law Matters' in Larry Diamond and Leonardo Morlino (eds), *Assessing the Quality of Democracy* (John Hopkins UP) 8; Gráinne de Búrca, 'Developing Democracy beyond the State' (2008) 46 Colum J Transnatl L 221, 230; Carolan (n 28) 27.

[43] Tasioulas (n 12) 117. See similarly Daniel B Rodriguez, Matthew D McCubbins and Barry R Weingast, 'The Rule of Law Unplugged' (2010) 59 Emory LJ 1455, 1458.

[44] International Law Association (n 29) 1–2.

[45] Peter Rijpkema, 'The Rule of Law beyond Thick and Thin' (2013) 32 Law & Phil 793, 795; Michael Sevel, 'Legal Positivism and the Rule of Law' (2009) 34 Austl J Legal Phil 53, 53–54.

one particular kind of social order from the diversity of orders to which the name 'law' might be applied'.[46] To the extent, for example, that a regime does not have rules of general application or prospective impact, the procedural view of the rule of law might be used as an analytical concept to deny that the regime warrants the label of a legal system at all. This is the use made of the concept of the rule of law in many domestic systems, where rule-of-law requirements are often elevated to become binding secondary rules of recognition, including through constitutional entrenchment.[47] For such systems, the failure of any particular law to comply with a rule-of-law requirement will render that law devoid of binding effect: it becomes in effect no law at all.

Where it is invoked, by contrast, as a 'principle of governance', the rule of law is used to define the qualities that should be manifested by a good law or legal system.[48] The concept of the rule of law under this use is evaluative and aspirational. A procedural conception of the rule of law might, for instance, prioritize the exercise of power by public officials 'in accordance with the limits defined by reasonably clear and stable law in a way that restricts their discretion enough to prevent the tyranny of arbitrary action'.[49] Where public officials make decisions that fail to comply with such requirements, their decisions are not deprived of the status of law as they are when the concept is used as a 'principle of law'. They will instead be treated as laws that hold less authority because they reflect deficient or undesirable forms of governance. The rule of law thus becomes, as a principle of governance, a statement as to whether a given law, or a given legal system, is a 'good' or a 'bad' law or legal system. The rule of law as a principle of governance might encompass a variety of procedural or substantive elements, reflecting the two conceptions of the rule of law that have been introduced in this section. Whether a given system of law or governance is considered to be 'good' will depend upon which rule-of-law values are emphasized.[50]

The difference between the use of the rule of law as a principle of law or a principle of governance boils down to a distinction between invoking the concept 'either a minimum standard which something has to meet in order to be law or as an aspirational standard identifying what it means to be good law'.[51] On the latter use, the rule of law is used to articulate a view as to how public officials should exercise their authority. This makes it possible to connect the rule of law to adjudicative decisions about deference. Standards of review, in particular, are one way in which adjudicators might articulate their view of the rule of law as a principle of governance. International investment tribunals use standards of review to determine when the decisions of States (be they from judicial, administrative, executive, or legislative actors) ought to attract deference from international adjudicators.

---

[46]   Terry Nardin, 'International Pluralism and the Rule of Law' (2000) 26 Rev Intl Stud 95, 104.

[47]   See International Law Association (n 29), generally, for a discussion of different domestic rule-of-law requirements.

[48]   See Rijpkema (n 45) 795, generally, on the connection between the concepts of 'good governance' and the rule of law; Benjamin Guthrie, 'Beyond Investment Protection: An Examination of the Potential Influence of Investment Treaties on Domestic Rule of Law' (2013) 45 NYU J Intl L & Pol 1151, 1160; Iutisone Salevao, *Rule of Law, Legitimate Governance & Development in the Pacific* (ANU Press 2005) 5; S Jayakumar, 'Applying the Rule of Law' (2009) 43 Intl Law 83, 83; Sattorova (n 1).

[49]   Reitz (n 18) 435–36.

[50]   See eg Juanita Olaya, 'Good Governance and International Investment Law: The Challenges of Lack of Transparency and Corruption' (2010) Society of International Economic Law, Online Proceedings, Working Paper No 2010/43, 2; European Commission, European Governance: A White Paper [2001] OJ L 287/1, 10; Patrick McAuslan, 'Law, Governance and the Development of the Market: Practical Problems and Possible Solutions' in J Faundez (ed), *Good Government and Law: Legal and Institutional Reform in Developing Countries* (Springer 1997) 27.

[51]   Rijpkema (n 45) 795.

Standards of review articulate the qualities arbitrators think decision-making should reflect in order to be recognized as authoritative and thus attract deference.[52] Decisions about deference thus articulate normative criteria about how decisions should be made, or about who (which institutions) ought to have the final say in respect of those decisions.

The rule of law might be relied upon by adjudicators as a principle of governance to determine when the decisions of other actors should attract deference. International adjudicators might, for example, elect to give weight to domestic decisions if they are made through particular procedures or on the basis of rational or reasonable grounds. The criteria selected to identify decisions worthy of deference will disclose the international adjudicator's views on how States should exercise their decision-making authority. A procedural approach, for example, indicates that the adjudicator values particular procedures for decision-making, or decisions exhibiting particular procedural qualities. Tribunals might, by contrast, adopt a more substantive vision of good decision-making, according to which domestic decision-makers will only be afforded deference to the extent that their decisions exhibit substantive reasonableness, fairness, or proportionality. Arbitral approaches to standards of review articulate, in effect, 'judicially-created criteria for proper lawmaking'.[53] Such criteria impose differing burdens on domestic decision-making, and reveal what qualities international adjudicators value in domestic decision-making.

Concepts associated with the rule of law may therefore inform the standards of review used by adjudicators to examine deference to domestic decision-making in practice. Theories about a separation of powers between international and domestic actors are particularly well adapted to inform investment arbitrators' approaches to deference. Such theories indicate where decision-making authority should rest in a given legal system. They thus recognize that some decision-makers may have a better claim vis-à-vis others to the expertise or legitimacy to make certain decisions. In such circumstances, an international tribunal might defer to a domestic actor due to a recognition of the domestic actor's superior authority on a given matter compared to that of the tribunal and, in so doing, implicitly create a particular separation of powers between itself and the domestic actor. Such authority could derive, in particular, from the domestic actor's superior expertise or legitimacy vis-à-vis the tribunal to determine a particular topic. Where an adjudicator uses such considerations to defer to other actors, they implicitly endorse certain views about the separation of powers between the decision-makers comprising the regime in which they are operating. Standards of review in investment arbitration, in particular, articulate adjudicative views about the relationship between investment tribunals and national authorities.

B. Connecting the Separation of Powers to Deference in Investment Arbitration

This section examines two different ways of structuring the connections between separation of powers theories and deference in investment arbitration.[54] Section 1 considers how a formal approach to the separation of powers might prompt international adjudicators to adopt particularly binary approaches when deferring to domestic actors. Under a formal

---

[52] See Shirlow (n 4), for a more elaborated development of this point.
[53] Ittai Bar-Siman-Tov, 'Semiprocedural Judicial Review' (2012) 6 Legisprudence 271, 278.
[54] The section builds on Shirlow (n 4).

approach, particular tasks are considered to be inherently suited to particular types of institution. This view of how powers ought to be separated relies upon an a priori formal categorization of a matter which produces a particularly binary approach by the adjudicator to assessing whether it—or another actor—is institutionally more suited (due to considerations of expertise or legitimacy) to determine the matter. Section 2 explores an alternative, functional approach to the separation of powers and demonstrates how it might prompt more nuanced analyses. A functional approach is more nuanced because it looks at the particular qualities of available decision-makers in order to determine which is the best equipped to make a given decision. This produces less binary, more gradated, approaches to setting the applicable standard of review for a given decision.

1. Thinking formally about the separation of powers

A formal approach to the separation of powers allocates particular tasks to particular institutions.[55] According to such a view, a separation of powers is present where decision-making is divided between 'distinct organs independently exercising power'.[56] Most States, for example, divide their decision-making powers roughly between 'executive', 'legislative', and 'judicial' structures. Under a formal approach to the separation of powers, each institutional structure is conceptualized as holding decision-making expertise and/or legitimacy over particular subjects. Whereas, for example, a legislature might be vested with 'political' decision-making powers, an administrator might hold 'expert' decision-making capacity, and a judicial actor might be particularly equipped to exercise 'adjudicative' functions. As Rebecca Brown notes, such an approach to the separation of powers 'depends upon a belief that the legislative, executive and judicial powers are inherently distinguishable as well as separable from one another'.[57]

Such an understanding of the separation of powers may inform particularly binary approaches to adjudicative standards of review. Where a decision can be classified as political, for instance, a formal approach to the separation of powers might indicate that the decision is best allocated to a legislative or executive, as compared to judicial, actor. Under such a theory, an investment tribunal confronting a political question might be minded to defer entirely to a legislative actor's views about that question. As Eoin Carolan notes, using such a model:

> When faced with a question of disputed competences, the formalist court or commentator is concerned chiefly to identify and classify the task at hand. Once characterized as a legislative, executive, or judicial function, the task is allocated to the appropriate institution. The initial classification effectively exhausts the formalist enquiry.[58]

Such approaches to deference adopt the perspective that there are certain matters which a court or tribunal ought not to consider at all. The approach thus relies on 'an a priori classification of forms or functions' to ground standards of review analysis.[59] Such approaches to

---

[55] Carolan (n 28) 23–25.
[56] ibid 18. Carolan notes that distinct organs have 'not been wholly reproduced in the institutional architecture of any modern state'.
[57] Rebecca Brown, 'Separated Powers and Ordered Liberty' (1991) 139 U Pa L Rev 1513, 1524.
[58] Carolan (n 28) 23.
[59] ibid 201.

deference will often take a binary form according to which deference becomes an either/or issue, including by prompted deference in the form of approaches that resemble domestic justiciability doctrines.

Many States responding to investment treaty claims have leveraged such formal understandings of the separation of powers to contend that particular categories of decision should always attract deference from international adjudicators. In *Pope & Talbot*, for example, the respondent State argued that the tribunal ought to accord it complete deference in respect of measures 'in the form of regulations'.[60] States have similarly requested, albeit with varied success, that tribunals defer to domestic decisions concerning sovereign debt restructuring[61] and currency devaluation;[62] the conduct of banking regulators during a financial crisis;[63] legislative acts;[64] taxation measures;[65] measures related to environmental regulation;[66] and prosecutorial decisions.[67] Such requests for deference expressly or implicitly invoke a formal separation of powers as their basis. The *Paushok* tribunal, for example, declined to decide whether a State had acted for a 'public purpose', noting that: 'the definition of public interest ... is more a subject for political debate than arbitral decisions'.[68] These approaches to deference adopt a formal conception of the functions of international tribunals vis-à-vis domestic actors, based upon institutional design or the subject matter of a given decision to which deference might attach.

A number of investment tribunals have endorsed such a view to hold that policy choices and administrative decisions ought to attract deference from international adjudicators. Investment arbitrators have, for instance, declined to conduct *in abstracto* review of domestic legislative[69] or policy[70] choices. The ICSID tribunal in *Enron* stated to this effect that it:

---

[60] *Pope & Talbot v Government of Canada*, UNCITRAL, Interim Award (26 June 2000) para 99.

[61] *Abaclat and ors v Argentine Republic*, ICSID Case No ARB/07/5, Decision on Jurisdiction and Admissibility (4 August 2011) paras 548–50; *Alemanni and ors v Argentine Republic*, ICSID Case No ARB/07/8, Decision on Jurisdiction (17 November 2014) paras 318–20.

[62] *El Paso Energy International Company v Argentine Republic*, ICSID Case No ARB/03/15, Award (31 October 2011) para 222; *National Grid v Argentine Republic*, UNCITRAL, Award (3 November 2008) para 96.

[63] *Renée Rose Levy de Levi v Republic of Peru*, ICSID Case No ARB/10/17, Award (26 February 2014) paras 156–58.

[64] *Achmea BV v Slovak Republic (No 2)*, PCA Case No 2013-12, Award on Jurisdiction and Admissibility (20 May 2014) para 251; *Paushok v Government of Mongolia*, UNCITRAL, Award on Jurisdiction and Liability (28 April 2011) para 298; *Lemire v Ukraine*, ICSID Case No ARB/06/18, Decision on Jurisdiction and Liability (14 January 2010) paras 240–41, 315.

[65] *Jan Oostergetel v Slovak Republic*, UNCITRAL, Final Award (23 April 2012) paras 236, 259; *Feldman v United Mexican States*, ICSID Case No ARB(AF)/99/1, Award (16 December 2002) paras 112–16; *RosInvest v Russian Federation*, SCC Case No 079/2005, Final Award (12 September 2010) paras 574–80; *Renta4 v Russian Federation*, SSC No 24/2007, Award on Preliminary Objections (20 March 2009) para 179.

[66] *Bilcon of Delaware et al v Government of Canada*, PCA Case No 2009-04, Award on Jurisdiction and Liability (17 March 2015) paras 595–97.

[67] *Ahmonseto v Egypt*, ICSID Case No ARB/02/15, Award (18 June 2007) para 254; *Rompetrol v Romania*, ICSID Case No ARB/06/3, Award (6 May 2013) para 152.

[68] *Paushok* (n 64) paras 328, 337. See further *Blusun v Italian Republic*, ICSID Case No ARB/14/3, Final Award (27 December 2016) paras 317–18; *Guaracachi America v Bolivia*, UNCITRAL, PCA Case No 2011-17, Award (31 January 2014) para 437; *Parkerings-Compagniet AS v Republic of Lithuania*, ICSID Case No ARB/05/8, Award (11 September 2007) para 411.

[69] *Merrill & Ring v Canada*, ICSID Case No UNCT/07/1, Award (31 March 2010) para 218; *Renée Rose* (n 63) paras 161–62; *Anatolie Stati*, SCC Case No V116/2010, Award (19 December 2013) para 1135.

[70] *CMS Gas Transmission Company v The Republic of Argentina*, ICSID Case No ARB/01/8, Decision on Jurisdiction (17 July 2003) paras 25–33; *LG&E Energy Corp, LG&E Capital Corp and LG&E International Inc v Argentine Republic*, ICSID Case No ARB/02/1, Decision on Jurisdiction (30 April 2004) para 67; *El Paso Energy International Company v Argentina*, ICSID Case No ARB/03/15, Decision on Jurisdiction (27 April 2006) paras 97–99; *Saluka v Czech Republic*, UNCITRAL, Partial Award (17 March 2006) para 337.

will not sit in judgement over the general tax policies pursued by the Argentine Republic or the Provinces ... This is a matter exclusively appurtenant to the sovereignty of the Argentine Republic.[71]

Adjudicators have on similar grounds declined to second-guess certain administrative decisions or the factual basis for domestic decisions. The *Enkev* tribunal, for instance, observed that:

this Tribunal is not an appellate court inserted into the Polish legal system. Nor is it entrusted by the Parties with the general task of judicially reviewing the legality or reasonableness of administrative acts by Polish state entities under Polish law ... In particular, it cannot act as the ultimate town planner for the City of Lodz. It is certain that this Tribunal is no more fitted to decide issues of town planning in the City of Lodz than its town planners are fitted to apply and interpret the Treaty as an international arbitration tribunal: each has different roles.[72]

An international adjudicator may thus decline to assess the correctness of domestic legislation or policy as a matter of economics, politics, or domestic law. The adjudicator thereby abstains from interfering with the freedom of States 'to adopt the policies that they choose', instead focusing on 'the manner in which policies may be changed and implemented, not on the policies themselves'.[73] Such approaches to deference have the effect of articulating (and creating) a formal separation of powers between (international) adjudicative and (domestic) policy functions.

Investment tribunals have also been particularly receptive to requests for deference to domestic court decisions on matters of domestic law. This may include deference to domestic decisions concerning the interpretation of particular domestic laws,[74] or matters of domestic constitutional law.[75] The tribunal in *Grand River*, for example, observed that '[b]oth parties apparently would have the tribunal resolve [a] highly contested question of U.S. domestic law'.[76] The tribunal, however, noted that it was:

loath to purport to address these delicate and complex questions of U.S. constitutional and Indian law ... These issues of national law belong in national courts, not in an international tribunal.[77]

Tribunals on a similar basis have deferred to domestic courts by emphasizing that they do not operate as courts of 'appeal'.[78] The *Arif* tribunal, for example, emphasized that

---

[71] *Enron v Argentina*, ICSID Case No ARB/01/3, Decision on Jurisdiction (14 January 2004) para 29.

[72] *Enkev Beheer v Republic of Poland*, PCA Case No 2013-01, First Partial Award (29 April 2014) para 327.

[73] *Achmea BV v Slovak Republic*, PCA Case No 2008-13, Award (7 December 2012) para 294.

[74] See eg *AES v Republic of Kazakhstan*, ICSID Case No ARB/10/16, Award (1 November 2013) paras 306–07, 318–29; *Petrobart v Kyrgyz Republic*, SCC Case No 126/2003, Award (29 March 2005) 84; *Arif v Moldova*, ICSID Case No ARB/11/23, Award (8 April 2013) para 441; *International Thunderbird v United Mexican States*, UNCITRAL, Award (26 January 2006) para 160.

[75] *Plama v Bulgaria*, ICSID Case No ARB/03/24, Award (27 August 2008) paras 219, 280–82.

[76] *Grand River v United States of America*, UNCITRAL, Award (12 January 2011) para 139.

[77] ibid 234.

[78] *Anatolie Stati* (n 69) paras 1223–24; *Middle East Cement v Egypt*, ICSID Case No ARB/99/6, Award (12 April 2002) paras 159–61; *Mondev v United States of America*, ICSID Case No ARB(AF)/99/2, Award (11 October 2002) paras 126, 136; *Loewen v United States of America*, ICSID Case No ARB(AF)/98/3, Award (26 June 2003) paras 51, 242.

'international tribunals must refrain from playing the role of ultimate appellate courts', including by refraining from substituting their 'own application and interpretation of national law' for domestic interpretations.[79] For the *Arif* tribunal, such substitution would 'blur the necessary distinction between the hierarchy of instances within the national judiciary and the role of international tribunals'.[80] Such deference has been justified on the basis that international adjudication does not provide an 'appropriate forum' to decide 'contentious' or 'technical' questions of domestic law.[81] This creates a separation of powers between international adjudicators and domestic actors, insofar as it is left to domestic courts to interpret domestic law. In *Perenco*, for example, the tribunal held that deference to a domestic decision-maker was needed in order to 'recognise the allocation of competencies between adjudicatory bodies at the national and international levels'.[82] All such approaches are similar insofar as deference follows from the categorization of a given matter as suitable (or not) to determination by an international tribunal as compared to the organs of a State. Such approaches to setting the standard of review follow a view that adjudicators, and international investment tribunals in particular, perform a role different to that performed by particular domestic actors in respect of particular topics or decision types.

2. Thinking functionally about the separation of powers

A formal approach to the separation of powers has been criticized on the basis that the functions performed by different organs might overlap or be indistinguishable in practice.[83] This has prompted the development of less formal, more functional, approaches to the separation of powers. While a formal approach to the separation of powers allocates decision-making powers by reference to the formal structure of an institution, a functional approach allocates power by reference to an actor's institutional qualities and capacities. This could include the specific procedural powers of an international adjudicator compared to domestic organs, the specific expertise of individual adjudicators compared to specific State officials, or the capacity of the international adjudicator to apply law—as compared to some other normative system—to resolve the given issue. Functional approaches to the separation of powers recognize that each institutional type is comparatively stronger (or weaker) at making particular types of decisions than others. Each institutional type will also be comparatively stronger (or weaker) at making decisions vis-à-vis investment tribunals. This view of the separation of powers adopts the perspective that the capacities of different decision-making organs will differ and that, in an ideal system, these decision-makers would 'dovetail' with each other to leverage their respective decision-making strengths and minimize their respective weaknesses.[84] Deference—and adjudicative standards of review—'provides a means by which the strengths and weaknesses inherent in institutional

---

[79] *Arif* (n 74) para 441.

[80] ibid.

[81] *Yukos v Russia*, PCA Case No 2005-04/AA227, Final Award (18 July 2014) para 499; *Lauder v Czech Republic*, UNCITRAL, Final Award (3 September 2001) para 287; *Saluka* (n 70) paras 433, 442–44; *Tokios Tokelės v Ukraine*, ICSID Case No ARB/02/18, Award (26 July 2007) paras 128, 131.

[82] *Perenco v Ecuador*, ICSID Case No ARB/08/6, Decision on Jurisdiction and Liability (12 September 2014) para 583.

[83] Carolan (n 28) 19.

[84] Henry M Hart Jr and Albert M Sacks, *The Legal Process: Basic Problems in the Making and Application of Law* (Foundation Press 1994) 158; Andrea C Westlund, 'Deference as a Normative Power' (2013) 166 Philosophical Studies 455, 467.

design can be appraised and accommodated on a case-by-case basis'.[85] Adjudicators adopting a functional approach will engage in more detail with the decision-making context when deciding whether—and how—to defer to a given decision. This entails analysis of a range of matters relevant to determining whether the deferring adjudicator or the actor to which deference might be given is the most appropriate decision-maker for the given issue.

A functional separation of powers might, for example, allocate decision-making powers by reference to whether an institution is well-equipped to make the particular decision at issue. The adversarial structure of adjudication or the deliberative approach of an international tribunal might, for instance, make it less equipped to locate and review a wide variety of inputs into a given decision-making process.[86] An adjudicator also typically assesses disputes retrospectively, and operates under tighter timeframes when appraising information.[87] It may also be constrained by restrictive rules of evidence that permit it to engage only with certain legally relevant inputs into its decision-making process. A domestic administrative body, by contrast, might be better able to 'continually monitor a situation, gather evidence about it, or seek information from more diverse stakeholders'.[88] Such bodies may also have differing access and capacity to appraise sensitive or scientific information. They may also have greater ability than courts or even legislatures to 'revise decisions' on an ongoing basis.[89] The evidence-gathering and decision-making processes of these organs thus differ. Such features might make some institutions better adapted to make particular decisions than others. These actors also employ different reasoning processes. Habermas suggests that the separation of powers between various institutional types reflects a 'distribution of the possibilities for access to different sorts of reasons'.[90] Legislatures typically adopt decisions by reference to normative, pragmatic, or empirical reasons, whereas the judiciary is largely confined to legal discourse.[91] A legislature might therefore have better capacity than the judiciary to analyse issues involving political, normative, or moral components. The adversarial procedures of adjudicators may mean that polycentric disputes implicating interlocking interests are also inherently more suited to settlement through other institutional structures.[92]

The proximity of an actor to a given situation may also impact its capacity to make particular types of decisions. Investment tribunals, for instance, may be less adept than domestic actors at evaluating local circumstances and may be less 'acquainted with local issues, sensitivities and traditions' than domestic decision-makers.[93] They may also have

---

[85]   Shirlow (n 4) 22.

[86]   Yuval Shany, 'Toward a General Margin of Appreciation Doctrine in International Law?' (2005) 16 EJIL 907, 918; Jeffrey Jowell, 'Judicial Deference and Human Rights: A Question of Competence' in Paul P Craig and Richard Rawlings (eds), *Law and Administration in Europe: Essays in Honour of Carol Harlow* (OUP 2003) 73; Paul Daly, *A Theory of Deference in Administrative Law: Basis, Application and Scope* (CUP 2012) 90.

[87]   Shany (n 86) 918; Jowell (n 86) 73; Thomas Raine, 'Judicial Review under the Human Rights Act: A Culture of Justification' (2013) 1 NELR 81, 102; Daly (n 86) 90.

[88]   Shirlow (n 4) 23.

[89]   Daly (n 86) 95.

[90]   Jürgen Habermas, *Between Facts and Norms: Contributions to a Discourse Theory of Law and Democracy* (Polity Press 2015) 192.

[91]   ibid. See also: Ronald Dworkin, *Taking Rights Seriously* (Duckworth 1977).

[92]   On the distinction between 'monocentric' and 'polycentric' disputes, see Lon Fuller, 'The Forms and Limits of Adjudication' (1978) 92 Harv L Rev 353, 353.

[93]   Caroline Henckels, 'Balancing Investment Protection and the Public Interest: The Role of the Standard of Review and the Importance of Deference in Investor-State Arbitration' (2013) 4 JIDS 197, 205. See also: Machiko Kanetake, 'The Interfaces between the National and International Rule of Law: A Framework Paper' in Machiko

fewer resources to make fact-heavy assessments than comparatively better resourced domestic actors. This might mean that domestic administrators or legislatures, with better access to information and in closer proximity to a given situation, will be better adapted to make decisions about that situation than other actors, including international tribunals.[94] Conversely, international adjudicators may have greater capacity to interpret and apply international law compared to domestic actors. Distance from a given situation may also enable them to reach decisions on certain matters from a less biased (or subjective) vantage point.[95]

The selection of standards of review and approaches to deference that reflect these considerations implicitly endorse a functional separation of powers between international tribunals and domestic actors. Such deference may mean that an international adjudicator still assesses domestic acts for compliance with international law, but may in some cases influence them to limit the extent to which they do so. In invoking such considerations, international tribunals manifest a view that certain decisions—or certain aspects of those decisions—are more expertly or legitimately made in domestic systems and, as such, should not be second-guessed by international adjudicators. The qualities of domestic decisions that signal to an adjudicator a need for some deference might be derived from different accounts of the rule of the law. An adjudicator might be particularly willing to defer, for instance, to independent, non-arbitrary, or procedurally appropriate decision-making.

Some investment tribunals have adopted standards of review which focus upon the functional qualities of individual decision-makers to analyse whether deference is due to their decisions in the context of a particular case. Instead of deferring to domestic actors qua domestic actors, such tribunals require some additional proof that an institution's particular strengths have been brought to bear in its decision on a given matter. The *Fraport* ad hoc annulment Committee, for example, emphasized the importance of deference to domestic interpretations of municipal law, given that 'the Tribunal had not been chosen for its knowledge of Philippine law'.[96] The Committee emphasized that such deference did not mean, however, that domestic interpretations would be 'necessarily dispositive'.[97] Instead, it accepted that they 'may need to be scrutinised very carefully by an international tribunal', which 'would need to satisfy itself, *inter alia*, as to the impartiality of the relevant decision-maker'.[98] The *Tatneft* tribunal similarly adopted the view that 'deference on the part of international tribunals requires the clear perception that domestic courts are independent,

---

Kanetake and André Nollkaemper (eds), *The Rule of Law at the National and International Levels: Contestations and Deference* (Hart 2016) 21; Caroline Henckels, 'The Role of the Standard of Review and the Importance of Deference in Investor-State Arbitration' in Lukasz Gruszczynski and Wouter Werner (eds), *Deference in International Courts and Tribunals: Standard of Review and Margin of Appreciation* (OUP 2014) 123; Carolan (n 28) 144–45.

[94] Carolan (n 28) 144.

[95] Andreas Føllesdal, 'Much Ado About Nothing? International Judicial Review of Human Rights in Well-Functioning Democracies' in Andreas Føllesdal, Johan Karlsson Schaffer and Geir Ulfstein (eds), *The Legitimacy of International Human Rights Regimes: Legal, Political and Philosophical Perspectives* (CUP 2013) 19; Henckels, 'Balancing Investment Protection and the Public Interest' (n 93) 13.

[96] *Fraport AG Frankfurt Airport Services Worldwide v Philippines*, ICSID Case No ARB/11/12, Annulment Decision (23 December 2010) paras 117, 236.

[97] ibid 242.

[98] ibid.

competent and above all clear of suspicion of corruption'.[99] The *Glamis* tribunal simi-larly emphasized a requirement for decisions to exhibit procedural reasonableness to at-tract deference. In that case, the tribunal noted that the respondent State's decisions had been informed by 'cultural studies and the guidance of professional archaeologists and re-searchers'.[100] The tribunal opined that, in such circumstances:

> it is not for this Tribunal to assess the veracity of evidentiary support for domestic governmental decisions; the Tribunal may assess only whether there was reasonable evidence, and thus the government's reliance on such was not obviously and actionably misplaced.[101]

Thus, the analysis of appropriate standards of review might not operate formally (by ref-erence to institutional category) but instead functionally (by reference to institutional design). Of course, a criticism that could be made of this functional approach is that it leads to greater unpredictability (which may itself be a rule-of-law concern). However, it produces potentially more fine-grained and principled analyses than a formal approach. Over time, an adjudicative regime may also—through functional approaches—articulate the standards or types of decision-making that will be valued and as such that will attract deference. To that extent, then, functional approaches—where properly explained by the deferring adjudicator—may in fact enhance the predictability and coherence of deference over time. Such approaches to deference are also better adapted to recognize distinct in-stitutional strengths, and minimize institutional weaknesses.[102] Functional approaches can be used to appraise the strengths and weaknesses of decision-making organs not by reference to their (formal) institutional designation but instead by reference to the 'com-parative institutional qualities' of different decision-makers vis-à-vis particular types of decisions.[103] This makes the analysis of deference more nuanced. Under such an approach to the separation of powers, deference is no longer an either/or enquiry but becomes in-stead a question of more/less. This prompts comparative assessments. Such functional ap-proaches to review convert deference into a function comparing the investment tribunal's expertise and legitimacy to make a particular decision with that of domestic actors. More deference will be accorded where a domestic actor is assessed to have greater expertise or legitimacy to make a particular decision than the adjudicator, and vice versa. Elected legislatures may, for example, be more legitimate decision-makers in respect of issues that need to be decided in a manner that is responsive to public opinion. Non-elected adjudicators may by contrast be more legitimate decision-makers on technical matters of law or in respect of issues necessitating decision from an unbiased, or non-majoritarian, perspective.[104]

---

[99]   *OAO Tatneft v Ukraine*, PCA Case No 2008-8, Award on the Merits (29 July 2014) para 476.
[100]   *Glamis Gold v United States of America*, UNCITRAL, Award (8 June 2009) para 781.
[101]   ibid 786.
[102]   Carolan (n 28) 183.
[103]   ibid 200.
[104]   Allan (n 14) 189; de Búrca (n 42) 230; Schmitter and Karl (n 42) 24.

IV. Using Theories about the Rule of Law and Separation of Powers to Inform Standards of Review in Investment Arbitration

Different theories of the separation of powers may thus impact how adjudicators appraise and defer to the decision-making efforts of other organs. This means that theories about the separation of powers can be used to inform the analysis of intersections between the decisions of different organs in a legal regime.[105] Adjudicators might, in particular, use separation of powers theories to inform their analysis of whether—and how—they ought to defer to the decisions of other organs on topics relevant to the matters brought before them for adjudication. This raises the question as to what the appropriate separation of powers is between investment tribunals and domestic actors, and how tribunals might use separation of powers theories to inform their analysis of deference in practice. Carolan has developed a particularly useful account of the relationship between the separation of powers and standards of review under domestic law. Examining how this account might apply to investor-State arbitration indicates how this or other theories about the separation of powers might be used to inform adjudicative approaches to standards of review in practice.

According to Carolan's approach, a separation of powers indicates that the various governance organs within a polity should approach each other's decisions with both 'deference and distrust'.[106] This theory is informed by a view that each institution has an input into the process of governance that 'is both legitimate and provisional'.[107] The stance of 'deference and distrust' makes governance an 'ongoing and collaborative process to which all of the institutions may potentially contribute'.[108] Institutional separation of powers (including under a formal theory) might supply the basis for a starting presumption of deference. The provisional nature of such deference indicates, however, that more functional approaches should follow as a second step. As Carolan explains, the understanding that any institution's decision-making power is contingent 'logically suggests that these assessments of non-suitability ought to be based on a flexible appraisal of the institution's own limitations, rather than on an *a priori* classification of forms or functions'.[109] Practically speaking, the application of Carolan's theory to the relationships between adjudicators and other organs recognizes that the 'particular skills of each institution make them more equipped to perform particular tasks, but these outcomes can be reviewed by other bodies'.[110]

Adapting Carolan's theory to investment arbitration entails three key consequences. First, any claim to decision-making authority is contingent and contestable. Thus, when a tribunal is confronted with a domestic decision to which deference is requested, the starting point under Carolan's approach would be for the tribunal to presume that the domestic actor has brought their expertise and legitimacy to bear in deciding that issue. This presumptive starting point might refer to the domestic actor's formal institutional status or their specific decision-making competencies. Investment tribunals should thus not 'simply continue to insist that power should be exercised only in accordance with their views'.[111]

---

[105] The connection between deference and the structure of the relationship between the domestic and international legal systems is explored in more length in Shirlow (n 4).

[106] Carolan (n 28) 187.

[107] ibid 183.

[108] ibid 186.

[109] ibid 201.

[110] ibid 183.

[111] ibid 188.

While tribunals might thus start from a presumption of 'deference', they must also imbue their analysis of whether deference is due with an attitude of 'distrust'. This indicates that the starting point of presumptive deference will always be provisional. Complete deference to a domestic actor will no longer be appropriate insofar as the investment tribunal itself holds capacities that could be applied to improve a given decision.[112] A tribunal must, nevertheless, at the same time 'have regard to its own relative limitations so that it can identify when a matter may be more appropriately dealt with by a different branch'.[113] A tribunal might be more or less inclined to defer to or to distrust decisions from domestic institutions. The balance struck by an adjudicator between these attitudes of deference and distrust will impact the operation of deference in practice. Such balance cannot, however, be resolved in the absence of an overarching theory concerning the appropriate separation of powers between investment tribunals and domestic actors.

Second, the standards of review appropriate to mediating a separation of powers between investment arbitrators and domestic actors cannot be fixed in advance.[114] Instead, deference can only arise where a decision has been made by the application of a domestic actor's capacity, and provided that this capacity exceeds that of the investment tribunal.[115] The procedural features and institutional qualities of domestic actors vis-à-vis international investment tribunals may mean that certain types of decisions are more likely to attract deference than others. This might include, for instance, interpretations and applications of domestic law or technical, moral, or scientific assessments. However, as the capacity of investment tribunals increases or wanes over time, different mediations of their relationship with domestic actors will follow through deference and standards of review.[116] It is thus not possible to 'fix' the appropriate standard of review and thus the appropriate level of deference between investment tribunals and domestic actors. While a framework for such decisions may be developed, the outcome of applying that framework will differ by time and context. The relative nature of the enquiry means that deference cannot be fixed in advance for all relationships and contexts.[117]

Third, deference under Carolan's theory of the separation of powers entails a responsibility for each actor to justify the basis for its decisions, such that other actors can appraise whether such decisions should attract deference or not.[118] Deference is therefore not unidirectional. It instead entails certain responsibilities for the actor seeking deference. As Carolan notes:

> Where one institution has the advantage of better or more relevant information, for example, it should explain and identify that advantage so that the other institutions can subsequently take account of it in making their own independent judgements.[119]

---

[112] ibid.
[113] ibid 200.
[114] ibid 187.
[115] Shirlow (n 4) 258.
[116] ibid 266.
[117] ibid 267.
[118] Carolan (n 28) 188–89.
[119] ibid 188.

Such an approach to deference might, in turn, reinforce the separation of powers. As David Dyzenhaus observes, by requiring each actor to 'justify the exercise of its power', and by requiring deference where a 'reasonable justification' of greater expertise or legitimacy is provided, 'the roles each branch plays are made clearer'.[120] This approach would require both international tribunals that defer to domestic actors, and domestic actors seeking deference from international tribunals, to clearly articulate the basis upon which decisions about deference are being made. This would, in turn, contribute to more express statements as to the relative institutional qualities enjoyed by, and appropriate separation of powers between, international tribunals and domestic actors.

V. Conclusions: Standards of Review and Rule-of-Law Problems and Lacunae

This chapter has explored how a core component of the rule of law—the separation of powers—might inform adjudicative standards of review in investment treaty arbitration. It has explored the connections between the rule of law, separation of powers, and standards of review in order to consider how these concepts might inform whether, and how, investment arbitrators defer to domestic decision-makers in investor-State arbitration. The discussion indicates that (at least some) investment tribunals are (at least implicitly) using standards of review to endorse a particular view as to the separation of powers between domestic and international actors. While it is possible to investigate such approaches for what they reveal about the de facto separation of powers between investment tribunals and domestic actors, such approaches are not currently informed by any express overarching theoretical framework concerning the role of the rule of law or separation of powers in setting the appropriate standard of review. This indicates that there may be some scope to draw more expressly from rule-of-law theory to inform analyses of deference in investment treaty arbitration. The chapter has suggested some initial ways in which such approaches might be developed, including developing a basis for stakeholders to evaluate the approaches towards the standard of review adopted by tribunals in practice against rule-of-law considerations. Through this analysis, the chapter has demonstrated how investment tribunals may use standards of review to articulate their views as to the appropriate relationship between investment tribunals and domestic actors. Standards of review might thus reinforce, or even create, a separation of powers between international and domestic actors.

---

[120] Dyzenhaus (n 24) 255 (referring to the executive providing a justification for the exercise of its power, and the judiciary seeking a 'reasonable justification' for that exercise).

14

Risking the Rule of Law?

The Relationship between Substantive Investment Protection Standards, Human Rights, and Sustainable Development

Steffen Hindelang, Patricia Sarah Stöbener de Mora, and Niels Lachmann[*]

I. Introduction

The relationship between international investment law (IIL) and the rule of law is much debated, particularly in the appreciation of decisions of investor-State arbitral tribunals.[1] Some commentators stress IIL's role as a 'tool to enforce the international Rule of Law' by the means of a neutral tribunal, limiting the arbitrary exercise of sovereign powers towards investors.[2] But in turn, criticism targets what would be an insufficient attention by IIL and arbitral tribunals to international legal regimes that reflect essentially non-economic interests competing with those of an investor,[3] especially human rights and sustainable development concerns.[4] Recent studies have found tribunals tending towards 'evasion' of relevant human rights concerns other than those relating to the investor,[5] or towards adopting a 'pick and choose' approach that 'does not lead to a thorough, substantive cross-regime consistency' across the human rights and investment law regimes, 'but rather serves as a form of window-dressing',[6] or towards prioritizing investor 'rights' over others' 'aspirational' human rights and sustainable development concerns.[7]

Rule of law is—in this contribution—understood as defined by the United Nations (UN):

a principle of governance in which all persons, institutions and entities, public and private, including the State itself, are accountable to laws that are publicly promulgated, equally

[*] The authors gratefully acknowledge the feedback on earlier drafts by the editors of this volume as well as by the members of the ILA Committee on the Rule of Law and International Investment Law present at the Paris meeting in 2019. Errors remain our own.

[1] See Thomas Schultz and Cédric Dupont, 'Investment Arbitration: Promoting the Rule of Law or Over-Empowering Investors? A Quantitative Empirical Study' (2015) 25 EJIL 1147.

[2] Velimir Živković, 'Pursuing and Reimagining the International Rule of Law Through International Investment Law' (2020) 12 HJRL 1, 8–9 with further references.

[3] See José E Alvarez, *Public International Law Regime Governing International Investment* (Brill 2011) 93 and 373–78.

[4] See Stephan W Schill and Vladislav Djanic, 'Wherefore Art Thou? Towards a Public Interest-Based Justification of International Investment Law' (2018) 33 ICSID Rev—FILJ 29. As the relationship between human rights regimes and sustainable development is beyond the scope of this chapter, for simplicity, we opt for the term 'human rights *and* sustainable development'.

[5] Johannes Hendrik Fahner and Matthew Happold, 'The Human Rights Defence in International Investment Arbitration: Exploring the Limits of Systemic Integration' (2019) 68 ICLQ 741, 747–49.

[6] Silvia Steininger, 'What's Human Rights Got to Do with It? An Empirical Analysis of Human Rights References in Investment Arbitration' (2018) 31 LJIL 33, 55.

[7] Tomer Broude and Caroline Henckels, 'Not All Rights Are Created Equal: A Loss–Gain Frame of Investor Rights and Human Rights' (2021) 34 LJIL 93.

Steffen Hindelang, Patricia Sarah Stöbener de Mora, and Niels Lachmann, *Risking the Rule of Law?* In: *Investment Protection Standards and the Rule of Law.* Edited by: August Reinisch and Stephan W. Schill, Oxford University Press.

enforced and independently adjudicated, and which are consistent with international human rights norms and standards. It requires, as well, measures to ensure adherence to the principles of supremacy of law, equality before the law, accountability to the law, fairness in the application of the law, separation of powers, participation in decision making, legal certainty, avoidance of arbitrariness and procedural and legal transparency.[8]

From this understanding, it follows that, beyond formal process-oriented notions, normative foundations in human rights are essential to the rule of law. Therefore, this contribution proceeds from the assumption that frameworks relating in particular to international human rights norms and standards are intrinsically linked to the normative foundations of the rule of law, and that IIL should be in accordance with them. Indeed, arbitral tribunals' decisions should take into consideration all relevant international legal regimes, not only IIL, but also eg the rules on environmental protection or on indigenous peoples' rights, where they are affected —in their substance—reflecting and further detailing human rights norms and standards and, thus, the normative foundations of the rule of law. If in a legal appreciation of a certain factual situation, any one of the applicable legal regimes remains unconsidered or inadequately taken into account, the respective concerns will not have the adequate bearing on decisions. An arbitral tribunal would then even reconfigure on account of their own standards the very foundations of the rule of law, and eg effectively mute certain human rights. If that risk materializes, IIL would, as this contribution puts it, loosen its bonds with the rule of law, as IIL does not contain a mandate of those charged with its enforcement for such reconfiguration that should in any event at least require State consent. In that case, IIL might expose itself to the criticism that 'so-called rule of law, without respect for human rights, can be used as a tool for the arbitrary and oppressive exercise of power'.[9]

This contribution first discusses the formal and normative aspects of the rule of law and how IIL and its substantive protections standards could entail potential risks in relation to the rule of law's normative foundations (Section II). It then shows that there are mechanisms in place to mitigate the risk of IIL loosening the bonds with these normative foundations through arbitral decisions (Section III). Indeed, even if the relevant international investment agreements (IIAs) do not—unlike increasingly is the case in recent years—explicitly refer to human rights or sustainable development, arbitral tribunals in any case have to be aware of and possibly take into account such concerns in accordance with the principle of systemic integration codified in Article 31(3)(c) of the Vienna Convention on the Law of Treaties (VCLT).[10] The contribution's focus then shifts to a discussion of selected decisions by arbitral tribunals where human rights and sustainable development were at stake, with a focus on more recent ones, in order to assess both whether the risk of IIL loosening its bonds with the rule of law has materialized in problematic decisions, and the utility of the risk mitigation mechanism (Section IV). As the tribunals' recent trend towards a more adequate taking into account of human rights and sustainable development concerns has not cleared the relationship between IIL and the rule of law of ambiguities and unevenness, we

---

[8] United Nations Security Council, 'The rule of law and transitional justice in conflict and post-conflict societies, Report of the Secretary General' (23 August 2004) UN Doc S/2004/616, para 6.

[9] United Nations General Assembly, 'Strengthening and Coordinating United Nations Rule of Law, Report of the Secretary General. Addendum' (11 July 2014) UN Doc A/68/213/Add.1, para 15.

[10] Vienna Convention on the Law of Treaties (opened for signature 23 May 1969, entered into force 27 January 1980) 1155 UNTS 331 (hereafter VCLT).

raise questions about factors conducive to this situation, and efforts to overcome it (Section V), before concluding (Section VI).

II. A Risk for the Normative Foundations of the Rule of Law Inherent in the Substantive Protection Standards in IIAs?

The rule of law contains, on the one hand, formal process-oriented notions. On the other hand, the rule of law has its normative foundations in human rights and even in sustainability concerns. As the UN General Assembly stated: 'Devoid of the human rights framework, the rule of law is merely "rule by law", a term describing legal or rule-based frameworks, without a normative underpinning to secure substantive justice.'[11]

The international human rights and sustainable development framework, as part of the normative foundations of the rule of law, reflects and is determining interests or values, including respective priorities, governments wish to pursue. Human rights and sustainable development regimes typically further define public, supra-individual interests that for the purposes of this contribution are termed 'social justice'. They relate to and further detail the normative foundations of the rule of law and legitimize interests to be pursued by a host State. Human rights and sustainable development are thus critical for a state's relationship with an investor, both when protecting private property and when restricting the investor's economic freedom. The normative agenda they provide allocates a certain value and priority to a certain interest. Government is though left with a wide margin of appreciation when exercising its regulatory powers.

Human rights and sustainable development–related international regimes mainly determine and (de)legitimize the social justice interests to be pursued by the host State. In turn, the substantive protection standards in IIAs secure that these interests are pursued in a certain process, ie based on non-discrimination, due diligence, procedural fairness, proportionality, etc. IIL, to a large extent, helps secure a process-oriented notion of the rule of law, and provide protection for investors (ie to police the process of how certain interests, and priorities attached to them, are pursued and achieved by the host State).[12] In this sense, its substantive standards can be said to 'run in parallel' with the functions of the rule of law as regards foreign private property.[13]

However, substantive protection standards in IIAs may interact with the normative foundations of the rule of law in certain ways, including in a manner that entails the risk of IIL's application by arbitral tribunals' decisions loosening the bonds with these foundations. This holds true especially for the fair and equitable treatment (FET) standard, the rules on expropriation, and the full protection and security (FPS) standard.

The FET standard is said to be an 'embodiment' of the rule of law-serving functions of IIL.[14] This standard requires the State parties to an IIA to uphold legal security and

---

[11] UNGA (n 9) para 15.

[12] Pierre-Marie Dupuy and Jorge E Viñuales, 'Human Rights and Investment Disciplines: Integration in Process' in Marc Bungenberg and others (eds), *International Investment Law* (Nomos 2015) 1739, 1746–51.

[13] Stephan W Schill, 'International Investment Law and the Rule of Law' Amsterdam Law School Legal Studies Research Paper No. 2017-18 & Amsterdam Center for International Law No. 2017-15, 6 <https://ssrn.com/abstract=2932153> accessed 23 July 2021.

[14] Stephan W Schill, 'Fair and Equitable Treatment under Investment Treaties as an Embodiment of the Rule of Law' IILJ Working Paper 2006/6.

predictability, legal certainty and transparency, to uphold the principles of legality, to protect legitimate expectations, to guarantee some degree of due process in administrative, legislative, and judicial proceedings, to act proportionately, and to avoid arbitrariness and discrimination.[15] The FET standard largely contains elements of the rule of law that can be described as securing the process of the operation of law, safeguarding the observance of laws and procedures in the host State.

Nevertheless, the more the FET standard is enriched by sophisticated notions of what is perceived as good governance in legislative, judicial, and administrative practice,[16] the stronger notions of social justice are conveyed by the standard. This can have an effect on those parts of the normative foundations of the rule of law which relate to interests other than those of the investor. Bolstering the FET standard may impact the relative weight and balancing of the investor's interest vis-à-vis other interests, to the point where the latter could be completely overshadowed. Especially relevant is the triggering of the FET standard because of the frustration of an investor's legitimate expectations. That possibility has been deemed to have a 'chilling' effect on host States taking action that could affect investors negatively, or even impeding states to prioritize interests other than investors'.[17]

One of the criticisms of the application of the FET standard relating to the protection of legitimate expectations of an investor 'is that the openness of the standard can lead to its interpretation as an "umbrella clause" for the investor's complaints'.[18] Understood in such a broad fashion, the FET standard may secure the observance of commitments by the host State towards the investor; even more so than 'classic' umbrella clauses, which have become rarer in recent treaty-making practice. The FET standard then hardens and shields certain commitments undertaken by the host State against subsequent unilateral interferences through the use of sovereign powers. While this—rightly—secures legal certainty, it is easy to see how an extension of the scope of the FET standard through interpretation may come to affect the normative foundations of the rule of law if the FET standard is understood too broadly. Areas of regulation covered by such a broad reading of the FET standard would be exempted and could not be adapted to new real-world challenges, which may require other interests, possibly reflecting other human rights, to be prioritized, without having to compensate for legislative change.

The rules on expropriation describe how the use and possession of property can be brought to an end by government.[19] While process-oriented, their application may also touch on social justice notions by drawing dividing lines between compensable taking and non-compensable regulation,[20] defining the extent of the social function of private property. According to decisions of arbitral tribunals, an investor is not entitled to compensation

---

[15] Campbell McLachlan, Laurence Shore and Matthew Weiniger, *International Investment Arbitration: Substantive Principles* (2nd edn, OUP 2018) 296–329.

[16] Andrew D Mitchell, Elizabeth Sheargold and Tania Voon, 'Good Governance Obligations in International Economic Law: A Comparative Analysis of Trade and Investment' (2016) 17 JWIT 1, 12–19.

[17] See Krista Nadakavukaren Schefer, *International Investment Law: Text, Cases and Materials* (3rd edn, Edward Elgar 2020) 401–50. The standard's application has hence triggered various IIA reform efforts, for example with the aim of ensuring another balance of interests in such situations; see United Nations Conference on Trade and Development 'Investment Policy Framework for Sustainable Development' (2015) UN Doc UNCTAD/DIAE/PCB/2015/5, 83, 97–98.

[18] Nadakavukaren Schefer (n 17) 456.

[19] McLachlan, Shore and Weiniger (n 15) 360.

[20] Nadakavukaren Schefer (n 17) 261.

for the mere loss of profit due to regulatory activity, but neither is a host State shielded from a finding of compensable exproporiation by merely referring to a regulation in the public interest.[21] Therefore—as in the case of the FET standard—there is the potential for an expansive reading of an expropriation clause which, in turn, might touch upon the normative basis of the rule of law with regard to concerns other than the protection of private property. The risk is that an expropriation clause may become one of the ways through which an IIA entails a 'lock-in' of regulation that provides for certain investment conditions,[22] including tax incentives and (potentially lower) environmental or labour standards, as the host State cannot afford to pay compensation for indirect expropriation. Host States might fear that reducing incentives for investors and catering for other interests may trigger investors' claims and, thus, could refrain from introducing respective legislation. In turn, certain human rights norms and standards that also take part in the normative foundations of the rule of law could end up being disregarded.

The FPS standard, according to its 'prudent' reading, obliges the host State to protect a foreign investor and its investment against physical interference, and to punish perpetrators of such interference.[23] It thus formulates certain normative criteria, ie social values to be protected under local law. Like the FET standard and the expropriation clause, the application of the FPS standard may raise questions regarding IIL's relationship with the normative foundations of the rule of law. For example, in relation to cases of squatting, it has been pointed out that a host State's 'over-commitment to upholding its FPS obligations has the potential to threaten human rights'.[24] The tribunal in *Houben v Burundi* found the standard breached on account of Burundi's failure to prevent the squatting of the investor's property. It did not address the investor's claim that the failure to expel the squatters would (also) constitute a breach.[25] Scholars pointed out that challenging questions about human rights had followed if the tribunal had addressed that part of the investor's claim and not discarded as irrelevant Burundi's related defence based on concerns for the human rights of the people to be expelled.[26]

Risks in the relationship between IIL's substantive protection standards and the normative foundations of the rule of law show when a tribunal only takes into account the IIL standards and turns a blind eye to other international legal regimes to which a host State subscribes. Problematically, the tribunal would then engage in an exercise of policing whether its own notions of social justice are properly implemented by the host State, rather than those expressed by the obligations that State has taken up.

---

[21] McLachlan, Shore and Weiniger (n 15) 403–06.
[22] Kristina Bodea and Fangjin Ye, 'Investor Rights versus Human Rights: Do Bilateral Investment Treaties Tilt the Scales?' (2020) 50 Brit J Pol Sci 955, 955–63.
[23] For a brief assessment of the 'prudent' reading that limits the standard to *physical* security and host State action against perpetrators and the 'expansive' reading that includes legal protection and security as elements that a host State can be held accountable for, see McLachlan, Shore and Weiniger (n 15) 334–36.
[24] Nadakavukaren Schefer (n 17) 400.
[25] *Joseph Houben v Burundi*, ICSID Case No ARB/13/7, Award (12 January 2016) para 168.
[26] Fahner and Happold (n 5) 744–45, referring to *Houben* (n 25) para 177.

III. The Effects of the Legal Framework for Arbitral Tribunals' Decision-Making on the Relationship between IIL and the Normative Foundations of the Rule of Law

International investment tribunals owe their very existence to the fundamental concern for investors' rights that underlies IIL. As argued by scholars, this may lead to a situation in which a tribunal 'does not have a real choice which treaty to apply in case of a norm conflict: it must prioritize the treaty it is charged with applying, since it is only because of that treaty that it has jurisdiction to determine the dispute at all'.[27] This makes it necessary to look at the legal framework building the basis for arbitral tribunals' decision-making: the IIAs themselves, which have been criticized for their lack of receptiveness to other international legal regimes that are a part of the normative foundations of the rule of law. Scholars have gone as far as to argue 'that BITs contribute to a worsening of human rights practices' through a 'lock-in' of regulation that provides for attractive investment conditions while running counter to citizens' rights and well-being.[28]

Yet, recently concluded IIAs might be more conducive to an adequate consideration of human rights and sustainable development concerns by arbitral tribunals. Starting in the 1990s, preambles and specific provisions of IIAs increasingly have stated their parties' 'right to regulate', which can be conceptualized as 'an affirmation of states' authority to act as sovereigns on behalf of the will of the people'.[29] Among the first concerns addressed were health, labour rights, and better living conditions.[30] Recent multilateral agreements, such as the United States–Mexico–Canada Agreement that is to replace the North American Free Trade Agreement (NAFTA), or the Comprehensive and Progressive Agreement for Trans-Pacific Partnership, and the typical design used by the EU for its free trade and investment agreements, have confirmed this trend: they have notably established that not only investor expectations, but also the character of government action has to be taken into account when distinguishing between the exercise of the right to regulate and expropriation.[31]

Overall, in more recent IIAs, there is a growing connection between IIL and such international legal regimes that relate to sustainable development, responsible business conduct,

---

[27] Fahner and Happold (n 5) 758, referring to Arbitral Tribunal constituted under ch 11 of the North American Free Trade Agreement *Grand River Enterprises Six Nations Ltd, et al v United States of America*, UNCITRAL, Award (12 January 2011) para 71.

[28] Bodea and Ye (n 22) 956.

[29] Lone Wandahl Mouyal, *International Investment Law and the Right to Regulate: A Human Rights Perspective* (Routledge 2016) 8.

[30] See eg Treaty between the Government of the United States of America and the Government of the Republic of Georgia concerning the reciprocal encouragement and protection of investment (signed 7 March 1994, entered into force 10 August 1999) TIAS 97–817, preamble; Agreement between the Government of Hong Kong and the Government of New Zealand for the Promotion and Protection of Investments (signed 6 July 1995, entered into force 5 August 1995) NZTS 1995 No 14, art 8.3; Treaty between the Federal Republic of Germany and the Federal Democratic Republic of Ethiopia concerning the Encouragement and Reciprocal Protection of Investments (signed 19 January 2004, entered into force 4 May 2006) 2771 UNTS 215, art 3.3.

[31] Agreement between the United States of America, the United Mexican States, and Canada (signed 30 November 2018, entered into force 1 July 2020) Annex 14-B: Expropriation, pts 3(a)(ii), (iii), 3(b) <https://investmentpolicy.unctad.org/international-investment-agreements/treaty-files/6008/download> accessed 23 July 2021; Comprehensive and Progressive Agreement for Trans-Pacific-Partnership (signed 8 March 2018, entered into force 30 December 2018) Annex 9-B: Expropriation, pts 3(a)(iii), 3(b) <https://investmentpolicy.unctad.org/international-investment-agreements/treaty-files/5673/download> accessed 23 July 2021; European Commission 'Transatlantic Trade and Investment Partnership. Trade in Services, Investment and E-Commerce. Chapter II - Investment, draft text TTIP—investment' (September 2015) Trade Document No 53807, arts 2.1–2.2, Annex I, 1 and 3 <trade.ec.europa.eu/doclib/docs/2015/september/tradoc_153807.pdf> accessed 23 July 2021.

and human rights standards.[32] On environmental matters, the links between respective international legal regimes and IIAs started in the 1990s, with NAFTA recognizing the parties' exercise of their regulatory power because of 'environmental concerns',[33] and have become broadly established.[34] Sustainable development is the explicit aim of many, especially more recent IIAs.[35] There are however still diverging approaches to the inclusion of references to human rights in particular.[36] Most IIAs that explicitly mention human rights are clustered around specific contracting parties being involved, particularly the EU and Canada.[37] Africa might be on its way to become another 'hub of human rights references' in IIAs, the 2016 Morocco–Nigeria BIT exemplifying that trend.[38]

If the right to regulate to achieve other public interests is, in this way, mentioned in an IIA, especially if not only in the preamble but in a specific provision, it forms part of elements to be considered when interpreting the substantive protection standards according to Article 31(1) of the VCLT. Hence, arbitral tribunals would have to consider it as a limitation on the interpretive unfolding of IIL's substantive protection standards. Where IIAs further operationalize the right to regulate, eg by defining what would qualify as unfair treatment or an indirect expropriation,[39] the balancing process eventually to be undertaken by arbitral tribunals is pre-structured in even more detail. Therefore, there is less risk of decisions which do not account appropriately for other human rights or sustainability concerns and, hence, also reduced risk of loosening the bonds of the rule of law.

However, the impact of the described change in treaty language on arbitral tribunals' decision-making is still limited, as, in most cases, tribunals will still have to decide disputes on the basis of 'old' IIAs which do not mention the right to regulate, human rights, or sustainable development concerns explicitly. Nonetheless, the absence of explicit treaty language does not relieve tribunals from taking into account human rights and

---

[32] See Steffen Hindelang and Carl-Philipp Sassenrath, *The Investment Chapters of the EU's International Trade and Investment Agreements in a Comparative Perspective* (European Parliament 2015) 113–66; Jason Rudall, 'Green Shots in a Barren World: Recent Developments in International Investment Law' (2020) 67 NILR 453, 455–58; and the earlier conclusions from empirical analyses by J Anthony VanDuzer, 'Sustainable Development Provisions in International Trade Treaties: What Lessons for International Investment Agreements?' in Steffen Hindelang and Markus Krajewski (eds), *Shifting Paradigms in International Investment Law: More Balanced, Less Isolated, Increasingly Diversified* (OUP 2016) 142, 176; Kathryn Gordon, Joachim Pohl and Marie Bouchard, 'Investment Treaty Law, Sustainable Development and Responsible Business Conduct: A Fact Finding Survey' (2014) OECD Working Papers on International Investment 2014/01, 25.

[33] North American Free Trade Agreement (signed 17 December 1992, entered into force 1 January 1994) (1993) 32 ILM 289, art 1114.

[34] VanDuzer (n 32) 157.

[35] The IIA Mapping Project database hosted by the United Nations Conference on Trade and Development's Investment Policy Hub lists currently 78 IIAs where sustainable development figures in the preamble, while 241 overall would refer to the notion <https://investmentpolicy.unctad.org/international-investment-agreements/iia-mapping> accessed 23 July 2021.

[36] A discussion of the relationship between human rights and sustainable development and a more thorough disaggregation of the latter's aspects in case studies is provided by Sheng Zhang, 'Human Rights and International Investment Agreements: How to Bridge the Gap?' (2019) 7 Chin J Comp L 457, 464–74.

[37] As follows from a search in the IIA Mapping Project database (n 35).

[38] See Niccolò Zugliani, 'Human Rights in International Investment Law: The 2016 Morocco–Nigeria Bilateral Investment Treaty' (2019) 68 ICLQ 760, 762, referring to the Reciprocal Investment Promotion and Protection Agreement between the Government of the Kingdom of Morocco and the Government of the Federal Republic of Nigeria (signed 3 December 2016) <https://investmentpolicy.unctad.org/international-investment-agreements/treaty-files/5409/download> accessed 23 July 2021.

[39] Gebhard Bücheler, *Proportionality in Investor-State Arbitration* (OUP 2015) 136–41. Annexes such as those establishing a distinction between right to regulate and expropriation in recent multilateral IIAs (n 31) are part of a treaty's text, see VCLT (n 10) art 31(2): 'The context for the purpose of the interpretation of a treaty shall comprise, in addition to the text, including its preamble and annexes'.

sustainable development concerns. Indeed, tribunals have to interpret IIAs in accordance with the VCLT's rules of interpretation that codify customary international law, including the requirement in Article 31(3)c that beyond wording, object and purpose, and context of a treaty, 'shall be taken into account ... any relevant rules of international law applicable in the relations between the parties'.[40] The State's right to regulate is essentially the sum of its rights and obligations to act in the pursuit of public interests mandated by human rights and other international obligations of said State. In arbitral practice this concept of a State's right to regulate has appeared through reference to a State's 'police power(s)'.[41]

The VCLT's requirement of 'systemic integration'[42] applies—of course—also to the relationship between an IIA and other international legal regimes relating to, eg human rights and sustainable development.[43] It should prevent IIL, and more specifically arbitral tribunals, from loosening the bonds with principles that are part of the normative foundations of the rule of law.[44] Systemic integration allows (and obliges) taking into account the normative environment of an IIA more widely and could lead to a more integrated interpretation of IIL and other legal regimes.[45] It should lead international investment tribunals to a harmonious interpretation that takes adequately into account all concerns at stake in a case.[46] Neither the interests of investors, nor other public interests, can be regarded as per se more important. As stated by the tribunal in *Noble Ventures v Romania*, 'it is not permissible, as is too often done regarding BITs, to interpret clauses exclusively in favour of investors'.[47]

---

[40] The customary status of the provision was stated by Mark E Villiger, *Customary International Law and Treaties: A Study of Their Interactions and Interrelations with Special Consideration of the 1969 Vienna Convention on the Law of Treaties* (Martinus Nijhoff 1985) 269, and since by the International Court of Justice, Certain Questions of Mutual Assistance in Criminal Matters *(Djibouti v France)* (Judgment) [2008] ICJ Rep 177, para 112 and Maritime Delimitation in the Indian Ocean *(Somalia v Kenya)* (Judgment on Preliminary Objections) [2017] ICJ Rep 3, para 89.

[41] See *Philip Morris Brands Sàrl, Philip Morris Products SA and Abal Hermanos SA v Oriental Republic of Uruguay*, ICSID Case No ARB/10/7, Award (8 July 2016) para 292 with further references; *Técnicas Medioambientales Tecmed, SA v The United Mexican States*, ICSID Case No ARB(AF)/00/2, Award (29 May 2003) para 119.

[42] See Campbell McLachlan, 'The Principle of Systemic Integration and Article 31(3)(c) of the Vienna Convention' (2005) 54 ICLQ 279; Panos Merkouris, *Article 31(3)(c) VCLT and the Principle of Systemic Integration: Normative Shadows in Plato's Cave* (Brill 2015); Daniel Rosentreter, *Article 31(3)(c) of the Vienna Convention on the Law of Treaties and the Principle of Systemic Integration in International Investment Law and Arbitration* (Nomos 2015).

[43] Bruno Simma and Theodore Kill, 'Harmonizing Investment Protection and International Human Rights: First Steps towards a Methodology' in Christina Binder and others (eds), *International Investment Law for the 21st Century: Essays in Honour of Christoph Schreuer* (OUP 2009) 678, 691–702.

[44] See Katharina Berner, 'Reconciling Investment Protection and Sustainable Development: A Plea for an Interpretative U-Turn' in Hindelang and Krajewski (n 32) 177.

[45] See International Law Commission, 'Fragmentation of International Law: Difficulties Arising from the Diversification and Expansion of International Law. Report of the Study Group on the Fragmentation of International Law. Finalized by Martti Koskenniemi' (13 April 2006) UN Doc A/CN.4/L.682, 209. See also eg Berner (n 44); Simma and Kill (n 43); Tamar Meshel, 'Human Rights in Investor-State Arbitration: The Human Right to Water and Beyond' (2015) 6 JIDS 277, 302–04; Luke Eric Peterson, 'Human Rights and Bilateral Investment Treaties: Mapping the Role of Human Rights Law within Investor-State Arbitration' (2009) Rights & Democracy (International Centre for Human Rights and Democratic Development) 22; Attila Tanzi, 'Public Interest Concerns in International Investment Arbitration in the Water Services Sector' in Tullio Treves, Francesco Seatzu and Seline Trevisanut (eds) *Foreign Investment, International Law and Common Concerns* (Routledge 2013) 318, 329. See also the arbitral decisions in *EDF International SA, SAUR International SA, and León Participaciones Argentina SA v The Argentine Republic*, ICSID Case No ARB/03/23, Award (11 June 2012) para 909; *Tulip Real Estate and Development Netherlands BV v Republic of Turkey*, ICSID Case No ARB/11/28, Decision on Annulment (30 December 2015) paras 86–92; *Urbaser SA and Consorcio de Aguas Bilbao Bizkaia, Bilbao Biskaia Ur Partzuergoa v The Argentine Republic*, ICSID Case No ARB/07/26, Award (8 December 2016) paras 1193–1210.

[46] Fahner and Happold (n 5) 749–56.

[47] *Noble Ventures, Inc v Romania*, ICSID Case No ARB/01/11, Award (12 October 2005) para 52.

When assessing the host State's balance of interests within the scope of the substantive protection standards in the specific case, the tribunal then has to make an assessment on the basis of proportionality.[48] Proportionality entails notably that '[a]ny changes to laws and policies or inconsistent administrative treatment of investors must be justifiable on the basis of public policy'.[49] Important in this balancing exercise is that none of the legal areas concerned can per se be regarded as inferior: public international law protects investors and their property rights as well as human rights other than those that are in the investor's interest. That is why an adequate balance exercise needs to respect each one of them and try to make both as effective as possible on a case-by-case basis.

If an investment tribunal in such a balance of interest fails to take into account all of a host State's human rights or sustainable development obligations, this would not only be methodologically unsound. It may also risk arbitrarily reconfiguring the normative foundations of the rule of law, thereby delegitimizing certain interests pursued in regulation. However, it must be stressed that, while one can be critical of the outcome in individual cases, as long as the relevant investment tribunals faithfully follow the methodology provided in public international law, particular in the VCLT, there is no issue with the normative foundations of the rule of law. Such critique would then be of a political rather than legal nature. Investment tribunals do not need to address each and every issue somehow related to the case but only issues necessary to decide on the admissible claims presented before it; otherwise it would risk acting *ultra petita*.

IV. Human Rights and Sustainable Development Concerns in Arbitral Tribunal's Views

With the interpretive tools that public international law offers in mind, we now scrutinize how arbitral tribunals reconciled the different interests at stake when resolving investor-State disputes. Thereby, we evaluate whether the risk of IIL loosening its bonds with the normative foundations of rule of law materialized in certain decisions. The trend in IIAs to more effectively protect States' right to regulate and address human rights and sustainable development concerns is recent. As long as 'old' IIAs remain the basis for tribunals' decisions, a particular attention to systemic integration between the said concerns and investor interests is critical.

In the mid-2010s, a commentator suggested that 'arbitration tribunals are uniquely placed to strengthen and promote important human rights norms ... that may be negatively impacted by investment protection measures', were these tribunals ready to become 'more sensitive not only to the interests of foreign investors'.[50] In fact, arbitral tribunals are more and more showing that sensitivity: eg the tribunal in *Continental v Argentina* ruled that only an interpretation of IIAs 'that accommodates the different interests and concerns of the parties in conformity with its terms accords with an effective interpretation of the treaty'.[51] And as found by the tribunal in *Urbaser v Argentina*, this is even more the case

---

[48] Caroline Henckels, *Proportionality and Deference in Investor-State Arbitration. Balancing Investment Protection and Regulatory Autonomy* (CUP 2015) 74.

[49] Bücheler (n 39) 132–36.

[50] Meshel (n 45) 278.

[51] *Continental Casualty v Argentine Republic*, ICSID Case No ARB/03/9, Award (5 September 2008) para 181.

where the IIA itself instructs the tribunal to make its decision, where appropriate, by reference to other treaties in force between the parties as well as general principles of public international law.[52]

As we show in our analysis of selected arbitral decisions below,[53] the situation appears not quite so clear-cut when it comes to balancing and reconciling competing interests in foreign investment disputes. We address human rights more generally (Section A); indigenous peoples' rights (Section B); health (Section C); the right to water (Section D); environment protection (Section E). In conclusion, we provide a comparative perspective of the treatment of these public interests by investments tribunals (Section F).

A. Human Rights

Traditionally very few, if any, investment protection agreements mentioned human rights,[54] and investor-State arbitral tribunals do generally not have jurisdiction to hold States liable for breach of their human rights obligations.[55] Nevertheless, investor-State arbitration is not 'splendidly isolated from the dynamics and tensions of the rest of the legal universe'.[56] Arbitral tribunals are increasingly relying on human rights, and, in a number of cases, have anchored their assessment in international human rights regimes or judicial decisions stemming from those frameworks.[57] This reflects a general acknowledgement that respect for human rights is of importance also for investors, even if human rights are binding only on States or other parties to the relevant treaties and do not create obligations on companies. According to the United Nations Guiding Principles on Business and Human Rights (UNGPs), private entities have the 'responsibility to respect human rights', but only States have a 'duty to protect'.[58]

For example, where investors' claims of human rights violations by the host State are raised as part of an alleged breach of the substantive protection standards in an IIA, they have often been accepted by arbitral tribunals as falling within the scope of their jurisdiction.[59] Also, States may rely on human rights obligations as a defence to an investor's claim if the human rights of other persons than the investor cannot be protected otherwise.[60] The tribunal in *Suez v Argentina*, for instance, stressed that Argentina is subject to both

---

[52] *Urbaser* (n 45) para 1201, referring to art X(5) of the underlying BIT.

[53] For an example of a more systematic analysis of human rights references by arbitration tribunals, see Steininger (n 6).

[54] Marc Jacob, 'International Investment Agreements and Human Rights' (2010) INEF Research Paper Series: Human Rights, Corporate Responsibility and Sustainable Development 03/2010.

[55] Peterson (n 45) 25.

[56] Bruno Simma, 'Foreign Investment Arbitration: A Place for Human Rights?' (2011) 60 ICLQ 573, 576.

[57] See Steininger (n 6) 38–45; Filip Balcerzak, *Investor-State Arbitration and Human Rights* (Brill Nijhoff 2017); Pierre-Marie Dupuy, Francesco Francioni and Ernst-Ulrich Petersmann (eds), *Human Rights in International Investment Law and Arbitration* (OUP 2009); Dupuy and Viñuales (n 12); Jacob (n 54); Meshel (n 45); Peterson (n 45); Simma (n 56); Jorge Daniel Taillant and Jonathan Bonnitcha, 'International Investment Law and Human Rights' in Marie-Claire Cordonnier Segger, Markus W Gehring and Andrew Newcombe (eds), *Sustainable Development in World Investment Law* (Wolters Kluwer 2011) 53, 78–79.

[58] Office of the United Nations High Commissioner on Human Rights, 'UN Guiding Principles on Business and Human Rights: Implementing the United Nations "Protect, Respect, and Remedy" Framework' (UN 2011) Principle 11.

[59] *Grand River Enterprises* (n 27) para 219; Meshel (n 45) 280; Filip Balcerzak, 'Jurisdiction of Tribunals in Investor-State Arbitration and the Issue of Human Rights' (2014) 29 ICSID Rev—FILJ 216, 224.

[60] See Meshel (n 45) 280–81.

international obligations, human rights, and investment protection, and must and can re-spect both of them.[61] In *EDF v Argentina*, the tribunal confirmed that it 'should be sensi-tive to international jus cogens norms, including basic principles of human rights' and that human rights could have 'potential significance or relevance' in connection with IIL.[62] The tribunal approached the question of human rights as a factor in the balance of interests to be established in order to find a compensable violation of the substantive protection stand-ards in an IIA. But both in this case and in a number of other cases arising from the 2001–02 economic and social crisis in Argentina, the host State's human rights defence was rejected for lack of evidence that human rights were at stake, and the tribunals did not consider Argentina's measures justified on that basis.[63]

In *Urbaser v Argentina*, the tribunal addressed a counterclaim by Argentina. The tribunal rejected first 'that the BIT is to be construed as an isolated set of rules of international law for the sole purpose of protecting investments through rights exclusively granted to investors'.[64] Turning to the question of human rights obligations, referring explicitly to the UNGPs, as well as to the 1948 Universal Declaration of Human Rights and the 1966 International Covenant on Economic, Social and Cultural Rights (ICESCR), it held that 'it must neces-sarily ... be ensured that no ... individual or entity, public or private, may act in disregard of such rights'.[65] With reference to the systemic integration principle contained in the VCLT's rules of treaty interpretation, the tribunal then stated that:

> the BIT cannot be interpreted and applied in a vacuum. The tribunal must certainly be mindful of the BIT's special purpose as a Treaty promoting foreign investments, but it cannot do so without taking the relevant rules of international law into account. The BIT has to be construed in harmony with other rules of international law of which it forms part, including those relating to human rights.[66]

By contrast, commentators who criticize arbitral tribunals for not analysing human rights arguments[67] point to other cases in which arbitral tribunals failed to engage at all with human rights. For example, in *Houben v Burundi*, the investor claimed in relation to the FPS standard that Burundi not only should have prevented the squatting on the investor's prop-erty, but it should also have endeavoured to expel the squatters.[68] The tribunal did not ad-dress Burundi's argument that expelling the squatters would arguably have been in breach

---

[61] *Suez, Sociedad General de Aguas de Barcelona, SA and Vivendi Universal, SA v Argentine Republic*, ICSID Case No ARB/03/19, Decision on Liability (30 July 2010) para 240.

[62] *EDF* (n 45) paras 909 and 912.

[63] ibid paras 912–14; *CMS Gas Transmission Company v Argentina*, ICSID Case No ARB/01/8, Award (12 May 2005) para 121; *Siemens AG v The Argentine Republic*, ICSID Case No ARB/02/08, Award (6 February 2007) para 79; *Sempra Energy International v The Argentine Republic*, ICSID Case No ARB/02/16, Award (28 September 2007) para 332. One tribunal found, however, that temporary measures could have been justified: *LG&E Energy Corp, LG&E Capital Corp and LG&E International Inc v The Argentine Republic*, ICSID Case No ARB/02/1, Decision on Liability (3 October 2006) para 267.

[64] *Urbaser* (n 45) para 1189.

[65] ibid para 1196. See also ibid para 1195 (referring to UN Guiding Principles (n 58) Principles 11–13, 23) and para 1196 (referring to UN General Assembly, 'Universal Declaration of Human Rights' (10 December 1948) UN Doc A/RES/217(III), arts 1, 21(2), 25(1) and 30; and para 1197, referring to International Covenant on Economic, Social and Cultural Rights (opened for signature 16 December 1966, entered into force 3 January 1976) 993 UNTS 3 (hereafter ICESCR) arts 5(1), 11(1), 12).

[66] *Urbaser* (n 45) para 1200; cf *Tulip* (n 45) paras 86–92.

[67] Taillant and Bonnitcha (n 57) 77–79; Fahner and Happold (n 5) 749.

[68] *Houben* (n 25) para 168.

of Article 17 of the International Covenant on Civil and Political Rights,[69] and rather considered that it was only Burundi's failure to 'prevent, *a priori*, these usurpers from taking possession of the land' that was to be assessed.[70] Critics see this as an example of 'evasion', being a common and frequent response to human rights defences in investment arbitration.[71] A scholar has concluded that arbitral tribunals 'adopt a quite consistent approach with regard to the *non*-significant role of international human rights law in investment disputes',[72] even though the same tribunals recognize the significance of other international law frameworks.

Nevertheless, whether there still is such a degree of consistency underpinning tribunals' decision can be questioned. Even if a tribunal, like in *Urbaser v Argentina*,[73] concludes that no fundamental human rights were at stake and, thus, could not legitimize the host State's measures, that does not necessarily reflect a lack of concern for human rights. As mentioned, in the tribunal's reasonings, the concern for human rights was clearly present, as different international human rights regimes were referred to, and it was stressed that no actor should disregard human rights. However, States wishing to restrict the right to property in order to protect other human rights must demonstrate that it is not possible to pursue both objectives at the same time, for example by less restrictive means. As the tribunal in *von Pezold v Zimbabwe* found, it is not acceptable to fail to dislodge squatters and even violate *erga omnes* obligations on account of what amounts to racial discrimination against investors, even against the background of retribution and reparation for previous racial discrimination suffered by the majority of the State's citizens.[74] A fair balance of all interests involved must be ensured.

On the whole, arbitral tribunals are increasingly relying on human rights and are open to take into account human rights interests of actors other than investors through systemic integration and harmonious interpretation. It remains to be seen whether tribunals will follow this lead in the future in a consistent manner. So far, arbitral tribunals have been too often too reluctant concerning the protection of human rights, thereby potentially exposing themselves to the critique of loosening the bonds with the rule of law.

B. Indigenous Peoples' Rights

Regarding the rights of indigenous people, tribunals have not always engaged in depth with these rights and their protection under public international law. In *Glamis Gold v USA*, the tribunal was aware of the interests of indigenous peoples, and the 'tension sometimes seen between private rights in property and the need of the State to regulate the use of property'.[75] The award even referred to the World Heritage Convention as an incorporated part

---

[69] International Covenant on Civil and Political Rights (opened for signature 19 December 1966, entered into force 23 March 1976) 999 UNTS 171, art 17.

[70] *Houben* (n 25) para 177, as translated from the French original by Fahner and Happold (n 5) 745, n 21.

[71] Fahner and Happold (n 5) 749.

[72] Moshe Hirsch, *Invitation to the Sociology of International Law* (OUP 2015) 139.

[73] *Urbaser* (n 45) paras 1210, 1220.

[74] *Bernhard von Pezold and ors v Republic of Zimbabwe*, ICSID Case No ARB/10/15, Award (28 July 2015) paras 638–57.

[75] Arbitral Tribunal constituted under ch 11 of the North American Free Trade Agreement in accordance with the United Nations Commission on International Trade Law (UNCITRAL) Arbitration Rules *Glamis Gold, Ltd v United States of America*, UNCITRAL, Award (8 June 2009) para 8.

of the applicable domestic law.[76] Still, the tribunal came to conclude that it was 'not required to decide many of the most controversial issues raised in this proceeding',[77] even if they were somehow related to the case.[78]

By contrast, in *Grand River v USA*, the tribunal discussed indigenous peoples' rights. It did so in light of a claim related to the FET standard that the respondent had 'an obligation of non-discrimination against special or disadvantaged groups', one of the investors being a Native American citizen of a foreign country, and that a duty of proactive consultation and to attempt to 'ameliorate' the impact of respondents' measure would follow therefrom.[79] The tribunal found that a duty to consult may exist as part of customary international law and as an obligation for States stemming from the UN Declaration on the Rights of Indigenous Peoples.[80] Even if the customary status of this regime and more specifically the provision on consultation had been disputed by the respondent, the tribunal stated: 'It may well be … that there does exist a principle of customary international law requiring governmental authorities to consult indigenous peoples on governmental policies or actions significantly affecting them.'[81] In particular, this would have been relevant in relation to the governments of the Native American tribes or nations 'whose members and sovereign interests could, and apparently are, being affected' by the respondents' measures to regulate commerce in tobacco.[82] However, this obligation would not apply to the investor individually.[83] The tribunal's approach was thus one interpretation of the IIA's substantive protection standards in light of the respondent's international commitments to protect indigenous rights, and then to establish what it meant for the investor. Thereby, the tribunal followed the methodology of systemic integration.

In *Bear Creek v Peru*, which concerned a mining project in an area close to indigenous communities and notably the question whether the investor had obtained 'social license' to proceed with the project, the award stated that while 'the concept of *"social license"* is not clearly defined in international law, all relevant international instruments are clear that consultations with indigenous communities are to be made with the purpose of obtaining consent from all the relevant communities'.[84] By establishing that international legal frameworks protecting indigenous rights are to be taken into account when assessing not only the host State's conduct, but also the investor's, this finding alone already shows the impact of systemic integration. While the majority did not find that the relevant international regimes as such establish a duty and potentially a failure to comply by the investor,[85] *Bear Creek v*

---

[76] ibid para 84, referring to Convention for the Protection of the World Cultural and Natural Heritage (opened for signature 16 November 1972, entered into force 17 December 1975) 1037 UNTS 151, preamble and arts 5 and 8–11 (World Heritage Convention).

[77] *Glamis Gold* (n 75) para 84; see the critique of the exclusion of the concerned indigenous people as a 'mischaracterization of human rights stakes' by Julien Cantegreil, 'Implementing Human Rights in the NAFTA Regime—The Potential of a Pending Case: *Glamis Corp v USA*' in Dupuy, Francioni and Petersmann (n 57) 367, 385–89.

[78] Fahner and Happold (n 5) 748.

[79] *Grand River Enterprises* (n 27) para 205.

[80] ibid paras 210–11, referring to UN General Assembly, 'United Nations Declaration on the Rights of Indigenous Peoples' (13 September 2007) UN Doc A/RES/61/295, art 19.

[81] *Grand River Enterprises* (n 27) para 210.

[82] ibid para 212.

[83] ibid paras 211–13.

[84] *Bear Creek Mining Corporation v Republic of Peru*, ICSID Case No ARB/14/21, Award (30 November 2017) para 406, referring to United Nations Declaration on the Rights of Indigenous Peoples (n 80) art 32.

[85] *Bear Creek Mining*, ibid, para 664.

Peru has contributed further to the debate about foreign investors' obligations to comply with human rights and sustainable development regimes.[86]

Even if there are still only a few cases where arbitral tribunals have shown awareness of indigenous rights, there seems to be an increasing openness to take note of such rights, which in turn reduces the risk of loosening the bonds with this part of the normative foundations of the rule of law. However, as shown in *Glamis Gold v USA*, awareness does not necessarily mean that investment tribunals take indigenous peoples' rights into account.

C. Public Health

Investor claims in relation to public health measures, namely in relation to tobacco products, have raised fears of 'regulatory chill', meaning that host States might be hesitant to regulate in favour of public health for fear of facing a potentially costly investment claim.[87] The perspective on claims relating to tobacco has changed since the late 1990s and early 2000s, where public health concerns were not accounted for in tribunals' decisions, as respondent States at that time hardly ever justified the disputed measures by those concerns.[88]

More recently, however, in *Philip Morris v Uruguay*, the tribunal established that the matter was 'to be decided on the basis of the BIT itself and other applicable rules of international law'.[89] When assessing whether the FET standard had been breached, the tribunal noted that the Uruguayan measures 'were adopted in an effort to give effect to general obligations' under the World Health Organization's Framework Convention on Tobacco Control (FCTC).[90] Dismissing all the investor's claims on the merits and burdening the investor with all costs, the tribunal's decision has been seen as 'an important turning point in investment arbitration case-law' because of the engagement of the tribunal with human rights in general and the human right to health in particular.[91] The tribunal's assessment of the FET standard's scope also appears as methodologically apt, taking into account other international obligations of the respondent connected to human rights. In *Philip Morris v Australia*, the tribunal decided that the investor's claim was inadmissible[92] and did not directly address the FCTC.[93] However, the tribunal upheld entirely the respondent's claims on

---

[86] Jean-Michel Marcoux and Andrew Newcombe, '*Bear Creek Mining Corporation v Republic of Peru*' (2018) 33 ICSID Rev—FILJ 653, 658–59, referring to *Urbaser* (n 45) para 1199.

[87] Elizabeth Sheargold and Andrew D Mitchell, 'Public Health in International Investment Law and Arbitration' in Julien Chaisse, Leïla Choukroune and Sufian Jusoh (eds), *Handbook of International Investment Law and Policy* (Springer 2019) 13.

[88] Valentina Sara Vadi, 'Reconciling Public Health and Investor Rights: The Case of Tobacco' in Dupuy, Francioni and Petersmann (n 57) 452, 466, referring to *Marvin Roy Feldman Karpa v United Mexican States*, ICSID Case No ARB(AF)/99/1, Award (16 December 2002), where the concerned tax legislation in fact could according to the analysis be qualified as a support for 'health dumping' since its aim was to encourage Mexican tobacco exports.

[89] *Philip Morris v Uruguay* (n 41) para 179.

[90] ibid para 401, referring to WHO Framework Convention on Tobacco Control (concluded 21 May 2003 and entered into force 27 February 2005) 2302 UNTS 166.

[91] Monica Feria-Tinta, 'Like Oil and Water? Human Rights in Investment Arbitration in the *Wake of Philip Morris v. Uruguay*' (2017) 34 J Intl Arb 601, 624–25.

[92] *Philip Morris Asia Limited v The Commonwealth of Australia*, UNCITRAL Case No 2012-12, Award on Jurisdiction and Admissibility (17 December 2015) para 585.

[93] *Philip Morris v Australia*, ibid, Australia's Response to the Notice of Arbitration, 21 December 2011) paras 16–17, referring to WHO Framework Convention on Tobacco Control (n 90).

costs, in view of 'in particular the relevance of the outcome in respect of Australia's policies in matters of public health'.[94]

From these decisions, it can be deduced that the protection of public health has been recognized as an important public interest which can justify State measures interfering with foreign investors. The protection of public health, and more particularly the protection against the hazards of tobacco consumption, therefore, is the clearest example so far of a development where the risk of IIL loosening its connection with the normative foundations of the rule of law has been minimized.

D. The Right to Water

How arbitral tribunals dealt in the past with the right to water has been found to exemplify arbitral tribunals' reluctance to take human rights into account when it is the respondent State that raises human rights as a defence.[95] The *Urbaser v Argentina* decision has, however, been identified as an indication that tribunals are seeking to move away from this reluctance and engage more fully with the right to water as a human right.[96] The tribunal in that case recognized the human right to water and sanitation and that this right corresponds to the duty of the State to provide all persons living under its jurisdiction with safe and clean drinking water and sewage services.[97] It referred to the ICESCR where 'State Parties recognize the right of everyone to an adequate standard of living for himself and his family, including adequate food, clothing and housing, and to the continuous improvement of living conditions'.[98] According to the UN Committee on Economic, Social and Cultural Rights, 'the right to water clearly falls within the category of guarantees essential for securing an adequate standard of living, particularly since it is one of the most fundamental conditions for survival'.[99]

However, the *Urbaser v Argentina* tribunal did not consider that a private investor was, or could be, obliged to ensure the population's access to water on the basis of international law, as the acceptance of a concession contract could not have the effect that the obligations arising out of this contract should become—in addition or in parallel to the host State's obligations based on international law—an investors' obligation under international law. An obligation to provide water and sewage services can only be based on the host State's domestic law, and contracts with the investor or concessions granted to it.[100] Therefore, an investor failing to fulfil a contractual obligation would not be committing a human rights violation. The tribunal in *Urbaser v Argentina* can be found to have applied the dichotomy between private actors needing to respect human rights but States having to protect these rights.[101] This approach also may be said to reduce the risk of substantive investment

---

[94] *Philip Morris v Australia* (n 92) Final Award Regarding Costs (8 July 2017) para 101.

[95] See Meshel (n 45); Tanzi (n 45) 320–23.

[96] Feria-Tinta (n 91) 626–29. Acknowledging this engagement but seeing it as an 'overcomplication': Edward Guntrip, 'Private Actors, Public Goods and Responsibility for the Right to Water in International Investment Law: An Analysis of *Urbaser v. Argentina*' (2018) 1 Brill Open Law 37.

[97] *Urbaser* (n 45) paras 1207–21.

[98] ICESCR (n 65) art 11(1).

[99] United Nations Economic and Social Council, 'General Comment No. 15 (2002) The Right to Water (arts 11 and 12 of the International Covenant on Economic, Social and Cultural Rights)' (20 January 2003) UN Doc E/C.12/2002/11, para 3.

[100] *Urbaser* (n 45) para 1220.

[101] Guntrip (n 96) 52–59.

protection standards becoming disconnected from the normative foundations of the rule of law.

E. Environment

Arbitral tribunals' decisions involving environmental issues have been of particular importance to underline that, in general, non-discriminatory regulatory action does not amount to expropriation and, thus, does not entitle an investor to compensation.[102] But even if the scope for police powers to be exerted to protect the environment seems rather generous as such, in many cases arbitral tribunals have rejected the arguments of the respondent State, as in *Tecmed v Mexico*.[103] In turn, the tribunal in *Glamis Gold v USA* did not see itself required to decide on environmental issues because of its case-specific mandate.[104] It acknowledged however the legislator's attempt to balance on the one hand the respect for mining claims and availability of as much public land as possible for mineral exploration and development with, on the other hand, other potential uses for the land and the need to protect its scenic, scientific, and environmental values against undue impairment and pollution.[105]

In *S.D. Myers v Canada*, the tribunal proceeded to interpret the relevant IIA provisions in light of the VCLT's general rule of interpretation,[106] and while it did not mention explicitly Article 31(3)(c) containing the principle of systemic integration, it reviewed the respondent's international commitments relating to the environment.[107] This analysis became relevant in the assessment of whether the measures that gave rise to the claim were discriminatory in a way that they would contradict the standard of national treatment.[108] The tribunal considered that Canada pursued a 'legitimate goal' consistent with one of the international environmental regimes it had committed to, but that the method of pursuing that goal did indeed breach the protection provided to the investor.[109]

By contrast, in *Chemtura v Canada*, concerned with the prohibition of the sale and use of a certain chemical ingredient in a seed treatment product, the tribunal stated not only that Canada acted in accordance with Canada's international obligations,[110] but

---

[102] See *Tecmed* (n 41) para 119; *SD Myers, Inc v Government of Canada*, UNCITRAL, Partial Award (13 November 2000) paras 281–88; *Saluka Investments BV v The Czech Republic* UNCITRAL, Partial Award (17 March 2006) para 262; *Chemtura Corporation v Government of Canada (formerly Crompton Corporation v Government of Canada)*, UNCITRAL, Award (2 August 2010) para 266; *Methanex Corporation v United States of America*, UNCITRAL, Final Award of the Tribunal on Jurisdiction and Merits, 3 August 2005, pt IV, ch D, para 7.

[103] *Tecmed* (n 41) paras 119–51.

[104] *Glamis Gold* (n 75) para 8.

[105] ibid para 48.

[106] *SD Myers* (n 102) para 201.

[107] ibid paras 204–21, referring to the Agreement between the Government of Canada and the Government of the United States of America concerning the Transboundary Movement of Hazardous Waste (signed 28 October 1986, entered into force 8 November 1986) CTS 1986/39; the Basel Convention on the Control of Transboundary Movements of Hazardous Wastes and their Disposal (concluded 22 March 1989, entered into force 5 May 1992) 1673 UNTS 57; North American Agreement on Environmental Cooperation (opened for signature 14 September 1993, entered into force 1 January 1994) CTS 1994/2.

[108] *SD Myers* (n 102) paras 252–57; see Nadakavukaren Schefer (n 17) 376 for a definition of the standard.

[109] *SD Myers* (n 102) paras 255–56.

[110] *Chemtura* (n 102) paras 138–43, referring to Protocol to the Convention on Long-Range Transboundary Air Pollution on Persistent Organic Pollutants (opened for signature 24 June 1998, entered into force 23 October 2003) 2230 UNTS 79.

moreover concluded that the measures 'constituted a valid exercise of the Respondent's police powers'.[111] The tribunal thus assessed the scope of the FET standard as restricted by the State's compliance with its international obligations.

More recently, decisions taken in the wake of *Urbaser v Argentina* seem to indicate that arbitral tribunals have become more receptive to host States' counterclaims on environmental issues and the argument that also investors should be subjected to international law obligations.[112] In *David Aven v Costa Rica*, while it has been pointed out that 'the obligations enforced by the tribunal had their origin in national rather than international law',[113] part of the national law in question consisted in incorporated multilateral environment treaties.[114] The tribunal found that the relevant IIA provision could be interpreted as meaning that an investor ignoring or breaching host State environmental protection measures would commit 'a breach of both domestic and international law' and that such 'provisions impose affirmative obligations on investors'.[115] In accordance with this point of view, the tribunal stated 'that the enforcement of environmental law is primarily to the states, but it cannot be admitted that a foreign investor could not be subject to international law obligations in this field'.[116] This would mean that investors have an implicit obligation flowing from public international law to abide by and comply with environmental regulations in the host State.[117] The tribunal's conclusion that, nevertheless, there were no 'affirmative obligations' imposed by the IIA upon investors,[118] seems contradictory,[119] or at least confusing.[120] In the end, the decision raises more questions about the extent to which investors actually can be held to have international law obligations regarding environment protection than it provided useful answers.[121] Still, in general also arbitral tribunals' decisions concerning environmental issues confirm a development towards a more open approach to take into account both the substantive protections in IIAs and other international legal regimes.

F. Findings

The short analysis of selected decisions by arbitral tribunals where human rights and sustainable development concerns were at stake shows that more and more of those decisions demonstrate that arbitral tribunals are mindful of rights and obligations stemming from

---

[111] *Chemtura* (n 102) para 266.

[112] Andreea Nica, '*David Aven v. Costa Rica*: An Aftershock of *Urbaser v. Argentina*?' (*Kluwer Arbitration Blog*, 12 December 2018), commenting on *David R Aven and ors v Republic of Costa Rica*, ICSID Case No UNCT/15/3, Award (18 September 2018); and referring to *Burlington Resources Inc v Republic of Ecuador*, ICSID Case No ARB/08/5, Decision on Counterclaims (7 February 2017); *Perenco Ecuador Ltd v The Republic of Ecuador and Empresa Estatal Petróleos del Ecuador (Petroecuador)*, ICSID Case No ARB/08/6.

[113] Rafael Tamayo-Álvarez, '*David Aven v Costa Rica*: A Step Forward towards Investor Accountability for Environmental Harm?' (2020) 29 RECIEL 301, 306.

[114] *David Aven* (n 112) para 423(b)–(c), referring to the Convention on wetlands of international importance especially as waterfowl habitat (opened for signature 2 February 1971, entered into force 21 December 1975) 996 UNTS 245; Convention on Biological Diversity (opened for signature 5 June 1992, entered into force 29 December 1993) 1760 UNTS 79.

[115] *David Aven* (n 112) paras 734–35.

[116] ibid para 737.

[117] Tamayo-Álvarez (n 113) 305.

[118] *David Aven* (n 112) para 743.

[119] Nica (n 112).

[120] Tamayo-Álvarez (n 113) 305.

[121] See Nica (n 112); Tamayo-Álvarez (n 113).

other international legal regimes, protecting human rights and other aspects of sustainable development. This is true also for disputes on the basis of IIAs which do not mention explicitly the right to regulate and/or rights and interests that compete with those of investors. While various public interests, in particular human rights, have figured in arbitral decisions in different ways, systemic integration and harmonious interpretation of various legal regimes involved in an investor-State dispute, as required by the VCLT's Article 31(3)(c), is becoming more and more commonplace amongst arbitral tribunals.

It should, however, be noted on an empirical level that not all tribunals then considered human rights or sustainable development issues relevant for their decisions, or that an acknowledgement led them to decide in favour of the State. For example, as much as *Urbaser v Argentina* is considered a landmark decision, the tribunal clearly—and following our analysis correctly—stated that the investor's interests could not be held to include a State-like obligation to provide for sustainable development elements like water, housing, and infrastructure.[122]

Notwithstanding the limited scope and selectivity of the discussion of arbitral decisions in this chapter, the cases suggest that more 'classical' human rights, such as the right to life are more easily and more favourably considered by tribunals than issues like the rights of indigenous peoples and the right to water. Indeed, other scholarship has likewise found that economic and social rights as well as third-generation human rights play a more limited role in investment arbitration.[123] However, one needs to keep in mind that in regard to these rights also the corresponding States' obligations are anything but clearly established and, it is to be recalled, that investors are not obliged in the same way as States, if at all, to protect these rights,[124] even less if human rights addressing economic, cultural, and social concerns are in question.

V. Risks for the Rule of Law? Ambiguity and Unevenness

From our review of arbitral decisions, when it comes to the question of potential risks for the normative foundations of the rule of law, a somewhat mixed picture emerges.[125] It is clear that a tribunal would no longer state, as has happened in the past, that since its 'competence is limited to commercial disputes', 'other matters—however compelling the claim or wrongful the act—are outside this Tribunal's jurisdiction'.[126] Yet, arbitral decisions, including recent ones such as *Urbaser v Argentina*, *Philip Morris v Uruguay*, or *David Aven v Costa Rica*, while showing an awareness of the need to take into account relevant human rights and sustainable development concerns, are not necessarily without their own ambiguities.[127] Not without reason have scholars pointed out that arbitral tribunals so far 'have

---

[122] *Urbaser* (n 45) para 1220.
[123] Steininger (n 6) 56.
[124] UN Guiding Principles (n 58) Principles 1 and 11.
[125] See similarly the conclusion by Schill and Djanic (n 4) 53–55.
[126] *Antoine Biloune and Marine Drive Complex Ltd v Ghana Investments Centre and the Government of Ghana*, UNCITRAL Award on Jurisdiction and Liability (27 October 1989) para 61, quoted by Steininger (n 6) 44.
[127] See similarly Rudall (n 32) 461–67.

not developed a coherent methodology for evaluating the human rights dimensions of in-vestment disputes'.[128]

Arbitrators can be justifiably presumed to be both competent and willing to apply the principle of systemic integration and a harmonious interpretation of relevant treaty com-mitments. But the tribunal decisions they contribute to have not always shown it when ad-dressing the relationship between IIL, on the one hand, and human rights and sustainable development concerns, on the other. One aspect might be sociological: the professional background of arbitrators has tended to be one where human rights concerns have not been a major focus in their careers, while the relationship between IIL practitioners and human rights law practitioners has appeared somewhat adversarial in the past.[129] As scholars have recently advanced, this sociological factor might lead to a bias by arbitrators to view in-vestor rights as endowments and other human rights and sustainable development con-cerns as 'aspirational'.[130]

Another reason might have more fundamental implications for IIL and its application by arbitral tribunals: the asymmetric enforceability of different international legal frame-works.[131] Acknowledging this issue—rather disturbingly—goes to the heart of why IIL is depicted as one of the strongest parts of an 'international rule of law': the strength of its enforcement mechanisms, especially through investor-State dispute settlement (ISDS).[132] Revealingly, when human rights frameworks allow for judicial decisions like the European Court of Human Rights, it 'certainly facilitates the transfer of norms and legal standards enshrined in case law'.[133] However, the institutionalization of a legal framework—its ap-pearance of 'solidity'—should not determine whether it is being taken into account. This is the case when arbitral tribunals improperly draw upon other well-established legal regimes whose notions come in handy to approach specific issues.[134] But even more relevant in light of this contribution is the risk that tribunals ignore the relevance of other legal regimes that appear less 'solid'. Such ignorance is especially a danger when IIL is wrongly approached as some sort of a self-contained regime.[135]

Even if an arbitral tribunal considers other legal regimes reflecting non-investor-related interests, these interests might still find themselves placed at a fundamental disadvantage compared to the investors' in the tribunal's prioritization.[136] Unlike 'evasion' of human rights and sustainable development concerns, 'prioritization' addresses them, and its out-come might eventually not differ from what a harmonious interpretation would have led

---

[128] Vivian Kube and Ernst-Ulrich Petersmann, 'Human Rights Law in International Investment Arbitration' in Filippo Fontanelli, Andrea Gattini and Attila Tanzi (eds), *General Principles of Law and International Investment Arbitration* (Brill 2018) 221, 245.

[129] See Hirsch (n 72) 128–56.

[130] Broude and Henckels (n 7) 105.

[131] This passage reflects feedback by the editors on a previous draft, which is gratefully acknowledged.

[132] Živković (n 2) 10–12.

[133] Steininger (n 6) 48.

[134] See as an example the critique of an arbitration tribunal's resort to World Trade Organization law by José E Alvarez, 'Beware: Boundary Crossings—A Critical Appraisal of Public Law Approaches to International Investment Law' (2016) 17 JWIT 171, 195–203, discussing *Continental Casualty* (n 51).

[135] The (self-)perception of IIL as being such 'solid' legal framework may also have contributed to arbitrators' willingness to consider previous decisions from other arbitral tribunals as de facto precedents, discussed critically by Steffen Hindelang, 'Study on Investor-State Dispute Settlement ("ISDS") and Alternatives of Dispute Resolution in International Investment Law' in Pieter Jan Kuijper and others, *Investor-State Dispute Settlement Provisions in the EU's International Investment Agreements. Volume 2— Studies* (European Parliament 2014) 66–69.

[136] See Broude and Henckels (n 7) and Fahner and Happold (n 5) 758.

to.[137] Yet, as an approach, prioritization might bias outcomes to be different from what a harmonious interpretation would induce. One example for such a bias is pointed out by scholars: tribunals would tend to treat human rights and sustainable development concerns other than an investor's as 'aspirational', take them into account differently from investor interests, or let investor interest prevail when in competition with the said concerns.[138] Supporting that argument is another scholarly finding that while investor's interests can be operationalized through IIL's apparently clear-cut, more 'solid' legal framework, this is, for example, more elusive for indigenous peoples' rights or cultural heritage.[139] The international legal regimes addressing the latter concerns might accordingly fail to create crystallized, palpable decisions to which a clear legal 'value' can be attributed that could then be operationalized in an investment arbitration. In such a situation, arbitrators may be seen as simply reluctant to deal with human rights or sustainable development concerns of which the manifestation at international level tends to be legally more elusive than decisions of established human rights courts or of arbitral tribunals which are more easily at hand to be referred to.[140]

What can be done to address evasion or biased prioritization that may risk compromission of the normative foundations of the rule of law through tribunals' application of substantive investment protection standards? First, it should be noted that IIAs have only recently started to explicitly state the relevance of human rights and sustainable development concerns. If included in IIAs, such provisions stress and reaffirm the duty of arbitral tribunals to consider human rights and other legal frameworks on sustainable development when solving a dispute. Our findings suggest that while tribunals theoretically can be expected to apply eg the VCLT's rules of interpretation, making IIA references to the VCLT superfluous,[141] empirically they might benefit from clearer guidance provided by IIAs on how an investment protection obligation should be interpreted and understood in light of human rights and sustainable development commitments.[142]

Were one to aggregate the approaches found in recent IIAs in terms of integrating IIL and human rights and sustainable development concerns into a model IIA,[143] the starting point remains the right of the contracting parties to regulate as the general vehicle for such integration, as mentioned in IIAs' preambles and increasingly further operationalized in specific provisions. On that basis, the scope of IIL's substantive protection standards can be defined in reference to human rights and sustainable development concerns as legitimate interests to be pursued by the host State. References to such concerns can be more firmly anchored by mentioning specific legal instruments. For example, the 2019 Netherlands Model BIT links environmental protection to the Paris Agreement, labour standards to the fundamental ILO Conventions, and human rights to the Universal Declaration on Human

---

[137] Fahner and Happold (n 5) 758–59.
[138] See Broude and Henckels (n 7).
[139] Valentina Vadi, *Cultural Heritage in International Investment Law and Arbitration* (CUP 2014) 232–33.
[140] See Berner (n 44).
[141] As pointed out by one of the editors in a comment on an earlier draft.
[142] See Rudall (n 32) 467; Peterson (n 45) 45; Meshel (n 45) 300.
[143] A related suggestion of 'model clauses'is made by Pia Acconci, 'The Integration of Non-Investment Concerns as an Opportunity for the Modernization of International Investment Law: Is a Multilateral Approach Desirable?' in Giorgio Sacerdoti and others (eds), *General Interests of Host States in International Investment Law* (CUP 2014) 165, 188. The findings result from a search in IIAs and Model BITs in UNCTAD's IIA Mapping Project database (n 35) for human rights, sustainable development, environment, and labour rights references, as well as references to the VCLT.

Rights.[144] Even commitments binding upon the investor to fulfil international obligations with regard to human rights and sustainable development have appeared.[145] Lastly, IIAs increasingly reference and stress the application of the VCLT, notably its rules of interpretation and thereby its systemic integration approach.[146]

However, these recent developments in IIAs are in themselves not sufficient to address the challenges relating to the integration of IIL with international human rights and sustainable development concerns. In fact, those developments are ambiguous, and only some States and the EU have rather vigorously pursued them. Neither have many IIA parties so far followed the lead provided by the work of the UN Conference on Trade and Development (UNCTAD) on updating the IIL regime, also with a view to strengthen its contribution to sustainable development. UNCTAD's roadmap of 2015 considers safeguarding the right to regulate while providing protection to investments as well as enhancing systemic consistency as priorities.[147] Another issue addressed by UNCTAD is the interpretation of IIAs.[148] A Working Group of the UN Commission on International Trade Law has been discussing the need and possible options for an ISDS reform since 2017,[149] including questions of contracting State parties' involvement and control mechanisms with regard to the interpretation of IIAs.[150] A multilateral framework at near universal level could be an appropriate way to address integration between IIL and other international legal regimes.[151] However, such a framework is still a work in progress with (very) uncertain prospects as it appears to be extremely challenging to achieve consensus around it. It is, therefore, still critical that arbitral tribunals foster systemic integration in practice in order to keep the connection between IIL and the normative foundations of the rule of law appropriately ensured.

VI. Conclusion

IIL and its substantive protections standards entail potential risks in relation to the rule of law's normative foundations. Even with recent IIAs referring increasingly to human rights and sustainable development concerns,[152] currently arbitral tribunals have to address

---

[144] Netherlands Model Investment Agreement: Agreement on Reciprocal Promotion and Protection of Investments between … and the Kingdom of the Netherlands (adopted 22 March 2019) art 6.6 <https://investmen tpolicy.unctad.org/international-investment-agreements/treaty-files/5832/download> accessed 23 July 2021, referring to Paris Agreement (concluded 12 December 2015, entered into force 4 November 2016) <https://treat ies.un.org/Pages/ViewDetails.aspx?src=IND&mtdsg_no=XXVII-7-d&chapter=27&clang=_en> accessed 23 July 2021, and Universal Declaration of Human Rights (n 65).

[145] Morocco–Nigeria BIT (n 38) arts 15 and 18. Such commitments, however, could also serve as a tool to exclude well-founded investor claims.

[146] This is especially the case of the EU and the post-Brexit United Kingdom, as results from a search with the terms 'Vienna Convention' in the IIA Mapping Project database (n 35) show.

[147] United Nations Conference on Trade and Development, *World Investment Report 2015: Reforming International Investment Governance* (United Nations 2015), 127 and 128.

[148] United Nations Conference on Trade and Development, 'Interpretation of IIAs: What States Can Do' IIA issues Note No 3, December 2011, 9–10.

[149] See the website <uncitral.un.org/en/working_groups/3/investor-state> accessed 23 July 2021.

[150] United Nations Commission on International Trade Law, Working Group III (ISDS Reform), 'Possible Reform of Investor-State Dispute Settlement (ISDS): Interpretation of Investment Treaties by Treaty Parties, Note by the Secretariat' (17 January 2020) UN Doc A/CN.9/WG.III/WP.191.

[151] Acconci (n 143) 166.

[152] See, however, Wolfgang Alschner, *Investment Arbitration and State-Driven Reform: New Treaties, Old Outcomes* (OUP 2022) who is sceptical about whether the new language will bring about change in arbitral practice.

claims made mostly on the basis of IIAs that do not mention human rights or sustainable development explicitly. For the time being, we might just be left with 'muddling through', ie ambiguity and unevenness in tribunal decisions when addressing human rights and sustainable development issues. Critical scrutiny certainly continues to be warranted to identify and single out flaws in the approach of arbitral tribunals to systemic integration. On a positive note, in recent times, arbitral tribunals have tended to gradually overcome evasion and biased prioritization that are detrimental to human rights and sustainable development concerns. If this path is consistently pursued, and systemic integration and a harmonious interpretation that accounts for all relevant international legal regimes achieved, IIL can indeed be an effective tool to enforce the international rule of law, understood in a substantive fashion, based on normative foundations linked to human rights and sustainable development concerns.

15

International Investment Agreements, Investor Obligations, and the Rule of Law

Susan L. Karamanian[*]

I. Introduction

International investment agreements (IIAs) have been criticized for being pro-investor, as their sweeping promises to protect foreign investors, and their investments, are not matched by an equally rigorous set of investor obligations.[1] Many IIAs enable investors to sidestep national courts and pursue claims in arbitration against host States for breach of the IIA investment protections.[2] In investor-State dispute settlement (ISDS), host States face potential liability with limited, if any, involvement of their respective national judicial systems.[3]

Is a legal regime dedicated to foreign investors that lacks uniform and rigid investor obligations at odds with the rule of law?[4] Is it sufficient to counter any gap under international law by deferring to national legal systems, as surely a host State can enforce its laws regarding investor obligations in national courts? Yet, even if national systems can define and enforce investor obligations, why not consider IIAs as an additional means for host States to regulate foreign investors consistent with the former's governance obligations?

One could look at the original purpose of IIAs, namely, to encourage investment by protecting the investor as it deals with an uncertain, perhaps unfriendly, foreign legal landscape, and readily appreciate why IIAs should have no bearing on investor obligations. Yet, the text of many IIAs signals the regime is not only one-way. Considered within the broader

[*] Thanks to participants in the HBKU College of Law Research Forum, particularly Professor Ilias Bantekas, Professor Georgios Dimitropoulos, and Professor Damilola Olawuyi, for their insights and comments on a previous version. Thanks also to Johannes Tropper for his diligence and patience in handling administrative aspects of this submission.

[1] See eg Gus Van Harten, 'Five Justifications for Investment Treaties: A Critical Discussion' (2010) 2(1) TL & D 19, 26–27 (identifying pro-investor features of IIAs). See also Yulia Levashova, 'The Accountability and Corporate Social Responsibility of Multinational Corporations for Transgressions in Host States through International Investment Law' (2018) 14 Utrecht L Rev 40, 42 (describing IIA asymmetries).

[2] See UNCTAD, 'Investment Policy Hub' (providing access to IIAs) <https://investmentpolicy.unctad.org/> accessed 13 March 2022. See generally, Taylor St John, *The Rise of Investor-State Arbitration: Politics, Law and Unintended Consequences* (OUP 2018) (discussing the history of ISDS).

[3] Paul Michael Blyschak, 'State Consent, Investor Interests and the Future of Investment Arbitration: Reanalyzing the Jurisdiction of Investor-State Tribunals in Hard Cases' (2009) 9 Asper Rev Intl Bus & Trade Law 99, 134.

[4] Given the world's varying legal traditions, defining the 'rule of law' poses multiple challenges. International Law Association, 'Rule of Law and International Investment Law: Sydney Conference (2018)' <www.ila-hq.org/images/ILA/DraftReports/DraftReport_Investment_RuleofLaw.pdf> accessed 13 March 2022, 2. At its core, however, the rule of law reflects 'a government of laws, the supremacy of the law and equality before the law' ibid 3 (quoting Simon Chesterman, 'An International Rule of Law' (2008) 56 Am J Comp L 331, 342). For an argument that ISDS is not 'fair, rules-based' and is not 'something that advances the rule of law', see Gus Van Harten, 'Investment Treaty Arbitration, Procedural Fairness and the Rule of Law' in Stephan W Schill (ed), *International Investment Law and Comparative Public Law* (OUP 2010) 627.

Susan L. Karamanian, *International Investment Agreements, Investor Obligations, and the Rule of Law* In: *Investment Protection Standards and the Rule of Law*. Edited by: August Reinisch and Stephan W. Schill, Oxford University Press. © Susan L. Karamanian 2023.
DOI: 10.1093/oso/9780192864581.003.0015

framework of international law and national law, the actual or potential influence of IIAs on obligations of investors is expansive, as evidenced by host State counterclaims against investors. Further, ISDS is not risk-free as investors face possible imposition of costs and fees and a reduction in damages if they are found to have violated investor obligations.

This chapter first examines traditional IIAs, which typically do not impose obligations on investors, and identifies the rule-of-law implications of this absence. The situation, however, is nuanced. As explained, the lack of express investor obligations does not render them irrelevant to IIAs or arbitral awards. Various IIA clauses could open the door for an analysis of investor obligations, as ISDS typically operates under the umbrella of international law and even national law. The chapter's second part examines responses of States and arbitral institutions and tribunals to the gap. The analysis and conclusion foreshadow an ongoing adaptation of IIAs and ISDS to a continued rule-of-law critique.

II. IIAs and the Rule of Law: An Overview

This section first establishes the contours of the rule of law, recognizing that the concept includes procedural and substantive principles. Applying the principles to IIAs and ISDS under them, it identifies two potential shortcomings as to investor obligations: (1) fearing an investor's claim under the IIA, a host State could elect not to regulate foreign investments to the full extent of the law; and (2) an arbitral tribunal constituted under an IIA may lack the authority to resolve issues relating to the investor's obligation although the case before the tribunal implicates or informs the latter.

As further discussed, both shortcomings, which are identified as gaps, are nuanced. IIAs are far from uniform, so generalizing about them is a trap for the unwary. Decisions of arbitral tribunals add further complications to the landscape.

A. The Rule of Law in a 'Thick' Sense

At a minimum, a legal system comports with the rule of law if it has impartial and independent judges, public accountability, and uniform application of the law.[5] Yet, for many, the rule of law extends beyond procedure and has a normative component. For example, a 2012 report of the UN Secretary-General recognized that the law's consistency with international human rights law is an essential component of the rule of law.[6] Similarly, the publisher of the leading index on the rule of law, the World Justice Project (WJP), defines the rule of law as the 'framework of laws and institutions that embodies four universal principles': accountability, just laws, open government, and accessible and impartial dispute resolution.[7] The concept of a 'just law' recognizes that the law protects 'fundamental rights,

---

[5] See eg Tom Bingham, *The Rule of Law* (Allen Lane 2010) 8 (under the rule of law, 'all persons and authorities within the state, whether public or private, should be bound by and entitled to the benefit of laws publicly and prospectively promulgated and publicly administered by the courts').

[6] UNGA, 'Delivering Justice: Programme of Action to Strengthen the Rule of Law at the National and International Levels: Report of the Secretary General' (2012) UN Doc A/66/749, para 2.

[7] World Justice Project 'Rule of Law Index 2019' (2019) <https://worldjusticeproject.org/sites/default/files/documents/WJP-ROLI-2019-Single%20Page%20View-Reduced_0.pdf> accessed 13 March 2022, 9 (WJP Index). The WJP is an 'independent multidisciplinary organization working to promote the rule of law worldwide'. See World Justice Project, 'About Us' <https://worldjusticeproject.org/> accessed 13 March 2022. For an analysis

including the security of persons, contract and property rights, and certain core human rights'.[8]

Robert McCorquodale has applied the rule of law to the international system by advocating an 'international rule of law', or a 'thick' approach, which is founded on procedural standards and substantive ones such as 'equality of application of the law; [and] protection of human rights'.[9] In other words, a comprehensive understanding of a regime's rule-of-law implications necessitates a critique of its effect on substantive rights as well as traditional due process considerations.

B. The Rule-of-Law Gap

1. The gap defined

Do IIAs and arbitration under them enable foreign investors to shirk their legal obligations? Answering the question implicates the values of accountability under the law and the substantive norms promoted by the law.

State parties to IIAs regulate activity within, aimed at, or under the control of, their respective jurisdictions. They may impose civil and criminal sanctions against those engaged in prohibited conduct. National legal systems may also authorize individuals or legal persons to bring civil actions for equitable relief or damages based on a variety of obligations, whether in contract or tort. Further, many States have constitutions setting forth broad-sweeping individual rights and a municipal judicial system for their enforcement.

The range of laws applicable to a foreign investor could be sweeping and depends upon the host State's values and priorities. Various national laws have come into play in ISDS, including those concerning the environment,[10] health,[11] taxation,[12] and procurement.[13] These laws mandate specific compliance and thereby impose obligations on investors.

Although foreign investors are not exempt from most national laws, and the associated duties under them, in numerous instances they have argued that a State's enforcement of the laws violates the IIA's protections. The investor's contention may take various forms, such as enforcement being at odds with the State's promise not to expropriate the foreign investment or engage in activity tantamount to expropriation absent due process and appropriate compensation,[14] or enforcement running afoul of the requirement to provide fair and

---

of a thick definition of the rule of law in the context of investment treaties, see Stephan W Schill, 'International Investment Law and the Rule of Law' in Jeffrey Lowell, J Christopher Thomas and Jan van Zyl Smith (eds), *Rule of Law Symposium 2014: The Importance of the Rule of Law in Promoting Development* (Academy Publishing 2015) 81.

[8] WJP Index (n 7).

[9] Robert McCorquodale, 'Defining the International Rule of Law: Defying Gravity' (2016) 65 ICLQ 277, 292.

[10] See eg *Lone Pine Resources Inc v Canada*, ICSID Case No UNCT/15/2, Notice of Arbitration (6 September 2013) (challenging environmental law that revoked investor's exploration licence); *Pac Rim Cayman LLC v El Salvador*, ICSID Case No ARB/09/12, Award (14 October 2016) (alleging respondent's implementation of de facto mining ban violated the Central American Free Trade Agreement).

[11] See eg *Philip Morris Asia Limited v The Commonwealth of Australia*, UNCITRAL, PCA Case No 2012–12, Award on Jurisdiction and Admissibility (17 December 2015) (denying investor's claim challenging Australia's Plain Packaging Act 2011 and related regulations).

[12] See eg *Yukos Universal Ltd v Russia*, PCA Case No 2005–04/AA227, Award (18 July 2014) (challenging Russia's enforcement of tax laws).

[13] See eg *ADF Group Inc v United States*, ICSID Case No ARB(AF)/00/1, Award (9 January 2003) (denying investor's claim arising out of a bid on a highway construction project).

[14] See eg *Burlington Resources, Inc v Ecuador*, ICSID Case No ARB/08/5, Decision on Liability (14 December 2012) (denying investor's claim that Ecuador's windfall profits tax was an expropriation); *CMS Gas Transmission*

equitable treatment (FET).[15] ISDS tribunals have grappled with the interplay between the host State's compliance with its national laws, the IIA protection standards, and the conduct of the host State and the investor.[16]

Thus, a rule-of-law gap could arise when an investor's threat of a claim under the IIA causes the host State not to regulate foreign investments or be cautious in doing so.[17] The upshot is that an investor's obligations under national law would be rendered hollow.

Also, under a law-based system, surely the investor must be accountable for not adhering to national regulation,[18] yet the arbitral tribunal could lack authority to resolve issues relating to non-compliance with investor obligations.[19] So a second rule-of-law gap could occur when the tribunal is powerless to resolve issues arising out of, or relating to, the investor's obligation due to shortcomings in the IIAs and the arbitration rules. A dispute resolution system, such as ISDS, that enables an investor to pursue a claim against the host State for breach of the IIA without facing consequences in the arbitration proceeding for having violated national laws is difficult to reconcile with the fundamental principle of accountability.

2. The gap in context

This section critiques the rule-of-law gap in IIAs and ISDS. It examines applicable law, standard provisions in IIAs, and arbitration rules to establish that arbitrators have the tools to recognize and give effect to certain investor obligations. The analysis below explains why one should proceed with caution in generalizing about IIAs and ISDS, particularly as to the perceived pro-investor bias.

a) Text and interpretation

IIAs are subject to interpretation under the Vienna Convention on the Law of Treaties (VCLT) Article 31(1), which requires arbitral tribunals to interpret IIAs 'in good faith in accordance with the ordinary meaning to be given to the terms in their context and in the

---

Co v Argentina, ICSID Case No ARB/01/8, Award (25 April 2005) (denying investor's claim that Argentina's limit on and ultimate denial of investor's ability to adjust gas tariffs constituted an indirect expropriation).

[15] UNCTAD, *Fair and Equitable Treatment: UNCTAD Series on Issues in International Investment Agreements II* (United Nations 2012) 39–59 (analysing ISDS cases involving claims for violation of fair and equitable treatment, including ones based on State regulation).

[16] See eg *Methanex Corp v United States*, UNCITRAL, Award (3 August 2005) (denying relief to Canadian investor that alleged breach of NAFTA ch 11 due to California's regulation of gasoline additive).

[17] Australian Government, Productivity Commission 'Bilateral and Regional Trade Agreements: Research Report' (November 2010) <www.pc.gov.au/inquiries/completed/trade-agreements/report> accessed 13 March 2022, 271 (referencing Professor Van Harten's observation about the 'documented withdrawal by Canada of a proposal to impose cigarette plain-packaging regulations following the threat of ISDS arbitration'). See also BBC, 'Is Democracy Threatened if Companies Can Sue Countries?' (31 March 2015) <www.bbc.com/news/business-32116587> accessed 13 March 2022 ('opponents of ISDS argue that the fear of [ISDS] awards makes many poorer countries hesitate before implementing policies that might benefit their populations').

[18] See Vera Korzun, 'The Right to Regulate in Investor-State Arbitration: Slicing and Dicing Regulatory Carve-outs' (2017) 50 Vand J Transnatl L 355, 360 (observing that 'international investment agreements and the ISDS regime have empowered foreign corporations to interfere with a state's ability to regulate for the benefit of the public at large').

[19] See eg *Roussalis v Romania*, ICSID Case No ARB/06/1, Award (7 December 2011) paras 869, 876 (recognizing that the applicable BIT 'does not provide for counterclaims to be introduced by the host state in relation to obligations of the investor' and thus finding that the counterclaim is beyond the tribunal's jurisdiction).

light of its object and purpose'.[20] Along with context, tribunals are to take into account 'any relevant rules of international law applicable in the relations between the parties'.[21]

Under VCLT Article 31(1), tribunals analyse the evidence presented to them under the treaty objectives and give effect to them and defer to the host State when its regulations are non-discriminatory and made in good faith.[22] Tribunals have interpreted key provisions of IIAs, such as preambles, exception clauses and necessity clauses as well as the substantive protection measures, such as FET and the prohibition against expropriation.[23] Further, substantive provisions of IIAs may be governed by international law, which include other treaties governing human rights, the environment, labour standards, and anti-corruption.[24]

Key provisions in first-generation IIAs have enabled arbitral tribunals to scrutinize investor conduct, signalling that IIAs are not a one-way street. Absent treaty text, tribunals have relied on international law and national law to assess investor conduct.

The first bilateral investment treaty, which was between Germany and Pakistan in 1959, required the host State to admit investment 'in accordance with its legislation and regulations'.[25] Similarly, in defining 'investment' that is entitled to protection, numerous IIAs require that it have been made 'in accordance with the laws and regulations' of the host State.[26] These clauses require investors to ensure that they and their investments comply with host State law to at least be admitted into the host State or to be eligible to assert a claim under the IIA.[27] In other words, they impose duties on investors.

Arbitral tribunals have examined language requiring compliance with host State law, particularly in the context of the host State's challenge to the tribunal's jurisdiction on the basis that the investor engaged in corruption or bribery as to the investment.[28] Their analysis is far from consistent, as some tribunals have required serious wrongdoing, such as 'noncompliance with a law that results in a compromise of a correspondingly significant interest of the Host State'.[29] Other tribunals have overlooked minor

---

[20] Vienna Convention on the Law of Treaties (opened for signature 23 May 1969, entered into force 27 January 1980) 1155 UNTS 331 (VCLT) art 31(1).

[21] ibid art 31(3)(c).

[22] See eg *Philip Morris Brands Sàrl, Philip Morris Products SA and Abal Hermanos SA v Oriental Republic of Uruguay*, ICSID Case No ARB/10/7, Award (8 July 2016); *Saluka Investments BV v Czech Republic*, UNCITRAL, Partial Award (17 March 2006).

[23] For a discussion, see Silvia Steininger, 'What's Human Rights Got to Do with It? An Empirical Analysis of Human Rights References in Investment Arbitration' (2018) 31 LJIL 33, 46 (discussing reference to human rights in elucidating expropriation standards).

[24] See eg The Reciprocal Promotion and Protection of Investments between the Argentine Republic and the State of Qatar (6 November 2016) <https://investmentpolicy.unctad.org/international-investment-agreements/treaty-files/5383/download> accessed 13 March 2022, art 14(5); North American Free Trade Agreement (opened for signature 17 December 1992, entered into force 1 January 1994) (1993) 32 ILM 289, 645, art 1131(1) (NAFTA). Treaties are a principal source of international law. Statute of the International Court of Justice, Charter of the United Nations, Annex (opened for signature 26 June 1945, entered into force 24 October 1945) 1 UNTS XVI, art 38(1)(a).

[25] Treaty between the Federal Republic of Germany and Pakistan for the Promotion and Protection of Investments (signed 25 November 1959, entered into force 28 April 1962), 457 UNTS 24, art 1(1).

[26] See eg Agreement between the Government of the United Kingdom of Great Britain and Northern Ireland and the Government of the Republic of Indonesia for the Promotion and Protection of Investments (signed 27 April 1976, entered into force 24 March 1977), 2262 UNTS 75, art 2.

[27] *Salini Costruttori SpA and Italstrade SpA v Morocco*, ICSID Case No ARB/00/4, Decision on Jurisdiction (23 July 2001) para 46 (recognizing that the clause's purpose is 'to prevent the Bilateral Treaty from protecting investments that should not be protected, particularly because they would be illegal').

[28] See eg *Plama Consortium Ltd v Bulgaria*, ICSID Case No ARB/03/24, Award (27 August 2008) para 138; *World Duty Free Co Ltd v Republic of Kenya*, ICSID Case No ARB/00/7, Award (4 October 2006).

[29] *Vladislav Kim and ors v Republic of Uzbekistan*, ICSID Case No ARB/13/6, Decision on Jurisdiction (8 March 2017) para 398 (emphasizing that the violation 'depends on the seriousness of the law viewed in concert with the seriousness of the violation'). See also *LESI SpA. et al v Algeria*, ICSID Case No ARB/05/03, Decision on

indiscretions.[30] Another twist is whether the host State law must relate to investment regulation. For example, in *Saba Fakes v Turkey*, the tribunal dismissed Turkey's claim of illegality as to the investment as the alleged non-compliance arose out of competition law and telecommunications regulatory law, which were not 'host State's domestic laws governing the admission of investments in the host State'.[31]

Absent treaty text, are foreign investors impliedly obligated to conform to national law or to another standard, such as one under international law?[32] *Phoenix Action, Ltd v Czech Republic* answered this question in the affirmative.[33] The tribunal in that case considered whether an investment by an Israeli entity controlled by a Czech national, who was subject to a tax and customs duty evasion investigation in the Czech Republic, was protected under an IIA between Israel and the Czech Republic as well as the ICSID Convention.[34] The Czech national had fled to Israel and established the Israeli entity, which purchased assets of the Czech entity and a related one in which the Czech national had been CEO.[35] The Czech Republic challenged jurisdiction as the investor established the company 'to create diversity of nationality'.[36] In response, the tribunal noted that it lacked jurisdiction over acts or omissions occurring before and after the claimant had made the investment.[37] As to acts or omissions occurring while the Israeli investor owned the investment, general principles of international law, including good faith, precluded the investor from benefiting under the IIA.[38] The tribunal was concerned that the investor had invested solely to invoke ICSID jurisdiction.[39] According to the tribunal, the investment 'is not a bona fide transaction and cannot be protected investment under the ICSID system'.[40] The conclusion was reached although no violation of Czech Republic law was alleged.[41] Instead the tribunal recognized that 'conformity of the establishment of the investment with the national laws is implicit even when not expressly stated in the relevant BIT'.[42]

The tribunal in *Phoenix Action* further recognized that obligations under international law could constrain the investor. Specifically, it stated that 'the ICSID Convention's jurisdictional requirements as well as those of the BIT cannot be read and interpreted in isolation from public international law and its general principles'.[43] It then observed, by way

---

Jurisdiction (12 July 2006) para 83; *Desert Line Projects LLC v Yemen*, ICSID Case No ARB/05/17, Award (6 February 2008) para 104; *Rumeli Telekom AS v Kazakhstan*, ICSID Case No ARB/05/16, Award (29 July 2008) para 319 (recognizing that investment protections apply unless the investment was made 'in violation of fundamental principles').

[30] See eg *Tokios Tokelés v Ukraine*, ICSID Case No ARB/02/18, Decision on Jurisdiction (29 April 2004) para 86 (holding that alleged minor corporate filing errors did not render the investment in noncompliance with the law).

[31] *Saba Fakes v Turkey*, ICSID Case No ARB/07/20, Award (14 July 2010) para 119 (noting that the applicable BIT required the investment be 'established in accordance with the laws and regulation').

[32] For a discussion of these clauses, see Rahim Moloo and Alex Khatchaturian, 'The Compliance with the Law Requirement in International Investment Law' (2011) 34 Fordham Intl LJ 1473.

[33] *Phoenix Action, Ltd v Czech Republic*, ICSID Case No ARB/06/5, Award (15 April 2009).

[34] ibid paras 22, 26–33.

[35] ibid.

[36] ibid para 34 (quoting Respondent's Memorial on Jurisdiction).

[37] ibid paras 68–71.

[38] ibid paras 75–78, 91–93. The Tribunal quoted VCLT art 31(1). ibid para 76.

[39] ibid paras 92–95, 113

[40] ibid para 142.

[41] ibid para 134.

[42] ibid para 101. See also *Mobil Corp v Bolivarian Republic of Venezuela*, ICSID Case No ARB/07/27, Decision on Jurisdiction (10 June 2010) (finding abuse of process when, after a dispute had arisen, the investor restructured its investment to procure IIA benefits).

[43] ibid para 78.

of example, that the ICSID Convention could not be interpreted to protect investments in violation 'of the most fundamental rules of protection of human rights, like investments made in pursuance of torture or genocide or in support of slavery or trafficking of human organs'.[44] Implicit in this observation is the obligation of the investor not to engage in the prohibited conduct.

The tribunal's decision in *Phoenix Action* is not without its critics[45] yet it is aligned with decisions of other tribunals.[46] Indeed, in *Churchill Mining PLC v Indonesia*, the tribunal ruled that the investor's claims were inadmissible as they arose out of an investment 'based on fraud or forgery which a claimant deliberately or unreasonably ignored'.[47] Further, a person representing the investor, and not the investor itself, engaged in the alleged forgery of documents.[48] The tribunal relied on international law to conclude that fraudulent conduct breached 'the principle of good faith' and constituted 'an abuse of right' and 'abuse of process'.[49] Hence, in *Churchill Mining* the tribunal drew on entrenched international legal principles, grounded in public policy, to ensure that the investor would not benefit from a fraud perpetrated by a third party.[50]

Further, various States have largely maintained the status quo and rely on arbitral tribunals to harmonize investment and other objectives within the existing language of treaties and governing law. Commentators have urged use of a wide range of international law tools, mainly through VCLT Article 31(1), to accomplish this end.[51] Indeed, the area of public health is a prime example in which tribunals have deferred to States and in doing so effectively imposed obligations on investors. For example, Uruguay required warnings on tobacco packaging and prevented producers for using their trademarks to advertise.[52] Investors alleged that the regulations constituted a taking, among other things, in breach of applicable IIAs.[53] In *Philip Morris v Uruguay*, the tribunal deferred to the police power of the State to uphold Uruguay's measures, and in doing so used Article 31(1) of the VCLT to harmonize international public health norms with investment protection.[54]

b) Counterclaims

A growing body of law regarding counterclaims in ISDS lends support to the argument that investor duties may form part of the applicable law under IIAs. In *Urbaser v Argentina*,[55] the

---

[44] ibid. Similarly, another tribunal denied jurisdiction, finding lack of good faith, due to the investor's fraudulent misrepresentation of credentials in a bid for a government contract. *Inceysa Vallisoletana, SL v El Salvador*, ICSID Case No ARB/03/26, Award (2 August 2006) paras 230–39. See also *Methanex* (n 16) para 24 ('a tribunal has an independent duty to apply imperative principles of law or jus cogens and not to give effect to parties' choices of law that are inconsistent with such principles').

[45] See eg Joseph M Boddicker, 'Whose Dictionary Controls?: Recent Challenges to the Term "Investment" in ICSID Arbitration' (2010) 25 Am U Intl L Rev 1031, 1060–62.

[46] See eg *Plama Consortium* (n 28) para 135 (finding that the substantive protections under the Energy Charter Treaty were inapplicable when the investment violated the law).

[47] *Churchill Mining PLC v Indonesia*, ICSID Case No ARB/12/14 and 12/40, Award (6 December 2016) para 508.

[48] ibid para 485.

[49] ibid paras 491–506.

[50] ibid para 508 (holding that 'claims arising from rights based on fraud or forgery which a claimant deliberately or unreasonably ignored are inadmissible as a matter of international public policy').

[51] See eg Barnali Choudhury, 'Spinning Straw into Gold: Incorporating the Business and Human Rights Agenda into International Investment Agreements' (2017) 38 U Pa JIL 425; Campbell McLachlan, 'Investment Treaties and General International Law' (2008) 57 ICLQ 361, 364 (recognizing that 'the content of the treaty obligation may be informed by general international law' and arguing for 'a structured process of treaty interpretation').

[52] *Philip Morris* (n 22) paras 74–134.

[53] ibid paras 9–14.

[54] ibid para 290.

[55] *Urbaser SA v Argentina*, ICSID Case No ARB/07/26, Award (8 December 2016).

tribunal considered whether investors, as opposed to States, owed obligations as to their investment. In that case, a Spanish entity that had a water and sewerage concession with the Province of Buenos Aires, along with some of its Spanish shareholders, filed an arbitration claim against Argentina under the Spain–Argentina BIT.[56] Claimants alleged financial loss when Argentina imposed emergency measures to address the 2001–02 economic crisis.[57] Ultimately, Buenos Aires terminated the concession.[58] Argentina asserted a counterclaim, alleging that the entity violated the human right to water by not investing in the project as per the concession.[59] The tribunal recognized that under the BIT and arbitration rules, it had jurisdiction over the counterclaim[60] yet denied relief under it.[61]

Of note, the tribunal in *Urbaser* did not reject the merits of the counterclaim on the ground that the investors were not subjects of international law and therefore had no duties under human rights treaties. According to the tribunal, such an approach would have ignored that 'international law accepts corporate social responsibility [including compliance with human rights] as a standard of crucial importance' to multinational corporations.[62] Instead, the tribunal defined its task as follows: 'contextualizing a corporation's specific activities as they relate to the human right at issue in order to determine whether any international law obligations attach to the non-State individual'.[63] It recognized that there is a human right to water and sanitation under international law;[64] the issue was 'whether such right is completed by a corresponding obligation on part of Claimants as investors'.[65]

In holding that the investors owed no duty under international law to provide water and sanitation, the tribunal focused on the source of the investors' relationship with the State, the concession contract, which did not impose this duty on investors.[66] Further, the Spain–Argentina BIT, although expressly subject to international law, did not impose a human rights duty on investors.

An interesting statement in the award concerned the nature of the right to water. In *Urbaser*, the right was allegedly a positive one, namely, the investors were to have provided water. The tribunal observed that if a negative right were involved, such that the investor owed a duty not to interfere with an individual's right to water, the analysis would have differed.[67] The tribunal analysed international human rights sources, including the Universal Declaration of Human Rights and its recognition that no 'State, group or person' can act to destroy the rights and freedoms set out in the Declaration.[68] The tribunal linked the right to

---

[56] ibid para 34.
[57] ibid.
[58] ibid.
[59] ibid para 36.
[60] ibid paras 1153–55.
[61] ibid para 1221.
[62] ibid para 1195.
[63] ibid.
[64] ibid para 1205.
[65] ibid para 1204.
[66] ibid paras 1206, 1208. As the Tribunal observed, '[t]he human right to water entails an obligation of compliance on the part of the State, but it does not contain an obligation for performance on part of any company providing the contractually required service'. ibid para 1208.
[67] ibid para 1210.
[68] Universal Declaration of Human Rights (opened for signature 10 December 1948 UNGA Res 217 A(III)) (UDHR) art 30.

water to the 'human right for everyone's dignity' and the 'obligation on all parts, public and private parties, not to engage in activity aimed at destroying such rights'.[69]

Since *Urbaser*, tribunals have recognized counterclaims, including awarding relief to the host State due to an investor's failure to comply with a local environmental law.[70] In another case, the tribunal found that the host State had not complied with a technical requirement to assert the counterclaim but otherwise could have pursued it based on the investor's failure to comply with a standard in the applicable investment treaty regarding the environment.[71]

c) Costs and damages

This interpretive approach and reliance on rules to allow counterclaims, however, has not satisfied vocal critics. In their minds, the arbitrators themselves are the problem[72] as they have 'prioritized the protection of the property and economic interests of transnational corporations'.[73] The rule of law, under this reasoning, would require elimination of ISDS due to its bias in favour of foreign investors.

The assertions of bias, however, are belied by empirical studies.[74] Further, arbitral tribunals have proven adept in imposing costs against non-prevailing investors when the facts warrant. For example, in *Methanex*, in which the United States prevailed, the tribunal ordered the non-prevailing investor to pay to the United States nearly US$3 million in legal costs as well as US$1 million in deposits that the United States had paid.[75] In *Churchill Mining*, the tribunal ordered the investors to pay 75% of respondent's US$12.3 million in costs, particularly due to the fraud and forgery linked to the investor.[76] In other words, parties to ISDS have obligations shaped by the arbitration rules and fundamental principles, and investors, merely due to their status, are not free from them.

In assessing damages, an arbitral tribunal can consider and hold the investor accountable for its own conduct.[77] If indeed investor obligations were wholly irrelevant in ISDS, this fundamental principle of the law of State responsibility would ring hollow.

As Section II has established, the mere fact that IIAs do not expressly impose investor obligations does not make the latter irrelevant to ISDS. Applicable law and arbitral rules equip

---

[69] *Urbaser* (n 55) para 1199. Compare *Roussalis* (n 19) para 871 (recognizing that the referenced BIT 'imposes no obligations on investors, only on contracting States').

[70] *Burlington Resources Inc v Ecuador*, ICSID Case No ARB/08/5, Decision on Counterclaims (7 February 2017).

[71] *David Aven v Costa Rica*, ICSID Case No UNCT/15/3, Award (18 September 2018). The applicable treaty did not 'prevent a Party from adopting, maintaining, or enforcing any measure otherwise consistent with this Chapter that it considers appropriate to ensure that investment activity in its territory is undertaken in a manner sensitive to environmental concerns'. Dominican Republic–Central America–United States Free Trade Agreement (opened for signature 5 August 2004, entered into force 1 March 2006) art 10.11 <https://ustr.gov/trade-agreeme nts/free-trade-agreements/cafta-dr-dominican-republic-central-america-fta/final-text> accessed 13 March 2022 (DR-CAFTA).

[72] See eg Letter from Professor Erwin Chemerinsky and others to Senator Mitch McConnell and others (11 March 2015) (urging, 'to protect the rule of law', that investor-State arbitration not be included in the then proposed Trans-Pacific Partnership and Transatlantic Trade and Investment Partnership as unaccountable private lawyers are arbitrators) <https://studylib.net/doc/18661490/isds---public-citizen> accessed 13 March 2022.

[73] Gus Van Harten and others, 'Public Statement on the International Investment Regime' (31 August 2010) <www.osgoode.yorku.ca/public-statement-international-investment-regime-31-august-2010/> accessed 13 March 2022.

[74] See eg Susan D Franck and others, 'Inside the Arbitrator's Mind' (2017) 66 Emory LJ 1115.

[75] *Methanex* (n 16) pt V, para 13.

[76] *Churchill Mining* (n 47) paras 551–52.

[77] See eg *Burlington Resources, Inc v Ecuador*, ICSID Case No ARB/08/5, Decision on Reconsideration and Award (7 February 2017) paras 576–85 (recognizing that under the law of State responsibility a State is not responsible for wilful or negligent acts of the investor causing damage to the latter, yet not finding the facts of the case warranted a reduction in damages).

arbitrators to examine the conduct of investors and may enable them to consider the conduct in resolving a dispute. Nevertheless, the lack of clarity and consistency as to investor obligations, which are fundamental to the rule of law, is a legitimate concern.

III.   The Shifting Landscape of IIAs and ISDS

States have taken specific measures in response to the uncertainty surrounding investor obligations, and the critique of IIAs and ISDS due to it. This section sets out and analyses the response with a focus on the growing public engagement in shaping international investment law. Understanding what has transpired, both in terms of a broader public engagement in and with ISDS that led to a focus on pro-investor aspects and the twists and turns of addressing the concerns, is relevant for numerous reasons. First, as this section shows, public engagement has infused a third element in the process beyond the investor and State. This added dimension, while creating uncertainty as to the role of investor obligations, is aligned with transparency and accountability. Second, the willingness of certain States to leave or threaten to leave ISDS has given them leverage vis-à-vis investors if they elect to exercise it.

This section examines the public's emerging role in ISDS and assesses whether States have enhanced or undermined the rule of law, particularly in the context of investor obligations.[78] State responses include systemic adjustments and treaty reform. Included in the former are the withdrawal of States from IIA or the key treaty that supports ISDS, the Convention on the Settlement of Investment Disputes between States and Nationals of Other States (ICSID Convention)[79] and the elimination of ISDS, either completely or in favour of an international investment court. Within treaty reform are a broadening of preamble language to introduce objectives beyond traditional investment ones, an expansion of the regulatory space exempt from review, a recognition of a broader obligation of States as to imposing heightened standards as to investors, and an express delineation of investor obligations. Coupled with these adjustments is a more active engagement of arbitral tribunals in interpreting IIAs to give full effect to a broader object and purpose as well as relying on international law to elucidate investment norms.

A.   Accountability

1. Transparency

The increase in the number of ISDS arbitrations with high-profile issues sparked public interest in IIAs and the arbitrations. In 2004, the United States adopted a new model BIT, which required public disclosure of key documents relating to ISDS under the BIT.[80] In 2006, ICSID amended its Arbitration Rules to open arbitration hearings to the public,

---

[78] Professor Anthea Roberts has classified the responses as incremental, systemic, or paradigmatic. See Anthea Roberts, 'Incremental, Systemic, and Paradigmatic Reform of Investor-State Arbitration' (2018) 112 AJIL 410.

[79] Convention on the Settlement of Investment Disputes between States and Nationals of Other States (opened for signature 18 March 1965, entered into force 14 October 1966) 575 UNTS 159 (ICSID Convention).

[80] 2004 US Model BIT, art 29 <https://ustr.gov/archive/assets/Trade_Sectors/Investment/Model_BIT/asset_upload_file847_6897.pdf> accessed 13 March 2022.

absent a party's objection,[81] and to allow arbitral tribunals to accept written submissions from amicus curiae, after receiving input from the parties.[82] In 2014, the UNCITRAL Rules on Transparency in Treaty-Based Investor-State Arbitration were adopted.[83] In 2017, State parties to the Mauritius Convention authorized application of the UNCITRAL Rules on Transparency to treaties before 1 April 2014.[84] Many other model IIAs now impose a transparency duty on States both as to their laws and regulations as well as to arbitration under the treaty.[85]

With public disclosure about the ISDS process has come intense scrutiny from those directly or indirectly affected by the arbitral cases yet not parties to them, including human rights activists, politicians, and legal scholars.[86] Their work has raised fundamental concerns about IIAs, including the perceived lack of focus on investor misconduct and its implications. For example, the Columbia Center on Sustainable Development and others have documented how in ISDS the State's interests may not be aligned with those of interested citizens, particularly as to investor obligations.[87] In addition to promoting legitimacy, the emphasis on transparency has enabled citizens and affected stakeholders to shape substantive norms, such as investor obligations.[88] And the emphasis on transparency has extended beyond the State as newer IIAs have imposed transparency obligations on investors.[89]

2. Consistency, coherency, and predictability

Reform has extended beyond efforts to enhance the transparency of and broaden participation in ISDS. In 2017, UNCITRAL established Working Group III: Investor-State Dispute Settlement Reform. Working Group III (WGIII) has identified three areas of procedural concern: lack of 'consistency, coherency and predictability' of outcomes; qualifications of arbitrators; and costs and duration.[90] While its work is ongoing and focused principally on procedure, WGIII is proposing recommendations such as a multilateral advisory centre to advise States to address 'interpretation and related questions', a draft code of conduct

---

[81] ICSID Arbitration Rules (amendment entered into force 10 April 2006), art 32 <https://icsid.worldbank.org/sites/default/files/ICSID%20Convention%20English.pdf> accessed 13 March 2022.

[82] ibid art 37.

[83] UNCITRAL Rules on Transparency in Treaty-Based Investor-State Arbitration (opened for signature 1 July 2013, entered into force 1 April 2014) <www.uncitral.org/pdf/english/texts/arbitration/transparency-convention/Transparency-Convention-e.pdf> accessed 13 March 2022.

[84] United Nations Convention on Transparency in Treaty-based Investor-State Arbitration (opened for signature 10 December 2014, entered into force 18 October 2017) <www.uncitral.org/pdf/english/texts/arbitration/transparency-convention/Transparency-Convention-e.pdf> accessed 13 March 2022.

[85] See Status: United Nations Convention on Transparency in Treaty-based Investor-State Arbitration (New York, 2014) <www.uncitral.org/uncitral/en/uncitral_texts/arbitration/2014Transparency_Rules_status.html> accessed 13 March 2022 (listing treaties applying the UNCITRAL Rules on Transparency).

[86] Esmé Shirlow, 'Three Manifestations of Transparency in International Investment Law: A Story of Sources, Stakeholders and Structures' (2017) 8 Go JIL 73.

[87] See eg Columbia Center on Sustainable Investment and others, 'Third Party Rights in Investor-State Dispute Settlement: Options for Reform' (15 July 2019) <https://uncitral.un.org/sites/uncitral.un.org/files/media-documents/uncitral/en/wgiii_reformoptions_0.pdf> accessed 13 March 2022.

[88] Kelly Garton, Boyd Swinburn and Anne Marie Thow, 'Who Influences Nutrition Policy Space Using International Trade and Investment Agreements? A Global Stakeholder Analysis' (2021) 17 Global Health 118 (discussing the role of civil society organizations in shaping public health aspects of IIAs. See also Shirlow (n 86) 77–79, 96.

[89] United Nations Conference on Trade and Development 'Transparency: UNCTAD Series on Issues in International Investment Agreements II' (United Nations 2012) 30–35 <https://unctad.org/system/files/official-document/unctaddiaeia2011d6_en.pdf> accessed 13 March 2022.

[90] Siobhán McInerney-Lankford and Manuela Corredor Vasquez, 'UNCITRAL WGIII and Human Rights: Towards a More Balanced ISDS System?' (*EJIL:Talk!*, 8 October 2020).

for adjudicators, a strengthening of dispute settlement mechanisms outside of arbitration, such as mediation, and standards as to counterclaims.[91] Various of these areas could implicate investor obligations. For example, proposed 'clear guidance on the application of international law norms'[92] could enable full effect to preambles that recognizes the need for foreign investment to conform to environmental and labour standards. Or as another example, WGIII has recognized that its work 'should not foreclose the possibility that claims might be brought against an investor, where there was a legal basis for doing so' and it urged consideration of 'formulating provisions on investor obligations which would form the basis for a State's counterclaims'.[93]

Another example is the broad approach of the United Nations Conference on Trade and Development (UNCTAD) as reflected in its Reform Package for the International Investment Regime.[94] The Reform Package, which acknowledges that assessment of IIAs and ISDS should be ongoing, is focused on procedure, substantive standards of protection, and system-wide factors.[95] Guiding the recommendations is alignment of IIAs with sustainable development, recognizing that IIAs 'have underused potential as an instrument for sustainable development objectives'.[96]

B. Systemic Adjustments: Withdrawal from IIAs, Denouncing the ICSID Convention, and Eliminating ISDS

The perceived pro-investor approach of IIAs has prompted some States to take substantial measures, such as terminating IIAs, denouncing the ICSID Convention, or eliminating ISDS. These actions, while not imposing specific duties on investors, reshuffle power and could fundamentally change investor duties.

For example, Ecuador and India have withdrawn from or terminated existing IIAs.[97] In 2010, after thorough study, South Africa withdrew from existing BITs and prohibited entry into new ones absent 'compelling political or economic reasons'.[98] Instead, the Protection of Investment Act 2015 recognizes South Africa's 'sovereign right to regulate investments' in a broad sense[99] and protects investment under South African law, such as the Constitution and legislation.[100]

---

[91] UNCITRAL Working Group III (Investor-State Dispute Settlement Reform) 'Possible Reform of Investor-State Dispute Settlement (ISDS): Note by the Secretariat' (30 July 2019) UN Doc A/CN.9/WG.III/WP.166/Add.1.

[92] ibid.

[93] UNCITRAL Working Group III (Investor-State Dispute Settlement Reform) 'Possible Reform of Investor-State Dispute Settlement (ISDS): Multiple Proceedings and Counterclaims, Note by the Secretariat' (22 January 2020) UN Doc A/CN.9/WG.III/WP.193, paras 32, 41.

[94] UNCTAD, 'UNCTAD's Reform Package for the International Investment Regime' (2018) <https://investmentpolicy.unctad.org/uploaded-files/document/UNCTAD_Reform_Package_2018.pdf> accessed 13 March 2022.

[95] ibid 11.

[96] ibid 17.

[97] International Institute for Sustainable Development, 'Ecuador Denounces Its 16 Remaining BITs and Publishes CAITISA Audit Report' (12 June 2017) <www.iisd.org/itn/en/2017/06/12/ecuador-denounces-its-remaining-16-bits-and-publishes-caitisa-audit-report/> accessed 13March 2022; Alison Ross, 'India's Termination of BITs to Begin' (*Global Arbitration Review*, 22 March 2017).

[98] Xavier Carim, 'Lessons from South Africa's BITs Review' (25 November 2013) 109 Columbia FDI Perspectives 2 <https://academiccommons.columbia.edu/doi/10.7916/D8930R39> accessed 13 March 2022.

[99] Protection of Investment Act, 2015 arts 4(b), 12 (SA) <www.gov.za/sites/default/files/gcis_document/201512/39514act22of2015protectionofinvestmentact.pdf> accessed 13 March 2022.

[100] ibid art 6(1).

Another approach, taken by Bolivia, Ecuador, and Venezuela, has been to withdraw from the ICSID Convention. While generating substantial discussion, this step has not gained traction; in fact, Mexico recently ratified and Djibouti also recently signed the ICSID Convention.[101] Further, in 2021, Ecuador has re-signed the ICSID Convention.[102]

A third step is to eliminate ISDS. For example, in negotiating IIAs, Australia considers whether to include arbitration 'on a case-by-case basis in light of the national interest'.[103] Hence, the Australia–United States Free Trade Agreement, while providing standard protections to foreign investors, does not include ISDS.[104] A more aggressive approach is the substitution of a court for an arbitral tribunal, such as under chapter 8 of the European Union–Canada Comprehensive Economic Trade Agreement, which calls for the establishment of the Investment Court System, a tribunal consisting of 15 permanent judges with expertise in public international law and ideally in international investment law, international trade law, or international dispute resolution.[105]

Withdrawal from IIAs or the ICSID Convention could signal a host State's lack of receptivity to foreign investment. This perception would not be unfounded, particularly when other States continue to embrace IIAs. Establishment of rigorous national standards that impose duties on foreign investors and eliminate ISDS could be a hollow victory if investors flee or simply elect to invest elsewhere.

Second, when IIAs are considered part of international investment governance, and a way for States collectively to address societal problems through strength in numbers while continuing to attract capital, a State's disengagement from IIAs could minimize the ability of that State to influence international investment norms.[106]

Further, as a State loses foreign investment, it may need to 'prioritize specific efforts to attract or keep foreign investment notwithstanding consequent harms to global commons'.[107] The race to the bottom to attract and maintain foreign investment could have negative consequences for the people within that State as well as in other States.

The backlash against ICSID has likely contributed to ICSID's re-engagement with States to examine for a fifth time its Rules and Regulations.[108] In the proposed new Rules and Regulations, transparency again has received attention. Specifically, under proposed Rule

---

[101] ICSID, 'Database of ICSID Member States' <https://icsid.worldbank.org/about/member-states/database-of-member-states> accessed 13 March 2022 (listing contracting and signing States).

[102] ICSID, 'Ecuador Signs the ICSID Convention' (21 June 2021) <https://icsid.worldbank.org/news-and-events/news-releases/ecuador-signs-icsid-convention> accessed 13 March 2022.

[103] Australian Government-Department of Foreign Affairs and Trade, 'About Foreign Investment-Investor-State Dispute Settlement' <www.dfat.gov.au/trade/investment/investor-state-dispute-settlement> accessed 13 March 2022.

[104] Free Trade Agreement between Australia and the United States (opened for signature 18 May 2004, entered into force 1 January 2005) <https://investmentpolicy.unctad.org/international-investment-agreements/treaty-files/2682/download> accessed 13 March 2022.

[105] Comprehensive Economic and Trade Agreement between Canada, of the one part, and the European Union and its Member States, of the other part (signed 30 October 2016, provisionally applied since 21 September 2017), art 8.23(2), (4) (CETA).

[106] Emma Aisbett and others, 'Rethinking International Investment Governance: Principles for the 21st Century' (Columbia Center on Sustainable Investment Books 2018) <https://scholarship.law.columbia.edu/cgi/viewcontent.cgi?article=1000&context=sustainable_investment_books> accessed 13 March 2022, 78 (noting that 'relying only on domestic political autonomy will not address all of the problems caused by capital mobility' as 'international economic governance can decrease the risk premiums which hosts may otherwise have to pay to attract investment').

[107] ibid 79.

[108] ICSID, 'Proposals for Amendment of the ICSID Rules' (2019) <https://icsid.worldbank.org/sites/default/files/amendments/WP_3_VOLUME_1_ENGLISH.pdf> accessed 13 March 2022.

44, a party is to have consented to publication of awards and annulment decisions unless it withdraws consent within 60 days after dispatch.[109] This type of reform aligns with the rule-of-law principle of transparency and accountability as discussed above.

Leaving the ICSID Convention does not equate to withdrawal from an international approach to foreign investment. For example, in Latin America, two new dispute settlement initiatives have been under way, with one, under the Union of South American Nations (UNASUR), establishing draft procedural rules for investment disputes.[110] Whether the UNASUR approach will materialize is unclear but it signals an engagement of the States to fill an international void.

Removing ISDS may not translate into an enhanced accountability of investors to third parties (private or public) in the host States. The critical aspect would be the procedural rules under which the new proceedings would operate, such as enabling the host State to impose a counterclaim against an offending investor.[111]

C. Reform of IIAs

The steps most likely to have a profound influence on investor obligations involve amending IIAs. These measures range from less direct efforts, such as including preamble language to reaffirming that foreign investment satisfies stated requirements or to require States to encourage investors to meet standards, to more aggressive moves, such as expanding the space for States to regulate without fear of an investor claim or even imposing investor obligations. In between is new treaty text that obliges States to adopt various laws and policies that invariably would impose obligations on foreign investors.

1. Broadening IIAs' object and purpose

The preambles of a growing number of IIA identify the objectives of the treaties beyond the unbridled protection of the investor. They reaffirm that investment should be consistent with promoting public health, labour, human rights, environment laws, sustainable development, and even the rule of law itself.[112]

For example, the preamble to the EU–Canada Comprehensive Economic Trade Agreement (CETA) reaffirms the States' commitment to democracy and fundamental rights under the Universal Declaration of Human Rights and recognizes the 'importance' of 'democracy, human rights, and the rule of law'.[113] The preamble to the Netherlands Model Investment Agreement of 22 March 2019 reaffirms the commitment of the State parties 'to

---

[109] ibid.

[110] See Melida Hodgson, 'Reform and Adaptation: The Experience of the Americas with International Investment Law' (2020) 21 JWIT 140. Hodgson discusses key features of the final draft of procedures for investment dispute resolution, including exhaustion of local remedies, excluding arbitral jurisdiction over specific economic sectors, and an appellate mechanism akin to that of the WTO Appellate Body.

[111] See Stephan W Schill, 'From Investor-State Dispute Settlement to a Multilateral Investment Court? Evaluating Options from an EU law Perspective' in European Parliament Directorate-General for External Polices, 'Workshop Report: EU Investment Protection after the ECJ Opinion on Singapore' (2019) <www.europarl.europa.eu/RegData/etudes/STUD/2019/603476/EXPO_STU(2019)603476_EN.pdf> accessed 13 March 2022, 38.

[112] UNCTAD, 'IIA Issues Note International Investment Agreements: Taking Stock of IIA Reform: Recent Developments' (June 2019) <https://unctad.org/system/files/official-document/diaepcbinf2019d5_en.pdf> accessed 13 March 2022, 2.

[113] CETA (n 105) preamble.

sustainable development and to enhancing the contribution of international trade and investment to sustainable development'.[114]

The CETA preamble goes a step further by recognizing a light form of investor obligations as follows:

> ENCOURAGING enterprises operating within their territory or subject to their jurisdiction to respect internationally recognized guidelines and principles of corporate social responsibility, including the OECD Guidelines for Multinational Enterprises, and to pursue best practices of responsible business conduct.[115]

Tribunals have referenced preamble text to interpret IIA investment protection measures, such as to FET.[116] The protection of the investor's legitimate expectations, which has been recognized as an element of FET,[117] is shaped by the host State's 'specific undertakings and representations … to induce investors to make an investment'.[118] A foreign investor that seeks protection under CETA, for example would be hard pressed to claim that a new host State regulation mandating specific responsible business conduct in line with international standards runs afoul of the investor's legitimate expectations.

2. Encouraging or mandating investor conduct

In chapter 22 of CETA, entitled Trade and Sustainable Development, the State parties agree to promote trade by 'encouraging the development and use of voluntary best practices of corporate social responsibility by enterprises, such as those in the OECD Guidelines for Multinational Enterprises, to strengthen coherence between economic, social and environmental objectives'.[119] CETA also imposes an obligation on State Parties to respect, promote, and realize key labour standards and reaffirm their commitments as members of the International Labour Organization.[120]

Yet CETA hedges in imposing a direct obligation on investors. First, it takes the conventional angle of acknowledging that the treaty is a creature of States and binds States, not enterprises although the latter benefit from the treaty. This take is consistent with the arbitral award in *Urbaser*.[121] Second, it imposes on States the duty to 'encourage' enterprises to engage in certain conduct. Third, it identifies that conduct be voluntary in nature.

Other treaties have taken a similar approach to encourage but not mandate investor compliance with corporate social responsibility (CSR). For example, in the EU–Peru–Colombia

---

[114] Netherlands Model Investment Agreement (22 March 2019) (Dutch Model BIT 2019), preamble <https://investmentpolicy.unctad.org/international-investment-agreements/treaty-files/5832/download> accessed 13 March 2022.

[115] CETA (n 105) preamble.

[116] See eg *MTD Equity Sdn. Bhd and MTD Chile SA v Chile*, ICSID Case No ARB/01/7, Award (25 May 2004) para 113.

[117] See eg *Rumeli* (n 29) para 609.

[118] *Philip Morris* (n 22) para 426.

[119] CETA (n 105) art 22(b)(3). See also Dutch Model BIT 2019 (n 114) art 8(2) (State parties are to 'encourage investors operating within its territory or subject to its jurisdiction to voluntarily incorporate into their internal policies' international CSR standards).

[120] CETA (n105) art 23.3 (1).

[121] *Urbaser* (n 55) para 1210.

Free Trade Agreement the parties agree to 'promote best business practices related to corporate social responsibility'.[122] Similarly, the Canada–Mongolia BIT provides:

> Each Party should encourage enterprises operating within its territory or subject to its jurisdiction to voluntarily incorporate internationally recognized standards of corporate social responsibility in their practices and internal policies, such as statements of principle that have been endorsed or are supported by the Parties. These principles address issues such as labour, the environment, human rights, community relations and anti-corruption. The Parties should remind those enterprises of the importance of incorporating such corporate social responsibility standards in their internal policies.[123]

In chapter 8, which covers investment and the ability of an investor to seek a remedy for breach of the investment protection measures, CETA clarifies that an investor cannot submit a claim 'if the investment has been made through fraudulent misrepresentation, concealment, corruption, or conduct amounting to an abuse of process'.[124] This language supplements the requirement that the investor comply with local law. Under CETA, an investor who has lied, cheated, engaged in bribery, or misused the court system cannot avail itself of a remedy against the host State for alleged breach of CETA's investment protection measures.

Similarly, the Dutch Model BIT 2019 includes language that mandates the States to ensure that their investment laws and policies 'provide for and encourage high levels of environmental and labor protection'.[125] They are to remove 'barriers to women's participation in the economy' and be committed to promoting 'equal opportunity and participation for women and men in the economy'.[126] In all of these respects, the IIA is serving to mandate specific municipal laws and policies, which would ultimately impose obligations on foreign investors.

3. Expanding the regulatory space

In the late 1990s and early part of the twenty-first century, various tribunals had ruled in favour of investors that had complained that State regulation breached the IIA.[127] The cases, while limited in their success as to investors, generated concern that IIAs were preventing States from regulating in the public interest.[128]

A decade later, a major outcry occurred when a Swedish investor filed a request for arbitration against Germany due to the latter's decision in August 2011 to phase out nuclear

---

[122] Trade Agreement Between the European Union and its Member States, of the one part, and Colombia and Peru, of the other part [2012] OJ L354/3, art 271(3).

[123] Agreement between Canada and Mongolia for the Promotion and Protection of Investment art 14 (titled Corporate Social Responsibility) (signed 8 September 2016, entered into force 24 February 2017) <https://investmentpolicy.unctad.org/international-investment-agreements/treaty-files/5373/download> accessed 13 March 2022.

[124] CETA (n 105) art 8.18(3).

[125] Dutch Model BIT 2019 (n 114) art 6(2).

[126] ibid art 6(3).

[127] See Vicki Been and Joel C Beauvais, 'The Global Fifth Amendment? NAFTA's Investment Protections and the Misguided Quest for an International "Regulatory Takings" Doctrine' (2003) 78 NYU L Rev 30 (discussing decisions under NAFTA ch 11 in favour of investors).

[128] ibid.

power, which was prompted by the nuclear power facility meltdown in Fukushima, Japan.[129] Germany, an economic powerhouse with a well-established legal regime, was seen unable to regulate nuclear power without facing a multibillion-dollar arbitration demand.[130]

General exception clauses, akin to exceptions under GATT Article XX and GATS Article XIV, started to appear in IIAs in the 1990s,[131] and became more frequent thereafter. An example is Article 22.1(3) of the Australia–Korea Free Trade Agreement (FTA), which enables the host State to adopt certain measures so long as they are not arbitrary, unjustifiably discriminatory, or a disguised restriction on trade or investment. Specifically, under Article 22.1(3):

> … nothing in this Agreement shall be construed to prevent a Party from adopting or enforcing measures:
>
> 1. necessary to protect human, animal or plant life or health;
> 2. necessary to ensure compliance with laws and regulations that are not inconsistent with this Agreement;
> 3. imposed for the protection of national treasures of artistic, historic or archaeological value; or
> 4. relating to the conservation of living or non-living exhaustible natural resources if such measures are made effective in conjunction with restrictions on domestic production or consumption.
>
> The Parties understand that the measures referred to in subparagraph (a) include environmental measures to protect human, animal or plant life or health, and that the measures referred to in subparagraph (d) include environmental measures relating to the conservation of living and non-living exhaustible natural resources.

Other clauses carve out specific measures from the IIAs, such as various forms of tax-related ones[132] and tobacco restrictions.[133]

In addition to defining the protected regulatory space, the Dutch Model BIT 2019 confirms that a State's regulation that 'negatively affects an investment or interferes with an investor's expectations' is not a violation of the agreement.[134] In other words, an investor will be subject to local law and the State's enforcement of, or even changes to it, cannot give rise to a claim against the State.

---

[129] Diane Bailey, 'When Free Trade Takes on Democracy' (*Windpower Monthly*, 29 May 2015) <www.windpowermonthly.com/article/1349268/when-free-trade-takes-democracy> accessed 13 March 2022.

[130] Germany settled the arbitration claim. See Cosmo Sanderson, 'Germany Settles with Vattenfall' (*Global Arbitration Review*, 5 March 2021) <https://globalarbitrationreview.com/germany-agrees-settle-vattenfall-case> accessed 13 March 2022.

[131] See Céline Lévesque, 'The Inclusion of GATT Article XX Exceptions in IIAs: A Potentially Risky Policy' in Roberto Echandi and Pierre Sauvé (eds), *Prospects in International Investment Law and Policy* (CUP 2013) 363, 363, n 3.

[132] See eg NAFTA (n 24) art 2103; CETA (n 105) art 28.7.

[133] See eg Comprehensive and Progressive Agreement for Trans-Pacific Partnership (opened for signature 8 March 2018, entered into force 30 December 2018) <www.international.gc.ca/trade-commerce/trade-agreements-accords-commerciaux/agr-acc/tpp-ptp/text-texte/29.aspx?lang=eng> accessed 13 March 2022, art 29.5 (allowing a State party to elect to deny investment protection as to claims challenging a tobacco control measure).

[134] Dutch Model BIT 2019 (n 114) art 2(2).

The broadening of the areas within exception clauses, and entrenching the right of the State to regulate and reform, gives the State a potentially powerful tool to defend against certain investor claims.[135] Their ultimate value in enabling a State to fulfil obligations under human rights treaties, however, depends on the ability of a tribunal to interpret them consistently with the entirety of the treaty text under the VCLT.[136] While not imposing an affirmative duty on investors, these restrictions serve to constrain the latter's investment activities.

4. Imposing investor obligations

Certain IIAs have been more aggressive in imposing a duty on the foreign investor. Notable in this respect is the Morocco–Nigeria BIT of 2016.[137] This BIT's tenor differs from others as reflected in its preamble, which highlights investment's role in promoting sustainable development, including 'furtherance of human rights and human development' and the importance of a State's ability to regulate investments so that the appropriate balance of 'rights and obligations among the State Parties, the investors, and the investments'.[138] From the outset, the Morocco–Nigeria BIT signals a level of mutuality and equality between the two States and a collective commitment to sustainable investment that is lacking in other treaties.

The Morocco–Nigeria BIT reflects a cooperative spirit. Although an aggrieved investor can pursue investor-State arbitration, it can only do so after the investor's home State participates in a dispute prevention procedure under which a joint committee of representatives designated by both Morocco and Nigeria (Joint Committee) assesses and attempts to resolve the matter.[139] Absent resolution, the investor must exhaust local remedies in host State courts before pursuing arbitration.[140]

The significance of the Morocco–Nigeria BIT goes beyond the tenor and establishment of an inclusive supervising body. In particular, after reaffirming their committee to labour rights,[141] the States recognize that it would be 'inappropriate to encourage investment by weakening or reducing' labour protections or 'to encourage investment by relaxing domestic labour, public health or safety'.[142] These provisions are not novel[143] and immediately

---

[135] See eg Karen Halverson Cross, 'Converging Trends in Investment Treaty Practice' (2012) 38 NC J Intl L & Com Reg 151, 196–97; Levent Sabanogullari, 'The Merits and Limitations of General Exception Clauses in Contemporary Investment Treaty Practice' (*Investment Treaty News*, 21 May 2015) <www.iisd.org/itn/2015/05/21/the-merits-and-limitations-of-general-exception-clauses-in-contemporary-investment-treaty-practice/#_edn5> accessed 13 March 2022 (contending that 'a host state's defence profile can potentially benefit greatly from the possibility of invoking [a general exceptions clause] in arbitrations involving the public interest').

[136] Caroline Henckels 'Should Investment Treaties Contain Public Policy Exceptions?' (2018) 59 BC L Rev 2825, 2829 (noting that it is unclear whether an exception clause 'operates as a *permission* or as a *defense*') (emphasis in original).

[137] Reciprocal Investment Promotion and Protection Agreement between the Government of the Kingdom of Morocco and the Government of the Federal Republic of Nigeria (signed 3 December 2016) (Morocco–Nigeria BIT) <https://investmentpolicy.unctad.org/international-investment-agreements/treaty-files/5409/download> < accessed 13 March 2022.

[138] ibid preamble.

[139] ibid art 26. Details about the establishment and responsibilities of the Joint Committee are in Article 4, titled 'Institutional Governance'.

[140] ibid.

[141] ibid art 15(1) (acknowledging their 'obligations as members of the International Labour Organization (ILO) and their commitments under the ILO Declaration on Fundamental Principles and Rights at Work and its Follow-up').

[142] ibid art 15.

[143] See eg Susan L Karamanian, 'Human Rights Dimensions of Investment Law' in Erika de Wet and Jure Vidmar (eds), *Hierarchy in International Law: The Place of Human Rights* (OUP 2012) 237, 245 (identifying BITs with comparable language).

after them is the commitment of the each State to 'ensuring that its laws and regulations provide for high levels of labour and human rights protection appropriate to its economic and social situation' while striving to improve them.[144] Further, the States are obligated to have their 'laws, policies and action' conform to international human rights treaties to which they are parties.[145] This last provision is important as enactment of human rights obligations within the State's domestic laws would force the investor to comply with applicable human rights standards and its failure to do so could be grounds for denying protection under the treaty.[146]

The key distinguishing feature of the Morocco–Nigeria BIT is the imposition of duties on investors, both pre- and post-establishment.[147] For example, investors are required pre-investment to 'comply with [applicable] environmental assessment screening and assessment processes', whether required by the host State or the home State, whichever is 'more rigorous'.[148] This provision does more than impose a duty as it addresses a concern that the law of the investor's home State should have relevance when the investor goes abroad.[149] In addition to submitting an environmental assessment, the investor or the investment 'shall conduct a social impact assessment' based on standards established by the Joint Committee.[150] Also, pre-establishment, investors and investments that engage in corruption are deemed to have breached the domestic law of the host State.[151]

Post-establishment, the BIT obligates that investments 'maintain an environmental management system'.[152] Further, '[i]nvestors and investments shall uphold human rights in the host state' as well as comply with ILO labour standards. In their operations, investors and investments 'shall not ... circumvent[] international environmental, labour and human rights obligations to which the host state and/or home state are Parties'.[153] Again, the BIT recognizes that if the home standard is more demanding, it follows the investor and its investment. The BIT imposes other obligations on the investors and their investments, particularly as to corporate governance, such as transparency and accounting practices.

What are the consequences if an investor breaches the duties set forth in the Morocco–Nigeria BIT? Under Article 20, if the investor's conduct causes 'significant damage, personal injuries or loss of life in the host state' the investor shall be subject to suit for civil liability in its home State.[154] This provision enables any person or entity that can establish damages due to the investor's conduct in the host State to assert a claim for civil liability in the courts of

---

[144] Morocco–Nigeria BIT (n 137) art 15(5).
[145] ibid art 15(6).
[146] See nn 171–83 and accompanying text.
[147] This approach is also reflected in the Supplementary Act A/SA.3/12/08 Adopting Community Rules on Investment and the Modalities for their Implementation with ECOWAS (opened for signature 19 December 2008, entered into force 9 January 2009) <https://jusmundi.com/en/document/pdf/Treaty/IIA-3547/en/en-supplementary-act-a-sa-3-12-08-adopting-community-rules-on-investment-and-the-modalities-for-their-imp lementation-with-ecowas-ecowas-supplementary-act-on-investments-friday-19th-december-2008> accessed 13 March 2022.
[148] Morocco–Nigeria BIT (n 137) art 14(1); the precautionary principle is to apply to the environmental assessment (art 14(3)).
[149] See Robert McCorquodale and Penelope Simons, 'Responsibility beyond Borders: State Responsibility for Extraterritorial Violations by Corporations of International Human Rights Law' (2007) 70(4) MLR 598.
[150] Morocco–Nigeria BIT (n 137) art 14(2).
[151] ibid art 17(2), (4).
[152] ibid art 18(1).
[153] ibid art 18(4).
[154] ibid art 20.

the State where the investor is situated.[155] Recognition that the foreign investor could face liability in its home State for acts in the host State fills a critical existing gap. The home State may previously have declined jurisdiction over claims by foreign plaintiffs as to acts that occurred and damages that were incurred in the host State based on a presumption against extraterritoriality. Article 20 reverses that presumption.

Finally, Article 24 of the Morocco–Nigeria BIT, entitled Corporate Social Responsibility, recognizes that investors and their investments 'should strive to make the maximum feasible contributions to the sustainable development of the Host State and local community through high level of socially responsible practices'.[156] Shaping the CSR concept are the priorities of the host State and the UN Sustainable Development Goals.[157] Further, investors 'should' follow the ILO Tripartite Declaration on Multinational Investments and Social Policy and other appropriate standards for responsible conduct.[158] Unlike the obligations to perform environmental and social assessments, not to engage in corruption, and to uphold human rights, the CSR obligation is in terms of 'should'.

The Brazil–Guyana CIFA, signed on 13 December 2018, takes a similar approach to the Morocco–Nigeria BIT.[159] In this agreement, States recognize that investment is essential to 'promoting sustainable development' and they reaffirm 'their regulatory autonomy and policy space'.[160] The treaty requires investors to comply with all laws concerning the investment, bars investors from engaging in bribery, and imposes an obligation on investors to provide information about the investment and investor per applicable legislation.[161] The Brazil–Guyana Cooperation and Investment Facilitation Agreement (CIFA) also includes a CSR clause, in which investors and their investment 'shall strive to achieve the highest possible level of contribution to the sustainable development of the Host State and the local community, through the adoption of a high degree of socially responsible practices'.[162] The agreement then describes 'voluntary principles and standards for a responsible business conduct' to which the investor 'shall endeavour to comply'.[163] Like the Morocco–Nigeria BIT, the CSR obligation in the Brazil–Guyana CIFA is not mandatory.[164]

---

[155] Southern African Development Community (SADC) Model Bilateral Investment Treaty Template, art 17(2) has a similar provision with more clarity as to the obligations of the home State:

> Home states shall ensure that their legal systems and rules allow for, or do not prevent or unduly restrict, the bringing of court actions on their merits before domestic courts relating to the civil liability of Investors and Investments for damages resulting from alleged acts, decisions or omissions made by Investors in relation to their Investments in the territory of the Host State.

[156] ibid art 24.
[157] ibid.
[158] ibid.
[159] Cooperation and Investment Facilitation Agreement between the Federative Republic of Brazil and the Co-operative Republic of Guyana (signed 13 December 2018) (Brazil–Guyana CIFA). See also Cooperation and Investment Facilitation Agreement between the Federative Republic of Brazil and the Republic of Suriname, Preamble, arts 14–15 (signed 2 May 2018).
[160] Brazil–Guyana CIFA (n 159) preamble.
[161] ibid art 14.
[162] ibid art 15(1).
[163] ibid art 15(1)–(2). The voluntary principles and standards included respecting 'internationally recognized human rights of those involved in the enterprises' activities', encouraging local capacity building, and refraining from discriminatory practices. ibid art 15(2).
[164] See also Reciprocal Promotion and Protection of Investments between the Argentine Republic and the State of Qatar (signed 6 November 2016) art 12 ('Investors operating in the territory of the host Contracting Party should make efforts to voluntarily incorporate internationally recognized standards of corporate social responsibility into their business policies and practices') <https://investmentpolicy.unctad.org/international-investment-agreements/treaty-files/5383/download> accessed 13 March 2022.

The Dutch Model BIT 2019 is another example of an IIA that imposes investor obligations. Specifically, it requires that investors and their investments comply 'with domestic laws and regulations of the host state, including laws and regulations on human rights, environmental protection and labor laws'.[165] Yet presumably the investor would be required to comply with municipal law, the treaty aside!

In March 2015, India revealed a Model BIT with obligations to comply with all host State law, including human rights and environmental law.[166] The draft also required the investor to comply with transparency, anti-corruption, and tax obligations.[167] The March 2015 Indian Model BIT authorized the State to bring a counterclaim for breach of the positive obligations.[168] Yet in late December 2015, after obtaining feedback on the March 2015 Model BIT, India launched a new BIT, which did not impose duties on investors.[169] Instead, the new BIT, known as the 2016 Indian Model BIT, carved out a broad exceptions clause to prevent application of protection measures to a wide range of government conduct and it limited investor-State arbitration until after the investor had pursued claims in the courts of India for at least five years.[170] As of today, only Cambodia has signed a BIT modelled after the 2016 Indian Model BIT and, in the meantime, as noted, India has terminated 58 BITs based on earlier models.[171]

States have multiple tools to address the human rights gap in IIAs. Some of them are less effective than others. For example, a State that disengages from IIAs abdicates power in the face of other States that may be wielding their power to lure in foreign investment. Another form of abdication would be for the State to remain idle with hopes that tribunals will sort through the human rights aspects of IIAs, absent some reform of the latter. States have the authority to refine standards and processes, whether through new IIAs or by way of advisory bodies along the lines proposed by UNCITRAL.

As the next section discusses, reforms of IIAs that broaden the State's regulatory authority and exempt specific State action from the investment protection measures or include explicit reference to obligations of investors, have the potential to hold investors to a greater level of engagement in respecting obligations.

D. Interpreting Treaties: Filling Gaps and New Challenges

What does refinement of IIAs mean for investor obligations? First, in a general sense, today's conversation about most IIAs cannot ignore investor obligations, yet this was true in a limited sense in 1959 as the first IIA required that the investment be in accordance with

---

[165] Dutch Model BIT 2019 (n 114) art 7(1).

[166] Model Text for the Indian Bilateral Investment Treaty (Model Text), art 12 <www.mygov.in/sites/default/files/master_image/Model%20Text%20for%20the%20Indian%20Bilateral%20Investment%20Treaty.pdf> accessed 13 March 2022.

[167] ibid arts 9–11. See also Jesse Coleman and Kanika Gupta, 'India's Revised Model BIT: Two Steps Forward, One Step Back?' (*Investment Claims*, 4 October 2017) <https://scholarship.law.columbia.edu/cgi/viewcontent.cgi?article=1111&context=sustainable_investment_staffpubs> accessed 13 March 2022.

[168] India Model Text (n 166) art 14.11.

[169] Coleman and Gupta (n 167).

[170] ibid.

[171] Nishith Desai, 'Why India's Model Bilateral Investment Treaty Needs a Thorough Relook' (*Mondaq*, 13 February 2019) <www.mondaq.com/india/x/780336/Inward+Foreign+Investment/Why+Indias+Model+Bilateral+Investment+Treaty+Needs+A+Thorough+Relook> accessed 13 March 2022.

host State law. Language aside, tribunals have used international law to prevent investors from using ISDS to benefit from their wrongful conduct.[172]

As to treaties in which the preamble states that the parties expect that investment will further goals beyond investment, the potential for engagement with a range of issues looms large. Under VCLT Article 31(1), a statement about the treaty's purpose could inform a tribunal's interpretation. Although arbitral tribunals have not given substantial weight to preamble text, as it has largely been quite vanilla,[173] with language that links foreign investment to objectives beyond investment itself, they have the tools to evaluate pre- and post-establishment conduct. For example, the preamble to the 2012 US Model Bilateral Investment Treaty provides that the treaty's investment objectives are to be achieved 'in a manner consistent with the protection of health, safety, and the environment, and the promotion of internationally recognized labor rights'.[174] Surely a tribunal could interpret this text to recognize that foreign investment at odds with a State's safety measures would not be protected under the treaty. As a result, the 2012 US Model BIT, while not expressly imposing a duty on the investor, implicitly does so given the recognition that the treaty seeks investment consistent with mandated safety measures.

Whether tribunals will use the tools available them to give full effect to IIAs is another issue. As observed, States have 'chosen to remain silent on many important matters that influence their treaty obligations or dispute settlement procedures'.[175] With States realizing that treaties and arbitration rules could afford them the right to assert a counterclaim, however, a tangible and potentially rewarding incentive is on the table.

Further, non-parties, such as individuals or non-governmental organizations, whose rights could be affected by an investment or the investor's dispute against the host State have a greater degree of engagement in investment disputes under various treaties. Even as to IIAs in which reference to non-investment goals is merely a reaffirmation, such as in the CETA preamble, those affected by a dispute have the potential to appear before the new court and present both oral and written submissions.[176]

Beyond the preamble, the critical substantive areas of change in IIAs have been in the imposition of express duties on investors. The Morocco–Nigeria BIT is unambiguous and exposes the investor to a claim in its home State for non-compliance of obligations. As to other treaties, such as the Argentina–Qatar BIT and Brazil–Guyana CIFA, the obligation, while directly on the investor, is to comply voluntarily with CSR standards. The language should not be ignored as it must have legal significance beyond words of encouragement. For example, an investor that ignores CSR and expressly refuses to consider any policies would run afoul of the treaty. On the flip side, an investor that adopts a CSR policy as per these BITs but then disregards the policy at least could be negligent as the policy establishes a minimum standard of care.

---

[172] See above nn 42–50 and accompanying text.

[173] Ole Kristian Fauchald, 'The Legal Reasoning of ICSID Tribunals—An Empirical Analysis' (2008) 19 EJIL 301.

[174] 2012 US Model Bilateral Investment Treaty (preamble) <https://ustr.gov/sites/default/files/BIT%20text%20for%20ACIEP%20Meeting.pdf> accessed 13 March 2022.

[175] Kathryn Gordon and Joachim Pohl, 'Investment Treaties over Time-Treaty Practice and Interpretation in a Changing World' (2015) OECD Working Papers on International Investments, 2015/02 14 <www.oecd.org/investment/investment-policy/WP-2015-02.pdf> accessed 13 March 2022.

[176] CETA (n 105) art 8.38(2).

A vexing issue is the legal effect of the State's duty under the treaties to encourage investors to comply voluntarily with various CSR standards. The treaties impose this obligation on the State, not directly on enterprises. In CETA, the recommended CSR standards for investors are those in the OECD Guidelines for Multinational Enterprises, and the Dutch Model BIT 2019 likewise references these and other international standards. The OECD Guidelines, aptly titled, are 'non-binding principles and standards for responsible business conduct consistent with applicable laws and internationally recognized standards'.[177] Nearly all State parties to CETA were already bound to them as OECD members. Drawing on the UN Guiding Principles, the OECD Guidelines recognize that enterprises have obligations in countries where they operate. As under the UN Guiding Principles, enterprises are to respect human rights and 'address adverse' consequences that they have caused.[178] Various duties, however, such as the duty to protect human rights, however, ultimately rests with the States.[179]

Nonetheless, *Urbaser* signalled that international law has recognized that CSR obligations of corporations are of 'crucial importance'.[180] At the same time, as even *Urbaser* acknowledges, merely acknowledging the importance of these obligations does not elevate them to the level of international legal duties of investors. The key is for the IIA to unambiguously delineate the obligation.

Another perplexing approach is Article 15 of the Morocco–Nigeria BIT, which calls on each State to take action, such as 'high levels' of 'human rights protection' and ensuring that 'laws, policies and actions' conform to obligations under human rights treaties. This language begs the question why each State has not done so already if indeed human rights treaties impose such a duty on the State. Second, the obligation under the treaty is not limited to laws affecting foreign investors. In short, an inventory of the entirety of the State's laws enforcing applicable human rights standards would be required. After the assessment, the State would need to adopt and enforce the laws. Such a lengthy and consuming process could be overwhelming. Instead, each State, perhaps through the Joint Committee, established under Article 4, could prioritize areas of human rights and submit proposed laws to the States. Ultimately, the burden should be on the State, as opposed to the investors, to ensure the recognition and protection of human rights.[181]

Equally unclear is the legal significance of the obligation that '[i]nvestors and investments shall uphold human rights in the host state'.[182] The absence of specificity as to the human rights at issue could render the obligation hollow. Second, under human rights treaties, the State, not investors, bears the legal obligation. Another part of the Morocco–Nigeria BIT refers to the investor's compliance with specific standards, such as the 'core labour standards' as reflected in the ILO Declaration on Fundamental Principles and Rights of Work, 1998, or anti-corruption measures. The treaty should delineate the standards that the investors are obliged to follow. Further, it should delineate the means for compliance with these standards.

---

[177] OECD, *OECD Guidelines for Multinational Enterprises* (OECD 2011).
[178] ibid ch IV.
[179] UN, 'Guiding Principles on Business and Human Rights: Implementing the United Nations "Protect, Respect and Remedy" Framework' (2011) <www.ohchr.org/documents/publications/guidingprinciplesbusine sshr_en.pdf> accessed 13 March 2022, I.A.
[180] *Urbaser* (n 55) para 1195.
[181] I am grateful to Professor Andrea Bjorklund for her insights on this issue.
[182] Morocco–Nigeria BIT (n 137) art 18(2).

Third, as noted, the Morocco–Nigeria BIT establishes a mechanism for institutional governance, the Joint Committee. The Joint Committee has substantial authority, the application of which could be at odds with fairness and predictability. For example, before an investor can file an arbitration demand it is required to first seek amicable settlement of its dispute before the Joint Committee. Settlement of disputes through mediation is highly desirable; yet, having representatives of the State parties as mediators could cause undue political influence in the process.

The soft approach of Article 24 of the Morocco–Nigeria BIT, CETA and other treaties of encouraging investors to engage in specific conduct has the advantage of sidestepping legal process. The downside is the absence of any reliable means to assess progress towards accomplishing the intended goals. Without such, the commitment to obligations, while laudable, could be meaningless, and even counterproductive as all participants take comfort in the treaty language. At a minimum, the treaties should set out specific steps for investor compliance with the CSR obligation and identifying objective standards for evaluating their progress.

Concerns about the host State's ability to hold investors accountable for their failure to adhere to obligations under the law of the host State could be minimized by a requirement that the home State commit to have its courts exercise jurisdiction over the investors as their overseas activity. This approach is not unprecedented, as evidenced by the US Foreign Corrupt Practices Act (FCPA).[183] Under the FCPA, acts of bribery committed by US actors, for example, can be prosecuted in US courts, regardless of where they occurred.[184]

Finally, more corporations are adopting codes of conduct, in which they commit to adhere to standards in a range of areas, such as compliance with anticorruption, data privacy, human rights, and intellectual property norms. For example, the Nike Code of Conduct entitled 'Inside the Lines' provides a long list of 'laws, regulations and company policies' that apply to its employees.[185] Nike pronounces the following simple rule: 'Don't bribe anybody, anytime, for any reason'.[186] At a minimum, this rule, coupled with the detailed analysis Nike provides of it, establishes that bribery is a serious wrongdoing. As noted, tribunals have found serious wrongdoing to establish the basis for holding that the foreign investment based on it undermines a tribunal's jurisdiction.[187] Nike also mentions that it adheres 'to safety, health, environmental protection and labeling requirements for products in compliance with all applicable law'.[188] A tribunal could rely on this language to establish the importance to Nike of its overall commitment to environmental laws, arguably including ones enacted after Nike has made an investment, to establish the contours of FET. Another approach would be for the tribunal to consider an investor's noncompliance with its own standard of care in deciding compensation, which would be in line with an approach set out in the Dutch Model BIT 2019.[189]

---

[183] Foreign Corrupt Practices Act 1977 15 US Code §§ 78dd-1ff.

[184] ibid.

[185] Nike, Inc, 'Inside the Lines: Nike Code of Conduct' <https://s1.q4cdn.com/806093406/files/doc_downloads/2021/02/Inside-The-Lines-Code-Of-Conduct-November-2020.pdf> accessed 13 March 2022.

[186] ibid 17.

[187] See n 29 and accompanying text.

[188] Nike (n 185) 19.

[189] Dutch Model BIT (n 114) art 23 (in deciding compensation, a tribunal 'is expected to take into account non-compliance by the investor with its commitments under the UN Guiding Principles on Business and Human Rights, and the OECD Guidelines for Multinational Enterprises').

As Section III has documented, the landscape as to IIAs is fluid with the concept of investor obligations becoming more critical in defining it.

IV. Conclusion

Gone are the days when reference to investor obligations in ISDS would lead to silence or a short, perfunctory dismissal of the statement. New IIAs have put development goals, eliminating corruption, securing the environment, and promoting human rights in the mix and even on par with the aim of protecting the investor and its investment. IIAs have expanded the scope of areas in which host States can regulate. VCLT Article 31 equips tribunals with legal authority to interpret IIAs to give effect to investor obligations consistent with the treaty objectives.

For the foreign investor, understanding the full implications of its investment is critical. Each situation may be unique, depending on the IIA, yet an investor should tread cautiously in assuming that if the IIA does not impose a specific duty that it is not otherwise relevant. Even when the treaty encourages the investor to comply with CSR standards, for example, it signals that the investor will need to act. In the years to come, treaties with such soft language could usher in new domestic investment laws requiring CSR compliance.

For the rule of law, the 'rebalancing' as well as other developments as to IIAs reflect a reconciling of two perceived competing interests, reflecting values of powerful constituencies. Instead of shying away, the differences should be addressed head-on. The new generation of IIAs does just that. They have launched a discussion that will likely lead to further rebalancing, and yet again, after further trial and error, even more rebalancing.

16
Domestic Investors, the Rule of Law, and Equality

Krista Nadakavukaren Schefer

I. Introduction

The international investment law regime—by which I mean the bilateral, plurilateral, and multilateral investment protection treaties and the institutions to resolve investor-State disputes arising out of them—has been under sustained criticism for nearly two decades. Significantly, the system has vigorously taken up these criticisms with dozens of conferences, committee and working group meetings held, expert reports written, and steps taken to discuss the perceived failings and propose repairs or replacements. While both the criticisms and the proposed solutions have been avidly led, accompanied, and followed by the scholarly investment law community, one fundamental aspect of criticism has remained a shadowy figure despite its popularity among political debates on the regime. This is the question of how to justify the preferential treatment the system gives to foreign investors as opposed to national investors vis-à-vis the host State: the equality issue.

The equality issue is not new: the Argentinian scholar Carlos Calvo had argued for equality in the nineteenth century—that foreigner investors should be treated as nationals in every respect: no worse, but also no better.[1] But neither is it getting much traction in the twenty-first-century investment community. Not that it has been overlooked or completely ignored, but with our attention firmly on the 'international', most of us are concerned more with how States address the alien or to what extent the public goods of environment, health, and fundamental labour rights can be regulated without the State incurring liability towards the foreign investor than with how national investors fare. The treatment of national investors, after all, is an issue of domestic law and with the system evolving so rapidly, there is plenty to write about on the international law aspects. Or maybe we do not ask the question too loudly because if investor inequality is recognized as a problem, resolution of the problem will not be one of tweaking the system. It will be one of ditching it.

The editors of this volume are courageous for including a chapter on equality of investors in their work on rule of law. Yet, when they asked me to contribute my thoughts on this, it was with what I now admit as an ignorant pleasure that I agreed. I, like many, have harboured some doubts about whether a specific area of law known as foreign investment law is essential to fostering development[2] and even if it is normatively

---

[1] See generally Ahmed Kamal el-Din Izzeddin, *The Calvo Doctrine and the Hull Formula: Prospects for Harmony* (BookVenture Publishing 2017) 15.

[2] Much of the 'do BITs work?' literature is focused on asking whether the special treaty-based regime for offering investors protection achieves the promise of stimulating investment flows between the State Parties. The results are notoriously ambiguous. While Salacuse and Sullivan's early look at the question detects a strongly positive

Krista Nadakavukaren Schefer, *Domestic Investors, the Rule of Law, and Equality* In: *Investment Protection Standards and the Rule of Law*. Edited by: August Reinisch and Stephan W. Schill, Oxford University Press. © Krista Nadakavukaren Schefer 2023.
DOI: 10.1093/oso/9780192864581.003.0016

desirable;[3] like many, I have serious doubts as to whether the investor-State dispute settlement (ISDS) mechanism is an essential part of the investment protection regime;[4] and like many, I recognize the dangers of the moral hazard of offering foreign investors engaged in businesses that may profit from a foreign government's lack of effective human rights, labour, and environmental protection a way to protect their businesses when these same governments violate the investor's rights.[5]

I did not, however, doubt the fundamental character of the regime as adhering to basic rule-of-law standards. I, too, have written that the regime of foreign investor protection is, at its best, one part of improving overall governance, both international and domestic.[6] Asking about the equality issue specifically, however, raised further questions of whether my normative doubts about the system should impact what I analyse in terms of how the investment regime interacts with the larger conception of the rule of law. To do this analysis, I needed to be clear about both what the rule of law is and what equality means and how they relate. This definitional work led me to conclude that there is no single answer—that the multiple answers are heavily dependent on our legal culture's view of rule of law and our personal differences in what we see as the goals of equality.

The limits of space do not allow for an exhaustive exploration of all angles of the relationship between rule of law, equality, and investment law. The concept of 'rule of law' deserves a much deeper treatment than is found here. Even my initial research efforts into the subject uncovered firm evidence of the fundamentally different approaches taken by German, US, French, British, and Swiss legal scholars as to what the rule of law aims to ensure and what

effect of bilateral investment treaties on investment flows, others question reliance on the available data, and more innovative methods reveal little to no positive effects. Compare Jeswald W Salacuse and Nicholas P Sullivan, 'Do BITs Really Work: An Evaluation of Bilateral Investment Treaties and Their Grand Bargain' (2005) 46 Harv Intl LJ 67, 95–111; with Jonathan Bonnitcha, Lauge N Skovgaard Poulsen and Michael Waibel, *The Political Economy of the Investment Treaty Regime* (OUP 2017) 158–76 and Jason Webb Yackee, 'Bilateral Investment Treaties, Credible Commitment, and the Rule of (International) Law: Do BITs Promote Foreign Direct Investment?' (2008) 42 Law & Soc Rev 805, 818–27. See also Jason Webb Yackee, 'Do Bilateral Investment Treaties Promote Foreign Direct Investment?—Some Hints from Alternative Evidence' (2011) 51 Va JIL 397.

[3] Critics of the investment law system as a whole include Schneiderman and Sornarajah. See eg David Schneiderman, 'Investing in Democracy? Political Process and International Investment Law' (2010) 60(4) UTLJ 909, 940 (asserting that the 'investment rules regime' promotes a 'nexus between robust democratic practice and the suppression of alternatives'); David Schneiderman,*Constitutionalizing Economic Globalization: Investment Rules and Democracy's Promise* (CUP 2008) 225; M Sornarajah, *The International Law on Foreign Investment* (5th edn, CUP 2021) 2–6 (describing investment law as the result of policies imposed by developed States on developing states and that conflicting views of investment law remain ones of 'power confronting justice').

[4] George Kahale, III, 'Rethinking ISDS' (2018) 44 Brooklyn JIL 11, 45 ('one has to question whether the outcome of [the ISDS] reform process, even if "successful", would be worth the investment of time and effort necessary'); Sergio Puig and Anton Strezhnev, 'The David Effect and ISDS' (2017) 28 EJIL 731, fn 12 and accompanying text.

[5] The clash between the international investment protections offered corporations and the gaps in corporate accountability for environmental and human rights accountability are core elements of much of the United Nations Committee on Trade and Development (UNCTAD) and civil society activity in the area of investment law. The International Institute for Sustainable Development and the Columbia Center on Sustainable Investment each have contributed heavily to the literature. See Elisabeth Tuerk and Faraz Rojid, 'Towards a New Generation of Investment Policies: UNCTAD's Investment Policy Framework for Sustainable Development' (2012) 1(3) Investment Treaty News 7–9 <www.iisd.org/itn/en/2012/10/30/towards-a-new-generation-of-investment-polic ies-unctads-investment-policy-framework-for-sustainable-development/> accessed 14 October 2021; Columbia Center on Sustainable Investment and the United Nations Human Rights Special Procedures Working Group on the Issue of Human Rights and Transnational Corporations and Other Business Enterprises, 'Impacts of the International Investment Regime on Access to Justice, Roundtable Outcome Document' (CCSI, September 2018) <www.ohchr.org/Documents/Issues/Business/CCSI_UNWGBHR_InternationalInvestmentRegime.pdf> accessed 14 October 2021.

[6] Krista Nadakavukaren Schefer, 'State Powers and Investor-State Dispute Settlement' in Shaheeza Lalani and Rodrigo Polanco Lazo (eds), *The Role of the State in Investor-State Arbitration* (Brill 2015) 15–21, 19.

elements constitute a rule-of-law system.[7] These different views of rule of law could lead to substantially different results of an analysis of offering foreign investors access to international investment protections than the results set out here. The present chapter is much less ambitious, as I adopt the editors' choice of rule-of-law definition—that set out in the 2004 United Nations Secretary General's statement and considered a statement of what the 'international rule of law' means.[8]

The question of how to approach the question of 'equality' in investment law is also underexplored, given the complexity of the topic. The object of philosophical and legal (and legal philosophical) study for millennia, the core notion of 'equality' is its setting forth of a relationship between non-identical objects that are similar in certain ways but different in others.[9] For this chapter, I take a view of equality that mainly looks at formal, or Aristotelian, notions of equality: that which demands like be treated as like and unlike treated as unlike. I do, however, refer to an alternative vision of equality that deserves further study in the investment law context.

The chapter thus proceeds as follows: Section II describes how the rule of law is defined as a guiding concept for the international community. Section III takes up the concept of equality and argues that it may be seen as either an element or consequence of rule of law, but that differential treatment on its own does not violate either. In Section IV, the rule-of-law–equality relationship is set within the investment law context, highlighting the cases in which domestic courts have examined the distinction between foreign and national investors and ruled on whether distinct privileges offered to foreign investors by international investment agreements violate national norms of equality of treatment. Section V concludes, suggesting that further work on the rule-of-law–equality relationship in investor-State interactions needs to examine more deeply other views of rule of law and other concepts of equality.

II. Rule of Law

The definition—and therefore the content—of rule of law varies over time and legal system.[10] The conventional legal approach to rule of law is to consider it a proposition that

---

[7] Even if one accepts the contested characterization of rule of law as a legal principle and that it is a principle intended as one of self-restraint—one that applies to a sovereign's use of its own legal power as judged by the sovereign itself—what this means in any particular legal system depends on the specifics of that system. These various views on rule of law are based in the differences in the notions' development through the legal history of the different systems in which similar—but not identical—norms arose. Thus, any discussions of rule of law in the international investment law context—including discussions relating to whether equality is a necessary element of the rule of law—are going to be coloured by the legal background of the participants (and audience) and, just as importantly, its use is going to be necessarily transposed by the very existence of an external adjudicator of the State's actions. See eg Ernst-Wolfgang Böckenförde, 'Rechsstaat' in Joachim Ritter and Karlfried Gründer (eds), *Historisches Wörterbuch der Philosophie* (Schwabe 1992) 332–42; Jeremy Waldron, 'The Concept and the Rule of Law' (2008) 43 Ga L Rev 1. Even these conceptions of rule of law remain within the Western legal conceptual frameworks addressing rule of law. Other frameworks would need to be examined for a fuller analysis. See eg Randall Peerenboom, 'Varieties of Rule of Law: An Introduction and Provisional Conclusion' (2004) <http://ssrn.com/abstract=445821> accessed 14 October 2021.

[8] UNSC, 'The Rule of Law and Transitional Justice in Conflict and Post-Conflict Societies: Report of the Secretary-General' (23 August 2004) UN Doc S/2004/616.

[9] See Stefan Gosepath, 'Equality' in Edward N Zalta (ed), *The Stanford Encyclopedia of Philosophy* (Spring 2011 Edition) <https://plato.stanford.edu/archives/spr2011/entries/equality/> accessed 14 October 2021.

[10] Even within the same legal culture, many different views are also apparent. There are, for example, scholars who emphasize formal elements, those who look to procedure and application, and those who would require

calls for all persons within a legal system to be subject to the laws and to respect the laws, and for those who do not respect the laws to be held accountable for their violations.[11] Studies on the rule of law, however, diverge beyond this basic approach.[12]

The concept of 'rule of law' as it is often described in international settings has a natural affinity to the nineteenth-century Germanic idea of the *Rechtsstaat*.[13] At its heart, this idea does not question the right of the ruler to make laws, but rather stipulates that the government must set out in writing the rules which it would apply to govern society.[14] The legitimacy of these generally applicable rules are the sole basis for governmental interference in the individual's liberty and right to property. The international rule of law, similarly, does not question States' right to their sovereign power. Rather, it tries to constrain the unprincipled use of that power.

The following describes two approaches to the international rule-of-law discussions that have influenced thinking in the investment context: the World Bank's Rule of Law concept and that of the United Nations. The World Bank's early discussions of rule of law were firmly focused on the use of legal systems to adequately protect private property and allow economic growth and development. With the growth of the human-development agenda, the international community began to give more attention to the necessary supporting functions of governments. That is, in addition to protecting existing property rights, governments would need to ensure access of their citizens to food, education, and healthy environments. The UN's adoption of a rule-of-law programme in the new millennium therefore added to the formalistic approach by including 'elements of "thick" definitions'.[15]

---

substantive content to rule of law. Jeremy Waldron, 'The Rule of Law' in Edward N Zalta (ed), *The Stanford Encyclopedia of Philosophy* (Summer 2020 Edition) <https://plato.stanford.edu/archives/sum2020/entries/rule-of-law/> accessed 14 October 2021.

[11] Peerenboom notes that despite the variety of views regarding rule of law, there is a 'broad consensus as to its core meaning and basic elements' (n 7) 2.

[12] See Guido Pincione, 'Rule of Law: Theoretical Perspectives' in Mortimer Sellers and Stephan Kirste (eds), *Encyclopedia of the Philosophy of Law and Social Philosophy* (2019) 1–8 <https://doi.org/10.1007/978-94-007-6730-0_135-1> accessed 14 October 2021 (including a comparison of numerous theorists' views of the requirements of the rule of law); Waldron (n 10) ('[I]t is controversial what the Rule of Law requires. This is partly because the Rule of Law is a working political idea, as much the property of ordinary citizens, lawyers, activists and politicians as of the jurists and philosophers who study it'); Leander Beinlich, 'International Procedural Rights, Domestic Legal Systems and the International Rule of Law' (2019) ESIL Conference Paper Series, Conference Paper No. 1/2019 6 (commenting that '[t]here is little more than a minimum consensus on [rule of law's] core requirements' and that the 'matter gets even more difficult when turning to the international level', leading to debates on not only the content of, but also the existence of, international rule of law).

[13] The term *Rechtsstaat* is one that is literally translated: law-State. The history of the concept is tied to the history of Germany under the absolutist Holy Roman Empire. See Eberhard Weis, 'Enlightenment and Absolutism in the Holy Roman Empire: Thoughts on Enlighted Absolutism in Germany' (1986) 58 J Mod Hist S181 (describing the struggles between the aristocrats and the emperors and noting the changing views of the emperor's relationship to the State). The *Rechtsstaat* concept of rule of law plays a dominant role in international discussions. Indeed, former Advocate General of the European Court of Justice and former Spanish Supreme Court judge Cruz Villalón notes, 'in the EU legal order rule of law is not understood as the counterpart par excellence to the sovereignty of parliament (see Lord Bingham), but as part of a whole set of values ... akin to the German notion of Rechtsstaat. In a word, we say rule of law where we largely understand Rechtsstaat' (emphasis in original). Pedro Cruz Villalón, 'Rule of (German) Law? On Legal Hegemony in the EU' (2020) MPIL Research Paper Series No 2020-43, 11–13.

[14] Moshe Cohen-Eliya and Iddo Porat, 'The Administrative Origins of Constitutional Rights and Global Constitutionalism' in Vicki C Jackson and Mark Tushnet (eds), *Proportionality: New Frontiers, New Challenges* (CUP 2017) 103–29, 114.

[15] Kenneth J Keith, 'The International Rule of Law' (2015) 28 Leiden JIL 403, 408.

A. The World Bank's Liberty-Oriented International Rule-of-Law Approach

The goal of liberty has often been seen as conducive to economic growth,[16] making the liberty-oriented view of rule of law one that has numerous proponents among the international community dedicated to increasing production and global incomes. The World Bank's use of rule of law is a prime example of the liberty approach.

While the law and development movement of the 1960s and 1970s had promoted using legal changes to incentivize economic productivity, the recognition of weaknesses in the governance of developing countries dampened enthusiasm for relying on law to help generate economic growth in World Bank client States by the 1980s.[17] By the 1990s, in fact, global events were demonstrating that laws could be used to prevent economic changes as well to foster them. It was then that the World Bank began to adjust its law-development approach and refer to 'the rule of law' and pursue legal reforms as an integral part of development policy.[18]

As experiences with attempts at legal reform through the simple transplanting of legal rights found in the strong Western economies revealed the weaknesses of believing that strong markets and privatization could rely only on 'good laws', the World Bank (and other institutions) began altering their view of rule of law. As Trubek puts it, '[o]fficial ideas about the "rule of law" become complexified', and a number of social aspects of economic life were taken up as additional aspects of the rule of law and formalism was increasingly questioned.[19] The basic belief in 'the nature of law, the relationship between law and development, and the relevance of Western models, however contextualized' remains, however.[20]

The definitions used by the World Bank under different general counsels[21] evolved from purely formalistic ones to statements including values such as democracy, legitimacy, and poverty reduction. Still, 'at the heart of the Bank's ROL remains a stark formalism'.[22] The Bank explains rule of law as indicating 'perceptions of the extent to which agents have confidence in and abide by the rules of society, and in particular the quality of contract enforcement, property rights, the police, and the courts, as well as the likelihood of crime and violence'.[23]

The World Bank's concept thus appears to aim at ensuring that individuals are both free to pursue economic activities, and secure in their belief that the government will not violate their property rights if they do so. The criteria by which the Bank assesses these perceptions are consequently those of the efficiency and efficacy of the courts, the level of corruption, the control of violence and crime, as well as the rules regarding expropriation, the State's adherence to contracts, and the protections offered to land and intellectual property.[24] Using

---

[16] Javier Alfonso-Gil, Maricruz Lacalle-Calderón and Rocío Sánchez-Mangas, 'Civil Liberty and Economic Growth in the World: A Long-Run Perspective, 1850–2010' (2014) 10 J Institutional Econ 427.

[17] Gordon Barron, 'The World Bank & Rule of Law Reforms' (December 2005) www.files.ethz.ch/isn/137920/WP70.pdf accessed 14 October 2021, 5–8.

[18] ibid 9–10.

[19] David Trubek, 'The "Rule of Law" in Development Assistance: Past, Present, and Future' in David M Trubek and Alvaro Santos (eds), The New Law and Economic Development: A Critical Appraisal (CUP 2006) 74–94, 90–91.

[20] ibid 93.

[21] ibid 13–14.

[22] ibid 15.

[23] World Bank, 'Rule of Law' <http://info.worldbank.org/governance/wgi/pdf/rl.pdf> accessed 14 October 2021, 1.

[24] ibid.

the label 'rule of law' to continue to aim to create conditions under which economic actors can engage profitably is perhaps the best the World Bank can do—observers have pointed out the quixotic goal of promoting rule of law without violating the Bank's own prohibition on acting 'politically'.[25]

B. UN's Development-Oriented International Rule-of-Law Approach

The United Nation's international rule-of-law definition goes beyond a liberty view, specifying that the laws a State promulgates are to be 'consistent with international human rights norms and standards'. This chapter follows the volume editors' request that authors adopt the description of the international law rule of law as that set forth by the United Nations (UN) Secretary-General in 2004 as a starting point. Then Secretary-General Kofi Annan described the approach as follows:

> The 'rule of law' ... refers to a principle of governance in which all persons, institutions and entities, public and private, including the State itself, are accountable to laws that are publicly promulgated, equally enforced and independently adjudicated, and which are consistent with international human rights norms and standards. It requires, as well, measures to ensure adherence to the principles of supremacy of law, equality before the law, accountability to the law, fairness in the application of the law, separation of powers, participation in decision-making, legal certainty, avoidance of arbitrariness and procedural and legal transparency.[26]

The next section describes the procedural demand of the international rule of law as a governance mechanism (Section 1) and its material requirement of generality (Section 2).

1. Rule of law as a way to govern

As 'a principle of governance', this conception of the rule of law emphasizes how law is applied and enforced. This means that in the international system of sovereign States, the United Nations' view of rule of law is not a legal demand, but a (preferred) way of using State power. The statement lists substantive goals (including equality before the law) as elements of an international rule of law but does not dictate the processes or organizational forms by which States are to achieve them.

Thus, the rule of law as put out in the 2004 UN Report (and seemingly intended in the 2012 General Assembly Resolution)[27] appears to make mainly process-oriented demands on States. This is useful because the heterogeneity of the governmental forms represented by the UN membership (absolute and constitutional monarchies, as well as dictatorships join democracies as members) is not directly challenged. Moreover, it fully accepts that

---

[25] Barron (n 17) 32 ('the need to focus on purely economic legal institutions necessarily imposes on the Bank a very restricted view of the legal system and the ROL, and severely limits its ability to "build" the ROL').

[26] UNSC (n 8) para 6; see also August Reinisch and Stephan W Schill, 'Introduction' (in this volume) 1, 4–6.

[27] UNGA Res 67/1 'Declaration of the High-level Meeting of the General Assembly on the Rule of Law at the National and International Levels' (30 November 2012) UN Doc A/RES/67/1. The Declaration in fact contains no definition of rule of law, rather emphasizing its importance and noting that rule of law is 'interlinked' with democracy and human rights. ibid para 5.

States are sovereign—both in terms of being equal as States and as possessing full power within their territories—another important criteria for the UN, given the Charter's commitment to an international system characterized by independent and equal States.[28] The UN's rule-of-law notion in fact supports the sovereignty of States by asking governments to make the law supreme to a State leader's fiat (suggesting that the leader's will could, otherwise, be a source of ultimate power) and by asking State officials to notify the existence of the laws to those who are subject to them.

From the perspective of rule-of-law 'thickness', it is the normative elements of the UN's rule-of-law definition that are its most interesting: the call for laws to be consistent with international human rights and that the application of law is to be fair. These criteria are unusual, and add some viscosity to the concept that international investment law should not ignore when considering the compatibility of offering foreign investors special protections with the rule of law.

The substantive content of the definition is clear because the report itself (although its particular emphasis was on rebuilding post-conflict societies) exemplifies what can be called 'spillover thinking' about development,[29] which arose in the 1990s. This was the belief (shared by the World Bank) that the liberty-enhancing civil and political human rights, supplemented by a push to promote economic and social human rights, would lead naturally to development. It was a way of addressing what Trubek calls the 'triple shift' in the paradigm of international development that was occurring in the wake of the end of the Cold War: 'from state to market, from internal to export-led growth, and from official capital flows to private foreign investment'.[30]

To ensure buy-in by the growing human rights community, 'rule of law' replaced the idea of 'law and development' as a goal of placing law at the core of the international development agenda.[31] The demands of the UN rule of law therefore go beyond the 'thin' view of rule of law, which asks only for regularity and publicity, and adds to it a call for the generality of laws.[32]

2. Generality as an equality element in the rule of law

Generality itself is considered an egalitarian principle by some of the most significant legal theorists, but its exact meaning is disputed.[33] The concept of 'generality' is also an element of the UN view of rule of law, and the two elements together are significant for the compatibility of the relationship between foreign and domestic investors and the rule of law.

The principle of generality demand that laws be written without the legislature knowing a particular case to which it will apply, that the rules be written at some level of abstraction, and that laws apply to legislators as well as the public.[34] It also requires like cases to be treated alike by law enforcement and judges.[35] However, like equality, generality allows for

---

[28] See also ibid para 3 ('We rededicate ourselves to support all efforts to uphold the sovereign equality of all States, to respect their territorial integrity and political independence').

[29] Trubek (n 19) 90.

[30] ibid.

[31] ibid.

[32] Paul Gowder, 'The Rule of Law and Equality' (2013) 32 Law & Phil 565, 566.

[33] Andrei Marmor, 'The Rule of Law and Its Limits' (2004) 23 Law & Phil 1, 9–15 (describing the complexities of 'generality' as an element of the conditions for a rule of law).

[34] ibid (setting out Hayek's views of generality, citing Friedrich von Hayek, *The Constitution of Liberty* (U Chicago Press 1960) 150–55).

[35] Gowder (n 32) 603 (citing HLA Hart, 'Positivism and the Separation of Law and Morals' (1958) 71 Harv L Rev 593, 623–24; John Rawls, *A Theory of Justice* (Harvard UP 1999) 237).

laws to apply only to certain groups, as long as the line-drawing of subjects/non-subjects is justifiable.[36]

To the extent generality and equality coexist, the Secretary-General's Report's reference to equality and fairness as elements of rule of law adds a dimension that is noteworthy. The 'thickness' of rule-of-law views that include generality rests on the aim of not only ensuring a vertical equality (State–individual), but also a horizontal equality (individual–individual) within the State.[37] Where the vertical equality of (weak) rule of law means that States 'cannot easily abuse their power, and individuals can be fairly secure in their legal rights against the state', horizontal equality strengthens the rule of law by making individuals 'genuinely equal under the law'.[38]

The rule-of-law element of generality requires that 'officials ... substantially satisfy the principles of publicity and regularity *and* only use the state's coercive power in accordance with laws that do not draw irrelevant distinctions between individuals (that is, general laws)'.[39] That means that States must not only ensure that all individuals know about and are subject to laws (unless there are justifiable distinctions among the individuals) but that all individuals have the same rights and duties under the law (unless there are justifiable distinctions among the individuals).[40] The reason that generality is important is to ensure that likes are treated like in receiving societal benefits and in taking on societal burdens.[41]

3. Equality as an element of rule of law?

Whether equality is necessary for a rule of law is open to debate. Joseph Raz, one of the foremost theorists on rule of law,[42] 'denies that the rule of law has anything to do with equality'.[43] Shocking to some, this statement is nevertheless plausible to the extent that equality before the law (that is, equality of those subjected to the law)[44] is distinguished from equality of (or under) the law (that is, the equality of the standards applied[45]).[46] Under this view, even systematic discrimination is not incompatible with the rule of law.[47]

As we have seen, however, the UN's conception of rule of law does view equality as a constituent element.[48] If equality is an element of the rule of law, does this mean that States offering foreign investors benefits (or burdens) that are not offered national investors are

---

[36] Gowder (n 32) 603.

[37] See ibid.

[38] ibid 566.

[39] ibid 601–02.

[40] ibid fn 86.

[41] ibid 602.

[42] William Lucy, 'Equality Under and Before the Law' (2011) 61 UTLJ 411, 414 fn 4 and accompanying text (naming Raz and Lon Fuller as the 'most influential modern accounts' of rule of law).

[43] Gowder (n 32) 604 (citing Joseph Raz, *The Authority of Law: Essays on Law and Morality* (OUP 1979). Raz's idea has powerful explanatory value for the questions of the 'equality'—or not—of foreign and domestic investors, because the concept of equality is different from that of non-discrimination.

[44] Lucy (n 42) 416.

[45] ibid.

[46] Another critic of considering equality essential to rule of law is Paul Gowder. Gowder sees the equality as a consequence of the rule of law and not as an element of it. As such, equality is key to the latter's moral relevance. The rule of law, however, could exist without equality. See Gowder (n 32).

[47] ibid 604.

[48] See also Ivar Alvik, 'The Justification of Privilege in International Investment Law: Preferential Treatment of Foreign Investors as a Problem of Legitimacy' (2020) 31(1) EJIL 289, 291 (claiming that equality before the law is 'an indispensable element' of the rule of law).

violating the rule of law? Not necessarily. In fact, not even probably. Our answer will depend on what equality is. We turn now to that.

III. Equality

As was shown above, rule of law is a contested concept. However, rule of law seems an almost simple concept when compared to that of equality. Literally thousands of years of philosophical inquiries precede our continuing discussions and disagreements among and across disciplines as to what equality is, whether it is a moral imperative, and how to determine its existence or its absence in any particular situation. The following gives a basic overview of how equality is considered in general terms (Section A) before looking at international law perspectives on equality (Section B). I then turn to answering the questions of what equality in international law requires of States (Section C) and the separate, but related, question of who may demand equality (Section D).

A. The Basics of Equality

Equality is a relational view on the world that sets out the quantitative or qualitative similarities of the elements making up the real world.[49] This unavoidably requires line-drawing to the extent of defining the relevant markers of similarity and difference. Whether the marker is the existence of a particular substance (such as a banned chemical), a particular method of production (the involvement of forced labour), the belonging to a social group (such as nationality or citizenship), or the membership in a species (the measure used for most human rights), it is the predefined similarity or difference that permits discussions of equality in the first place.

In legal discussions of equality, the goal of determining the equality of objects (including individuals) is to use the equality or inequality to assess the treatment each receives under the law. While equality before the law has long been held as a legal maxim,[50] it was the Enlightenment and the rise of liberal thought that established the ideas of human equality extending beyond the privileged few and it was not until the twentieth century and the rise of international human right law that all humans were deemed morally equal.[51] Yet, moral equality does not secure the same legal rights for every individual, regardless of context. As Gosepath clarifies, 'no conception of just equality can be deduced from the notion of moral equality'.[52] Rather, equality today is only widely accepted as indicating the same rights

---

[49] See Gosepath (n 9).
[50] Daron Acemoglu and Alexander Wolitzky, 'A Theory of Equality Before the Law' (2020) 131 Econ J 1429.
[51] Jessica Lynn Corsi, 'Article 5: Equality and Non-Discrimination' in Ilias Bantekas, Michael Ashley Stein and Dimitris Anastasiou (eds), *The UN Convention on the Rights of Persons with Disabilities: A Commentary* (OUP 2018) 140–70, 142. The Enlightenment's vision of equality before the law was viewed as equality within social strata rather than across them. See Maimon Schwarzschild, 'Constitutional Law and Equality' in Dennis Patterson (ed), *A Companion to Philosophy of Law and Legal Theory* (2d edn, Blackwell 2010) 160–76, 160–62. See also Acemoglu and Wolitzky (n 50) 1 (citing Douglass C North, John Joseph Wallis and Barry R Weingast, *Violence and Social Orders: A Conceptual Framework for Interpreting Recorded Human History* (CUP 2009)); ibid 4–6 (describing different societies' moves from elite domination to full equality before the law; Lord Bingham, 'The Rule of Law' (2007) 66(1) CLJ 67, 73.
[52] Gosepath (n 9).

among those to whom the law applies—and not equal rights or equal protection more generally.[53] As Westen writes:

> All legal regulation involves classification ... In order to decide whether a state classification treats differently people who are [legally] deemed to be 'alike', however, we must first possess a [legal] standard for distinguishing those people who are alike from those who are not. We cannot find such standards in the formula that 'likes should be treated alike', because the equality formula presupposes anterior [legal] standards for ascertaining 'likeness' and 'unlikeness'.[54]

Thus, it would be entirely within the rule of law to treat investors differently based on nationality as long as the State had legitimately distinguished the different types of investors in laws, correctly so-called, by officials authorized to implement said laws, and in a way that treats the investors within each group equally.

The practice of promoting equality before the law brings with it enduring complexities because of the relational nature of equality. These theoretical and practical complexities are of tremendous importance in discussions about equality because they colour the precise relationship between rule of law and equality in any specific context. (In fact, according to Westen's famous account, the 'conceptual confusion' caused by trying to apply the various notions of equality to legal rights discussions leads to the conclusion that '[e]quality ... is an idea that should be banished from moral and legal discourse as an explanatory norm'.)[55]

B. Egalitarianism and International Law Views on Equality

As the international law system took on the law of human rights, a strong strand of egalitarianism emerged. Egalitarianism is the promotion of equality—an idea that more equality (and less inequality) is preferable to less equality (or more inequality). It is, however, 'a shifting target'.[56] It shifts, because, as David Miller observes: 'There is no single cause that egalitarians favour, no one motive that drives them to the views they hold ... we are all egalitarians on some issues, inegalitarians on others'.[57]

The differences in views of egalitarianism can be significant and in multiple respects[58] because they have different views on the proper aspect of equality that should be assessed. Most of the traditional egalitarians focus on an equal distribution of goods, with equality

---

[53] Lucy (n 42) 417.

[54] Peter Westen, 'The Empty Idea of Equality' (1982) 95 Harv L Rev 537, 560.

[55] ibid 542. See also ibid 578, fn 140 (citing Polyviou, Honoré, and Ely as others who have written on the emptiness of the concept of equality).

[56] David Miller, 'Equality' (1989) 26 Royal Inst Phil Supps 77–98, 78.

[57] ibid 79. As an example of the varying views on equality, Miller points to market economies. These are fundamentally egalitarian in the aspect of exchange, given that two persons freely enter into a reciprocal relationship based on an implicit acknowledgement of their own equality to give and receive items of a presumptively equal value. Yet, the market actors' own differing stores of assets in fact foster further inequality of consumption and production because the free market exchange results in one of the actors' greater ability to further consume or produce. ibid 81.

[58] See Richard Arneson, 'Egalitarianism' in Edward N Zalta (ed), *The Stanford Encyclopedia of Philosophy* (Summer 2013 Edition) <https://plato.stanford.edu/archives/sum2013/entries/egalitarianism/> accessed 14 October 2021.

of resources and equality of welfare two opposing subcategories.[59] Newer approaches look to equality in relations.[60] I take these up in turn, starting with describing equality as a way to distribute units of utility, then describing how complex equality differs from equality viewed from a single dimension. Third, I turn to the view of equality that ignores distribution and focuses instead on relationships.

1. Equality as a principle of distribution

As a topic of study, differing views on the elements and aspects of equality have been traditionally categorized as discussions of formal, 'simple', or 'numerical' vs proportional equality.[61] Formal equality requires that the legal system treat each like the others unless there is a legally relevant justification for treating them differently. The rule finds reflection in the law most prominently as the concept of equality before the law, where laws apply to all persons within the jurisdiction.

Proportional equality adjusts formal equality by treating cases differently in proportion to their difference in a particular quality. An offshoot of numerical equality, the proportional equality retains the idea of treating persons equally, but adjusts the amount of what they receive as a result of—and in an amount relative to—the individual's difference to others. Here again, a legal system that attends to a 'rule of law' may find justice in granting certain additional benefits to individuals that are deficient in a particular quality without running afoul of the principle of equality or justice.

Gosepath observes that ' "[e]quality" and "equal" are incomplete predicates that necessarily generate one question: equal in what respect?'.[62] It is this question that remains wide open in international investment law—are we to measure equalness in regard to actions and operations, to access to remedies and influence on policymaking, or to nationality? Any is possible, but each leads to different answers as to whether equality is achieved.

2. Unidimensional vs complex equality

Asking 'in what respect' a comparative analysis must be made, moreover, brings up a further differentiation in views of equality: unidimensional versus complex equality. Unidimensional equality measures equality along a single vector: wealth, power, status, etc. The difficulties, as mentioned above, rest with agreeing on in which respect to measure and how to measure the 'amount' of this possessed/enjoyed by the relevant individuals.[63]

Yet, even if there can be agreement on how to measure equality, there are those who consider that a pluralistic society requires equality in many, if not all, dimensions of life. As Dworkin points out, '[t]here is a difference between treating people equally, with respect to one or another commodity or opportunity, and treating them as equals'.[64] The insight here is that because there are various aspects of life that people value, and might value having an equal share in, people are not true equals if they are equal in only the one aspect considered

---

[59] See Ronald Dworkin, *Sovereign Virtue: The Theory and Practice of Equality* (Harvard UP 2000) 12.

[60] Elizabeth Anderson is the most prominent theorist of relational equality. See in addition to the works cited above in nn 66–74, Nathan Heller, 'The Philosopher Redefining Equality' *New Yorker* (New York, 7 January 2019).

[61] See Gosepath (n 9).

[62] ibid (citing Douglas Rae and others, *Equalities* (Harvard UP 1981) 132f).

[63] A simple description of measurement issues that arise can be found in Tania Burchardt, 'Foundations for Measuring Equality: A Discussion Paper for the Equalities Review' (June 2006) CASE/111 <https://core.ac.uk/download/pdf/7119231.pdf> accessed 14 October 2021.

[64] Dworkin (n 59) 11.

morally relevant by the measurer. At the same time, looking at 'complex equality' allows for individuals to be unequal in many respects, but still socially equal as long as the inequalities do not interact.[65]

3. Equality as a principle of social relations (relational equality)

A fundamentally different perspective of looking at equality arises out of critical enquiries into the ultimate purpose of promoting equality. Elizabeth Anderson argues that the aims of equality are not those of offsetting bad luck and protecting desserts, but rather 'to end oppression'[66] and 'to create a community in which people stand in relations of equality to others'.[67] The result of seeing equality in this way is that the measure of a society's adherence to it is 'that its principles express equal respect and concern for all citizens'.[68]

Relational (or, in Anderson's words, 'democratic')[69] equality thus looks at equality as 'an ideal of social relations' that aims to place each individual in a position of equality with regard to others in the society.[70] Unlike equality concepts that focus on how many goods different individuals (or groups) have or should receive, social relations equality is not about distributing anything. Rather:

> the only comparisons that fundamentally matter are among those who stand in social relations with one another and in which the goods of equality are essentially relations of equal (symmetrical and reciprocal) authority, recognition, and standing.[71]

Relational equality explicitly recognizes that private relationships can be as oppressive as public measures are, and it protects the individual's responsibility for using (or not) opportunities that arise.[72] Anderson stresses that the guarantees of relational equality are limited to 'effective access to levels of functioning [only] sufficient to stand as an equal in society'.[73] This leads to a positive dimension of relational equality (to accompany the negative dimension of ending oppression): the creation of a democratic, non-hierarchical, community of persons that each has the right to participate in discussions about the rules to which the community will be subjected and each has the obligation to listen to the others' views.[74]

Without engaging in a thorough analysis of the implications of this view of equality on investment law, one can still recognize that a consideration of what a participation-based commitment to equality would demand in the way of protecting investors from different communities (domestic and foreign) may alter the outcome of how 'equality' interacts with rule of law in the investment context.

---

[65] Miller (n 56) 93 (relating Walzer's ideas set forth in Michael Walzer, *Spheres of Justice* (OUP 1983)).
[66] Elizabeth Anderson, 'What Is the Point of Equality?' (1999) 109(2) Ethics 287, 288.
[67] ibid 289.
[68] ibid.
[69] ibid.
[70] Elizabeth Anderson, 'Equality' in David Estlund (ed), *The Oxford Handbook of Political Philosophy* (OUP 2012) 40–57, 40.
[71] ibid 41.
[72] Anderson (n 66) 313–14.
[73] ibid 318.
[74] ibid 313.

C. What Does the Basic International Norm of Equality Demand?

The requirement of equality set forth in the UN's definition of international rule of law rests with the call for ensuring that legal subjects are equal 'before the law'. That is, unless the State has justifiable grounds for denying the equal treatment of individuals when applying and enforcing the law, each person is to have the same rights to enforce her rights in court as all others (equal access), that parties to a dispute are given the same opportunities to present their case to the judge (equality of arms), and that similar complaints are heard in similar types of proceedings (equality of proceedings).[75]

Equality beyond the law (in addition to equality before the law) is implicitly integrated into the international rule of law to the extent that the 2004 UN definition of the rule of law makes reference to the conformity of laws to human rights norms.[76] Equality in this sense extends not only to non-discrimination on the basis of 'race, sex, language, or religion',[77] but also to the inherent dignity that equalizes all humans on account of their 'reason and conscience'.[78] While it may well be that the rule-of-law elements of generalization and publicness support the broader principle of equality on a more general scale, the UN leaves explicit explanation of further substantive requirements aside in its considerations of what the rule of law requires. (Justice, which the report discusses alongside rule of law, encompasses the substantive outcomes of the rule of law.)[79]

Focusing on equality before the law, these UN requirements of the rule of law are flexible enough to give States the ability to circumscribe the groups to whom they will offer equal treatment. This is possible because of the justifiability of discrimination on grounds other than those specifically prohibited. That is, equality is generally demanded, but inequality can be justified. Thus, if there is a legitimate reason to write a law that limits a certain category of persons' access to (or exclusion from) a particular type of proceeding, the restriction of the persons' access will not be contrary to the rule of law as long as the restriction itself is administered in a way that is transparent, even-handed (given the distinct categories), and predictable.[80] The need for equality before the law is fulfilled because as long as the particular legal proceeding is intended to offset inherent disadvantages (or inherent advantages) that the category of persons would otherwise suffer (enjoy) in the generally available proceedings, the inequality is justifiable. As long as this 'exception' to the law's generality is known (or knowable) by the relevant audience of interested persons, and as long as its reasoning can be explained and administered fairly and consistently, there is nothing in the concept of equality before the law to prevent such differential treatment.

More generally, the international rule-of-law's demand of equality before the law does not determine *how* States are to determine the relevant subjects of a particular law. While the UN report suggests generality by demanding that laws are to apply to 'all persons', legal rules will rarely be universally applicable. The 'all' is therefore open to definition by the

[75] See generally Lucy (n 42).

[76] UNSC (n 8) para 6.

[77] Charter of the United Nations and Statute of the International Court of Justice (opened for signature 26 June 1945, entered into force 24 October 1945) 1 UNTS XVI (hereafter United Nations Charter) art 1(3).

[78] Universal Declaration of Human Rights (adopted 10 December 1948 UNGA Res A(III) (UDHR) art 1 ('All human beings are born free and equal in dignity and rights. They are endowed with reason and conscience and should act towards one another in a spirit of brotherhood').

[79] UNSC (n 8) para 7.

[80] See generally Westen (n 54).

lawmaker. If the lawmaker only addresses one category of persons, there is no breach of the rule of law solely by virtue of that limitation. (This is different from addressing a particular group or individual, which generality usually would not permit.)

Neither is the fact that a law is not universally applicable a problem with equality if there are no 'likes' to treat 'alike'. This was the reasoning of the ICJ in its 1956 Advisory Opinion on the question of whether its limited jurisdiction (allowing only States or international organizations to bring cases to it) violated the principle of equality. The Court denied any such violation, explaining that the jurisdictional limitation 'does not in fact constitute an inequality' because the limitation 'is antecedent to' the relevant focus of the required equal treatment.[81] That is, the lawmaker *predefined the relevant category of those who have standing* to be 'states and international organizations' and those who do not as 'individuals'. The categorization makes the two unlike, so the demands of 'equality' do not require equal treatment across the categories. (We will see this argument used more recently by the Court of Justice of the European Union (CJEU) when it faced the question of whether the right of foreign investors to access international arbitration violated the right of European investors to equality.)[82]

D. Equality for Whom?

A final aspect of the concept of equality is that of its reach. Who must be treated equally is a critical question that one must address if equality is to be applied as a legal principle. It is a particularly important question for investment law, where the basic question has two sub-questions. First, do the rights to equality extend to corporations (Section 1)? Second, do the demands of equality require States to give foreigners treatment equal to nationals and nationals treatment equal to that offered foreigners (Section 2)?

1. May corporations claim rights to equal treatment?
As we have noted, equality is distinct from identity—in fact, it demands non-identity of targets. Yet, there must be some overlap of characteristics that can validate the target's right to equal treatment. Do the 'persons' that are widely discussed as the objects of equal treatment demands include corporations or are they limited to natural persons? This is an important first question because the real differences between natural persons and legal persons sometimes lead to legal differentiation, but investors can be either.

In philosophical writings on the topic and in most discussions of equality among legal theorists, there seems to be a presumption of individuals as the point of interest.[83] The natural person basis is particularly true of relational equality theories, but even theories of distributive equality and complex equality are mainly seen as morally justified because they enhance an individual's well-being or underline the individual's dignity.[84] These goals are deeply human—they cannot be easily transcribed to fit a corporation.

---

[81] Judgements of the Administrative Tribunal of the ILO upon Complaints made against UNESCO (Advisory Opinion of 23 October 1956) [1956] ICJ Rep 77, 85.
[82] See Section IV.B.2 below.
[83] Gosepath (n 9) (pointing out that contemporary debates continue over the question of equality relating to groups).
[84] See ibid (explaining that individuals are the main bearers of responsibility).

The equality before the law concept, however, does not wholly dismiss claims of equal treatment by corporations. In relation to how the law is administered and how the law is enforced, courts often accept that corporations have the same rights as natural persons.[85] This equality, however, is more granted than accepted because corporations are creatures of the law as much as they are subject to the law. Corporations cannot have intrinsic rights stemming from 'dignity', and therefore will enjoy only those rights that are offered them.

The extent of offers of corporate rights is a matter of expedience rather than of morals:[86] where investment law generally permits 'investors' to be either natural or legal persons, this is based on the will of the States and reflected in treaty texts. While it is fully within the rights of a host State to consider an offer of access to the benefits of an investment protection agreement open to natural person investors and corporate investors, the principle of equality itself—even as equality before the law—does not require the State to offer benefits of a treaty to legal persons equal to those it secures for natural persons.

2. May foreigners claim a right to equality?

The second question is the extent of the circle of those to be treated equally. Specifically, in determining to whom the State owes equal treatment, one must know if the principle extends to all individuals within its jurisdiction or if it may delineate a subgroup to be the relevant focus of equal legal treatment.

On its own, the principle of equality says nothing about the extent of its reach. Neither, moreover, do egalitarians necessarily demand equality for every person even in a single dimension.[87] Because equality is a relational concept, it only can reasonably extend to those in some form of a relationship with each other.

Thus, even if a State offers each of its citizens and corporations equal treatment as regards, for example, the right to contribute to political campaigns, the principle of equality's fundamentally relational nature means that the State can refrain from offering non-citizens the same right on the basis of foreigners not having a (desirable) relationship with the policy-making branches of government. Equality may be bounded by making the relevant factor of comparison citizenship.

The same reasoning permits States to limit equality before the law to those sharing a particular nationality, whether the State's own or another's. While the basis of international human rights law and the core idea of minimum international standards of treatment of the alien define all humans as 'alike' for purposes of the enjoyment of some basic rights, even these—the strongest expressions of equality—permit differential treatment of individuals on the basis of their status. This means that both prisoners and non-citizens may be denied the right to vote, and that military personnel and non-residents may be denied the right to appear before all courts, even though the treatment is clearly unequal. The State can limit the equality of result and opportunity and still be treating persons 'legally' because the demands of equality simply do not extend to the particular group (eg to prisoners, immigrants and refugees, or military personnel).

---

[85] Frederick Green, 'Corporations as Persons, Citizens, and Possessors of Liberty' (1946) 94 U Pa L Rev 202, 203 fn 3 and accompanying text.

[86] See Nikolas Bowie, 'Book Review: Corporate Personhood v. Corporate Statehood' (2019) 132 Harv L Rev 2009 (discussing Adam Winkler, *We the Corporations: How American Businesses Won Their Civil Rights* (Norton 2018)).

[87] See discussion of the definition of equality above pp. 335–338.

Equality as a principle of law does not specify who has the authority to compose the groups within which equality should extend. Philosophical studies of equality are generally concerned with the moral relevance of the distinctions drawn by those in a position to offer the questioned treatment. The law, on the other hand, generally presumes the lawmaker's right to circumscribe its jurisdiction, worrying more about overextensions than the opposite.

International law in particular defers to the State's sovereignty in promising benefits to foreigners. The widespread use of national treatment and most-favoured-nation treatment clauses in economic treaties (as well as the need for international human rights treaties) is witness to the majority view that international law does not impose duties of equal treatment of persons on a State without its consent. If a State, then, wishes to restrict its offer of equality to its own nationals, it may do so to the extent it has not contracted itself into a duty to act otherwise. If it wishes the treatment of the foreigners to be preferable to that of its nationals, international law will be even less relevant.

IV. Rule of Law and Equality in the Investment Context

Seeing the investment law regime as fundamentally a tool for protecting foreigners from the power of the State is one of the most prominent views of those considering the investment system as a rule-of-law system. It is quite convincing for those of us who see investment law as holding the promise of improving governance.

Stephan Schill's work is perhaps the most thorough on this topic. His paper on the rule of law in the context of investment law sets out very thoroughly the reasoning behind seeing international investment law as both a reflection of and a tool for advancing the rule of law.[88] Investment agreements' substantive protections of investors, says Schill, cover the range of elements that 'thick' rule-of-law definitions require: binding the State to its own rules, accountability for violations, publicity of the law, independent adjudication, legal certainty, and transparency.[89] Reading 'rule of law' as a tool for development, Schill shows how the objectives of investment agreements 'parallel' those of the liberal ideal of the *Rechtsstaat*— namely, in 'decreasing political risk' stemming from the State's sovereign authority over the resources within its jurisdiction.[90] He also explains in detail how the material elements of investment agreements are the same as those of the rule of law. Focusing in particular on the interpretation of the fair and equitable treatment (FET) provision, Schill highlights how tribunals have determined that FET requires predictability, legality, due process, transparency, and proportionality.[91] Finally, the investor-State dispute settlement mechanism contained in most international investment protection instruments can be viewed as a way to ensure that a State's rule-of-law obligation to ensure access to justice is achieved.[92]

---

[88] Stephan W Schill, 'International Investment Law and the Rule of Law' in Jeffrey J Lowell, Christopher Thomas and Jan van Zyl Smit (eds), *Rule of Law Symposium 2014: The Importance of the Rule of Law in Promoting Development* (Academy Publishing 2015).

[89] ibid 5 (quoting the definition of rule of law from the 2012 UN Secretary-General's report, UNGA, 'Delivering Justice: Programme of Action to Strengthen the Rule of Law at the National and International Level' (16 March 2012) UN Doc A/66/749, para 2).

[90] ibid 6.

[91] ibid 9.

[92] ibid 11–13.

Alternative views on the relationship between investment protection and the rule of law consider the failures of national rule-of-law frameworks when confronted by the State's foreign investment protection obligations. Gus Van Harten, whom Schill uses to contrast his own views, points to the domestic rule-of-law results of investment protection rules. Investment treaty obligations, says Van Harten, limit the possible responses of the State to issues of public import (including environmental or social threats):

> The system delegates to arbitrators the power to define what activities are sovereign and what are not, to decide whether sovereign actors have acted improperly and unlawfully, and to direct the payment of public money or the seizure of public assets on behalf of private actors ... [I]nvestment treaty arbitration involves not only the review of decisions that affect the claimant in a specific and discrete way. It extends to polycentric legislative, judicial, and executive decisions and often engages matters of general significance.[93]

The view of rule of law reflected by the investment regime critics, it seems to me, are as valid as the arguments of Schill—but they are seeing rule of law from a different perspective. The fear of the critics is essentially one of dissociating the State from its sovereign, the *people*. David Schneiderman's extensive work on the interaction of the investment system with democracy puts this contrast in views bluntly:

> If the investment-rules regime has been described as contributing to 'good governance' practices, such as the promotion of transparency and respect for due process, investment treaties and international investment tribunals charged with interpreting these treaties have not had a lot to say about the operation of democratic processes.[94]

This is the view of rule of law that I will label the legality view. Unlike the idea of rule of law set forth in the 2004 UN Report, legality sees the rule of law as a way to ensure that the State exercises only the authority it is given by its citizens.

This view is also implicit in the critiques of ISDS as removed from local interests. Marc Poirier points to the problems of international tribunals deciding matters of tension between what policies host State citizens have called for and what investors desire.[95] Here, the rule-of-law approach is that of a legality grounded not only on the generality or publicness of a law, but on the citizen's right to argue about how a law is to apply in a particular context. The democratic element is key to this concern—and is equally valid as a rule-of-law consideration.

What the relationship between rule of law and investment is, then, depends on the view of rule of law taken. In international law, the context of the foreigner–State relationship is much closer to that of the citizen within the authoritarian State than to that of the sovereign citizen of the democratic State. It is not surprising, therefore, that the conventional view on rule of law (including that espoused by the UN Secretary General's report used here) is closer to that of the *Rechtsstaat* than to legality. It is not that democratic values and the need for individual justice do not play any role in international law in general (of course they are

---

[93] Gus Van Harten, 'Investment Treaty Arbitration, Procedural Fairness, and the Rule of Law' in Stephan W Schill (ed), *International Investment Law and Comparative Public Law* (OUP 2010) 627, 632 and 637.

[94] Schneiderman (n 3) 914.

[95] Marc R Poirier, 'The NAFTA Chapter 11 Expropriation Debate through the Eyes of a Property Theorist' (2003) 33 Envl L 851.

widely protected by human rights treaties), but these are arguably not part of the genetic makeup of the international rule of law as *Rechtsstaatlichkeit* as they are for rule of law as legality.

A. The Investment Law Context

The relationship of rule of law to equality is diffuse to begin with and gets more blurry in its application to investment law: where some say equality is 'inherent to' rule of law,[96] others, we have seen, fear that claims about the rule of law can undermine equality.[97] What seems certain is that the content of a rule-of-law principle (to the extent it is accepted in the UN statement) only necessitates procedural equality. This is a very small slice of the larger concept of equality, and itself may (in the long run) be only secondary to egalitarian concerns.

The role of egalitarian thinking in investment law, too, is complicated. The regime itself is in some sense an equalizer—but to whose advantage? As Sergio Puig and Anton Strezhnev note, this depends on who is looking:

> This debate about ISDS' role and purpose within a global governance system can be framed as a tale of two types of underdogs: relatively weak governments fighting corporate power or defenceless private actors fighting arbitrariness. Of course, which account is more accurate depends on one's perspective.[98]

The national–foreign distinction is unmentioned in this scenario, perhaps because the equality view on that relationship is not a one side or the other is the underdog, but one of whether the investment rules repair an inequality (the disadvantageous position of the foreigner's access to justice relative to the national) or whether they create an inequality (the regime denigrates the national by giving the foreigner additional avenues of protection and relief).

B. Equality and Investment Law's (Non-)Treatment of National Investors

When addressing the question of the inequality between national and foreign investors that is reflected in the current and proposed investment legal regimes from the conventional view of rule of law and the common understanding of its demands of equality, the unavailability of treaty protections, and special dispute resolution procedures is neither a failure of the rule of law nor of equality. As set out above, while the rule-of-law's demand for equality before the law means that the legal system offers access to authoritative redress for alleged violations of laws, the international rule-of-law's demand of generality allows the lawmaker to define categories to which a particular law will apply. If the lawmaker chooses nationality as the basis of the categorization, the rule of law is not violated so long as there is an articulable reason for the law being written this way.

---

[96] See Green (n 85).
[97] See Schneiderman (n 3) 914.
[98] Puig and Strezhnev (n 4) 732.

The recent court responses to cases challenging the investment regime of the Comprehensive Economic and Trade Agreement (CETA) between Canada and the European Union demonstrate two approaches that can discredit claims of alleged violations of equal treatment principles. In each of these cases, the background to the proceedings was CETA's chapter 8 on investment protection. That chapter guarantees Canadian investors the standard (though updated) protections from any EU Member State government's unwarranted interference in their activities. It also has an investment court system (ICS) system that provides Canadian investors with the right to lodge an arbitration request in an investor-State proceeding should the investor consider that one of the Member States had violated one or more treaty provisions. The claimants in these cases (one before the French Conseil constitutionnel, one before the CJEU, and one before the Colombian Constitutional Court) argued that both the protections and the ICS violate the principle of equality before the law.

1. Case before the Conseil Constitutionnel

The first Court to respond was the French Constitutional Court. In July 2017, the Conseil Constitutionnel decided that there was no indication that the protection standards would unequally favour foreign investors because there were assurances that the standards were to only offer national treatment (and not better-than-national treatment) to foreigners.[99] The more important question was that of whether the ICS provisions of the Canada–EU free trade agreement are compatible with the French Constitution's guarantees of equality before the law.

The Court noted that French law guarantees that 'the law must be the same for all',[100] and agreed that the offer of ICS only to foreign investors and not to French investors in France results in 'une différence de traitement'.[101] This difference in treatment did not, however, violate the equality principle because in the Court's eyes it was justified by a public interest:

This difference in treatment between Canadian investors and other foreign investors in France, however, responds in two ways to the objective of general interest, on the one hand by reciprocally creating a protective framework for French investors in Canada and, on the other hand, attracting Canadian investors in France.

This objective of general interest is directly in line with the purpose of the Agreement, which is to favour exchanges between the parties, the stipulations of Chapter 8 may thus introduce a procedural mechanism of conflict resolution that may apply, in regard to investments made in France, only to Canadian investors.[102]

---

[99] Conseil constitutionnel, Decision No 2017-749 DC (31 July 2017), Accord économique et commercial global entre le Canada, d'une part, et l'Union européenne et ses États membres, d'autre part <www.conseil-constitution nel.fr/decision/2017/2017749DC.htm> accessed 14 October 2021.

[100] ibid para 35 (quoting the Declaration of 1789, art 6).

[101] ibid para 37.

[102] ibid paras 38–39. The original reads:

38. Cette différence de traitement entre les investisseurs canadiens et les autres investisseurs étrangers en France répond toutefois au double motif d'intérêt général tenant, d'un côté, à créer, de manière réciproque, un cadre protecteur pour les investisseurs français au Canada et, de l'autre, à attirer les investissements canadiens en France.

39. Ce motif d'intérêt général étant en rapport direct avec l'objet de l'accord, qui est de favoriser les échanges entre les parties, les stipulations du chapitre 8 pouvaient donc instituer un mécanisme procédural de règlement des différends susceptible de s'appliquer, s'agissant d'investissements réalisés en France, aux seuls investisseurs canadiens.

Justification, then, can allow a government to treat likes unlike without violating their obligation of equality. The government's view of the advantages to the public interest of greater flows of foreign investment was considered an adequate reason to consider foreign investors differently from domestic investors, essentially weighing the presumed benefits of investor protection more heavily than the benefits of having the same treatment for all investors.

2. Case before the CJEU

The CJEU used a separate analysis in an opinion requested by Belgium, asking the same question about CETA, this time on the grounds of EU legal guarantees of equality. In its April 2019 Opinion 1/17,[103] the Court did not need to look for a justification for unequal treatment because it did not find Canadian and EU investors to be like to begin with.

Part B of the Opinion sets out a very different view of the equality of the EU and Canadian investors than does the French decision, but with the same end result.[104] The CJEU first states that equal treatment is a part of equality before the law, and that it 'requires that comparable situations must not be treated differently and different situations must not be treated the same way, unless … objectively justified'.[105] This is not problematic. Then the Court continues, explicitly noting that '[i]f the situations are not comparable, a difference in the treatment of the situations concerned is not in breach of equality before the law'.[106] It uses this—also unproblematic—statement to find that differently treating Canadian and EU investors does not violate the principle of equal treatment:

> [I]t is clear that, while Canadian enterprises and natural persons that invest within the Union are, in the light of the object and purpose … of inserting in the CETA provisions concerning non-discriminatory treatment and the protection of foreign investments, in a situation comparable to that of enterprises and natural persons of Member States that invest in Canada, their situation is not, on the other hand, comparable to that of enterprises and natural persons of Member States that invest within the Union.[107]

The sparse analysis of the 'different situations' opens the Court's opinion to criticism on this respect,[108] but at least the equality concept behind it is clear. As the requirement of equal treatment only adheres to like subjects, an initial finding of unlike subjects negates any need to consider the treatment itself further. If the lawmaker defines nationality as a relevant difference between investors, it does not violate the equality requirement because foreigners and domestic investors are not 'alike' in the first place. With no violation of the equality principle, there is also no violation of the UN's procedural view of the rule of law.

---

[103] CJEU, Opinion 1/17 (*CETA*) [2019] ECLI:EU:C:2019:341.
[104] ibid paras 162–88.
[105] ibid para 176.
[106] ibid para 177.
[107] ibid para 180.
[108] One might, for example, like to know if the Court is assuming that the idea of 'European-ness' has overcome any latent nationalism within Member States, such that non-host State EU investors do not face nationalistic discrimination before courts of the host State.

3. Case before the Colombian Constitutional Court

In Case C-252-19,[109] the Colombian Supreme Court reviewed the constitutionality of the France–Colombia bilateral investment treaty.[110] Like the French and Belgian claims, some of the experts asked for inputs by the Colombian Court alleged that the investment treaty's substantive and procedural provisions offered foreign investors advantages that were not offered domestic investors, and thereby violated the equality guarantees of the Constitution. Specifically, one intervener argued that formal equality ('*igualidad formal*') was violated by, for example, the provision protecting foreign (but not national) investors from uncompensated indirect expropriations.[111] By allowing compensation for the State's infringements on the investor's expectations rather than her property, the competitive equality of the marketplace is undermined.[112] The access to dispute settlement that provides for compensation not tied to the State's capacity to pay ('*sostenabilidad fiscal*') was also a formal inequality in the eyes of the claimant.[113]

More interesting was a second charge: that material inequality ('*igualdad material*') resulted from the treaty's protection of foreign investors.[114] In the intervener's view, the treaty elevates foreign investors to being a group receiving special protections despite the fact that, far from being vulnerable members of society, are, in fact, 'powerful economic actors'.[115] It thereby violates the non-discrimination principles of the Colombian Constitution's Article 13 without a legitimate need for affirmative action:

> [t]he treaty converts the investor into a subject of special protection unmentioned in Article 13 of the Constitution. As a result, the affirmative action given to the investors changes this principle from supporting the general interest to supporting the particular interest of the investors.[116]

The Court's considerations of the equality claim were strikingly more thoughtful than those of the French Conseil or the CJEU's. Rather than giving a simple declaration of compatibility or not, the Court recognized that the question of the State's treatment of foreign and domestic investors implicates both equal treatment and non-discrimination principles.[117] These, it underlines, are separate (even if similar) matters.[118] Separate, too, therefore, are the responsibilities of the State under these principles. One 'mandate' is to provide foreign investors equal treatment under the law, so as not to disadvantage them vis-à-vis national

---

[109] I would like to acknowledge the generous assistance of Dr Rodrigo Polanco in the analysis of this case.

[110] Constitutional Court of Colombia, Judgment C-252/19 (6 June 2019) (MP Dr Carlos Bernal Pulido) <www.corteconstitucional.gov.co/relatoria/2019/c-252-19.htm> accessed 14 October 2021).

[111] ibid para 90. The intervenor, Magdalena Correa, is the director of the department of Constitutional Rights at the Universidad Externado de Columbia. ibid para 11 and accompanying table.

[112] ibid.

[113] ibid.

[114] ibid para 91.

[115] ibid.

[116] ibid. The Colombian Court had upheld the constitutionality of affirmative action (for women) in Case C-371/00. In that decision, measures of affirmative action are permissible if there is demonstrable discrimination and if the measures taken are both reasonable and temporally limited. See Felipe Jaramillo Ruiz, 'Colombia's Constitutional Debate on Gender Quotas: The Link between Representation, Merit, and Democracy' (2019) 31 DESAFÍOS 19 <https://doi.org/10.12804/revistas.urosario.edu.co/desafios/a.6723> accessed 14 October 2021.

[117] Constitutional Court of Colombia (n 110) para 110.

[118] ibid.

investors.[119] This, the Court said, is what the treaty requires as well as what Article 100 of their own Constitution demands.[120]

The second 'mandate' is just as important, however: the Court emphasized the other 'constitutional mandate addressed to the public authorities that consists in not discriminating against national investors and their investments in treating foreign investors and investments'.[121] This second requirement stems from the Constitution but is not expressed in the treaty.[122] Thus, the Court determined that while it could uphold the treaty in principle, it must condition its finding of constitutionality.[123] The Court noted that constitutionality would only be maintained if the government could conclusively clarify that nationals will not be subject to lesser protections than investors of the other party.[124] The president, therefore, was warned that prior to ratification, appropriate steps would need to be taken to ensure that future interpretation of the treaty provisions will uphold the equality of domestic investors.[125]

The Colombian Court, therefore, forged a third path in the equality debate regarding the substantive provisions of investor protection. Unlike the CJEU (but like the French Court), it presumed foreign and national investors to be equals in regard to substantive investment protections. The nationality of the investor was not a sufficient ground to legitimate finding them subject to different laws. Unlike the Conseil, however, the Columbian judges rejected any justification of different treatment on the basis of benefits to the public interest. Rather, it saw a potential of unequal treatment of equals, determined this to be a threat to its national conception of permissible grounds of discrimination, and accordingly demanded that actual equality of local investors be guaranteed:

> [T]he Court considers it indispensable, in order to adjust the treaty ... to the Constitution ... and in particular to its Article 13, to declare it conditionally enforceable, in order to avoid unconstitutional interpretations of its clauses, given the explicit lack of protection of the equality of national investors and their investments in Colombia. Thus, the Court will declare the conditional enforcement of this treaty ... subject to the understanding that none of the provisions that refer to substantive rights will result in more favorable unjustified treatment towards foreign investors with respect to nationals.
> This conditioning is indispensable. This, in order to guarantee equal treatment of the investor and local investments in relation to French investors and investments in Colombia. In particular, this conditioning seeks to prevent the provisions of this treaty from being interpreted in such a way as to grant more favorable unjustified treatment to the French investor and to the national investments in Colombia, for example, in relation to the scope and protection of its legitimate expectations [Articles 4 and 6 of the BIT], the content scope

---

[119] ibid.

[120] ibid.

[121] ibid ('De otro lado, la Corte resalta que de dichos artículos se deriva otro mandato constitucional dirigido a las autoridades públicas que consiste en tratar en condiciones de igualdad a todos los inversionistas y a todas las inversiones nacionales en Colombia respecto de los extranjeros y de no discriminación en contra de los inversionistas y las inversiones nacionales').

[122] ibid para 112.

[123] ibid para 121.

[124] ibid paras 121–22.

[125] ibid para 122 ('la Corte advertirá al Presidente de la República que, si ... decide ratificar este tratado ... deberá adelantar las gestiones necesarias para propiciar la adopción de una declaración interpretativa conjunta con el representante de la República Francesa respecto del referido condicionamiento').

and limits of compensation [Article 15 BIT] or the conditions of payment thereof [Articles 6 and 15 BIT]. In other words, this conditioning seeks to guarantee that all investors, local and foreign, in Colombia are subject to the same protection of their investments, rights and legitimate expectations, and, therefore, that no international responsibility is derived for the Colombian State as a result of actions that guarantee this mandate of the principle of equality.[126]

Intriguingly, for all its caution in ensuring that foreign investors do not receive better treatment than Columbian investors in terms of the treaty's substantive protections, the Columbian Court did not seem to see an inherent inequality in the treaty's investor-State dispute mechanism. Its discussion regarding the existence of ISDS is striking. Here, the Court has the same view as the CJEU: equality is maintained because the comparator groups are not Colombian investors and French investors in Colombia, but rather Colombian investors in France and French investors in Colombia. From this perspective, the Court saw no reason to question the existence of a separate dispute settlement mechanism as equal:

> The Court also notes that the [ISDS mechanism] is in accordance with Article 13 of the Constitution. Far from what is asserted by the claimant, this rule does not violate the right to equality of national investors by granting privileged treatment to foreigners. This, since ... *the criterion of comparison applicable to this rule is the scope of the rights granted to foreign investors of both States. Therefore, the comparable groups for purposes of this rule, are French investors in Colombia and Colombians in France*. Faced with this criterion of comparison and in relation to these comparable subjects, the Court finds that the treatment provided for in paragraph 4 of this article is equal (art. 13 of the CP).[127]

The Court's words about dual citizens are also significant. It points out specifically that a Columbian-French dual national investor must, in order to ensure the equality of the treatment, subject herself to national courts:

> In turn, the Court evidences that precisely the rule ... according to which the investor who has dual citizenship can only go to the local courts, seeks to ensure proper use of this clause and, therefore, to avoid any discriminatory treatment against the national investor who does not have the aforementioned dual citizenship. For this reason, this rule is also in accordance with the Constitution.[128]

This clarification underlines the comparability of the subjects of the equality principle: foreign investors in a foreign country and national investors in their own State.

A final note on the Colombian case arises from the separate statement of a judge who disagreed with the majority.[129] According to Justice Linares Cantillo, the majority was wrong

---

[126] ibid paras 120–21.

[127] ibid para 377 (emphasis added).

[128] ibid.

[129] Constitutional Court of Colombia (n 110) Aclaración de Voto y Salvamento Parcial de Voto del Magistrado Alejandro Linares Cantillo (much of the disagreement stemmed from Linares Cantillo's dissatisfaction with the Court's interjection of itself into executive matters and its—in his opinion misplaced—reliance on ISDS decisions interpreting treaties other than the one at issue in the case).

to subject their findings on the equality of the substantive provisions to further negotiations. In his statement, he contends that 'the Court is wrong in trying to impose on the two States a particular vision of the important principle of equality' because in his opinion, the national treatment provision takes care of the constitutional concerns of equal treatment and non-discrimination.[130]

Arguably, however, this is precisely the question requiring study, because the equal treatment issue for investment protections revolves around the comparators used. If the foreign investor and the national investor are considered the relevant comparators for equal treatment, the differential protection offered by national treatment (to the advantage of foreigner investors) would be problematic for equality. If the foreign investor and national investor are not comparable, no equality questions arise, and the different treatment would be permissible to the extent that non-discrimination on grounds of foreignness is not violated (ie to the extent the foreign investor is not disadvantaged). Here, then, the majority had the clearer vision of the equality issues underlying investment law protections.

V. Conclusion

Under the international view of the rule of law, the State is constrained in its actions towards its own citizens. Despite sovereignty, a State may not use its otherwise unlimited legal powers in a way that undermines the notions of regularity and publicity. Equality, requiring a conscious delineation of its scope, is a normative idea which the State must define along multiple dimensions. It does not exist in general—it exists only to the extent the State declares it to exist. Whether equality and equal rights under the law are an inherent part of the rule of law is debated, but it is clear that the international law concept of rule of law permits the State to declare who and what will receive equal treatment. This does not mean equality cannot be violated, but it does mean that violations of equality can only be determined in regard to the standards of equality already established by the State.

For the investment law regime, there is no violation of a general commitment to equal treatment before the law when the State offers foreign investors certain substantive standards of protection and a path to international arbitration and domestic investors none, because the State simply does not extend its definition of 'equal investors' to include foreigners and nationals. Consequently, the rule of law is upheld as well—because if the State created the equality rule to only cover foreign investors and it follows this rule by ensuring that all foreign investors are offered the same conditions of dispute settlement, the State has not abused any of its powers.

If this analysis is difficult to accept, it may be because the conventional conception of the rule of law accepted by the international community does not demand an original legitimacy of the source of laws to be implemented. That is, it fails to demand democratic origins of State power and the argumentative rights of the citizen. At the same time, equality's own normativity prevents differential access rights of domestic and foreign investors to treaty protections from violating the requirements of the rule of law.

---

[130] ibid para 9.

Considering the ambiguity of the concepts of both rule of law and equality, it cannot be a surprise that the relationship between domestic and foreign investors resulting from the international investment regime can be declared neither unequal nor a breach of the rule of law. It can be so declared because the rule of law as defined above is one focused on the liberal and rational constraint of the State's absolute power over those within its jurisdiction. To this extent, it demands neither democratic rulemaking nor conceptions of justice that reach beyond the prohibition on abuses of power. To the extent that equality is a law-based concept, it relies on the distinguishing of categories by a decision-maker and demands only that those within each category be offered treatment equal to that of another in that category.

This analysis might change, however, if the conception of the rule of law and/or of equality were altered. Using either a conception of rule of law which incorporates democratic notions of limited powers granted to the State or a relational (rather than distributional) equality perspective would give a gloss to the characterization of the foreign–domestic investor relationship which is otherwise absent. The importance of democratic consensus to both legality and relational equity raises the need for the broader societal aspects of the differential treatment of foreigners in the marketplace to be considered before declaring foreign investors' exclusive access to international arbitration legitimate in principle. A fuller investigation of the relationship between the rule of law and equality–egalitarianism in investment law would be welcome.

17

The Impact of Investment Protection Standards on the Rule of Law

Strengthening or Weakening the Domestic Rule of Law?

Mavluda Sattorova

I. Background

Historically, the international investment regime has its roots in a system that was designed to protect interests of foreigners abroad. The more recent narratives, however, argue that the fast evolving international investment treaty regime and its investor-State dispute settlement (ISDS) mechanism benefit not only foreign investors but also various constituencies in host States.[1] This is because of the so-called positive spillovers that investment treaties and investment arbitration jurisprudence generate. Although the primary objective of the investment treaty regime is to maximize the protection of foreign investment and thus facilitate economic growth, the regime can arguably play a significant role in strengthening the rule of law in host States, in particular developing countries.[2] Key investment protection standards contained in investment treaties—ranging from the fair and equitable treatment to the guarantee against uncompensated expropriation and sanctity of contract clauses—have been construed as rule-of-law requirements.[3] These rule-of-law requirements, albeit designed for the benefit of foreign investors, may arguably 'spill over into domestic law and may set new standards also for the domestic legal system'[4] and 'provide a powerful incentive to review and modernize'.[5] By enshrining these standards in investment treaties and enforcing them through investor-State arbitration, the function of investment treaty law is to 'reinforce and on occasion to institute, the rule of law internally' in host States.[6] Investment treaties and investment arbitration jurisprudence thus 'embody norms that all

---

[1] See eg Stephan W Schill, *The Multilateralization of International Investment Law* (CUP 2009) 377; Roberto Echandi, 'What Do Developing Countries Expect from the International Investment Regime?' in Jose E Alvarez and Karl P Sauvant (eds), *The Evolving International Investment Regime: Expectations, Realities, Options* (OUP 2011) 13; Thomas W Waelde, 'The "Umbrella Clause" in Investment Arbitration: A Comment on Original Intentions and Recent Cases' (2005) 6 JWIT 183, 188.

[2] Kenneth J Vandevelde, *Bilateral Investment Treaties: History, Policy, and Interpretation* (OUP 2010) 119; Jonathan Bonnitcha, *Substantive Protection under Investment Treaties: A Legal and Economic Analysis* (OUP 2014) 43.

[3] See eg Velimir Živković, 'The Use of Investment Treaty Standards to Enforce Other International Legal Regimes and Domestic Law' (in this volume) 193.

[4] Peter Muchlinski, Federico Ortino and Christoph Schreuer, 'Preface' in Peter Muchlinski, Federico Ortino and Christoph Schreuer (eds), *The Oxford Handbook of International Investment Law* (OUP 2008) vi.

[5] Rudolf Dolzer, 'The Impact of International Investment Treaties on Domestic Administrative Law' (2005) 37 NYU J Intl L & Pol 953, 972.

[6] Bonnitcha (n 2) 31, referring to James Crawford, 'International Law and the Rule of Law' (2003) 24 Adel L Rev 3, 4.

Mavluda Sattorova, *The Impact of Investment Protection Standards on the Rule of Law* In: *Investment Protection Standards and the Rule of Law*. Edited by: August Reinisch and Stephan W. Schill, Oxford University Press. © Mavluda Sattorova 2023.
DOI: 10.1093/oso/9780192864581.003.0017

countries committed to the rule of law should follow' and can therefore 'contribute greatly to institutional quality in host countries'.[7] The rule of law does not mean that investment treaty prescriptions need to be treated as supreme or given precedence in relationship to domestic (constitutional) law, but rather that an effort should be made to implement them and to comply with them domestically. The unintended but nonetheless significant function of the regime is arguably to compel host States to act in compliance with the rule-of-law standards in investment treaties which require governments to embrace transparency, stability, predictability, consistency in government decision-making, and to ensure effective administrative and judicial remedies.[8]

Unsurprisingly, there are also distinct strands in the literature on investment treaty law which contend that rather than promoting the domestic rule of law, investment treaties and their investment arbitration mechanism adversely affect the rule of law, in particular in developing countries.[9] For instance, one UNCTAD report questioned the rule-of-law effects of investment treaties by arguing that the open-ended and broad interpretations of investment treaty standards would pose considerable challenges to host State agencies that interact with investors: '[i]f the State and its subnational entities do not know in advance what type of conduct may be considered a breach of a treaty, then it cannot organize its regulatory and administrative decision-making processes and delegation in a way that ensures that its conduct will not incur liability'.[10] In more trenchant terms, Ron Daniels argued that investment treaties 'enfeeble host state governments', thus 'discrediting the normative legitimacy of the BIT as a rule of law project'.[11] To Santiago Montt, investment arbitration and its tendency for 'the relatively free invention of new rules without proper methodological foundation' undermines the rule-of-law legitimacy of the system.[12] Tom Ginsburg argued that foreign investors' ability to bypass domestic institutions and thus exit the domestic legal regime entrenches weaknesses in the rule of law because host governments are no longer incentivized to improve domestic governance mechanisms and practices.[13] Jonathan Bonnitcha too is sceptical of the positive impact of investment treaties on the domestic rule of law: mandating governments to compensate foreign investors for their losses, while not extending similar privileges to domestic business actors, is likely to lead national decision-makers to overvalue the interests of foreign investors.[14]

Does the investment treaty regime and its ISDS mechanism strengthen the rule of law in host States? Does the regime 'assist developing countries in promoting greater effectiveness

---

[7] Kenneth J Vandevelde, 'Model Bilateral Investment Treaties: The Way Forward' (2012) 18 Southwest JIL 307, 313.

[8] See eg Stephan W Schill, 'Fair and Equitable Treatment, the Rule of Law, and Comparative Public Law' in Stephan W Schill (ed), International Investment Law and Comparative Public Law (OUP 2010) 154–61.

[9] For an overview of this literature, see Susan D Franck, 'Foreign Direct Investment, Investment Treaty Arbitration and the Rule of Law' (2007) 19 Pac McGeorge Global Bus & Dev LJ 337, 365.

[10] UNCTAD, Fair and Equitable Treatment: A Sequel (United Nations 2012) 12.

[11] Ronald Daniels, 'Defecting on Development: Bilateral Investment Treaties and the Subversion of the Rule of Law in the Developing World' (23 March 2004) University of Siena 3, discussed at Franck (n 9) 366.

[12] Santiago Montt, State Liability in Investment Treaty Arbitration: Global Constitutional and Administrative Law in the BIT Generation (Hart 2009) 153.

[13] Tom Ginsburg, 'International Substitutes for Domestic Institutions: Bilateral Investment Treaties and Governance' (2005) 25 IRLE 107, 121.

[14] Jonathan Bonnitcha, 'Outline of a Normative Framework for Evaluating Interpretations of Investment Treaty Protections' in Chester Brown and Kate Miles (eds), Evolution in Investment Treaty Law and Arbitration (CUP 2011) 128.

of the rule of law at the domestic level'?[15] Where both proponents and detractors of the rule-of-law claims converge is the fact that until recently any theories about the impact of investment treaty law remained hypothetical and untested with empirical data. While the narratives postulating a positive impact of the investment treaty regime on the rule of law in host States have been steadily proliferating, they are commonly underpinned by a set of assumptions as to how States *should* respond to investment treaty disciplines. It is presupposed that investment treaty law will have certain deterrent and transformative effects on sovereign behaviour: not only is the host State expected to refrain from mistreating foreign investors in the future, but it is also expected to take positive steps to change its legal and bureaucratic practices (which supposedly are lacking and therefore lead to investor-State disputes). The aim of this chapter is to situate these narratives—and the normative assumptions on which they are premised—within a small but growing number of empirical and comparative case studies.

The principal question the chapter seeks to address is whether investment treaty law can exert a positive influence on the domestic sphere by fostering greater State compliance with rule-of-law standards contained in investment treaties. In doing so, the chapter relies on the notion of rule of law as expounded in the writings of Ibrahim Shihata, the then Senior Vice President and General Counsel, World Bank; Secretary-General, International Centre for Settlement of Investment Disputes. Why Shihata's vision of the rule of law, the reader might ask? Not only was Shihata among the first to articulate the meaning and relevance of the rule of law in the context of investment treaty law, but he also was one of the key figures behind the World Bank's well-documented efforts to promote investment treaties globally.[16] While locating its roots in laws restraining the power of monarchs in twelfth- and thirteenth-century England, Shihata described the modern incarnation of the rule of law as an embodiment of 'the principles of law-abiding governmental powers, independent courts, transparency of legislation, and judicial review of the constitutionality of laws and other norms of lower order'.[17] In the particular context of foreign investment, Shihata supported the view that 'the establishment of the rule of law attracts private investment, to the extent that it creates a climate of stability and predictability, where business risks may be rationally assessed, property rights protected, and contractual obligations honored'.[18] For the purposes of the World Bank and its work in both financing rule-of-law reforms in developing countries and assisting foreign investors through its dispute settlement mechanisms, Shihata narrowed down the scope of the rule of law to a system of law bearing the following hallmarks:

> a) there is a set of rules which are known in advance, b) such rules are actually in force, c) mechanisms exist to ensure the proper application of the rules and to allow for departure from them as needed according to established procedures, d) conflicts in the application of rules can be resolved through binding decisions of an independent judicial or arbitral

---

[15] Roberto Echandi, 'What Do Developing Countries Expect from the International Investment Regime?' in Jose E Alvarez and Karl P Sauvant (eds), *The Evolving International Investment Regime: Expectations, Realities, Options* (OUP 2011) 13.

[16] See Taylor St John, *The Rise of Investor-State Arbitration: Politics, Law, and Unintended Consequences* (OUP 2017).

[17] Ibrahim Shihata, 'The Role of Law in Business Development' (1997) 20 Fordham Intl LJ 1577.

[18] Shihata (n 17) 1578.

body, and e) there are known procedures for amending the rules when they no longer serve their purpose.[19]

Shihata's rule-of-law hallmarks reflect Razian minimalist conception[20] and the idea of a 'thin rule of law' that underpins a significant swathe of investment arbitration jurisprudence and scholarship. For instance, in one of his earlier writings on investment treaty law as a vehicle for promoting the rule of law, Schill defines the latter in a manner largely mirroring the thin conception with its emphasis on procedural fairness and due process.[21] Yet it must also be acknowledged that the rule of law remains an essentially contested notion,[22] and it is beyond the scope of this chapter to engage with an extensive and still growing body of scholarship that has critiqued or otherwise parsed the conceptual foundations and effects of the rule of law on those who it intends to benefit. Instead, the aim of this chapter is to highlight the emerging empirical data which unveils the effects of investment treaty law on the domestic rule of law.

By drawing upon Shihata's articulation of the rule of law, the chapter does not seek to either endorse or challenge any particular understanding of this distinct social phenomenon but rather highlight its peculiar historical origins and their echoes in contemporary investment law discourse.

II. Examining the Interplay between Investment Treaties and the Domestic Rule of Law: Using an Empirical Lens

At the core of this contribution are the findings of a recent project which sought to evaluate the hypotheses underpinning the rule-of-law narratives with the aid of empirical and comparative insights obtained through interviews with government officials in developing states and the analysis of national legislation. The project was carried out between 2013 and 2018 and focused specifically on the views and perceptions about investment treaties and their effects in host States that have been parties to investment treaties and had acted as respondents in investment arbitration cases. An overview of this empirical project and its findings were published as a monograph and subsequently built upon in further investigations.[23] In total, the case studies comprise comparative analysis of national legal and policy documents and eight sets of country-specific qualitative interviews conducted in Georgia, Jordan, Kazakhstan, Kyrgyzstan, Nigeria, Turkey, Ukraine, and Uzbekistan (74 interviews in total).[24] Interviews were carried out with government officials who work or have worked

---

[19]   ibid.

[20]   Joseph Raz, 'The Rule of Law and Its Virtue' in J Raz, *The Authority of Law: Essays on Law and Morality* (Clarendon 1979) 214–18.

[21]   Stephan W Schill, 'Fair and Equitable Treatment, the Rule of Law, and Comparative Public Law' in Schill (n 8) 154.

[22]   Jeremy Waldron, 'Is the Rule of Law an Essentially Contested Concept (in Florida)?' (2002) 21 Law & Phil 137, 140.

[23]   See Mavluda Sattorova, *The Impact of Investment Treaty Law on Host States: Enabling Good Governance?* (Hart 2018).

[24]   Some of the earlier findings from case studies in Nigeria, Turkey, and Uzbekistan have been discussed in Mavluda Sattorova, Mustafa Erkan and Ohio Omiunu, 'How Do Host States Respond to Investment Treaty Law?: Some Empirical Observations' in Akbar Rasulov and John Haskell (eds), *International Economic Law: New Voices, New Perspectives* (2020) EYIEL 133.

in the ministries and agencies that have had involvement in investment treaty-making and dispute settlement, as well as government officers who interact with foreign investors outside the context of investment treaty law and dispute settlement, ie in the process of making, implementing, and otherwise applying national laws in domestic, not international, settings. The respondents were drawn from a variety of agencies and ministries responsible for inter alia economic development, energy and natural resources, financial regulation, justice, municipal administration, State prosecution and internal affairs, as well as the legislature and judiciary. The interviews were conducted using a snowball-sampling method. In order to provide a broader and more accurate picture, the empirical findings have been corroborated with the analysis of the relevant national statutory material and judicial practice as well as other published empirical studies to date.

In addition to those empirical case studies, the chapter will also draw on other recently published qualitative analyses of the relationship between investment treaties and the domestic rule of law, including most notably the works of Jonathan Bonnitcha and Josef Ostřanský and Facundo Pérez Aznar respectively, which make a valuable contribution to the scholarship by expanding the geographic focus of empirical studies and raising novel analytical questions. Bonnitcha's recent case study focuses exclusively on Myanmar.[25] Through a combination of semi-structured interviews and analysis of legal and policy documents, Bonnitcha examines whether investment treaties promote the rule of law at a domestic level. A recent empirical case study by Ostřanský and Pérez Aznar focuses on the similar normative claims but with a focus on India, evaluating the rule-of-law impact of investment treaties with the aid of ethnographic research, including interviews and documentary analysis.[26] Both studies supply the hitherto missing and crucial empirical context by illuminating views and experiences of those who deal with foreign investors—government ministers, advisers, lawyers and other officials in the extended government machineries.

By drawing on this growing body of empirical insights in evaluating the rule-of-law impacts of investment treaties on domestic constituencies, the primary objective of this chapter is to reveal some of the on-the-ground perceptions and experiences that often remain unseen behind conceptual framings of international investment law. Guided by this modest objective, the chapter will introduce four key findings from the recent empirical work, each finding presenting a set of factors that appear to be currently shaping the ways host States learn from their experience of participating in the investment treaty regime. This will be followed by a discussion of what, if any, conditions should be present for investment treaty law and arbitration to positively influence the rule of law in host States. The chapter thus focuses on a very specific dimension of the relationship between international investment law and the rule of law: the ability of international investment law to generate positive spillovers at a national level for the benefit of domestic constituencies on the ground.

---

[25] Jonathan Bonnitcha, 'The Impact of Investment Treaties on Domestic Governance in Myanmar' (8 November 2019) <https://papers.ssrn.com/sol3/papers.cfm?abstract_id=3644056> accessed 20 December 2021.
[26] Josef Ostřanský and Facundo Pérez Aznar, 'Investment Treaties and National Governance in India: Rearrangements, Empowerment, and Discipline' (2021) 34 LJIL 373.

A. Finding No 1: No Rule-of-Law Effect Due to Limited Awareness

If investment treaty law indeed operates as a mechanism encouraging or otherwise compelling host governments to ensure compliance with the rule of law—both in their dealings with foreign investors but also more broadly—it is essential that 'all levels of government and agencies that interact with foreign investors understand the scope and consequences of the commitments under investment treaties and the practical implications for their day-to-day activities'.[27] As Bonnitcha has presciently observed in his writings, the hypothesis that investment treaty law promotes compliance with the rule of law at the domestic level rests on three assumptions: 'that lawmakers and decision-makers are aware of investment treaties; that they are concerned to avoid liability under investment treaties; and know that greater compliance with [rule-of-law] principles will reduce their likelihood of breaching investment treaties'.[28] These assumptions are 'theoretically coherent, intuitively plausible and generally accepted',[29] yet they remain unsupported by empirical evidence.

One area where empirical data becomes particularly relevant is awareness. Now that many host States have experienced the effect of investment treaty law and its arbitration mechanism in a respondent capacity, the principal question is: to what extent are government officials actually aware of and influenced by investment treaty disciplines in their subsequent daily practices?

Even before the rise of empirically oriented approaches to analysing the interplay between international investment law and national decision-making, doctrinal scholars argued that government officials—particularly those in administrative agencies of developing states—who do not have direct or regular dealings with foreign investors are unlikely to be aware of international investment agreements (IIAs) and their prescriptions.[30] As a consequence, such decision-makers are unlikely 'to internalise the constraints of investment treaty protections'[31] in exercising their day-to-day decision-making powers vis-à-vis foreign investors. This argument resonates with findings from case studies conducted by this author as well as Bonnitcha's work in Myanmar[32] and Ostřanský and Pérez Aznar's study of India's experience.[33] The interviews show that the first exposure to investment arbitration claims entailed some rise in the levels of awareness of investment treaty law among government officials who were directly involved in regulating and implementing foreign investment projects and ISDS (ie ministries of energy and natural resources, justice and foreign affairs). However, lack of awareness has also been observed among officials in other branches of the government (ie the judiciary, legislature, public health and environment protection ministries, municipal authorities, anti-corruption agencies, financial regulation authorities, State prosecutor offices). The low levels of awareness about investment treaty law and its rule-of-law prescriptions could be explained by the fact that government officials

---

[27] UNCTAD, *Best Practices in Investment for Development: How to Prevent and Manage Investor-State Disputes: Lessons from Peru* (Investment Advisory Series, Series B, no 10) (United Nations 2011) 11.

[28] Bonnitcha (n 6) 138.

[29] ibid.

[30] Jack Coe Jr and Noah Rubins, 'Regulatory Expropriation and the *Tecmed* Case: Context and Contributions' in Todd Weiler (ed), *International Investment Law and Arbitration: Leading Cases from the ICSID, NAFTA, Bilateral Treaties and Customary International Law* (Cameron May 2005) 599.

[31] Bonnitcha (n 6) 122.

[32] Bonnitcha, 'Impact on Myanmar' (n 25) 5, pointing to a low level of awareness about investment treaties beyond the key nodes of government with direct responsibility for treaty negotiations.

[33] See Ostřanský and Aznar (n 26) 31.

tend to be guided by national law and regulations in exercising their regulatory, administrative, and judicial powers in cases involving foreign investors.[34] Some respondents pointed out that although international investment treaties might occupy a higher place in the constitutional hierarchy of legal norms, such treaties rarely if ever were considered in governmental decision-making in dealing with day-to-day aspects of foreign investment activities, such as taxation, environmental control, and financial markets regulation.[35] Neither are investment treaty prescriptions directly effective or otherwise transposed in national legal orders. When prompted to elaborate on the reasons why the country's engagement with international investment law remained unknown to government officials, a number of interviewees pointed also to a lack of communication and coordination between various government ministries and agencies. As one respondent put it, '[e]veryone works autonomously, everyone is by himself'.[36] One respondent lamented the lack of not only awareness but also of 'shared vision' between officials in central government agencies and regional/municipal authorities: 'It is as if we are on opposite sides of the barricades'.[37] The lack of interagency dialogue and coordination has also been found in Ostřanský Pérez Aznar's case study of India.[38] Findings from Bonnitcha's case study in Myanmar also points to a lack of legal capacity as a wider cause for the lack of awareness of investment treaties within the government machinery.[39]

B. Finding No 2: Awareness Is Not Always Translated into Rule-of-Law Reforms

For international investment law to have a preventative effect and, moreover, to strengthen rule of law in host States, it is crucial that all levels of government that interact with investors are aware of the scope and consequences of the State's obligations under investment treaties and their practical implications for day-to-day activities of the relevant agencies.[40] Furthermore, the host government should acknowledge the importance of, and commit to, necessary reforms. The case studies suggest that investment treaty law tends to be internalized by government officials in host States but not necessarily as postulated by the proponents of the rule-of-law narratives.

The emerging qualitative data shows that, even after the host State had the experience of investment arbitration and the relevant government officials gained some awareness of investment treaties and their liability implications, such knowledge did not necessarily

---

[34] See eg Sattorova (n 23) 65–70.
[35] ibid.
[36] ibid.
[37] ibid.
[38] Ostřanský and Aznar (n 26) 28.
[39] Bonnitcha (n 25) 17.
[40] See UNCTAD (n 27) 11. Internalization throughout the government machinery is important because legislation alone is not sufficient to ensure effective compliance with the rule of law; rather what is required is an effective implementation with the law in daily legal and bureaucratic practices. As some empirical analyses have shown, a large proportion of investment disputes arise in connection with the actions of the executive. Host State administrations are thus a primary site for evaluating the rule-of-law failings and successes. See Jeremy Caddel and Nathan M Jensen, 'Which Host Country Government Actors Are Most Involved in Disputes with Foreign Investors?' (28 April 2014) Columbia FDI Perspectives no 120 <http://ccsi.columbia.edu/files/2013/10/No-120-Caddel-and-Jensen-FINAL-WEBSITE-version.pdf> accessed 20 December 2021.

motivate the government to treat foreign investment projects in line with investment treaty rule-of-law prescriptions. Instead, as some earlier studies have indicated, after experiencing the first bite of investor-State arbitration[41] the host country may endeavour to scale back its investment protection commitments. Some States sought to retroactively limit access to investment arbitration through constitutional review of the relevant national legislation.[42] In one country, an informal guidance was issued by a ministerial body instructing government officials to prevent the inclusion of arbitration clauses in agreements involving foreign investors.[43] But the same government did not embark on any reforms to improve the domestic rule of law. Our interviews reveal that, in some cases, despite their awareness of the State's previous exposure to investment treaty arbitration claims, government officials chose to ignore the risk of a new claim which their treatment of a certain foreign investment project could entail. One interviewee, for instance, referred to an incident where a high-ranking minister disregarded legal advice about the potential risk of investment arbitration. The minister reasoned that even if in breach of international investment law, the governmental action at issue was 'economically significant' and therefore ought to be maintained despite other considerations.[44]

Other countries continued to actively sign investment treaties, but have taken no significant steps to address the root causes of investment disputes and to strengthen the rule of law domestically. Some host governments created special government agencies tasked with defending the State interests in investment arbitration, yet no measures were taken to improve institutional norms and practices. As one interviewee put it: 'national laws are good, we just have problems with enforcing them and generally with a legal culture'.[45] Or, in the words of another respondent: 'We have a perfect Constitution, perfect laws; it's just they don't really work'.[46] This view was shared by a number of interviewees from other countries also, and my other case studies, including Bonnitcha's in Myanmar. Among other things, Bonnitcha finds that conclusion of a new treaty does not trigger any process to review the consistency of existing laws and government practices with the treaty'.[47] Nor was there any instances where the conclusion of a particular investment treaty had led to ad hoc changes in Myanmar's laws or regulations.[48]

This finding raises the question that has long animated debates in law and development scholarship: to what extent can the mere incorporation of rule-of-law benchmarks into national legal frameworks result in actual transformations in national legal cultures?[49] The interview responses also point to a shared scepticism about the potency of either international law and national law to effectuate any significant changes in legal and bureaucratic *culture* on the ground.[50] The interviews and analysis of the national legislation in countries

---

[41] Lauge N Skovgaard Poulson and Emma Aisbett, 'When the Claims Hit: Bilateral Investment Treaties and Bounded Rational Learning' (2013) 65 World Pol 273, 282.

[42] See Mavluda Sattorova, 'International Investment Law in Central Asia: The Making, Implementation and Change of Investment Rules from a Regionalist Perspective' (2015) 16 JWIT 1089, 1105.

[43] Sattorova (n 23) 72.

[44] ibid 73.

[45] ibid 75

[46] ibid.

[47] Bonnitcha (n 25) 10.

[48] ibid.

[49] See eg John Hewko, 'Foreign Direct Investment: Does the Rule of Law Matter?' (2 April 2012) Carnegie Endowment for International Peace Rule of Law Series, Democracy and Rule of Law Project, Working Paper No 26.

[50] See Ginsburg (n 13).

covered by the case studies reveal that none of the governments in the case study has made efforts to introduce or strengthen existing legal frameworks on accountability of individual officials or government agencies for financial harm caused to the State as a result of investor-State disputes caused by their actions.

C. Finding No 3: There Are Rule-of-Law Reforms But Unrelated to the Investment Treaty Regime

A number of countries in the case study have recently introduced a series of reforms aimed at the improvement of the investment climate. Some of these involved the creation of national investment ombudsmen. A salient example of this trend is the case of Kazakhstan. Here, the investment ombudsman is vested with responsibility for eg (1) solving issues related to rights and interests of foreign investments during implementation of investment projects, (2) mediating settlement of disputes between investors and State authorities, (3) offering support in legal proceedings, (4) where problems cannot be solved under the existing legislation, designing and submitting proposals for the improvement of the legislation to the competent legislative organs.[51]

However, the respondents in our interviews did not expressly link the creation of the ombudsman with Kazakhstan's experience in investment arbitration. Rather, the initiative was reportedly sponsored by the World Bank and supported by other international organizations.[52] Nor is the institution of ombudsman seen as a promising development in the sense of its capacity to transform legal and bureaucratic practices on the ground. One interviewee suggested that there is a sense that the ombudsman 'does not have competence to do much, mostly to issue recommendations. It needs prerogatives to impose obligations and other executive powers.'[53] Nevertheless, despite this institutional disadvantage, the ombudsman is seen as capable of making effective one-off interventions in an effort to prevent investor-State controversies from escalating into investment arbitration disputes. This type of intervention, however, is ad hoc, very informal and, as one interviewee put it, 'may have no basis in law'—in cases where existing laws provide only limited or cumbersome and protracted solutions.[54] A similar disconnect between the creation of the ombudsmen and the prior experience with investment arbitration and investment treaty law in general can be found in other countries included in the case study, in particular Georgia, Jordan, and Ukraine. Likewise, Bonnitcha traces the genesis of Myanmar's Investor Grievance Mechanism back to institutional reforms in the justice sector spearheaded by the International Finance Corporation (IFC), not the government's realization of the need to avert investor-State disputes and to comply with investment treaties.[55]

Another pertinent policy development featuring across a number of countries is the emergence of national investment promotion agencies. These usually are conceived as independent, non-governmental investment advisory boards tasked to work closely with the

---

[51] See eg Law No 373-II On Investments, Republic of Kazakhstan, 8 January 2003, as amended 12 June 2014, art 12(1).

[52] Interview IDM1.

[53] ibid.

[54] Interview IDM1, AFM1.

[55] Bonnitcha (n 25) 26.

relevant government ministries and other bodies. Although vested with no formal powers with respect to dispute settlement, investment promotion agencies are expected to act as informal facilitators and thus complement the role currently played by investment ombudsmen. Neither do these agencies have the power of legislative initiative to initiate reforms to address domestic rule-of-law issues affecting foreign investors. Rather alarmingly, it transpires that some agencies have a mandate to support foreign investors of a certain calibre only.

The proliferation of national investment ombudsmen and investment promotion agencies demonstrate that some investment reforms are indeed taking place across developing countries. These reforms are aimed at the improvement of national investment climates and as such can ultimately strengthen the domestic rule of law, potentially benefiting a broader range of stakeholders. However, the emergence of these agencies appears to be entirely isolated from the relevant countries' participation in the investment treaty regime and investment arbitration. None of these initiatives have been explicitly linked to investment treaties and to the respective government's learning from its brush with investment arbitration but rather appear to have been advocated and sponsored by international organizations, such as the EBRD, OECD, and World Bank. Furthermore, some of the interviewees working at these new-fangled national bodies showed minimal or no awareness of the investment treaty regime and its impact on their respective countries.[56]

D. Finding No 4: Some Rule-of-Law Reforms Tend to Overprotect Foreign Investors at the Expense of Systemic Improvements

Long before the emergence of empirical studies on the impact of investment treaty law on government behaviour, some scholars had persuasively argued that '[r]equiring governments to compensate foreign investors for their losses, while not extending equivalent protection to other private actors, is likely to lead decision-makers to overvalue the interests of foreign investors'.[57] Holding the host government liable for failing to treat foreign investors in a certain manner may translate into pressure to treat foreign investors better than other businesses, as opposed to changing the generally prevailing governance culture and practices that had led to liability in the first place. This argument resonates with findings from our empirical case studies. Rather than embarking on comprehensive and systemic reforms of domestic institutions and practices, some host governments appear to opt for short-term localized solutions aimed solely at safeguarding special treatment of foreign investors and optimizing the defence of State interests in investment arbitration disputes. Furthermore, the empirical data indicate that by enabling foreign investors to benefit from stronger protections, international investment law might in fact hinder the formation of a domestic business constituency that would agitate for the stronger domestic rule of law. This, in turn, only contributes to the sense of scepticism already prevalent on the ground, especially in developing states, about international norms as a force for change.

---

[56] See Sattorova (n 23) 77–79.
[57] Jonathan Bonnitcha, 'Outline of a Normative Framework for Evaluating Interpretations of Investment Treaty Protections' in Brown and Miles (n 14) 128.

An overwhelming number of respondents in our case studies revealed that the improvement of investment climate is often seen as synonymous with creating legal enclaves for foreign investors. As one respondent (a former judge) recalled, the government would frequently issue formal and informal executive orders demanding that foreign investors be accorded special protection in judicial proceedings.[58] Interviews also point to the growing popularity of practices whereby national foreign investment promotion agencies as well as investment ombudsmen specifically tasked with providing 'a tailor-made, door-to-door' protection to foreign investors. When interviewed, one representative of a newly established investment promotion agency told us that the privilege of a 'door-to-door' protection will be extended only to foreign investments of a certain size and in strategic sectors of economy.[59] An interviewee from one national ministry recounted the government's intention to introduce an overarching framework which would, among other things, enable an expedited visa and entry clearance procedures for foreign investors and their personnel.[60] To this end, agencies responsible for border control and internal affairs would work closely with the ministries and departments responsible for the promotion of foreign investment. Another respondent mentioned the government's intention of introducing a ranking system whereby heads of municipal authorities would be rated for their success in attracting and retaining foreign (not domestic) investments within their respective jurisdictions.[61]

One prominent example of such trend is the recent launch, in Kazakhstan, of the Astana International Financial Centre (AIFC), a special economic zone to promote foreign direct investment (FDI), facilitate the privatization of State-owned enterprises by foreign investors, and generally foster the improvement of the local financial system, human and technological capital, and cementing Kazakhstan's role as the financial and logistics hub of the Eurasian region.[62] A particularly noteworthy feature of this initiative is the fact that the newly created AIFC has been conceived as a special jurisdiction with independent commercial law inspired by common law. According to Article 13(2) of the Constitutional Law of the Republic of Kazakhstan 'On Astana International Financial Centre', the AIFC Court must be independent in its activity and not be a part of the judicial system of the Republic of Kazakhstan.[63] Even more notable is the fact that Kazakh law is not to be the applicable law; rather, the Court will be governed by rules 'based on the procedural principles and norms of England and Wales and (or) standards of the world leading financial centres'.[64] The interviews with Kazakh government officials revealed the intention to appoint judges on the basis from foreign experts with professional reputation and an established track record of previous experience in common law jurisdictions.[65] The underlying idea is to afford foreign investors with special privileges by insulating them from national law and the national judicial system.

---

[58] Interview THS. This claim was corroborated by interviews HSG and HSK1.

[59] Interview IK1. Similar testimony found in interview IU1.

[60] Interview IDM1.

[61] ibid.

[62] Constitutional Law of the Republic of Kazakhstan 'On Astana International Financial Centre' (entered into force 1 January 2017).

[63] ibid; the full text is available at <http://www.kazembassy.org.uk/en/pages/page/88> accessed 20 December 2021.

[64] ibid art 13(5)

[65] Interview MFA1.

The emerging picture suggests that, in an effort to improve national regulatory environment, some host governments have been favouring not a systemic reform that would result in 'better rule of law for all', but rather solutions that overprotect foreign investors by creating special legal enclaves and thus insulating foreign investors from the vicissitudes of doing business under the same rules as local investors. The fact that international investment protection norms may lead to host States overvaluing the interests of foreign investors yet again shows that governments do not always respond to international sanctions and incentives by embracing rule-of-law reforms. Furthermore, the empirical insights support what other scholars refer to as rule-of-law 'enclaves' or 'bubbles'[66] exist for a certain class of foreign investors. The rule of law here is the rule of market.[67]

III. 'What If', or How to Enhance the Rule-of-Law Effects of the Investment Treaty Regime

The foregoing discussion has sought to elucidate some of the insights into the effects of investment treaty law on the domestic rule of law. These findings paint a somewhat bleak picture and cast doubt on the narratives that postulate a positive impact of investment treaties and arbitration on sovereign behaviour. BITs bite but not in a way that leads to improvements in domestic rule of law. Across the globe, developing States have been carrying out rule-of-law reforms aimed at the improvement of national regulatory and bureaucratic environments for investors, but these reforms tend to be unconnected to the IIA regime. Host States do draw lessons from their participation in the investment treaty regime, but these lessons do not necessarily translate into rule-of-law improvements.

As acknowledged from the outset, the aim of this contribution is not to examine the very notion of the rule law but rather to test the existing claims about the (positive) rule-of-law spillovers of the investment treaty regime. With a nod to a sizeable body of literature which offers a rich seam of sophisticated critiques of the rule of law, and admitting that engaging with such critiques is beyond the scope of this chapter, one is invited, for a moment, to side with those authors who believed that the rule of law 'may achieve its promise of substantive equality and justice'.[68] If the rule of law were, as it is argued, an 'unqualified human good',[69] could the investment treaty regime play a positive role in promoting justice, equality, and fairness at the domestic level? What conditions would need to be in place for international investment law to fulfil its promise of strengthening the domestic rule of law?

---

[66] See Anil Yilmaz Vastardis, 'Justice Bubbles for the Privileged: A Critique of the Investor-State Dispute Settlement Proposals for the EU's Investment Agreements' (2018) 6 LRIL 279.

[67] Tor Krever, 'The Legal Turn in Late Development Theory: The Rule of Law and the World Bank's Development Model' (2011) 52 Harv Int LJ 288, 307.

[68] ibid.

[69] EP Thompson, *Whigs and Hunters: The Origin of the Black Act* (Pantheon Books 1975) 267, cited in Krever (n 67) 309.

A. Openness about the Rule-of-Law Mission

The bulk of IIAs do not expressly refer to their rule-of-law mission. Instead, most of the rule-of-law narratives of international investment law are premised on the idea that it is primarily through the interpretation and enforcement of certain investment treaty prescriptions by investment arbitration tribunals that the regime can discipline the sovereign and thus strengthen the domestic rule of law. It is therefore not surprising that these narratives are seen as an attempt to ascribe a certain societal function to the investment treaty regime and thus assuage concerns over its legitimacy. Unlike investment treaties and investment arbitration tribunals, other regimes and judicial bodies have been more forthcoming and thus more convincing about their ambitions to alter domestic legal environments. Consider, for instance, some of the recent EU cooperation and trade agreements which not only expressly acknowledge their rule-of-law mission but also feature provisions concerning the steps the contracting State parties commit to undertake to improve the rule of law on the ground. A commitment of the parties to strengthen the respect for democratic principles, the rule of law, and good governance is not explicitly stated in the treaty preamble but is also elaborated in a standalone clause whereby the signatories commit to cooperate 'in strengthening the functioning of institutions, including law enforcement, prosecution, the administration of justice and the prevention of, and fight against, corruption'.[70] Of course, it could be argued that these provisions are declaratory at best and are not accompanied by concrete mechanisms to facilitate and monitor compliance. Nevertheless, unlike international investment treaties, trade and cooperation agreements of this kind are open about their broader mission. They also outline some processes and institutional arrangements which the contracting State parties are committed to develop as part of their shared ambition to strengthen the rule of law.

The clarity about its purported rule-of-law promise might also have helped contracting State parties, as the key actors of the investment treaty regime, to concentrate their efforts on implementing the relevant rule-of-law safeguards as opposed to being preoccupied with ISDS. If the strengthening of the domestic rule of law were indeed an important part of the investment treaty regime's broad array of functions, it would need to be supported by a clear set of provisions elaborating the ways in which investment treaty norms could be effectively translated into the daily work of domestic legal, bureaucratic, and judicial bodies. The recent generation of comprehensive trade agreements increasingly feature provisions on notification, reporting, and monitoring compliance yet the bulk of investment treaties remain silent on this very important aspect of compliance and implementation. Outside trade, a glance at the experience of other international treaty regimes also reveals that reporting, data collection, and monitoring serve as a means of familiarization with and internalization of investment treaty laws by domestic actors.[71] In the words of Chayes and Chayes, it is there that 'domestic officialdom begins to translate the treaty law into the daily work of administration and to define the level of commitment to it'.[72]

---

[70] See Enhanced Partnership and Cooperation Agreement between the European Union and its Member States and the Republic of Kazakhstan (signed 21 December 2012, entered into force 1 March 2020) art 235.

[71] Abram Chayes and Antonia Handler Chayes, *The New Sovereignty: Compliance with International Regulatory Agreements* (Harvard UP 1995) 155–60.

[72] ibid 136.

B. Redesigning Investment Treaty Regime's Rule-of-Law Mechanisms

Openness about the rule-of-law ambitions would admittedly entail some introspection about the regime's design, in particular the working of its key rules and the design of its remedies. First, if the investment treaty regime were to help strengthen the domestic rule of law, it would need to lead by example. This, in turn, would require addressing internal rule-of-law deficits that beset the functioning of investment treaties and their investment arbitration mechanism. The rapid rise in the number of investment disputes over the last three decades has exposed numerous deficits in the original drafting of investment treaty standards and their interpretation in investment arbitration practice. When analysed through the lens of the existing theories of compliance, the capacity of the investment treaty regime to generate positive spillovers for the domestic rule of law hinges on three primary factors: (1) determinacy—'the ability of the text to convey a clear message, to appear transparent in the sense that one can see through the language to the meaning';[73] (2) coherence—the rule must treat like cases alike and relate 'in a principled fashion to other rules of the same system';[74] and (3) procedural fairness—the rule must emanate from a fair and accepted procedure,[75] and be 'closely connected to the secondary rules of process used to interpret and apply rules of international obligation'.[76] The regime featuring these hallmarks can exert the so-called compliance pull.[77] Yet, many of the regime's critics from across the scholarly community and civil society groups would concur that the investment treaty regime is yet to address its internal rule-of-law deficits.

In his critique of the rule-of-law narratives of the regime, Gus Van Harten points out that '[i]nvestment treaties generally do not establish coherent, non-contradictory rules that are capable of being known and thus followed on a reasonably reliable basis, but rather a set of broadly framed ideals that have in turn been assigned different and at times conflicting meanings when interpreted by arbitrators'.[78] Although these shortcomings of investment treaties and arbitral jurisprudence have become the focus of the recent and ongoing reform efforts, one cannot help but agree that there are still profound concerns about a lack of predictability and ensuing uncertainty in the functioning of investment treaty law. As acknowledged in one UNCTAD report, such uncertainty poses a significant challenge to host states and their agencies that interact with investors: 'if the State and its subnational entities do not know in advance what type of conduct may be considered a breach of a treaty, then it cannot organise its regulatory and administrative decision-making processes and delegation in a way that ensures that its conduct will not incur liability'.[79] Until these deficits are fully addressed, the rule-of-law prescriptions of investment treaties are unlikely to be effectively internalized and transposed into the daily practices of national institutions in host States.

---

[73] Thomas M Franck, 'Legitimacy in the International System' (1988) 82 AJIL 705, 713.

[74] ibid 741.

[75] Chayes and Chayes (n 71) 127.

[76] Oona A Hathaway, 'Do Human Rights Treaties Make a Difference?' (2002) 111 Yale LJ 1935, 1959; Franck (n 73) 41–46.

[77] Franck (n 73) 705.

[78] Gus Van Harten, 'Investment Treaty Arbitration, Procedural Fairness, and the Rule of Law' in Schill (n 8) 627, 628.

[79] 'Fair and Equitable Treatment: A Sequel' (2012) UNCTAD Series on Issues in International Investment Agreements II (New York and Geneva, United Nations) 12.

Not only do the norms and processes of investment treaty law require some fundamental rethinking, but if one is serious about the rule-of-law mission of the investment treaty regime the often-overlooked investment treaty remedies also merit close attention. Of particular relevance here is the primacy of monetary relief in the investment treaty regime's arsenal of available remedies. It is often assumed that the financial pain of damages awards granted to foreign investors would have a deterrent effect on respondent host states compelling them to revisit their legal and bureaucratic practices and improving their rule-of-law compliance. Such assumptions are, however, belied by a welter of evidence produced by law and development scholars, in particular those studies that have highlighted the limitations of financial pressures and incentives in fostering rule-of-law reform in developing States.[80] Among other things, such studies show that transformation through coercion (including financial sanctions) tends to be less effective than initiatives based on persuasion. Financial sanctions leave no room for internalization of rule-of-law reforms.[81] While questioning the effectiveness of coercive measures in fostering rule-of-law reforms,[82] the literature on law and development suggest that remedies might produce the desired effect on State behaviour but only if carefully designed. For instance, to achieve a desired outcome, sanctions need to be designed so as to exert pressure on specific decision-making elites or entities they control, or against specific activities.[83]

Are investment treaty sanctions designed so as to compel host governments to abide by the rule of law at the domestic level? The significant flaw in the design of investment treaty remedies is the fact that investment treaties and arbitration have traditionally been concerned with providing redress to disaffected investors, not with incentivizing host States to respect the rule of law. Damages, as a principal investment treaty remedy, are aimed to retrospectively undo the harmful financial effects inflicted upon the investor by a non-compliant host government. It is useful to compare the investment treaty regime with WTO law. One of the key goals of the WTO dispute settlement mechanism is that of inducing compliance with the primary norms contained in the multilateral trade agreements.[84] In alignment with this goal, the principal remedy for a breach of WTO norms is the withdrawal (or modification) of an offending measure.[85] Compensation is also available but not as an alternative to withdrawal; rather, compensation can be used as a temporary remedy in cases where the respondent State failed to withdraw or modify the offending measure.[86]

What is the primary objective of investment treaty remedies? Is it to induce State parties into compliance with the rule of law, or to rebalance economic interests of parties to a dispute by compensating the aggrieved investor? Can investment treaties strengthen the

---

[80] See eg Celine Tan, 'The New Disciplinary Framework: Conditionality, New Aid Architecture and Global Economic Governance' in Celine Tan and Julio Faundez (eds), *International Economic Law, Globalization and Developing Countries* (Edward Elgar 2010) 100.

[81] See eg Frank Schimmelfennig and Ulrich Sedelmeier, 'Governance by Conditionality: EU Rule Transfer to the Candidate Countries of Central and Eastern Europe' (2004) 11 JEPP 669, 674.

[82] Michael J Trebilcock and Ronald J Daniels, *Rule of Law Reform and Development: Charting the Fragile Path of Progress* (Edward Elgar 2008) 351.

[83] ibid.

[84] Yuval Shany, *Assessing the Effectiveness of International Courts* (OUP 2014) 195.

[85] Understanding on Rules and Procedures Governing the Settlement of Disputes, Annex 2 of the Agreement Establishing the World Trade Organization, 1994, art 3.7.

[86] ibid ('The provision of compensation should be resorted to only if the immediate withdrawal of the measure is impracticable and as a temporary measure pending the withdrawal of the measure which is inconsistent with a covered agreement').

domestic rule of law if investors primarily seek, and tribunals continue to use, damages as a principal remedy (as often prescribed by investment treaties)? Law and development studies and scholarship on rule-of-law reforms[87] have long questioned whether the pain of monetary payouts incentivizes host States to adjust their domestic legal orders in line with international benchmarks.[88] By contrast with damages, orders of injunctive relief and specific performance 'purport to constrain the manner in which a government may exercise its powers'.[89] Yet specific performance and injunctive relief are not commonly sought by claimant-investors and granted by arbitral tribunals in investment treaty practice.[90] The prevalence of monetary remedies in investment treaty arbitration may thus diminish the regime's overall capacity to deliver on its rule-of-law promise. Further still, with its focus on retrospective sanctions for a breach of investment treaty standards, investment treaty law does little to foster the creation of domestically situated frameworks to ease *the entry and operation* of foreign investors in host States. The fact that the international organizations are pushing for investment treaty protection while also advocating the parallel reforms on investment facilitation and dispute prevention at a national level could also be seen as tacit acknowledgement that investment treaty law does not automatically lead to 'learning' and improved domestic rule of law in host States.

C. Capacity Issues

One principal shortcoming of the rule-of-law narratives of the investment treaty regime is a misplaced assumption that developing countries have the capacity to undertake domestic rule-of-law reforms but only need an external push to launch them. The case studies of recent developments in Colombia, Kazakhstan, Peru, and Ukraine show the key role played by external agencies such as the World Bank, EBRD, UNCTAD, and the EU missions in funding the design and rollout of the relevant domestic reforms aimed at the improvement of the investment climate and the prevention of investor-State disputes.[91] Interviews also confirm that these initiatives owed their origins to external technical support. The fact that dispute prevention and management frameworks in Peru and Colombia have been funded with the help from external actors resonates with international relations theories which tie changes in government behaviour with the availability of resources. Again, of note here is the scholarly work on compliance by Chayes and Chayes who argued that the process of facilitating State compliance with international rules should involve informing states of their international obligations and building State capacity to comply.[92] One could take this stance further and argue that capacity-building support is needed not just to help developing States learn about their international obligations but to support domestic constituencies as primary drivers of sociopolitical change internally, in a bottom-up rather than top-down manner.

---

[87] See eg Ngaire Woods, 'Order, Justice, the IMF, and the World Bank' in Rosemary Foot, John Gaddis and Andrew Hurrell (eds), *Order and Justice in International Relations* (OUP 2003) 83; Trebilcock and Daniels (n 82) 342.

[88] For more detail, see Sattorova (n 23) 109–18.

[89] Bonnitcha (n 2) 60.

[90] Christoph Schreuer, 'Non-Pecuniary Remedies in ICSID Arbitration' (2004) 20 Arb Intl 325.

[91] For more detail, see Sattorova (n 23) 77–85.

[92] Chayes and Chayes (n 71) 25.

The issue of capacity is closely intertwined with resource constraints which have long been recognized as one of the key impediments besetting external efforts to transform domestic institutions and practices in developing States. The rule-of-law narratives of international investment law need to be cognizant of the fact that a failure to maintain transparency, stability, predictability, and consistency for which developing States are held liable under investment treaties is often the direct consequence of resource constraints. These cannot be alleviated by merely imposing additional (and often crippling) financial liabilities on host states. Although contentious in its own right, technical assistance as well as financial incentives (as opposed to financial sanctions) might be better geared towards building domestic capacity and generate internal support for rule-of-law reforms. It is also crucial that capacity building for rule-of-law reforms should not be used as a pretext to interfere with the domestic affairs of developing States.

D. Commitment to the Systemic Reform, or 'Rule of Law for All'

One might argue that the emerging trend to create national agencies tasked with the prevention of investment disputes—such as national investment ombudsmen and one-stop shops for investors—is a manifestation of the positive effect of the investment treaty regime on the domestic rule of law. However, the causal link between such developments and the functioning of the investment treaty regime is belied by the empirical data. Furthermore, even if one were to concede that the prevention of investment disputes is evidence of a growing commitment to the rule of law on the ground, a close analysis of the existing prevention strategies raises some important questions. Currently, most of the dispute prevention agencies appear to be concerned with pre-empting individual disputes from escalating into fully blown investor-State arbitration cases. Arguably, such strategy is unlikely to be conducive to an improved adherence to the rule of law in the daily operation of a multitude of government agencies. Unless the prevention of investor-State disputes comprises some form of wider learning and internalization of the relevant norms and practices, foreign investors are likely to become the only constituency to benefit from such early detection and dispute management policies. The disadvantage of the recent emphasis on the prevention of investment disputes through timely intervention from a central government agency is that such pre-empting strategy is unlikely to bring about changes in daily practices of the host State's legal and bureaucratic institutions. The preoccupation with the prevention of investment disputes instead of transforming a wider legal and bureaucratic culture might sidetrack the central government from the pursuit of a broader, meaningful, and more systemic reform aimed at the overhaul of the lacking domestic institutions and practices.

Likewise, the recently established national investment ombudsmen and investment promotion agencies tend to opt for ad hoc, informal solutions to avoid lengthy legislative and bureaucratic changes.[93] They do not possess effective institutional powers to propose and implement long-term systematic reforms. Their current operational framework is underpinned by the idea of a centralized, tailor-made, 'door-to-door' support of individual

---

[93] Interview responses reveal that such agencies do not have requisite powers to propose and initiate more comprehensive reforms and instead are expected to intervene on a case-by-case basis, favouring investors of a certain calibre. See Sattorova (n 23) 78, 85.

investment projects through maintaining focal points of contact, rather than diffusing knowledge about investment treaty law and its rule-of-law prescriptions. The creation of separate regimes—legal enclaves—for foreign and domestic investors removes the incentive for foreign investors (and powerful domestic constituencies) to lobby for institutional reforms at a national level.[94] By prioritizing foreign investment protection over a comprehensive change of national legal and bureaucratic landscape, such policy solutions do little to meet interests of the domestic business community and are therefore likely to hamper the emergence of legal and regulatory innovation that would benefit a broader range of domestic stakeholders.

One overarching observation which can be distilled from the existing empirical insights is that for investment treaty regime to exert positive effects on host State compliance with the rule-of-law standards in the domestic sphere, the regime must address its internal issues, including the clarity of purpose, consistency, capacity-building, and a coherent approach to investment climate reforms. Some of these issues have been recently pushed to the forefront of the reform agenda at the UNCITRAL Working Group III.

IV. Conclusion

The aim of this chapter was to offer a fresh contribution to a debate about the interplay between investment treaty law and the domestic rule of law, especially in developing host States. In particular, it has focused on the impact of investment treaty law on State compliance with the rule of law in the domestic sphere. Drawing on emerging empirical data, this chapter has sought to identify various preconditions that need to be in place for the investment treaty regime to be successful in its purported mission to improve the rule of law on the ground. The key takeaway is that a causal relationship between the functioning of the investment treaty regime and improvements in the domestic rule of law is very complex. The original features of the regime, including the thrust of its core rules, remedies, and dispute settlement provisions, are not sufficiently geared towards influencing host State behaviour. Although the awareness about international investment law on the ground is growing, government officials in developing States do not always translate lessons from their encounter with the regime into concrete changes in the way the government machinery operates in its daily life. The empirical data also show that across developing States a number of far-reaching reforms are taking place with a view to improving national investment climates. While such reforms can ultimately lead to strengthening the domestic rule of law, these are not linked to investment treaty law. Some of these reforms are also narrow in their focus on facilitating the entry and operation of foreign investors into host States. For the investment treaty law to have a positive impact on the domestic rule of law, the regime must be clear about its mission and the tools to accomplish it. It needs to lead by example and tackle the existing rule-of-law deficits of its own. Whether these deficits could be addressed is open to debate.

---

[94] Soumyajit Mazumder, 'Can I Stay a BIT Longer? The Effect of Bilateral Investment Treaties on Political Survival' (2016) 11 Rev Intl Organ 477, 478.